Fire and Ice:

The Meth Bible

written by

Boston Bornagain

editor: Sandra Lee
cover art: Steve Oliver

Dedication: For Misty…go after all your dreams.

Special Thanks: To Sandra…I couldn't have done it without you.

Contents

Chapter 1 Virgin Lungs

Chapter 2 High School High

Chapter 3 Demise

Chapter 4 The Driver: Stakes is High

Chapter 5 The Greatest Love of All

Chapter 6 Angels and Signs

Chapter 7 Till the Wheels Fall Off

Chapter 8 Movie Magic

Chapter 9 Orange is the New Whack

Chapter 10 Dark Days Asylum Nights

Chapter 11 The Open Road

Chapter 1

Virgin Lungs

The smoke pulled into my virgin lungs, charring the outer membranes. THC lined my blood cells and the feeling of tranquility hit me like a five o'clock train. Snowbanks and naked trees canvased the scene, a blanket of arctic chill held us captive under the bridge in suburbia. Reading was the city. We were a band of clowns and outcasts. Twelve-year-old fools enjoying life to the brink. We laughed our days away.

These boys helped mold me. I was in awe of their comedic skills and ability to mask the pain that laid just below the skin. My youth was about to take a turn down a hard road this fateful day. Weed was something I had heard about but never had the stones to try…until now. We marched down the tracks like storm troopers. Our mission was to get blown.

Young hearts raced as the stolen half joint sat in a used pack of Parliament Lights. Our feet clad with cheap snow boots. Our parents were on a budget. We didn't live on the rich side of town. But even us poor kids had it made in the shade. Our dads were working. Our moms were either lonely housewives or working nine to five to pay for the patriarch's beer tab for the month.

The dope was stolen from the mother of the gentle giant. Buddy was bigger than the rest. Larger than life too. I met him on the first day of sixth grade. He wore a big baggy t-shirt, jeans, and the freshest pair of Reeboks you have ever laid eyes on. Bright African colors of yellow and hunter green donned with peace signs on the side. I took one look at this monster and knew we would be compadres till the casket dropped. I approached him right away. Fat kids gottta stick together, and this guy was a bruiser. He had a foot on us all and looked like he could already play nose tackle for the New England Patriots.

      We hit it off right away, our sense of humor and interest in gangster rap music bonded us like steel beams on the Tobin Bridge. His mom was a cool hippy chick. They came from half-White and half-Japanese descent. Buddy's grandma was a one-of-a-kind lady. Growing up during World War II in Japan, she overcame some of the greatest adversity and turmoil one could go through. She was there when the Enola Gay Boeing B29 Superfortress dropped the bomb. She was awesome. During the beginning of our friendship, we would all sit around and eat Chinese food as she told old stories and showed us that we should be grateful for having been born Stateside.

      His house was truly a refuge for me when times were rough at home. The congregation of troubled teens started almost immediately after school began that year. Misfit kids of all shapes and sizes wearing JNCO jeans, knit caps, and Fila sneakers ascended on the house like locusts while Ma Dukes was at work.

      We all shared one thing in common, we came from dysfunctional families that allowed us to do as we wished. Some were single parents, some married. Our parents all grew up in the Sixties and Seventies. The hard-partying, fast-living attitude was a way of life. All our parents worked extremely hard. Blue-collar and lower-end White-collar jobs ate up most of their time, so getting away with murder was easy.

      It was a boxy-looking house with a basement

underground and a one-level living space. Two bedrooms, an old-timey kitchen with cherry floors from around the time "Leave It to Beaver" was a smash, and a living room in the front that faced Main Street in Reading, Massachusetts. There was a long cheap couch facing an old tube TV in the front room. Buddy had a set of red metal bunk beds in his room, the style with a twin on top and full on the bottom. A ghetto blaster boombox with a six-disc changer sat on a wooden table. Tupac, Biggie, and Cypress Hill were the soundtrack to our lives. The cast of characters grew like a sunflower after spring rains.

  Drug use was common among our parents. They worked hard. They played harder. In the Just Say No era, these party animals were totally saying yes. The roaring Nineties were in full swing. With our folks all in their forties, hard drinking, pot, and other pills and powders were accepted as normal after work remedies for the working-man blues. We started to become curious cats. The feline persuasion that would sniff around top drawers, old cigar boxes, and winter coat pockets for money, cigarette lighters, and whatever other interesting contraband we could claw up.

  One day, on top of a flimsy, black card table, the sort with the faux leather top, Buddy and I stumbled upon a half joint perched in a black plastic ashtray. Fat with stinky, pungent greenery. The forbidden fruit was ripe as a Georgia peach. The smell wasn't so foreign though. We weren't dummies. We smelled the familiar odor wafting from bathroom doors and behind garages since we were knee high to a corn stalk. This was herb, man! We looked at each other with devilish grins. All fear dissipated as Buddy growled with authority, "We're doing it, Boston." When Buddy gave an order, it wasn't so much fear that got me to comply, it was that I just liked him so damn much. We devised a plan that took three days to hatch. We asked around about how long the effects would last, how we would act, and the big enchilada...would we die?

#

After school, we abandoned all other activities to trot to a remote location. We headed for the bridge above the railroad tracks. The snow was probably a foot high. The train acted as a plow, so if we walked the tracks themselves then we could cruise to our destination, interrupted only by the commuter rail that would pass every forty-five minutes or so. Cold whipped across our young skin, razor burn that blushed our cheeks to the point of a raspberry tint. Pigeons squawked above, flapping filthy wings. Passing cars were overhead; circular tires gripped the asphalt, throwing a high-pitched crackle through the air.

His hand reached in his pocket to brandish the goods. A navy Bic lighter was our source of heat. His thick thumb gives a flick, and it was all systems go. The fire ignited the blackened end of the spliff and within a matter of seconds, he was ripping his first hit of ganja.

A stream of smoke hit the arctic air that loomed in our surroundings. A gurgling cough that mirrored bronchitis roared from his barreling chest cavity. Gagging, he passed me the broccoli stem, rolling the zig-zag paper off his fingers and into mine. It was go-time, and I was nervous. That's when I hit it.

#

The walk home was a strange trip. Icicles on tree limbs were vivid. Blackbirds prancing on snow mounds looked prehistoric and firm. The giggles hit. We would catch each other's eye from time to time and burst out laughing like we were watching Rodney Dangerfield do stand-up.

We burst into town like psychedelic Vikings. Our wool caps kept the heat from leaving our dreamy heads. There was a local Burger King in the distance as we crossed the plane back into society. The smell of French fries permeated the December air as if Willie Nelson's biofuel tour bus had just passed us by. Hitting the cold glass door, a wall of heat glued our feet to the floor tiles. Approaching the counter was nightmarish. A dark-skinned Pakistani gentleman greeted us with a grimace. My clan of degenerates were always harassing this man. Years of abuse and juvenile jokes had obviously taken its toll on his patience for our gang…and that is what we were, a band of jesters.

"How can I help you?" was met with a great deal of laughter. Our chubby faces were gutters for tears. Streaming eyeballs poured like April rains. The fluorescent bulbs showcased the crimson shade of our peepers.

We had purchased Clear Eyes after hearing it would mask the red-eyed effects of dope. Ben Stein would be proud. But you can't benefit from it if you forget you bought it in the first place, so it sat in my inner breast pocket safe and sound and completely unused.

Our order was large. A choice was made to sit in the very back near the ball pit in case anyone that knew us happened to stumble in. We were trying to avoid a "Cheech and Chong" episode, seeing this was our maiden voyage.

Unwrapping the Whopper with cheese was amusing. The wax paper crinkled flat as I stared at this artwork with a carnivorous thirst. I loved food, but today something was different. The sesame seeds had meaning. The soft bread was buttery and unique. The grease that dripped from the all-beef patty had an aroma of pleasure. The lettuce was crisp and fresh pickles draped over a plump slice of a fire engine red tomato. The vinegar in the pickle slices gave off that tang that made your taste buds perk up instantly. Mayonnaise was spread across the top bun perfectly; the amount was exactly measured to my liking. The first bite made me feel as if I had a virgin orgasm. We were both silent, aside from the near-sexual moans we were letting off and the chomping effects from our newly permanent incisors. This was the most spiritual piece of cow I had ever encountered. The carbonation in my soda thoroughly wet my whistle. Bubbles popped in my esophagus like firecrackers in a Chinese New Year parade. Food had never been like this before.

  I always enjoyed talking with Buddy, but today the conversation was deep and dreamy for two twelve-year-old morons. I felt the changes in my world. Our bounty sat in our bellies while feelings of contentment comforted my soul. I was at peace. At this moment, my spirit was calm and tranquil. The herb's natural effects were opening doors in my mind's eye that I never thought were possible.

  Winter glaze attached to my skin once we stumbled out into suburbia. Hardtop met the soles of my boots and walking had a certain fun about it. One Video Place was our hometown video store. Remember those? The shop was a stone's throw from the Burger King we had just visited. We spent a good hour picking out the films we had already planned on watching.

  The porno section was in the open. A middle-aged man stood on the felt green carpet in front of this section. We pictured these ordinary Joe's with trench coats on and hairy palms, but mostly it was our classmates' fathers and construction workers looking for a hot date on a Saturday night. We were peeking at the taboo videos as the cougar behind the counter rang us up. The employees were dressed in white tuxedo shirts and black slacks. They looked like caterers at a wedding.

  Finally, we made it home. We plopped down on the grey-blue poly blend couch. The TV tube crackled as the power was turned on. We laughed like a couple of stoned hyenas as some low-rent slapstick comedy played. Time ticked by slowly. The effects of this lucidity we had experienced were wearing off like anesthesia in a recovery room. We could never go back to the way things were before we shared that first joint. Pandora's box was blown wide open. The curse had been put on; the spell arranged. The spirit of addiction was fully invited into our lives, and we wouldn't realize it for many moons.

#

We stole the herb as much as possible after that. Our taste for getting high and creating foolishness was becoming an everyday aspiration. In our group, we all came from troubled lives. The escape of marijuana was a perfect break from whatever was going on at home.

Childhood trauma, fighting, and whatever caused the pain to surface like a nuclear submarine, the weed calmed the storm. Just down the street was a block we referred to as the hood. This area consisted of Warren Avenue and Center Avenue, which ran parallel. Sal and Ricky lived on Warren Avenue and Donnie's house was on Center Avenue. The fences were touching with two rickety wooden ladders, attached so we could travel back and forth. Every goofball and knucklehead kid for miles around would lurk to see what kind of trouble they could get into.

My crew was full of talented, funny guys. Ricky was a natural athlete. He was a star soccer player, fastpitch baseball legend, and the fastest runner the town of Reading, Massachusetts had ever seen. He was one hundred and forty pounds of pure muscle and adrenaline, with the wit of a young Jim Carey. Ricky was fun to be around. Girls flocked to him, with even the prettiest girl in school fighting to get an ounce of his time. His little brother, Sal, was a blond bulldog. Short, stocky, and a star wrestler. He was a year behind us in school but kept up with the best of them. Equally as funny as his big brother, just in a different way.

Seeky also lived on Warren Avenue. He was a rail thin, tall drink of water with a short haircut. A truly funny guy in every sense of the word. Known for doing impressions and breaking balls, he was a hoot to have on the squad.

Manny was also a skyscraper of a dude. He was built like a house, with blond hair and a face more animated than a looney toons double feature. He loved hip-hop music. Manny was a talented artist; the kid could dream up some epic stuff, even back in those early times.

Moose was one of Sal's buddies. A Korean whippersnapper. He had jet black pin-straight hair combed over neatly to the left with handsome coin-slot eyes, and a heart the size of Central Park. He was a natural stoner. He would laugh at everything and always come up with a deep conversation that would blow your mind.

Donnie was our resident boxer. Not the most lethal fighter, but he had the heart of a lion. Donnie would fight anyone who stepped up. There was a photo shot of all the people Donnie had fought from sixth to eighth grade. It looked like an all-male class picture. There had to be fifty lads! He was muscular; his hair cut in a bald fade. That was the look for our crew, clean cut with short hair. His thick Boston accent and quick mind made him a comedic force to be reckoned with. He had a twin sister named Darla. Though they were twins, Darla was a natural beauty who looked nothing like Donnie…thank God.

Fort D was the dilapidated garage that was lumped behind Donnie's ranch-style home. Off-white vinyl siding gave way to lines of windows. This place was decked out, equipped with a wet bar and pool table. Donnie's parents were as cool as the flip side of a pillow. Kids from all over town began showing up there by the end of seventh grade. Fort D... what an iconic place in time! The peeling green paint covered long planks of cedar. The roof was made of tar shingles, folded up from years of winter exposure.

The doors had been taken off the front of the garage years ago. This left two square gaps where the elements and local teens would blow in at all times of the day and night. Two window frames were on each side of the structure, totally busted out. You could step up on the sill and jump right through if you needed to make a fast exit.

The roof pitched up almost like a church. Dirt floors kicked up dust like you were in a Saharan sandstorm on dry summer days. Mighty oak trees surrounded the yard, allowing shade to offer a cool refuge in the August heat. Fort D was quickly becoming a hot spot in town. All of us guys from Parker Middle School were the core of the operation.

#

By this time, we were dealing weed. Times were good. We were all still in school, healthy and enjoying the carefree life of middle schoolers. We had part-time jobs to support our extracurricular activities. I was the real clown of the bunch. My ice-blue eyes, chubby cheeks, and fast-talking tactics could charm the pants off a nun.

We all strived to be womanizers. Darla was a year behind us in school. So, she offered a streamline of younger, cute dames for us to put on our arms as trophies. On weekends, the old wooden shack turned into a freak show tent at the circus. The traffic could be compared to Route 128 at rush hour on a Friday night. Kids knew where the party was at, and they all showed up. Donnie's father, David, was the best guy ever. A strapping man in his early forties, he had a big mustache and glasses that looked like he had two 22-inch TV screens hanging in front of his eyes. That was the style back then. My dad had a pair as well. David worked nights. He would get home and enjoy a few ice-cold Bud Lights, catch a healthy buzz, and pass out. He was one of the hardest working guys you would ever meet. Noontime might as well have been midnight to David. We referred to him as "The Bear."

Almost every day, the most ruthless Whiffle ball games would pop off. Home run hitters from Parker Middle School would swing for the fences in the dirt lot that sat next to the garage. The small yard was perfect.

Flattened beer boxes made up the bases. The home plate sat right in front of the ladder leading to Ricky's house. We would fire over the roof, the plastic ball with air holes landing on Center Avenue. Some days there would be twenty fired-up teenage boys screaming full blast. The sounds in the air would remind you of Fenway Park during a Yankees playoff game. Weed smoke rose to the treetops. It smelled like the Allman Brothers Band was holding a concert on site.

A crash, then the sliding door on the elevated baby blue deck flung wide open, "Donnie! What the HELL is going on out here?"

"The Bear's" frustrated screams sounded out like a foghorn. Kids scattered like German roaches when the lights get cut on in a Hell's Kitchen apartment. When "The Bear" came out of his cave, it was time to roll. Donnie would be left alone, holding the bag for us all. That poor kid would have to take the wrap, and this was more than a common occurrence.

#

The Fort was becoming legendary. Word spread to our rival, Coolidge Middle School. We hated them. This was a rivalry that began between the hood kids and the more affluent Coolidge crew. The Coolidge kids were viewed as preppie, stuck-up rich guys. We did however welcome Coolidge girls. But don't think we neglected the hood girls. They were an awesome group of young women that had our backs in every way. We dated them, smoked with them, and had an all-around blast in their company. This group consisted of Darla and all her friends.

    The parties became so prevalent that we had to move them into the woods down the street. A group of thirty or more juvenile delinquents would sneak down a thin path canvassed by huge oak trees.

    The cover acted as a canopy, giving the maniac crowd stealth as we fired up doobies and started to experiment with booze. My first drink ever was in those very woods. I'll never forget that moment in my life, as it was the single turn that defined my addiction and downfall that would come in the very near future.

    It started with the arrival of my friend, Sullivan. Sullivan was a true pal. He was tall with sandy blond hair and the goofiest Irish smile you have ever seen. He was a guy I would put in my best friend category. In his tattered backpack lay cradled some stolen Underwood and Pierce vodka. The 1.75-liter bottle was clear plastic with a black and red label. This one memory is the type that is still burned in my mind to this very second. An odd day it was. It was a midsummer afternoon as we walked on the wooded path alone. Two pals that were soon to be drinking buddies in an especially important landmark moment. We walked good-naturedly as flies buzzed around our heads. Both of us were dressed in jean shorts and baggy t-shirts. There was a fallen tree that crossed a babbling brook. The cool water was music while the smells of green grasses made these

July memories nostalgically and forever imprinted in our minds. The air was hot and sticky, the stale and absence of wind made the sitting spot a Massachusetts sweat lodge. Rusty dirt clung to our kicks. Plopping down on the massive log provided a much-needed break. We pulled a half-full gallon of a spiked orange juice from the backpack. The generic plastic bottle had sweat beads that ran down it as we unscrewed the cap to the blended beverage. The mixture was yellow in tint. The amount of spirits Sullivan incorporated into Florida's most exported product was abominable. The juice was almost transparent.

  I grabbed the bottle and shook it like a paint shaker in Home Depot. We were about to get down to business. The blue snap-top came off the fusion of poison. I looked at Sullivan and "cheers" was all I said. Two hands cradled the vile concoction. My lips felt the wetness and burn that only alcohol can produce. The liquid sloshed down my throat. I was in shock. A slight gag at first made me worry. I gasped for air as I handed my Irish friend the bottle. With the first pull finished, a slow and ember-like burn hit the lining of my stomach. A complete rush! A real and absolute chemical reaction took place within my body. I was morphing. Whatever this strange potion was, I was in love. I think back and my first thought as this change took place was *That's what I am talking about. This is the way I want to feel all the time.* We both got as tall as Georgia pines. The conversation was deep and colorful. Spirits consumed my fragile young mind; feelings of invincibility and grandeur overcame me in biblical proportions. Bulletproof armor cloaked my body. Jokes poured out of my mouth colored in fountains of knowledge and creativity. I was lovestruck as the leaves blew above, with a light rustle shifting cool wind through my fine hair.

  Earlier we had acquired a pack of Old Gold cigarettes. I

took a drag, and the stolen smoke filled my lungs like a death chamber. The nicotine enhancing the low buzz in my noggin. This relaxed feeling was from the evil one. His presence was clearly in our homemade mixture. Seduction was in full swing. Anything this tempting and powerful can't be of God.

Too young to realize the event at hand, I glorified it right away. Drinking became an instant passion of mine. My Celtic genes bonded to the foreign substance. The chemicals released in my brain had all cylinders firing. We drained the bottle like sands of time in an hourglass.

After stumbling through romantic visions, dreary and vivid, the sadness finally took hold. Hours passed as we talked about the dark days we had already lived through and survived. Brothers in every way. A new bond between us, inseparable, a drunkard caricature of Laurel and Hardy.

Swaying as we left our self-proclaimed drinking hole, we shuffled our way out of the pitch-black woods. A single streetlamp projected a beam upon us at the entrance. It was a scene from Close Encounters. I was waiting to be transmitted into a Martian ship and taken to a faraway galaxy. The block was empty. Time was absent and fear was light-years from us. Walking home, it dawned on me that my new love affair was with booze. Craving for the brew had already begun to set in. I was an alcoholic after the first sip. It amplified every attribute that I liked about myself, and that wasn't a long list. I was extremely funny, and the boldness and carefree effects of the hooch made my speech uncensored. All filters were torn down like scaffolding at the end of a construction project.

Ash Street was a straightaway. I cruised to my destination with half-hearted vigor. Home was where the hell was. Mercury faithfully rises after nightfall, and so did the stress level in my childhood home. My blood was thin with cheap vodka, my breath stinking and vile. I walked up the elevated area to the house on the hill.

My home was a tall two-story mini mansion that Barry, my father, acquired in 1982. It was his pride and joy. I waded through the summer dew, stumbling around like a bull in a China shop. Three massive oaks that dated back to the Revolutionary War provided the backdrop to this magnificent home. It was snow white, contrasted by black wooden storm shutters. The house was built in 1929. A hand-laid stone foundation bordered the bottom where the basement met the pine structure.

A matching stone wall elevated to the backyard where a woodshed that we dubbed "The Little House" sat. Another white building sat at the back. This was our two-car garage that proudly stood under one of the mighty trees. A brick-laid patio was fashioned into the ground between the home and the stone wall in the rear.

The patio is where I would make my sneaky reentry. There was a black set of double doors that opened into a spooky basement, pitch as a raven. The boiler room smelled of home-heating oil even in the summer months. The furnace was from the Sixties and wasn't airtight. The basement was a half-finished project. Sheetrock walls draped down to greet the plywood flooring. The dampness would hit you like a ton of bricks. An old crap-brown refrigerator stood against the wall overlooking the haunted staircase, leading up into the main living quarters. I felt my way up the walls like a blind man in new surroundings. My drunkenness was worsening with every movement I made.

I busted into the kitchen around midnight. Avocado appliances dated this room; the Brady Bunch would be proud. An old TV with push-button channel changers sat on a white linoleum countertop. The windows overlooked the back patio and yard. Everyone was asleep. My younger brother, my mother, and my father were all in separate rooms on the top floor. Creeping like a disabled cat burglar, I centered myself as I climbed the curved staircase. Careful not to wake a soul, my uncoordinated left hand clutched the old shellacked wooden banister with a life and death urgency.

If Ma got up, World War III would break out. The ferocious beatings I had already taken for coming home blown on ganja had left a bad and literal bloody taste in my mouth. I crept into my room and closed the oak door. It was the sort that opened with a skeleton key, cherry tinted and strong. The queen mattress engulfed me; quicksand feelings surrounded my mind. The room was dark and quiet. A Motley Crew poster flagged the wall, how appropriate for a lost youth diving into addiction head on. Tomorrow was Saturday. It had begun. The total transformation had taken place and my innocence was lost. The weeks and months to come were defining.

#

The chase was on. Finding someone to buy alcohol was a full-time job. Older brothers and sisters of friends were hit up, raiding the liquor cabinets of classmates, and soon, even paying homeless tramps to score cold ones became commonplace. I was instantly hooked. Gin is a grotesque clear spirit made from the Juniper berry. I discovered it soon after my first attempt at drinking like a gentleman. One September night at Buddy's house, I got a taste for the stuff full force. I had acquired a pint of Mohawk Gin and decided once again orange juice would be the mixer. Keep in mind, Snoop Dog had just released a smash by the name of "Gin and Juice" not long before. I mixed a half bottle into an old soccer player's water jug, with a thick, clear rubber tube acting as a straw. The ice melted slowly, cooling the acidic alcohol-laced liquid that pooled within. I sucked on the straw like a toddler on the nipple of a milk bottle. Grimacing faces were animated and scrunched. Christmas flavors and hints of pine needles hit my taste buds and ran down the back of my throat, slow burning and insidious. My eyes widened; the world looked as though it was through a fisheye lens.

    This was not like the other varieties of alcohol I had been trying. Somehow it was causing a powerful and God-like affiliation within myself that can only be described as eloquent. I sat in the kitchen listening intensely as Al Green's "Let's Stay Together" blasted on Buddy's mom's sound system. The daze was welcomed as all problems floated off like a hot air balloon at the Montana State Fair. I was numb to any outside strife. Undercurrents of sadness blanketed my weary teen spirit. School was beginning and my already terrible scholastic enthusiasm was nose diving to an all-time low. Thinking as I sipped the potion, my future seemed fragile and pointless. There was no interest in playing baseball, a sport I once adored. I quickly found that alcohol and childhood trauma were like napalm and a lit match. In the recesses of my mind that night, I realized that drinking was going to play a major part in my future.

    Some girls from school arrived at the shack. Buddy invited them in, and we partook in heavy drinking and flirting. I loved the way booze opened me up and lowered my inhibitions. This was no longer the shy fat kid that would be asked to do the "truffle shuffle" every five minutes. This was now the sophisticated funny man, interesting and cultured. My comedic timing and cunning wit were attracting a crowd. The attention I received from my drunken antics and shenanigans made me hungry for more. This gin I had discovered made me who I had always wanted to be. Funny, confident, and on point.

As time marched on, the parties got bigger and more brazen. The crew expanded and shit-shows became more frequent. One of the neighborhood girl's moms worked as a house manager and event coordinator for the Stephens Estate Mansion, a massive sprawling estate in North Andover, Massachusetts that had a deep history. We were invited to overnight there as a gift to us for helping around the house, as this lady lived right next to Donnie. Moose, Ricky, Sally boy, Buddy, Sullivan, I, and a slew of others all made our way up the long curvy drive, pine trees danced above, and the cool September air filled the lungs of the puberty-stricken brood. Over the hill revealed an enormous brick and mortar monstrosity. It was three stories high, equipped with a brick carport and church arches. Doors that appeared ten feet tall stared us in the face as we gasped in wonder. Slate shingles appeared miles high to our young perspectives. The drive circled around the back and down the hill sat the Carriage House. This was an ancient structure that served as a horse barn and storage for the buggies that were once pulled. The place was old, early Nineteen hundreds by my best guess. An eerie feeling emerged as soon as we set foot on the property. A blackness that had the baby hair on the back of one's neck standing straight up. It was nighttime during transitional fall in New England. The spookiness was bad enough without being thrust into a haunted house that looked like it came from the mind of Stephen King.

      We traveled into a living room where time seemed to stand still. Oriental rugs and cherry antiques furnished a massive great room fully stocked with old portraits and stained-glass lamps. I felt like we were on the set of a Vincent Price movie. Astonished teens strained their necks looking at the soaring ceilings and Victorian artifacts that were on display.

The air was stagnant and aged. Faint hints of mothballs and cigar smoke from fancy parties' rich people had here still suspended in the air. Crystal ashtrays and candy dishes sat atop on what seemed to be countless one-of-a-kind pieces. Queen Ann chairs sat in all four corners with lion claw feet that supported them in all their splendor. The commercial kitchen was just down the hall. Stainless appliances with matching countertops and a massive farmer's sink brought the room together. The padlock on the old wooden door signaled us that there was booze inside. Our overnight bags were stuffed to the hilt with Southern Comfort, Captain Morgan Spiced Rum, and Aftershock.

We all hurried to the second floor to stow our belongings in the sleeping quarters. Fifteen separate rooms lined the massive hallway. On both sides of the aisle were well-made doors that opened to decent-sized bedrooms, each with two twin beds and a private bath. The bedspreads were crimson, and the walls were a paisley tan. White porcelain sinks and deep tubs met white tile with black grout in the lavatories. Manic teens ran and screamed like children on a playground. The crew was pumped! With our chaperone downstairs, we began to hit the bottle with great enthusiasm. This party was coed…let the games begin.

#

Teen sexuality ran wild. Couples paired off and went to different rooms to fall in temporary love. Infatuation that was only for a moment, as we were young, and life was about to warp us into strange and far away paths that only God knew. My love had lips that were soft as Asian silk. Her long hair whipped in my face as she straddled my eager lower half.

The whiskey we shared pulsed through our hearts,

barreling through each chamber as it coursed its way to our already euphoric minds. Living in the moment, we were drunk with cheap Canadian Club and passion. Time faded. My transformation as a romantic came bold and sudden. My heart burst through with affection and sentiment. Taken aback, blown away with sudden emotion and admiration, she made me realize that I was not meant for this earth. I was better suited for some far away interplanetary solar system built on the emotions of the heart. A realization that I didn't love as other people did, suddenly coated me as hard as the candy shell that wraps an M&M.

Soon the bottle was dry as a Utah creek bed. The hunt for more was on. The dark wood and dim lights made the hallway look like a tunnel of sadness. Something Stanley Kubrick would dream up in one of his legendary films. The dull moans of girls rang in the distance. It was an underage orgy. I am certain Sodom and Gomorrah were blushing in comparison. I stumbled upon Moose. He was in the same pickle. We met in the kitchen where a naked lightbulb hung from a cloth cord. A large knife was extracted from the butcher's block. Our eyes darted at the padlock on the liquor room in unison. We cackled like drunkards as he pried the cheap True Value bolt off the rotted wooden frame of the cabinet door. Eureka, we entered the holy grail. Bottles of all types stared us down. We took choice top-shelf liquor bottles and jammed them into a pillowcase with the urgency of contestants on Supermarket Sweep. The alcoholic traits were already seeping out. We had booze upstairs. But to us, there was never enough.

The scream room was downstairs in the basement. The room was infamous because, in legend, five of the Steven's family committed suicide with a noose and swayed there for days before the cold corpses were found by the help. It was rumored to be haunted. There were running bets that no one could sleep in it overnight. The bet was turned down by every tough guy in the place.

As the night moved on, the group funneled into the basement like a bunch of tourists being led into King Tutt's tomb, torches and all. The stairs creaked as terrified teens marched single file into the grasp of the witch's den. You could feel the evil at once. The stone foundation made up the walls. A loose dirt floor was underfoot. With a damp Bostonian must in the air, dripping sounds chimed with cold September wind that screamed through the cracks of the aging structure. A horror scene, the girls held the arms of their protectors. Something not of this world joined us. The grim feeling that we were not alone smashed our psyche. This was a séance even though a Ouija board was absent as we ventured into the black unknown. The historic nature of the dwelling left us trembling as thoughts of the five souls that took their own life ran through our half-cocked minds. Even drunk, this was a scary trek. There was no electric lighting in this portion of the mansion. We relied on Bic lighters to guide us.

Right as we huddled in the very middle of the room, two loud voices came stalking out of the shadows. A loud roar! The whole lot of us ran like banshees, up the stairs, blind and falling over one another like a fire in a crowded theater. I went back to the door to slam it shut, the loud crash of two beer bottles froze me in place. Buddy and Donnie were howling in concert. Those bastards. We were so drunk that we missed the fact that those two practical jokers were missing during the basement excursion.

#

Months flew by. We were having fun. Weekly hood games were conducted. At this point, we were training for the regular occurrence of running from the Reading police. Fence hopping was one such competitive event. One that Seeky had in the bag. His body looked like a daddy long legs on steroids. He would gallop a few steps, then his stilt-like legs would hit the chain-link fence and he would catapult over with the greatest of ease. No one could even come close. An event that served him well on many occasions. He would even taunt the Reading police officer rookies to chase him just to save his chubby, turtle-like compadres.

Seeky ran like the wind. One time they surrounded him by Washington Park. He was cornered as we all watched from across the railroad tracks. He sprinted down an alley between some houses and dove on the pavement before the fuzz had even turned the corner. With them out of sight, he threw the empty pack of Marlboros that contained an eighth of dank Cali bud behind the tire of a parked car. After a quick search, the cops brought him home where he took his lickings, then snuck out of his top-floor window, cut through the park, and successfully obtained the discarded weed.

The administration at Parker Middle School, along with the Reading police, were now aware of what went on at Fort D. Parking bikes in the front of the house was now off limits. We had lookouts after dark watching for headlamps to beam. If the cops rolled up, a signal was thrown, and any party activity halted at once.

Twenty youngsters would huddle inside the crumbling walls, just out of sight. Seeky had dug a secret hole in the dirt floor where weed, booze, and graffiti paint could be stashed. An old couch we found on the side of the road was plopped on top of the makeshift floor-safe just in case the cops got nosey.

The girls would sit there looking pretty, acting as paperweights so the loot couldn't be confiscated. Drugs and alcohol now played a major role in our daily life.

#

The Hemp Fest was a huge production put on by MassCann, a pro-marijuana legalization group. They would pull permits for the biggest open space pro-pot rally in all New England. Besides Humboldt County, California, I think this was the biggest one at the time. A bunch of us left Buddy's house on Main Street and proceeded through the Hood to the Reading Depot. The Purple Line commuter rail is an above-ground train that will take you from Reading to Boston in about thirty short minutes. The great big silver train approached in the distance. There was an ear-splitting noise from metal-on-metal grinding let out from the massive wheels below. The engine stopped; the conductor was a lesbian-looking lady with short hair. She hopped off the staircase and onto the hardtop as she signaled us to board the train, a huge crowd of stoner rejects. Long hair hippies, rockers, and high school kids all stoned from various pre-game gatherings waded in.

As I stepped over the yellow line onto the stairs that led up to the train car, my heart raced. This was my first festival and during a time when pot was still illegal. We had heard tales this event was free reign, a day where cops turned a blind eye to toking up. It was a massive protest-style rally where the people took the power back by using the sheer force of numbers. There were more of us in one spot than law enforcement could handle. The two-person seats were the color of plums, almost a maroon tint that had a leathery smell that embedded in my brain. Old newspapers riddled the rare, but empty, seats. The train quickly became standing room only. It felt like an eternity before we took off.

Right before departure, the ticket taker shouted, "If anyone smokes on this train, I'm going to throw you off and the police will be waiting for you at the next stop!" And then we took off.

After the second stop, the locomotive halted in the middle of a densely wooded area about halfway to the city. The ticket taker appears and gives a shout, "Ok, spark 'em up!"

We couldn't believe our ears. Instantly the smoke started to billow. Huge glass bongs came out of backpacks. Blunts were lit, joints ignited like tinder. My ocean blue eyes began to burn as if we were in tear gas training at boot camp. I stood up. The car was a fog chamber. I could not see in front of me. The visibility was a matter of inches. I had not even put a spliff to my lips and I was feeling tall. The train was a sea of burnouts of all ages and backgrounds. It was a circus freak show that rivaled any tent in the old-time state fairs. A psychedelic vibe took over. There were tie-dye t-shirts dancing with distant music. Preppies, jocks, band geeks, and metal heads were all engaging in peace, all in the name of drugs. What a concept! People of all shapes, sizes, and financial status were partying together while sharing smoke, snacks, and anything else they had on hand. This was a true commune. I realized then two key things about drugs. One was that substance abuse does not discriminate, all people are subject to its enchanting and destructive power. The second was that controlled substances were here to stay in America. We are raised with an entitlement to have a good time.

The Boston Common, where the festival was taking place, was blasting in technicolor. Lush and electric green grass covered the sprawling hills. Smells of peanut vendors and a purple haze infiltrated the soul with great pleasure and understanding.

The black metal one hitter I carried with me was pulled from my pocket as Seeky generously packed my bowl. Flick went the Bic, and I was blazing in public without a care in the world. Upper-class college students with dreadlocks danced to reggae music, goths were seen dropping acid, and some poor and misunderstood wasted youth inhaled plump balloons of nitrous oxide. A stage was set up on an elevated hill with oak trees behind it. A passionate speech from the podium preached pro-pot rhetoric, reminiscent of some of the Sixty's protests.

The movement was in full swing. A gathering of the fringe. Freedom from government oppression, our voices were great and strong. Most were there to get high, but one thing was for sure. In 1996, the seeds of political change were being sown for the full legalization of recreational marijuana. What felt like an impossibility was soon to become a firm reality in the not-so-distant future.

With the September sun beating down on the festival grounds, this stoned version of Central Park was literally alive and breathing. Bongo drums beat, circles of hippies searching for enlightenment smoked fine greenery in Phish t-shirts and Birkenstock sandals. My friends and I sat on manicured blades of grass. "Spill the Wine" by The Animals blasted as a Rastafarian hit a massive whalebone ganja pipe. His lengthy dreads and colorful Rasta cap blew me away. He passed me the piece while my inexperienced and fragile mind was trying to understand how this eclectic group could melt together like butter and onions in a sauté pan. Beams of sunlight reflected off an onyx bust of Paul Revere, a massive statue that towered over one of the oldest landmarks in our great nation.

Boom! A single shot rang out. A drunkard with a gun fired off a round into the sky. People ducked and scattered into the recesses of the park. It wasn't long after that the short attention spans of the self-proclaimed protesters forgot all about this pre-September 11 act of violence. The world was a different place in those times. Columbine had yet to happen. Gun violence and mass shooters were few and far between.

Mounted police trotted through; steel boots clanged on the hardtop path that sat right behind our makeshift camp. Some cute skater chicks conversed with Buddy and me. Donnie held court under a distant oak tree. His spiky black hair and piercing eyes seemed to have his listeners in a trance. One of these prima donna girls pulled out a smooth slide-out weed container. Beautiful choice buds with crystal hairs and red strains intertwined with plush-green leafy explosions. After pooling our money together, we purchased an eighth. This purchase was for later that night. We surely couldn't go home without some foreign products! Finding this kind of top-notch Lodi Dodi was a score and a half in those days. We now had our special reserve for a post-game hemp fest celebration.

Live music began on the main stage. Alternative rock, reggae, and new age jammed out of the huge Marshall stacks that appeared to stand miles high. Mushrooms, pills of all varieties, plus strange and inviting powders circulated in the black market around us.

It was time to get going. Exhausted, we began rounding the troops up. Reading, Massachusetts bound, we walked back to the Purple Line in a desolate fog. Familiar surroundings were just what we needed.

Pale Irish skin contrasted with bloody eyes, a dead giveaway that we had just come from the biggest pot-smoking extravaganza this side of the Sunshine State. A blast was had; new friends were made. Thank God this was before the days of YouTube, all presidential hopes would have been crushed.

We arrived at Buddy's crib at dusk with a new badge of honor upon our chests. We made our first HempFest a great success. We guzzled Mike's Hard Lemonade and Jack Daniels

Lynchburg. Cute honeys flocked as "Thug Life" and "Total Devastation" blared from the six-Disc CD changer on the old wood floor. Laughter and fellowship, a clear understanding of friendship, and a brotherhood bound by blood were creating a group of life-long chums. We were a crew. We were each other's therapy. We were made men.

  The night turned to early morning. Crisp twilight sky encompassed this September folly. Girls paraded back before curfew and the crew dwindled. Laramy, a hilarious newcomer with a shaved head and an epic schnoz, along with Buddy, Seeky, and me were all that remained after this fairy-tale day of drug use. Buddy alluded to the fact that it was time to blaze. An old honey container, in the shape of a bear, with the top removed, was our go-to pipe. Tinfoil and elastic bands wrapped around and gave an airtight seal to this makeshift bowl, while pinholes pricked into the foil allowed smoke to enter its chamber. A spot was melted into the front where the label once was. A hollow body of a pen was stuck in, acting as a straw where the smoke was to be inhaled. Buddy, always the pot-perfectionist, even colored red lines in this bear's eyes. His twisted sense of humor never ceased to amaze me. This creative homemade bong was dubbed "Honey Bear."

  The bowl was loaded with today's score. A cheap gas station lighter ignited the crystal hairs and colorful leaves of nature's escape. Smoke rolled in the atmosphere, each stoner ripping huge hits, then choking with tears of joy running down our faces. This session was a nightcap. The vibrant colors of a Lava lamp cascaded the cheap walls, while within its insides, there were blobs of purple plasma floating in suspension within the alien-like glass container. With a blacklight plugged in, ultraviolet illumination uncovered every imperfection in the room. Posters activated by the Seventies-era UV light appeared to blow off the wall. You know, the kind that looked harmless in their normal form, but under a black light, they were a full-tilt experience for the avid stoner. We laid in awe. The bunk beds, the couch, a makeshift pallet on the floor. It was a teen flophouse with a hallucinogenic twist. Strange feelings that I was floating up into the air took over my thought process. It was as if I was Reagan from "The Exorcist." Immaculate levitation occurred in my mind. This went on for a good ten minutes that might as well have been an eternity.

"Does anyone else feel like they are floating?"

My question made Buddy sit straight up in bed like a commuter awakening to a six in the morning alarm clock.

"Oh my God, I can't believe you just said that" he exclaimed.

The other boys all burst out in gagging laughs. We chuckled as we realized the drug's bizarre effects were the same for all of us. We talked and compared what we were experiencing. This wasn't an ordinary bag of grass. This mythological batch was forever dubbed "Floater Weed."

High school started the next week. In the past few years, we had become a unit. Hood kids, warriors of weed. Drunk Dons of Parker Middle School and absolute legends in our little hometown of Reading, Massachusetts. There were a million stories in between, too many to name. These were just some examples of the times we shared in middle school. The next leg of the tour was just as defining. A whole new world was about to materialize The girls got hotter, the drugs much harder, and the drinking became local folk-lure that still burns in the ears of aspiring party animals to this very day. All aboard passengers! The crazy train is about to leave the station.

Chapter 2

High School High

Reading Memorial High School was a brick monstrosity that sat on Oakland Road in Reading, Massachusetts. If you are not daydreaming too hard, it is about a thirty-minute walk from Buddy's house. The first day of ninth grade kicked off with a bang. Some of the crew spent the night at Buddy-Boy's, making sure we had enough time for a wake and bake before we ventured into this brand-new situation. Buddy, Laramy, Sullivan, and I lit up some White Widow before meeting up with a larger band of loonies down in the hood. New jeans, kicks, and Starter football jackets gave us the appearance of an all-white disgruntled version of N.W.A., the hip-hop group popular during the start of our high school days.

       The joints burned continually as we made the voyage on foot. Stoned was the way of the walk. Fearless of upperclassmen, we strutted up the busy sidewalks of Reading proper acting like fools. The cemetery sat in the shadows of a landmark church in Reading Square, a massive, old, white building with an enormous steeple that practically erected into the clouds.

At the very top was a bell the size of a Volkswagen that bonged at the top of each hour, reminding the good people of Reading exactly what time it was as they went about their day. Reading Square was full of restaurants, storefronts, and local pharmacies. A sleepy suburb that was full of soccer moms, businesspeople, and law-abiding citizens. The scene was Rockwellian. A perfect place to raise your family just outside the rat race that was Boston, Massachusetts. This picturesque little village was the perfect deception, a façade, a sugar-coated top layer that masked the devious and drug-filled world that lay just underneath the skin.

    The cemetery was elevated. Long paved paths divided grave plots that dated back to the Revolutionary War. Ghosts were among us. Even during the day, fragments of the afterlife would shine through on the right of the main road that leads through this morbid resting place. A family site of three graves stood up on the grass with a stone border. Two crumbling gravestones with words you could barely make out sat on each side of a five-foot statue of a young girl holding her hands out like the Virgin Mary, palms to the sky. Jenny Penny was someone from a past life. A youngster that left before her time, keeping a watchful eye over all the guests that passed through her dreary and permanent home. Sitting in front of her, smoking gas, and telling stories, we would all pay the toll to Jenny. We placed shiny one-cent pieces in her palms as she sat stone-silent and proud. We were stoned ourselves. Lab chimps that had escaped a THC testing facility, on the run and full of teenage energy that would blow the socks off any adult who dared to test us.

    Walking through the back-parking lot of the school was odd. There were tons of new faces and we watched as many of our classmates' puffed cigarettes and were sipping SoBe as they collected their morning thoughts. We cruised around to the front entrance. The doors flung open, and we walked right dead smack into Mrs. O, the hard-hitting assistant principal that was just transferred in from the big city. She stood all of four feet and eleven inches tall, dirty blond hair, bangs covering her large forehead. A brown knit dress, too tight in my opinion, draped her tiny but intimidating body.

"Where are you boys off to?" she asked.

We froze like a team of geriatric lawn jockeys. Mouths dropped open; saucer-size glazed eyes hit the floor like sad puppies who just peed on the carpet. The green and white checkered floor couldn't save us. No matter how bad we wanted to keep staring at it, her voice loudened, and she meant business.

"Ok, where's your first class, gentlemen?" she sneered.

Laramy thought this would be a great time to inject some humor into the situation. "Well, I'm looking for Rocket Science 101!"

Daggers! She looked like she was going to rip his oversized Adam's apple right from his scruffy throat.

"We're holding that class right down at the main office. Mister?" She was asking for his name. She got it. He quickly cowered at her response.

"I'll be watching you boys," she threw her fingers to her big green eyes and pointed them back at us. This first impression was not good, planting a seed of hatred she had for us that would grow into an all-out loathing of anything hood for years to come.

Even at our young age, we had made a dominant splash in Reading's party scene. Older kids and faculty alike knew who we were. Parker Middle School administration had even gone as far as making some phone calls to Reading Memorial High

School to let them know there were a batch of bad seeds on their way to wreak havoc.

The girls? Wow! These Bostonian queens were mind-blowing. Blonds, redheads, outspoken Italian princesses, and Nubian goddesses. We traveled the halls in bewilderment. This felt like a new beginning. A stage was set for us that we could have never dreamed of. The realm of high school had a feel to it only described as unchartered waters. It was like one of the Seven Wonders of the World. The mystery of it all blew us away.

Classes were intimidating. I had fallen out of academics years ago. My pot-smoking rampages and booze-fueled diatribes were a thing of legend, even for a middle schooler. By this time, I had taken a great interest in drinking. Months would pass by like zooming cars on the Autobahn in Germany without me turning in my homework or cracking a book open even once. As a child young in addiction, I played it off as most do. I was just a boy having fun. Society in Reading told us we were just partying. I met new and exciting playmates, a pig pen of hurting and lost souls who were also swirling into the beginning stages of addiction. We were oblivious to the defects of character, spiritual sickness, and demonic possession that was beginning to spawn in us.

#

The back-parking lot was the land of the lost. It was an elevated flatness filled with Honda Civics, Buick Regals, and a variable plethora of other buckets of bolts that sat in waiting. This was a melting pot of future addicts and burnouts. Comedians, musicians, and street performers all shined like lamps, setting the stage for so many crazy times.

Love showered. The importance one feels when accepted by our older peers is paramount. The back-parking lot was where I was introduced to a sparkling group of young women that became lifelong friends: Charla, the two Claire's, and NaTiana. They were all uniquely placed into my life, presented with friendly faces that welcomed me with open arms. I was hilarious to them. My chubby cheeks and outgoing personality, the fearlessness of my comedic delivery, and my wacky sense of humor sparked their interest at once. They were truly kind.

Charla was wearing a pea soup green Adidas tracksuit, five times too big. She was a carrot top, fire-infused with ghost-white Scottish skin embedded with millions of beautiful freckles and the eyes of happiness. Claire One was a tall drink of water. Long, dark, reddish-brown hair, a cherubic face, and big eyes that all the boys loved. She had a style that crossed a hip-hop vixen with a dancing day's hippy gal. She was an American sweetheart just below the surface. Clair Two was one-of-a-kind. She had long pin-straight brown hair with a Boston accent that would stop traffic, and a smile so big and beautiful you couldn't help but fall in love, even if just the platonic kind.

Then she arrived. Natosha was a Jewish gem. Short and stunning with the most intimate voice in Reading history. She was cool and trendy. A pop-culture phenomenon.

She loved music. The Band's "The Weight" was a staple song in her metallic blue Chevy Nova. Standing there, denim from head to toe, she projected class and eloquence like no other. When Nat spoke, it was like watching "The Beautician and the Beast." She was Fran Drescher with a cool tint to her aura. These ladies introduced me to Reading's hippy counterculture.

They brought us to the sprawling back entrance of the high school, where the sound of skateboards clanged as the trucks ground the rails on the steep hill to hell. There we met a hard-drinking bunch of ragtag characters whose fair-haired dreads held the stench of cloves and Patchouli oil. A mixed bag, this crew mirrored the collage of folks at HempFest, except the ages were closer in proximity.

Mikey was in my grade, his Sid Vicious tee made him an instant brother. A mane of curly black hair draped to his neck, he was a master impressionist and rogue scholar. He was always deep in thought. Emilia, an eccentric goth and photographer lived a stone's throw from the back-parking lot. A big breasted ninth grade recluse, she was reserved and used sarcasm as a second language. I instantly drew to her. Her adopted sister was a warrior girl named Honey. And that's her government name all day! She was a photographer in the making. Smoking and picture snapping on the screened-in porch ate up many moons.

#

Mikey and I started a drug relationship right away. My introduction to amphetamines came in the form of pharmaceuticals. Ritalin and Adderall were prescribed as an ADD medication to troubled teens. Parents agreed to dose their children in return for some sort of peace and hike in grades. In my experience, all the kids on these pills hated taking them. It made them zombies with math skills.

The opportunist that I am, friending these tools was an easy way to score. I fell in love with the speedy draw. Mikey and I self-educated ourselves on the inner workings of speed in art class. In plain sight, we would huddle, sucking the time-release coating off a twenty milligram of Ritalin. A dollar bill's fine linen texture was perfect to fold over the pill and use a quarter to press it into a powdery mix.

As the teacher would draw example pieces with Sketch crayons, Mikey and I would be lining up rails. A dangerous ballet with tense moments of need. As the underpaid teacher turned his back, the chunky pharma was sucked into a jagged McDonald's straw, funneling the dry payload into our pink and irritated nostrils. The drip was half the fun. A putrid, stale burn that invaded our taste buds. The drugs mixed with the mucus membranes in the throat. Chemical flavors chaffed young tissue. The pupils dilated almost at the point of impact. Awake, alert, and creativity undefined. My back thrust into the placid seat behind. Angel eyes glazed, twitching like two shaking balls of jelly, scanning side to side as air conditioning cooled the lenses.

  A new high, a frantic feeling of dopamine-induced primal rage. Sexual fantasies outshined rational thought. The room melted away; petite classmates became future pornography, saving them for after class when I could skip and find alone time in post-puberty self-abuse. Amphetamines, for me, were sex in powder form. While high, I was a useless pervert even in the infancy of my use. I was scoring zip locks full on a bi-daily basis. Distribution became a means to obtain my favorite amount...more. I found myself shifting around to different groups within the microcosm. The hood gents one day, hippies the next. I was shocked to see the doors that drugs were opening, even the jocks were giving me invites to gatherings within their clique.

  Sullivan and I started to branch out. His mother was a full-blown heroin addict. Oxycontin is a powerful narcotic. We were about to cross the plane. He had scored some of these from the matriarch. Eighty milligram tablets sliced into quarters...morsels of doom. The apartment was dead across from Burger King on Main Street. He lived on the towering third floor. A gruff beige staircase led up to the devil's den.

  She lay in the back room, on the nod from huge doses

of Afghani brown. Nervousness clouded; a dim kitchen light cast enough illumination to navigate within. The old TV flickered; a strategically placed boom box flattened on the shag carpet. The white plastic blinds twisted closed. The air conditioning was turned to absolute zero. Breath took gas form as it hit the frozen atmosphere.

    A glass coffee table had a mirror reflection. A cheap crystal ashtray, nothing like the ones in my parent's house, held half-lit buts and an orange syringe cap. My drinking confidant was about to transcend into something much different and sinister. His boney fingers wielded a steak knife, ever so gently crossing lines in the precocious pill. The quarters were minuscule and ominous. He displayed a tutorial of how to properly ingest this deadly spirit. His thumb and index finger pinched the pebble with absolute care. He placed it between his top and lower front teeth. Chomps of silence, the gritty substance was foul tasting and so small was the piece that the experience was over as soon as it began.

    "That's it?" Sullivan sprang up and turned on "Dark Side of the Moon" by Pink Floyd. On TV, "The Wizard of the Oz" was paused at the exact moment the lion on the MGM promo roared the second time. Lots of thought went into this trip we were about to go on.

    Simultaneously the tracks played. Audio and visual. The sound to the TV muted so Floyd would complement the movie like chocolate and peanut butter. We started to float. The slick black leather couch was buttery. Marlboros smoldered as the opioids slowly burned in my twisted belly. It was dark, lethargic, and unforgiving.

    Pinned pupils rejected the light. Migraine melodies danced like marionettes. Mental strongholds crumbled; this drug was the strongest narcotic encounter to date. The control was absent. For the first time, I felt my resolve slip away, a demon. Opiate tranced, time was still as Oz turned to color. The Tinman stood cold. His oiled jaw moved in vain.

Dashing to the bathroom, I struggled to lift the seat as I vomited a dark cola like substance into the internal outhouse of the low-income apartment. For such a tiny mass, the monstrous drug produced an acidic rank in my stomach. Liquified lining clung to the bowl. The smell was like a screwdriver, thick and yellow. Bile was all that remained. I returned to the living room with the remnants of death dribbling from my chin. This was not for me. I peered at Sullivan. His experience was much different. Nodding and scratching his skin to its third degree, he reveled in the beast. Pleasure points in his face indicated he was in the clutches of a spirit that had a deep hold on his fading soul. The first dance was sweet for him.

The road forked for us at this very moment. His speech slurred; attitude scarred from the substance. His chest rattled with enlarged organs and nicotine. I hated what my friend had become from the gate. I was not with this shit. The credits rolled in unison with Sullivan's vacant eyes. The heavy oak door slammed behind me as I escaped from an opium den. He didn't even notice I had fled. Moving around was my only option.

#

The old town dump was now grown over. A long path led up to rocky gravel and sandstone visions. We traveled as a pack, like wolves on a hunt. The hippies were gathering. The path gave way to a narrow opening, tall blades of grass bent in the March wind.

The trail descended into an opening that resembled a Renaissance fair. Piping flames clawed to the heavens. Loose sundresses on teen dreams swirled in a celebratory dance. As we leveled into the pit, smoldering fires crackled in tune.

Smokey notes intruded the sense of smell, clinging to one's clothes, weaving into the fabric. Leaving evidence of your whereabouts to anyone in arm's reach. A keg of ice-cold brew was the main attraction in this masquerade. Grunting heathens lifted the rare prize into a plastic trash can full of freezing cold ice cubes.

The bread line was open. A five-dollar fee was needed to partake in the evening festivities, collected by an elder of the tribe, scruff and mature. Red solo cups cradled the social lubricant that summonsed the brood. This was a brand-new experience, never before have I encountered this pagan ritual. I paid for two cups. Standing toe to toe with drinking legends, I filled my chalices, then was on my way back to the end of the line. The cold carbonation gurgled in my throat. A black hooded sweatshirt cloaked my freshman profile, a stoned druid, instantly intoxicated and gleaming with pride. Jokes were hurled, deep banter spat by street theologians. Athletes reflected upon past victory. Loser stereotypes with glazed eyes stared into the fire, dampened by life's sorrows, dreaming of better days. Drink flowed like Hawaiian waterfalls, crisp and clean. Stars above speckled the night sky, mighty oaks swayed, tarnished by darkness and flickering with an orange glow. Electric waves, an eclectic jargon mystifying the scene. I took in the evening with a boldness I had never allowed. This was home. Love present, bonding and deep. I was part of something much greater than myself; it felt beautiful. My heart burst with acceptance.

Outcasts found their way. The hour of need had passed; new paths opened as I freed my mind. Hashish cooked in water pipes, chugging and strong. Youthful lungs choked greasy smoke, leaving blood cells pregnant with inspiration. We fed Buddy's dog, indulged her with Hornsby's Hard Cider. She was lapping from a charcoal grey doggy dish. She stumbled, half-lit, a terrier with a ball of harnessed energy. The drunkenness' cultivated hilarity within our teenage rage.

A used-up tire was thrown into the dying flame. A plume of raven smoke escalated into a vibrant night sky, rubber fumes cloaking smells of marijuana and cigars. Plastered underclassmen were sent on a firewood expedition, being under the Claire One and Two's wings ensured me with VIP treatment. I had it made with my female connections. No troublesome chores or fraternity initiation tactics were used on me. In Reading's party scene, it was all who you knew.

Flashlights beamed over the early morning hills. Screams of warning, like thwarted zebras alerting the herd, outshined by beats of bongo drums. We were busted. Lashing groups of partygoers ran hard in every direction. Confusion set in on the aging overweight Reading police. Off-trail escape routes were pre-mapped and rehearsed. We retreated over the failing chain-link fence at the Lakeview Apartments. Waiting chariots picked us up. Sullivan, double fisted with beers, pogoed on the broken fence, flying straight up, landing directly on his face. The hardtop shattering his nose and splitting his upper lip open. It looked like the skin of a plum, blood streaming thin and plenty. He staggered to his feet. Muddy jeans gave him the appearance of a homeless man.

"I didn't drop 'em!" he exclaimed. The alcoholic in him refused to party foul the last drinks in the arsenal. Addicted pride and fear of sobriety lunged him into injury. One hard-drinking son of a bitch, he was.

Clair One and I mastered the art of party throwing. On Thursday afternoons we would both start calling multiple facets of Reading's social class. Crisscrossing conversations, cunning and repetitive. Plans were hatched like farm fresh eggs. The plan was to call every different group and proclaim that "I heard there's a party at Stage Fort Park this weekend." By Friday evening, the whole lot of fantastic freaks would make the forty-minute drive to Gloucester, Massachusetts. A sleepy coastal secret, Gloucester overlooked a prime area for commercial fishing on the Bay States' outer limits. Summer months closed in. Stage Fort Park was a pin-drop sized cove. Long curved staircases made of concrete and stone-dipped alphabetical letter C's facing each other like fighters at the weigh-in. They ended abruptly upon a light cocoa-colored beach. The cove was a half-moon shape, completely tucked back, out of sight, a small dwelling shrouded in privacy. A trippy attraction, waves breaking, sea salt water in esoteric motion. The summer air hung low and firm. Samuel Adams popped, Bic lighters replicating bottle openers. Magic Hat Number Nine erect in Coleman ice chests, bottles of Goldschlager relaxed and neat.

    Button mushroom caps bulged with a blue flame, infiltrating the magic. Grown in Vermont cow patties, the illicit drug was rare but a sought-after find. I purchased a half ounce with speed proceeds. I munched down three gargantuan caps and two regulatory stems. I immediately guzzled an ice-cold Rumplemintz straight out of its textured, glassy bottle. The fix was in.

    In thirty minutes time, the poison entered my bloodstream. Staring out to sea, a blurry soiree of electric color and shape took my thought to its most primal place. Psychedelic pharma, tripping balls in the warmest sense. A funky kid, I wore a black t-shirt, jean shorts, and a half-tilted back Atlanta Braves fitted cap. The earth's natural gravitational pull lured me sneakily near the water's edge.

    This particular beach had a strange phenomenon

buried just beneath the surface. Where the water met the sand, once retreated, if one were to step hard on the dampness, a green light would glow around the footprint. Local bacteria grew on the beach. The sudden impact would ignite a chemical reaction, giving the appearance of this glow. It looked like when the floor lit up under Michael Jackson in the "Billy Jean" video. Tie-dye t-shirts took on a vibrant life. Are His works not amazing?

Faces melted like wax of a candle in horrifying delight. A strange mood. Ocean smells berated the senses, seagulls cawed, and the footprints of a crab's pitter-patter in the dim moonlight. Waves of energy stunned my vision. Curving lines of a spectrum that flowed down from sky to ground. Artistic dreams manifested as the blowing wind cut violently. The souls around me drank and danced to classic rock music. An understanding of the earth. A nod from the Lord, revelations of mystery, a drug-induced ceremony. The great bubble was shown, an atmospheric depth, I saw how far the universe was spread.

This trip was the moment I realized how huge this all is. How egotistical and fragile the human condition is. It's all an illusion, the energy transferred into bone and blood that will die as we escape into the vast. We will never comprehend. Moments like these are a Spirit-driven gift. Too much for a fifteen-year-old mind to fathom, any mind really. I went home feeling we are not alone for the first time in my life.

#

Klonopin sales were up. Sullivan and I were beaming. I got them a dollar apiece, sold them for two, plenty of wiggle room for a now full-blown addict to eat up all the profits. Scalding amounts were ground up and then dumped into Hawaiian Punch. Walking and drinking this benzodiazepine cocktail was always an adventure. A dangerous drug similar to Xanax, it affects the same part of our brain as alcohol. I must have looked like a bear coming out of a cave in spring. Heavy breathing, sweats in the summer sun. Main Street, Reading was a track of shame at this time. Families passed in minivans as my docile eyes rolled in my orbits. Young and addicted, a travesty.

    Keep in mind that I wasn't trading one addiction for another. I was adding to the grocery list of problems in my short and devilish life. Seeds of self-hatred and spirits of darkness were summoned. Still drinking heavily, I recognized that booze was the starter. It opened the gates of my rage.

    Enter cocaine.

#

    The bathroom was white and pristine. A short man, a hippy counterpart, dumped the rocky white powder onto the water tank of a crisp toilet. A filthy dollar bill was rolled into a tube, the tool to snap up the creator of energy. Placing it to my nose, I snorted like Snuffalupagus. Vacuumed force, my head snapped back into writhing motions. A numbing drip coated my alcohol-filled throat. I gagged as tastes of diesel and gas purged my esophagus. Feeling as if I was falling down an elevator shaft, my stomach was full of butterflies.

    The line was crossed. The sixteen beers ingested suddenly had no effect. Rejuvenated, I burst through the bathroom door with a lion's roar. The partygoers greeted me like a star! Screaming my name in unison, I had arrived. I was stumbling drunk moments before. Ready to call it a night. Suddenly the night was reborn, a new beginning. It was as if I had just walked in the door. This was deadly. To find a drug that meshed with alcohol, unlike the speed pills which made your bile burn, was a recipe for disaster.

#

Weeks passed. Weekend cocaine use spiraled. I planned the party at Barry's mansion. My childhood home was to be opened to all. My parents were going out of town. My baby brother was to stay with my aunt. Dumb with trust, they left the jester alone to his devices. Days leading up to their departure, I put out an open invitation to every high school student on campus. Rumors swirled; plans set.

My mom and dad were going to two separate spots for vacation. My mom was flying to Myrtle Beach; my dad driving to Vermont on a golf trip. Friday approached and came with the force of a comet. They were dropping me off in front of Reading Memorial High School when the old wood panel station wagon sputtered to a complete stop in front of the school.

The engine struggled to turn as Barry cranked the key in anger. My heart was punching out of my chest. I had hundreds of people showing up to this thing. My dad says he's calling a tow truck. One last turn and old Betsy fired up! It was like being drunk behind the wheel and the cops flying past you with the lights on. Whew!

I snorted thirty milligrams of Ritalin in the bathroom after lunch and decided to ditch sixth period to get a head start on the partying. I got a ride with an older girl. Running up to my bedroom, I dashed for the coke. One gorilla finger-sized line was laid out for each. She hit first and made way for me. I high-fived my Motley poster and screamed "Paaaarty" before snapping the hog leg up into my brain. I started doing shots of tequila.

The hardcore guests started to funnel up the driveway like Boomtown tramps. The music on my father's huge stereo blared as the festivities kicked off. All varieties of people started to fill the house. Lumpy green carpet, a brick fireplace, and cherry wood furniture rounded out the room. Snow-white walls, tan couches, and crystal lamps made a target for drunk vandals. The slightest screw up could get me busted. Buddy and some of the crew showed up with enough beer to have the Russian army singing a sad song.

I was already super-duper high. A nervous wreck, high on pharmaceutical speed, cocaine, and booze. I was staring out the window more times than not looking for the Reading police. By nightfall, there had to be one hundred crazies in my unsuspecting parents' house.

Some girls showed up with some green Versace X pills. The lime green pill had a Three-D face that extended out with a Versace impression. The snakes on these medusa pills seemed to be moving. I popped one and was angry because two was the dose I usually started with. But X is like a wave that hits. It crashes all at once, overshadowing the booze and any other mind-altering substances you happen to be on.

I stood in the melting blades of grass on the elevated lawn in the backyard. DMX blared as the X suffocated my spirit. A jiggle ran from head to toe, the whole body feeling a low vibration that made me a good kind of queasy. The MDMA in the X pills opened my serotonin valve wide as the Grand Canyon. Sex thoughts painted porno pictures. A body high that inspired romance and pure love. Platonic at times, animalistic sexuality at others. My heart raced as the X, coke, booze, speed, and pot raced in my bloodstream. I was ingesting as many and as much as my pocketbook would allow. Since this was my party, if you didn't bless me, you were hitting the bricks. Sanctuary gave me a great bargaining chip, and I knew it. Nightshade and torchlight filled my optics. The Tiki lamps that sat on the old stone wall gave off a luau vibe. Fire reflection on glassy eyes, the warmth of the drugs burned just beneath the skin's depth. Ice cold beer gripped in my hand; a sea of people moving as ash in the sky.

Everything was slow; I could literally feel the wind flow through my body. It entered through the fibers of my clothes. It ran its fingertips over my skin and slipped through my skeletal core, the wind had taken the form of seduction.

I was frozen. In awe of my surroundings. I didn't realize the fiery redhead next to me was having a full-on conversation with me. I opened my arms and hugged her. Glow stick people whirled as dancing liquid, hands moved circular, seemingly fast and choreographed. Candy necklaces and flared out jeans, house music jamming broad and loud. This had turned into an all-out rave.

Cali shows up, pocket full of truck-stop speed, whipped up in his mom's kitchen. We retreat to my room, careful not to alert anyone to the presence of non-sharable drugs. The substance hit the dinner plate on my nightstand, submarine yellow, stuck with humidity. The razor chopped out some thin lines; he cautioned me that this batch was of deadly strength. I made two fat ones and told him to "stop being a little girl." I was hell-bent. Overdose thoughts never present, ten feet and bulletproof. He looked like a soldier, crew cut, tall, and thin. His eyes were as grey as the May sky. Snorting it was a pain. It felt like a steak knife had been shoved up into my mind. The taste was a crude, soiled flavor. It created a chemical bubbling in the throat. The instant sexual drive gave me the look of a rapist Hell's Angel in a singles bar. People pounding on the oak door, the ringmaster was being summoned.

There had to be one hundred and fifty partygoers at this time. Music pumping and the cocktail of drugs distorted my reality. Laughter and distant screaming was the soundtrack. I felt if I ingested anything else, I would not be able to handle it. I was at the high watermark. I was a teenager; put that on paper for a minute. A kid, I looked twelve. On five drugs, full of alcohol, and scheming on unprotected oral sex. This is what your child could be doing. Yes...you.

Days had passed. The party was still in full swing. Day three was lethargic. The number of illegal drugs I was doing was colossal. Fifty people present at ten on a Sunday morning. Sitting in the corner, the living room overflowing with dancing girls and horny teen boys, I sat disgusted with myself. I hated all things Boston. I loathed the way I looked. I hated how I acted. Everything in the mirror was evil to me. Doing impressions of myself was common, negative self-talk and rage turned inward. I walked into the bathroom. The streaked mirror had splattered blood all over it. It looked like a cocaine nosebleed sneeze.

This type of self-degradation played in my head for most of my days. Drilled in me from a young age that I was no good, fat, and a problem. I stared at myself, a bottle of vodka in my grasp. I wanted to attack the image. Talking into the mirror made the hate burn in me. Alone, frustrated and insecure, I started to punch myself in the face. This practice was a relief. I wasn't a cutter, but I sure was a puncher. I beat my own left eye to a pulp. Drunk and crazy, still a kid, unsupervised, and wild with anger. I left that bathroom morose. However, self-abuse and rageful masturbation were my only release after the booze and drugs reached a plateau point. After all, you can only get so high. Being the life of the party is a full-time job. The class clown is, most of the time, not so happy. The funniest, most cheerful people are in the most pain. I needed to be accepted in social situations at this age. I would go way out of my way to make others laugh. I would get in trouble, make a fool out of myself, and bring a lot of unneeded attention towards me just so people would like me. I saw the people laughing.

I also saw them going on without me.

My classmates started to pass me by. The funnyman, the energy in the room, I was just a big joke. I knew most people my age felt sorry for me. They laughed with me, at me, and behind my back. There were holes in my heart. I could never place it. An empty void that never filled no matter how much substance was poured in. An endless pit of nothing.

Walking through life on drugs and alcohol, I felt relief. Moments in between self-hatred were welcomed, sweet and savory. High fives, pounds, and greetings were given freely. My homeboys loved me, and I loved them. I am willing to bet a lot of them felt the same as I did inside. The shame keeps you silent and awkward. The party was to end by dawn on Monday. It was a holiday weekend, and my parents would be home by five that evening. Sunday night was a jam.

The eight ball of coke I had been doing all weekend was not mine. A girl in my class had me middle it for her mom. A kindergarten teacher. They were supposed to be at my house at eight p.m. Around seven that evening, I went to the medicine cabinet to find some vitamins to cut the coke with, replacing what I had already stolen. My mother had taken it all with her. They were on the way to pick up the drugs they ordered, and I couldn't produce. I scrambled. Drunk reasoning led me to the pantry of all places. The only thing I could come up with that remotely even resembled cocaine was powdered milk!

I mixed a small amount of strong cocaine with the dehydrated dairy product. Guzzling vodka and doing speed, I mocked the unsuspecting customers, one of the most infamous burns in Reading's drug history, still talked about to this very day.

She came in, had a beer, and received the two-gram bag of barnyard powder. This was the addict in me; even at the early stages, I was breaking rules to use more than I could pay for. I heard later that they loved it. I thought these people would be blowing bubbles. They had no clue. The rip off was a total success.

  Sunday night tapered into madness. The hardcore and insane showed up. This crowd was full of maniac kids that had stamina; three days of getting wrecked was normal to them. Cars ran down the whole driveway. The sidewalks lined with vehicles. My golden retriever was going batty. She was old at this point. As nuts as these people were, my friends were really loving and respectful and treated my house and animal with care. I was so proud that no damage was done.

  The evening pushed on. The large amounts of Adderall that I had ingested and snorted had my hands shaking. No matter how much I drank, I couldn't come down. I disappeared into my bedroom; self-loathing consumed my underdeveloped mind. I took four Klonopin and headed to bed with a new awareness of the depths of addiction. I knew then that the devil had me in his slimy palm.

#

  Break Heart was a reservoir located in the town bordering Reading. A canopied, mystifying landscape of green trees and crisp fresh water. Massive rocks, as you would find in a quarry, rose out of the crystal-clear watering hole. Gazing down one, you could see a patch of summertime beaches, wood grain, and sparkling water.

  Summer wind blew in matrimony, orchids sent out heavenly smells, love was in bloom. Young admiration between couples, laughter, dancing, all the fun of those younger days. We skipped class near the end of the year, celebration sweet for hard work left undone. None of us were students. Clanking away on the keyboard of addiction, writing sad tales,

Nostradamus predictions, omens undefined. As summer approached, scholastic failure was imminent. Some of us knew summer school was a sure thing.

Honey and I loved the ambiance. Puffing bowls of ganja and reassurance for one another was an everyday thing. I loved Honey, my platonic counterpart. Romance was never a thought; she was my sister. The bonds among the wounded, lost and scared. It was a family, functioning in much more peace than the one we feared at home. We explored the possibilities, a group of ten or so of us. A summer retreat for the tortured.

The paths leading to the diving rocks were made of tar. The gravel parking lot was where we unloaded coolers, towels, and lawn chairs. An old boom box and D-batteries powered the soundtrack to our youth. The climb to the rocks showed where the world reached apex and was as steep as it was memorable. The path bumped over the crest. Miles of the horizon, the span of the great divide. The bluest sky, sweet metallic glow, a cool breeze patted the faces of stoned kings and queens.

The rock at the top of the path opened to a stage. Flat, an observation deck that God had placed there just for us. Here is where we were taught great lessons in love and friendship. The coals of self-hatred and rage extinguished by the cool waters of fellowship and laughter.

The Lord knows when your soul needs a break, and He always provides. This was a place to get away from the terror of reality. A basking spot, tan bodies were youthfully fit and clean, soaking up mellow rays of the sun. Memories for a lifetime produced with the eloquence of Hollywood dreams. You couldn't write the times we lived. The cast was eclectic and firm. The tightness of the group was snare-like and well thought out. Peering back, God assembled us. We needed each other. Ignorant to the future, the players would fade in loss, souls taken too soon, snatched from the world we knew.

Diving from the rocks was daring and courageous. The girls preferred to walk down, while the apples of their eyes dove to what seemed to be a sure death. The screams were not of fear, but exhilaration. Hard-bodied athletes fell headfirst with the posture of Olympians. The swim to the water's edge was short and calming. An old wooden raft was in line of sight, head just above the water, sunfish leaping all around. A mastodon oak tree, roots extending over the edge into the lake. A hang man's branch extending far out from its trunk, a tattered rope hanging limp and frayed. The bottom had a massive knot where bare feet clung. This rope swing accounted for countless hours of joy and adventure. Tarantula teens flying over and over off the rope like a nine-year-old at an amusement park. A hill sat behind the trees back. With the rope in hand and feet in place, the takeoff was immense. The stretching in the line as the arch peeked was scary. Noises of failure painted disastrous pictures of falling friends. It never broke. Tailor-made, this rope held up through harsh winters. It stood the test of time, mirroring the friendships taking shape that summer. Bonds never to be broken, not by addiction, time, or lust.

With the trust forthcoming, we built everlasting foundations, relationships unlike I have ever experienced. There is something about those childhood friends that never fades. The times shared are treasures tucked in the past, making you who you are, ever reminding of where we came from. This place, Break Heart, is etched in the inner workings of my past. As addiction grew, it was a shrine of healing.

Dark times touched the body of water and one fateful day the dream ended. Our African American friend from out of town joined for a day to remember. No one could see what was to come next. Bodies splashing, flailing arms, and feet like piranhas of the Amazon.

A scene out of Jaws, the onyx boy sat far from the school of unsuspecting fish. Attention lacking, the group failed to see the struggle. His head dipped below. A panicked bobber on the end of a loose line. He disappeared into the nothing below. It wasn't till after his soul escaped that he was noticed. Dreary darkness drained the light of summer's day. Finality and fatality intersected; his life cut short by the water we held so dear. The drowning marked the end of these pleasurable times.

His body was rescued by onlookers. Lifeless and cold, ebony skin smooth as silk. Chest left motionless. His heart stopped like a masterful Swiss windup watch. This was the first-time death had visited. It certainly wouldn't be the last. This was the seal breaking, the cherry of doom bursting open.

In retrospect, the gates of hell opened below Reading Memorial High School. He wasn't part of our crew in the nuclear sense. However, I feel this was the devil himself stumbling upon a flock of God's children. Surprised like a hunter in a field of ten-point bucks. Children of light, vulnerable and nude. The Dark Prince saw the chinks in the armor.

The spots in us that allowed the shadows to creep. The people in my life at this point were special. Gifted and dangerous to the evil one. Still lost, we were targeted. The curse had been put in place. The seeds of death, a crop that would reap barns later on were planted that day. He had found us. The towering beast had his feast, and we had no clue what was coming to pass.

Break Heart was viewed as a graveyard. No longer would the youths be submerged. The good days there had ended, and the locust needed a new site to congregate. The Dump and a new lot called Blueberry Hill were the choice locations to sow our wild oats.

#

My drinking and drugging took a dark turn. That August marked a place where it all stopped being pure fun. My depression was fueled by my alcohol abuse. My blood work could tell the tales. The chemical makeup in my brain was forever changed. The clasp of the demon was already strong. Scientifically, I was a full-blown alcoholic. The uppers were purely a tool to combat the effects of drinking. All I wanted to do was guzzle more.

School in September had a dreadful deadline. I hated it. Girls were starting to lose their appeal. I had lots of girlfriends in the years leading up to this. I stopped looking for puppy love after I realized any sweet girl, anyone of substance, would be horrified by my activities. A crying shame. I started to see relationships crumbling by my tenth-grade year. Countless blackouts and midweek benders were taking a toll on anyone in my bubble.

I flat out gave up on scholastics. Sports were totally out of the question, as my grades were listed as Ds on the high end. Incompletes and failing classes were becoming the norm. I had zero interest anyway. I hated myself. Not for failing in school, but for simply existing. There was something beneath the surface I just couldn't place. Facing the depth of my issues wasn't even registering. I knew I had a problem but didn't know I had a problem. Insanity.

Reading, Massachusetts culture screamed otherwise. I was just hardcore. A battle-tested version of who I once was. The people I drank with started to change. I was still maintaining my hood friendships and my place in the hippy realm; however, I began to move around more. Day drinking on the weekends, the characters grew darker.

Dicky wore a ratty old Red Sox cap that sat on his devilish head. Long face and a Lucifer goatee rounded out space for his angelic eyes. An older cat who drank with the younger crowd because people his peers would no longer put up with him. A great guy, a gypsy with notes of a traveling Jerry Garcia.

Faded jeans and a Dead Head patch on his denim jacket made him a sight to see. I started hanging with him during select times. Day drinking and late nights after the parties were long over. The first to arrive and the last to leave. As they slept, we would pick the fridge clean like buzzards on a Death Valley corpse. There was never enough to drink. A desert within, unquenchable and rare. Thirty racks of Bud hybrids dissipated into our bellies. Belching long into the night, staggering shells of people who once had souls. Dicky would drop acid and smoke pot, but drinking was his passion. He was just like me. A fan of all things "more".

I remember one night. Dicky and I had surpassed the herd. Once everyone entered slumber, "Touch of Grey" faintly played in the backdrop of a gloomy apartment. The gross couch I sat on overlooked a dusty wing chair. He engulfed the stained fabric, peach and brown. His old boots had muddied the surrounding carpet. Daylight shone through the chipped and broken blinds, layers of soot caked the panels that used to be white, now a dark splattered mess. Brown Coca-Cola stains covered the textured ceiling. The ghosts of fistfights and domestic violence remained.

I sputtered over to the flimsy black dormitory refrigerator that held the last two beers in the house. Piss warm, small roach droppings were around the rim. Neither of us bothered to wipe them clean as we cracked them open and put it to our lips. They smelled of skunk expulsion; most likely they had been rotting in there for months. Savoring the flavor, eyes droopy and sad like a couple of over-the-hill basset hounds. Sticky skin ran with sweat and grime. The tips of my own fingers were yellow with nicotine and a stinky sour stench that almost made me vomit. Dicky had nearly killed his beer in three short pulls. Seven a.m. blackness.

Out of smokes, we started lighting up half-used snipes. Bright pink lipstick stains from a promiscuous barfly imprinted stale Virginia Slims. There was a stench in the air, the face of alcoholism weathered. Sitting upright, alcohol poisoned and gagging back bile, I thought of bursting through the front door and running all the way home to the safety of my bed.

Dicky went into sheer panic mode. A terrorizing look of despair and rage as he realized the booze had run dry. Stores were not open yet and what difference did it make? We were both flat-broke and busted.

He gleamed across the bottle boneyard, a glass coffee table, smeared with grease and cigarette ash. The look in his eyes was a strange mix of delight and shame. He staggered over to the far end of the table. Hidden in the chaos was a three-quarter full, single-serving size bottle of Sutter Home White Zinfandel. Cap off and room temperature. The prize? A half-killed Marlboro Ultra-Light floating like a turd in a punch bowl sat at the bottom of the bottle.

A grimace, followed by a sinister smile, "Down the Hatch." Dicky winked at me and tilted the filthy bottleneck to his chapped flaking lips. The pink wine glugged as air bubbles rose inside. Determined to get every last drop, he allowed the rancid tobacco product to plop into his mouth. After shaking the bottle into his wide-open hole, he spat the cigarette onto the trash-filled coffee table. His saliva raining onto an empty McDonald's bag that stood half-cocked. He oozed back down into the chair, dust plummeting up in a cloud around his Carl's

Moving t-shirt. Repeated burps of skunky beer and wine released from his rotted stomach lining. He was a full-blown alcoholic, as I was. He just had a good four-year jump on me. He was in a chronic phase, knocking on death's door right before my eyes.

#

Back at school on Monday, I was severely hungover. More so than usual. I needed to start going to classes. I had back-to-back suspensions for skipping school. My parents took turns getting me back in, meetings with Mrs. O were now regulatory. Trouble was following me like my shadow. My father would drop me off on his way to work. I would walk through the front door, out the back, cut through the back-parking lot, and head home to nurse my hangovers watching "Martin" and "Jerry Springer."

In class, my need for acceptance got shameful. Project Achieve was the only class I could function in. This was only because the percentage of severely troubled pupils was one hundred percent. This day's class was a zoo. The barnyard folly got out of control and Mrs. M started screaming in frustration. I was the only student not participating in the madness. Everyone sat down firm as she threatened to bring the principal up to manage things. In the midst of her threats, silence took the class by surprise. I raised my hand and she called on me by name.

"Mr. Bornagain?" she asked.

I looked her square in the face and replied, "Your authority means nothing in my world."

For what reason? I had nothing to do with the class being in trouble. I was too sick from the night before to even think about getting loud. But I was addicted to laughter. That three second burst of acceptance from my classmates. The attention spans were short. How soon they forgot my sacrifice. I was hauled into the office and given three days for insubordination. Another failure in the drama that was my addicted life.

Sadness overtook me on most days. I had no dreams. The classes I did like were pointless. The rest of my schedule was full of failure; I couldn't enjoy what I loved. Any passion or interest I once had by this time was dead.

The thoughts of becoming a dropout were sounding better every day. My mother had the pleasure of getting me back into school this time. Mrs. O was at the end of her rope. They sat and argued as if I wasn't in the room. The grouchy assistant suggested that I may want to leave school to pursue a job. I was sixteen years old. My mother's heart broke before my eyes. She called Mrs. O a bitch and walked out for the last time.

#

I was working in a women's shoe store part time. I excelled at salesmanship. Selling shoes to mail order brides and lonely housewives was my specialty. I had a few dudes come down to the store and threaten me because I would send their wives home with five hundred dollars of pumps, week in and week out. I was made a floor supervisor almost right away. The forty-five-year-old that missed the promotion was not happy with me. I was always polite to him. I didn't agree with it. How can I boss around a poor guy three times my age? I always sent him to the back to chill while I did his side work, out of the kindness of my heart. I was a junkie alcoholic, but even then, I had a big heart for others.

My mom would hit me up to pay the electric or the cable bill from time to time, but mostly my pay went to drugs and booze. I was raging. I started dating a nice punk rock girl named Kelly from the neighboring town of North Reading. She had short hair and big full lips. I really liked her. She partied hard and liked to fool around. My kind of gal. Over the next few months, I dated Kelly and kept the party alive even though I wasn't in school.

The hood kids were still my buddies, the hippies too. Pretty much all my contacts and drug connections were the same. My depression was deepening. I felt like a loser. Watching everyone I came up with in school from grades K through tenth grade pass me by in life silently took its toll.

I started using pills more often. The blackouts were an everyday thing. However, I never mixed substance with work. Something my dad instilled in me from an early age. How would I get wasted if I lost my job? Everything in life revolved around using.

Kelly had given up. She had addiction issues also and I was too out of control for her. I started to see myself coming forward as the worst in any group. No matter how many times I switched settings per week, I was wearing out my welcome everywhere. I had a full bottle of pill-laced Kool-Aid in my hand. I was sitting on Sullivan's couch when Kelly spat on me and walked out. She got tired of me passing out at five in the evening. I laughed as she stormed down the barren staircase and out onto Main Street. The laughter once again masked deep pain and discomfort. I started losing things, and people. I really valued her, and this was the last time I would see her again. Inside, the blackness took shape. The beginning of a dark period.

#

I got a new job at a full-service gas station. I would tell girls I was a Petroleum Transfer Technician. I just pumped gas. I was always joking to take the focus off the sad life I had created. I felt like a drowning man. The canopy that hovered over the pumps would shelter me from the icy winter mix that Reading is all too famous for. Customers loved me. My people skills shined. It was all I had to survive. I honed my craft. Addicts are master manipulators to begin with. I genuinely cared for people and together, that became a winning combination. People handed me five and ten-dollar spots. Tips, always building a rapport with the local clientele. Nat's dad would come into gas up his taxi every morning like clockwork.

Mel, Burt, and Kenny were the owners of the mechanic shop attached to the gas station. I watched some of the hardest working men I had ever seen. They let me change bad tires, fix flats, and help with lube oil filters when gas sales were slow.

These guys knew my problems and took me under their wings. It was a real family. They always made sure I had hours, money in my pocket, and a place to hang out if I was sober. They became a real positive influence in my life. They were so funny too.

Mel, a Viking man standing over six feet and built like a Chicago Bear, had hands like a baseball mitt. He held a torch up to the tailpipe of a cherry-red Ford LTD. The lift suspended the beast overhead as the bolt he targeted turned white-hot. He used the torch when the salt from the streets would fuse metal on metal to deep rust. He held his hand out like he was catching raindrops. He smirched and said, "look at this." The glowing bolt dribbled into his palm, almost liquid in form, a hot-red disc. He closed his hand almost as if he were doing a magic trick. Thick white smoke scorched callused skin. A smell of meat filled the air. Everyone looked in wonder. He was a cyborg. He cackled, head up and mouth wide open. No one could believe their eyes.

#

As I look back, examining my relationships with

women, I was not in any healthy relationships. At this age is when one learns to build trusting and wholesome relationships. I was not doing so. Sexual selfishness and gratification were present at this time. I would lie and use girls to get what I wanted sexually, as well as emotionally. I would seduce them to feed my huge yet damaged ego.

Plans, plots, and schemes. Not one bond I entertained was based on truth or love. In all my affairs, I was fueled by substance and true addict thinking. The seeds were not planted, but trees were full-grown and sky-high. Master manipulation was my forte.

I could guilt, persuade, and coax people into doing almost anything I desired. These times set the stage for damaging and destructive behaviors that later ruined everything in my life. All my principals were routed in the gutter. When your spiritual foundation is built on trash, you will reap rubbish in all you do. False promises and shame were major tools of the trade. Not only in my love life but every other aspect of me as well. My cute and bubbly exterior made it easy for me to slither into situations others could not. I got what I came for. Period.

As time passed, I cooled it on illicit drugs. I remained drinking fifteen beers a night on the low end. Poker was an everyday attraction. I gambled with drinking buddies to caulk the holes that coke and speed left in my heart. My weight was out of control; I ballooned to over two hundred and sixty pounds. At the urging of a good friend, it was decided the gym and a sensible diet would benefit my life. I started going every day. An hour of basketball, one hour of weightlifting, and a full hour of cardio were all on the menu. I starved myself from all food to achieve my weight loss goals. Health was never the true motivation. The true purpose of this transformation was to look good so the quality and quantity of women would increase exponentially.

I started getting in tip-top shape. I was running and lifting full time. I was eighteen years old. The Lord put it in my heart that I needed to totally change my life, retreat from drugs altogether, and become a police officer. I wanted to help others and have an exciting and dangerous career.

The drug life always fascinated me; my goal became to transpire into an undercover narcotics officer. The path I saw was to join the military's National Guard. Go to boot camp and pivot into law enforcement.

I went to a recruiter's station and signed up. I knew I was about to become government property. I drove with an officer to take the ASFAB aptitude test. I passed with a mid-grade and qualified as a military police officer. I went into downtown Boston to get a physical.

Something in me rebelled. Right before I was set to sign my papers for enlistment, I decided that my comedic talents would make me a shoo-in for stand-up comedy. Friends were heading to Vegas, and I wanted in. The Las Vegas club scene was one step before the famous Comedy Store in Los Angeles. The couple I was to move with were great friends, consisting of one of the Claire's and her longtime boyfriend. All the hard work and a year of intense training for the National Guard and plans to be a cop were now history. A whim thinker and free spirit, a runner from problems, I took off. I had a bus ticket and fifty bucks in my pocket. Young and fearless, a two-thousand-mile bus trip while completely broke didn't seem that bad. Long before my reliance on Jesus Christ, I looked at this as an adventure. Survival and the journey were things that would manifest themselves.

The bus pulled up to a dilapidated bus station in

downtown Vegas shortly after five p.m. on a Tuesday. After riding on a cramped sweaty bus with our nation's low-income travelers, I was ready for a shower. A friend from back home set me up with a temporary home out there, as Claire and her man wouldn't be there for another month to meet me.

 Jerry was a short-statured, spiky-haired Texas transplant. He stormed up in a massive white Chevy truck covered in desert dust and mud. He hollered "Howdy" as he signaled me into the rig's cab.

 We shuffled through heavy traffic in Las Vegas's grid-like street system. We pulled up to his second-floor condo, air conditioning blasting as the Valley sun beat down from above.

 Plush white carpet and romantic artwork hung from nails in snow-colored sheetrock. Couches tan and inviting, a clean crisp kitchen in plain view of the living room. My first Vegas evening was to kick off hard. Party Town USA; Sin City; When in Rome, we do as the Romans do. A fridge full of Budweiser Red, three packs of cowboy killers on the counter, and a special treat that sat in Jerry's pocket, gave this season opener all we needed to get it going.

 I guzzled beers as he gave me a personal tour of the community pool outside. Gorgeous cougars were bathing in the sun. Tan skin glistening with perspiration. My vision was distorted by booze, I fell in love with this place immediately. Back inside, we sat on the deck as the solar system darkened. Vegas lights and strip sounds lit up the horizon like a Roman candle. As night marched on and drunkenness set in, Jerry's demeanor changed. He had a hunger in him, a starving man like I have never seen.

 "Don't judge me," he barks as he reaches in his top drawer in his glamorous bedroom.

 A new toy. Resembling a baby rattle, a glass piece of

wonder and shame appeared in his hand. A bubble end with a straight stem for sucking. He pulled a zip baggy from his shirt pocket. An enchanting substance that resembled rock candy made the bag plump and glowing.

"Ice anyone," Jerry asks.

I felt fear for a moment. Then he dropped the shards in the glass structure. It made a clanking that rang loud and burley. A sound like no other on this planet. The cheap gas station lighter erupted in flame. A safe distance from the glass, it cooked up the crystal into a brown oil that swished in the bowl as he twisted it in perfect rotation. He ripped it like a Hoover. He opened his mouth like a twisted demon in an exorcism. Face to the ceiling, he sprayed a thick blue, white cloud toward the hot lightbulb above. The look in his eyes glassy and full of lust. He stood in freezing stillness as he let the rush kick him square in the brain.

He brought the bowl, putting it to my lips never trusting a first-time smoker with his glass. He put the stem to my lips and rolled. The vapor hit my throat with stealth and comfort. A cool cloud with an inviting aroma, a taste that one can only describe as chemical. I gagged as smoke flooded my nostrils and mouth. I had succumbed. The realization that I had just hit a crystal methamphetamine pipe for the first time had me writhing in shame.

The initial feeling was lacking. Then in seconds, the molecules traveled in my blood, to the brain, and mind explosions erupted. This was Ritalin on steroids! The same wired-up madness, after my sixth hit I lost total interest in ice-cold beer. Jerry and I swapped stories as we tweaked. Motor-mouthed and dangerous, we devised plans to take over the world and decided to take on every female sexual conquest in our wildest dreams.

Jerry got out his laptop and started to watch porn on the adjacent couch. He signaled me to take the pipe to my room and retire for the evening. Masturbation was unlike anything I have ever experienced. Parts of my body tingled and writhed in sexual debauchery.

    I thought of every woman I had ever had a sexual thought about. The old, young, and indifferent. Women working in stores, old pornographic images from years past. Prior sexual trysts with strangers, lust personified. Everything from Catholic schoolgirls to librarians seduced my toxic mind. Flailing hand on my beet-red member, my body soaking through the mattress with sweat and rage. Hours passed by like moments. Self-shame and abuse became something of grandeur. Fantasies of hookers and nymphomaniac street dwellers felt like reality. Vivid and deep, I was in a new world of self-induced pleasure. Body lotion lubricant subserviently coated my skin. Rubbing, tugging, and moaning in my own disgusting slime. The queen mattress a desecrated place of deviance. A sexually abused body lifted off the cushion. Covered in hair conditioner and moisturizer, sweaty and weak.

    Cracks of morning light bent through the blinds; a night wasted in evil masturbatory pain. Breathing heavy, seven in the morning and sore. I gazed into the clean bathroom mirror and saw myself in a twisted, distorted view. Something had changed me. Pupils swarmed, hair wet and curly. A hot mess in the truest sense of the word. I had never felt sexuality in such a raw and dark sense. It was an outside force like no drug I had ever ingested. This was my first dance with Beelzebub. The darkest demon. The one who would later rule and consume me with complete abandon.

    That's when it hit me, this wasn't high school anymore.

Chapter 3

Descent

The Light of the Lord was in me all along. I couldn't see the illumination through the cloudy despair, rage, and trauma. Vegas is where the winds of change shifted. This is where I found myself as a true salesman. Looking back, the shoe store, the gas station, all of it was the light within shining through. My life in ruins, total lack of education, and lust for substances had ruled out most options to make a living at that point. The lack of funding was a major problem too. I went out broke, a hobo with a big smile and boyish charm. I sucked people in and got them to like me. Stand-up comedy was a dream, but I needed that real paper.

    I met Claire's brother at the t-shirt shop just after eight in the morning. Hungover and smelling of stale Budweiser. We hopped into the brand-new Yukon Denali. Big chrome rims, deep navy-blue paint, and butter-soft gray leather interior, this ride was pimpin' in a big way.

    We departed from the shop where he screen-printed cheap shirts and boxed up Chinese-made lighters and bathing suits. He had a string of stores in the Casino malls all over the Vegas strip. Very lucrative and completely exciting.

    He needed a dependable delivery driver and salesman. So, there I was, putting the bright lights and stage on hold. A funny man's career would have to be in my spare time; I needed to get paid in a major way. Not only was rent imperative, but I also had to eat, and most importantly, get rocketed into oblivion.

The Denali coasted down Las Vegas Boulevard, slow-motion rolling in the summer heat. August air streamed over dramatic paint, squiggle lines rising, one fifteen Fahrenheit. Freeze blasted out of factory vents. The sound system bumping some classic rock tune that slips my mind completely. Passing the Luxor: The Dark Pyramid of Las Vegas, jet black as the night sky. In the dead of night, this world wonder shot a laser beam of light far into the atmosphere. A beacon of hope for every degenerate gambler in a hundred-mile radius. Passing streetlights, running intersections with no regard, Claire's bro headed toward the great lions of the MGM Grand. The Vegas Strip was popping midday, the hustle of horny husbands and sadistic bachelorettes, taking the streets by storm. Crowds flowed, honking horns of yellow taxis blew like revelation trumpets. I was starstruck. Showgirls marched in high top sneakers. Rowdy college students slapped each other's caps off and joked like immature hooligans as illegal street crossing commenced. I was about to get a tour of the shops. I needed to learn every store, service entrance, and employee so I could restock the kiosks with merchandise.

We pulled into the Aladdin Hotel and Casino. A great sandstone building that was embedded in the heart of the Strip. We burst through the service doors into a tunnel. Rat traps every few feet to ward off any dumpster-dwelling vermin. Cold dry air entered my lungs, fluorescent bulbs burned in unison. When we entered the casino mall, I fell into shock. The ceilings were a baby-blue sky color, clouds etched into art; it was an Arabian reality like I have never seen.

This was the magic carpet version of the Sistine Chapel.

Huge stone slabs naturally and strategically placed made up the floor. A burnt-earth tint, it felt like a Middle Eastern marketplace straight out of Bollywood.

Genies danced; street performers breathed fire into controlled rolls. It was a false reality, a perfect escape for excommunicated tourists. A short foreigner bumps my shoulder, a bottle of cold Crystal in each hand, open and sipping, he jaunted on his way. The most beautiful female creatures I have ever laid eyes on pranced alongside seventy-year-old millionaires. Vegas was a playground; a sinful palace awaits. High-end call girls camouflaged by evening wear from the night before clicked in heels to their hotel destinations. I was nineteen. This opened my eyes to the lure of Vegas. The devil's playground was warm and inviting.

The kiosk stood in the dead center of the madness. A tall Black man in a purple snakeskin bodysuit was putting on a show within arm's reach. A contortionist by trade, he slithered through hoops the size of tennis rackets as middle-aged couples dropped twenties into a top hat that sat near his bare feet. The t-shirts and novelty hot sauces were flying off the shelf. People in Vegas are dying to go broke. Buying cheap crap for their loved ones back home as they dumped the rainy-day cash on slots and dice. Guilt spending, they were happy to drunkenly shell out dough on anything that caught their bloodshot eyes. The short Hawaiian dream that worked the register shook my quivering hand. She stood four-feet-and-eleven-inches tall, and her Asian eyes gazed into my blue ones. A quick hello and we were off. I was there to learn the route.

Cruising on, we made stops at The Palace, the Fashion Show mall, and lastly, The Stratosphere, a mile-high space needle that had red roller-coaster rails spaghetti bowling the glass observation deck. This was the tallest structure west of the

Mississippi at the time.

We screamed up the service elevator. The force lifted you off your feet. I felt like a NASA chimp during pre-flight testing. At the top, elevator doors opened to the mall. Water massage machines, oxygen bars, and food all left the shopper dazed in amazement. This place was famous for having the best blackjack odds on the strip. Through the back window sat one of the worst ghettos in the country, stoking in the shadows of a towering money machine. I started driving my route the very next day. I drove the Denali as my company truck. Big balling for a nineteen-year-old. They let me take the truck home. It was a gesture I didn't expect.

About two weeks had passed before the Dark Prince showed his face in America. A vulgar display of power for all the planet to consume as they woke on September 11, 2001. Vegas was three hours behind the Big Apple. I woke at seven in the morning to the phone ringing off the hook. Claire and her man had just moved into the new apartment; we didn't even have furniture or a TV set yet. I stumbled out of my room, walking on the cold floor, hungover with stale breath. The voice on the other end was my boss's wife screaming. "We're at war!" She proclaimed there could be as many as fifty thousand dead; they had hit the World Trade with commercial planes.

A transistor radio sat on a snow-white carpet. Bare walls deflected reverb sounds and frantic reports of flames and death. You could hear the terror in the broadcaster's voice as he painted a foul picture of manifested evil thrown upon the earth. Satan invaded the radio waves. I called my dad, as he was at work in New Hampshire.

The phone rang one time; a pre-recorded message that all circuits were busy began playing in my ear. The tape had stretched from wear. It was demented, distorted and made a melting sound as if the phone were oozing out of my hand. Total shock ran through me.

  The radio was speculating that foreign terror was to blame. Whatever this was, it was from Hell. I had to work, Hell or highwater. The Denali barreled down Flamingo toward the Strip. In the midst of a Middle Eastern terror attack, where was God sending me? The Aladdin.

  The population inside was brown. Turbines and burkas were all I could see. A panic-stricken crowd walked in a daze; their zombie eyes stared blankly. The first image I was to see was the South Tower collapsing on a jumbotron system. They panned in as humans leaped to their death, avoiding the furnace prowling out of the windows behind them. City streets clouded with contaminated ash like Mount Saint Helens overtook Manhattan. Blood streamed onto the suit of an African American woman victimized by violence. Shouting, broken glass, the sound of twisted steel and jet fuel ignition. Towering inferno tales; freakish mid-air family phone calls. Begging, dreary, and choatic to a fault. Nothing would be the same after this day. People were crying as they walked by the empty shops in the Persian backdrop.

  Pentagon bombs, Pennsylvania field fires. A nation wounded, deep to the veins. Vegas is a valley surrounded by a mountain range. Everyday McCarran International Airport circles countless planes before landing. This day? The sky was silent as I walked through the dark parking garage. The nose of the truck pulled onto the Strip on a perfect Tuesday, unaware of the apocalypse. The world had a stillness, unlike anything I have ever experienced.

  Life in slow motion, serrated silence jagged and sharp. I bit into the moment with an apple sweetness. The bitter after taste of blood and war coated my throat as I entered the city streets. The area was gridlocked; streams of cars made their way home. A wondrous September afternoon, every window was down as we sat at a stoplight. Reverb noise, a stadium echo as the President spoke to the nation. Deliverance, war drums pound, his voice filled with anger.

Talk of soaring gas prices and malicious destruction filled the airwaves. I look left, then right, the scene was the same everywhere I turned. Tears streamed down the faces of mothers, children seemed shocked, cars sat a stand still.

I found sanctuary. The apartment was quiet and lonesome. I had my roommate buy me an eighteen pack of Budweiser the night before, not knowing the brew would serve a much deeper purpose as it drowned my sorrows. The beer gurgled faster than usual. I extinguished the fires of my consumed rage. Ethyl alcohol exploded like jet fuel in my mind. America was furious and so was I.

The weeks following 9/11 were times of danger for the establishment. The men who run the world had to sit back and watch as the country united. Middle Eastern hatred brewed like coffee. The innocent retreated in fear of hate crimes and shame. Anyone who resembled someone from that distant part of the world needed to be careful. American hate and ignorance forced Indians and others into the gallows. A new enemy, one face came to be the symbol of evil on earth. Bin Laden.

#

I flew home as the smoke cleared. I was to testify in Barry's defense during my parents' divorce. The plane was empty. Some feared flying. In all honesty, it was the safest it's ever been. Barry met me at the gate in New Hampshire. He was dressed to the nines that day. A stout man, longer hair, a jet-black suit, white shirt, and a gold tie. My old man dressed well. I will never forget his warm smile as he sat looking like a million bucks. The military's presence was thick with fatigued warriors, carrying loaded machine guns ready to kill. Barry approached as they began to wand him for contraband.

The excessive security prompted Barry's quick wit. "What do I look like, I'm in the Taliban?"

"Dad, you can't say that!" I shouted.

Even the soldiers burst out in laughter. Just like my dad, hurling a gut-busting bomb of inappropriate humor at the exact wrong time.

I was to spend a week in Boston. I linked up with the hood guys soon as I touched down in Reading. The air was different at Donnie's. The basement was filled with people. This night was glum. The static electricity of the party atmosphere was absent. The soulless eyes of my past classmates were pinned and weak. A former football player cringed on the sofa. Withdrawals from Oxycontin ravaged his core. Cold sweat and fear coated his facial structure. Contorted and restless, he had tears streaming down his cheeks. His Irish face flustered. A Puerto Rican with a cane entered the room. He was the dealer, man of the hour, and the devil's henchman they were all waiting on.

Drug prices soared as the opioid epidemic hit New England with dark force. An eighty-milligram pill was selling for a dollar a milligram. This put the drug out of reach for almost any addict.

The football player begged the evildoer, "Please man, I got eighty."

"The price rose to one twenty," the dealer said unmercifully.

Supply and demand always rules in the game. If you can't pay, someone else will. The pigskin hero shelled out all he had and borrowed the remainder. He sucked the time-release coating off like a stone-cold junkie. His Massachusetts driver's license crushed the whole load. A straw slurped up the stagnant death, instant pleasure for the wanting man. A grave feeling came over me. The light above the red-felt pool table beamed onto a group of addicted souls. I sat at the wet bar snorting cocaine and drinking. An old friend stoned on junk gave me this speech. "Bornagain, if you hadn't left, you would be dead." The seriousness hit like a snare drum. They knew me, they also knew the severity of the local drug problem. An infestation was so deep that it had our class's top students stealing and selling their bodies. The demons crept in. The dollar signs were too steep for the wicked. Heroin had arrived. The Captain Morgan and mushrooms I had ingested were peaking.

 Derrek showed up. It was his birthday. A pagan drug celebration, an excuse to use more than other days. He signaled me into the bathroom. The finished basement was set up like a clubhouse , an opiate addict's dream. We locked the balsa wood door behind us as he chopped two massive lines of coke on the countertop. A second baggy was pulled from his pocket. October madness, a bittersweet moment when the wax bags imprinted with Bin Laden's face were sliced open. The face of the enemy was used to market the pure Afghani brown.

 "Gimme the Osama's," the birthday boy hollered.

 Derrek was a punk rock god. Huge nose and tatted skin, dripping with the sleaze of a young Nikki Sixx. Speedball warriors. The chunky cocaine folded into the light brown of the dope. Intense and striking. The moon's glow filtered through the basement window of the bathroom. The bulb above blasted white-hot light as I tripped. The rum on my breath, loaded and ready. He warned me of its strength as he sliced mounds. Gorilla fingers of poison laid in wait. The crisp twenty came out of my pocket. Rolled up and clean. Derrek blasted off, head cocked up and eyes splattering with delight. He choked on the drip. A toxic cocktail of cocaine and heroin slid down his throat. I snapped up in likewise fashion. I tasted a wintery mix of fuel and disease.

    I plopped on the velvet couch as the drugs took hold. The rum, the shrooms, the coke, and smack. I could feel the black in my eyes constrict from the light. Holes to my soul, closing in protection as evil invaded spaces that I never knew existed. My stomach turned. I felt my hands become pillows. Dreamy dizziness and warmth slid over my body like a silk sheet. Spooning with Satan, I lounged in his arms. The quiet whisper of the dark prince was in my eardrum. This was the watermark. The highest I had ever been. My liquid body dripped in sexual aggression. I could barely speak. Throat caved in, numb from cocaine abuse. The brown I was overdosing on made my heart slow and saturated. Figures were standing in a shadow. They surrounded me as I slurred out a dull response. They were selfishly checking if I had life in me. A pulse determined if I would be revived, robbed, or tossed on the side of the house like third-world trash. The alcohol's depressive effect met the heroin with a sluggish gleam.

    I was carried to the bathroom where Derrek made me up possibly the largest rail of cocaine in the history of man. The disco rail; the legend. Medicinal and needed, a counteraction for my fading pulse. The coke would speed up my heart and pull me from hell. I could barely wrap my head around the thought of taking more drugs. However, the free ones were not going to escape my grasp. I shoveled in three key bumps as Derrek laid out the mastodon. New level shit, I screamed as the razors tore my brain. The coke made me gag. I was numb. Onlookers couldn't believe a man in my state could even finish a line of that size. This only added to my legend. The beast from the east.

A short leg on the tour and it was back to Vegas.

I saw hell, life was forever changed. In the scope of things, the world was matching the horror of September 11. Addiction was rampant and swelling. Manifestations of war looming, people just didn't want to see the road ahead. Planet shattering prophecies, I watched my old stomping grounds sinking into the depths of heroin. The doctors wrote prescriptions recklessly. The bonus money from pharma reps was too tempting to pass up. It was no mistake that the US was sliding into opioid dependency, as the greatest opium conquest the world has ever seen, kicked into high gear. The war in Afghanistan was about treasure. Not men with box cutters.

The fields were bare as Taliban henchmen, propped up by the post-cold war CIA, burned the bulbs under the guise of Allah. Doctors wrote the scripts for the opiates, the addict sunk into poverty, and heroin was born again. A re-emergence of the brown sugar that once plagued America's ghettos and jazz musicians.

What middle America didn't see was the needles filling the gutters, the body bags in record numbers. The carnage that would consume White suburbs and college dorms. The fix was in. The devil knows no bounds; the evil running the world doesn't care who you are. The backs of the poor were about to be used as stools for the ultra-rich who designed America's war on drugs. Vegas bound; I had seen enough.

#

Landing gears fell as the screeching tires hit the tarmac back in Sin City. I was back to work and drinking harder than ever. I made a fool of myself at my boss's house. Clair had given me a gag gift. A huge martini glass intended for change and car keys. Of course, I filled it with apple puckers and vodka and guzzled gargantuan drinks of pure hard liquor. I urinated in the backyard, said obnoxious things, and acted like the town drunk in typical Bornagain fashion. That night I was insistent that I was perfect for the supervisor's position that had opened post 9/11. They gave it to me. I was off to supervise a multiple location operation.

As weeks passed, I realized how irresponsible I really was. Drinking half a handle of rum a night. I would drink till four in the morning, be up at seven for work. Our across-the-hall neighbors were a hard-partying couple. Her dad was a major computer innovator, him a heavy metal hanger-on. Her trust fund was endless. The supply of drugs never ceased. Her bank account drained as he would flip his long hair over his Iron Maiden t-shirt, throw on his leather bomber, and hit the road to score. Crack cocaine was their poison. Altoid tins filled with drugs. They had a similar apartment. Beige rug. Deco art hung from the walls. Marilyn Monroe posters overlooked us as he lit the water bong, refitted with a chore boy filled stem. Orange flames melted huge pieces of rock. The chamber of the pipe filled with choking amounts of pure coke.

I was signaled for my turn. I had never smoked crack. When one is about to ingest drugs with a stigma, pure shame and preventable regret tend to consume the user. But for me, it was just a passing thought as Budweiser and Xanax lubricated the decision-making process. I put the chamber to my lips as the debunked metal junkie lit the fuse. A strange taste, glue-like, filled my mouth and lungs. I ripped a massive blast. A bell ringer. I heard choo-choo trains chugging along and bells ringing. A Scarface version of "The Polar Express" ran down the tracks between my ears. The pair stood back as the cocaine passed through the chambers of my heart. My brain was cloudy and tranced. A racing pulse and beaded sweat resonated with a horny rage. The drug the Reagan administration warned us about in the "Just Say No" era. The first hit of crack cocaine is what the chase is all about. Every hit after is a wasted attempt where you will never reach the mountain top again.

I sat on the sofa staring at the wall. He spoke to me inquisitively. He wanted to get off to my first impression of the drug. "Gimme another" was my only cry. I popped a green Morphine Sulphate. A time-released heroin-mimic. The nod came within thirty minutes and overshadowed the cocaine as if a beanstalk sprouted up in place of the sun. Consuming daylight sparkled through the sealed blinds of the apartment. A loaded twelve-gauge teetered near the end of the sectional. A boulder the size of an adult front tooth was placed on the hot pipe.

It sizzled as it sat waiting. I approached the hit with the full intention of an explosion. I wanted to see how high I could get. The smoke filled the lining of my chest.

The opioids ceased momentarily. Black magic, my eyes filled with blood as oceans ran in my veins. Tumbling, the white walls melted away. Universal uncaring for my surroundings. I was at the apex. The distant drawings of satanic artistry bloomed. This was why mothers sold their children, why the murder spirit haunted every ghetto from L.A. to New York. This was the demon in cold flesh. I felt its spirit and fully understood this mind-bending addiction for the first time. This was the Granddaddy. I wanted a hit every few seconds. The man politely suggested I slow down. His boney hand slid the tin of stones from my possession. I knew he feared my overdose, not wanting to be bothered with cops or paramedics. It was time I made it home. High as a kite, sexually frustrated, and stoned, I proceeded to my bedroom, guzzling booze till I fell out.

#

The following month's ran together. Drug-induced depression and the depths of my alcoholism drained my spirit to an all-time low. Barry had been pushing me to come home. With my stand-up comedy dreams snuffed out like candlelight, I took the long road back. When I arrived, January wind was blowing into Boston. Barry worked for a company in the mountains of western New Hampshire. I was employed as a driver for the company men. They all stayed at an old barn house. They all came from out of town to work. They would stay the week and travel home on weekends.

  The divorce had Barry living here full time. His nights were spent at the City Pub, a college bar with billiards and karaoke on the evening's menu. I wouldn't drink. I drove for them. I was safe passage as some of the guys had already experienced a DWI. We had a blast.

  Bonding over three rolls of quarters, seventy-five cents a game. We shot pool and laughed all night. My old man was an accountant. He loved to drink and listen to tunes. He was a great man. Loved classic rock, the King of B sides. My dad loved the obscure, the stuff no one listened to.

  On the way home, we would stop at the gas station to get snacks and a huge amount of after-hours beer. The crew would dwindle. I stoked the great cast iron wood stove that heated the mountain chateau. This living arrangement got me away from drugs for the time being. Reading was over an hour and a half drive, and I really acclimated to the local college kids.

  My drinking was problematic. I would find myself passed out at the bottom of a steep staircase regularly. I had clearly fallen judging from the contusions all over my body. Rising off the cedar plank floor of the barn house was cringeworthy. Five A.m. was wake up time, the dead of winter in New Hampshire was never any fun, especially if you woke up on the floor. Walking back into the living room to stoke the dying flames in the stove, I would crash on the cheap black futon, pressing a bag of ice on my knotted flesh to bring down the swelling. This type of thing happened daily. Twenty years old and a full-blown, falling-down alcoholic.

One night after the guys were in bed, I got extra loaded on Heineken. Having gone outside to urinate, I walked upstairs to make sure my dad was asleep. Making my way downstairs, the snow that tracked in on my shoes had melted. I must have slipped. My feet went over my head; I felt myself levitating above the wooden staircase.

There was a slow-motion free fall, and I was lying flat in midair. The back of my head pinged off the dull wood, sounding like a Louisville Slugger cracking a pumpkin in half. My neck was next. Bone shattering force caved in on my spine. As the dust settled, I could only help but lay there and moan. Not having the energy to cry for help, my lifeless body slipped into a drunken slumber.

I awoke to my dad shaking me hard. He was used to a passed-out son by now, but this was quite different. My eyes opened to a blinding light and ringing in my ears. Sheer pain ran through every inch of my body.

"Boston, are you ok?"

I could barely speak in response to Barry's inquiry. He had to get to work. I limped into the living room. I lay on the futon and flipped on the tiny TV and VCR combo that sat on the filthy glass coffee table. Upon further investigation, I had blood running down the back of my skull. A large laceration in the middle of the back of my head, the point of impact where my body met the floor.

I lurched into the bathroom to assess the damage in detail. The mirror was stained with hard water. An ancient electric heater blowing hot greasy air filled the room with dust.

I flipped on the light. The image staring back at me was grotesque. My face battered from multiple falls in the days before. I turned my neck slightly. Faint clicking noises rattled my inner core. With every twig snapping noise that my body made, my jellied eyeballs shook in a quaking jiggle.

  I quickly realized as I shifted my back, the clicking was a byproduct of the absence of spinal fluid. I had sprung a leak. I had a major concussion. The headache felt like a hatchet attack. I bent over to tie my shoelace. Leaning forward, the blood rushed to my skull and blew open pain valves in the recesses of my nervous system. As I tried to stand up once more, I heard a loud pop! Dizziness ravaged my perception. The ringing in my ears was deafening. I grabbed the bathroom counter as I blacked out.

  After finally waking up, I stumbled to the fridge, a man in indescribable pain. The door swung open; the cold air came first, and then the lightbulb burst bright, blinded me. A migraine-type effect. I reached for a half-drunk bottle of chardonnay. My eyes met the shit-brown refrigerator. In my state, I could smell the color. The fermented grapes, putrid and depressing, made me gag. A large amount of vomit filled my unbrushed morning mouth. Knowing that if I committed fully to the puke, I would lose precious wine, I choked down my own throw up. Swallowing an acidic load of poisonous venom for the sake of fifty cents worth of stale week-old wine. The rest of the bottle helped me wash down six Aleve. The hunt was on.

  I nursed the last three Budweiser's floating in the cooler . My dad just got home for lunch and was genuinely concerned for me. I convinced him to go to the gas station. I proceeded to order a twenty pack of Bud bottles and two bottles of wine. Sighting pain and discomfort, what father wouldn't alleviate his hurting son. I sat on the futon. Smoking Marlboros and chugging booze. I kept toying with the stair print on the back of my head. Even with the swelling at its worst, I could feel a massive dent where the wooden object caved in a portion of my skull. I refused medical treatment one hundred percent. I couldn't help but think that if I had hit my neck first, I would have surely perished.

This dance went on for a good week. I couldn't move but to get up and use the restroom and get more alcohol from the fridge. I am no doctor, but I knew death was a real possibility. I had lost blood, spinal fluid, and a lot of self-respect. No one could tell me a thing. I lived by my own rules, addiction was my master.

At the end of January that year, I was to hit a milestone in my addiction. My twenty-first birthday. About to come of age to buy booze, bar hop, and go absolutely shit-house crazy. It was a freezing Thursday evening. The warm refuge of the City Pub welcomed us in. Barry, and friends drank the night away as usual. This night was about to be different. I caravanned them home at around half past eleven that night. Barry hands me a crisp one-hundred-dollar bill and wishes me a "happy birthday." My dad loved me very much. Best friends would be a gross understatement. He had set up my birthday night so that his friend Tommy would let me sleep over after parking the Jeep. His seedy apartment was in view of the Pub. At midnight I was to turn the legal drinking age and be able to bar hop and buy booze for the first time in my life.

A wretch, and an addict. I turned twenty-one on a Friday night, and I was in my first treatment center on Monday morning.

#

Walking in with a huge duffel bag of brand-new clothes, I hit the medical office for a blood draw. I was scared. I looked like I was twelve years old and felt eight. Arriving in the day room, I looked around to find a slew of misfit souls, severely weathered from the storm. Wrinkled faces and snaggletooth fronts, some teeth missing or black.

It was my first encounter with the demonic drug underbelly that existed in the mean streets. My first impressions of heroin, track mark bruises, and rail-thin patients infected with HIV and Hepatitis C. Black crack mammas, slick talking street demons, spitting game that my White suburban mindset couldn't even fathom.

I felt miserable in every way. Copious amounts of drugs and booze seeping from my pores, I was made to feel comfortable with a healthy dose of Ativan. I chopped it up with some twenty-something call girl, a Puerta Rican Mami from Mattapan, sweet and alluring. It was clear from day one that I wasn't going to take this seriously. I was there to take the heat off, an escape from it all till I can pull it together. Ninety percent of people in rehab are there just to shut up their family or appease the legal system in some way. People were laughing and joking. Fifty-year-old gangsters in the mix with doctors, lawyers, prostitutes, and soccer moms. A glimpse into the cold fact that addiction knows no color, age, race, or creed. A futuristic version of Hempfest. A fast forward to the grim realities of this progressive spiritual disease. The changing forms were obvious; similar stories where it starts out as pure fun and ends with the needles, failed livers, criminal records, and far worse.

The next couple of days were filled with classes and tormented speech from councilors that we mocked. Chow hall admirers, day room divas. Rehab romance bloomed for uncomfortable sex addicts and the desperate, who were both grasping at anything they could in the absence of their drug of choice. Addicts filling holes emotionally with false love, food, and dumb laughter.

It was high-school level behavior from people of all ages. A couple of horny middle-class fools, maybe in their fifties, caught moaning in delight in the bathroom. The married pair was shamed by staff and left to explain to their spouses why they got thrown out of rehab and back into the street. Discharged because they just couldn't keep it in their pants.

#

I was called into the doctor's office. I was informed that the MD had to see me about my blood results. His face was disapproving. This doctor informed me that my liver function was five times the norm. They had not seen this level of alcohol deterioration in someone my age in recent memory. My soul caved like a snow tunnel.

"If you continue to drink, you will not live to see twenty-five."

I staggered back to the TV room defeated. How could I live if I couldn't drink? I was a used up twenty-one-year-old bag of trash. I started spitting and snarling at the staff. I kicked over a trash can in pure rage. The day room stopped and stared as tears were flowing down my Irish face, plump and red. This was the first sign of the "king baby." The tantrum-throwing mess of a human being that laid just beneath some good-looking young flesh. How could this be? I was young. I couldn't dream of a life without controlled substances and booze. It was my way of life. It was my sex, my love, the inner workings of pleasure points that drove my everyday functions. I was psychologically dependent, one hundred percent. This ate at me like battery acid on baby skin. I built deep resentments toward the treatment facility, the incompetent doctors, and annoying patients.

Days passed. The "Great White" fire that claimed a shocking number of lives in a nightclub in Rhode Island played out on TV. We watched in collective horror as hundreds of people trampled each other to escape the inferno. I mentally blocked any type of logic and reasoning that the place tried to offer me. I spent the rest of my thirty day stay goofing off and making light of a grave situation. I flat out ignored the warning the medical team gave me. I pushed it into the recesses of my demented mind. Addicts are masters at masking reality. I invented my own truth. That's this disease. It tells you nothing is wrong. I finally escaped my first rehab. Back to the enabling arms of my father. The thirty-day certificate I got was my winning ticket, I was cured as far as my family was concerned.

My dad's job at the company had ended. A bad business deal by the evil company owner put my father in a major financial pickle with the IRS. After my grandpa died, we decided to relocate to Corpus Christi, Texas, the Sparkling City by the Sea. My grandpa left a three-bedroom house in the wake of his death. A perfect refuge for two broken Northerners, tired of the cold desolate environment of New England. The divorce had proved fruitful for Barry. The big house on the hill sold for a very handsome profit. We were free, had funds, and the open road called us. My second attempt at a geographical cure. I was leaving behind the shame, the regrets, and the failures. We hit the ground running. This was the starting point to the worst portions of my journey.

We arrived. It was now the year 2004. The eighteen-hundred-mile trip to South Texas was liberating. We entered the most epic drinking binges in Bornagain family history, and that says a lot.

Our new home had a large Seventies style living room with white textured ceilings, wood paneling, and a snow-white carpet. Matching white leather sofas, a brick fireplace, and a small wet bar rounded out the room. There was an old-school big-screen TV for all our drunken entertainment needs.

My Grandpa, Barry the Second, was a psychiatrist, an avid jazz pianist, and a violent alcoholic. His brother died of alcoholism at a seemingly young age as well. The smoking of Old Golds got Grandpa. My bloodline was poisoned deeply by addiction. As the line dwindled down, the drinking and self-loathing appeared to get worse.

Grandma was a sweet woman. She loved animals, an angel in many aspects. She was a nurse when she met grandpa. She was a vision. She looked almost like Ava Gardner in some of her old nursing pictures that sat on the shelves in the house. Years of watching his ramblings and affairs had wounded her sweet soul. An affair forced her to insist they move from their bright and successful life in Massachusetts in the Seventies. She couldn't live in the same city as the women he bedded down, gave jewelry to, and loved on the weekends. For years, she drank vodka straight out of the bottle. She was a blackout drinker for decades. The affair and move wakened an alcoholic gene that was lying dormant in her tiny body. The next generational line of us had it double bad, that genetic predisposition and spiritual curse that breeds addiction.

My dad's younger sisters were both alcoholics as well. My whole father's side of the family was affected by the rage that is alcoholism.

The brick home in Corpus Christi was one level. A Mesquite tree sat in the shallow front yard. The garage attached to the house was on its left. The kitchen had the same avocado appliances as the house in Reading.

I couldn't escape that puke no matter where I went. Beige tiles sat on the kitchen floor. Wood cabinets and white linoleum countertops gave this place a very "Brady Bunch" feel to it. The snow-white carpets were all over the house, the bedrooms, the long hallway. It was a doctor's home. Pristine.

We rolled over the services of my grandparents' maid, a sweet woman. She worked cheap, loving, and she did everything, down to folding laundry. This was a bachelor heaven. A certified pad where we could blast tunes, drink ice-cold beer, and generally go crazy without the judgment of anyone. Barry and I were the best of friends at this point. Our relationship looked more like a pair of fraternity brothers rather than your traditional father and son. We started hitting the bars and local strip joints as soon as we touched down.

I didn't resemble someone who just completed treatment in any way. We found different watering holes that all served unique purposes. We had pool bars to shoot billiards in. There was the strip club, a place for sexual debauchery. Night clubs to try to meet local singles and other dives for entertainment. Neither one of us were working. Living high on the hog from Barry's real estate windfall, we decided some time off was much needed in the Texas sun.

I started playing golf with my dad when I was twelve. Pre-addiction times were so much fun. Barry worked a ton, providing a life for my mother and me. He didn't get to make too many baseball games or school events growing up. When he brought home those clubs for me, I was thirsty for time with him.

Barry loved golf. It was his refuge from the day-to-day rat race that the business world thrust upon him. He always said it was the only thing that kept him sane. So, Saturdays he could be found with his buddies, chipping out of sand traps and drinking cold ones. I never blamed him for that. The man worked hard, and he needed an outlet.

We started bonding on the golf course. The hairdryer winds and fast greens made for some interesting rounds. My dad was awesome. Not the best golfer on earth, but a low eighties player whom I idolized. Barry was just a blast to hang out with. Watching him smile, his infectious laugh, long hippy hair blowing in the wind as he destroyed the links. I loved him. He had the best sense of humor. Crude as it was tender. I really got to know him in those early days in Corpus. The bond between us was super-glue strong. In Texas, out on the golf course, is where we became legendary buddies.

After the day was over, the drinking would kick off in full force. Playing golf was an everyday thing. Six days a week minimum. Like clockwork, we would return home, shower, and pop open a cold Budweiser. My drug connections far off, I was forced to compensate with larger amounts of beer. I was eating like a pig. Consuming gross amounts of food while hungover. Hitting the bar scene every night, coming home to drink more, and pass out cold. Repeat.

My weight ballooned very quickly to over three hundred pounds. Nightly rampages and next day food binges were a recipe for disaster. My insecurity consumed me. The early days in Corpus were filled with self-loathing. My self-image was that of funhouse mirrors at a carnival. I would see an oblong figure, swollen fat face, and sunken eyes.

Barry's fat jokes didn't help much, trust me. Ball busting was his second language, terms of endearment between two friends with family ties. However, it did affect me in the back of my mind. For the first time, I could see women laughing at me in bars and clubs. This only threw gas on the alcoholic flames roaring inside my brain. The fatter I felt, the more I drank, which meant the more I ate. Around and around, we go.

I am a different animal than Barry. When it comes to

partying, I am a time bomb. Barry would return home at around eleven and he would retire to the king bed my grandpa left behind. My rage was only beginning. I would jump in my grandpa's Suzuki Sidekick and leave, pocket full of cabbage and eyes full of beer. On the hunt for more drinks and hopes that I would find a woman desperate enough to sleep with a porker like me.

#

Enter the branching out period. This was the time I started cruising bars dead drunk. Making a fool out of myself nightly. Shots poured, beer was chugged, and new adventures felt grim. Drunk driving was reckless but felt necessary. Flying down the Corpus streets like I owned the road. Stumbling out of bars, blind drunk on cheap rum and drink specials. Not a care for anyone around me. Coming home in a blackout became the mantra. Daily trips to the garage were met with sheer terror, checking to see if the Suzuki even made it home, followed by a check of the front end to see if there was blood on it from a possible hit and run.

About a ten-minute trip from the house was a wild little bar called "The Laugh Shack". An improv comedy troupe took the stage for two shows a night on Wednesday through Sunday. My dreams of being a comedian still lingered in my soul. Being insecure and fat, I loved all the great ones. Farley, Belushi, and Kinison.

I dreamed of making people laugh and getting paid to do so. The place was a badly lit, poorly ran club in the depths of a strip mall. Black concrete floors, dim factory lights hanging from wires above, cheap black restaurant tables, and green leather-like cushions on black metal chairs. A small wooden bar held old chrome wells, beer and wine chilling as they didn't have a hard liquor license from The State of Texas.

The owner was a short Mexican man, pudgy in stature. After scoping out this spot for a few weeks, I got drunk enough to approach the owner for a job. I figured this could be my "in" for someday taking the stage in my grandiose debut. As a drunk, I lived in daily fantasy, always thinking there would come a day where I would be recognized for my unrehearsed talents. The owner needed a bartender. It was only slinging cold beer and pouring cheap wine to half-cooked patrons, so no experience was required. I got my TABC license online and I made my way into the club scene, this time as a world-class worker bee.

The club hosted karaoke on weeknights. This is where a rowdy lower-middle-class group of mostly Mexican Americans and low-brow cowboys who would get blinding drunk on the domestic brew. Carol was my new coworker, and she was a lesbian. Her tomboyish ponytail and sporty, yet spicy, attire made for a hauntingly sexy friend. We hit it off instantly. She thought I was funny. Big shocker there. I served with a smile. My insane Boston accent was at the forefront. Carol and I were a great pairing. She waitressed as I flung orders her way. Working the crowd was important. Working for tips was the perfect job for an expert manipulator, a people pleaser, and a laugh addict such as myself. I could crack a joke and a cool smile, and the fives and tens would rain into the tip jar like monsoon weather.

I was a notoriously hard worker. I never drank or used on the job. There are specific times for work and play. How else would you be able to keep a job to support your addiction? Up to this point in life, I kept this rule as law. After a few short weeks, my addiction reared its snarling beak into my work life in full force. One beer bought by a customer matched with a moment of weakness set off a chain of events that would shape the dark tale you're reading.

Night by night I slowly took the temperature of my boss. I felt out exactly the level of drunkenness he would tolerate as I worked behind the bar. As weeks passed, I let him slide on paying me the two and a half dollars per hour that he owed me on my check as per state law. As the debt racked up, my dark manipulative side emerged. Addicts know how to use any advantage to further their mission in order to get loaded. I purposely let him sink into debt with me, knowing full well he was barley keeping lights on in the joint.

After a good amount was built, I approached him with an idea. I told him that if he let me drink the beer free while on shift, we could call the weekly pay even. He agreed. This was my green light to start pounding as much of his profits as I could fit down my greedy throat. The partying got underway. The more I drank, the funnier I became. Customers loved me; I was building friendships every night. Regulars tipped well; the beer was now free…I had got myself into a beautiful situation.

That's when he walked in. He was a short, mustache-wearing Mexican. John worked in the refineries here in town. A low-level crony that worked hard and loved to drink Miller Lite. We struck up a friendship right away, both drinking more than average people and alcoholics always tend to find kindred spirits. He constantly hit on Carol. It wasn't so much that he didn't know she was gay, he just didn't care.

Friday nights were particularly crazy at the club. We were all half lit by midway through the second show. This night, as usual, John was highly intoxicated. He took his boney finger and signaled me to follow him to the rundown, filthy bathroom. Plywood walls and cheap stalls of cream made up the makeshift commode area. After further investigation, I realized John was about to open a door to evil I had been looking for since we arrived in the Lone Star State. Cocaine. A small plastic bag tied in a knot sat in his palm. My eyes were fixated as he unwrapped the Columbian coke. My mouth was salivating like a Doberman Pinscher looking at a juicy T-bone. His keys shot up from his jean coat pocket.

"Boston, do you get down?"

"Like James Brown," I replied wholeheartedly.

His Toyota key shoveled up the chunkiest yellow coke that I had never seen. He danced it up to my nose as the laughter of the crowd broke in the distance. I snorted with vigor. Wow. What was this alien substance? It numbed the whole sinus cavity and made me almost puke. Pure cocaine, as close to Mexico as you can get. This was an un-stepped on product straight from cartel sources south of the border. My eyes glazed over like jelly donuts. I pointed to the bag, he needed to even out this drip on the other nostril. I made my way back to the bar with a motor mouth. I rifled beers at patrons, Carol amazed at my newfound work ethic. Moments before I was a useless dip shit, drunk and lazy. I saw her go into the bathroom after. I knew then the three of us would become the best of friends.

#

After closing time, we negotiated a bag for purchase. I was amazed to find that this monster coke, twice as potent as back home, was also twice as cheap. I bought a forty-dollar payload and made my way home, wired. The computer room was my destination. Barry dead asleep in the master bedroom, this party was just getting started.

I laid out a monster line to get it going. A cut straw my weapon of choice, I ripped it like Whitney Houston on her birthday. I fired up the computer. I searched websites for hardcore pornography. Withered and dehydrated from days of drinking, I slumped into a black chair. The desk was a large office type that was surrounded by old bookcases. An antique clock sat on one of the top shelves. It would chime on the hour like a demonic church bell in a cocaine nightmare. I got naked and horny beyond belief. A masturbatory sex romp, sweaty and repulsive. My three-hundred-pound body dumped buckets of perspiration as I self-abused in a marathon session. Only a thin set of grey curtains were between my obese sexual carnage and a street full of eyes. I searched for the kinkiest porn you could find back then. I watched Black sluts and horny housewives in compromising situations with unusually hung guys. My pension for stimulants and sex had returned instantly, this time with dark undertones and feverish potency.

    The coke ran out at around six in the morning. I lurched into the kitchen and started slamming beers as the terror driven anger of a comedown consumed my every thought. I drank myself to sleep. This was the single evening that changed the course of my life. I now had a cocaine connection and money in my pocket. My shifts at the club became all about drinking and using. I was reckless.

    A normal occurrence would be finding me standing out in the open, in the grunge of the bathroom, shoveling key loads of pure coke into my snout. A pig in every way. Watching a family man's face as he opened the door to see a three-hundred-pound drunk using hard drugs in plain view of the general public was mind bending. My drug use became vulgar to new heights. Openly talking about, scoring, and using cocaine was a new way of life. I justified my usage in every possible way.

    A new kid came on board. He was a bar back to assist me with restocking beer, cleaning, and anything else for the day-to-day operations in the bar. Halloween night, we had a keg of beer. We served only bottles, so this was a new venture. The drinking started heavy right out of the gate. He asked me for a hit out of the blue. My reputation was starting to attract users of all types. He admitted he had never done cocaine before. I handed him a full forty bag and told him "One up each nostril, careful, it's strong." What a scumbag move. I knew it yet still I introduced this twenty-year-old kid to coke. I gained nothing from it. Not a sale. Nothing. Why? Misery loves company.

My Catholic upbringing left me with a taste of evil. If you believe in the Lord Jesus Christ, you must believe all of it. The devil, demons, angels. Cocaine is its own spirit. As is meth and booze. Every drug has a spirit. Sex has a spirit. Sometimes these spirits swirl together, leaving an inviting Neapolitan flavor. Sex and uppers are something that targeted two deep weaknesses that I reveled in. The high itself would mesmerize me into a voodoo trance.

Sexual degradation left me writhing in sin. The combination was a cocktail. It's why I did drugs at this point. Coke and pornography were enchanting. I worked and drank all night with the omnipresent thought that sexual deviancies were only a short time away. The few times I had real sex during this period were letdowns. The sex wasn't kinky enough. Cocaine birthed perversions in me that could never fully be described in spoken word. Staring at a computer screen. Coke drenched tongue flicking from side to side like a serpent. Laying in a chair naked, living out some Sodom fantasy that no real women in life would agree to or enjoy.

I became addicted to pornography and stimulants. The combination was an experience. One could not be had without the other. During this time, isolation was my utmost pleasure. After the bars and clubs, after daily life with others, I would retreat to this room. The chiming of the antique clock an hourly reminder of the self-imposed prison I had created. I loved every minute. My days off would become dark. Forty-eight hours of drinking, cocaine, and porn. I wasn't even talking to Barry anymore. He would knock on the door if he needed something. My shameful responses met with his concerned voice. If he knew what laid only feet away through the wood of a thin door, his heart would break.

A mess. Full-blown addiction at its worst. Months of chugging and snorting, masturbation parties, alone and afraid. I left a bar that was directly across from my job at the strip mall. I had an estimated twenty drinks in me as I blasted homeward. Arriving on Oakbrook unscathed, I entered the house without any cocaine. It dawned on me I had no smokes left. Jumping in the Suzuki, I drove to the market a stone's throw from the house. After buying some Marlboros, I got it in my head that it would be a wise choice to hit last call at Theo's Bar right down the road.

I swerved as the bubble gums lit up behind me. The blue and red lights flickered with the accompaniment of a siren. I was busted. They pulled me from the seat after asking for my driver's license. These cops meant business as booze reeked from my mouth. Click-clacking cuffs with my hands tightly behind my back. They latched them extra tight after the comment I made about the officer's mustache looking like a gay Seventies porn star. Off to jail I go.

#

This was my first DWI. I was taken to central booking at the city jail to be processed into the system. Staggering to the photo booth, I mouthed off in typical fashion. They snapped a bloated, shameful mug shot. I stood in the cold cell in my Georgetown Hoyas hockey jersey, looking anything but thin.

I got for my first taste of the rotten fruit that is Nueces County Jail. Sitting in the drunk tank in one of the Nation's worst county jails, doom started to sink in. This was a serious arrest, not just a simple public intoxication, certainly nothing to be taken lightly. Because I refused the breathalyzer, they could only charge me with a misdemeanor. This was before the days of mandatory blood draws. I sat for hours, turning down the pathetic bologna and cheese sandwich and cookies they threw at me. I made a phone call to Barry the next morning who promptly bonded me out and came Downtown to pick me up.

    My driving privileges were revoked by The State of Texas. I sat alone at the house, ashamed. Barry and I began drinking together a lot more. There were no golf games or bars. He knew I was becoming crazy.

    One day Carol, John, and I were all snorting coke in my living room. John made a call for our second eight ball. This dealer showed up. Short, Mexican, and a blue-collar worker like John. He wore a baby blue mechanic-style top and uniform pants, black, as they did in the refineries. I paid him, eighty dollars a ball was the going rate. John introduced us formally. My dad was out of town on vacation, so we were on a major binge. This dealer came back five times in the next two days. He knew what kind of customer he had right away.

    I knew his number by memory. I had now cut out John, the middleman. I wanted to use alone; I hated sharing cocaine with anyone. This was a sex-fueled, cocaine-induced, desolate retreat. I was using around the clock. I had quit my bartending job to get wasted full time. This dealer was a delivery man. A customer service genius. He barely spoke when dropping the product. I could ring his cell, and within an hour I had a big bag of powder.

    My dad was unknowingly funding my drug use. I would lie and tell him I drank it at the bar, bought clothes, whatever got him off my back. I started to run out of coke like clockwork at ten in the morning. I would call the dealer over, and over, and over. I could tell this guy was getting pissed at me.

He never said anything because I was dumping every penny I had into his very pocket. Leaving the garage door open, I would have him duck into the side entrance to the laundry room. We would do a handoff and I'd be off and running. His lunch breaks were now eaten up by serving me.

One day he had to weigh it out at my house, so he came in. We sat in the living room. I bought a gram and a ball for eighty. I was now getting player pricing because I was a frequent customer. He handed me the gram as he bagged up the ball separately.

I looked at him and said, "Watch this." I slammed back the whole thing in one line. The drip left me breathless. My throat constricted as I was breathing out of a straw. He looked on in pity. I remember thinking "I want to see how high I can get before I die."

I started interacting with this dealer more than anyone else in my life. It was a constant revolving door between the garage meetings and the pornography laced office. Life in ruins, I hated myself more now than any other period thus far. Calling him forty times in a row if he didn't answer was a regular thing. How could I stoop so low? The floor started to drop out financially. I was draining Barry for hundreds a week. He loved me. I used that love against him every chance I got.

The rage inside me emerged on days that he refused to pay. I would hold him hostage in his own home for hours. Screaming at him in demonic language, pushing him. I made life a living hell for that man until he met my demands. In the end, I always got my way. I would cry when anger didn't work. Cocaine ruled me. I would try to stop every three days or so, only to fail when I would drink. Five beers into a binge, I was already calling this dope man on wheels. It was clear if I were to drink alcohol, cocaine was only moments away. I was possessed by the obsession to get high. Alcohol lowered all inhibitions.

My dad suggested we go to The Palace, a local strip club, one night. We ran an epic five hundred–and-fifty-dollar bar tab by the seven o'clock shift change. He had a younger Mexican stripper on his lap. Her eyes widened as she heard the total on the ticket. He paid with his credit card. Her black doll eyes investigated his.

Desperate for female companionship, he stuffed twenties into her hands as she performed derogatory lap dances. The grinding and pulse of the lights overtook my old man. I knew he was in trouble right then. The remainder of the evening's tab was another whopping eight hundred dollars.

We dropped an astonishing three grand in one sitting when you included the tips. Strip club decadence. A shameful night that we remembered for years to come. What a waste. These two exchanged personal numbers before we left that fateful night. Soon they were dating. This monster was now present at the house all the time. He was dropping big money on dinners, clubs, and clothes. I saw her for what she was. A professional hustler with a pension for old men with money. Her thick Mexican accent irked my last nerves. I hated her and all she represented from the start. Gia was the scum of the earth far as I was concerned, and she had Barry in her slimy clutches.

Barry had an inheritance from Grandpa. He needed to hide some of the money in an account he had opened for me at a local bank. I had full access to twenty thousand dollars. The IRS would seize anything my father had if they knew where it was. Currently, he was becoming incredibly angry with me in my addiction. Clashes with Gia happened daily, her in his ear telling him to get me out of the house. Barry approached me and told me she was moving in. A battlefield fight broke out that lasted a good five hours. She was to arrive with her things the next morning at ten. Before the bank closed, I walked in and withdrew five grand in hundred-dollar bills. I'd show him.

The Suzuki flew down the Cross-Town Expressway. I pulled into an ocean view hotel and checked in. I called the dealer and ordered a half ounce of blow. There was an Irish pub attached to the downstairs of the establishment. I had all I needed for an epic binge, smelling of suicide and sex.

I checked into the place under an assumed name...Christopher Wallace. The Notorious B.I.G.'s real name. No one will find me. I felt empowered by my stealth. I loved the feeling of sneakiness. The dealer arrived at the room for the exchange. Soon as he left, I unpacked my clothes and the sick amount of alcohol I had brought with me for after the bar had closed. Downstairs I went. The Irish Pub was cute. All antique wood flew in from Ireland. They had a small stage in the corner where classic Irish music played live.

The smell of the old bar was like sweet vanilla pipe tobacco. Woodgrain absorbed pale skin as I bellied up to the scene of the crime. Forty-seven hundred dollars in my jean pocket. My blood-red polo golf shirt made me pop against the dark interior of this majestic watering hole. The bartender was a dark horse behind the bar, looking like a vivid pinup. A long red dress with chunky matching high heels. Thin, tall and pale, her skin covered in traditional tatts that dripped from her canvas. She had big green eyes and wire-framed glasses. Her hair in big black curls, pinned to the top of her head, a long flowing curtain of locks made her look like she came out of some beautiful Fifties drama.

She started pouring me whiskey sours. The slow burn hit my throat like a seething leach, sucking my lifeforce deep within. My eyes grew wide and dreamy. The slapping of a stand-up bass pulsed in my veins, the heartbeat of the music rising like a morning star. Patrons of Corpus Christi's nightlife shuffled into the narrow entrance with great fervor. Smoke in the air gave the room a gleaming view. Reflections of faces chimed off mirrors on all sides of the dark wood encasement. I pounded the drinks. The shame of a thief sprang into my heart like a dagger. I tossed with self-hatred as I saw my dad's sweet smile in my mind's eye.

  Eight drinks in and the madness took hold. A ravished feeling like hunger or extreme thirst possessed my every thought. I was like a brimmed hat demon, a piece of Lucifer attached to every fiber in my soul. My legs started moving before my mind had a chance to give an order. I left my tab open with two hundred dollars behind the bar. I signaled hot stuff with a wave; I'd be back. They're always back. The hotel carpet was an acid trip. Squiggly lines that flowed together in the bright light of a Seventies chandelier. Reds and whites melted together as I stood in front of the black elevator doors. I entered the car buzzed, a stumbling baboon, sifting side to side in a sad dance. A short ride and I had my room key ready. One swipe separated yours truly from a pile of large porn dust.

  I burst through the door, a man in a rage. Tipping over the bag on the manila nightstand, I scrambled for a credit card to make out the line. I took the back of my hand and swept the hotel bible out of the way and onto the hunter green floor. As it dropped, I cringed. A whole life of Catholic upbringing, my baptism ruined, as it tumbled in total disrespect. Knowing Jesus is a double-edged sword. His arms are open and loving. However, when one is in the depths of sin? His eyes can feel disapproving. Moments of faith met with the darkest sin imaginable. It makes for one hell of an experience. The threads of His existence were weak in me. I practiced religion in appeasement for my parents and the approval of my extended family. At the same time, in moments of trouble, He was where I ran.

This sick line I was making out was a first. It was the time I realized I was conjuring something evil. Was it the blue leather bible slapping to the ground? Was it the images of the blood running down the feet of the Teacher?

Spirits were in that room. The goose pimple flesh on my arms gave me chills. The thin blood coursing in my heart. The air pressure dropped to a bariatric low that only "evil" can describe.

I gagged it back. The mirror behind me flickered white-spotted light as I whipped around in this cookie-cutter hotel that was generic at best. They all look the same, after all. Boxes of misery. Places away from family, where hidden sin is performed, and demons clung to cheaply papered walls. I put my palms on the TV stand at the foot of the bed and stared into the mirror at the image of a dark soul. It was upon me. Some force within…attached.

I slinked down the hall to the elevators. I ran down the shaft to the bar, my stomach in knots from the parasitic apparition in my innards. Reemergence into the pub was fleeting. The bar stool skidded across the floor, chalky and dry. Another round slides toward my claw as I converse with a stranger in slurred and elevated speech. My feet below felt like I had stepped onto a rowboat. A floating and remarkable feeling, falling in place. I stole a large sum of cash from the patriarch of my family, my best friend on earth. My defender, my enabler. How could I do this?

The more shame I felt, the more I consumed. The night rambled on with long life conversations with drunk out-oftowners and cougar dames. I solved world issues with complete arrogance and ignorance. Back at the room, I lined out ten good size rails. I snorted them like a pig in a trough. Daybreak hit the curtains, shattering all sense of safety. A new day was born. Another rotten chapter in the play that had become my life. I was alone and on the run from my own family. I couldn't even look at my own image in the bathroom mirror. I did some shots to put me on an even keel with the rest of the world, knowing full well I was to hit the streets for much-needed supplies.

The gas station down the street is where an epiphany hits. I was about five hundred in the hole, and I wanted to get even and head home. The gambling began. Scratch off lotto was the bright idea I came up with. I bought a hundred stack of five-dollar tickets and sat at a lunch table near the window. In the same sweaty, gross clothes from the night before, I scratched at the tickets like a mangy Labrador with fleas. Silver tin shavings from the ticket started to pile up on my pants. After losing on every single ticket, I leaped up and retracted a wad of cash out from my trousers. I bought two hundred more in tickets.

A uniformed cop walked in. Old and looking like he was a desk jockey at the station. He sat and talked with the overweight female clerk with a curly perm, looking like a stuffed sausage in her blue uniform top and black slacks. He kept peering at me in curiosity. I won forty-five dollars on the two-hundred-dollar investment and quickly went up to cash in. As I took my seat and started the pitiful act of losing, he approached. He sat down next to me as I was stinking of whiskey, cinnamon schnapps, and beer.

"Looks like you're in it to win it?"

I looked up with glassy eyes and nodded. I was sniffling like an Ebola patient in a Nigerian village. He knew exactly what I was involved in. He got up and shook his head as he walked away.

Back at the hotel, I rang my dealer. There was no running out of coke on this outing. I had just paid for another two nights; five p.m. couldn't come fast enough. The bar was breathing when I walked in. Cocaine markers were in my blood at toxic levels, and I shook uncontrollably. The new clothes and cologne I wore were no match for the punishing abuse I had just endured.

I knew I looked sick. Everyone in the place stared at me in horror as I did shooters and made small talk with the band. Beads of sweat rolling down my forehead. My curly hair was way overdue for a cut. Saturated and slick, I ran my cigarette-stained digits across the bar. The dealer showed up. A quick bathroom handoff and I was on my way back to the den.

The cocaine had me sexually deprived. Looking for paid dates before the days of internet dating sights and online brothels is nothing like today. I picked up my local yellow pages and looked under escorts. A faint-voiced woman answers and takes my order. I wanted a Mexican, older. The lady obliged and I started to clean up the room and hide the drugs and paraphernalia in case it was a sting operation.

About an hour passes and a soft tap at the door startles me. She came in and we had sex to the tune of two hundred dollars. The funds were dwindling down fast. Huge bar tabs, hookers and cocaine. It was all adding up. The guilt of what I had done to my father was eating me alive. A three-day bender had come to pass. One of great shame.

I limped back home to find my father seething. I blew the whole five grand. I started crying and sobbing like a baby. I admitted I had a major drug problem for the very first time. Hearing the words come out of my own mouth really changed everything. We had an unusually long talk. A trip down to the bank to withdraw the rest of money in cash happened. My dad completely cut off my money supply for the very first time. I was officially on the wagon.

#

Gia was there with Barry. Soon I relapsed. My dad viewed alcohol as a staple in our house. His famous line was "Switch to beer man."

If I wasn't insane on hard liquor or drugs, I was pretty much allowed to get drunk, if it was beer. Me not working and spending money all became a problem for Gia. Deep, dark resentment and jealousy grew inside her core. We hated each other. I started wearing thin my welcome at the Bornagain home. I knew my days were numbered. A big blow out fight between myself and the former stripper left my father having to choose. Who do you think he picked? Young tail or a bloated, money-sucking alcoholic addict as myself?

I called back home. I quickly decided to return to Boston. This was around the 2005 mark. I called my friend, Buddy. He would welcome me with open arms. I had plans to reemerge into a new apartment. Get a job and start a new life. Buddy had no idea the depths of my drinking, my damaged thoughts or depression. But I was on my journey. My mom bought me a Greyhound ticket one way. The trip from Corpus to Boston was painful. It was much worse than my bus trip to Vegas, most likely because the lights of youth and wonder had drained from my eyes. I felt old even in my early twenties. I had a lot of time to think on the trip. I was mentally preparing myself for a period of "getting my shit together." I needed to buckle down and show my family that I could pull it together and survive after years of failure.

Claire and her hubby picked me up from the downtown bus station. The first night back I was drinking within a few hours. What would be a Bornagain arrival without a welcome home party?

A lot of old hippy friends from the dump days came over and we did our formal meet. Claire and her husband owned a quaint little two-bedroom condo in North Reading. We partied for about two days straight. Just alcohol, but still, the volume is the key factor here.

I was completely hungover when I got the call from Buddy. It was time to go look at our new apartment. His grandma took us out for Chinese food in Wakefield just a few minutes down the road. After a hearty meal full of Chinese chicken wings and noodles, we arrived at the Four Plex Apartments on Water Street.

The building towered, a two-story brownish aluminum-sided monstrosity. Green trim and matching wrap around wooden deck. The driveway was gravel, dusty, and country looking. Hardwood floors graced the interior hallway. The door opened to a kitchen, bedroom, and bathroom in the rear. The living area was in the front overlooking Water Street. It was a one-bedroom. Buddy's grandma was paying the first and last on the joint, so he obviously got the bedroom. Buddy's uncle lived in the back apartment. They had a huge community garden set up for summer. Everyone in the Four Plex would pitch in and pick fresh produce.

After securing the lease, we moved a three-seat couch into the living room. A drab grey thing with oversized pillows. We had an entertainment center that held a huge old school TV. We moved the cheap kitchen table into the center of the living room right away. It was cramped, but how else were we supposed to play Texas Hold 'Em?

Now I was under the gun to look for a job right away. So, the second day at our new place I took off on foot to gain employment. I came over the cusp of the hill on Water Street, not even three blocks from the house. A five-minute walk if you were taking your time. Big oak trees with canopies of lush green leaves shaded the sidewalk. A massive sign, "S&M Liquors."

I walked into the building that was erected sometime in the Sixties. Shelves of glass bottles that seemed to go for miles stretched to the back of the dated store. A huge Boston Red Sox display that was themed around their epic 2004 World Series win sat above the doors of the beer cooler that made up the whole back wall. Neon lights were everywhere and were blinking; they sold every kind of beer and booze one could name.

Green and white checkered flooring with fiberboard ceilings. The counter in the front of the store stretched almost the whole length of the place. Pints and halves, airplane bottles, smokes, candy, everything a drunkard's dream is made of. On the floor of the main sales area was the strangest oddity I had ever seen in a liquor store. A lazy boy recliner! A medium-size TV older than me sat up above the beer coolers. If you were sitting in the old polyester brown chair and you looked up, you would get a great view of the daily Sox games. The bell on the door alerted whoever was in the back.

I heard a deep voice, "I'll be right there," he pronounced with the thickest Boston accent you ever heard. Out came a tall hunched over man sporting a horseshoe bald spot with a bowling ball shine. He wore brown slacks and penny loafers. A white button-down shirt with short sleeves. "How can I help you?" he stammered.

I walked up to the man and extended my hand and introduced myself politely. I was a very respectful young man. I told him my intent, gave him my retail sales background, and filled out an application. This was Darold. He was Rodney

Dangerfield reborn.

As I am doing the paperwork, he popped a squat in his recliner. He explained to me that he had cable and satellite. Back then satellite was unheard of. He explained that he was the biggest Sox fan on this planet, and no matter what, he was going to catch the game. If one outlet went down, he had a backup. Darold was drinking water. I could tell he didn't drink booze. He agreed to hire me and started to show me around the place.

We started off way upstairs. It was an attic-like compartment with a flimsy staircase. Red shaggy carpet that stunk of mothballs was below our feet. The carpet ran back to a massive ice maker, and a big wooden table to bag ice on. A steel basket to carry the full bags of ice around was sitting on the tabletop. It was hot as a hash pipe up there. No central AC, no windows, only a small FM radio. It was dark except for one hanging light that had a linen pull switch. The Jetsons were on when this thing was installed. Most likely the same bulb too.

We made our way to the basement. This dark damp concrete dungeon was eerily interesting. A conveyor belt ran down the side of the old wooden stairs. The ceiling was super low. You had to watch your head as you walked through. Old ceiling joints above would really crack your coconut if you were not careful. All the beer that was to be stocked into the walk-in beer cooler was down here. It sat warm. That was what the conveyor belt was for. When the distribution trucks came to deliver, we would put it on the belt, send it down to a man waiting, who would then stack the cases neatly on the floor.

After the grand tour, Darold told me to come in the following day at ten a.m. sharp, an hour before the store opened. When I got in the next day, I came to do work. A big delivery was to come in and this was my chance to really prove myself. Darold introduced me to Nova.

A hippy chick who looked exactly like Janis Joplin. Turns out, she was obsessed with Janis. She wore a long flowing skirt, black with a witchy print. She had bare unpainted feet with old sandals. Her hair was onyx and stringy. A large nose and sunken in eyes. She wore far too many rings on her long fingers. After meeting her for ten minutes, I decided she was the nicest girl ever. John was another balding Dr. Phil look-alike. Younger, forty years old as an estimate. He was a typical nerd. Goofy running shoes, tan cargo shorts, and a stained t-shirt. White gym socks pulled directly to the knees. He was an avid PC gamer. When he told me he had kids, I was a little shocked. I didn't think he could pull a one-nighter, never mind a full-on relationship.

The order came in and it was my turn to stack beer downstairs. I worked at a breakneck pace. I really had something to prove. I stacked beer for hours as John ran the conveyor. Darold watched sports comfortably in his chair, right underneath the AC vent. Nova worked the register. She served early-morning alcoholics. They are all the same. They come in and buy the bare minimum. A half-pint, maybe a single beer. They would come back ten times a shift. The alcoholic in some cases will lie to themselves all day. Only buying what they think they need to keep off the delirium tremors, no more, no less.

Darold was overly impressed. So much so that he ordered me to take the lead on bagging up all the ice to fill the coolers on the floor. I was spent by the day's end. He was incredibly happy he hired me. I loved the store. I left that day and looked at the landmark S&M sign. It was a Wakefield trademark. It was the original from the Sixties and the town couldn't tear it down because the monster was grandfathered in.

#

Back at the apartment, the crew was gathering. Buddy had Antonio, and a few others over already. The card game was in full swing when I arrived. D was a bald redhead. A good ten years older than us. He worked for a local sales company and had his stuff together, pretty much. The hands were dealt as a plate of powder was passed around. A line for each, including me. I sat down and was dealt-in immediately. The Red Sox Game was on, beer was in hand…this was heaven.

At this time, with all the male company, the coke didn't make me sexually crazed. We played for an hour. The funky dealer that Buddy had was a riot. A professional coke dealer in his late forties named Bronson. He had combed over black hair and a big black caterpillar mustache. He donned huge TV screen prescription sunglasses with a blackish purple tint in the massive lenses. He flung the door open like Kramer from TV's "Seinfeld." Sneak Attack! He bucked in the apartment like a whole bull in a China shop. He had a black compact disc holder. He converted this one into a cocaine store. Eight balls, teeners, crack. We referred to it as soft and hard. He always had both. He dropped a chunky eight ball on us. It was double Texas prices and half as strong. Bronson did some product and hit the door, blowing out like a manic wind.

This was Groundhog Day. Months had gone by like feet marching down an ever long road. The partying intensified daily. My drinking was fueled by my job at S&M. Darold started letting me run a tab midweek, paying him back on Fridays. His concern for me prompted comments, him saying things like "It's the same as letting a fish work in a water store." Even D's decline was evident. He cashed in his retirement plan and put the whole thing right in Bronson the dealer's pocket. Years of savings pissed away like raindrops in the city drainage system.

I drank more than anyone in the group. Buddy had started lashing out. He would call me an alcoholic at the worst possible times, cutting deep as a saber blade into buffalo flesh. My performance at the store was poor at its finest. I was staying up all night, with no sleep, then coming into work. I was lax, lazy, and downright criminal. You could find me some days sleeping in the beer cooler as the others would cover for me. I used my friendship with my coworkers to further my irresponsibility. Dreaming of cards, nose cemented with poisonous snot form cocaine abuse, my days were filled with misery. I started slipping on my portion of the rent. Traffic at the house was dangerous. I was wearing my sneakers to sleep so if the cops kicked in the door, I could jump out the window and have a running chance.

Buddy and I started to disagree. This was in no way my friend's fault, and I knew it. It was time to go. I just vanished. I left all my clothes, my job, and pride back at the apartment. This was one more failure in the life of Boston Bornagain. I took the bus to Reading Square. I was looking for anyone who would take pity on me. I couldn't go to the hood because Buddy would surely find me and put a whopping on me for leaving him in the lurch on the rent. Claire and that whole crew were leery of my behavior at this time, so I struck out once again.

#

I found myself uptown with nowhere to go. I called my aunt and uncle. My aunt was not happy with me, getting full reports of my behavior in Texas. After a sob fest, she agreed to let me come and stay with them. There was to be zero drug and alcohol use. Facing the streets and being broke, I agreed. My arrival was followed by a long, painful come to Jesus meeting with my uncle. The groundwork for a clean and sober life was laid down with firm guidelines. One slip and I would be put out on my ass.

  Soon as the dust settled, I was taken shopping. My uncle was a bonified millionaire. No expense was spared. I had never been treated like this in my entire life. Barry made me work for everything I ever had. They lived in a brick palace in a wealthy Boston suburb. My cousins had angel hair and blue eyes. Everything from the outside looked like peaches and cream and smelled even sweeter. My Aunt was recently clean and sober and militant in her march for change. I had to follow all the rules, pitch in, and pull my weight. They had a maid, so pulling my weight just meant cleaning up after myself and not getting loaded.

  My cousins were good students. My oldest cousin and I loathed one another. She was snotty and stuck up, but she was family, so I tolerated her. We bumped heads, so for safety's sake, I stayed far out of her way. The middle one was a sweet girl, the sweetest you could imagine. My little cousin was funny as can be. He and Barry knew all the great lines from "The Three Stooges" by heart and would always recite them at parties. He was a lively kid, full of love and laughter. I settled in nicely. I had cut all ties with anyone from Reading, knowing full well my weakness for drink and drugs.

  As time passed, I got a job working at a local Italian food spot. I started working the door. I had to wear a business suit, so my uncle bought me three to get started. I loved it. My bubbly personality and creative problem-solving mind made me a perfect fit for a door attendant and host. I seated guests, held the door, all while the elite of Wesley, Massachusetts, one of the nation's wealthiest communities, shoved crisp tens and twenties into my coat pocket. I started to want to better myself and my life in general. I was upwards of two hundred and eighty pounds. I started a crash diet and dropped a considerable amount of weight right away. I was twenty-three years old. Newly clean and sober for the first time in a decade.

  Auntie's best friend moved into the house, running from a bad marriage and love lost. She was from a different state and knew my aunt and uncle since the early Seventies. She was short. Thin as can be, small-breasted. The legs of a dancer. She was cute. She was also fifty-three years old at the time. We became quick friends. I lived upstairs in the loft apartment with her, in a bedroom off the kitchen. Days drifted as Christmas time fell. She and I went to the mall to go Christmas shopping for everyone, even one another. Our friendship bloomed during this period. It became very flirty, it had sexual tension with a razor's edge. Neither one of us would think about it, how could we? She was married and I was a kid compared to her.

  Christmas Eve was filled with food and song. The great brick fireplace roared in the living room. Expensive furniture, the lap of luxury. The family shuffled up to the top floor and their respective bedrooms at around midnight. She and I went to talk on her bed in her room, door open, only the night air between us. The window behind her delicate face made the scene picturesque, snow in bounds, cotton white backdrop, cold, and tempting. The bed cover melted us in, talking and laughing, looking into one another's eyes as an in-depth bond formed. We were about to exchange gifts. I got her a small token of appreciation. Her husband had some serious money; what could I get her that she didn't already have? The card I gave her was personal and sweet. I saw that her mature heart was melting as she read words of admiration and kindness. She looked up as she handed me a small box. I unwrapped it, Lacoste Red. A wonderous scent, crisp and clean. I leaned in and hugged her long and meaningfully.

  The hug trailed like the end of a Steely Dan jazz epic.

My thick fingers on her bare arms. Her black silk top was a turn on in every way. I looked into her big eyes. My youthful lips went in and locked on her. My hand gently touched her face as we kissed in the sweetest embrace. Chemical reactions I had never felt were firing like a Fourth of July spectacle. Raw emotion and a breeze overcame my heart. I cupped her left breast as soft moans and creeks of love spewed from our vocals. She pushed me away like a cat on water. Her eyes were huge and terrified.

"What are you doing?" she asked.

My response, "What are YOU doing?"

She began having remorse and panicked. I left that night devastated. Regret and shame had filled my mind. But I also went to bed with a smile. I was falling for her, and she knew it.

Weeks of lunches. Hallway kisses, slow and grinding bodies in forbidden love. We stole away every chance we got. We began meeting in privacy. Finding ways to be home alone, fairy-tale trips in the car that ended up in city parks and school parking lots long after acceptable hours. Late-night hot tub trysts. This was a full-on affair, unlike any relationship I had experienced. I was a clean and sober adult male for the first time ever. I didn't have the mask of alcohol clouding the meanings of love. I could feel something for someone else for the first time. I became obsessed with her touch. I lived every moment to please and serve her wild extramarital fantasy.

#

I got the results I was looking for, two hundred and fifteen pounds and solid. I was looking great. Now I had a closet full of suits and ties. The owner of the eatery came in and saw something in me. He saw my hustle and respected it. He threw me in headfirst as I entered their management training program.

    I would be working in Boston's swanky Back Bay neighborhood. I started to take the same commuter rail line that the HempFest journey took place on, only this train ended up at South Station. A quick walk down Newbury Street and I was at work. Rich European college students and businesspeople of all types made up the lunch crowd at this new location. This was a trial by fire. I was making a new salary of forty thousand per year. That was great money for a twenty-three-year-old man at that time. I was well on my way to a promising career in the restaurant business.

    My cousin was around thirteen. He was smoking tons of weed with his friends in the basement of the brick mansion. It all started back up. I would sneak into the boiler room with his young friends and toke up. A grown man hanging with teenagers in secret. My aunt and uncle knew what was going on. Coming from the hippy counterculture, weed was harmless. They eased up on the idea of me smoking marijuana. In typical Bornagain fashion, I fucked up. I had money to burn, literally. I was paying zero rent and all my food was provided. Big bags of bud were bought on a weekly basis. My affair with the older woman was no longer in motion. I was smoking nonstop from the time I got home till the time I slept, and around the clock on my days off.

    The twelve-hour workday matched with the two-hour train commute was wearing me down, it was six days a week. I had to memorize the whole menu for food allergy purposes. A front of the house manager had to become food safety certified by the state in order to run the establishment. It was a massive amount of information. The Cesar salad dressing alone had a million ingredients. I needed to know each one and how much of the ingredients were listed in the chef's cookbook. The grueling schedule broke me. I started to show cracks. My brain was in full relapse mode before I ever realized it.

I got off work at seven p.m. Another joint they owned was right up the street from the training restaurant I worked in. My feet moved once again before I could think. My expensive dress shoes scuffed the cold sidewalk as I ripped open the door, overcoat tail blowing in the wind. I was blank. Throwing it all away is what I was programmed to do. The fatigue, the fight I had with my lover that day. It all mounted. Really just excuses for what was about to take place. I sat at the bar. I ordered a double Appletini. A chilled martini glass hit my hand with a frosty nip. I lifted it by its frozen stem and peered into the potion. The dark wood of the bar beneath, the chatter all-around, the happy hour crowd unwinding. Time stood still as my lips hit the cold rim. A tangy-sweet tartness. A candy-flavored burn, charring my throat. This was the first drink all over again. My lengthy sobriety stint had me feeling like a virgin. The bar staff looked on in concern as I slammed the double like a shot. I ordered another immediately. My eyes were on the clock as I knew the last train home was at ten minutes past nine.

My verbiage was belligerent. I was raising my voice after the fourth drink. Eight shots in a matter of moments. No food in my belly and nine months of meaningless white-knuckle recovery. People looked on in shame. They felt bad for me. My coworkers knew I was loaded. It was an unknown fact that I wasn't drinking. The walk up the stairs at home was scary. Knowing full well if I got caught, I was done for at the house. I passed out cold.

At work the next day I got a ton of angry stares from other trainees. I guess I had told some people off in anger. I was mortified. It died down after about a week or so. Well, until the next catastrophic event. I walked into the same bar. The same bartender stood before me.

This time I went with two other guys at the training program. We started drinking heavily. Shots. Beers. They were going to take me home, so the clock wasn't running against me. I had met a girl in a chat room about a week before. I was texting her as the night progressed. She was a big girl. How big I didn't yet know. I was talking super loud at the bar about hookers, cocaine, and other rubbish. Everyone in sight could hear my diatribe. Embarrassing scenes of degradation in career-ending proportions. The bartender had enough. She cut me off and threw me out. I started shouting obscenities at her. Anyone else who got in the way got it too. With my coworkers horrified, we sifted down to the car. I called the big chick right away. I insisted these guys drive me forty-five minutes away to her house.

Upon arriving for this drunken one-night stand, she appeared in the doorway. In full view of my coworkers, she stood almost four hundred pounds. They were laughing at me as I stumbled up the drive in the saddest manifestation of shame. They were just relieved to be rid of me. A drunk, a general problem to others, a nuisance. I went into the house and immediately started a vile escapade with this complete stranger. Driven by sexual lust and self-hatred, I demeaned myself. This is someone I would on no other circumstance give myself to. Not that she was a bad person or wrong in any way. I just wouldn't be attracted to someone that had her features. Just not my cup of tea.

I never slept. Still shattered when the sun came up, I knew I needed to be at work at eight a.m. sharp. I was a forty-five-minute drive from there and she didn't have a vehicle. The commuter rail ran from her place to North Station in

Downtown Boston. I ran. Same clothes on. My stinking booze teeth were rotten and ripe. My hair twisted and matted with dried sexual sweat and God knows what else.

I ran into work forty-five minutes late. I didn't even call as my cell phone was dead as a doornail. The first few hours were fine. After lunch, I returned to find the whole kitchen looking at me. I was working with the chefs to learn the menu. They shunned me like a leper. Eyes pierced me like daggers. I heard the snarling laughs from the shadows. They mocked me in private. Upper management had heard the whole tale.

They fired me. My promotion gone; I was devastated to nothing. I was crushed. My family was in shock. I was nothing. Suffering a total loss of identity and the world around me had ended like a bad movie. Roll the credits. I went on a bender. I found comfort in the drink like never before. Upon returning home, I was asked to go to treatment once again. My work insurance covered it and off I went. This time it was in the Greater Boston area.

#

I hated myself in ways I couldn't have dreamed. My days in treatment were taken as seriously as a slapstick film. I made friends with loser rejects, demons in every way. The spirit of heroin was alive. One prostitute I met was a particular driving force. She flirted, seduced, and enticed male clients. Me being one, I was sad to see her walk out the door. She gave me her phone number before she left. The runner in me decided to walk out the door three short days after she departed. I called her at a Boston train station from a payphone with the last two quarters I had.

She picked up. I explained that I was broke, desperate, and wanted to get high. The train took me to the heart of the ghetto. I walked up to the address she gave me, a two-story white house with a brown lawn made of dirt and dead grass.

A group of Black males greeted me at the porch. They looked at me with evil eyes and demonic faces. They knew I was coming; the devil has a funny way of announcing you. I was introduced to the portly Black lady who ran the trap. She talked to me like I was a rodent. Stern and direct.

"Sit over there and shut up."

I sat on the roach-infested couch and waited. I was offered a hit of crack and I blasted off. The small Italian hooker strolls in fresh off a trick. She sits with me, hugs me, and kisses me on my lips. She goes into detail about the trick she had just finished. An old man who paid her for oral sex. He paid her extra to be able to finger her rectally. I was shocked, grossed out, and turned on. She left me to hit the liquor store.

The hardwood floor was filthy, cakes of dirt and boot prints from the muddy front yard. Wallpaper peeled off stained sheetrock. A gaping hole in the ceiling where pink insulation poured out. A smell of crack smoke and death. Zombie men and women shuffled about; this was purgatory personified. The prostitute returned with four bottles of Red Mad Dog 20/20. I started chugging like a suicidal man dying of thirst. After the alcohol took hold, the demon spirits were swirling, I asked the house mother for another hit. She said I was going to earn this one.

Her eight-year-old son took me by the hand to the back of the house. The back yard was encased by a broken, rusted chain-link fence. The grass was a mile high, masking a sun-faded plastic playhouse. A discarded old lawn mower sat rotting. A black cat stiff in rigor. Like a shank board, feet straight out and dead mouth wide open, covered in horse flies. Its sharp white teeth snarling to the sky. Eyes wide open and whited over with rank film. The boy instructed me to bury it. I asked for a shovel. He hands me a toy spade. One that kids would have on family beach outings.

"Mamma said she gone hook you up after."

I was shaking. The ground was hard and dense. The plastic spade bent like lemongrass as I piled dirt aside this feline grave, shallow and cold. I dug a foot-deep hole. Grimacing, I laid my hand on the cat. A sack of rotting animal flesh, bile, and blood. I gently laid the carcass in its final resting place. The spade now snapped in half. I covered the cat with my bare hands, the earth tinted my skin shit brown. I patted it as flat as I could. Its stiff tail sticking up like a headstone, emerging from the ground. The tail, a marker of death for all to see. I couldn't even bury a household pet the correct way. The son took my dirt coated hand and we walked back inside. His young face was unphased by what just happened. The death of his pet. The morbid half-assed burial. None of it touched this little broken human being. I got the dime piece hit Big Mamma gave me. I lit it in a used, shared community crackpipe, handed to me by a transient with fever blisters on her chapped bleeding lips. I was alone in the room, drunk, afraid, tears in my eyes. I ripped it in one hit. Laying back, thinking. *Where did it all go? How did I get here? Is this who I am?*

The prostitute now sitting beside me, grinning. The crack smoke deep on my mind. I got horny as hell. I asked her politely to perform oral sex on me. We moved to the bathroom, out of eyeshot of the kids playing on the dirty crack-house floor in the living area. I entered her used mouth raw, no protection for this careless act. Empty feelings of sexual slander. I hated myself but reveled in the evil, swindling lie of the flesh. Sucking sounds, serpent slurps, and moaning music. I couldn't contain myself any longer. She spits unmade children onto scum-laced tiles. The floor riddled with bloody panties and kids' pajamas.

The baby blue walls closed in. She sat on the cruddy commode and cooked herself up a massive shot of smack. I left and told her "Save me some."

I sat on the couch, fleas covering my arms and jeans, eating me alive as I sat in rage. She returns with a new mask on. A face of heroin, black as pitch. Her sweat-drenched top and black stretchy pants made me want to vomit. Her eyelids heavy, black-pinned orbits looking right into my soul. She hands me an uncapped needle. Full of brown sludge. I moved to sit on the toilet, the first needle use of my life. I sat down as the broken fixture shifts on rusted bolts. She pulled down my pants, covered in flea larva. The toilet seat stuck to me like car leather in summertime . She started giving me head as I poked the pin through my blue virgin vein. I drew back my pure blood into the rig. A satanic force helped me push the white plunger inward. The warm blanket of dope covered me from head to toe. The rush made me climax without warning. She gagged and laughed in unison. I threw the used needle on the floor, uncaring for the children in the house. We both stumbled to the couch. I sat in a bug-infested pile of shame. My stomach burned with pleasure. I looked at the fallen angel. Her face contorted and twisted like Detroit steel.

Smirking devilishly, she said, "I have Hepatitis C. Now we can share everything."

This hell can't be described. She took pleasure in my panic. She let out a soft laugh as she touched my head. Moments later the reality of what I had done made me throw up off the side of the sofa. I passed out in Lucifer's arms. They let me sleep a while as they looked on. I was a fresh kill. I was mocked and laughed at.

What have I done?

I woke to her stringy black hair on my chest. It was only

an hour or so after my fix. Still mesmerized by the smack, I nudged her. She woke up and I demanded a hit of rock.

She pulled the broken stem from her purse. She passed me a preloaded hit and a crack lighter. I smoked it feverishly. I held it in until I choked. We lurked to the back bedroom. High on blow, we started French kissing in a demonic dance. Twirling around as my tongue flipped in the mouth of a prostitute. I ripped her clothes off. With no panties on, and covered in beads of liquid, I threw her onto the carpet, matted with dog hair. Navy blue and stinking of smoke and kerosene. Dirty clothes now strewn about, we lay stark naked. I entered her body. Rough sex ensued with hateful passion. We loathed one another. I took out the madness I felt from her Hepatitis C admission in the form of sexual punishment. I pinned down her arms as she squirmed, hundreds of puncture wounds leading to black tracks that ran the length of her collapsed veins.

There was no way this was me. I could feel my soul fading like a hologram. Invaded by a shadowy brim-hatted figure. A glowing set of eyes within my own. Cocaine and the evil of heroin mixing like cement in a truck, thick and chunky. I had her legs over her head as I rammed as deep as science would allow. Her devilish moaning made me hate her even more. I pumped as fast and hurtful as I could, despair met with even more delight. She rubbed the bumps on my chest, pleasure centers that when high, make you explode. I announced my finish. I remained in her womb as I pulsed with enticing homicide.

I stood as she lay in puddles of slop. Panting and screaming inside. She got dressed as I sat in the corner. Then she left the room. Never to see her again. Shortly after, Big Mamma threw me out. I had nothing to offer, and I could tell I made her sick. I walked back to the train broke, tired, and stinking of perverse sex and bodily fluid. Within an hour I would be back to the wholesome doorstep at home. Exile awaited me.

#

My aunt let me in just to yell at me. Missing and lost in more ways than one. They allowed me to sleep it off upstairs. First, I showered in the hottest water possible. Scrubbing imaginary herpes from my skin in terror. The fear of the HIV and HEP-C that I believed to be raging in my organs consumed me. I wept as the steam clouded the glass on the expensive shower door. I went from an inner-city crack-house to upper-class suburban America in the blink of an eye. What a vast contrast. I had sunk into the bed in horror. Sweet dreams, Boston. New demons were born to haunt me. Death, sex, and disease.

Days passed; it was just too much. I stole huge piles of change from my uncle's dresser. I left to buy a large jug of Carlo Rossi wine. I sat behind the liquor store near a dumpster. With the hot garbage stinking and the sun beating down, I drank it as fast as possible. Staggering back to the house, I decided this was it. I knew the jig was up. I lunged past my aunt. Locking myself in the bathroom, I dumped two whole bottles of psych meds down my throat, washing it down with cold tap water. The door popped open. She looked on as I attempted suicide. Long time coming.

Taking one's life in their own hands takes balls. Not a cry for help, I wanted my soul to eject from my body and soar out of the atmosphere. I needed death.

#

The sirens wailed; the back of the meat wagon was hectic and chaotic. EMT's screaming, saying my name, telling me to hold on. The ER scrambled to prep a table for me. I was pumped full of charcoal. After about twenty minutes, I regurgitated a thick black tar from my mouth, a molten petroleum product like I had eaten a runway.

    I laid in bed, the doctors explained to me that I was lucky to be alive. The amount of medication should have fried my already taxed liver and kidneys. They admitted me to my first psych ward. A mandatory seventy-two-hour hold for all suicidal patients. While here, my older lover broke it off all the way. Hurt, and self-hatred killed my mind. They contacted Barry. I was to return home after this. I was their problem no more. I caused havoc in my family's home. I disrespected their trust. I broke every rule.

    Addiction had a new purpose. It was now a slow road to suicide. Its face changed. Demons had me and I knew it. The childhood trauma. A fresh wound of love. Loss of my job. Another pearl on the string of massive failures. I was about to return home to Texas. A broken man, more so than ever before.

    Happy for me to be home, my dog ran and jumped in my arms as I came up the drive, duffel bag in hand. Barry was all smiles. After all the hell I caused, I was welcomed with nothing but love. I had made some major waves for Gia. My aunt demanded she move out of the home, and she did.

    That is when I moved into my own place down the street. I got a job at the Republic of Texas, the nicest steak house in all of Corpus Christi. I worked at the door. Wearing a suit, I was tipped handsomely. Within a few days, I was drinking every night after work and calling the same dealer from before. He would deliver cocaine to the apartment upon request. I was back at it. I ran out of money. I called him and traded him my pappa's gold ring. He was dead. Years before, my mother's father gave me the ring, which had an onyx plate with a diamond in the center. His love for me was incredible, and I traded the only memento he left me for an eighty-dollar sack of powder that I shoved up my nostrils in five hours. It deeply affected me.

I was miserable. I found myself in a terrible spot. I wanted to change. I gave AA a shot for the very first time. A real shot, with an open heart and mind. New Phoenix Group was in a mall next to one of my favorite strip clubs called Aloha. The building was canary yellow. Three steps lead to a porch with white trim. The glass French doors swung open into a drab old room from the Seventies, a crowd of smokers outside ripping butts and drinking Folgers. Just like you would see in a movie. Chairs in a row, steel and folding. Couches lined the walls, the lone table at the front with the Big Book sitting in full view. The meeting started with the Serenity Prayer.

"God, grant me the serenity to accept the things I cannot change, the courage to change the things I can, and the wisdom to know the difference."

I listened. People of all types, just as you see at parties, all sharing experiences of strength and hope. How they got sober, how they stayed that way. My heart was in it. I witnessed the smiling faces of people free from drugs and booze. They had what I wanted, and I was willing to work to get it.

I went to meetings for a couple of weeks. I was a little bashful about talking to others. I was so blacked-out drunk all over town for so long, I didn't know who my enemies were. Once I got up the courage, I started talking to some older guys who had substantial clean time. Jax and Devin were great guys. They took me to meetings, lunch, and invited me out hunting on the ranch. We built friendships. I asked Jax to sponsor me and started working on the world-famous Twelve Steps.

I couldn't wrap my head around the process. We walked into it slowly. Admitting I had a problem. Admitting there was a power greater than myself that could save me from this addiction.

I always knew there was a God. I had serious doubts in the back of my mind though. Childhood trauma. The rage within. All these emotions mixed with the numbing effects of the substances blocked out the Light of the Lord. I was willing to try. I was finally open to a new way of life because my way had become hell on earth.

The fellowship was amazing. Alienated from almost everyone, I was glad to have made a new group of friends. A network of contacts that I could call in those dark and trying moments when the demons came. I saw a transformation over the next few months. I was growing fond of the new me. I was able to look at myself in the mirror. The hate-filled self-talk, the doubt…it all started to fade as my tender mind cleared like ash settling after a volcano eruption.

#

I needed a real, stable daytime job, away from alcohol and drugs. I started at a grocery store in Corpus Christi. Once I applied, it was only a few days before I was hired to work in the small takeout style restaurant inside its massive walls. Work was great. I was prepping food and serving customers, what I do best. I made a ton of new friends. Life was getting sweet. After a few paychecks, I put a deposit down on a new place in a better part of town.

There she was, sweet, long brown hair, and a nice smile. I wait about a week after talking and flirting a bit. I ask her out and she says no. Crushed, the next day I played it super cool and told her, "I really just needed someone to show me around town." The next day, she asks me out; we kiss. She moves to my new place with her four-year-old daughter.

I married her four months later. We moved to Port

Aransas, Texas soon after. I got a job at a vacation rental company as a person who answered calls and pitched them back to the sales team. I was paid very little, to the tune of ten dollars an hour. We moved into a tiny apartment right on the beach with a pool out the back door. A boardwalk to the sand. Life was excellent.

My family life will be kept private. The next part of the story will detail my rise and fall in the business world. I will say in short, some important things that you, the reader, should know. I had three children. The little four-year-old girl whom I loved at first sight and later adopted. I had a bouncing baby boy, half Irish, half Mexican, and then his little sister. We shared everything that life had to offer. Out of respect for them, I will only touch on them briefly to explain my lineage. To let you know I was once a proud father of the best kids in the world. The pitter-patter of sandy little beach feet and laughter. The sounds of baseball games and soccer matches that shaped my life for a decade. The school plays, the award ceremonies, the date nights, and anniversaries. Happy birthdays and BBQs that made us smile.

I woke to joy every day. Chubby babies are as funny as can be. Inside jokes and special dishes of food. Holding my children in loving arms, I lived my life for them. They were my everything. The four people I loved more than anything in the world. I would have done almost anything for my family. I say almost for a reason. The fact is that I loved drinking more. We will get into that.

#

I worked at the largest company in town. At that time, they managed one hundred and fifty premium vacation rental homes on the Texas Gulf Coast. We rented luxury condos, million-dollar houses, and everything in between.

The office had a front counter where guests would check in. A wall behind had two sales desks with big windows that overlooked the front where I was working. The paint was beige, a black and white marble countertop, and a computer to look up reservations. Dark, hardwood trim and molding made this a classy place to work. I remember wearing a business suit on my first day. I was told "Never wear that again" by the owner. This was the beach! Island Time as the locals declare. Island time is a term describing the fact that no matter what, everyone shows up thirty minutes late, to everything.

Port Aransas was a drinking town with a fishing problem. Everyone there was a party animal. The local IGA grocery store was in full agreement with two-piece bathing suits and flip flops on dripping wet bodies of tourists. I mean hell, even the computer repair guy didn't even wear shoes when he would come into the office. It was laid back beyond your wildest dreams. Golf carts are street legal; they have gigantic tires to roll on the sand. Beach-cruiser bikes sail down city streets past the Ice Cream Shop and Winton's Candy Store. Salt in the beachy air, horns honking in summer traffic, from Memorial Day to Labor Day the place was full of families and the Texas elite.

The main street had huge souvenir shops, one with a massive plaster shark where kids could pose for pictures inside its mouth. Nightfall comes, taxicabs burn fuel running from bar to bar, pouring out tourists at destinations unknown. It was a place like I have never known. Carefree to a fault. The town wouldn't let in chain stores or eateries at this time. It had the feel of a little village by the ocean. Dreamers, painters, and bird watchers came in droves. Beatniks and artists, musicians of all types, Parrotheads, and people on the run, all found their home in little Port A.

After a short time, my big-city work ethic started to shine like the North star. In Port Aransas, if you showed up sober and on time, you were destined to be a superstar. I pitched calls, asked questions, and started to learn the locations of all the homes. I went into the field and saw the properties firsthand. Coastal décor, expensive furniture, all the comforts of home for the sandy and drunk traveler. I had an extensive sales and customer service background. I was starting to get the attention of all my coworkers.

One day a salesperson called in from work, playing sick, I am sure. It was high season; an empty sales desk meant the loss of big reservations for the company. I was asked to fill the slot. This day was a landmark moment in the career I was to build. I was shown the ropes by Luke. He taught me all I needed to know about the software to book reservations for guests. Back then it was a DOS system. Extremely low tech, so I caught on fast. I took my first big sale within an hour. It was a rush. I can only compare it to gambling. The excitement of it all grabbed me in like a Maine lobster claw. I gave directions to the guests upfront, so I knew the exact proximity to the water, the number of beds in the houses. I had all the info the client would need, and this destined me to be a great salesman.

I was clean, sober, and on fire to make that all mighty dollar. The strange part was that I didn't make a commission. I figured if I made the company a lot of money, they would reward me. I got a small pay bump to go into sales full time. I instantly made enemies within the company. I was doing well and the sales game in vacation rentals was incredibly competitive. I set the bar. I was the top salesman right out the gate. I became cocky right away. I felt so inferior in my life, especially without booze or drugs, that I felt it necessary to cut others down and stomp on them while on my way to the top.

In a matter of months, I had relapsed. The first of a thousand in my very turbulent marriage and career in this town. As soon as the booze poured down my throat, my ego exploded like a Molotov cocktail. I was working hard all day, then hitting the local club and bar scene at night. I drove drunk, got belligerent in bars, and soon built quite the reputation. Not a good thing in a tiny town with an even smaller police force. At season close, I was way ahead of the pack. I had racked up impressive numbers. Numbers they hadn't seen in that rental pool before. I was an east coast Yankee hustler to these folks.

My boss would joke that I was a "used car salesman." My addiction was a perfect tool for this job. I was selling vacations. The manipulator in me took the wheel. I was smooth-talking old ladies in Austin, schmoozing Dallas soccer moms, and breaking the bank of family men in San Antonio. I loved every minute. I was not in competition with my coworkers at this point. I had set my sights on them though. I was in bars singing "We're the best company in town!" Close of the year, I had done a million in gross sales for the vacation rental company.

My head was the size of a hot air balloon. It was my wife, me, and the little 4-year-old girl living at the condo. I was drinking every night, gaining tons of weight, and becoming more and more miserable. This was 2009. Balling on a budget was my style. I would hit the liquor store and pick up a liter of the cheapest gin I could find, some tonic or OJ, a bag of ice, plus a pack of smokes. I did this daily. My poor wife and child were subjected to watching me get blinding drunk, behaving obnoxiously, and then pass out...every night of the week.

The fighting started. And rightly so. My wife informed me that we were expecting our first child. He was a St. Patty's Day production. Big shocker there.

She was full of hormones and fed up with my terrible behavior. I had just gotten off work and had a big brown bag, my liquor store starter pack. Voices raised like barn frames and the child starts to scream. My wife took the bottle of rotgut out of the bag and smashed it on the white, grouted tile floor. The world stopped as I looked at the event in complete bewilderment. I stared at her wildly.

"Why did you do that?" I screamed.

The fumes escaped off the flooring and entered my breathing space. The pungent aroma of pine needles and rubbing alcohol permeated the entire room. I flew into a rage. Stomping around the apartment like a baby whose rattle was just snatched from their chubby hand. The yelling, spitting, and snarling began. It was the last of our family's money. I spent the last pennies I could find in the house on that swill. It hit me like the stench of the gin that had me choking. *This is what I put through my system every night?* I depressingly thought. It had me disgusted. My wife was not happy with me. My young daughter was not happy with me. I was not happy with myself.

I drank all throughout her pregnancy. I worried her and made life a living hell. The look on her face every time I walked in the door with that brown paper bag makes me cringe to this day. She loved me and saw me excel at work yet fail every day in my addiction. I would binge at night, mess up, and then plead with her every morning, promising that I would never drink again. Such shame.

The birth of my son happened, and I was doing great at work. We had moved into a Fourplex on Sixth Street in Port Aransas. A closet two bedroom with the cheapest faux wooden floors you could imagine. We were cramped. I hadn't been doing drugs at this point, but I had scored some crack at Shorty's, a local bar, Port A's oldest and friendliest.

I was in my car hitting a tinfoil pipe that I had made on the fly. My wife approached me with such great anger and rage. She flew off the handle when she learned what the pipe contained. This lady was not accustomed to hard drugs. A major fight took place. I went to the rental office at around two in the morning and got a key to an unrented hotel we managed for the owner.

I put the key into the door, and I opened it. I woke the people inside, no one was supposed to be there, but the owner had a friend staying in the room that I had chosen to squat in. I was confronted by the terrified guests and stormed off. I returned home, riddled with shame and remorse, high on crack and drunk. I never returned to work, lost my job, and moved in with Barry in Corpus Christi so I could re-group. Finding a job was tough. But something in the paper caught my eye.

I showed up at the club at two in the afternoon. A tiny ad in the paper that said, "Club manager wanted." That was all. It ended up being a local strip joint I knew all too well, Aloha. I wore a business suit to the interview. A white shirt and blood-red tie. An Irish gangster walking into the belly of the beast. The Greek owner met with me and hired me on the spot. I knew my wife would be mad, but anything to pay the bills at this point.

The club was dark and seedy. Burgundy carpet with white track lighting to guide the waitresses in complete darkness. A stage lit up by a devil green spotlight. A metallic pole where temptresses would swing and gyrate, the alluring trance of sex. Three chairs surrounded each shiny black circular club table. About twenty in all. The sound system blared Texas rap and hip-hop hits, as dangerous vixens dove deep into hell. It stunk of cigarette smoke and alcohol.

"Your main job is to turn waitresses into strippers," he sneered in his thick Greek accent.

Off we go. The carrousel of death began to roll. From the jump, I was drawn into the darkness of it all. I loved watching naked dames dance in slick seductive motion. I loved the slimy clientele, bikers, gang members, junkies, and perverts. Demons retracting in the shadows, corners of the club filled with diamond eyes, fleeting and driven. I reveled in the madness. Grain alcohol shots poured down the throats of patrons, dark spaces illuminated with delight. Money being thrown in the air, raining down on strippers engaging in lesbian acts upon a moonlit stage. There were brutal fights and exchanges of drugs almost everywhere you looked. The back-dressing room was shocking. The black satin curtains peeled back, revealing a room of nakedness. An orgy of drug use, snarling comments, and lies. The speech about the customers was horrifying. The total hatred for the men shoveling money into their lace panties was frantic. They schemed and plotted, they raged with resentment. The evil one was with us in his purest form.

As weeks passed, I began to become desensitized to the whole vomit-filled experience. I remember walking in the dressing room multiple times per night and catching a stripper with a needle dangling from her vein. I would say "Twenty bucks or you go home." They would always stare up with child-like eyes, full of fear. They didn't have the money to blow but if I sent them home, they made zero. They reluctantly shelled it out. My sleazy palm greased by sick addict women, and I could care less.

I started snorting coke nightly. Drinking on the job was an unsaid rule. Gentlemen fresh out of prison buying shots for me, strippers giving me hits of X in my office. It was Rome in the finality of its existence. A pregnant dancer of eight months was seen smoking, drinking, and partying her way through life.

I had to break it to her that she had to stop dancing. Customers were more turned on by the mother-to-be, feeling her belly any chance they got. She cried as I told her. I demoted her to a waitress for the duration, till she popped.

I rehearsed a speech to entice waitresses into dancing.

"Hey honey, you can make a hundred bucks a night, or a thousand bucks a night, it's up to you."

Nineteen-year-old girls driving new mustangs and gangster men made up the workforce. The money was fast and the life was a dead end. But it sucked them in anyway.

Set Stage. A Black girl of eighteen dancing alone on the stage at two in the afternoon as we opened. Not a soul in the bar. The steel doors swing open like a draconian movie. Light shattering darkness, Texas sun cutting through clouds of the fog machine. An old Mexican man with a ball cap comes in bragging how his wife dropped him off. He was there to get his jollies. The two disappear into the shadows. I go about opening the bar after pouring him a Miller Draft on special for a dollar. A scream roars out from a corner unseen. I bolt from behind the bar and rush to the ebony girl's aid. I find him in the middle of a full-on sexual assault. His hand inside her barely legal panties. I grabbed him by his shirt and opened the front door with his face.

I walked back and asked, "You ok, we got to call the cops!"

"No, please! I got warrants," as tears streamed down her brown face.

She was powerless. She let it go. A victim of a sexual assault, only asking for a handful of drink tickets to numb her pain. Wasn't the first time, won't be the last.

#

This was not the job for a family man with a new baby. I would come home shattered at five in the morning, high, smelling of strawberry sin with glitter on my pants. The perverse dance I was taking part in took its toll right away. She told me she was leaving me. I was informed of the divorce lawyer, the papers, the whole nine. I begged and told her I would go to rehab, anything she wanted. She declined my offer. *How dare she?* She left and moved to her parents. I was devastated.

But I stayed at the club. Loving every minute.

#

Tiffany was my new girlfriend. A thin blond dancer with a thick Ohio twang. I would be on shift watching her twirl upon the pole in a neon green two-piece. I would stare blankly as she would grind the laps of the elderly, the gang member, and the guy in wind pants with no underwear. I didn't care for her. But I loved her demonic sexual nature, her hustle, her addict mind.

I was soon fired. Tiffany was naked, on top of me at a table on my night off. I was banned from the club and soon began drinking and using full time. Tiffany would turn tricks and dance all night. She would return in a cab after half past two in the morning with a massive bag of coke, X pills, and a sex drive that rivaled a porn star. I had a place to stay. Barry was disgusted by my actions, loving my wife as his daughter. I was downing a case of Bud Light Lime, an eight ball of coke, and five X pills a day. Every day.

I woke to find Tiffany in alcoholic delirium tremors. She began to seize as I called paramedics. When they arrived, they asked her "Who is the President?"

She replied, "That Black dude."

It was Obama at the time. She started drinking as soon

as the EMT's left the house. A knock at the door; my wife was in a rage. I was seen in the store where we had met, shopping with the bleach blond. My old coworkers had called her to tell her the heartbreaking news. She almost killed Tiffany. I wouldn't let them fight. My wife asked me to choose her. I sent her away. I chose drugs over her and it broke her heart.

    I threw out Tiffany days later and went to my dad. I told him I needed to go to treatment. I was fat, bloated, and depraved. The scars of losing my family were deep and sore. I walked into Charlie's Place Drug Rehab right after Christmas 2009. I rang in the New Year in treatment. Another trip down the sunshine highway. Another shot at getting clean and sober. I was single. On my way to a divorce court and totally damaged. Days went by as I clung to life. My emotional state wreaked of loss and depression. I started to seek the Lord in total desperation.

    My Birthday was in February. Barry came to give me gifts, some new clothes, and other small tokens of love that made my whole day. A few days later I was searching. I went to my room, and I prayed on my knees for my family to return. I stood up and walked down the stairs out to the gazebo. A tall Black client walked up to me and said, "Hey man, your family is here." I was sure he was mistaken. My wife wasn't even talking to me. Not even on the phone. I walked into the building. There they stood. My wife, flowing brown hair, holding my baby son and the little girl was wearing a cute pink backpack. All smiles.

    The wife looked up at me, "Hi."

    "What made you come here?" I said with awe on my face.

    "I don't know, an hour ago I just felt the need to bring the kids to come see you."

    God knew my heart before I even prayed. He saw my

love and desperation before I spoke it. He is always around you. Always.

Repair started. I finished up the program and left a new man. Clean and sober. Fixing things with my wife, I was happy. One more chance. Another shot at a life with the ones I loved most. We all moved into Barry's, and I started work doing hydro blasting in the refinery. I was so scared to do this kind of job. I had no experience and was terrified of heights. I worked hard. The labor had me losing weight like crazy, feeling good, and looking even better. I would climb three hundred feet in the air on towers to clean out drums and do other jobs involving high-velocity water. Very dangerous. I did what I had to for my family, risking life and limb was never an issue for me.

One day at work I got a call from an old coworker at the vacation rental company. She explained to me that the company was in dire need of a great salesperson. They were getting their clock cleaned by a new company down the street and wanted to compete. Months and months of hard labor left me tired. The four a.m. wake ups and late nights were killing me. The lady told me the owner was willing to forgive my terrible behavior. The power of money will never cease to amaze me. I went and talked to my old boss and was offered the job. I talked to my wife, accepted, and back to Port Aransas we went.

#

I came back on fire. New software, new phones, and new computers all excited the salesman in me. A new start-up company down the road from us was taking our house contracts in big numbers. The company was at death con five. The problem was sales. I was brought on to sell the owners the fact that Port Aransas' best salesman was now on payroll, and it was a true statement.

I was fearless. Booking vacations like never before.

Racking up huge numbers, reeling in new house contracts and retaining old business all at the same time. I was of sound mind, clean, sober, and had nothing else to do but work. I started at eight a.m. and left at eleven p.m., shifting addictions from drugs to getting paper. I was on a weak bonus program plus hourly pay. I got a ton of overtime and paid extra for doing after-hours emergency calls. My wife heard me doing reservations while dreaming. Talking in my sleep.

 I gained a reputation fast all over town as being the number one guy in property management. I was a sales guru, a master problem solver, and I could make any unhappy customer smile no matter what the issue may be. I had a natural talent for the business. I was brought into meetings with new clients as a pitchman. I would sell homeowners on our services. I couldn't lose. We gained property, which in turn boosted sales and drove morale through the still-growing company. We claimed the top spot in town and showed no signs of letting up.

 I stayed clean, I stayed on my grind, and in one year's time, I built the reputation. The largest home builders in town started seeking advice on how to build the most marketable homes in the vacation rental industry. Real estate agents were banging down the door for me to give them advice on rental income projection numbers. I was an expert. I could look at a home and let potential buyers know within a few dollars how much the home would bring in. Life was the best I could remember. Nothing could touch me.

 We found out we were pregnant once again. I was the happiest I had ever been in my life. Time went on and business was booming. We were now living upstairs at the same Fourplex on 6th Street where we lived before.

#

The climb of my career came too fast. One trip to the beach with coworkers led to a major relapse. A bottle of Jack, did me in. I was drinking in full force.

My wife was out of town, and I got nailed and fell fast asleep while cooking hot dogs. The little apartment filled with smoke. A pound at the door turned out to be the local cops. I answered and refused to let them in. The fire department was there. I got wild in rage. They arrested me for interfering with a public servant and an old warrant I didn't know I had. Work knew I had a drinking problem from the incident at the hotel. I was not supposed to be drinking as part of the conditions of my re-hire. The jig was up, so I thought. But I was making so much money, soon I figured out I could do anything I wanted and keep a job.

My ego blew up like a Zeppelin on fire. I was taking pills all day, getting drunk all night, and was fast gaining a reputation as the town drunk. I was thrown out of every bar in town. I was mouthing off about work. Telling anyone that would listen of how unstoppable I was. Acting like a millionaire cokehead on a rant. Number one and only gaining steam.

The more I drank, the better I became at my job. I woke up every day and looked in the mirror. I would say out loud "You are the best; you are the King of Vacation Rentals," a character I created to compensate for how bad I felt on the inside.

My daughter was born as I detoxed in a hospital room chair, shaking and rambling on. I was angry I had to even be there because it interfered with my drinking. All until I saw her little Irish Mexican face. My angel. I loved her beyond words. The baby of the family. My bouncing little girl. We took her home in the dead of winter. The family was complete.

#

I was unhappy with my job. I had put pen to paper and realized my worth versus what the company was paying me. I was making them a ton of cash and I was working for pennies. Ego running wild, I started to clash with the headstrong owner. My phone rang at my sales desk. The owner of the up-and-coming company was on the other end. They offered me a huge sales position. After-hours pay, a huge bonus structure, and room for advancement included. They also offered to match my hourly rate, so it was a huge pay bump. I would receive a bonus for each property I signed to their pool.

I went to my boss and offered her to match it. She went crazy. Started screaming. Threatening to fire coworkers. Hire new people. It was a huge scene. I printed a client list with phone numbers and email addresses, left my key in my coffee mug on my sales desk, and that was that. A new chapter in my life.

Shock waves went through the rental community. I went right to work the next day. I learned the software at the new company and in my first week did seventy thousand in gross sales. I was number one once again without blinking an eye. I made a thousand calls. Ego driven, money hungry, and locked-in to proving I could do it all over again.

The homeowners started jumping ship like rats off a burning boat, record-breaking numbers. I was the best, and they knew it. They only cared about the money. No loyalty in that business. I was signing two big houses a day. It seemed like it went on forever. It was a hostile takeover. A siege of power and treasure. The town knew my name and I rolled like a feeding gator. The domino effect happened. Once you get a few, you get many. I was so proud of myself. My old boss was having plenty of sleepless nights. I chalked it up to "it's just business."

I took this new company to the next level. The biggest

homes in town were now crossing over. They had nice stuff already, but now they were getting homes in the very high-end beachfront communities. I was meeting new people. The biggest builder in town gave us an exclusive deal on all his new construction. He liked my new boss, and with the top pitch and salesman on board, he would not consider anyone else. Things were taking off like a rocket.

Then the letter came.

I got a certified letter delivered to me at work. It was from a lawyer representing my old boss. A cease-and-desist letter telling me that I better stop taking customers from his client base before I ended up getting sued. My new boss was worried. Her partner flat out told me to stop. However, my new boss was as greedy as I was, and secretly told me to keep going. I knew from being in the know that this lawyer was used because he was cheap. He had a sex charge under his belt from being with an underage hooker, and he was a registered sex offender. I sent one email explaining I would expose him and continued my raid.

Unstoppable doesn't begin to describe my momentum. As we acquired properties, my sales skyrocketed. The house got nicer, the cars far more luxurious, and life became a great place to be. I was drinking full board. My weight again ballooned to three hundred and eighty pounds. I was soon in a Five-X shirt. BBQing every night of the week. I started to drink an eighteen pack of Bud cans, a pint of Jager, and three Red Bulls a night. I was smoking a pack of Marlboros as well.

My blood pressure was in the two hundred's if I didn't take my pills. Years later, I assessed my food intake at this time in my life and I was consuming ten thousand calories a day. It was out of control. The more hungover I was, the more sales I would do. I could act as I pleased at my new company, cash was king, and I brought it in by the wheel barrel. I would leave work at three in the afternoon and put my beer on the ice every day of the week.

I won a Yeti cooler in a sales contest. It was a four-hundred-dollar cooler. It held my beer every day for years. I was on top, yet totally out of control. Money changes the way people see you. I was doing ok, but I was not rich. The key was that I made millions for other people, the ones who called the shots in town. The taxes my sales brought the town of Port Aransas gave me a free pass with the cops and everyone else. My bad behavior all over town was widely known and accepted. I dropped cash in bars, clubs, and restaurants. I was drunk whenever I wasn't at work. I had contractors do all the after-hour jobs. I would answer the phone totally loaded and send someone else to do the dirty work.

I was tearing it up in all areas. I did a million three that year. I was consulting with real estate agents, doing business with the mayor, and shining like a lamp to all who looked on. Year two was epic. We were now closing in as the largest company in town. The money was pouring in. Not one client was leaving us. In a cutthroat business where a better deal was a green light to switch companies, losing clients was a normal thing. We didn't lose one. They had the best and they knew it.

I got my wife hired on as we put the kids in daycare. I showed her the ropes, and we made the best team. I now also had a personal assistant. Me being me, I started to abuse my coworkers with my role as the King of Vacation Rentals. I would put down others in order to build myself up, more so than ever. I could feel resentments building. I had an attitude where I viewed things as "If you don't like me, beat me." I knew they couldn't even come close. I was number one, the number two person in town worked with us as well, and I had doubled their sales numbers every month.

My marriage was bad. We fought like most couples do, well maybe a little more often and fiercely, but all was seemingly well to others. What a difference some money makes. The kids were in all types of sports, we coached teams, went to events, and they were all doing well in school. I wasn't doing drugs at all. Just drinking my socks off and working a ton. We were attending Catholic church every weekend; the kids were in CCD classes. Life was surprisingly normal.

I was always a person who believed in the bible, just not with a whole heart and mind. Most likely because I was living a life away from the Lord. Our priest explained to me that I had a demon on my shoulder. It had been there my whole life. *A metaphor for addiction? Or something far more sinister?* Back then I thought he was talking about my disease, turns out it was much more the latter.

Barry was growing proud of me. I was gaining the approval of my dad for the first time in my life. He was a businessman. He respected what I was doing. He would come to my house during this period quite a bit. He was seeing how I was being received in town and in my career. I was so happy to see him smile.

He was my best friend. We were playing golf, hanging out; he spent time with the kids and myself. We would party together. We had lots of laughs. The BBQing. We made whole weekends out of watching Netflix, drinking ice-cold brew, and listening to our favorite music. I loved him so very much.

Things at the company started to get a little hairy around this time. I was doing so well, and my head got so big that I demanded to be put on salary. Factoring in my bonus for the last few years, I was making a good chunk of change. I twisted their arm and they had to comply. It created huge resentment with the greedier of the two owners. She was frequently calling me a diva, telling people I was "grossly overpaid." Deep down, she hated me. She stopped showing up for work. I took the reins as a figurehead. I was meeting with all the owners and doing a lot more than sales. I was doing my job plus her job on most days. Resentment grew on my end. In my mind, I figured I should be brought in as a partner.

The company had gone from eighty properties to over two hundred in my brief time there. It was now raking in over six million in gross rental sales, not counting fees. They were netting huge checks and I felt robbed. I could see my exit on the horizon. I wanted to own my own vacation rental business, I wanted the big money, the accolades, the respect. It was all alcoholic ego. It was all for show, part of my identity, the mask of success. I needed my career to be accepted. Without that, I was a no-good degenerate drunk. I would be deemed worthless, and I knew it. I had no degree; I was all in. I needed to make something happen, but how?

#

Another lady owned the third-place company in town. A small-time operation that we publicly laughed at. There was no way she could even touch us. No one took her company seriously. She came in one day and said "hi" during an unrelated real estate transaction, as she was an agent. We parted ways with a smile.

About a week later I was called to her home for a talk. I was offered my matching salary plus a ten percent backend piece of the pie. I would be a full-fledged stake holding owner in a vacation rental business in the town where I reigned as King. One more meeting took place to sew it all up. And before I knew it...Done Deal. I just needed to work at the old place for another month.

As stated, things had been at a boiling point with the company I was with. The owner and I were continuously butting heads. She was full of ego to the point of insult. Talking down to housekeepers, not looking people directly in the eye, that type of arrogance. A major blowup between my wife and the boss took place. This one event put us on the chopping block. I knew it was only a matter of days before we were to be fired. Unfortunately, I was about to do our annual family staycation in Port Aransas. Every year, I would get a million-dollar beach home gifted to me on Labor Day weekend. I would celebrate the end of the season by getting a keg of draft beer and invite Barry and anyone else who would enjoy it.

I called the new boss up and struck a deal to come over and start right away, instead of waiting for the originally planned timeframe. She asked what it was going to take to get me over there. The planned vacation, that's what! She agreed to give me a three thousand dollar signing bonus to help fund my booze-filled weekend and pay rent and bills.

There it was. Soon as I had the cabbage in hand, I left work at lunch and never returned. I was about to do it all over again. I helped build and run a six million a year vacation rental management company, became an expert vacation rental agent, and was at the top of my game. Some respected me more than the owners because I was doing all the work. I worked the late nights and answered the phones. I put the money in the bank as they sat back collecting huge checks.

#

The weekend went well. Until the phone call. My friend had passed. She succumbed to addiction. I won't go into any details because I love her family so much. But the Lord called her home. I received the call from a mutual friend from the dump crew. Natosha was one of my best friends from back in the day. I loved her very much. She was like a true sister to me. No one will ever know the true dynamic of our friendship, but it was close to sibling level. I knew her from the time I was fourteen years old. Thousands of conversations. Hundreds of incredible nights of laughter and times at school. I know her parents, brother, and sister very well and I love her whole family. The news smashed my core. I collapsed on the side porch of this million-dollar beach home. The life knocked out of me. Tears streaming down my face. Surrounded by family and friends.

The Texas sun beat down on the tan stucco home as I wept in fear and anger all at once. If I remember right, it was around nine in the morning when the call came in. I was at the top of the world in my career. People in my family had flown in as part of the celebration for this new promotion. It was supposed to be a glorious time in my life. It was as if the devil reached his slimy clawed hand into my world and twisted a double-edged blade in my heart. I fell to pieces, shattering like lightbulb glass inside a cold bathtub. I died a little at that moment. This one event touched my life in the blackest of ways. Addiction tearing a beloved person from existence. I was left screaming inside, *"Why not me? Why was I spared?"* Feelings of guilt, shame, sadness, and rage buried into the dark staircases that lead to my broken heart.

Bare feet crept down the stairs to the garage. I couldn't take the private elevator within the home. I staggered past it with veiled eyes, writhing in pain. I saw the keg floating in the icy water of a plastic grey trash barrel. I examined a red solo cup and decided it was time to self-medicate in a big way. Dr. Feelgood was in and he was prescribing beer. I poured five consecutive Miller Lite drafts and pounded them in one chug. My belly was full of alcohol. Still saturated from the night before, my organs swelled instantly, and my brain began to drift. I knew at this moment that there would not be enough booze to fill the hole that this loss had dug. By ten in the morning, I was dead drunk and not even thinking of slowing down.

I came up the stairs broken and battered. My whole family looked on as I turned the keys to a suicidal door. They went about their day. I went about mine. My children went to the pool. Everyone ate a nice lunch. I drank and drank and drank. This was the first time that death had really hurt me. I was bleeding from a broken heart. I poured down countless shots of room-temperature rum, top-shelf. I turned fine liquor into homeless swill. I was looking classy, feeling Skid Row.

My poor wife looked on throughout the day as the dark side of me emerged. I sat poolside near the private boardwalk at Port Villageo in Port Aransas, Texas. Sun rays blaring on my milky white skin. I was turning lobster red and didn't even care. I was wheeling a cooler around full of hard liquor and brew. It was medicinal at that point.

It was as if I was a cancer patient walking down a hallway in the ward, toting a bag of IV fluid on a rolling pole. The booze was not to leave my side. I drank and cried intermittently. I would go from a laughing jolly fool to a crying three-hundred-and-eighty-pound blob in five seconds flat. I was putting on the mask. The alcohol was devastating. I smelled vile. My organs must have been saturated with toxic fluid. I could feel my liver swelling. Nowadays, if I binged like this, I was experiencing pain on my right side.

#

After the weekend, the family flew home. The party had ended, and the pain had just begun. Right away at work, I was under extreme pressure. They hired me to steal clients. Period.

They watched my last employer get rich and they wanted a repeat. They thought I was dumb, but I knew full well why they wanted my services. There was a raid about to take place. The biggest single-power shift in the Port Aransas vacation rental industry. Millions of dollars changing hands. Big scary changes for all involved and the whole thing rested on my shoulders. I was an insecure, self-hating, overweight alcoholic.

  Everyone in town knew I was a drunk. However, I was really entering the darkest of days. I was starting to get sick. I could feel the toll of my lifestyle. I would find myself at a property, walking up three flights of stairs, completely winded and choking. My liver hurt all the time. Swollen, my face was the size of a beach ball. I was taking blood pressure pills so I wouldn't have a heart attack. Without them, I was in the red zone. Headaches, pressure behind the eyes. I was smoking and drinking like I wanted to die, because I did. The pills were causing major cramping in my muscles. My children looked on regularly as daddy leaped off the sofa in agony and ran around the room with Charley horses. You could hear the muscle snapping like a rubber band. My body was severely scarred from the way I consumed substances and food.

  I had to start contacting ex-clients. It was the promise I had made. To bring the company one million dollars of new sales in two seasons. I was shooting for the stars, possibly way higher than that. I needed to take them all. The phone started ringing, emails came pouring in. I began to sign contracts right away. The more I signed, the more I drank. My wife working by my side, we set up the same software as my previous employer and the third-rate company started to take shape as a true force to be reckoned with. My internal thoughts were a pressure cooker. Screaming silently, I waded through days scared and motivated only by my conceited self-talk and ego.

Big houses started to come over. I was winning. The plague spread; the dominoes fell across the board. Months had passed, work was done, we soared passed previous projections. I started to dabble in methamphetamines. I met a maintenance man at the last company who was an addict. He lived in a one-room shack behind a free-standing home in Old Town, Port Aransas. I was getting drunk at night and would bike over to his house. I started buying twenty-dollar bags of ice. This is how it all started. The slow road to destruction. A descent of epic proportions.

#

After the ice drained down my sinuses and into my throat, after the family went to bed, the sadistic dance of pornographic viewing began. I was staying up all night watching porn. The sunlight would creep through the shades and that signaled that it was time to get in the shower. No sleep, up and dressed to the nines before the kids were awoken.

I was still playing the role of a great dad. Still a husband and a provider. A member of the community and a shining star in the local business world. No one knew the darkness in me. People couldn't see the struggle within. I was making so much money for people, they were blinded to my descent. Using maybe three days a week, it was manageable. Snorting the drug to forget my problems. Sniffing into sexual pleasure, huffing demons into my body to pacify the confusion in my mind.

I was partying with this guy who was a housekeeper at the previous company. He started to work for us at the new place. I would buy meth from him too, on the cool, in the shadows, so no one in town would know. What was to happen next was the first true supernatural experience that I remember. This happening was very real and very scary, a moment that would foreshadow the epic journey to come. The

Evil One. He sent one of his demons to let me know he was there.

I was at my sales desk. My wife, my boss, and others were all working. My boss just had the office blessed with holy water the week prior. The office was small and cramped. My desk sat next to a big window and looked at the front door, which opened to the right, facing the street. At around four in the afternoon, the door swung open. The office had grey-blue paint on the walls, dark hardwood trim lined the place. Low lighting and closed shades gave the building an eerie feel.

The girlfriend of the housekeeper I was buying meth from was there. Her stringy blond hair snarled as she cocked her head through the door. She was growling, eyes wide and full of flame. She wore slinky black bicycle shorts and a skimpy tattered white t-shirt.

"Get out here, Boston," she shuddered in a raspy venomous tone.

Spit rained out of her jowls as she hurled insults and curse words. She tried to put forth her filthy white sneaker to step inside. She retracted her foot as if there was a force field, she couldn't step inside. The more she tried, the angrier the serpent grew. It began to scare the women in the office. I got up and headed for the door. She paced backwards on the hot tar boiling from the Texas heat, the wind felt like a hairdryer. I have never really spoken to this thing in person. She was new to me. As I stood closer, I realized this being wasn't a person in the traditional sense.

I went outside because she was disrupting business. Looking back, if I knew fully what this was, I never would have walked outside. I wasn't spiritually smart back then. Suddenly, it was upon me. It was sweating and grinning, laughing like a demonic toy. Her movements were that of a puppet on a set of old rusted and wiry strings. She jerked around in break dance motions.

"AHHHH, I know what you do," she snarled with a liar's tongue.

I could feel an evil presence. I had never felt evil like this in my life. Not even in the trap houses. This was far more sinister.

"I'm gonna tell your wife", she screamed in a violent and boisterous tone.

Her voice scratched like an old mono record with a dusty needle. Snot ran from the nose of the demon, or whoever this girl was. I couldn't breathe or speak.

I finally mustered up a voice, "Go ahead, tell her."

She growled and let out some more vicious lies, and some unspoken truths of mine. I felt it knew my innermost secrets. My porno nights, my meth-fueled masturbation. The things under the rug I couldn't expose to the world. The demon tried to inflict fear on me. It was targeting me directly by name. It came to see me specifically.

"I'm not scared of you, bitch! Get outta here before I call the cops, you're high!" I yelled.

I tried to throw a carnal explanation on this spiritual encounter taking place. It screamed as it slithered back to the beat-up Ford truck filled with dirty clothes and cleaning supplies.

I composed myself. I was checking my underpants for feces as I had never been so scared in my life. This was a ninety-pound junkie female. The presence of the demon, the voice of the deceiver, and the knowledge of my indiscretions. It was all earth shattering. I was leaking sweat off my brow. The fear imploded my mind.

I reentered the building in shock. We all sat and

discussed the event. My boss explained that her husband had blessed the whole office. He took the holy water and traced the door as he prayed. He blessed the place in the name of Jesus, the Highest. The body of the afflicted couldn't break the plane.

#

The success of the company continued as I spiraled out of control. I was signing homes like a mad man by day, raging in addiction by night. I was very involved with my children, still present during events, and loving them every minute. To tell the truth, I was also detached and angry at the same time. My addiction was the source of all the fighting, all the ugliness within our marriage and the home. I was too stressed out to deal with the kids after the games. I found myself sending them to their room more and more.

My wife and I went to new technology trade shows for the vacation rental industry. We were pioneering new ideas in the business, making great strides in sales and marketing; all the while my addiction grew worse and worse.

#

The owner's daughter came to town. She was a small-town girl who married big. She flew in on a private jet. That's how big she married. She came and saw the new potential for the company and wanted it all for herself. We were dealing with a family business. Blood is way thicker than water. Mommy found out her daughter's desires and it was the beginning of the end.

I hadn't been sober enough to see my own accomplishments. I promised a million in new sales in two seasons. I ran the books and found that I had personally signed one and a half million dollars in new business in just over nine months. They had what they needed. I had only shaken her hand on this deal. I could feel the danger coming my way. They had promised me I would be a part of their successful company. But they weren't going to give it up. I asked to have my contract signed. They pushed a pile of dung over the table, calling me a manager, not an owner.

I consulted Barry on this bogus contract, and he advised me to use the specific word "unacceptable." I asked for a revised contract with our original agreement in it. Then, the big bang. The day that rocketed me into the worst possible experience a human could have. A fall into a long-suffering for the record books.

I was called to a private home that we managed. A poolside meeting with my partner's husband. The Warlock as I called him. He sat me down poolside. After setting his wife up, after bringing them to be the number two company in town, he informed me I was being suspended for being an alcoholic. He dipped into a diatribe about his own past drinking issues. He was seventy years old, pretentious as hell, and he meant business. This was a sham. I was never late, not once. Not one writeup, not even a verbal warning. This was no suspension, and I knew it.

He sent me away. I walked back to the street where I was parked. I felt high. It was a dream-like feeling that punched me right in the guts. Barely breathing, I returned home to break the news to my wife. Panic came over the house. I cried and screamed. I drank twenty-five beers and a whole bottle of Jager. No matter what I did, it was over. They kept her on for about two weeks before deciding to let her go as well.

We went from making ninety thousand a year to zero in two seconds flat. The fear of it all was paralyzing. I had major overhead. Two vehicles, phones, lights, insurance, all the daily operations of a life built over eight years. I started to drink from the moment I woke up. I was buying twenty-four of the sixteen-ounce aluminum Coors at a time. I drank as fast as I could. When my eyes were open, I was ruled by fear and anger. I couldn't believe what happened to my career. My ego was so big, I thought I was indispensable. I was very wrong. Passing out at around noon, I would sleep for about three hours and get up to start all over again.

My wife was disgusted. Friends were stopping by to see how I was doing, only to find a sad shell of a person. They looked on with deep concern and pity. My phone was dead silent for the first time in years. No work calls, no coworkers. I quickly learned that my job was my whole identity. As days went by, I had sunk deeper into depression. The meth stopped because I could no longer afford it. All my cash was for the bottle. I can't tell you how many times over the years, I took the last of the family money and spent it on alcohol, but it was a thing every few days at this point. Borrowing, no intention of paying people back, it all became a desperate House of Cards. I was useless to the world. A hopeless drunk.

My wife took a job in town to help pay bills. Under the pressure, I pulled it together and took a job at the local IGA Grocery. The deli is where I landed. In a small town like this, I ran into every person I had ever met. Old customers, neighbors, and friends. The single most shameful experience of my life. When you put other people down for a decade, trample on them with your own ego and pride, and tell the whole world how great you are, people tend to love to see you fail. I was a zoo animal. They came to the deli just to see the sad dying tiger, through the frosted glass, behind the counter, tired and weak.

My competition was coming in. People from all the different companies I worked for. I'll never forget this day long as I live. A lady I worked with came in and ordered some sliced items. She made a joke about me losing my job and I walked to the back and broke down in tears. The ice-cold air in the deli department made it hard to breathe. I blubbered and sighed heavily as tears rolled like big raindrops down my swollen fat face. I walked back to the counter defeated and drained. She gave me a devilish smirk as she looked into my beet-red eyes, fighting every notion of breaking down again as I handed her the ham and cheese that I sliced. Suicidal thoughts jammed my brain. I had images of shoving my wrist in the deli slicer. I pondered if I could sever the mainline in my wrist and bleed out fast enough before the EMT's arrived. This would be no cry for help. I honestly wanted to die every second that I was awake.

Killing myself was the only thing I thought about during this time. My wife would be at work on my off days. Ships purposely passing in the night. She was falling out of love with me. Rightly so. I wasn't even me anymore. This wasn't the person she married.

I was a monster. An angry jackal who was verbally abusive to everyone I encountered. I was leading my family into a toilet. I didn't have the money to get a lawyer and fight the company on my contract. They knew it. I walked away quietly and planned to kill myself with booze and drugs.

I took the deli job to provide basics for my family, to keep the lights on. I worked hard at that store. In the freezer, slicing meat, carrying boxes. I ate my pride because I loved them. But the night shift really cut into my drinking. I asked to switch to the morning shift. My manager saw right through me. I would need to be a door key holder for the opening shift, and they were not comfortable with that. I was told I would remain on the same shift. I quit. Another blowup, one more massive bad choice. It's heartbreaking to realize that I loved booze more than my family.

I began drinking around the clock. More strain on an

already dying marriage. More fighting. I was not only letting my family down. I was downright hurting them. I was shameful. Embarrassing scenes out in the yard. Yelling and swearing. My oldest was ashamed to know me.

#

I needed money in a major way. I started looking on Craigslist. I considered sucking human feces out of porta-potties, but even they refused to hire me. I finally got a job digging graves, of all things. I was to be the guy that lowered people in the ground after we dug the six-foot hole that would be their final resting place. This job would end up being a big part of the reason why I am still alive today. I was still drinking tons, but the early four a.m. wakeups and grueling hard work would slow me way down. I started taking whole nights off from booze. Only drinking a six pack in a fifteen-minute timespan on some nights. I was making progress.

Putting people in the ground. Seeing the loss and pain in the eyes of the children. Seeing the brokenness in parents burying babies. The victims of cancer, AIDS, murder, suicides, and just all the death in general, began to set in my mind the true finality of it all. I started to question if I really wanted to die. I started to enjoy my job. As dark and sad as it was, I was learning a lot about life. I saw that we only get one shot at this thing. I began to lose weight. It was a miracle time. One day, I realized I was three days sober. I went on a massive diet. I lost sixty-four pounds in sixty days. No booze or cigarettes. I was doing better than I had in years. The job paid a living wage, offered life insurance, and health insurance.

#

I started feeling better every day. Months went by and life continued to get better. The bills were maintained. We were still fighting but nothing like before. The poor girl was really trying to love me. Then another bad choice. I was burying someone in Alice, Texas. I saw an old homeowner I used to manage a property for. I made this guy a ton of cash over the years. He waited until I was lowering his grandma into the earth when he whispered "Wanna start a company?" in my ear. I finished up what I was doing at the funeral, and we set up a meeting. I went home and told my wife. To be honest, I didn't want to do it. I was just coming to terms with the fact that my career in Port A was over. I was settled into a new life, a new job, and I was feeling strangely stable. We talked. I felt like she thought I should do it.

Over the next few weeks, this guy and I negotiated the money part of the deal. I asked for one hundred thousand dollars as the initial start-up capital to get the business off the ground. He agreed. We got a lady to partner with us, a former housekeeper I had worked with. The plan was set, and I secured one of the nicest rental offices in town.

I quit digging graves. I started pulling the same salary as I was making burying people. We were on our way. I went to real estate offices, called old clients, and sent emails. I met with homeowner associations; I set up some important meetings with influential people.

I started drinking again.

My partner put on a good show. He seemed like he trusted and respected me. But all he wanted was my signing power. He wanted me to bring in business and do the sales. He lied to me. After about a month, I learned he was having his own assistant sign checks, yet I wasn't allowed to touch any of the money. With my back against the wall, I just ate the insulting bullshit and pushed forward.

#

I had just bought an affordable standard-gear truck. I

had never driven a standard before. The story goes that I was day drinking one afternoon during spring break. The town was completely full of tourists. The drinking began at home. Once I was good and drunk on my cold beer, I headed down to the local bar for the afternoon dollar specials. I had about ten drinks there and thought it was a good idea to learn to drive the unfamiliar truck up at the city park. So off I went. Three sheets to the wind and behind the wheel of a new pick up with no clue how to drive it.

  The town had built a dog park for the community. A chain-link fence encased the area where pet owners walked Fido for fun. I pulled in with one eye closed. I was sluggish, stinking of beer, and had no business driving, not even close. It was about four in the afternoon. The dog park was bustling with people. An older couple with a poodle, a younger couple with a black Lab, and a schoolteacher-looking lady with a pair of golden retriever puppies were all playing inside the brand-new fence.

  The lush green grass was accented by the sky, a baby-blue canvas of puffy white clouds; the weather was perfect as a cool wind blew between radiant sunbeams. I slouched in the leather of the truck like a lounging sloth in a banana tree. I threw it into gear on the hardtop. The wheels spun as I hit the gas. Smoke plumed into the March sky as the little white truck darted forward. I hit the clutch and slipped into second with a quickness. The tires gripped the pavement and I started to fishtail; the back end darted toward the brand-new fence line.

  People were screaming, diving onto the perfectly manicured grass. The shock on their faces was unforgettable. The rear taillight of the passenger side slammed into the gate. I hit the gas even more to correct the spin. I veered into some tall seagrass where the fence ended. The truck skidded to a stop on the sandy terrain. The quaking rearview mirror revealed a group of disturbed and angry citizens. Dusting themselves off, covered in grass stains, the group lurched near my truck like a starving group of zombie freaks. Everything was in slow motion.

I threw it back in first and plunged the gas pedal to the floor, trying to escape. The tiny truck had rear-wheel drive and sunk in the sand like a pond stone. The tires then zipped sand into the faces of the dumbfounded crowd. More shrieks as I gunned the engine three or four times in my futile attempts to flee. It was clear the truck was stuck like Chuck. I poured out of the front seat. At three hundred pounds, I must have appeared monstrous to all that looked on. A sad drunk, breathing heavy as I stared in their direction.

An older man yelled, "Don't you run!"

My mind raced with indecision. *What to do?* Well, I ran. I lived two blocks away. I sprinted away from the park looking like a super-sized Olympic runner. My jean shorts falling as I retreated from all responsibility. I had no clue that an onlooker had called the local cops. Being spring break, the state police helicopter was circling above as the report of a hit and run blew through the airwaves.

I outran the chopper and flung my front door open. I had a past misdemeanor family violence dispute during a drunken disagreement with my wife. I pleaded out on the charge even though I had never hit her. I wasn't supposed to be around firearms at all under federal law via the Brady Bill. Under our married bed lay a fully loaded, black tactical shotgun. I had the spring out of it, that is illegal. It held six deer slugs with one in the pipe. I ripped the firearm from its hiding place. It was purchased by my wife after a string of break-ins in our neighborhood.

I cocked the shotgun. I remember thinking *I can't go to jail*. I was drunk and instantly suicidal. I blew it all: the marriage, the family, the new company. Every single bit of it. I thought of putting the cold black barrel in my mouth. The gun was short enough to pull the trigger. Then I got the insane thought of having a shootout with the Port Aransas Police Department. I was scared out of my mind. Just so happens, they called my name over the police scanner and people in my wife's office let her know they were looking for me. She worked nearby; she beat the detectives to the house.

They pulled up as she locked the door. She poked her head out and said, "Let me talk to my husband." They knew me from the vacation rental business. Not knowing there was an intoxicated and highly suicidal madman with enough ammo to take on the US Marines, they agreed to let her talk with me first. She entered the room to find me red-eyed and crying with the loaded Goliath.

A swat team presence surrounded our little duplex apartment on Avenue D. I peered out the blinds and fear took hold like a killer's grip around the throat of an enemy. My wife pleaded with me. "We will get a lawyer; we will fix this." She loved me even then. Loved me enough not to let me ruin the little broken life that I had left. I slid the gun under the bed and headed outside. There was no struggle, no yelling. They asked me to put my hands behind my back, and we were off to the little city jail.

My wife called a lawyer who worked in town. He met me at the jail a few hours later to inform me of the charges. I can only guess that because I had made the town so much in taxes, they once again let me go. Well, pretty much. What should have been a hit and run DUI and felony evading arrest charge, was sweetly replaced with "Striking duty over Two-

Hundred-Fifty Dollars." My lawyer had never even heard of the charge. It was a glorified traffic ticket. I was signed out by my lawyer and went home to sleep it off.

The local paper listens to the scanner. They were at the scene within minutes and snapped a front-page photo of the damaged fence and my little battered white truck. My name was plastered all over the paper. Once again, I had failed. I almost killed people. My business partner was understandably livid about the incident. I could feel the disappointment in the room as we met to discuss day-to-day operations. But I chalked it up to being no big deal. I was once again drinking within three days.

Next month I went to court and the charges were dropped after paying twelve hundred dollars in restitution for the fence. I got away with it...again.

#

Since my wife was helping us set up the business software, she gave me tips on the financial aspects of our daily operations. She went to link the bank account with the computer software and was blown away.

"Boston, there is only twenty-six thousand in this account."

Surely that was a huge error. There must be another account with the rest of the start-up money...not true. My frantic calls were met with a response explaining that I was to sign fifty houses before any more funds were to be dispersed. I was screwed over once again. The nightmare had started all over. All the meetings I had set up, the new software, the HOA meetings I was pitching to. All dust in the wind.

Can you guess what happens next?

Yes, I drank my brains out. I couldn't lie to clients. I couldn't risk people's homes, I decided to close the company.

The place was doomed, and I knew it. So, there it was. The final chapter was closing for my time in the vacation rental business, which I truly loved very much. Heartbroken all over again, I slammed every ounce of alcohol I could get my hands on for weeks. Now a one-income family household, leaving my wife to pay all the bills, I accepted my failure.

  I went to Barry in shame. I wanted so badly for him to be proud of me. I thought this was going to be my ticket. All the revolutionary ideas I had. All the fire I had for taking the industry by storm. All went by the wayside. My dad was so sad for me. He saw the pain deep within. He knew what it was like to fail in business and how deeply it can affect a man's self-image. I already hated myself to the core. This was just one more thing on an awfully long and dark list.

  I didn't know what to do. Saturated by booze and tuned up on meth once again, I lost all drive. I was lost, broken, and depressed. I took some time off from searching for work. I got into my weight loss goals hard. I thought if I lost the pounds, I could like myself again.

  I put the plug in the jug, and for three months I ate nothing but chicken breast and veggies. I drank nothing but water. I lost another eighty pounds about as fast as a human could. I did water aerobics at the town pool with the elderly. I was too fat to jog, so it worked. Finally, I started to look amazing again. Well, in my eyes anyway. It fed my ego. I overcompensated for my failures by telling everyone how great I looked. I acted as cocky as ever, deepening the divide in an already distant marriage.

  What happened next was the single darkest period of my entire life. This next job I was to take led to a road in hell that most could never fathom. I was looking for work, but I didn't really care to do a real job. I found an opening at a local taxi company. A driver.

    Keep your eyes on the road passengers. The ride is about to get very bumpy.

#

Trigger Warning

The next parts to this story are some of the most gruesome tales of addiction that will enter your mind. The previous stories pale in comparison. My life was about to take a very dark turn into the abyss. I feel the need to warn you, as some of you are addicts. I know the struggle of addiction. The triggers, the thoughts, and the fantasies. Sometimes reading or viewing certain things can make you want to use again. There is substance to this story. It's all exactly how it happened. God felt it was necessary to remove the shame and guilt from my heart so I could write this book. To help others see the darkness of drugs. A firsthand account of how meth sucks you in, how it removes the people and things you love, and how it destroys anything good and holy from the lives of the involved.

The following will make you feel vile shivers of disgusted and pity. This was really my life. I will take you into the filthy recesses of the trap houses, places of prostitution, and the sex-laced under belly of Corpus Christi, Texas. What you're about to read is happening all over the world tonight while you sleep. You may see yourself or someone you love in the upcoming chapters. This may open your eyes to a loved one's addiction. You may wince at the reality within these pages. It will be hard for the non-addict to understand why I put myself through this living hell.

The drugs were a tool in a very thought-out form of slow suicide. I knew full well I was killing myself. The drug use is graphic. The sex is lude and gross in every single way. The whole lifestyle is an entrapment put upon us by the Evil One, from the inception of our first use. Reckless abandon is an understatement. I couldn't possibly write about the thousands of drunken nights, drug-induced parties, and experiences I had been involved in since I was twelve years of age to now. Just know, I had to leave out a lot. I drank and did drugs almost every day of my life. Only brief stints of sobriety existed from the mid 1990's to 2015. Just know I was far sicker than I let on in the previous chapters. I only skipped over things because the madness was very repetitive, and you as the reader would be overloaded.

Take heed as we enter the ice age of this story. The following trip into the methamphetamine counterculture will be bloody, murderous, and entirely sad in every way. The risks were huge, the behavior selfish and weak. It may seem at times like I am glorifying drug use. Keep in mind that I was being sucked in. I tell it as I saw it at <u>that</u> exact time. I do this to show how the drug life grabs you, why we stay, and how hard it is to leave. If drugs were not fun in the beginning, none of us would do them. This book has two purposes. One is to show God's true existence, and the other is to show addicts everywhere, no matter how bad the case...we do recover.

You will read about supernatural happenings. The reader can decide what caused these occurrences. I will only tell what I saw with my own eyes. It's all true, and I could pass a lie detector on anything in this book. No matter what you believe, no matter your stance, you will see that strange happenings are very real. You can call them "The Unexplained." I choose to use terms such as "Miracle" or "Demon." Just know that *Fire and Ice* is all real...and God is real.

I want kids to hear these tales and never want to try drugs. I hope my story prevents Satan from taking even one more soul. Just remember, when reading the ugly parts of this story, God comes in a big way. Love always trumps hate. God always wins no matter what the scorecard looks like. So, buckle up and enjoy the ride as we coast into the caverns of the cold. The ice game is not for the faint of heart. Don't get lost as we drive along passengers.

Chapter 4
The Driver:
Stakes is High

A small family-owned taxi company operated in the tourist trap that was Port Aransas, Texas. A short chubby man owned the outfit and I heard he was desperate for help during the night shift. I needed a job, so I decided to make a quid pro quo agreement. One hot afternoon, I waltzed up to his home. It was around spring break, and the town was shaking with college-age party animals and all types of rejects, swilling cold beer in the dunes off the sweltering Gulf of Mexico.

"I heard you needed a driver," I said with enthusiasm.

The man nodded. We talked a bit and before I left, we filled out the regular papers. I left with a contract, as I had intended.

Livery laws deal with a vehicle that is for hire to the public. Port A was unregulated as far as these laws were concerned, therefore no permit was needed to become a licensed cab driver. The owner had heard some bad things about me from his friends at the Port Aransas Police Department dispatch unit. My slew of run-ins with the local law almost cost me this job. But being the con man I was, I slithered in on a probationary deal.

I started my first overnight shift, which lasted twelve hours. I was so excited and couldn't wait for seven to roll around, which was my evening start time. I always loved the nightlife in Port Aransas, and now I would get paid to see the madness unfold. Even though I couldn't drink, the adrenaline of watching others get plastered, as well as the huge number of tips I received, well made up for it. The first few hours were a sluggish crawl. Old women back and forth to the grocery store, a few kids here and there. Nothing to write home about. Then the party started roaring all in one moment, like a flash; static air surrounded my space.

I drove a fifteen-passenger van. Big groups meant more money as we got extra for anything over eight people. The city streets were jammed with traffic. The meth I had snorted in the bathroom of the corner gas station had my blood pumping like a steam train. My eyes wide, senses heightened, and my urge for speed was in full tilt. Baby boomers stinking of booze and expensive department store perfume filtered in and out of the taxi for hours. In the cab business, I was to keep half of what is on the meter, plus tips.

I couldn't believe my eyes. It was all about the Benjamins and I was rolling in wads of cold hard cash. This was the easiest money I had ever made. Shooting the breeze with drunks, going to all the familiar condos. I knew this town like the back of my hand, so I was fast, dependable, and smart by my first night on the job.

I was doing key bumps of crystal periodically, every hour on the hour. Thrills ran up my back as the night progressed. A group of frat boys with board shorts, backward hats, and sandals started brawling outside The Flats, a dive bar off Cotter Street. One of my all-time favorite haunts.

A very tall muscular gentleman started throwing

haymakers at a large group of drunk college students. He nailed a female onlooker square in the nose with a Tyson style right cross. Blood poured in fountains out of both nostrils. The crowd hissed as he kicked her in the ribs and shouted obscenities. I leaned up against the white van, one foot behind me on the fender. Just like the Marlboro man with his cowboy hat tilted down. I was enjoying the show.

Blue and red lights from police cars and first responders beamed through the night sky. The March air doused with the iron smell of plasma, a fight for life in the shadows of the beach. They picked up the poor girl with a backboard. Her neck was stable but most certainly injured. The EMT's black boots crumbled the gravel beneath. The whole scene was a haggard mess, undeniable that alcohol reared its ugly head.

I chopped it up with the police officers on the scene. All my past indiscretions seemed to be water under the bridge. I pulled away with a newfound respect for how the taxi game worked. The hierarchy of the road went as follows: cops, firemen, EMT's, and cabbies. The cops respected us. They let us get away with speeding and running red lights. Far as they were concerned, we were helping the flow of drunks get home safe. Kings of the road. It is where I got my first taste of the hustle.

Driving was the new drug. Well, an addiction to excitement that was fueled by ice. The action can't be put into words. Booze was in the rearview. Ice was fun and new. My depression was slipping away as I got lost in this new life of fast driving and snorting lines. My home life was drifting away. I was working all night and pretending to sleep all day as my wife and three children went about normal wholesome life activities without me. The truth is that I was developing a nasty pornography habit, worse than ever before as I secretly simmered in my dim-lit bedroom.

#

The tan painted walls were covered in dark shadows from bamboo shades, covering a lone window. Eight a.m. couldn't come around fast enough. As soon as the front door slammed and the faint voices of my children dissipated, the demonic sexual ballet would begin. The queen-sized bed had become an altar of sin. Once a sacred place for my wife and me, it had now become a doormat in hell where my dehydrated body dripped sweat and sexual fluids. The cherry wood chest of drawers acted as a shrine to meth and deviancy. A plate my family ate breakfast off would be covered in a pile of shards. My driver's license was coated with a white film made of lithium traces and camping fluid. Meth now consumed me. I was no longer in control.

My clothes would be torn off instantaneously. Beach towels draped over the comforter, catching the sludge of various baby oils, lotions, and lube that made masturbation a wet, vile activity. Free internet porn was glowing in the glass of a damaged cell phone, searching for the raunchiest, unique sexual situations on The World Wide Web. Shocking fantasies and sick thoughts warped me as I laid strewn in a makeshift den of Satan.

Naked, I leapt to my bare feet. The air conditioning vent splattering a cold breeze upon my oil coated skin. A blood-soaked twenty-dollar bill was in one nostril as I ripped the chemical glass up my nose. Gagging on foreign material, I crawled back to my place of self-abuse and sexual torture. Rubbing my whole body for effect, finding places of untapped sexual gratification. I was with the sex demon. Its slithering, writhing characteristics were frightening. The flicking tonged repetition as I stroked my way into madness.

This is where I found a practice called edging. It ate up time in my life like a wolverine on a day-old corpse. Edging is where one masturbates to the point of climax, then denies oneself the orgasm right before it happens. Going to the edge, building the sexual rage and anticipation. I reveled in the pain. Aching testicles and raging hormones, mixed with the greatest sex drug known to man was a mind-bending escapade.

Hours ticked by as the demon took hold. The dancing, swirling presence of evil filled the room like bubbles in a warm bathtub. The smell of body odor, semen, and coconut oil gave the tabernacle of sin the essence of a peepshow gone array. The day was pasted together like a torn dollar bill. The dread of watching the digital clock, knowing full well I had a whole night of driving and customer service ahead. Luckily, my passengers were so drunk they barely knew I was there. One of the perks of driving a cab in Port Aransas.

The horrors of watching hardcore bondage and humiliation would ensue as I realized five o'clock was rolling around. The slumping realization that it was time to peel myself off the crusts of the towels, the damp bed of sin, and begin the coverup. It was a daily clean up job that mimicked that of a serial killer.

First, the towels go into the wash. Then a scrub of my demonic hands to prevent leaving oil stains on everything I touched. The leftover dope would be bagged up to keep me going for the first part of my shift, till I scored once again. I would then Lysol the whole room as if a gunshot victim met their bloody end. The bed was sprayed heavily with Febreze to rid the smell of immorality before my kids returned to play amongst the crime scenes.

The pillows would be fluffed, and I was off to the showers. My body was covered in lint and slime. The water was turned on as hot as one could stand. The steam molten hot. The mirror fogging as I hop in to reconcile the last eight hours. Lathering up with soap, I would scrub the shame off with whatever nervously bitten fingernails I had left. The film of the devil washed half-heartedly down the drain. My swollen red penis was throbbing. Still not drained in orgasm, the sexual tension and thoughts continued as I dried off. One last look to make sure the home looked like the family had left it. I dressed and shook off the insanity as I hugged my babies when they walked in the door. This was my off time. Day in, day out as I was paid to drive. Team No Sleep had a new captain.

#

Hopping in the van was rejuvenating. The smell of pine air freshener and dashboard shiner filled one's spirit with the hopes of cold hard cash. The money was getting huge. Pulling in twenties and fifties like autumn leaves in a rake. I was ready for the night. Sin was among the riders. They blew into the taxi like Ontario storm clouds and raging waves.

I started to see the devil working in the people I drove. Rich housewives were the worst. Spilling in the van seats after a long hard night of partying, a group of women would be telling stories of cheating and sin. The college-age local boys they had with them horny from cheap rum. The dance floor sweat still on their exposed breasts; I stared in the rearview in envy as the young men French-kissed the women old enough to be their mothers.

Pulling up to the Luxury condo they would be retiring too, one couple decided to stay back.

"Wanna let him watch?" The sunburnt blond of fifty-five years mumbled in a white-wine voice.

She slipped me a twenty out of her high-end purse and told me to swing around to the dumpster. I did. As her top slid off, I pulled into the shadows. My heart raced as she performed oral sex. His drunk face lost in the evil. My eyes glued to the rearview as the sexual nature of this trip hit a pitch point. She had on an off-white mini skirt and matching heels. His khaki pants slid to the floor as she sat on top of him like a cowgirl on a stallion.

She pumped up and down on his unprotected shaft, moaning as the spirit of Jezebel slid in her veins. She had her left hand on his bare chest. The massive H-class stone of her engagement ring twinkled in the beams of a distant streetlamp. The prisms of light danced as she jumped in decadence. My erection was solid as my hand wandered. I was panting as the mistress so freely gave her naked insides to this lucky stud. The final moments, a tense roller coaster of slime and profanity, high heels clicking as he came deep inside her, raw as a clam. They dressed as goo ran down her thighs, the bright inner dome light illuminated his greasy semen on her manufactured tan. She threw me another twenty and gave me a devilish smile as she slithered into the confines of her building. The young buck was passed out drunk in my rear seat. I slammed the breaks as we pulled up to the dingy meth filled trailer park he resided at. A sad night for her marriage indeed.

The cab was a rolling reality TV show. The conversations and scenarios were grotesque at times, but always an adventure. My marriage was crumbling. I was captivated by the late nights and easy money. Sitting at the table after a summer Friday night, I counted stacks of green totaling over six hundred dollars. This was the life I craved. Sex, drugs, and rolling on the city streets. Feeing the pulse of the night, metallic stars above, guiding me into the abyss.

I got drunk on my night off. We fought. I went to my dad's place on a three-day bender and got fired. But the fix was in, driving was where I wanted to be. I was "outta there."

#

Out of respect for my family, I am going to skip over the details of the rest of my marriage. This account is only to show the power of Jesus and his remarkable and unmatched power. Yes! Believe it or not, the book you are reading is about Jesus Christ more than anything else. Kind of shocking, huh? Just stick around, it gets a lot worse before it gets better. The marriage was over. I was out of the house, and I was away from my children for the first time in their life. Panic, shame, and regret ruled my every moment and tortured my dreams. Living at Barry's, I once again ventured out to my new passion…the street.

I found an ad on Craigslist for a driver. A guy who owned a cab hired his own drivers and leased it through the second biggest cab company in town. He lived down the street from my dad's on Oakbrook Road in Corpus Christi, Texas. We met, and in an instant, he said I was hired. I just needed to go apply for a cabby's license. This was the big city now, a whole different animal. There was a taxi inspector who oversaw all the drivers in town. This inspector issued suspensions, tickets, and kept everyone in the industry in line.

I paid a hundred and fifty bucks out of pocket and waited for my background check to come in. In about a week or so I was approved and ready to hit the ground running. I showed up at the cab stand at half past six in the evening, ready to drive. I was nervous, the size of the city was massive compared to Port A. Corpus being one of the most violent cities in Texas, more guns than a vine got grapes, I had a shiver running cold up my spine.

I got the keys and was shown how to work the cab's

outdated radio to receive jobs. We would hear our cab number, mine was number four, and we would go to the address given as fast as possible. The cab game in Corpus was all about the bucks. Cops don't stop you for speeding, the same respect applied here as it did in Port Aransas, only more so.

While in Port Aransas, I had made an ice connection in Flour Bluff. This was a small, tight knit, mostly White part of Corpus Christi. The plug was a guy who I struck up a quick friendship with. He was in his fifties but looked more like sixty-five. Thin as a rail, long stringy blonde hair, and a smile that was satanic and sweet. He ran a trap out of a duplex, dilapidated and snarling with the underworld dwellers of the methamphetamine counterculture.

I made a pit stop on the night of my first shift to pick up two twenties of the cold. I was getting the drug at a point-for-point price. Point-for-point is a term in the meth world describing the price of the drug versus the weight on the scale. For instance, one point is ten dollars, and so on, and so on. You end up paying a hundred dollars a gram. This is the price all newcomers pay in the game. I wasn't a hot chick or a somebody worth knowing, so that's the price I paid.

The crystallized shards hit the surgical steel plate on the top of the scale. The plug made small talk as the icy material bounced lightly before settling. The scale read four. I gave him two of my twenty-dollar bills. His boney sun-worn hands gripped the currency as he laughed. He had no shirt, old tattoos, and he looked like a jaded pirate of modern day. His ripped jeans were dirty from doing construction work on the property. It was a complex of about five duplexes where he was the live-in manager.

"Well, I gotta get going back out to the car" I said nonchalantly.

That was my terrible Boston accent shining through. The room all burst out laughing.

"We're going to call you Boston from now on," he chuckled. Even though that was my name.

There were three female bag chasers in attendance. Females in the game show up at trap houses with trash bags of clothes in tow, looking for free drugs in trade for sexual favors. I looked around the room, the women all had on sexy cutoff jean shorts and skimpy crop tops. They each had filthy tennis shoes and no socks. I didn't want to leave. I couldn't stay long as I was on a signal five, cabbie radio lingo for a five-minute break. The girls all said "Bye Boston" at once as they laughed. I headed for the door, through the gravel of the dusty parking lot, and back into the refuge of my air-conditioned taxi.

I pulled right out of the parking lot and sped away. This place was hot at as a Louisiana baked potato, and I was terrified of getting arrested at this point. I kept the bags in my mouth as I took off. A soda cup ready to go in case I had to swallow them during a traffic stop. My heartbeat slowed as I turned the corner. I was in the clear. I transferred the bags from my mouth to the bank bag I kept my cash in, and I was off to work.

I pulled into a church parking lot. It was still daylight and rush hour drive time. I took out a small mirror from my cab bag and crushed up a ten-dollar sized gagger. I had a rolled twenty-dollar bill ready to go, and I blasted off. A call scratched over the radio for cab four. I wrote the address down in my notebook, plugged it into my GPS on my phone, and I was making money.

#

City streets cascaded with lights as the sun went down. My pupils were wide and eager for action. I started to pick up various people all over the city.

This was not what I was used to. The city is full of the Mexican culture and vibes of the border. Hot chicas that looked like Selena Quintanilla hopped in and out of my back seat. I drove vagrants, hustlers, drug dealers, and pimps. My clientele spoke openly about where they were going and told me the everyday struggles they were going through.

On my first night at the job, I discovered the importance of the prostitute. I swung into the local Motel 6 off Lantana. I had a call to take a female all the way back to Flour Bluff, which was the whole length of Crosstown, the highway running through the heart of Corpus. This was about a forty-dollar ride. She hopped in looking like a Mexican Barbie doll. Cut off t-shirt, waist exposed, jeans so tight they looked like they were airbrushed on like artwork on a low rider.

Her eyebrows were sky-high, cheekbones highlighted with brown warpaint, and full plump lips that made my pants tight in the crotch. I looked at her in the rearview as we pulled off…"Where to?"

She gave me the address and I plugged it in. She chatted on her cell for a few minutes, haggling prices of some sort. She hung up angrily. "Fucking white boy," she barked as she hit the end button on her phone. "Why are you gringos all so damn cheap?" Then she gave me a chuckle.

The smell of high-grade weed plumed off her exotic skin. She flipped the long ponytail that was on the center of the top of her head. Her pin-straight hair and cocoa complexion drove my senses wild. I was lit and a horny pulsing mess. We talked, laughed, and hinted around the fact we both knew what time it was as far as drugs go. She explained she was a working girl and she made damn good money turning tricks.

I couldn't take my eyes off the gorgeous ink she had covering her arms. Gold earrings dangling like door knockers on an old Pueblo mansion. We pulled up to the trailer. Nighttime darkness illuminated by a single porch lamp. The trailer park bustling with activity, she told me to hold up as her trick was paying for the cab. She ripped the door open and started yelling. Soon after, a fat White male about thirty years her senior came out and asked how much the meter was. I told him and made his change. He didn't leave a tip. With it being such a good trip, I started to throw it in reverse and leave a happy man anyways.

Mama stomped back out the trailer in her chunky high heels yelling for me to hold up.

"Hey white boy, you had it written all over your face."

She placed a fat sack of crystal in my palm and gave me a big smile. She must have seen me lusting after her flesh the whole trip and recognized my drug of choice. The old man was most likely a dealer and got the stuff damn near free.

"What's your name on Messenger?" I asked her.

We could link up on social media whenever she needed a ride. I could call in a personal call to dispatch. She liked me. She knew I used drugs and guessed that she could probably trade oral sex for a ride if she ever got in a jam. She guessed right.

I made twenty dollars on the ride, got a fat sack on top of the payload I already had on deck, and I made a new friend, Daniella. This right here was what I was looking for. The street, the drugs, the sex. I was blown away by this chance encounter.

I gave a ton more rides. The South Texas sun came up over the horizon. I snorted some fat lines in the bathroom at the carwash where I cleaned up the taxi for the next shift. I sprayed foam and water on the sleek white paint of cab number four. I vacuumed the inside. The meth released sexual rage in me that had my mind in guttural places that were unspeakable.

I got back to the cab office. At the taxi stand, I broke bread with the company. After their half, I had raked in almost two hundred in cash, that fat sack of ice, and a pack of unopened Newport's someone left in the back seat. What a night. I glared at the dispatcher's legs as I walked out the door. Now it was time to summon some real demons.

I hopped in my personal car, a small black Mitsubishi Mirage. A tuna tin can of a car with tiny tractor wheels for tires. Fifteen bucks to fill the tank and it would roll three hundred miles. It was a standard, which I had gotten surprisingly good at driving. I was on a mission. I knew a little Asian market within the city limits that illegally sold porn DVD's under the counter. Daniella fresh in my mind, I opted to buy some Young Latina hardcore movies for a full day of masturbatory inclination.

I got back to the house and said a quick hello to Barry as he passed me on his way into work. It was perfect. I had cash, dope, and the whole house to myself. Snorting lines and making gross love to myself all day at full volume. This was exactly where my addiction had taken me, to look forward to this twisted dark sexual behavior.

#

Weeks passed. I was working seven days a week because, let's face it, my work wasn't really work. I was meeting people from all over town and all walks of life. People that take taxis are the poor, the downtrodden, the people of the night. The taxi was a safe passage for drug transactions and ways of prostitution. For a price, you could buy the silence of almost any taxicab driver in Crook City.

The cab company that currently employed me was outdated, way behind the times. Most cab companies today will have full video and audio setups in the taxi that record everything that happens within. I was digitally alone within cab four. So, I was able to meet the movers and shakers in the game unnoticed. Drug dealers of all types. I was making connections in the streets. My new "friends" were exciting, dark, and had anything you needed to get turned on.

I was loyal to my friends in the Bluff currently. I was still scoring from the old guy in the duplexes. He was a good buddy now and I always gave him my money first. I was making runs, picking up fares, and my list of personal calls were growing rapidly.

I got in a groove. The prostitutes I was meeting were by far the best paying, highest tipping clients I had. They took long rides and always paid cold hard cash. My phone book was growing by the day. At this time, I started to get lost in the seedy world of drugs and hustling

#

I was driving at the beginning of my shift when I met Charity. She was a middle-aged lady with a thick New York accent. I picked her up from the post office on a sunny calm afternoon. I happened to be one hundred percent of sound mind on this day, which was exceedingly rare. I just hadn't had time to run to the Bluff to score yet. We talked and she recognized my accent as well; we made fast friends that day. She gave me her phone number and we parted ways after the ride was over.

We texted back and forth for a few days just chatting about normal things, just small talk. I was high in my room not long after cruising through Craigslist in the personal ads, a site where sex was easy to find. Riddled with horny housewives, prostitutes, and any other kinky evil activity your mind could dream up.

There was Charity, draped over her bed in thigh high

stockings and a black silk nightgown. She had an add up for massages, one hundred and twenty dollars for half an hour. I was dumbfounded. We never talked about sex, drugs, or anything other than wholesome funny things. And here she was a working prostitute, servicing Johns out of the comfort of her own apartment, right down the street from my dad's house.

I was high as could be. I texted her right away. I told her I saw her ad and asked what she was up to? She invited me over right away. I pulled into the apartment complex with no drugs, but I had enough in my blood to last a lifetime. She answered the door with a big smile and a hug. We sat and talked a while and spoke about her choice of work. She had been in a terrible relationship in another city in Texas and had to flee. She was doing massages for older men, mostly in their sixties and seventies, for high dollar payouts.

She explained that most of her clients were elderly and only wanted the company. She never serviced young guys, as they wanted sex nonstop, and she was trying to get out of the game as fast as she could. I felt deep empathy for her. I told her what drugs I was doing and my own sexual experiences. She was very cool and understanding.

She opened her fridge and it was full of beer. She had on a pair of jean cutoffs and a tank top with her big gawky wireframe glasses. She had auburn hair and an older face, looking like a seventh-grade science teacher. She handed me a beer and we proceeded to get blindingly drunk. I hadn't drunk for a long time. Sitting there, I realized I had only a six-pack, and I was blitzed. This was a miracle moment in my life. I realized I hadn't had a drink in over a month. For me, that was a mountain mover.

Her apartment was nice. A huge leather sectional, brown and buttery. Big screen TV and onyx lamps that looked like they cost a pretty penny.

"You wanna get high?" she said with a motherly grin.

"Hell yeah, I wanna get high," I nodded with a slur in my words.

She took my hand and we stumbled into the bedroom. She had a huge pearl-colored chest of drawers with brass handles. A massive king-sized bed with a black comforter fit for, well, a king. She smiled as she retracted the top drawer of the pearl chest. I peered inside and was amazed. It was like looking at pirate treasure on a long-lost boat. Shimmering rocks of crystal meth, mountains of cocaine and pills. I couldn't believe my eyes. Cut straws and a mirror coated in various specks of dust sat right there for the taking.

She flipped her hair and said, "Take whatever ya want, kiddo," in her thick New York accent.

I picked up the mirror and placed it on top of the dresser. I laid out two huge lines of meth worth about twenty dollars apiece. When it's free, I spare no expense.

"What? Ya trying to kill me, Boston?"

We both chuckled as we sat on the edge of the great king bed. She handed me a cut straw. She blasted first. Her thin nose ripped the whole toxic pile up into her skull. Choking, she leapt up and started pacing the room in circles.

Nose to the ceiling, "Boston you are crazy?"

"You are the one who snorted that hog leg," I laughed gleefully.

I was up next. Still buzzed from the alcohol, I snapped back the whole pile in eager anticipation. It hit me like a sea wave, rouge and powerful. We sat on the bed talking about life, drugs, and sex.

She wasn't wearing a bra, so her nipples were standing straight up like top hats. I couldn't take my eyes off of her. An older White lady, her red hair, big lips, and glasses had me fantasizing about staying after class. I was at a good weight these days, so I felt kind of sexy myself.

I was in board shorts, white and baby blue with no underwear and a black t-shirt. My eyes were popping against the darkness of my shirt. She saw the lust dripping from my open jaw. The feeling of sexual tension mounted as the speed pulsed in our genitals. The poor lady tried over and over to switch the topic from sex, but I just wouldn't let up.

I got up and went to the top drawer once again. I laid out two massive gorilla fingers of coke.

"You sure you wanna mix those, kid?" she asked.

"I wanna mix it all," I said with lustful evil in my mind.

I sat back down and did mine first. The cocaine numbed my throat instantly. I watched her feverishly do her line. We both sat back, hands behind us, palms down.

She let out, "Wow, what the hell are you doing' to me?"

I laughed, got up, and went to her walk-in closet that sat in the master bedroom. She had tons of outfits, slutty in nature. Heels, lacey nighties, thigh-high socks. It was a mini sex shop sitting right in front of my eyes.

I pulled out a pair of red platform high heel stripper shoes and headed for the bed. She cocked her head with disparagement as I returned to sit beside her.

"What you think is going to happen here?" she asked.

At this time, the coke was really vibing with the ice we had ingested. I got us two X pills out of the drawer and some beers from the fridge. I placed the pill between two fingers, and she stuck out her long serpent-like tongue.

I placed it gently on her flesh as she slurped it back into the cavern of her pallet. Charity was a full-blown drunk and addict. I loved it. She loved it. The beer washed down the

MDMA laced pill into her belly.

As she sipped the brew, I could see the substance cocktail changing her spirit. She undressed in front of me as the club drug took her to outer space. She had on red-laced panties to match the shoes I had handpicked. She put them on slow, the sound of the fake leather straps popping made my pants a teepee. She had purposefully done this. I think me being younger turned her on tremendously. She was topless. She had one foot draped off the bed and the other foot bottom down on the black comforter. She looked like a sexual praying mantis about to slice my head off my torso.

She told me to take my shirt off and I eagerly listened to her. She was my elder, after all. If she wanted to be in control, I needed to listen. Her fifty-year-old fingertips were done in bright white paint, and she lightly scratched the skin on my chest and teased my nipples like a dragon seducing an altar server.

There was something very dark and evil in the room. I was in the pit of sexual rage. The slow tension of seduction reeled in my very being. I was lost. The X, ice, and coke all embodied the horniness I had been trying to feel my entire life. The dance, the ballet of lust. I couldn't get enough.

Charlotte started to play a sick game. She asked me to start spelling out my darkest fantasies in detail. I will spare you, the description I am laying out here is probably far more than you bargained for to begin with. I sexually spat lies and death. I told her my sick perversions as the ice and coke stimulated every inch of my body. The X gave me the whimsical feel of a romance novel. I preached degradation and sin in her ear as she touched me.

Her panties came off. Slow and sleek. Over the heels, the red lace ran as my breath left my body. I took off my shorts down to my ankles. She took the panties in hand, placed them on my shaft, soaking wet with her inner rivers. She stroked me up and down with them. The pained burning of the material, mixed with the soothing gel of her love, made for an experience that my soul had longed for. She continued as she flicked her tongue against mine. She kissed snake-like and fast. The meth controlling all sexual movements, the drugs fueling the whole tryst. She got on top of me and placed me inside her with authority.

  I was raw inside her. Her hips ground mine as I gazed at the defiled red panties beside my face on the bed. Charity moaned and spoke sexual abuse into existence without fear. I saw her facial expression swell with pleasure. My thickness filled the gaps in her heart. It was far from lovemaking, this was a lesson in lust from a dominatrix, her speech vile and controlling. My sweet friend from New York took my hands and placed them on her hardened breasts. I reached one hand to her throat and choked her diligently, upon direct order from the sexual demons within her soul.

  She spat on my chest, multiple times she shot venomous saliva at me in a show of force to degrade me. I hadn't had sex like this before. As turned on as I was, I was in shock. I envisioned my dead relatives' ghosts in the room watching me have unprotected masochist sex with a known prostitute. It turned me on even more. That was the power of hardcore stimulant drugs. The scarier the sex, the more you feel empowered, all inhibition's annihilated.

  Her heels clicked behind her head as the dark forces came to pass. I finished deep inside her, raw, unfiltered, and sad. My heart beating, a snare of depravity around my neck as my damaged hands released hers. She rolled off me and onto her back. I sat in wetness as my eyes stared at the top drawer.

We snorted drugs and drank until the sun dawned over the bay. The apartment stunk of sex and beer. I threw a Newport in my mouth and headed for the door. A soft kiss on the cheek from the schoolteacher massage therapist and I was in the Mitsubishi.

#

Our friendship bloomed. Charity and I started to spend a lot of time together. I was still driving the cab. With Daniella and friends throwing me a ton of business, life was exciting. I would take little vacations on my two days off. Through cab driving, I found the seedy strip that was North Beach. A tiny plot of land that sat in the shadows of The Sparkling City. It housed cheap drug motels, hookers walking the track, and more meth than a Tennessee drug evidence room.

It was here that a few moments would forever change my life. I found a cheap motel on the very end of the strip. I sought out the cheapest, most low-grade place I could find. I wanted to be close to all the action...the hookers, the cold, all of it. I would hit the little Indian owned liquor store that was inside a gas station. I bought a huge bottle of Fire Ball Cinnamon Schnapps, some beer, and then I hit the front desk of the motel.

Another Indian owner greeted me. He charged me forty dollars for the night and gave me the key to room 216. It was an end room. The strip in front of me, the water directly to the rear. The motel was bile yellow with red trim. I parked my little black car right in front of the door to the room so I could keep a close eye on it.

Entering the room, I saw a rancid paisley comforter, a cheap set of wood nightstands, and an old box TV on an ancient dresser. The carpet was almost the exact color and texture of a green felt pool table. It smelled of smoke and mothballs.

The bathroom had scummy white and pink tiles and a toilet fashioned with a wire coat hanger. This place was a total dump. Just what I was looking for.

I threw my smokes on the table, put the cooler full of beer on the nightstand next to the TV, and opened the bottle of liquor. Right away, I guzzled four huge gulps. I went back out to the car and grabbed my overnight bag and a big case of pornography DVD's.

At this point, I must have had two hundred hardcore titles with all ages, races, and genre. I had a taste of whatever sexual poison you could desire. My porn addiction was full time by now. Viewing even in the cab on my cell phone. I liked watching it hands-free on a larger screen, hence the massive DVD collection. As I returned, I looked up and saw a real-life vision of beauty. She stood five foot three inches, daisy dukes on, no panties. Bare trailer park feet, blond hair up in a bun. She had on a black tank top and gold hoop earrings.

She was outside smoking a cigarette, watching her son play. She lived there. I peeped in her motel room doorway, and it looked like an episode of hoarders. Trash bags full of clothes, toys, and food. I said "hey" to her and walked into my room. I left the door open. She strutted over and introduced herself as I lay the porn on the bed.

"Hey, you here to party?" she asked.

I nodded and she came in, leaving her son outside to play in the parking lot.

We chatted for a few minutes, feeling each other out. Mostly because I straight up looked like a cop and appeared as if I wanted to see what she was into. However, she quickly figured out I was on ice.

The conversation turned to drugs. She admitted she was a hooker and she quickly left for her room, yelling for her son to come inside where she put on an episode of cartoons. Then she returned.

"I got a pizzle," she said with a Jessabelle smile.

I had not smoked clear since Vegas, with my preferred method being to snort the substance. Something alluring struck me as she held the glass stem pipe with a bulb on its end. Charred remains sat in its bowl. I looked her up and down, staring at her dirty bare feet on the green felt carpet, arched in sex.

"I am Lettie" she urged.

From our previous words, Lettie knew that I had an eight ball of shards on me. Plenty to get off on for a two-day trip to North Beach. I took the bowl from her and loaded it with crystals. My Bic lighter ignited underneath the bulbous container. She jerked it out of my hand and shouted, "You gone burn it up, White boy."

Lettie was Mexican but her flesh was white as the driven snow. Her bleached hair gave her a White girl tint that turned me on in more ways than one.

She placed the stem to my lips; I was quaking as I was already high from a fat line I did in the car, plus the gulps of Fireball. The amber glow of the bulb lit the room in demonic illumination. The shards inside sizzling like a T-bone steak on an open grill. The solids quickly melted into a brown liquid, hissing and vaping into smoke as I inhaled slowly into my chest. I remembered to exhale right away to prevent the drug from crystalizing in my lungs. The cloud was enormous. Once again, my eyes danced in my skull.

She drew close and whispered in my ear, "See, that wasn't so bad."

We stood together, roasting hit after hit, till over a half gram was dispersed into our bloodstreams. Nothing too sexual was going on...well in my head, yes, very much so. I asked her if she had an extra DVD player that I could rent from her for a small amount of ice. She nodded and I bagged her up a dub sack as she went to her room to retrieve it.

She was taking too long for my liking, so I went and knocked on her door. A tall and very muscular White boy answered.

"Alright, alright, alright," he said in a dead ringer Matthew McConaughey impression.

He had reddish hair, high and tight. Huge arms with tattoos and a natural beach tan. He wore a grey tank top and navy-blue basketball shorts.

"Hey, you're the guy next door, huh? Boston?"

He told me his name was Larry. We chopped it up a few minutes before Lettie returned with the DVD player.

I invited Larry to my room to smoke him out. We hit it off instantly, talking about hookers and such. We laughed and had a grand time. Instant buddies. I dubbed him "The Matthew McConaughey of North Beach." Larry had a record of eighteen and zero on fist fighting at the beach. He schooled me to some things about the North Beach culture, its hard life and inhabitants. Some interesting characters started coming into my room. I had booze and drugs, so all the freeloaders started to act like my friend just to hang out.

One of which was Wheezy. A midwestern transplant, he had a masterpiece tattooed on his chest. Wheezy was a North Beach pimp. He was tall, covered in prison tattoos, and had a crew cut. His head was square shaped with a big nose curved outward. I also hit it off with him right away.

Everyone left for Lettie's room except Wheezy and me. We pounded the bottle of Fireball, drunk and reminiscing on Nineties' rap. Wheezy was a good connection. He could get ice, he knew working-girls, and he knew the ins and outs of North Beach like no one else.

He eventually stumbled into the shadows and onto the dark streets. I found myself alone in the room watching pornography and smoking ice out of the pizzle I pocketed from Lettie. I stayed locked up for forty-eight hours. The door swinging open on Sunday morning was a scene out of a vampire movie. My eyes were pained with potent beams of sunlight protruding through the smoky den. I had made some new friends, new connections, and fresh places to hide. My world was opening big time. The drug underbelly was about to find its latest minion. I was hooked up and now on that pipe.

#

I started to smoke every single time I used ice. The high was far more sexual and intense. I hadn't thought of my children in months. There were moments where their ghosts emerged in my mind. A deep sadness resonated within when this happened. I would hear childlike giggling and frivolous secrets from my bedroom on Oakbrook. I'd look out my door to find the house empty. I was being haunted by the happiness of my past. My kids reaching for me from a dimension unknown to the scientific world.

In general, the meth was known for causing forgetfulness. Anything you loved, the wholesome things, they all faded like ink from a magic pen. My new life had no place for family or real friends. It was driving, drugs, and sexual torture. As months passed, the pipe started eating at me. The amount of meth I was doing increased to epic levels.

I started linking up with a lot of local gang members and thug types. Being a lane of safe passage, my personal calls all started to become prostitutes or my other favorite customers, drug dealers. The rides were intense. I'd get a call on my cell for a job. The dealer was then instructed to call dispatch and book a ride requesting me directly. The cab had GPS so the meter would have to match the mileage of the run.

I would pick the dealer up from Point A, then either pick up a batch of drugs or drop off a delivery of drugs at Point B, and lastly return the dealer back to Point A. No fear of the cops pulling us over, no danger, just pure paper-chasing at its finest. Dealers in the ice game are infamous users. They are terrible with cash. The typical day for a dealer in the game is to pick up a shipment and "trap", meaning sell drugs to customers, then infamously do all their profits by using or trading the proceeds for sex. They were always broke. The only cash you would see them with was for the re-up. The re-up was the amount of cash needed to score the standard shipment that would reset the whole process. For instance, the dealer would buy a zip, which is one ounce of meth. Sell the meth at a much higher price to consumers. Then, they would keep back enough money to get another zip and smoke up the profits with bag chasers.

These dealers never had the money for the fare. A lightbulb went off in my head. I figured out that I didn't have to pay the company the money from the meter reading until the end of my shift. We would do a job, they would pay me in dope for the amount on the meter, and I would only be responsible for half of that amount in cash at the end of the night.

The drug dealing started to really take off. I had a group of gang members and street-level independents that now supported my ever-growing habit. A perfect job for a full-blown addict. I could come and go as I pleased. I was contract labor, so I could show up late, clock in and out for breaks whenever I wanted, and never hear "boo" from the cab company.

Days folded into one another. I was meeting new

women all the time. Watching pornography became a full-time thing when not behind the wheel on a job. I started to lose myself in the grim sexuality of the game. My soul was being darkened by the evil that surrounded me. All glimmers of Christ were gone, faded into the air like gun smoke. My whole being had changed. From family-oriented businessperson and a jolly soul to the stark raving sexual deviant that stoked in the shadowy streets of The Sparkling City by the Sea.

#

Charity was losing her mind. It was painful to watch and very annoying to be around. When I was done with my nighttime shift, I would spend hours at her house smoking up mounds of her supply. She became obsessed with a man who had raped her years before. She reached out to him to strike up some kind of a sick relationship with her attacker. I believe this was fully drug-induced. She cooked up this insane game in her mind. She would have me write out scripts, pretend to be a congressperson from DC, and then try to tell this guy he was going to be pardoned for the crime he had already done time for.

He was a dishwasher at a local eatery. I told him the government was to fly him to DC where he would speak on wrongful incarceration, giving this man all kinds of false hope for a newfound career. It was torture.

He bought every word I spoke. I was stooping to an all-time low, lying in some crazy nightmarish façade, all in an attempt to get high for free. She barely wanted to have sex anymore, so I knew I was about to make an exit from her life.

She was out of drugs. Her connect got so sick of her psychotic rants and demands, he blackballed her. She called me frantic looking to buy a quarter ounce of ice. The day before I had taken five grams, some of her last, and pre-bagged them up with the promise I would sell them and make her a healthy profit. I still had most of what I hadn't smoked left in my cab bag. I headed over and we had a chat. She opened the top drawer, empty besides the stacks of currency from her trick savings. A call came in. One of her clients was in the parking lot. I had to leave for an hour while she handled her business. I was enraged. I sat in the parking lot, roasting glass. It was high-grade. As the streets called it "the fire, bro."

    I saw the geriatric fool come out and get into his Audi. I rushed upstairs in a tweaked-out strut. She opened the door in a nighty. Hair disheveled and matted with the man's drippings. She fixed her glasses as we sat on the couch. By this time, I loathed her in every way. Still my friend but her mind was mush. She had three hundred dollars in her hand. She proceeded to give me some long Ted Talk on how she worked hard for her money and that if I ripped her off, she would never forgive me.

    I called the old man in the duplex. I set up a deal to buy a quarter for two hundred and fifty dollars. It was a total rip off, but I knew he could get it fast. He told me that it was already on the way, and I could meet the supplier at his house in the Bluff. I would then pinch a large amount out of her bag and keep fifty in cash for my troubles. Not to mention sit and smoke her stash with her for a good full day before she kicked me out.

    She was extremely paranoid by now. She was talking about the cops watching her former plug, looking out the blinds of her apartment every two minutes. She had me downright spooked. The large quantities I had toked up in my car had me really thinking extra this day. I cut her off rudely, snatched the three hundred from her boney old hands, and slammed the door behind me.

    I threw on my Locs sunglasses, opened my car door,

and plopped down in my seat. The air conditioning was thrusting dry hot air at my face as the car's system got going. Gears on the standard little car grinding as I blasted some Tupac for vibes. I sped down South Padre Island Drive on a mission to score. Paranoid, looking in the rearview for any signs of a tail. I was brilliant at checking my mirrors, always aware of my surroundings.

I pulled up to the trap house, dust from the dingy parking lot attaching to the onyx paint of my sled. Skidding to a stop on the gravel, I walked around the steel parking barriers that separated the parking spaces from the white wooden structures. My everyday ensemble of board shorts and a t-shirt with big black glasses and freshly gelled hair gave me the appearance of a bad undercover narcotics officer. I played the part of a tweaker stallion to a tee.

I rapped on the flimsy door of the apartment. I heard movement inside, like frantic roaches when a light is flipped on.

"Who is it?" yelled some derailed female voice.

"Boston," I squawked in a grumble.

To my amazement, the door swung open, and the old man was there with a large evil grin on his face.

"Come on in, man," he sputtered.

I reluctantly entered the trap. Every stick of furniture had been removed. There were heroin addicts squatting on the old hardwood floors where the couches and entertainment system had been. A sad group, all on a Jones for a fix. Tattered White girls with Mad Max apocalyptical haircuts full of pink or rainbow colors. Shaved scalps under strings of long hair gave them the essence of punk rock divas, with black tracks running up rail-thin arms. A couple of Mexican nationals that clearly didn't speak English sat shirtless and sick in filthy paint-covered dungarees. My plug's hair full of oils from lack of washing.

He informed me, "We are gonna have to wait for the guy to get here so just gimme the money and go sit in my room."

Panic ran through me like crap through a goose. The sheriff's deputy I passed in the church parking lot flashed in my mind. I could feel the energy of a set-up looming. I had a good amount of money and ice on me, and they could smell it. In the game, one of my carnal rules was "never trust a smack addict." Even the old man was all jammed out, which for him was completely out of character. Something wasn't right. In the drug world, you learn fast to always trust your gut. Addicts are creatures of extreme habit. If things don't appear normal…run.

I made an excuse to head back to my ride, citing that I left the cash in the car. I inched out of the apartment backward as the demons looked at me like a group of hungry dogs watching a piece of prime rib. Assuring them I would be right back, I hopped in and franticly turned the keys to carefully, but quickly, head down the road. My own paranoid thoughts were now a fear factory figuring that Charity had somehow set me up. This all burned wildly within me as I made a hasty exit. I was out of there.

Whatever was about to happen with this whole deal, it was not for me. I listened to my gut and decided to go to a familiar place of safety. North Beach. I hit the Harbor Bridge, watching my six. The steep terrain of the bridge's body led to an apex of wonder. Overlooking the USS Lexington, the water was Caribbean blue on this day. Twinkles of sun danced across a glass top sea, wrinkles of wind casting birds in the midday sky.

My descent onto the strip signaled that I was home free. I came to a screeching halt right in front of my regular room at Motel Hell, towards the end of the road. The inn keeper me signed in, so I hit the liquor store and bought two fresh meth pipes. This was the point where I turned off my cell phone, unpacked the porn and booze, and hunkered down for an epic binge.

#

I had just bounced on the old man, screwing up whatever deal he had in place for himself, and ripped off Charity on her three hundred cash. It was time to hide out for a while. I had about three grams of pre-packaged ice leftover, that apparently, Charity had forgotten all about. But I needed more. I sparked a half gram bowl of that fire and decided I would hit up Larry and Lettie next door.

There was Lettie, her friend Rain, and Rain's boyfriend Carlos, all smoking large amounts of crack. I told them I needed a quarter ounce of ice, and I would gladly smoke a ton of it with them if they hooked me up on the quick. I didn't want to reach out to any other dealers I worked with because I was so paranoid. I didn't want anyone knowing where I was.

I got the DVD player from her and was on my way back to my room. My overnight bags at this point contained some tweaker clothes, two cans of yellow brand butane fuel, and a handheld blowtorch. My torch was dressed up with decals of Bob Marley and some pot leaves.

I drank some Fireball, threw on a movie about older hot-looking schoolteachers, and blasted off into the speed stratosphere. I was incredibly sad currently. My life was sex and drugs, and that was it. I was starting to forget every fiber of who I once was. The heartbreak of my career ending, the children, and marriage over had all become faint memories that I seldom thought of. It was as if my mind shut those parts down in order to cope with their absence.

Hours slipped by. With the summer sunset over the coastal backdrop, diesel filled the calm air of the old motel room. Degenerates funneled in and out of my room. Starved for company, I lit up any homeless girl or friend of Lettie's that stopped by. The porn played on rotation as total strangers acted like my friends, smoking my stash and drinking all my liquor.

I was running out of dope just as a dark angel appeared in the doorway. He walked in standing all of five feet and five inches. Big baggy jeans and an oversized red t-shirt. A massive chunky silver chain swung from his neck, a fitted Chicago Bulls' hat on his little head. He introduced himself as Shorty. He was a short Mexican dealer with a high-pitched voice and scrunched up little face.

"Lettie told me you needed a quarter?"

He sat on the edge of the bed inquisitively. We talked for a bit and haggled the price. I explained that I was a cabbie and could offer him my services anytime he needed.

"Ok bro, you're getting wholesale prices over here from now on. You buy from me, you gonna get those playa prices."

Shorty sold me a quarter ounce of shards for one fifty. This was my first look at how cheap wholesale prices were. I was happy as a clam.

To grandstand even further, Shorty slowly pulled a loaded .38 caliber revolver from his jean pocket, placing it on the bed as cool as ice. He slipped a fat sack of crystals out and loaded my pizzle to the brim. The single biggest bowl I had ever seen.

He gave me his phone number and address on North Beach. He had it sewn up, this dude ran this place. The undisputed Don Dadda over this side of town. I had now made a quality connection. A great product at the best price so far. He popped on the torch and melted down the product, blowing thick blue clouds up to the light above. We chopped it up; he was friends with Wheezy, Larry, Lettie, the whole crew. I was in like Flynn. He took off to leave me to my own devices.

#

It was getting late, and I was dying for sex. A knock on the door proved to be Wheezy, he was hanging next door at Lettie's. He had a small handwritten note in his hand. I unfolded it as he sat staring at me with a shit-eating grin on his face. The note was a perverted version of a "do you love me: check yes or no" note. It was Lettie asking me if I wanted to have sex with her for fifty dollars. I thought about it and just couldn't do it. I liked Larry way too much. Even though I bet it was his idea to pimp her out to me, I just couldn't do it. I was the junkie sex addict with a heart of gold.

When I declined, Wheezy looked puzzled. I told him to go find me another streetwalker. He agreed and left after we finished off the massive pipe load Shorty had left for me. I smoked nonstop. There was no end to this session. I was exhaling massive amounts of gas practically by the minute.

Rain and Carlos knocked at around four in the morning. I let them in, and they explained that Lettie had a trick coming over and asked if they could kick it for a minute. They were a drug couple through and through. Addiction wreaked havoc on their relationship.

We sat and talked while watching porn together like it was the six o'clock news. This was the first time I was exposed to what drugs can do to a relationship.

They were bickering back and forth for what seemed like an hour, anger and resentment only divided by moments of awkward silence after a particularly mean insult. Carlos was fat and bald, wearing in a big black t-shirt. He continuously called her a whore as she sat looking at the pea-green rug below. He was Mexican and she was an Italian girl who looked like a weathered prostitute. It was clear she's had a hard life.

"Well, things go great until Miss Bitch over here disappears for three days," he rumbled.

He constantly abused her verbally, seemingly out of some sick twisted love, spawned by the ravages of what addiction does to its already fragile nature. She was taking off on him all the time. Whenever the drugs ran out, she would leave and come back after she'd had her fun.

He was a crack smoker. His anger brought on by the lack thereof. He had run out, blowing over a thousand dollars in less than two days. He was busted and thoroughly upset. She sat there as a demonic tongue flipped around in her boyfriend's mouth. He systematically cut her in pieces as I listened, eyes on the pornography the whole time.

He had never smoked ice before. In a last-ditch effort to calm his shattered nerves, I held the pipe to his lips and rolled the bowl ten and two as he inhaled, just as others had done for me in my infancy. Still not a pro, I put way too much heat on it and charred the bulb as he toked. He dove in headfirst. Ice doesn't have the blast effect that crack does. It's far different by design. I could tell it did the trick, he sat trance-like and dazed as the introduction into his blood was made. I sat glaring at Rain, watching her lick her crackpipe lips and flipping her long curly gelled up hair back and forth. This was a classic druggie love relationship, and it was disturbing to watch.

After they left, I continued this crazy binge for twenty more hours. Not a hooker in sight, Wheezy said the streets were dead as can be. The second night in the motel was very dark. I found myself unable to get any higher. I had reached a point where I had hit a plateau. No matter how much I smoked, the effect was the same. I was alone, sad, and kept all the lights off to match my mood.

The heatwave came upon us just mere hours before. It climbed to over one hundred degrees outside. I sat naked in an old wooden chair with a leather seat. The felt carpet was filthy and damp from spilled beer. There was the constant never-ending hum of a rusty motel air conditioner oozing cold air onto my naked skin. I sat paralyzed with an erect penis, staring at the flickering light of the pornographic images spewing from the junkyard television.

I had a scolding hot pipe and blowtorch nested on an end table that I had dragged next to my chair. A big bag of meth just waiting to be loaded up at a moment's notice. The air system moved the curtains in a way that made them look like they were breathing. The shadows danced on the dirty walls. There was an omnipresent smell of spent methamphetamine byproduct lurking all around the room.

I felt a wave of terror come over me. The wallpaper was crawling. Literally. The South Texas heat drove in an infestation of German cockroaches like nothing I had ever seen. Maybe someone next door sprayed a chemical. All I know is that thousands of small bugs were invading my room. I took four or five huge pulls off the pipe. Millions of roaches marching on every surface in the room. The bedspread nearby was like a living thing, moving before my eyes in the light of the TV.

None of this bothered me. I was not a human being anymore. I remember the horror of the roaches taking a back seat quickly as I continued to get high. This was far more important. I was swatting roaches off my baby oiled skin. Raking them out of my hair and shivering. I was careful not to drop the pipe or take my eyes off the nastiness on the screen. My demons had me so bad, that a biblical style pestilence couldn't take my attention off masturbating.

#

It was five in the morning. A quiet patter sounded on the door as I sprung up to investigate.

"I am a friend of Wheezy," a lady whispered.

I pulled the door back slowly, pipe in my hand, completely nude and erect. A short Mexican hooker, about forty-five years old stepped into the room. This was a very delayed reaction to the order I had put in a day prior. She was not even stunned by the nude White man smoking meth that answered the door.

She wore a ratty tank top and black bra. She had on daisy dukes and tennis shoes. Big green eyes and straight black hair in a ponytail. She was a run of the mill streetwalker. I shook as we talked about the sexual act about to take place.

We sat on the bed as she stated, "This is going to be a wham bam."

I was so high that I couldn't have sex. I felt like walking trash. Completely stuck in place. We agreed that she would use her hand on me. I had a bad feeling about having intercourse with this lady, so it came as a big relief to both parties involved. I gave her all the ice I had left in the bag and she slid out of her sweaty attire.

She grabbed the baby oil off the nightstand and put her barefoot on my thigh as I laid back. She greased up her hand and started working me slowly. We both glared at the hardcore images that were glowing on the box in front of us. Edging for days, I was swollen, beaten, and red. Full to the top and frustrated. I could barely breathe with the ice crystals that formed in my lungs. With the sheer number of drugs in me, I was panting as she stroked my manhood. Sweating, foaming, and gross, I proceeded to climax in her hand as hot semen flowed down her dirty knuckles. As soon as the orgasm subsided, a panic-stricken feeling of shame and hopelessness sprang me onto my feet.

I threw on some clothes as fast as my drugged-out body would allow. It's hard to put the feelings of terror and shame into spoken words. She dressed as I scrambled all over the room. I gave her all my pipes. I gave her the booklet with all my porn DVD's inside. She had all the drugs already and she even took the last shot of Fireball as I washed my hands in the bathroom. I gave it all away.

I was silently praying for the first time in as long as I can remember. I was thinking of God and how disappointed He must be in me. The hooker opened the door. There were lots of people coming in and out of the room as I gathered up the rest of my belongings. They were acting as if I wasn't even there. Dividing up my DVD's, begging her for meth. I pushed past them and made my way into my car. I started it up and left them all in my room, knowing full well they were going to steal anything that wasn't nailed down.

I turned the corner and hit the parking brake as I stopped. I broke down into deep salty tears. I was shattered. A broken man in every way. Thoughts of my beautiful children, the days at the park, benchmark moments in our life all ran through my head. I choked, phlegm gaging me as I reflected on my once wholesome marriage and life as a family. *How did I get here? What was I doing?*

I need to turn back.

I gathered my thoughts and pulled away from the curb in a hurry. Tears still dripping onto my cheeks. I was like a zombie, victimized by Satan, a shell of what I used to be. The nose of the car elevated as I hit the bridge. Damaged from two days of masturbation, self-degradation, and hardcore methamphetamine use, I felt my soul splintered by the destitution of my addictions.

As the Mitsubishi leveled at the top of the bridge, I made an internal promise for change and redemption. Instantly I swore off meth and sex in one fell swoop. I spoke out loud, "I am not doing this anymore." The car coasted to the bottom layer of the structure. When I hit the highway, almost right away I regretted my decision to give away all the dope and porn. I spun off the next exit and journeyed right back to score.

#

Shorty's number went straight to voice mail. The streets were empty and clear. The sea salt in the air was captivating and rich. The sound of gulls in the distance was music to my ears. Larry, walking the strip in the distance, looked tired and weak. With my windows down, I pulled alongside him and offered him a ride. He asked if I was hungry. I told him to just get in so he could connect me with a bag of dope.

"Here take this," he said.

He pulled out two safety green construction vests with bright orange trim. He directed me to pull into the parking lot of the Days Inn North Beach. We emerged out of the little black car and put on the vests. I was waiting for a punchline, or some sort of candid camera show to reveal itself as we did this.

"Well buddy, Imma show you how we eat out here on this beach," in his best McConaughey.

We walked in the side door of the hotel and headed right for the breakfast room, posing as local construction workers staying at the hotel. We had pancakes, cereal, muffins, and more. We made plates to go for the ladies of the night back at the motel. We laughed as we walked back to the ride. That's how it worked out there. Total hell, total pain, relationships between the sick that mimicked friendships. That one break in my suffering, that temporary laughter seemed to make it all ok.

I scored, I smoked, and drove home as if the whole horrifying event never took place.

#

I was using dating apps to meet women. I was on them all the time. Facebook was one avenue. I was getting lit up and sending hundreds of sexually charged messages to countless unsuspecting women. I offended many and scooped up quite a few as well. I was a sex fisherman. Throw out the line, use dope as the bait, and see who bites. That's how I met Tiana.

Tiana was a working girl posing as an angel on social media. A tall lanky Native American sweetheart. I met her in a hotel room off Leopard Street in Corpus on a stormy and dark night. I entered the room and Tiana was wearing sexy clothes and had her dog, a husky type breed, with her. We got super-duper high.

Tension in the air was looming. Something sexual, as always when meth is involved, but also something incredibly deeper. We talked about the darkest of fantasies. Evil stampeded our thoughts; Satan was between our souls. We went back and forth fantasizing about picking up a young hooker and sharing her among us. We went into significant detail, laughing as if it were a joke; all the while, underneath, the speed was manifesting thoughts of cruel sexual acts.

I was out of drugs before I even showed up. She was footing the bill for the whole night; something told me this was going to be a good friend. We didn't have sex. Not even close. I think our twisted minds made the other curious and interested. We laughed more than anything, and weeks later Tiana came to live with Barry and me on Oakbrook...doggy and all.

I was driving around the clock. The cab was a safe zone to get high in. I was mostly doing drug-dealer driving. I would get mad when I had to pick up regular fares or "flags", that's when a customer waves you on for a ride. Anything that got in the way of me hustling was a nuisance. I started to drive my personal car during the day for extra cash.

The demand for a White driver with a valid license and a new car was sky high, no pun intended. I was getting a million daytime calls on my cellphone. Team No Sleep was in full effect. Gang members, dealers, hookers, boosters, check cashing rings...these were all part of my clientele. I met a ton of new people in the taxi. A short chat and I had new business all day, every day.

This was my ritual. I would get home at around seven thirty in the morning. Circling the Mitsubishi making sure all the taillights and blinkers worked, looking for the brake lights in the reflection of my bedroom window. I would sound the horn and make sure all the fluids were topped off.

People paid me well to make sure they got home safe, and I was on point. Running a tight ship, I charged more per job than any other wheelman in the city. I wasn't some dime-store junkie with an expired license and a stolen vehicle.

I was getting so many calls I had to carry an extra charged battery for my phone. It was off the hook. I had to turn people away because business was so good. I had Tiana holding down the home base. She would do her business elsewhere, but she kept an eye on things at the house for me.

Tiana was on Craigslist one night when she met Tony. He took out an ad for like-minded people. She told him I would be showing up for the first meet, as she was leery of the whole situation. I think because I looked so much like an undercover cop, she thought it was funny to send me first to scare people.

I pulled up to the South Side apartment complex at around three in the morning. I hopped out of the ride and was greeted by a short Italian looking man with oily black hair and a hooked nose. He had moles and growths on his weathered face. With him was a pudgy older White man with snowy hair, a thick Chicago accent, ratty jeans, and a sleazy checkered black and white button-down collar shirt.

"You Boston?" Tony smirked.

"The one, the only," I said authoritatively.

We entered an empty two-bedroom apartment. White walls and a grey rug, a flimsy futon sofa, and a tiny TV that sat on a cardboard box on the floor. Something was off about this place. It didn't look like anyone really lived there.

There were drug-addicted vagabonds strewn throughout. The bathroom had a pair of sadistic looking Mexican girls shooting up speed with the door wide open. A back bedroom completely empty and shallow, a group of very tired looking youths squatting on a clean but lonely carpet. This place was a shell of a home. Evil lurked within. I loved it. *A new frontier? What was this place? Who are these mysterious people?*

"You do ice?" The older White man asked with a dark undertone and devilish smile

"Is the Pope a Catholic?" I returned with my east coast swag.

We plopped down onto the shag of the untouched rug, the older White man pulled the bulbous pipe from a stained gym sock that kept it free from debris. The bottom of the pipe filled with dope and the exterior charred.

"This is fire bro," I looked at him with amusement and glee.

Tony pulled a handheld torch off the ground and handed it to me. Free dope was something I was not used to. This immediately told me there were ulterior motives at work. I clicked on the blowtorch and swirled the pizzle in a circular motion while rolling it simultaneously over the intense heat below. The cracked shards within melted into a clear brown caldron. Smoke plumed in the chamber as I sucked the gas into my eager lungs. It was the fire alright. My eyes danced, heart raced, and the fix was in.

We sat and talked business, told stories, and joked around. The unease in the room was thick and plenty. The other addicts circled our smoke session like locusts. Tony shooed them away with quickness, almost as if they were embarrassing him in front of his new friend.

The two men treated me like a king. Anything I needed was at my disposal, all I had to do was say the word. The demon people sat in the dark shadows of the room, their eyes staring at me. Light reflecting off their orbits like rats in a tunnel, a yellow glow of evil beaming right at me as I smoked. I could feel the jealousy from all angles.

Then entered a pockmarked faced Mexican man. Leon was of average height, wore a button-down flannel and basketball shorts. He had tweaker written all over him, like a glow in the dark neon madness.

"Who the fuck is this, Tony?" Leon says with anger in his voice.

"This is our new friend we met online. Boston's a cabbie and has a car."

Now it became clear why I was getting the red-carpet treatment. It was just as I suspected. This was a front for an iced-out ring of thieves and their check-cashing operation. They were using Craigslist to recruit crash dummies, which are expendable people in the game. People who were brand new, as they call it, and dumb enough to cash fraudulent checks and return stolen items from stores with their Texas driver license.

Leon had a small bag with him like the bank bag I used

for my cab money. It didn't take me long to figure out what was going on. More minions showed up with laptops under their arms. We all went to the large living area and had a seat.

Tony and the older White guy were sort of the brains. They never let on who the boss really was, most certainly to protect the operation's key functions. They had top members of the crew present, such as Leon, his girlfriend, and others that ran the recruiting and day-to-day operations.

Leon was a mid-level methamphetamine dealer that supplied the ring with all the drugs they needed to work around the clock. A real Grade-A scumbag. From the first five minutes, we hated each other.

His girlfriend was shooting black tar heroin in the bathroom almost every hour. She nodded out at one point while she was sitting next to him on the floor. He smacked her in the back of the head.

"Wake up, you junkie bitch!"

He hit her hard. He was in his thirties, and she was about ten years younger. She was mousey, Caucasian, long brown hair with big circular glasses on. She started to cry in front of everyone in the place. Everything in me wanted to get up and smash his face in with the end of the torch I still had in my hand. But I knew what time it was. I was outnumbered by some peculiar and mean cats, and this was not an option. From that moment on I hated him.

About ten guys were now on the floor, at the kitchen table, and in the bedroom all on computers. Leon was really pissed that I was there. He was hesitant to talk about the workings of what was going on in front of me. He glared at me almost every minute, telling Tony openly that I shouldn't be there. Tony liked me right off the bat and basically told him to kick rocks. Tony knew I was about to serve a purpose. I was sticking around no matter how much Leon hated me.

Tony explained how it worked. The guys on the floor were hackers and check makers. They were getting into business accounts and printing fake checks. A bunch of junkies were about to show up at the apartment, collect said checks, and hit the check cashing places and grocery stores right as they open.

If they cashed ten or twenty checks before the Telecheck system recognized what was going on, this could be a very lucrative score. They did this week in and week out. The junkies all used their identification to cash the bad checks, knowing they would get busted. They were paid in shards, and they willingly took the charge when they got caught.

I watched as keyboards clanged and ice smoke filled the air as if we were at some demonic poker game. A young couple was having sex right there on the floor as the hackers clicked away. I had never seen anything like this in my entire life. I was awestruck. The sun was up, and I was very high. Overwhelmed by the whole scene I told Tony I was going home to get Tia. After all, she was the one who was supposed to meet him in the first place.

As I was heading for the door, Tony had a short talk with me. "You could make a lot of money with us. We got the women, the dope, whatever you need. We got jobs all over this city."

I told him I was down like James Brown.

Soon as I hit the door, Leon exclaims from the kitchen table "Keep your fuckin' phone on, we gonna need rides all day."

I gave him a snide nod and headed for the black Mitsubishi. I went home and threw on some porn and watched Tia as she slept as peaceful as a little angel. I was high as a kite.

The excitement of what I had just seen had me feeling like I had hit the lotto. I began masturbating. She woke from the feeling like she was sleeping next to a paint shaker at Home Depot. She giggled as she watched me right next to her. Once I finished, we smoked a fat bowl, and I told her of the new friends we had just made. A quick shower and we were right back to the apartment. I couldn't stay away if I wanted to. The allure of this new lick had me foaming at the mouth like Cujo in the Stephen King novel.

When the door opened it was a whole new scene. The checks had been cashed, there was dope everywhere, and there had to be twenty breathing souls flying high on meth and crime. Now there were a lot of younger people. Abercrombie and Fitch couples, rich White kids about nineteen years of age. These same kids were passing the pipe with hardened gang members covered in tattoos, all races and creeds on board. The back bedroom was an orgy. There were a couple of Mexican girls in their early twenties, naked and lying on the floor with a train of horny men just waiting their turn.

The computers were put away, but a new game was about to emerge. Tia was quickly introduced to the younger females. One of which laced her up on what was needed from us. Tia, being in the game a while, knew what to do. It was explained that we were supposed to take the younger ladies to the mall to return stolen merchandise for store credit. This was the beginning of a dangerous new racket for me called boosting.

Over the next few weeks, I drove the older White man to the mall and local Walmart stores in Corpus. There were three in the city and other retail businesses we hit up as well, as he was a master booster.

"Boston, the meth counterculture is very big in this city. Strange too, watch your back."

I listened to the old man's words carefully. I was doing the boosting gig as a daytime job after my shift ended in the taxi. If a big score were to take place at night, I would simply not show up to my cab job.

I had way too much going on. I had the hookers, the dealers, the regular taxi job, and now a full-time driving slot for a slightly dangerous check cashing ring. Where was I going to find time to have sex? That's all I cared about anyway. The driving was exciting, the money was good, but the whole mad dance was all so I could score dope.

The thing to remember is I was doing the dope because I was a full-blown sex and pornography addict and that was what was fueling it for me. Working around the clock, I started to fit the ice and sex into my schedule, no matter the cost. It was around this time that I started to see the forces of real evil creep in even more than before. I saw my old self fading away. Morals, character, and any resemblance of my former self was almost completely gone.

I finished my shift one morning and headed to Tony's. I rapped on the door to no end. I was supposed to pick up a girl who needed a ride to a local motel for sex with a John. When the door finally opened, the empty apartment had an evil stench. There was a big Mexican fella standing at the kitchen table with an older fat White man I had never seen before.

"Hey just take a seat, I'll shower really fast, and we'll go," said the biracial Mexican hottie.

I was pissed because my time was money. "Hey, this is gonna be extra, honey," I told her with authority.

She entered the bathroom in a hurry with her overnight bag of slutty clothes and high heels. I lit a bowl and took a few hits. The men at the table were counting money and staring at me like two hounds of hell guarding the gate to the abyss.

I noticed the bedroom door was ajar in the back hallway. Suddenly, a cell phone alarm went off on the table. The fat White man hit the snooze on it and grabbed for a little black nylon case. The two men walked off into the darkness of the hallway and into the pitch blackness of the bedroom. My curiosity was killing me. Since I could do anything I wanted at Tony's, I went to the kitchen to act as if I was getting some water. The bedroom doorway was now in full view and the light had been turned on. There was a young-looking Mexican girl in the bed, most likely twenty-one years old. Rail thin, with a sweaty pink tank top on, stringy brown hair, and a pair of hot-pink lace panties. She looked vacant and weak. She was under a spell of some sort.

The Mexican man sat next to her with a wife-beater muscle shirt, laying his tattooed hands on her leg. The fat White guy had her arm hanging off the side of the air mattress she slept on. He tied her off with a piece of rubber tubing you would find in science class. I saw the orange cap to a needle pop off the rig and land flush on the rug. She moaned as the surgical steel pierced her young skin, the fat White man shushing her like you would a baby who was fussing in a crib.

"Ok baby, just one more second and you will be ok," he said in an evil, creepy tone.

The rush hit her. Her body went limp and cold. I saw her small breasts rising and falling with every breath, she was barely alive. The smell of vinegar escaped the room from the black tar they had heated up in an old dirty spoon. She was a slave. A sex slave on a timed dose of smack, paralyzed by drugs. Her body a servant to sin, being sold by her captors to any horny junkie who had a few dimes to rub together.

I went and melted back into my seat on the floor. The ice entered my mind, but a fog of horror and disbelief overtook my thoughts. The fat White man emerged from the back room with the nylon case in his hand.

"Hey, you're driving Veronica today, right?" he said.

I nodded and gave him a shaky peace sign with two fingers.

"Well after he's done, you can give it a go," he said, pointing to his pal in the dark bedroom. "It's all gravy. Rubbers are on the dresser, just make it fast, you got to go soon."

The sound of grunting and a rubbery crackle from the stolen air mattress horned from the room like a satanic dinner bell. I was sick. But evil? Never.

The bathroom door opened, and the Mexican hooker burst out like a cumbia dancer.

"You ready, baby?" She said smelling like a strawberry field.

We hit the door. Business as usual. I drove down the road thinking of the girl. Her lifeless body being used up like chum in a shark tank. The train of meth addicts, hard and filthy, lining up to expel their sexually perverse seeds into her belly. Just another victim, another day in the game. I wasn't who I once was. And it was clear. Even to me.

#

Taxi screaming in the wet summer heat, the hardtop slick, beads of cool water hit my arm as it laid out of the open driver's side window. Nighttime fog cut by streetlight beams, a never-ending train of lost souls hopping in and out of the back seat. Cruising the strip club parking lots, honkey tonks, and bars.

The back-street scenes riddled with working girls and trap houses. Slick tires reflecting shadows of the gutter, rolling in urgency to every stop, never refraining from danger. A hodgepodge of characters leaping from seat to street, spilling their problems and sometimes their seed.

    The bulb of the pipe lit up in amber, ice blue flames lighting up my face like a ghastly Jack-O-Lantern. The taxi pushed on with a diligent force into the Corpus nightlife. The ferry of despair and sin. Coasting down South Padre Island Drive freeway, the diesel pouring from my mouth like a snarling dragon, the serpent beside me, invisibly present.

    Street noises like a symphony of darkness, moon rays bleed onto a windshield before Irish eyes. Cell phone static and radio crackle ring in my ear like a funeral bell sitting high in a New England church steeple. Day driving was a job. But the night, in the taxi…that was much, much more. It was gliding evil, a sleigh ride through hell. A meth driven carriage that burned with desire.

    Sleek paint reflected the lunar glow, highway curbs guiding tired eyes for a driver in dreams. Walking side by side with the Prince of Lies, I rode awake under the voodoo I craved with a black heart.

    It was a quiet night, all my dealings dry, late-night calls were few and far between. I rattled down the feeder road on South Padre Island Drive with sexual demons clawing inside my feeble brain. Broken inside, my life was a sexual nightmare. The darkest fantasies projecting onto the dash lights as I street sailed in the underworld of meth. This night was one of many. I drove aimless without a call, looking for the next fare, illegal job, or sexual tryst.

    I saw something in the distance. The night sky stale and illuminated by streetlamps corroded with turmoil. I pumped the brakes as I wheeled to the shoulder of the road in front of a cheap hot dog stand off Kostoryz Road. It was a wheelchair. An older woman had her feet on the curb, stuck, struggling to break the plane and get up onto the sidewalk. She was an older

Mexican woman, grey sweatpants, with a plain white t-shirt, dirty white Reeboks on her feet. Her hair of straw, black with strands of white running down to her shoulders. She sat breathing hard, fighting to get off the summer time street. I pulled into the parking lot of the restaurant. I hopped out of the taxi and rendered aid right away.

"Where you headed?" I said as I pulled her up over the curb.

"Walmart, but I ain't got no money," she said in a raspy voice with a hard accent.

I thought about it for a few seconds. I was on my way back to my dad's house to get more dope and smoke a quick bowl so I could wake up a bit. I had been up three days or more and I was in a trance. However, my heart was in the right place tonight. I saw an old woman, broke and needing help…so I helped. I offered to take her to the Walmart on Saratoga Boulevard right near my crib, but she would have to find her own way home.

She was happy to accept. I threw her wheelchair in the trunk, and we were off. My plan was to pull in my driveway, leave her out in the cab for a few minutes, and then I would take her to her destination free of charge. As I pulled into Barry's house on Oakbrook Road, I threw the car in park. The old woman begged to come inside with me, stating that she didn't want to sit alone in the dark. I assured her we were in the Country Club Estates and that she would be completely safe, but she wouldn't take no for an answer.

Not a sexual thought in my mind, I agreed to take her inside. My dad was fast asleep, and Tia was staying with friends this night, so I figured what the hell? She told me she had major health problems, but she could walk just fine if she took her time. We waddled into the dimly lit adobe quiet as mice, not wanting to wake the boss man himself. He wouldn't have been happy, even as cool as my dad was.

The dark hall led to the bedrooms. I was in such a fog that I forgot to turn the pornography off the last time I was in my room earlier that day. The moans of horny housewives echoed as we entered the drug den. She sat on my bed, surrounded by hundreds of empty drug baggies, needles that Tia was cleaning were laid in bowls full of bleach.

The overhead lightbulb exposed the depths of my addictions. The pipes, the porn, the paraphernalia all leading to the gateway of hell. I felt no shame. The old woman sat surprisingly calm in the midst of Junkieville. My thought process and sanity deeply affected, I had no problem with the elderly stranger sitting on my bed watching Slutty MILF #4, surrounded by enough meth residue in empty baggies to get you twenty years.

I lit up a massive bowl of high quality clear. The dragon expelled the plume into the sky, as I was always partial to doing, a bit of a show for the onlooker. Always a showman. The porn rolled as I took massive blasts off the pizzle.

"You wanna hit?" I asked politely.

"I've never messed with that stuff before, is it good?" she asked.

"Does it look good? I am high as a Georgia pine," I said with a big smile.

As I sat next to her on the bed, I lit the pipe for the grandma as I would for any newbie taking a pull off my glass for the first time. She and I talked for a good twenty minutes as we roasted a half gram of some of the best dope Corpus could offer. She was extremely high; she couldn't take her eyes off the two hot older women servicing the much younger stud on the old TV screen. She started to tell me that she hadn't had sex with her husband in years. He was too old; they had been married too long. The old woman was hinting for it.

        I didn't want to do this. It was unthinkable for me to sleep with an elderly woman in a wheelchair, I mean, come on now. At the same time, I found myself wrestling with the thoughts of sexual depravity.

        She was a warm body, just as the rest, and no one was looking.

        I couldn't! I would know and it would haunt me forever. I have morals, I am a good person, I could never do something like this.

        The battle of good and evil was waging within my ears.

        My boss was lighting up my cell phone, as I wasn't answering any calls on the radio. She laid back on the bed and lifted her shirt. She started to please herself to the naughty movie that blared before her. The ice had me crazy. I couldn't help it; I laid down next to granny and we started to make the most grotesque love imaginable.

        We were so high that we could barely move. Lusting sexual degradation consumed me as I stripped her naked, exposing wrinkled skin and aging pubic hair. I was disgusted with myself but could not stop. She had never smoked ice before, and I'd had her toking large amounts of the finest batch money could buy.

        The sexual demons swirled, she moaned as she rolled on top of me and thrust my manhood inside her very core. There was no condom being used, pure raw sex in the vilest of forms. Respecting my elders was out the window on this one.

        She hopped up and down on me as if she were possessed. The things that came out of her mouth are such that I can't explain, even here, so you know they would make Satan blush. I looked at the messages and missed calls stacking up on my cell, but I just could not stop. I wasn't in control of my actions. Sexual rage and impurity ruled the very muscles in my body. I climaxed inside of her, both of us pulsing and panting. She rolled over and started to cry. She felt so guilty for cheating on her husband that she lost it. She then explained she had been a smack addict since the seventies and there was a lot of pain in their relationship that they had repaired years ago.

The terror that poured into me for just having unprotected sex with a stranger who had been a lifelong heroin addict overshadowed just about any other thought at this moment. The room spun as every disease scenario rang in my head. I was mortified. Post-orgasm shame washed over me. Every wrinkle in her face showed, every grey hair, every imperfection became crystal clear...no pun intended. She was old enough to be my mother. I almost threw up in my mouth.

I hurried her up to get dressed, using work as an excuse to get her out of my room. The ride to Walmart was made in total silence. Just a short drive down the road, I dropped her in the parking lot and peeled out with the taste of guilt festering in my mouth, her insides coating my taste buds.

I pulled over at a car wash down the street. I banged my hands on the steering wheel in a rage, tears flowing down my chubby Irish cheeks. *What had I just done?* The radio and cell phone splattered with chatter. I dried up the tears and called my boss. I had three runs to Corpus Christi airport lined up for the next few hours, which meant big money. So, I needed to get a move on. I looked around the cab and found Granny's Texas ID. I rolled my window down and flung it into the parking lot like the whole nightmare never even happened. My sexual demons were taking me over. I was not well mentally. I hadn't one thought of my children or my prior life in months. They were ghosts of the past, fading in thought as I rolled down the city streets.

#

I was hitting the cab game hard, working and hustling from the Bluff to North Beach on the daily. I was moving around, different plugs, different connects, and different women all day, every day. I had a lot of traffic at my dad's house. Anytime I wasn't driving, I was at home smoking like a broke stove with Tia and a parade of ice users from coast to coast in Corpus.

I was now getting "playa prices" from a few different dealers. Tia hooked me up with a guy named Prince who was a dealer that delivered door to door in a shiny pearl Caddy. I was now paying half of what I used to pay. My use skyrocketed.

One night I picked up Tony. He needed to go meet Leon to score at a motel off Leopard Street. We made the drive across town late, around one in the morning. We picked Leon up and drove to a Westside trap house to re-up on some shards, as he was out. We made it back to the hotel and went upstairs so Leon could bag up the product for Tony.

When it came time to leave, Leon was being surprisingly nice, and he offered me a ten-dollar bill as compensation for the unexpected stop. He was pitching in for gas. As much as I hated Leon, he was Tony's plug, and out of respect for Tony, who was already paying me in ice for the trip, I politely declined to take his money.

Tony, being the salty son-of-a-bitch that he was, took the ten out of Leon's hand and we headed for the door. Somewhere along the way, we got a call from Sherry, a short chunky Mexican mamma who lived right down the street from my crib. We picked her up as we were all going to Tony's to get high, and she wanted a to-go bag from him as well. She spilled a bunch of ice in the back seat as she packed a bowl for us. We had a ton, so it wasn't the end of the world.

I thought she was cute; I was super-duper high, and her thick lips and thicker thighs had me like Ron Jeremy at a Viagra buffet. I was digging her. She was cute, a sweetheart, and best of all, she was knee-deep in the game, and at that time nothing could be sexier.

We did the do and dropped Sherry back off at home. Tony was out of smokes, and it was four thirty at this point, so we went to the gas station on the corner of Weber and South Padre Island Drive, right down the street from his apartment. He went in like a tweak box, stoned to the brim. I waited in the car, watching him close through the plate glass window.

He strutted out with a plastic bag in hand and right behind him was an angry clerk. She had her cell phone in her hand, about to snap pictures of my license plates on my car.

"Hey, what are you doing?" I yelled at her.

"Your buddy just gave me counterfeit money, that's what."

I was shocked. I told Tony he better go handle that ASAP. He went back into the store with the clerk. God protecting us, she screwed up by thinking that Tony had given her two fives, when he really gave her the ten that Leon had tried to give to me.

She was originally right, but during the dispute inside, Tony had convinced her he had given her two fives and she bought it. I looked at the back seat during this whole commotion and saw the shards Sherry spilled everywhere. If the cops had rolled up because of this, all they would have had to do was shine the Maglite in the car, find the ice, search Tony, find the eight ball he had on him, and we would have been off to the county jail.

Counterfeit bills carry a lengthy prison term, as well as a visit from the United States Secret Service. That was not something I wanted to get into. Not at all. I was pissed. The streets are heartless. Leon knew the money was fake. Upon later investigation, he had been printing small bills for some time. Passing them in drug deals with crash dummies, strip clubs, and convenience stores.

We walked away unscathed on this one. I learned a valuable lesson. Leon hated me, and he let his own friend leave with the fake money just the same. There are no friends out here, rule number one in Ice Game 101.

#

The cab was flourishing. My regular cash sales were booming around this time. Sitting outside all the bars, strip joints, and clubs were paying off. I started driving a lot of local dancers to and from work as well. Eye candy with cash, my favorite clientele.

My dad's house was a revolving door of users. I had new girls I would pick up like sticker burs on my socks. Friends would bring friends and BOOM! I would end up with a sexual plaything for a few days.

See, the game typically goes by its rules. Women would kick it with you if you had drugs. I had a place to stay and a car on top of that. I never paid girls for sex, not with ice at my continuous disposal. Never. However, I was far too selfish and way too addicted to part with any real amount of ice for sex. I would much rather throw a bag chaser out and watch porn, keeping all the tina for myself.

I had it made in the sex department. I was funny, I had all my teeth, and I was at a good weight, since I was eating food only two days out of the week. Ladies liked me. I had no problem finding a female to spend time with. The thing about ice heads is that about every three days they get antsy and want to find a new spot to hang at. This was perfect because right around that same time, I was getting sick of nailing the same girl. When honeys did stay with me, part of the deal was they could chill, watch TV all they wanted, shower, and all that. But they had to also clean, do dishes, and laundry. Barry didn't mind me having them there because the house was clean, and no one was eating groceries anyway.

My sexual demon was growing stronger. If she had a face, it would be a skull with snakes slithering from both eye sockets. The drug was the gate, the open crack to the spirit world that let this succubus wreak havoc in my life. I was spinning out of control in all areas. My taste for BDSM and bondage was a bittersweet dance with Satan. I found myself on my off time frequenting various porn theaters in Corpus, sitting in the bathroom snorting lines, and hitting the pipe simultaneously. The high of mixing the methods of ingestion would make you far hornier than just one or the other.

I could feel the evil all around. Straight porn was always playing on the big screen in a pitch-black mini theater on the outskirts of town. The clerk who took your eight-dollar entry fee always had a smirk on her face as you paid. The seats were benches you would find at a city baseball field, so high that I was quaking, I sat and watched group masturbation with men who were doing God knows what to one another in the shadows. The slurping sounds and sissy moans coming from all corners were enough to make you sick. A husband and wife sitting in the front row were letting men watch them play just for kicks. I loved the slime. Pleasuring myself in the dark, the puss-filled blackness made me feel right at home.

I was making my own schedule, working when I wanted to, making time for as much deviance as I could cram into my day. Around this time, I took a bit of a hit as far as driving drug dealers. There was an ice head chick who worked in the finance department at the local dealership. She developed a lick to where she would have the dealers come in, talk to a sales agent, and with a little cooking of the books, she would have it looking like they were the most stable employed dudes in town. Thus, in no time, every drug dealer in the Sparkling City was now driving a brand-new vehicle. The calls stopped coming as the dealers had their own fresh rides. But it was ok. I was still doing just fine. I needed a little break in the action.

  I found a kink and BDSM website, so evil I will not mention it by name in this book. They are nationwide and had thirty-five hundred members in the Corpus Christi area. I was high when I came across it, and it made me drool from more than one part of my body. I created a profile and was off to the races. I figured I could get all the demonic sex I could stomach, as well as drum up some driving business.

  I started getting messages right away. Any sick sexual fetish you could imagine was right at your fingertips. There were subs, doms, and dominatrix for hire. The pits of hell were full of sexual monsters of all shapes and sizes. They had a weekly get together called a munch. There was a bulletin board with the date, time, and location of the meeting. It was always at a restaurant or bar. If you went to the munch and they deemed that you were acceptable on Friday, you would get an email on Saturday morning inviting you to a private home play party later that night.

  The first munch I attended was at a local bar, held on the patio during the day in the sweltering South Texas sun. They were a cast of weird birds for sure. Plenty of swinging couples were in attendance. The most memorable was a dominatrix with a fake British accent. She was originally from the next town over, a total fraud to make her seem more mysterious. At three hundred an hour, she better be pretty damn mysterious. There were also a bunch of absurdly strange loners that showed up and were looking terrified and completely out of place. And then there was me. I sat at the table with a full beer, big black sunglasses on, high as a satellite, making jokes that were mostly only funny to me.

Networking in the sexual underworld of Corpus was strange. They made it really clear that drugs were a big no-no and could get you banned for life. So, I carried a water bottle with a thirty of fire diluted into it. You know, to stay below the radar. I had a blast. Well, as much as one could have, being submerged in a life of sexual torment and meth addiction. I always tried to keep my sense of humor. It was all I could do to forget the shattering loss of my career, marriage, and discarded children.

I had made a choice to live sexually liberated, with no guilt or remorse for my devilish activities. At the time, I thought this was my choice. Later I realized this was not a choice, outside of the self-inflicted drug abuse.

I was under a serious demonic attack, on a predestined journey to hell, being directly orchestrated by God himself. We will get into all that later. The "choice" was really the demon controlling my thought, just as a marionette would pull the strings on a puppet. I was demon-afflicted and had not yet realized it.

#

I went home and invited over a nasty girl that I knew from the streets. She was a hard needle user that loved sex. Seeing as I didn't have to pay, I was totally game. She was a White girl with short black hair and tatts all over her body. When she entered my room, the bondage porn was on, and I was half-naked. She kissed me with her seductive lips, the thought of where they had been the whole night before never even crossed my mind. After some devious talk, she was ready to "fuck me off." A term used in the ice game referring to one user getting another user to shoot up crystal. Not my first time with the needle, but the first with the flames. Ice, ice baby.

She sat me on the low bed in my room. White Christmas lights were hanging over the blacked-out window, the covering was a maroon sheet fastened with dollar store thumbtacks. The twinkle of lights gave the room an evil feel, the screen showing a female being worked on with a Hitachi Wand as she was strapped to a wooden table, hands tied up. My partner slipped her wife-beater off, exposing her A-cup breasts with pierced nipples. She sat facing me, on her knees with my legs wide open. I took my shirt off, nervous enough to vomit. She was a curvy phlebotomist, an expert at fixing lovers before sexual romps that blow the human mind.

The orange cap of the U-100 short point needle came out of her dingy rust-colored purse. The purse was most likely stolen from the mall on a boosting spree. She had some dope from a biker gang that was so strong, people on the street feared it.

She whispered directions showing me how to fix a shot directly in the rig without using a spoon, eliminating the risk of cross contamination. She dumped in a quarter gram. The dope had a blue tint to it that made the process erotic. She took an eye dropper and dumped the liquid in with care. She put the plunger back in the rig, tilted it right side up, and started to shake it.

"You ready, baby boy?" she whispered in the darkness.

I nodded as my eyes stayed fixed on the masked man inflicting sexual pain onto the inked-up girl on the TV.

She was gentle and soft as she took my arm in her hand. Milky-white flesh exposed under the freezing cold air conditioning vent, blowing with a dull roar. She flicked the medical plastic with her black-painted fingernails, bringing all the air to the top. She tied me off with a knock-off Gucci belt she'd had around her daisy dukes just minutes prior. My fist was balled up and squeezing as she instructed me to. By candlelight, she found a bulging artery. On her phone, she played "Black No. 1" by Type O Negative.

"Just relax, baby boy. You told me a huge shot, you gonna get a huge shot," she whispered.

She shifted as she pricked the ice blue vein that was popping out of my naked skin. I shuttered a bit; she had hit smooth the very first try. Her surgical touch made me feel safe, as well as aroused. The pin shifted as she drew back onyx blood in the gothic scene unfolding around me. The bondage, her unclad flesh, the needle dangling from my arm, as I lay there nervous and depraved. It was all so much. The shot was a sixty cc. That's a monster to begin with, never mind it was biker gang dope, never mind it's my first-time shooting shards.

I could feel the claws of the serpent behind me, raking my skin as the plunger began to push in.

The look on homegirl's face was that of a vampire viewing a cut jugular. Saliva dripping from thick lips, eyes of lust as the clear flames darted throughout my bloodstream. Exorcism touches, a levitation into sexual dreams one cannot describe in spoken word. The shot was almost three quarters done. I felt a warm flow, a satanic baptism being poured over me in buckets, from my head, all the way to my toes, passing over swollen testicles. A blanket of rage engulfed me with rapist qualities.

The plunger hits bottom, I leapt to my feet as the slutty doctor shivers in delight. I couldn't help but jump up and down. I keeled over and tried to breathe as a freezing cold breath exploded from my mouth, mentholated as if I smoked a freshly lit Newport. That's the fire, bro. That is where the term comes from. For the first time I knew, finally realizing this as I am bent over gagging like an alcohol-poisoned teen after prom.

 She was already undressed and, on my bed, getting ready to fix. She was done with the needle in what seemed to be seconds. I tore the rest of my clothes off with a quickness. She proceeded to lay on her back, thin as a bobby pin, much smaller than I was. I took the Gucci belt and fastened it around her frail neck. She lay with her head cocked so she could watch the madness gleaming out of the television. I tightened the belt to a point where she turned an eggplant color. Her pinching my chest as I got in a full mounted position. I was crazy with lust. This was the demon, I now recognized I was not alone for the first time. It was as if I was watching myself from another dimension. The power I felt was astonishing and scary. I turned beastlike, grunting and snarling. I teased her outside parts before I entered her raw. Her eyes wide with fear, she guided me to her forbidden place instead. Spitting on my hand and saturating myself with drool, I lewdly tormented her; her back door became invaded by a man possessed.

 The ravages of sexual bondage went on for hours with toys, images on the screen, the pale face of death living on her cheekbones. I drained her, pasting her onto the sheetrock as sweat poured from her scratched-up skin. Only breaking to inject more demon serum into our veins, the blaspheme of ages was happening, my sexual depravity leaking down her legs. I was not the same. A spiritual door had been blasted ajar, a gate that once opened, could never be fully closed. This experience was the beginning of the evil one, Satan himself, lurking into my life, a battle began.

 She left me sexually broken yet empowered to the point

of lunacy. As she departed my room, the ding of an email came through my phone. It was the group inviting me to the evening festivities. A private home party where Corpus Christi's most disturbed would gather and live out a sexual fantasy that can only be described as cosmic.

#

I had two grams of biker dope and another three of the uptown slime that I had acquired from other sources. Good in its own way, but nothing like the black-feathered shavings of fallen angels that baby had left behind. She had left me a ten pack of needles after I demanded she do so.

Hours passed as I sent hundreds of messages through their site, talking in a demon's tongue to anyone who may be in attendance. I wanted to make plans for pain well before I got there. No one was solid, most likely because I was far too perverted for their liking.

Another email came in about an hour before the event. By this time, I was ready to go, still reeling from the drugs. I took some shards and shelled them up in some Tylenol's that I had emptied out.

I could ingest these at any point at the home party while flying under the radar. It was basically my travel pack of ice in case I was having a really good time. I smoked a good size bowl of the biker dope to really send me over the edge just before departing, and off to hell I go.

My GPS took me to a very classy neighborhood not too far from my dad's house. As the nose of the Mitsubishi stared down the address, I was taken aback by what my eyes gazed upon. It looked exactly like Halloween in Salem. Vampire people clicking down the city sidewalks in black platform boots. Corseted queens in gothic gowns, skinny freaks with apocalyptic hair, and mayhem minds strutting in cold view for all to see.

I pulled up to the curb, still far from the address. There had to be a hundred people gathering. The walk to the house was surreal. A young Black goth chick appears on my arm.

"You going' to the party," she said with sharp teeth.

"Yea, this is gonna be a blast!" I said with excitement.

We walked up to the place with our arms still linked. A beautiful two-story home in one of Corpus Christi's nicest parts of town. A strange lady greeted us at the door. She was the homeowner, tall with hair in Lil' Bo Peep curls. She looked like something out of "Interview with a Vampire."

"Come in, meet everyone," she said in a ghoulish voice.

As I broke the plane into the living room, I saw naked people lounging around everywhere, drinking and talking jive. Women with ropes tied snug around their breasts, holding big goblets of crimson wine. This was a Transylvanian nightmare of epic proportions. The pendulum and the pit, this was Satan's brood.

Beer bottles clanged and the sounds of Oingo Boingo splintered my eardrums as I gave myself the grand tour. I walked out to the back patio. There was a concrete slab underfoot and a wood fence bordering the whole back yard. A wood terrace covering was above, with a matching shellacked two-person swing hanging from chains.

As there was a loud crack from behind me, I spun around toward the sliding glass doors that I had just walked through. I felt jaw-dropping excitement as I peered forward. There was a massive cherrywood Judas cross in the shape of a X. There was also a woman utterly naked with tattoos running up and down her body. One of them was a full pentagram canvased over her entire back. Black leather straps were used to bind her hands and feet. A masked man with no shirt and wearing leather pants flogged her with what looked like cat o' nine tails. Her raised skin was bruised, and crimson blood rose to the surface, a pain of pleasures all her own.

Walking back inside, I sat on a red velvet couch, a sectional full of strange and lovely monsters chatting away. A fat Black lady and her skinny White man were French kissing next to me. A group of the "Tied" were roped up and discussing world issues. Then I saw him. A man in his twenties in full leather garb. He was on all fours and wore a massive leather muzzle and sizeable leather floppy ears. He was acting like a dog, rolling over, letting people pet him and scratch his belly. This man never broke character all night. He even ate mini dog biscuits supplied by his owner.

I met and talked with some bizarre people. The girl who ran the social media page for our area was in no way hiding the fact that she obsessively practiced witchcraft and black magic.

In fact, after ingesting every one of the preloaded doses I had in the pill bottle, I spoke to a group of young women that flat-out admitted this whole group was part of a coven of witches. One of the girls owned a nude maid service operated by word of mouth, most likely a high-end prostitution ring.

There was a very satanic feel to it all, and I felt right at home. Shooting up, smoking, and ingesting meth all at the same time was one hell of a combo in an environment like this. I went room to room, looking around the indoors. I saw group sex, blood play, and masked men and women abusing one another. This was a portal to hell. And I willingly walked right in.

I met a three-hundred-pound sub, which is short for submissive. The sweetest woman who had a huge fetish for being perversely humiliated. I was so high, I played along. I selfishly only thought of myself, what I could do to her, get out of her, and use her for. We exchanged information and agreed to meet later that night. I left the party without taking part in anything strange. Well, some group masturbation...I didn't go for nothing.

#

Back at the crib, I stopped to have Tia fix me up with a half gram shot of biker dope. I had no clue how to shoot myself up and I was in misery. See, you can't overdose on meth, maybe a heart attack or two, a stroke here and there. But most likely you won't die. Well, that's the rumor on the street anyway. You can over-amp, a term for when you do so much meth that your brain turns off momentarily, and you pass out. I had no fear, I was on a suicide mission anyway.

She pushed in the shot, and I almost threw up.

I hopped in the shower and got stuck for a good twenty minutes. There is really no way to tell, I just stood there under the piping hot water staring at the wall. I threw on my usual tweak outfit of board shorts and a t-shirt. Finally, I headed to the sub's apartment, which was just a stone's throw from home.

When I arrived, she was wearing nothing but a dog collar. I was so high, I was slurping my tongue up and down the side of her cheek, making animal noises that could make a porn director blush. She was in no way attractive to me. If I weren't completely out of control, I would not be doing this. That thought paced in my head like an inmate awaiting his call to the electric chair. There were vibrators and nipple clamps us to use. Her imagination was that of a hell's kitchen playwright, and I don't mean the cooking show. The possibilities were endless.

At one point, I was leading her around the whole apartment with a leash, a hound of hell choking on my shaft, ordering her to masturbate. The dance controlled by drugs and demons, my actions vile and penetrating in every way. She loved it. Her fetish was for her partner to be devilishly mean, making fun of her weight and anything else that would cause her to cry. This was not in my nature. As sexually crazy as I was, I am to the core a nice guy. I don't think I could ever really lose that, not even to the demons possessing me. I don't like to hurt people.

    At one point she was begging to be humiliated. I fired off some insane speech, putting her down, spitting in her face upon request. Standing behind her while she was on her knees, I said "I am like a Sour Patch Kid. First, I am sour, then I am sweet." Just like they say in the candy commercial. I almost burst into laughter. I had to bite my knuckles, so I didn't ruin the moment.

    After we had intercourse, we laid naked and talked for a while. A sadness came over us both. The whole action was not right. In sexual madness like this, you find your consciousness of God when it is over. Your inner compass of morality that the Lord gives us to discern what's wrong from right suddenly awakens. Under all the bullshit, she was truly the sweetest girl I had ever met. The sub role she played was a mere front to find love. The poor girl just wanted an authentic relationship. The broken are always looking for love. That's the hole we fill with sex, drugs, and violence. That deep pit that nothing ever seems to fill, except through God.

    I felt horrible. Knowing full well that she was just a sex doll to me, never planning for her to be anything more than a trifling meat puppet, guilt consumed me. I got up and left, more dismantled than ever, higher than ever.

    I continued to have sex with her on and off for weeks. She was a Stage five clinger. She talked herself into an idea that we were a couple who was in a sexually open relationship. I would be so wrecked on drugs when I saw her that I just agreed to anything she said. The quicker I could get off inside her and jet the better. I was really getting sick of her. She had no clue that I was in the drug trade or the criminal underworld, none of it was known to her. She was a single mom with a cute kid. I only saw pictures. The kid was always with her dad when I showed up.

One night she sent me a text saying she had met a guy at a bar, and she had taken him home and had sex. This was my way out! I acted furious and jealous, then I broke it off with her. Finally, the million calls and texts would end, and I could go about my horrible life.

#

I was on day three of nonstop driving, working, and using like a mad scientist. I had to pay off some debts and make my tab with the meter right at the cab company, but I was dead broke. No dope, no money. I was busted and depressed. I got off shift early and was home by six o'clock in the morning. I slouched in the bed next to Tia. The sun was just coming up. We discussed our horrible situation, as she was also dead broke. The feeling of a major meth comedown is one that can put a user on the brink of suicide. The walls close in, your head starts to swell, and your skin starts crawling. I hadn't even tried to quit at this point, but if I didn't use it for four hours, I felt a major withdrawal from the drug to the point of insanity. It felt like palmetto roaches were festering under my clammy skin.

A text came in from the sub, she was begging me to get back together.

I looked at Tia and said, "Watch this."

I typed, "If you put two crisp hundred-dollar bills in my mailbox in the next fifteen minutes, I'll think about it."

Minutes had passed. I accepted defeat and tried to close

my eyes, knowing full well that there was no way in hell I would be able to sleep. The silent scream started in my head. Tossing and turning with beads of sweat running down my face. The text I had sent was simply a goof. I had written it off as a lost cause, and decided it was more of an insult to the poor woman. Hopefully, she would stop contacting me altogether now.

The rusty mailbox was attached to the very wall above our head, on the brick near the front door. Exactly fifteen minutes from the time I had sent the text, the old top to the mailbox crept open. The sound of the rusty hinges might as well have been the knock of Jesus Christ at the door.

Tia and I looked at each other in awe. Our eyes met and huge smiles appeared. I sprang to the window, removed the covering enough to watch the sub's car pulling away. I ran outside and opened the mailbox. Sure as silk, there were four crisp fifty-dollar bills inside! I came back to the room, jumping up and down, the lick of all licks, hit like a bullseye. I know it was only two hundred bucks. But to us, at that moment, it was as good as a ten-million-dollar score. We cackled like two witches in the October moonlight. Laughing and carrying on. This was the stuff of legend. The devil providing, we celebrated with great delight.

I called a dealer and had scheduled a quarter ounce of pure fire to be delivered. We scrambled to get our shoes on so we could go get smokes and some Pepsi before the drugs were to be delivered to the house on Oakbrook.

I sent a slap in the face text to the sub. "I said two hundred-dollar bills, not four of these fifty-dollar bills."

The scumbag that I was, I never planned on calling her back. A struggling single mom, looking for love in a satanic place, I had officially lost my morals.

I had struck a deal to sell stolen credit card numbers that I got from cab customers. This cab company was outdated with no machine to run the cards, so we would imprint them, write down all the info and call it in to dispatch to run the card for payment. Completely insecure. I would illegally take photos of the person's card front and back, message the person's billing information, and the pictures to the fence man. Then he would rip them off for whatever they could before the card was flagged as stolen. The fence man would pay me a gram of ice for each card I supplied him.

I pulled the taxi into the seedy trailer park to collect my earnings. On this day, about five grams in all. The taxi had a GPS on it. I was a blip on the radar, they knew my location. I took a signal seven, a lunch break, giving me enough time to collect and get high. The park was almost touching NAS Corpus Christi, the naval air station.

Half-grown pine trees forked through the small freshly paved roads. White trash strutted in cutoff shorts and Looney Toon t-shirts. Unwed mothers screamed at diapered children, strung out and sweating in the summer madness. Bag chasers, thieves, and tweakers made the layout look like some nightmarish Norman Rockwell painting. This was an all-Caucasian cell located in Flour Bluff. Long stringy hair and rock t-shirts were the uniforms.

The fence man was waiting outside his trailer. Wild hair, no shirt, and some cutoff jeans made him look extra sleazy. A fake gold chain hung from a hairy Robin Williams chest. Yellow ooze leaked from open sores on his picked-at face. He was a shooter, and that was clear. He would rake at his own face with blackened fingernails; his tweak was self-mutilation. Old blood on his five o'clock shadow dripped from dry cracks above his cheeks.

We entered the trailer, my cab bag in hand. The place was a mess. Motor parts, dirty laundry, and beer cans were strewn about the filthy travel trailer. The kind of trailer you tow behind a truck, yet there was no truck. I think he sold it. His lady was a chubby prostitute. Smack drained from her pores. Her heroin habit made her body wreak of Heinz vinegar. This demented Dolly Parton had a deep southern drawl, long brown hair, and she never wore a bra. Her nipples looked like turkey thermometers.

Her big frog eyes stared at me as I sat across from them at the small folding kitchen table. She could hit a vein like a Vietnam field medic, and I was about to employ her services. The fence and I did the deal and his old lady agreed to shoot me up. I gave her my last fresh rig and told her to put a half gram in it. She drew it up and tied off my arm after clearing away the homemade ashtrays and dead roaches on the checkered table.

The shot was thick as maple syrup. Yellow as Spic and Span. She plunged the needle into the blueberry tubing in my arm. Just as she drew the blood back, my phone went off, and she yanked it out of me. It was my boss. He was asking what the hell was taking so long. I had an emergency call to go to the damn airport. *What nerve, bastard interrupting my fix.*

I hung up the phone and threatened them, "I'll be back for that shot, don't you even think about doing it, understand me?"

They assured me it would be up in the cupboard until I returned. The needle was now full of blood and dope. The clock was ticking. You can only leave blood in a needle so long before using it. It could poison you.

I got super busy. I worked for the next twenty-four hours straight. Between the cab and drug dealing in the Mitsubishi, I couldn't make it back to the trailer for a full day.

When I returned, not much had changed. These two geeks looked like they hadn't even moved. He was on a laptop, working off a hot spot on a stolen cell phone. She was nodding out in the same spot at the table where I left her. I loathed these two. A gross pair with an even filthier home. Total addicts in every way. I guess I should have looked in a mirror occasionally. You always love to point the finger at how bad other people are so that you never have to look at one's own self.

    She grabbed the rig from the cupboard. Now jet black and even thicker. She tied me off with a greasy leather belt. Plunging to test the flow, she squirted a big clot of thick blood out of the end of the needle where it had coagulated. She pricked my arm, the now dull diabetic tool puncturing the bruised crease opposite my elbow. The blackness made it impossible to see the new blood register. She was an expert though. She felt my heartbeat at the end of the pin. The cold and filthy Coca-Cola concoction pumped into my main artery. I coughed, stood, and tasted hot menthol waves, followed by stinky iron-laced hints of human blood. I choked as the taste of cooked liver and onions coated the back of my throat.

    I grabbed my cab bag and stole a bag of short points from the pair. I had just shot a half gram of dope mixed with day-old blood. This was bad blood, the devil's work. I had more dope; I could have just mixed up a new one. But the thought process was that there was never enough ice for me. I wanted it all. Until my severed heart stopped beating. My family was gone, my soul sold, I didn't want to live. This nasty needle didn't even phase me. My level of grossness was what most humans will never fully grasp.

#

    Weeks later, I picked up the longhaired older man from the duplex in the Bluff. My first plug. I didn't buy from him anymore, but still chilled at his place because I loved him. A good friend. I knew a lot of people there and it was a family environment, sick as it was.

He needed a ride. Rain and thunder were pouring down straight from the heavens. I drove him to a trailer trap house on a dark back street in Flour Bluff. I backed the taxi into the driveway. I did this trip during cab hours because it was a re-up, the batch was big, and I didn't want there to be a chance of the bulls pulling us over.

Rain pounded the windshield as I waited outside alone. Fear always engulfed me in the Bluff. The Feds were watching these big trap houses. That was a fact. Wherever ice was cooked, you found heat within the flames. He returned in just a few minutes. We drove in the downpour back to the duplex. I dropped him off, and told him I would return, as I had the next two days off.

I came back later that day. I didn't have any drugs on me. I figured I would be in good company, and I had a few bucks on me. When I entered the trap, there were some new faces. A big southern dude and his girl. He was medium height with a crew cut. Older, maybe fifty. He looked like in his day he was a mean motor scooter. He was from a Southeastern state that I will leave unnamed. I was introduced and we hit it off right away. He was an ex-boxer, lethal from what I heard. He had a big fight against a pro boxer back in the day.

His girl was a vision. Taller than me, long flowing blond hair, she looked like a trailer park beauty queen, a fallen angel draped in icicles. She wore big cowboy boots and, of course, daisy dukes. A white wife beater and black bra rounded out her outfit nicely. We all sat and smoked, talked, and became fast friends. Then the voodoo came, the witches brew, shake and bake.

See, this guy was a cook. When there wasn't any crystal methamphetamine in circulation, this was the dude who could make that homemade. It's a yellow powdery version of meth that is cooked using over-the-counter cold pills that you can get at any drug store or grocery chain.

In the United States, they now limit you to three boxes of cold pills per month. A user can go into the store and buy one box at a time, hit three stores, and max out on the three boxes using their driver's license. The number on your ID is put into a computer, it goes directly to the DEA database, and is stored for data collection and monthly limits. Once you buy three in a thirty-day period, you are told you can buy no more for another month.

The United States government wants to be the only people cooking dope. If they are not making a buck, they sure as hell will make sure you are not either. They act like it is a weapon in the war on drugs. It's just to make sure Americans are buying the drugs from them.

I was sent to go on a run. They told me how it works, and I didn't see any problem with going to buy these pills using my ID. What the hell? I couldn't get in trouble, plus it was a brand-new kind of dope I had never tried, and I was to get paid a handsome bounty for my quest.

"You ready, Rockstar?" That's what I called her.

She was the most beautiful creature I had ever seen. She flipped her flowing mane of blond woven hair, spun in an angel's loom.

She looked up and said, "Hell yes doll, let's boogie."

Her accent was also from a very distinct Southern state, different from Captain Cooks.

We burst into daylight and exited the duplex parking lot on a mission for cold pills, six dollars a box for a quantity of ninety. That one box could make three and a half grams of the most heavenly truck stop crank this side of the Great Smoky Mountains.

I peered over to the passenger seat, eyes jiggly and weak. Her thick thighs ran down to those cowboy boots, the upper part sported the star of the Texas Flag. A debutant, a classy trailer park queen, sparkling with life and dancing with demons, showcasing a sexuality I had never seen. This chick was clearly off limits. One wrong look and her old man would pull the Tyson out and its night-night Boston.

We hit three stores using my ID, I am sure her ID was already maxed out for the month. I didn't even sweat it. We had enough cold pills to cook a large batch of the homemade. We returned to the duplexes in a hurry. This meal needed to get started.

On the counter sat all kinds of household chemicals, lithium batteries, and powders. It looked like an episode out of "Breaking Bad." Captain Cook may appear as your regular Joe, deep southern accent, tattered clothes, blue-collar working stiff from backwoods USA. He wasn't. See, this was an art form passed down from generation to generation. A birthright in the Great Plains and rural communities all over this country. A different kind of moonshine for the next generation. This moonshine still is much more compact and hidden, the product far more valuable.

Watching him was like seeing a mad scientist at work. Frankenstein, creating the monster, "It's alive." He crushed the pills in a blender, mixing the magical potion with great care and reverence. This was America in motion. Apple pie of the dope game. Cook started giving me a history lesson in meth as he did his thing. He told stories of how families passed these secret recipes down from father to son. Uncles showing nephew's how to cook in the flames of the woods, dodging the Fed's, and trafficking the dope to all in town.

A large empty Mountain Dew bottle was the centerpiece. It now held a clear and ominous liquid, a cast-iron pan sitting on the stovetop held warm water, which the bottle sat in during the shaking process. He explained that this was shake and bake, the process for cooking dope without the heat. Now we were cooking!

The small apartment had a feeling of danger. Something in the air that I had never felt in my million visits to this place. Something was very, very different. The good Lord warns you in times of grave danger. That inner voice that screams for you to flee in situations that you should not be in.

Cook started to explain the penalties for cooking as far as the United States Government was concerned. Hefty would be a great understatement. This could be a life sentence if the jakes were to kick the door in and raid us. They keep a watchful eye on the people that they believe hold the knowledge on how to create this evil and demonic substance. Once you're on the radar, they lay in wait like a lioness in the blades, just waiting to catch you slipping.

The green plastic bottle swelled like a tube of rotten meat in the sun. Bloating and puffing. He lifted it out of the water periodically to burp the vile gas, twisting the top ever so gently to avoid a traumatic explosion in the small apartment. This was a dangerous process in many ways. The cook itself could explode into blue flame; the cops could then put us away till there were flying cars like in "The Jetsons." All of it could be devastating.

Cook placed the bottle right side up on the faux granite countertop, the cold steel of the sink leaking in the distance. He peeled the shiny chrome wrapper off of a bunch of lithium batteries. Ribbons of death, party streamers to be dumped into the bottle, creating some sort of chemical reaction.

The dim light of the apartment glared off Cook's face. He walked the bottle over to a small half bath. He put his hands inside the bathroom, door cocked open.

"Boston, come over here, you gonna be higher than you ever been," he says with a jolly tone and deep southern drawl.

I walked over and stood by Cook's side while Rockstar was on the couch laughing, looking all sorts of beautiful. He twisted the white plastic cap to the Mountain Dew bottle a quarter turn. A potent hiss of sulfur and ammonia came pouring into the environment and assaulted my senses. The gas filled the spaces surrounding us. My lungs burned and filled with the traces of doom. We were not allowed to smoke anything during the cook for this very reason. The gas we were breathing was highly flammable. This was the same gas that cops wore HazMat suits for in meth lab raids on TV, and we were sucking it into our unprotected lungs.

My blood became thin and flowing. The gas form of the drug had me lucid and dreamy. I felt my heart race and a bulge began to rise in my crotch. The excitement of this whole experience had me in waves of joy. I was obsessed with the game. Anything new, I soaked up like dry lips and cherry Chapstick.

A Pyrex casserole dish sat on the counter. Cook then strained the clear product through some cheap dollar store coffee filters. This took out all the impurities of the cook. The liquid was then poured into the dish and thrown into the oven. This was the final stage. The heat dried up the liquid into a yellow powder. Wa-la, the homemade in the raw form. When this pie was done, we would get spun like a dreidel on Hanukkah.

About an hour later, Cook pulled the dinner from the oven. He used two credit cards to scrape the bounty off the glass. Caked and pretty, he scooped the brew into great piles. He plated the substance and got it ready for bagging.

The "boogers" were left at the bottom of the cooking glass. He scraped the pan for the scaled substance. He took a separate plate and laid out massive lines for snorting.

"These are some strong motherfuckers, Boston."

He was warning me of the strength of those boogers. They held a lot of potency. It only made me want to overdose on them.

We used all night and into the next dawn. Cook and I talked in detail about God. He was a man of deep faith at one time, excommunicated from his church for questionable extracurricular activities. He was a broken soul, as we all are in this meth game. A great man, troubled by the demons that come into us at a young age, the few and the chosen. As sun rays shimmered, he came to the kitchen table with a piping hot cup of java for me.

"Boston, this is going to be the best cup of Joe you have ever had," he said with a warm grin.

I started sipping. As high as I was, I could sense something starting to take hold of my innards. He used the filters that he strained the product through during the cook, procuring a rocket fuel pot of drug-laced coffee.

About an hour later I had to drive one of the bag chasers that laid with the plug. She needed a ride down the street. We walked to the car and took off. As I returned, my feet hit the rocky gravel of the desolate parking lot. The early morning moon looked pale and devious. Each footstep was work. I thought, *left, right, left, right,* as I strutted towards the door. I was so high, I literally forgot how to walk.

I sat and watched pornography on my phone, in a room full of people for a full three days, high as a kite from the ingested gas in that one cup of coffee. I burned up all the data on my phone. I lost seventy-two hours of my life in a drug-induced daze. I was stone-still as the trap house cycled around me. Hundreds of knocks on the door, visitors galore. They were just shadows to me. Moving pictures and voices that made not one difference to my sad, dark existence.

#

One thing I also learned from Captain Cook was that the body gets used to crystal meth once in the throes of a major binge. Your use will skyrocket in order to get the same effect. Once you change up to the homemade, during said binge, you will get high again. The key was to alternate the two forms of the drug in order to retain maximum effect, thus saving dope. I made it home and threw three grams of the homemade into my dad's freezer. Freezing the drugs suspends the potency and shelf life. You take it out as needed, once thawed, it's as strong as the day it was created.

A Xanax bar had me fast asleep, body ravaged, my soul-searching for rest. I needed to get back to work. The road was calling. My destiny, a dark trip through the nighttime palaces and caverns of Corpus Christi's underworld. I had so much going on. All the different traps, dealers, and associates, life was a maze of madness. The taxi was my home, the center of my universe, my refuge, and the meal ticket. I welcomed my return behind the wheel.

Remember Sherry? Tony's cute chubby friend? I struck up a true friendship with her. I began hanging at her house quite a bit when not driving. Her house was a known trap on Corpus Christi's southside, just minutes from home.

There were tons of traffic on this side of town. Her

father was an old man who resided in a hallway bedroom and never really emerged but to eat and use the restroom. I was using with her in her charming, decorated bedroom as much as I could.

Sherry was once straight, but now she dug women. We were getting high and fooling around. Yes, even though I am a man. I guess if you put me in some flannels and khaki shorts, I could easily pass for a butch lesbian. I kind of turned her on. She was known for keeping a plugin sex toy in her purse. It was nothing for Sherry to smoke a fat bowl, pull the power tool out of her purse, and drop her pants at the drop of a dime, no matter where she was. This thing was called a Hitachi, like the construction tool. This device would sound like a circular saw when powered on high.

Sherry would have me perform oral sex on her for hours, never reaching orgasm, because that damn tool had desensitized her to any form of human stimulation. I think she got off on forcing me down there. My jaw wide and raw, feeling like the bones in my face had snapped by the time she was done using me.

Sherry was famous in the game for bribing the infamous bag chasing ladies into going down on her for a fix of ice. Girls that were normally straight by choice, now forced into lesbian sex by this horny Mexican mamma. Watching their walk of shame out of the room as I would enter was a huge turn on, the smell of Sherry's love still in the air as I entered to do a drug transaction or two.

Sex addiction was omnipresent in the game. If you think I was the only freak in the street, you're crazy. The unspeakable parts of the game, the shameful nighttime secrets that are meant to stay in the shadows and told as fables. But guess what? I'll tell it.

I can't count how many times I would pick up transsexual divas at three in the morning and ferry them to a hardened gang member's home for late-night sex. His girlfriend or wife not home, the bedroom would turn into a homosexual tent of ooze. I have seen a lot of straight guys go "gay for pay," paid in ice to perform sexual acts that would ruin them in any gang circle for sure.

The drug does something to the destitute. I have seen acts of desperation that shake the common thinker to the core. The oral sex, the role plays for pay, the dark fantasies of the dealers who could afford to buy off victims and watch them squirm as they made the evil thoughts of the employer come to life.

The meth counterculture is all-afflicted by the same sexual demon that fuels the pornography industry as we speak. One devious spirit afflicting hoards of the addicted. It's a conjuring taking place on a worldwide scale. The Dark Prince sending legions to slowly torture and kill masses of God's children.

Driving the cab gave me a unique view of the people's bedrooms that hired me. They trusted me with great secrets, things that could get you killed out there. If the homeboys knew some of these dealers had "chick with a dick" servicing them sexually, that would be curtain call for that gang member.

I got love for the streets. I could go into detail on this matter, displaying dark sexual activities of the ones who paid me. But I seriously got too much love for those still in the game. I recognize the sickness, the possession by the dark forces that attack us in active addiction. I touched on it. I refuse to go into gruesome detail to sell books. The fact is, this stuff is very, very real.

It happens every day and lives are ruined. The shame,

guilt, and remorse these people feel after they come down is earth shattering. Then, some could care less. Nevertheless, it's none of my business. I would never out anyone for what they have done in their bedroom. Some things are better left unsaid. I am not trying to get anyone smoked with the writing in this tell-all book. Just telling the game, as it is, is enough of the ugly truth.

This is also to prevent the newcomer from falling into the traps of the evil one. The gay sex, prostitution as gay or straight, the orgies. All darts are thrown by the Dark One to enslave you using the black desires of the heart. Hidden by silence, but present, nonetheless. Meth makes you do things you normally wouldn't do. So, the lesson is, don't open the gate for this sexual spirit. It will grab you, break you, and leave you diseased, shamed, and begging to die.

Sitting at trap houses between drug deliveries was particularly depressing. Lines of single moms, in scantily clad dress, parading in and out after having sex with dealers. Shame faces and soggy tears would erupt as some of these broken women would leave the devil's den in the back of the house. Knowing full well, they just participated in some strange kinky fantasy for forty dollars worth of dope. It sinks you back in your chair.

Sometimes they would bring the kids along. On more than one occasion, I was babysitter to toddlers as Mom moaned in the next room. Vile speech and noise clanged through ventilation shafts for all to witness, even the children. I would turn the TV up as loud as it would go, sheltering these tots from the demonic activities taking place just feet away.

Single mothers would sell the only food stamps they had for pennies on the dollar, otherwise known as stampias in the Mexican community. Hungry children waiting with grandma back at home, Mom getting fifty cents on the dollar, in trade at a point-for-point price, swindled twice. These were solid gold rip-off prices in the dope world. The devil was sitting in the traps as all morality was removed from the addicts doing business there.

Uncles selling toys they originally bought for Christmas for nieces and nephews, never even making it under the tree. Well, they did. The dealers' kids were always rocking something high fashion, in-style, and cool. I saw the descendants of cancer patients, the people who cared for their sick and dying family member, trading pain pills to dealers at next to nothing rates, in order to acquire crystal meth. How could they? Where were their heart and soul? Keep this one act of heartlessness in mind. It will play a major role later in this story.

Hot merchandise was everywhere. Boosters had it all. Trap houses were like Toys R Us and Best Buy had a baby. You could get anything cheap. Clothes, auto parts, construction tools. It was a flea market for junkies. I remember thinking at one point, *I have not used cash to buy anything but smokes and Pepsi for three months.* Hell, I have never seen so many boxes of diapers in my life. Parents literally trading their own child's pampers and baby formula for a shard or two. The sadness in my life was devastating, watching the devil take souls right before my very eyes.

#

I was now wearing a full mohawk. An ode to Travis Bickle in the major motion picture "Taxi Driver." He played a street vigilante who happened to drive a taxi in the chaotic Seventies NYC. I looked crazy. But that was the point.

One night, I met some evil dude in a trap house. He said he had some fire back at his place and needed a ride home. He agreed to pay me a twenty sack upon drop off. We arrived at a shitty roach-infested apartment in the Bluff at around two in the morning.

The apartment had brown shag carpeting, tan walls, and Seventies furniture. Floral prints, brown and yellow, a combination that made the hairs on your neck stand up. The double-sided kitchen sinks full of rancid, food-caked dirty dishes. He asked me to get out a couple of beers from the fridge. I swung the door of the appliance wide open, also brown. This guy had shitty taste; no pun intended. Roaches crapping in the emptiness, not a lick of food. Just three tallboys of Miller Lite.

The imprint on the carpet where a big screen TV once sat told the tail of a pawn shop trip or trap house sales call. The entertainment for the family gone forever, up in smoke. I thought we were the only one's home. The noise of a distant TV sounded like a video game. Peering down the dark hallway, strewn with trash and dirty clothes, sat a little boy, maybe ten years of age. The man, his father, had left him alone all night with a bag of Cheetos and a Mountain Dew, of all things. Must be the sponsored beverage of Flour Bluff. I felt so bad for the kid. The man didn't even announce we were home.

He had greasy long black hair pulled back in a ponytail, a hook nose, and brown skin that matched the rug. He sat in an evil light beaming on a broken couch. I pulled up an old wooden kitchen chair and we lit a bowl, blowing clouds in the air, never thinking of the virgin lungs just down the hall.

"You wanna fuck him?" he said with a grin.

"What the fuck you just say to me, asshole?" I shouted back in anger.

He explained that he wanted to tag-team the kid, for both of us to have sex with his own ten-year-old son. I almost puked. This is where I drew the damn line. I saw red. Something came over me at this moment. I stopped arguing with the man and headed for the door. Well, after politely collecting my payment for the trip.

I exited to the driveway where my Mitsubishi sat cold and luring. I went to the hatchback in a blind rage, feeling paralyzingly tall from the meth I had just smoked. I flipped up the trunk. I pulled the shiny chrome tire iron from the hull at the bottom of the floor. I gripped it hard in my hands. The first time I had thought of my own children in months. Tears of anger streamed down my cheeks. The tire iron quaking in my clenched fist.

I was going to kick down the door and beat him to death. I had made up my mind. I was going to cave his Mexican skull in, grab the kid out, and pull him to safety. Call the cops and lie, saying the guy attacked me. I had the whole court defense played out in my mind in a matter of moments. Then the realization hit me that I was high. The fact I had dope in my cab bag, the fact I probably wouldn't be able to keep the story straight once the cops got there. I wasn't going to prison for this piece of shit. As much as I wanted to help that kid, I couldn't do it. That is a night I will always regret. A night that I knew this child would be molested if I decided to pull back out onto the street. I peeled out in tears. I headed straight back to my house on Oakbrook.

At sunrise, I called a friend's wife. She worked as a detective in the Department. I knew this cat before the game. Snitching in any way, shape, or form will get you killed. However, this was something I had to do. Kids are off-limits.

I hate child molesters with a passion, always have, always will. As sexually sick, twisted, and demon afflicted as I was, hurting a kid never crossed my mind, not even once. I am not wired for that kind of sin. Praise Jesus.

I gave her the address of that shit hole and the whole

lowdown on what was going on. I never heard anything back. To tell you the truth, I really didn't want to. Satan is real, his mark was on that whole scenario. Anyone who can hurt a child, never mind their own, has got to be a walking vessel for the Dark Prince. I was shaken to my core from this event. As with the drugged girl at Tony's, it shocked me even more how easily I could go about my day afterward.

#

Downtown streets curvy and full of hills, a flash flood of zombies toking synthetic marijuana riddled the parks and sidewalks as the Crown Victoria rolled on past. I hit the freeway hard and fast, cab bag full of dope and syringes, an orange moon hung over the land like a harvest pumpkin.

I ran back to the southside to catch the beginning of the evening bar rush. I needed a fix; I had a monster eighty unit shot preloaded to get the party started. I wasn't in the mood to get out of the taxi to get my fix, so I pulled up on the crest of a hill in a Catholic church parking lot. I sat parked under a large mesquite tree, full of summer leaves.

Eighty units is a very large dose. You might not want to be driving people for hire on a large IV injection of that size. But I was a beast, and that's what was going to get the job done. The parking lot hardtop sat vacant and bare. Not a car in sight. There at the holy spot sat the devil and me, the Dark One conjuring the demons about to enter me through the eye of a syringe needle.

A cool wind blew through the cab's air conditioning system as I lifted my white and baby blue board shorts up, exposing the milky-white skin of my femur. I was in a hurry to feel the menthol rush of the serpent flood my veins and gag my breath. Instead of shooting up in my arm as I usually did, I decided to plug into the main artery of my leg. A bad choice.

Rupturing this artery during a swing could kill a man, popping it wide open and bleeding you out like a stuck pig. "Fuck it" was my lifestyle, no hope, was the way of the walk.

I flipped the cap off the rig, pointing the needle at the blueberry highway that zig-zagged under my skin. Foot tapping to the sounds of Danzig's "Mother" playing on hard rock radio. The dome light in the taxi illuminated the injection site perfectly, a devilish pale tone that floated in my eye's cornea. The plunger's end pointed toward the steering wheel; I was about to harpoon the vein.

A crack of beamed light exploded up over the hill and hit the tree line above me. A car had darted in the driveway of the church. The vision of a police car came into my brain. I flinched hard in terror. A cabbie caught shooting up crystal meth was sure to be top headlines on Channel Ten's "People Behaving Badly" segment.

The circular end of the plunger hit the steering wheel hard, forcing the needle under the skin, pushing almost all eighty cc's under the blanket of warm flesh. Immediately a chemical burn began to melt the meat and muscle in my leg. A huge knot of parasitic poison bloated up, hard and burly. This is called a miss. Missing is a strange phenomenon in the meth lifestyle. You miss, the chemical floats underneath, staying in a toxic puddle, your body rejecting its presence for the next week or so. Properly in the vein, the meth hits the blood flow and dilutes immediately, getting you high in a matter of seconds.

The headlights backed down the hill. Someone just turning around, not a cop coming to bust me as I originally thought. I flipped down my board shorts, pulled a smaller fifty cc pre-loaded shot out of the cab bag, and injected it in my arm. Off I went, lighting the pipe as I pulled out, steering with my knees. That miss was out of sight, out of mind…for now.

#

Flash forward three days, nonstop work, and use of my favorite drug of choice. The lack of sleep itself had me in a greasy daze. I hadn't showered, ate, or drank anything. I found myself in the apartment across the way, the duplex that my original plug lived in. He had rented it to Rockstar and Captain Cook.

The floors were hardwood and swollen with heat. It was summer and the white sheetrock was sweating beads of holy oil. Some old and donated couches and cloth recliners sat in the living room, with meth cooking ingredients in cardboard boxes.

Cook's pal from his home state came in for a visit. He was a thin White boy covered in tattoos. A White gang member on the run, hiding out to avoid another prison term that he was destined to do. This kid was a big-time tweaker, a needle-using speed demon with a bad reputation for taking no shit. The racial markings on his body told tales of prison, meth, and a walk with Satan. He was a Bad Mamma Jamma. I got along with him great.

We went into the back yard which was fenced in and secluded. The backdrop was the skyline in the Bluff. It was dusk and the sky full of orchid colors and rays of purple paint. The pale of the moon was fluid and full, masking the night sky and stealing the show as the midsummer sun drained into the abyss.

Cook and Mr. White had two trash bags they pulled from the kitchen. Mr. White held church as the blackness of the evening cloaked a humid sky.

"Ya know, the first place the fuckin' Feds look is in the garbage. They search the trash, find the evidence and you're off to do twenty, just like that, Boston."

They were lacing me up, schooling me on the harsh

realities of cooking. Both told tales of how the smallest evidence could get you life.

The trash bags held all the bar codes, all the wrappers, all the receipts on the purchase of cold pills, the empty battery cartons, the cook ingredients, and byproducts. Everything related to cooking meth, any trace that the pills were purchased, needed to be burned. I had to "put in work." They handed me a plastic garden trowel and told me to dig a good size hole.

Humidity and earth clung to my dehydrated hands; a pit swelled around the plastic trowel as I dug a shallow grave for the evidence of a crime. I stood to my weary feet. My leg was pulsing, my heartbeat felt loud in the depths of the sludge-filled wound on my femur.

There was something very wrong. The miss had come to reap what I had sown in sin. Mr. White and Cook dumped the trash into the hole. Cook squirted cheap BBQ lighter fluid into the pit, soaking the prison term with vigilance and laughter.

"Up in smoke it goes, that's that," said Cook with a grin.

Cook took a Bic out of his pocket and lit up a piece of cardboard. He threw it into the soaking fumes of destiny. The flames ignited, incendiary beings began to dance and howl like wolves in the deep tinder of a desolate forest. Demon faces eloped and held hands as the air around us became stale and still. The wind was absent, and the leaves of trees stood as ominous as the Grim Reaper.

The ash from the fire rose like bread, swirling in the starlit sky. Smoky hints in our nostrils gave a sweet scent of diesel smores. My leg was swelling by the minute. The flames died, I covered the ash with earth, and we flung the wiry porch door to the kitchen open and fell back into hell.

The four of us smoked homemade off tinfoil strips all night and into the day. Now the sun was baking the shingles on the roof, there was no air conditioning to alleviate the summer flames, and my leg was festering and plump. Sweat poured down my skin, all over my body was a feverish blaze.

Cook says "You look like shit, man. What's wrong?"

I pulled up my stinky board shorts and revealed the magma filled pocket of puss floating on my leg.

Looking on in horror, the three faces that perched over me were scared and fleeting. The "holy shit" look. What was underneath was straight from a science fiction novel. A bag of fluid poison floated in the exact shape of a fried egg. "Kids, this is your leg. This is your leg on drugs."

It burned like a cigar was being snuffed on the muscular tissue, no venting for relief. A bizarre bright yellow nipple protruded out of the direct center of the injection site. This Martian substance, this voodoo potion, took on a moving living form. We watched as the pool moved like a blob from outer space, shifting in circles.

With my body rejecting the mass of chemical pain, I began to run a high fever. They got a baby thermometer out of a cupboard, and it was over one hundred and two degrees. Cook, genuinely concerned, advised me to go to the ER. Instead, I placed an eight-pound bag of ice on my leg…frozen water of course, not shards. The cool touch of the ice gave me comfort, shivering in my own sweat and malice.

I sat and contemplated a trip to the hospital. This shit was not fun anymore. This was clearly a dangerous sickness that was killing me. The game had me in situations that were beyond dangerous and vile. It was starting to sink in that I was drowning in flames. I decided against it and opted to smoke a gram of "homemade" off tinfoil with a hollow pen stem. Dr.

Feelgood was back in, and this time he was prescribing an amphetamine solution.

I hobbled for the door. Shattered by drugs and sickness. I drove to Oakbrook to shower and vent. I showed up at the cab stand about five hours late for my shift. An angry lady handed me the keys to the minivan I was to drive. The road, a flaky wave-filled dream, a dangerous driver gripping the wheel with white knuckles and tired eyes. I was dying, poisoned in every way.

After this shift, I took a few days completely off. I stayed home smoking ice and icing down my wound. A week had passed, and the swelling finally went down. The nipple shrank and the drug seeped into my flesh, an event that will forever be etched in my mind. I almost lost my leg. I could feel it.

#

Back on the road...home at last. Days away from the cab felt like months. If I took my foot off the gas, I felt as if I was missing something important. The excitement of the city streets was a drug in itself and I was addicted. The cast of characters amazed me. The gossip, the sex, the forever madness.

Tia had robbed me. She unloaded a ton of my father's belongings and papers into her Jeep. She got pulled over and called me for help. She wanted me to drive her Jeep so the cops wouldn't tow it.

They found needles and evidence of prostitution during the bust. I pulled up with Sherry. Tia was sitting in the front seat of a state police car while the officer was typing in his computer. A sure sign that she was about to cooperate, weather she wanted to or not.

As the cops left with Tia to book her, I looked on in anger as I found all my stuff in her ride. We were best friends;

how could she do this? Sherry and I loaded up my car with my things and I headed home. Some of the missing valuables included my family's real silver plate collection and the car titles located in the strongbox, still all missing to this very day. I wanted to kill her.

I had her dog. She had left him at the house while she went to the store, that's when the traffic stop had happened. Days later she contacted me. We had a very heated discussion. I had invited a bunch of bag chasers over to my house. I let Sherry and the girls have all of Tia's things. A laptop, clothes, all kinds of goodies. They attacked the closet like piranhas on a prize cow. Picking the pile to shreds in mere moments. Tia was furious when I told her. I informed her if she didn't have the silver and the car titles, I was going to cut the dog's head off and throw it to the sharks off the pier of JP Luby Beach. She was in tears and that was the point. The stuff was gone, I knew it, and I agreed to meet her anyway.

We met at HEB Plus parking lot down the street from Barry's. She had big tears in her eyes. I released the pooch, who ran right into her arms. I was the junkie with a heart a gold, remember? I could never chop a dog's head off. I was just talking shit to get my things back.

That's how the game is. You do your best and fail almost every time. Violence is just part of it. Getting jacked and betrayed, screwed blued and tattooed, all common factors of daily life. Your best friend will stab you in the back then they twist the serrated blade in your unsuspecting flesh. Friends don't exist in the game. You got fake friends and associates, all trying to get one over on each other at the drop of a dime.

Tia got in a car with the dog, and just like that, our friendship was over. I sped away to go take a bunch of verbal shit from Barry. It was my fault we got robbed, after taking a broken girl off the street, never charging her rent. Feeding her, I split all my dope scores and licks with the broad, and I wasn't even having sex with her. I loved her as my sister. Plain and simple. I learned that day that betrayal is something that was going to happen. The closest people to you in the game also have the greatest opportunity to slice your throat.

#

When the bubble gums light you up, it's time to shine. This is why they paid me the big bucks. It was an occurrence that was seldom, but when it happened, you had to be on point. The shadow of the Fuzz stomping towards the driver's side, the palpitation of his boots approaching the car, the heavy breathing of the two-time felon packing a gun in the passenger seat were all factors into my response.

I was white, well spoken, and had a clean record. My car was registered in my ex-wife's name, and she never even had a parking ticket. All big wins for the squad. When the cops ran my plates, I appeared as Joe Somebody on paper. I also held a Corpus Taxi license, an almost instant written warning for any traffic stop.

A stop is something feared by all in the game. I was the best. I would have my Driver's ID, Cab ID, and insurance ready to go by the time the Jake hit the rear of the Mitsubishi.

"What's the problem officer?" trying to mask my out-of-state accent.

I had answers to any question they could ask. If I had a female with us, the drugs were already up inside her honey pot. They would need a female cop to search a female passenger, and most times they were too short-staffed to call one out to the scene.

See, the thing about the cops is they mirror the actions of those in the car. If your cool, they are cool. You start acting froggy, they are going to jump. So, I never let anyone drink in the car, that's an instant search once they smell the booze. No pipes of any kind ever. I kept the possibilities of them finding contraband to a minimum. All the drugs were to be kept in one spot; a forty-four-ounce soda kept three quarters full ready to have the dope dumped into it in the event we got pulled over. And no needles...ever. Not in the personal car. The cab was different, the cops never stopped us when in the checkers. Seat belts are rule number one. You sit in my ride, you strap in. You got a problem with that, take the bus, Gus. That's the easiest way to prevent a traffic stop.

In a conversation with the law, I reacted like a New York night club comic in the midst of a heckler. The higher I was, the more creative the response. I was quick on my feet, a verbal prizefighter, an improvisational actor who had an answer for anything. I knew the passenger's government name and where they lived. I had all the info I needed to talk my way out of a problem. You got to be sharp as a dagger when explaining why the Mexican gangster sitting next to you is in the car in the first place. You can't respond with, "This is my pal, Joker." Knowing the details is the difference between going home, and a life sentence in the dope game.

Guns are a huge part of life in Texas. It's normal to be packing, legally or not. Felons can't own guns, but that will never stop them. The game is unforgiving, you got to protect your neck, or end up getting smoked. The trap houses were a dangerous place. One minute everything is okey-doke, next minute some real shit could pop off, just like that.

The way the drug game works is as follows: the US government brings in drugs; there are huge shipments brought in by plane or boat directly by our government; the drugs find their way into the hands of top-level people in criminal organizations; they are then funneled all the way down to low-level street dealers.

The street dealers are nothing more than mere addicts themselves. These dealers are, for the most part, all associated with street gangs. So, you have drug-addicted, gun-toting gang members running the ice game at the street level. It's a powder keg waiting to ignite. There are robberies, scams, and horror around every corner.

Politics between gang members can get ugly fast. A difference in opinion or policy, fighting over women or scores, can all cause a beef. Fights within gangs over drug dealing practices, territory, and clout cause major issues. Jealousy, envy, and all the other sins are major causes of the deaths in the drug world in Corpus Christi, Texas. People get smoked like brisket in Crook City; that's just the way it is.

Picture me, a geeky white boy, never had a felony arrest, chubby with an East Coast accent. No gang ties or experience, no knowledge of the game, its pitfalls or language, thrown deep in the middle of a mostly Mexican run gang network, selling the most dangerous drug known to man.

A fish out of water was an understatement. I just didn't fit in. Rightly so, I was the opposite of most people operating in the game. Don't get it twisted, I worked for drug dealers and gang members, but I would forever be an outsider. I was White, dealing mostly with the Mexicans. I never worked for my own people because they were just too crazy. I knew dealing with the Whites would be a bad idea all the way around. They got high, they got paranoid, you get killed. The stories in the street were enough of a warning for me. The writing on the wall caked with the blood of the ignorant.

I was a for-hire wheelman, paid by the job. My only value to these people was getting them to and from drops. I had no protection from robberies or violence. I was viewed as a square, a nobody in the gang world, and that was fine by me. I was there to get paid, mostly in dope, meet women, and fund my sexual adventures.

There are undercover cops, snitches, and the most deadly, confidential informants, everywhere. The gangs fear being infiltrated by outsiders, anyone who could possibly be working for the cops. Even the gang member could find himself getting caught up, offered a deal, and becoming an asset for the Corpus Christi Drug Task Force or the Feds. Thus, turning on his own set, building a case against the top brass, ultimately sending the administration of the gang away for an exceptionally long time.

If there was even a rumor that you were "telling," it could get you smoked. These gangs didn't take chances. Being labeled a snitch was the worst thing in the game. Even other addicts hurled the term snitch or CI (confidential informant) around as the mother of all insults.

I saw it as similar to what happened in the Salem Witch Trials. If someone didn't like you or had a beef with you, all they had to do was start a nasty rumor that you were telling, and no one would fuck with you. You have been blackballed; that's a term that means to not deal with you, sell drugs to you, or associate with you. An addict does not want to be blackballed.

Your pipeline to meth, your connections, and even your very life could be snuffed out by the whispers of your enemies, like throwing a light switch. I looked, talked, and acted differently than anyone out there. I sounded like I had an education, I was respectful and upbeat. I was an out-of-towner, I drove a taxi, and I looked like a damn cop, as I have stated before. The big difference was that I drove like one too.

#

I was driving old cop cars. I had become an expert driver. I could lose tails, maneuver like a stunt man, and I could make a fast exit out of almost any situation. People started to talk within the drug world. I heard the rumblings. "Where did he come from? How long have you known that homeboy?" Sometimes during an introduction, they would say this shit right in front of me like I wasn't even there.

This was the root of a rumor that would later prove to be nearly fatal for yours truly. It all took a serious turn with that son of a bitch, Leon. I was at Sherry's, dealing ice with her out of her bedroom in a little venture that I funded. We scored a quarter ounce and with her clientele, we would continuously flip it, using a ton of product for free along the way.

It was about three in the morning when I got a call to go to Tony's. Just hours before I had seen Leon at the local gas station. I heard he was bumping his gums about me to a bunch of people. I decided to play it cool. I didn't check him on the spot; rather I took his temperature, felt his mood out. We locked eyes and he nodded his head at me in a hello gesture. He was alone at the time. I got my smokes and left without incident.

When the call to go to Tony's came in, they ordered an eight ball, which is three and half grams of meth. Sherry sent me alone, as she was going to stay in her room and serve customers. She was all about making sales. It was only three blocks away and Tony was my boy; I had no fear.

I arrived at the apartment and knocked on the door, all was quiet on the outside. The door swung open to a living room full of degenerate looking scumbags, about ten or so, with the ringleader of them all, Leon, front and center. As I stepped in, he announced in a cocky sarcastic tone, "Hey, who invited the swat team?"

I cut him in half with my eyes, "Where's Tone?" I asked with anger.

He pointed to the rear room, and I strutted back there at once. Tony paid me for the ice and mixed me up a massive shot. We sat alone in the room, both injecting a taste from the new batch I just had delivered.

"It's fire, Boston," Tony said with wide-eyed approval.

I grabbed my cab bag and headed out.

Leon burst in with a comment, "Hey, tell the DA we said hello."

"Fuck you, Leon!" I exclaimed, slamming the door behind me.

I heard the room explode with commotion as I walked to the Mitsubishi. Leon was inside going buck wild. I had insulted him in front of his whole crew of check-cashing henchmen. He was like a badger with rabies, screaming and snarling. *Fuck 'em, I wasn't going to just take that insinuation laying down.*

In the weeks after, I learned that Leon was furious with me. Telling anyone and everyone who would listen that I was an undercover officer, sent to take down people in the gang world. Leon was a low-level banger himself. He had a voice in the underworld, but not one that held water. He was a scumbag and people knew it. I was worth more to them with my ride and everything I could offer by driving it. Most people blew off his bullshit. But the seeds were forever planted in the garden of the game. Rumor seeds that would be watered along the way, growing evil roots and branches that started to follow me along the journey.

#

I had forgotten what love and family felt like. I had changed in so many ways by this time that thinking of my wholesome past felt extremely uncomfortable. My DNA was changing on a daily basis. The streets were eating me as Adam and Eve ate the forbidden apple. Consumed by sex and drugs. Burned by the evil flames of a lifestyle most can't even comprehend. I was lost in every way.

    I had always believed in God, Satan. However, I was now walking among the latter. I could feel a spiritual shift. My children were ghosts, memories of a past life that seemed further out of reach every second. The thought of calling them made me want to throw up. The mere image of their faces made me weep uncontrollably. Then I would dry it up, use, and forget. A vicious and hateful cycle. My own selfishness, looking back, was the worst I had ever seen. Three little ones, all they did was love me unconditionally, and I left them for dead.

    My dad's kitchen was a spiritual gateway. The first supernatural experience I had in that room was a lament. One of the saddest of my life. I had been up for about a week, working and smoking ice hardcore. I got some product from a new source, the poison had a different taste and feel than usual. My father had taken the day off work. He laid in his bedroom down the end of the long hallway in my grandparents' old home on Oakbrook.

    There was no one present this day, no parasites or bag-chasing women. I sat in the kitchen, avocado green double sink to my back, cheap white countertop glistening in the beams of sunlight coming in through the hanging plastic blinds on the window sitting above.

    I had the white-hot pipe resting on a dishtowel on the countertop. The fumes of a hit lingered in the still air of the room, billowing like a distant brush fire on a South Dakota farm. My wife and youngest daughter, about six years old at the time, walked into the room. I scrambled to hide the pipe behind the toaster that sat on the counter.

We talked and laughed about old times for a few minutes. I was in tears looking at their smiling faces. My wife looked so happy and forgiving, she was loving me with her big eyes and flowing mane of brown hair. Her presence was very calming, she was the exact opposite of all the women in my life currently. Waves of great shame and remorse had washed over me. If she only knew the sexual rampage that I had been on since our separation.

This whole addiction phase, the entire suicide mission, was all because I had lost my family and career. I felt broken and ashamed, but most of all, very alone. I couldn't stop using, not even for a few hours at this point. I needed help and I was screaming for it on the inside. I was in hell; the shadows of pain, the hand I needed to pull me from the flames was absent.

My daughter's brown skin and angelic face looking up at me, pigtail braids, and her cute little outfit. Her pink tennis shoes, all in technicolor. I started to ask my wife if we could talk about me getting some help and the possibility of a reconciliation. Mid-sentence they both gave me huge smiles and just walked away. They headed for the laundry room that connected to the garage through the kitchen. There was a bathroom back there, I thought maybe that's where they were headed.

"Hey guys, where ya going?" I asked in sadness.

They coasted through the door frame, disappearing around the corner into the laundry room, never glancing back to answer me. I was shocked. *Why did they just leave me talking to myself?* I was angry at first. I stomped into the laundry room and saw no one. I flew into the garage; *surely, they had gone in there to play or find something they left behind at Grandpa Barry's.* Nothing. A vacant room, cold and ghastly. I spun around and ripped the bathroom door open; *it is the only place they could have gone!* The room was dark and as empty as my soul. Sheer terror came upon me.

It was then I flicked on the bright 100-watt bulb that sat above in the restroom. The 1970's yellow paint and wood of the counters made me weep. A half bath, the toilet white and empty, the floor bare concrete where tile once sat. A massive square mirror sat mounted behind the sink with a green and white floral wallpaper aged and peeling. I placed both hands onto the speckled countertop of the sink.

My head hung low; I rose to stare at myself in the electric reflection of the old mirror. They were never here. Was it a dream? A drug-induced, sleep-deprived hallucination? A spiritual vision sent from the Lord? That part is what could stir up a debate, but in my gut, it was the result of the latter.

Looking back, hindsight always twenty/twenty, this was right around the time I had let go. The period where my family and past life truly vanished from my heart in the clouds of the drug-induced haze. They were ghosts, coming to say goodbye. The closure of a family and deep love between five people. My little hearts all disappeared into thin air.

Panic consumed me. Still hanging on to the fact I was just having a conversation with real people and not ghosts conjured up in my mind, I ran down the hall to ask Barry if he had seen them. The conversation I had with them was as real as it gets. Two human beings standing before me, speaking audibly and moving in third dimension form.

"Dad, I was just talking to the girls, the baby. They went into the laundry room and disappeared, Dad!" I said shaking.

He looked at me with great pity and sadness. "Boston, it's nine thirty in the morning on a Tuesday; your wife is at work and the baby is at school. Boston, they are in Port

Aransas."

I started to cry. I sat on the edge of the bed devastated, weeping uncontrollably. It was the sight of them that shook me. I loved them so deeply, the visons bringing me to a nostalgic place of deep remorse for the life I now lived. It's bad enough seeing your wife and daughter in the flesh after such a heartbreaking exit, but to entertain the fact that you may also be a lunatic is another thing altogether.

It was so real; how could my eyes deceive me in such a way? My ears as well. The experience was as mind bending as it was sad. Was I losing my mind? I wrestled with the thought that I may be going insane. The realization that this may have been a spiritual vision, an omen of things to come. God revealing to me the exit of my family in my life. I was on the road to hell. Deep in the dark woods already, but where I was about to go, was no place for them.

It is for you to decide if that experience was a vison from God. In this book, I just report observations and realities that have occurred in my life, as I viewed them at that time. My father never said too much about my addiction. He knew that I wanted to die. He saw me heartbroken, and shattered beyond repair. My father loved me. The drugs were all I wanted, the only thing that made living ok. This event changed everything. He was now deeply and genuinely concerned for my wellbeing in all areas, and he began to voice his opinion. He told me I needed help. That I needed to "Get off that shit" once and for all. He said I was losing it.

I sat and listened, knowing full well I was only going to push on and get worse. That was the plan from the beginning, to die, in my bed, alone, thus lifting the burden of Boston Bornagain from this cold and unforgiving world. I told him I would get help. A shush of sorts, I just wanted him to get off the subject. I had deep guilt because of what I was putting him through as my father, best friend, and my roommate who paid every bill.

#

Flashback a little, ok passengers? Right before I started with the cab company, my dad was diagnosed with cancer. He had a cough and low-grade fever for a year before the discovery. He had seen two different doctors, both told him he had an infection or some other bullshit they misdiagnosed. I kept telling him there was something very serious going on. He drank beer like a fish and smoked Marlboro Reds like a broke stove. However, this cough sounded like that of a dying man for some time.

When I moved in with him, I found flood damage at the house. The rugs were matted with dog hair and mold from these two ancient pets that my father loved more than life itself. Our fourteen-year-old golden retriever, and my eleven-year-old pit and Labrador mix I had rescued in Port A. Between the financial neglect and the two old mutts, the house was destroyed. I tore up all the old carpeting when my dad got sick, except in the bedrooms. The house on Oakbrook went from being a sprawling four-bedroom home in the Country Club Estates, my grandparents' home, to a shell. It looked exactly like a trap house on the inside. Raw, unstained, cracked concrete floors. Holes everywhere in the sheetrock. It now looked like a shithole. But it was home.

I had rented a thirty-foot dumpster to haul off all the old carpeting and trash that had accumulated inside. I filled the dumpster to the hilt. When Barry got sick, all the money flow in the house stopped. The dumpster was five hundred dollars to hauling off. I was so strung out on meth, I just let it sit there. It was a complete eyesore. Could you imagine owning a house in the Country Club Estates, and being forced to look at a massive, ugly, blue dumpster in your neighbor's driveway, mere feet from your front door?

My dad was scheduled to have his whole right kidney removed. We prepped for surgery. He was a solid man of about two hundred pounds, five feet and ten inches, stocky. Barry had long grey-brown hair down past his neck. We always broke his balls to get a haircut, but he was a child of the Sixties and Seventies. He was a hippy rock dude who loved to party, very set in his ways.

There was always a fridge full of Bud bottles. My dad was also an extraordinarily talented businessperson and accountant. He dressed classy, black trousers, black leather dress boots with a slight heel. He loved solid-colored button-down dress shirts. Bright red was his favorite. Barry wore his clothes pressed and dry cleaned no matter how broke he was. The house may have looked like a trap house, but he always looked like a million bucks.

He took some time off from the hospital, where he worked as an accountant. The weeks leading up to surgery were scary. His cough got worse, gagging up phlegm and bile. His fever burned and his only activities were watching "The Rockford Files" and going to the restroom occasionally. He hadn't eaten in a long time, his weight dropping like the main character in Stephen King's "Thinner." He dropped about fifty pounds as fast as a man could.

The day of surgery Barry stumbled into the hallway bathroom outside my bedroom and vomited into the sink. I watched it and thought, *If I don't get him to the hospital, he won't make it another day.* We went to the local Doctor's Regional Hospital, and he underwent the surgery.

I went home and got high, staying up all night while he

sat in the recovery room, not able to have visitors. I couldn't face my father being sick and possibly dying. After smoking a massive bowl of ice, I went to the hospital the next day, as he asked, to help him walk around. The surgery causes major air pockets to form within the body. Walking helps expel the gas.

I got to his room and found him drugged on morphine. His ice-blue eyes barely able to open. He sat thirsty and cold, the room dark, and an even sicker man lay on the other side of a thin curtain. I stroked his long brown hair between my trembling fingers.

I held ice chips up to his lips so he could suck on them, dripping water in his dehydrated mouth. I will never forget the twinkle of happiness in those eyes. I was his best friend. He loved having me there to comfort him. I encouraged him and told him everything was going to be ok. The doctors informed us that the surgery was a great success.

I helped him out of the stationary hospital bed. The TV was showing "Wheel of Fortune" as Barry stood up on two feet, hospital socks hitting the floor, you know those baby blue ones with white rubber treads. His blue and white flowered hospital gown hung open exposing his bare bottom. Having a laugh, we started to wheel the IV bags out of the room to go on our particularly important walk to expel gas.

My dad and I talked for two hours as we paced through the hospital wing, walking in circles, expelling the gas from the pockets within his vessel. That was a laugh too, farts were funny in our family. Barry made big strides. In one day, he looked better than he had in a year. His cough lifted immediately. It was as if God had touched him with loving hands, a medical healing of biblical proportions. We went home in a few days, and Barry was one kidney short, but rid of the lemon-sized tumor. Cancer caused all his ailments. With this gone now, he was a new man.

We were out of the woods for now. They do a six-month checkup to see if you are in remission. Barry was back to work, and I started driving. This was the cancer's first, and what we hoped, last appearance. My dad wasn't making a lot of money, the dumpster stayed, and even after I went back to work, all my money went directly to the dope man. I was useless to him in every way. Life went on as I began to drive. I couldn't deal with him dying…no way, no how.

Now flash forward, let's get on with the story, huh passengers?

#

After the event in the kitchen, I was shaken. In the back of my mind, I always had the feeling I may be going crazy. To make myself feel better, I chalked the hallucinations up to the fact that I had gone "bat shit" due to staying up for a week. It's not good to be dull out there in the jungle. You can get killed fast for making one bad choice. Your kids never seeing you again because the fools caught you slipping.

In October 2016, some shit happened that would rock the ice world and Corpus to its core. It was right around the time I very first entered the game as a driver. I am flashing back a tad, to show you the people we are dealing with. This is a look into verifiable events and people that lurk in the depths of this cold lifestyle, no pun intended.

Breanna Wood went missing October 11 of 2016. She was a twenty-one-year-old girl. She was known in the circles as your typical sweet girl with some bad friends. She did what she had to in order to survive out there. It's just the way the life eats up young women, sad but true. She was missing for months.

There is evil in the street. Straight demonic activity that really can't be explained. The Spirit of Murder is in full bloom in The Sparkling City by the Sea. Satan himself even makes an appearance from time to time, making sure his minions are taking souls.

Wood was dating a man named Joe Tejada at one point. Tejada was a gang member in the Corpus area. He has an ominous "13" tatted under his bottom lip down to his chin. His face is covered with ink, the kind that just stands out in the crowd. He had a shaved head, and you could see a tattoo that is a thick bold line accentuating his hairline. His eyes were huge and alien.

If someone played "The Devil" in human form in a Hollywood movie, Tejada would be a casting agent's dream. He looked like a villain. He was "wero," meaning of Mexican descent, but appearing White.

News reports tell the tale, that an inmate at the Nueces County Jail told a guard that he had information on the whereabouts of the body of the missing twenty-one-year-old Breanna. In the following days, he led them to an abandoned farmhouse, on none other than Route 666, just outside of the city. This was now January.

When the CSI unit got to the farmhouse, they found a sinister-looking oil field trailer. Inside a box covered with a white sheet was a ghostly cloth draped over Pandora. They found the decomposing remains of a female, in her early twenties. Wrapped in thick plastic, entombed and stuffed away into the nothing. The evildoers never wanted her found.

Days later another inmate at the Nueces County Jail started singing like a canary. He told authorities that Tejada confided in him that he had abused Wood's body. The remains in the box were confirmed to be Wood. The autopsy showed that she had been shot in the back of the head with a pistol. Word on the street was her arms and legs were broken to fit into the crate. He had shot her allegedly.

The part of the story that is unclear, even in the streets, was what Breanna did to cross her killer. News reports all admitted that Joe Tejada was allegedly told by an accomplice to kill his ex-chick or he, himself, would get smoked like a Christmas ham. He was also allegedly offered five hundred dollars as a bonus to take Breanna out.

There are rules to this shit. You rip off the wrong person or you cross someone with something to prove, you end up in a box on some abandoned piece of property, never to be seen again. It's so dangerous, in fact, that if some shot callers in a gang get way too high one night, and decide that you have seen something incriminating, if you knew too much…BANG! You're dead, cowboy.

This is the real deal Holyfield, boys and girls. Google that case. That was what was happening out on the street when I was a wheelman. The grim reality of the life all around, anyone working and living in the backdrop of the drug trade knew full well the cost for playing. Sometimes you pay with your life. No sleep. You gotta stay up!

#

My life was out of control, and I was not having fun anymore. Getting high had become a job and the way I was supporting my drug habit had become extremely dangerous, as had my sex life. I missed being a human being, living a normal life, and having people around me that cared if I lived or died.

But not enough to get help, that wasn't even in my mind. I couldn't let go of the pain, the resentment, and the loss. I needed the drugs to die. I didn't want to live anymore, but I didn't want to live like this either.

Uber and Lyft came to town, throwing the cab world into a tailspin. They were exempt from having cab licenses and received all kinds of other freedoms us traditional cabbies didn't enjoy. Plus, the fares were about half the price of those riding in a taxi. They were putting us out of business. I went from making about $200 a night in regular cash jobs to $30 for a twelve-hour shift after paying for gas.

I'd just had it. I decided to borrow eighty bucks from my boss, knowing I would never pay him back, and I quit. I decided I would just drive the Mitsubishi full time. My risk level went up a thousand percent not having the cab as a cloak from the cops. The big transports would all now have to be done in my personal ride but hey, "Fuck it," remember?

The life of a driver may sound glamourous at this point. It wasn't. I was always broke. I was spending every dime I had on dope. I never helped my father with one red cent for bills. I paid zero in child support, and I never spoke to my children. All my time was spent doing drugs, having sex, or watching pornography, and maybe, just maybe, once in a blue moon, I would get a few hours of sleep. You think that's a joke? I was sleeping two nights a week on average, and only for three hours a night. That's six hours of sleep in a seven-day period. I was only eating food twice a week and I barely drank water at all. The effects on my health were starting to show already. I was losing my shit. It's not as fun as it sounds.

I was out of a real job, out of control, and out all night. The ride gets bumpy from here on out passengers. I was the driver, and the stakes were about to get much higher, no pun intended.

Chapter 5
The Greatest Love of All

Love hits you like a runaway train. Or in this case, a taxi. Walking through these dirty streets, one may find a crosswalk where you think you are safe. Then, BOOM! You are lying flat on your back. That's the way it happens, during the madness, when you are not looking, there she is.

It was around eight in the morning on a weekday, I just got back to Oakbrook from a driving job when Tony hit me on my cell. I had been up for about three days, and I was lit. He said he was on his way to the southside, and he was with "the sisters." That set some bells off right away. He had my attention. Tony said there was a spot over on Everhart Road, an apartment where some people were kicking it and rolling some bowls. It was about three blocks from the crib, I headed back out to the ride and drove on over.

He had given me the apartment number but told me to wait until he got there to go up to the door. There I sat on the second floor of a high-end southside apartment complex, out in the exterior hallway balcony, overlooking a courtyard parking lot. I peered down with my arms resting on a black iron railing, stucco floor under my feet. The apartment was brick and mortar, the courtyard below landscaped with little spruce trees and ferns. The pop of the green against the brown mulch was soothing to my high, tired eyes.

They pulled up in a shit box on wheels. A red jalopy, the make and model so forgettable that I can't recall it even for this testimonial. Tony never drove, he didn't own a car so most likely it was stolen or a dope rental. Just another day, an insignificant detail, a minor crime which I had no business knowing the details.

The car came to a halt in a parking space below. The brakes squealing like a stuck Alabama pig. Hey, drive it like you stole it, right? I watched a life-changing, breathtaking moment in my life unfolding before my eyes.

#

She slid out of the passenger side of the ride like a king cobra, slithering in sex and beauty. Majestic mamma, pin-straight brown hair. A dark navy pencil skirt clung tight to every succulent, plump curve on her bodacious body. I heard her laugh for the first time as her sister joined her on the hardtop; my body quaked in the presence of a goddess. The three walked towards me. Tony gave me a wave as she melted my heart with the most glorious smile I had ever seen. They disappeared below as they made their way to the secluded stairwell that would lead up to my racing heart.

I was paralyzed, nervous, and weak. She came through the glass doors of the staircase first, bursting through the door like a star onto a red carpet. As she walked by, she cracked a smile that made my knees feel like a bowl of green Jell-O.

Flipping her shoulder-length follicles with her wondrous hand, fingers painted like the Sistine Chapel.

Her body passed mine, causing shivers of a love that hit me like a magnitude ten on the Richter scale. The other two souls she was with were almost invisible. I saw only her, my neck breaking as I followed the angelic body that captivated my every sense. She smelled of fresh roses and strawberry, the sound of her feet like the clicking revolver of a loaded .357 magnum.

I followed the three into the apartment, a broken shell of the man I was. I couldn't speak. I had never looked at a woman the way I looked at this exquisite creature. She wasn't even human. I looked on as she strutted into an empty three-bedroom flat.

The rugs, a warm beige, the walls shiny and white, perfect for a young professional couple or doctor. This place was swanky, but as it sat, totally vacant and bare. Grease from the coils of a refrigerator that used to sit there painted a story on the floor in the kitchen. I'd bet it is in a trap house somewhere in town keeping the beer and BBQ leftovers nice and cool for an undeserving dealer.

The living room was massive. Sky-high cathedral ceilings came to a pinnacle point at what seemed like miles above. Beams crisscrossed over my head, this was not your typical apartment, and surely not a place you would find a bunch of dope fiends squatting.

Turns out it was sublet to a guy named Ramiro, a familiar face at Tony's check-cashing den. The original renter was a cool lesbian chick that also cashed fraudulent checks and smoked shards like a madwoman. She had cancer, didn't really care for life much, another depressing tale. She was forced to move for whatever reason and still had a lease on the place. I am assuming Ramiro traded her some dope so that he could move in, never planning to pick up the remainder of the lease.

Ramiro was a menacing little fellow. He was five and a half feet with muscular shoulders and a black crew cut. A weird Mexican that looked like he came from the Philippines. He always wore the same thing, khaki cargo shorts, and a white wife-beater. Barefoot as always. He looked like a dude in a Kung Fu movie.

On the living room floor, there was a vast assortment of black and white trash bags, brought in by the bitches frequenting the place. Ramiro's chick was a short little prostitute. She also looked like a Geisha, pin-straight black hair down past her ass, little baby blue shorts, a slinky crop top to match, and some Jordan flip flops, stolen for sure. She sat on the living room floor with a bitchy look on her face, knee-deep in a coloring book, a favorite pastime for tweakers.

The living area was the middle room of the apartment. There was a master bedroom and bath on one end, at the other end of the house was another smaller bedroom with a bath in the hallway.

There was a passel of strung-out squatters in this place. Junkies, shooters, and smokers alike. The smell of fresh paint and gas fumes, hints of stale Marlboro Reds and cheap Walmart perfumes worn by the various hookers in attendance.

Ramiro led Tony and the girls back to the smaller bedroom. I followed like an icy caboose, trailing along, stoned and hyper. Ramiro's chick hopped to her Jordan's, not wanting to miss any free drugs.

"Get the fuck outta here!" Ramiro barked at some of the squatters sitting on the floor. The roaches scattered out to the living area to tweak, watching porn on a cellphone.

"I'm Bella," she whispered as she gave me a huge smile. She tapped over to the wall and put her back up against it. As she had her back to me, my eyes were glued onto the sexiest pair of legs I had ever gazed upon. Her calf muscles were thick and muscular, running up to plump brown thighs and hips that made me drool.

The girl was a certified dime. A street sassy, half-White and half-Mexican bombshell. It was like Dr. Frankenstein gave Demi Lovato the booty of a young Nikki Minaj and the rack of a Magic City stripper, natural and robust.

Her skin looked like the inside of a can of cocoa, perfectly pale with a hint of sear. Her face was warm in nature. Symmetry ran over her seductive cheekbone structure. Her eyelashes were like Venus's flytraps of onyx, fanning out over the biggest pair of brown eyes ever created by the Good Lord. Her eyes sparkled and shone, they reflected like mirrors in a plantation, hanging on the walls in the Deep South. Stories of pain and vulnerability sat behind windows to a complicated soul, serendipitous and sanctified.

Her movements slow and speculative, auras of azure and sapphire flared off her dress. She crouched down and sat on the floor, crossing her thoroughbred legs one over the other. We all circled around in the cipher; a big bowl of the finest shards was being passed around like a Hells Angel's old lady.

Dissemination of truths, lies, and other stories spat out of the mouths of the unholy. Ramiro was a known bisexual prostitute who would service Johns for shards whenever times got tough. The truth is he liked it more than he let on. His girl was ok with it, long as she profited, turning a blind eye as she exhaled serpent smoke out of her flaring nostrils.

"You don't remember me?" Bella hissed across the session.

I looked at her puzzled and fearful. "No, no I don't," I replied.

She went on to scare me, keeping her comment shrouded in mystery. Years of alcoholism left me brainwashed from memories. I spent the better part of the previous decade in a massive blackout. Panic took hold as she toyed with my emotions. A once relaxing morning, now a terror laced question. *How did I know this being, who was this?*

I pestered her for answers the whole time we smoked. She would only smile and giggle, whispering in the ears of her much younger and different looking sister. Gorgeous in her own right, little Brittany was much darker, a full-blooded Mexicana. Thick and curvy, her mane of thick dark-brown curls flowed over a cute chubby face with a unique button nose. She wore daisy dukes and a tight-fitting black t-shirt.

The dope was gone. The ladies looked disappointed as their thirst for ice was that of one on a pilgrimage through the Mojave Desert. These party girls were more known in the game for their drug use than anything else.

"I got some shit at my house, fire too," I said with authority.

"Well, let's go, big shot," Brittany retorted with a snide tone in her voice.

We bid farewell to our most gracious of hosts. Ramiro looked angry, as he didn't get an invite. I didn't like his ass and I was not about to invite that demon up in my crib. That says a lot about him because in those days, all were welcome.

We sifted into our cars and took off to Oakbrook. My house was gross, the bare floor, the smell of putrid pet dander, and the presence of matted dog hair throughout. But even the classy chicks in the dope game never bat an eye in a trap house, this wasn't these broad's first rodeo.

We entered my bedroom, and all sat around as I dipped into the top drawer of my dresser and loaded a bowl of crystal into a brand new pizzle. I rolled out the good stuff for this dope game Beyoncé I had in my midst. Brittany looked on in great jealousy and rage. She hated her older sister. Turns out that Bella was thirty at the time; Brittany was a mere twenty-two. You could tell her older sibling always got the guy, the attention, and the dope first, leaving Brittany with the leftover scraps and scrubs that Bella passed up. This pitted a deep resentment; her eyes told the whole story.

Brittany hurled insults and ball-busting comments my way for pretty much the whole outing. Bella just laughed and carried on as smoke plumed like a refinery smokestack in the South Texas sky. The pair had just arrived, and already looked like they wanted to leave.

"What? Are you guys in a hurry?" I asked.

"Dude, we on the clock," Brittany replied, insinuating that they were prostitutes because I clearly took a liking to her beautiful older sister, and I suppose she thought that would ruin it.

After a while Tony went to the restroom down the hall. I excused myself and followed him as the girls sat smoking. When he came out, I asked him "Who is this chick, man?"

He said, "That's Bella, my friend, I am kind of seeing her."

I was crushed. She was the perfect woman, haunting in every way. I had to have her, and now I was going to have to step on the toes of a friend, employer, and a good dope connect to get her. So be that shit, this was the game, and I was gonna go for mine.

We returned to the room to find the pipe empty, the two smoked it up in a jiff. "Well, how ya like it?" I asked with pride, knowing the dope was voodoo.

"It was trash," Bella shot back, launching a dart into my heart, crushing me to my core. She said she thought there was something wrong with it and stood to her feet.

The girls were ready to go. I thought maybe it was the grotesque condition of my father's house, but who knows? When these types of girls are ready to move around, they get squirrely. As Bella inched past me, she drew close. "Hit me on Messenger," she said, giving me the contact name on her account, making sure Tony wasn't paying attention to our exchange.

I shook Tony's hand, and they took off. Obliterated by Bella's departure, I hit the showers. I had business to attend to that day. Since I was no longer a cabbie, I had to go full on into the drug dealing aspect of the business to support my large and growing habit.

I was the worst drug dealer in the history of the game. I always used up my own product. The few times I tried to deal myself, I not only used up the profits, but I also used up the whole batch. So, I steered clear of being a drug dealer. I would only end up broke, or worse, deeply in debt to some mean mothers that would make life a living hell until I paid them off. Either way didn't work for me. I was a wheelman, a driver. I had no business working a scale for a living. I was a full-blown addict. The temptation was far too great. The opportunity for catastrophe too easy.

I used my noggin and thought of some creative ways to supplement my drug income. I had some out-of-town clients that were always looking for a good deal on fire shards. They would drive in from neighboring towns where the dope was far more expensive. Me, getting a playa price and quality product, would middle a deal for them. They would come to my house, give me the buy money, and I would go pick up the package. They would tip me handsomely for my trouble. A quick drive across town and I would have enough dope for the whole night. A tight deal.

Rosie was a big girl. I had been dealing with her for some time now. She drove over an hour to get a product from me. I don't know why. The chick had more connections than I did. She clearly didn't need me to middle a deal for her. One would assume that she liked me, using my services to somehow connect with me on a deeper level. My past sexual advances and her rejections, however, had me puzzled. She was a good client, she paid generously. Whatever reason she had to fuck with me was good enough left unsaid.

The day crept on, and I had a dealer named Noel meeting me at the house. This was unheard of because it would be suicide for me to have Noel and Rosie meet one another. This would leave the door wide open for me to be "sidestepped," a term used when a connection between the customer and the dealer is made, thus cutting out the middleman, which would be me.

I called Bella. I was smoking nonstop from the time she left, now on a full four-day bender with no sleep. I was dreamy. She wanted to kick it. It was damn near sundown when I agreed to drive the ten-minute trek to her grandparents' crib to meet her. She lived in a predominantly Mexican hood just off the highway. She sent me the address, which I plugged into my GPS. I was getting desperate to see her. Not so much sexually, I craved her soul. The mystery on how she knew me, her ambiguity, it was all eating me alive.

Rosie and Noel showed up at the same time after hours of waiting. I was fed up. Wrecked on crystal and not thinking clearly, I left the dope dealer and the customer at my house, in the driveway waiting to do the deal. My dad was inside. I didn't even care about my end in the deal or the sidestep that was about to take place. I jumped in the Mitsubishi and hit the gas. I was on a mission to score me the ultimate chick in the game. The crown jewel, the big enchilada…well, in this case, hot tamale. She was the one I wanted.

I pulled up to the crib shortly after. I messaged her as the South Texas sun drained into a deep pink sky. She came right out. She was now in a pair of faded daisy dukes and a white t-shirt. Her booty was banging. I had never seen anything like it in my entire time on this planet. Hanging out the seams, the frays of the denim dripping down her thick and creamy thighs.

I leaned over and popped the door with ease, she slid down onto the sleek vinyl seat like a margarita pouring into a cold glass with a sugared rim. The bitch was bad in every damn way. She smelled of lilies of the valley, her hair perfect and pressed.

"Hey there," she pouted. Her lips glossed in a cherry glaze; huge aviator Ray-Bans perched upon her head.

Bella was a class act. She was a superstar in the game. She was known by the hood, but she had a style to her that I had never seen. We talked for hours out in the driveway. Turns out Bella was raised in an all-white community outside of Corpus Christi. Her Corpus wasn't showing, and I finally knew why.

She opened up about her life and who she was. She finally told me the story that had ruined my mind the whole day. Years ago, I was separated from my wife, four years prior to this day. We were officially split up at the time. I was at Theo's Bar on the southside one-night drinking heavily. I had a coke connect, a prison gang member that would sell me small quantities as I shot pool.

 That night I got invited back to the house where those homeboys were chilling during after-hours. Bella claims that's where we met. She was eight months pregnant at the time. I was in a blackout apparently. We spent the night together; I had no memory of this. How could I forget her? While listening to this story, we went back to the very house I was sitting at that night. She said we had a great time together. Until something spooked me, and I freaked out and left. Bella said she had chased me down the driveway holding a plate of tacos she had made for me. I was about three hundred pounds back then.

 I thought she was messing with me, I couldn't remember one detail of this story. We flirted, I was unable to stop gazing into her beguiling eyes, until finally I leaned in and kissed the most beautiful succulent pair of lips I had ever touched. I bit the flesh of her bottom lip ever so gently. Our tongues met in a sweet loving embrace. My head exploded into chemically induced bliss. Her pheromones leaked off her skin and into my smell sense. I was in love. She was the single greatest version of the female body I had ever experienced. One kiss and it was all over. Many more were had out in the driveway.

 "Hey, you want me to spend the night at your place?" she asked timidly.

 I nodded, speechless and weak.

 "Ok, I will go get the baby and his things"

 The baby? What baby? I didn't see this one coming. She ran into the house before I could say a word. It didn't matter. She could have told me she was going to bring an eighteen-wheeler of homeless alcoholics and I would have let her.

She returned with a car carrier for a baby and some clothes. The baby was sixteen months old. A small child. I would normally be nervous to have a child with me, seeing I was a full-blown meth addict. Not now. I was with Bella and that's all that mattered.

She brought maybe three days' worth of supplies for the baby and clothes for them both. I paid it no mind. We coasted back to Oakbrook; the dealer and Rosie were gone. She never left me the dope for middling the deal. Surprise, surprise. That was sarcasm if you couldn't tell.

We put the baby down on my bed; he passed out right away. Bella and I retreated to the laundry room on the opposite end of the house. Out came the pizzle and two grams of dope I had stashed under the bathroom sink. I packed almost three-quarters of a gram and started roasting it up with a brand-new Bic lighter. Bella could smoke like a champ. Most people couldn't keep up with me when it came to doing drugs, but this girl was my match.

"So, are you dating Tony?" I asked quietly.

"Ah hell no," Bella coughed out with a laugh.

Now, if she was or not is another story. Far as I was concerned, I was going to take her word for it. The washer and dryer sat under a window, looking out to the driveway in the laundry room. We smoked until the bowl was spent. Super high, Bella began to moan quietly in pain. She had major pain in her legs from an accident where she had fallen down a staircase years before.

She kicked one of her legs up onto the washer with her short Daisy Dukes on. Her eyes closed, silky brown bangs over her forehead, whimpering gently and as high as a Colorado Rocky. I stood behind her as her foot rested on the washing machine. Her cheeks hung down and out of her shorts; there was no chance of containing all that jelly.

    I started rubbing her athletic shoulders, massaging her tight muscles with thick Irish fingers. I kissed the skin from her shoulder to her ear lobe, not missing one inch of her neck. My hands ran wild, a medicinal rub-down for this wounded mexi-white hybrid.

    Her foot hit the floor, not long after, her Daisy Dukes and black lace panties slid down her perfect legs, leaving her naked and dripping like a penthouse faucet. She whispered some captivating words of instructions as she propped her foot back up on the washer. It was like dancing with a hood ballerina, a sex-driven tango with an expert contortionist.

    She tilted her head back and French kissed me in a passionate twist. With my pants now on the floor, I entered the center of her warmth, feeling every muscle grip me under tender pressure. Her mouth wide open, panting like a dog in summer heat, she let out cries of pleasure in the most angelic of ways.

    The methamphetamines clinging to every pleasure center of our brains, animalistic rituals of love spells disintegrated any molecules of shame we may have clung onto. Exploring one another as pioneers of sin. I roved her flesh for complete discovery, intending to focus all my senses into hers so that she could achieve orgasm.

    I carried the naked living sculpture to a vacant bedroom, laying my prey on her back with precision. Delicate and deliberate, I took her thighs in my hand and positioned both feet over her head as I invaded private spaces. For hours we smoked while naked and made love in ways I never thought possible with conjoined human flesh. Searing vapor pouring in with our every breath, heathen mouths reciting poetic emotion. Speed drove our romance as if on the Autobahn de jour.

I was high and in a sick infatuation with her. Outside we sat half-dressed in the open door of the garage, smoking Marlboro Reds and trying to make sense of what just took place.

We talked with weak voices. I felt a high like an illicit drug, but far more potent and spellbinding. My head rose far into the clouds, feeling like a conquering army that just took a stronghold from an imperial enemy. Victorious ramifications filled my heart, alive for the first time in many moons. As a cold world spun around us, we discussed family and sad truths that existed within us.

Her ma and grandma were both sick and a far distance away at the time. Only months before, my father was in recovery from cancer, a helpless feeling of mortality poured over us like the rains of the Amazon. I played the acoustic version of "3AM" by Rob Thomas, formally of Matchbox 20. A haunting rendition of a song he wrote about a time when his own mother had cancer.

We sat on the cold concrete, her back on my chest, the keys of the Steinway he played hitting soul nerves in us both. I held Bella as she wept emotional tears. A noticeably quiet soul, not of many words, she had the greatest trouble expressing her feelings. I could feel her past under her skin, unable to come out of the lips. I just took the painful vibrations as the only language she knew.

We went inside to tend to the child; as he awoke, we both took care of him. A special little boy that I loved immediately, his personality and charm like no other, even in infancy. We took it easy, relaxing the rest of the day. The birth of a sick love in my heart that proved to be expensive and unhealthy.

#

Later that day I took her to her house to get more things. She clearly understood she was invited as a permanent Oakbrook resident.

Flashing back to the night before, images of Bella on top of me felt like the strangest Deja vu I had ever experienced. The way she moved, specific things she did while making love in that one position, solidified that I had been with her in my past. Vague memories started to surface. Then clearer and clearer. I remember leaving her house four years ago. I remember now changing my phone number the next day after I left. Thinking to myself, *I like this woman so much, if I don't run away now, I will never go back to my family.* I had small children, and this night with this mystery woman was the event that caused me to reconcile with my wife. How could I forget such an important detail? The alcohol had washed all recollection of Bella and her memory right out of my memory bank.

#

Was this shaping up to be a hood fairy tale or what? I mean, I met this woman and had a passionate night of lovemaking four years before while she was eight months pregnant, forgetting every second of it. Reader...what could go wrong? This could be one for Hollywood!

#

The next few days Bella revealed her "tweak." She loved to get high and clean house. She made instant friends with Barry, going into his room and cleaning up after the old dogs, scrubbing his shower and bathroom from floor to ceiling. She then proceeded to clean the entire house. It was in the best condition in recent memory. Bella, the baby, and I bonded deeply, acting as a family in all ways. However, there was a twisted paradox. We were both full-blown drug addicts.

Bella needed dope. It was without question a daily staple. An unsaid requirement of our relationship. I found out fast that our family grocery list was short but stupidly expensive. Dope was over a hundred bucks a day minimum, right off the muscle. Without cigarettes, she got moody, so that's another daily expense. Pepsi and Texas' own Big Blue soda were also a must. We needed diapers, wipes, and food. We had food stamps that helped, but things still went over budget. Gas and other expenses, all of it made it pretty clear that I needed to get back to work. Driving was all I knew now, so that's what I went looking for.

Turns out, Bella was not new to meth. She was into a raging seven-year addiction, deeply hooked. She was not using in massive amounts as I was, but very emotionally dependent on the drug. If a hardcore addict doesn't get what they need, things get ugly fast. So, going back to work was now an emergency situation.

I approached the rival cab company in town. Leary because of the drought since the rideshare companies came into play; I researched numbers on what other guys were making in cash per night. To my surprise, at this company, cabbies were raking in over two hundred dollars a night! I still held a valid cabby license and applied right away. I paid a fifty-dollar fee to switch the name of the company on my license, and boom, I was back on the open road.

Bella didn't want to live back home. Things were becoming a lot clearer as to why she moved in so fast. I was a meal ticket with a place to stay. The first major red flag, Bella knew how to get what she wanted from men. A honey catcher is a woman in the game who takes bag chasing to the next level.

Not only does a honey catcher smoke all the dope their little heart desires, but she also gets all her bills paid, a place to stay, and the situation is more long term.

The relationship was extremely complicated. Bella had feelings for me, more pity than anything else, but you could tell it was not a complete con job. Down deep she was a cool lady. The funniest girl around, she lit up a room like a lamp and she knew how to party. She was a ton of fun. The sex was amazing. Life was good, so long as I overlooked the part that she was using me and lying to me about loving me back. I was sick, weak, and I didn't really care. At this stage, I didn't know the extent of how fucked up things really were.

The first night at the new cab company was intense. They were crazy busy and had a ton of new technology I had to get used to. On top of the GPS system, there were front and back viewing cameras with full audiovisual. This was a scary situation on many levels. I knew what I was about to do and there was no going back. My mind made up, the new taxi job was going to become a full-fledged criminal enterprise.

The first three days, I was getting trained. I learned the high-tech credit card system, which was totally secure with no way to run a scam. I had a supervisor riding along with me to make sure I was learning proper procedures. Having experience, I caught on quickly. I was a beast behind the wheel, I knew Corpus and I knew how to make cash.

The company felt comfortable enough to cut me loose after three nights and I started my first shift alone on a busy Friday. I got super high before work. I had to feel out the routine to see how I could use on the job without getting caught. I went to the cab stand at a quarter to seven and picked up the keys to a new minivan. I was happy to drive it because the more passengers you carry, the more money you make.

Getting a minivan off the lot on a Friday night was like hitting the jackpot.

I turned the corner in the car yard and as I walked by the mechanic shop, who do I see? None other than Maybach, the drug dealer who used to deliver to me on Oakbrook before I was even in the game. We exchanged daps with a promise to talk more later. He was there visiting a buddy at work; he was always hanging at the stand.

I got behind the wheel and I did my preflight. I checked the gauges, recorded the miles on the odometer, and checked the camera system. They had a black box mounted near the rearview mirror that housed the double-sided camera. There was a tiny bulb on the bottom right of the box that would change color patterns every time you turned on the ignition. The reason for this was when you start your shift, you may get a solid green light.

If you did get the infamous green light, you noted that on your paperwork. It changed intermittently for the pretense that the driver never gets wise to when the camera was rolling. If you hit the brakes too hard, if there was a collision or other factors, the light would switch to a random color and flash and start recording. Remember, there was full audio as well, clear as a bell.

I did some testing on the opening of my shift, hitting speed bumps, braking hard, and by the grace of God, I found a glitch in the system. This would later prove to save my freedom and life on the daily. I found that when the camera clicked on, there was the faintest sound inside the box. A low-frequency buzz that injected into all my senses. I found the chink in the armor!

At the opening bell, my first calls proved to be big money. Forty dollar runs back-to-back paying cash. This was a good omen of things to come. There was a pole stand in the middle of the floor in the front section of the cabs, to mount the computer screen, a tablet-style computer that ran off Wi-Fi. It would ding and the address and details of your next fare would pop up on the screen. It all ran off GPS, so when a call came into dispatch, they would see who was in the area of said call and transmit the job right to your computer. They could see if you had people in the taxi already, all computerized and very well put together. You could also call your own signals. Meaning you could sign out for your breaks at the push of a button, thus taking you out of the rotation for calls. It was perfect.

There was no shortage of business. As soon as I would drop, the next ding would come across the screen, and I was off to the next pick up. The way it worked was if someone paid with cash, you owed half to the company. If someone paid with a credit card, the company would owe you half the fare.

So, at the end of the night, you wanted a good mix of cash and cards so you could walk away with your full pay for the night in cold hard cash. Things get a little more complicated when you start factoring dope rides into your meter. You would take dope in place of cash for the ride and owe the cab company half the fare in cash. Kind of complicated, but after some tweaking, things worked out just fine...no pun intended. It was just like the old company, only this one was computerized.

The night was going smoothly. Lots of cash in my bag and things just seemed to get busier as the night went on. An address popped on my screen that rang a bell. I paid it no mind as I plotted the course in my GPS. Upon arrival, I was shocked to see I knew the house all too well. It was one of the busiest trap houses in town. Ran by this crazy White boy, the kind covered in tattoos and threw the word "nigga" around like it was a nerf football.

He came out with a smoking hot redhead. A well-known, high-end prostitute, the type that makes a damn good living hooking, not your typical bag chasing honey. This guy was The Man, fifty grand. A true legend in the game, a guy you absolutely don't want to fuck with. He liked me. He was always super upbeat and glad to see me when I came around. I met him through some trusted mutual friends, and I had a decent rapport with the kid.

"Boston, what the fuck you doin' man!" he greeted me with that enthusiasm.

We chatted and I explained that I had just started with this new company, and it was my first night. This guy was not someone I drove dope for, mostly because of the racial rules I set for myself as a wheelman. I knew well enough not to mistake anyone's kindness for weakness, never mistake a smile for safety. These people were bad news. The nicer the guy, the bigger the body count.

We went on a run. I knew what time it was; we did a signal four. That's when you go somewhere round trip. He went in, did his business, and he came right back out to go home. We didn't talk about anything in the cab during this trip. I noticed that the camera clicked on right when his ass hit the seat at the beginning of the ride. I didn't want to be paranoid, so I didn't mention it. Really it was the first night on the job, the first time that this had happened, so at that point, I didn't think anything of it.

When the ride was over, I stepped out of view of the taxi. He paid me in cash, and we chatted some about a future arrangement of paying in shards for services rendered. Dangerous, yes, but having a connect with this guy was a major score. He could give me the best product at a playa price that would be the envy of the street. So, I agreed and took him on as a part-time client, agreeing to work on a job-by-job basis, only in the taxi, when he rang. I would pick up his phone call on my personal cell. He would call dispatch, request me, and I would show up. I fully disclosed that everything was on audiovisual, and nothing was to be discussed in the taxi. All the dope payments would have to be well hidden or done outside the cab to ensure we were not being watched. He agreed and I went on my way.

I was having a ball. A totally new experience! The cash flow was a river, and the kid was back in full force. I had Bella and the baby at home, life was as good as it could be for a junkie. I had stopped shooting up. I didn't want to go to that extreme anymore. Shooting up is a sex demon. I wasn't trying to watch porn for days or nail a thousand women in a week anymore. I still got high, I was still using truckloads, but my sexual deviancy was taking a back seat…no pun intended.

#

I was genuinely and one hundred percent in a sick relationship with Bella. No longer did any other woman exist in my eyes though. I wasn't going behind her back. I wasn't sneaking around. I was faithful even in the throes of a lethal meth addiction.

Bella knew everyone in the game. I never fully pieced that part together. How did she literally know everyone? Thousands of people from Corpus were friends with her on social media, and she knew them in person too. It was uncanny the number of people this girl knew.

I was taking a lot of breaks. The cab company couldn't say shit, so I did as I pleased, using my time to go see Bella and the baby. I would randomly pull into the driveway at Oakbrook. My bedroom window faced the driveway with a planter hanging underneath. I would creep up and open the window, cooing at the baby. His big smiles would brighten my whole world. A ray of sunshine in the dark addicted world I lived in. A return to innocence. He was the one thing that gave me hope that this cold world could be restored to sanity. He was special to me from the very start. Not remembering my own kids at all.

    Looking through the window was my favorite part of the day. Bella was motherly and sweet, usually right after her first cigarette of the day. We were a nocturnal family. Hell, we didn't sleep ever. I would baby talk to the boy, lean in for kisses on the cheek of my Bella. I was genuinely happy in these short, but important moments. The spring wind blew through the mesquite branches in the front yard, whispering sweet tales of hope and family.

    On the rare occasion I would take a night off, Bella and I would sit in our spot under the tree. We called it the "picnic spot," a small place where the lawn rose off from the driveway just a few inches, right under the branches of the tree in the center of the yard on Oakbrook.

    She was always stunning. She was very proud of her body. Sometimes she would strut out to meet me at three in the morning under the tree, and she would be wearing a nighty or something sexy. The old men in the neighborhood must have loved that!

    We would sit and stare at the glistening Texas moon. I would hold Bell like it was the last time I would ever see her. In my line of work, with what I was doing every day, it may well have been. She never spoke to me very often. She was quiet. She wasn't a loudmouth or a smooth talker like I am. The fact is I don't think she really enjoyed my company too much. These sweet moments we had were totally one-sided. We were great drug friends; but she just didn't feel the same for me romantically. I knew it deep down.

I made her laugh, I bought her what she needed; in turn, she told me she loved me back and gave me sex. On the surface, it appeared like we were a couple. In the recesses of the heart, it was a mere arrangement for both parties. I would have given anything in the world for her to love me the way I loved her. It just wasn't in the cards. As much as I knew this fact, I always had hope that it would change.

Not too far along, I realized that if I didn't break bread, and if I didn't provide the drugs she needed, someone else would. I had to go get it done...day in, day out. The fact was, I was so sick, I didn't look at it as a bad thing. I would work a whole shift, go hustle, do illegal activity, risk twenty years in prison, and come home to slap all the money, all the dope, and anything else I got on the dresser and say, "Whatever mama want, mamma get." It was a running joke. I always kept back way more dope than I gave her in secret; but when she ran out, I always had more. The addict in me just had to know it was in my pocket. Anything I had was hers for the taking.

#

Word on the street was that Noel was in on the theft at my house. He was said to have my dad's car title and silver plates in a lockbox at his crib off Leopard Street. A junkie acquaintance laced me up on the facts while smoking at my house one day. This set off a major beef. Noel was an associate of Tia, and it was said that he orchestrated the whole damn thing. Months after it all went down, this new information came out and had me heated. I confronted the homeboy on it and tried to set up a meeting.

I tried to meet him three times. Every single time he would no-show on me. He was always super high and thinking it was a set up with the laws, he would "go Swayze." I never talked to the police. In the game, something like that would get you cut off quick, or much worse. So, I tried to handle it off the books like a man and get my shit back. After he blew me off the third time, we had a heated exchange on the phone while I sat waiting in the parking lot of Home Depot off South Padre Island Drive. He made some threats, so I decided to post up at the house for the night, seeing if he would show up.

Sherry had a friend named Mercy, the chick was crazy as hell, and somehow Sherry dumped the broad off on me and Bella at the house. All night we waited; cars passed while we smoked bowl after bowl in the driveway. I never carried a pistol; I was a sitting duck. There is nothing like waiting for a drive-by shooting to happen at your dad's house with a baby inside the crib. Your heart races as every passing car rolls by. The higher the three of us got, the crazier the whole scene felt.

Once inside, Mercy went off on a tangent. She was an excommunicated preacher from a tiny town outside of Corpus. She had an inappropriate relationship with an eighteen-year-old man that she mentored at her church, and they kicked her ass out the door. Not illegal, but in the church's eyes, she fucked up.

She was known to spout off when she got super-duper high, claiming that she was a healer. When she laid hands on people, she claimed to have supernatural healing powers from Jesus Christ himself. A charismatic gift from God to entice the nonbeliever onto the believer ship.

Mercy had us all holding hands in my bedroom, Bella was in shock. We were all so high, we went along with this impromptu prayer service. She was good. Preaching like a pro. Asking the Father for protection. Praying that our enemies be diverted to other places far and away. A strange wind blew in my room that night. A feeling that we were not alone, a movement of the Spirit that one cannot fully put into words.

Afterwards, a calm air contained any worry that we had about an attack from Noel. We stayed up, smoking and cleaning the house, using the drugs as a ceremonial opening to spiritual gates of the unknown.

Noel never showed up. In fact, I would not see or hear from him for an awfully long time. We drove Mercy home the next day. She was bisexual nowadays; the drug twisting her morals and sexual tastes. I saw her looking at Bell like a T-bone steak. Mercy sat in the backseat as Bella drove; sitting forward she said, "You got the body of a Black girl," in an Ebonics twang. After we dropped her off, Bella and I laughed so hard we almost pissed our pants. We said that line almost every day moving forward using that same accent. A funny impression that was always good for a chuckle.

All in all, something very spiritual took place that night. The feeling in the air remained in the house for quite some time. As twisted mentally as Mercy was, she brought good with her. The Lord was with her in a big way, and I could feel it.

#

This is around the time shit started getting real...and real strange. There weren't as many weird people coming over the house the past few months since Bell had moved in. She just wasn't having that shit. She was the woman of the house and what she said went. She hated the group of cannibalistic crazies I was hanging out with when we met. So, I toned the partying down to keep her happy. Well, at least the guests; I was still using as hard as ever. Her, more so than ever. I was rubbing off on her in bad ways.

Three in the morning was a strange time in my house. This time is known as "The Witching Hour." The time of the devil. Bella's friends started saying strange things were happening. People were saying they were seeing and hearing unexplainable things. I thought they were all just way too high and wrote off the alleged happenings as a byproduct of too many drugs and too little sleep. Certain people would come over to party a couple of nights, never to return, citing that "the place was haunted."

There was a touch of evil in the air. The place was damaged, broken, and hurt, just as its inhabitants were. Spirits can attach to people, and for some time now, there were a lot of bad souls ferrying in and out of that house. A stop on the underground railroad of the meth world. At some point, a gate was opened to the spiritual realm. A point of no return had been reached with no going back.

In Corpus Christi, Santa Muerte, the Saint of Death, has a huge following in the Mexican drug culture. She is a skeleton wearing a black cloak with a hood. She looks like the grim reaper.

In trap houses where black mass and bruja take place, people pray to life-size statues of her likeness. A lot of the people I knew during this period were praying to her. A Satanic figure said to make deals with her children, their souls in exchange for wealth and status. Maybe this had something to do with the evil spirits finding their way under the cracks of the door. A false idol, a hater of God, being worshiped by the very people that employed me.

#

Chevelle was an associate of Bella's. She was a short thick Mexican in her mid-thirties. She had long, pin-straight, jet black hair and big jade eyes. She looked like an Asian madam. She wore jeans and high dollar tennis shoes. A straight gangster bitch, Corpus Christi, stone to the bone. I was introduced by Bella, and Chevelle and I struck up a partnership. Little did I know she was among the most feared female figures in this city.

  I met her for the first time at her mama's crib, a modest single-story home in an undisclosed part of town. She was silent at first. We sat and got high, and she began to open a bit. Cunning and calculating, Chevelle was the type to observe the newcomer. Sizing you up, checking your temperature, and weeding out the possibility that you were working with the cops. I respected that, so I played along.

  After talking a while, I realized we were there so Bella could give Chevelle a massage; Chevelle stripped off her shirt, and Bell took off almost all her clothes. Only then did Bella begin to rub down the deadly beauty with essential oils. I sat high as a kite in a chair in the corner of Chevelle's bedroom. A black light lit the room in a dark blue illumination that gave this kinky scene a draw of hedonistic allure.

  I was excited, but more jealous than anything. The massage ended and we started to heavily use drugs. Now, I had been around quite a bit, but there were still some things I had yet to see. The three of us sat around for a minute, then Chevelle broke out a mirrored tray and a fresh pipe.

  "You wanna do a hot rail?" she asked stirringly.

  I was puzzled, but quickly let her know I was down. Chevelle took a massive pile of shards and laid it on the reflective glass of the tray. Without a care in the world, she dumped over an eight-ball, icicles bouncing, some clinging to the glass. By icicles I mean clear shards of rock candy that look like they were harvested from the landscape on Planet Krypton.

  As I watched intensely, this local Succubus held the bulb of the pipe between her pointer finger and thumb, stem pointing out. A soldering torch was in her other hand. Her long, perfectly manicured fingernails were painted neon-slime green with white French tips. The massage oil was glowing on her coconut flesh, smelling of the tropics. She clicked down the ignition on the high-powered butane powered torch.

An electric blue flame shot out in a sharp thin beam, coming to a point at the end. The swirling gas burning at an intensely high heat sounded like a commercial toilet bowl flushing at a low frequency. Bella crushed the shards into a fine substance and then lined them up into massive rails on the mirror with a straight razor.

Chevelle placed the inferno onto the stem of the pizzle. The heat hit the glass and forked into a hissing orange explosion. She shifted the flame from top to bottom, heating the stem until it was white hot and glowing red at the mouthpiece. The pipe had a small hole in the bulb to allow for airflow.

She placed it to her nostril as she ran the mouthpiece of the stem across the mirror, allowing for intake of the drug in reverse, thus shoveling the methamphetamine inside the stem. As the icy powder touched the roasting hot pipe, the drug vaporized into a hot cloudy gas, and she was smoking the line up her nose. Chevelle exhaled out of her mouth, gagging out a mushroom cloud that engulfed the whole room, visions of Hiroshima projecting like a melted eight-millimeter film on the snow-white sheetrock behind.

Bella followed suit, staggering back as the cloud ravaged her lungs. When it was my turn, I looked at Chevelle and said, "Make mine the biggest you ever have seen."

"Suit yourself, White boy," she said as she doubled the dose in front of me.

There was over a half gram in this line. That's suicidal.

I snatched the torch from her as if I were a frat boy saying, "hold my beer," right before a stupid human trick. I depressed the ignition, the butane erupting like a Russian grenade. Gliding the stem with the molten jet stream, I held the hottest part of the flame as close as I could without shattering the glass. I wanted this thing as hot as the Great Lake of Fire.

You could hear the tiny shards climbing up the pipe as I took the hit. A faint sound of a lightbulb shattering down some ghastly hallway in an abandoned crack house. The smoke flashed mind-images of gas chamber showers in Nazi Germany, Zyklon B pouring out and into the lungs of women and children, unsuspecting and walking to their death.

My jaw seemed to detach and fold wide open, nearly breaking the hinge in my cheek. I felt as if I was mid-exorcism, a snarling demon climbing up my throat, slimy claws grabbing my face and pulling its thin starving body out of my mouth. The smoke billowed out of wounded air sacks, the ladies cackling like witches of Salem on a cold winter's night. The amazement that I had hit the whole pile blew their feeble minds.

I put one hand on the bed, seething from the inhalation of a lethal size hot rail. I was taken aback. Lightheaded, stupid, and entranced. This new way of smoking the drug was a feeling I had never experienced. I felt dumb to the point that all rational thought escaped my mind. I sat and stared into the nothing, a faint scream within, one of depression and enormity.

When the smoke cleared it was time for an interrogation. Chevelle sized me up in every way. Using jailhouse tactics and tricks of the game in devious ways, she was inquisitive in her dialogue. The drug also showed some of her weaknesses. She made an admission about her former driver. He was a friend turned lover that had some questionable activities.

She went on to confide in me, of all people, that this dude was on a ranch in the middle of East Bumfuck, Egypt, with a bunch of known gang members. The ATF, DEA, and Department of Homeland Security conducted a raid. Lots of people went to jail. It was all over the TV. She was extremely worried because this guy was allowed to walk away, even though he had outstanding warrants. This was a bad sign. He was most likely cooperating with one or more of these agencies. Some heavy shit to just lay on someone you just met, but it was clear that she trusted me.

We went home and I continued to drive the cab nonstop. Our drug habit had grown so enormous, so fast, that I was now starting to drive my personal car during the day again, as well. Clients from all over started popping up, including customers from my past.

#

Chevelle started to make regular appearances on Oakbrook. She was starting to call for rides almost daily. I loved driving for her. She was funny, she gassed up the Mitsubishi every time, and she paid me handsomely in some of the best quality crystal that The Sparkling City had to offer. She was shrouded in mystery. Bella made one thing clear to me when I started to do business with Chevelle. She was no joke. She could make one phone call and get you handled. Remember the plastic wrap and the abandoned trailer? Yea…one of those.

About a month after first meeting Chevelle, she approached me for a talk.

"Bosty Cakes, I want you to drive for me exclusively."

That's what she called me, "Bosty Cakes," not a venomous street name, but Bell called me Boston, so this fit. This proposal was shocking, as no one had ever put that on the table. I was making a decent "dying" from driving all these Cretins. I refuse to call it a living. But to only drive for one person may put a damper on my earnings tremendously.

"Look, I keep gas in that tank, cash in your pocket, and as much dope as you can smoke in the pipe. You got no reason to work for anyone else," she said with authority.

This was more of a direct order than it was a proposition. I really had no choice in the matter, but she liked me, so she let me think I had a say.

We started to ride. When I wasn't in that taxi, I was with Chevelle. I was to be on call 24/7. If I was in the cab, I would make it work. When I was off, I was on the clock for one of the most ruthless female criminals in the city. It was known that when the Queen Bee calls, you best pick up that cell. This was a drug hotline, and I was the wheels.

I got to know her fast. A unique perspective into one of the most interesting lives I have ever witnessed. Before, I knew the drug life and the way the game worked. I just didn't know the depths of sadness that lived in the hearts of these dealers. She was very secretive about who she was. Chevelle never told me who backed her, who her connections were, or where she got her large shipments from. Her shipments, at that time by my estimates, were so large that she didn't use a driver for a re-up. I can only imagine a drop-off of epic proportions. Some upper-level plug, the dead of night, a safe house tucked deep in the shadows of Corpus Christi.

Chevelle was a dangerous cocktail, sweet to the taste and deadly within. I saw her heart. There were many days where the two of us would leave Bell and the baby on Oakbrook and ride out into the apocalyptic sunset, never knowing our fate.

We met lots of unsavory addicts along the way. Chevelle was a strange cat, she would deal ounces, all the way down to dub sacks. She got a legit kick out of dealing drugs. The game was all she knew; this woman had never worked a regular job a day in her life. A straight hustler since thirteen, running a good size ice and coke operation from the time she was supposed to be in high school, she had never once cashed a paycheck from a legitimate employer. Real-life terrified her. The sweet wholesome things that we take for granted, scared her.

I watched her love life with great sadness. She was broken-hearted and alone, yet always surrounded by people, phone chiming like the dinner bell in a chow hall. A string of one-night stands and empty relationships gave her a sense of false hope. I got to see what no one else did. Vulnerabilities that would be viewed as a weakness in the game. These cracks in one's shell could get you robbed, killed, and stomped on by every rival dealer, gang member, and junkie on the street.

She had to be ruthless, feared, and respected. For me to roll with her was viewed as an honor on the streets. I saw jealousy and envy in the eyes of all we served. They wanted to know how this "nobody white boy" got to work directly with the Boss Mexican Bitch, enjoying all the fruits that came along with it. They knew the amount of drugs involved. Shards were nothing to Chevelle. It wasn't uncommon for her to make it rain glass in trap houses. Getting people high for free made her feel wanted and loved.

False friends and hangers-on made me sick. I was an employee; however, I felt a duty to protect her. I loved her in excess, too fast. I clocked these demons in their every move. They would stand around her cup, watching it overflow, salivating at the chance for a hit. She was far too generous.

We became real friends, close and trusting. It's strange, the relationship between a driver and a dealer, especially in an exclusive situation. You bond, you care, you see that these dealers are real people with hearts, souls, lives, and children. They become human, you start to see exactly where they came from and how they transformed into the hated figures they now portray.

Once again, there are rules to this shit, and you better not forget it. As much as our friendship bloomed behind the scenes, in front of others, while doing business, I had to play a specific role. She was scary. Anyone who bumped their gums to her learned real quick. She could dissect a person verbally, knowing every weakness, trait, and secret that would disarm and destroy them. I have seen full-grown, gun-packing gangsters shiver in her midst. Her legend didn't just emerge from falsehood. Her reputation came from hardcore drug dealing and heinous acts of random violence.

Occasionally, even if I didn't do anything wrong, she would slice me up in front of customers. She would be malicious and derogatory. Chevelle couldn't have people thinking we were equal in any way, shape, or form. It was imperative that she break me down from time to time. The street talks, it's a living breathing organism, a life form that whispers and speaks. You must feed it once in a while in order to cultivate and reap what you need to sow. She had to hurt me; it was a rule in the game of which she was far from a pawn.

Sinking back into my seat after such an event, I would remain silent and pouty. Chevelle would clap the passenger door and say something like, "I love ya, Bosty Cakes," as she threw an extra half-gram sack in my lap. Somehow, the dope made everything ok. I was a junkie and she knew it. She also knew that's what healed my wounds and comforted my broken heart. It was a form of love only an abuser would partake in. She would beat me hypothetically, then console me with a treat, almost like training a dog that you loved deeply.

Our relationship was ultra-complex. I knew she loved me as a friend and much more. She was a vixen. So beautiful and hood. She was a Kingpin princess that made me shutter in her very presence. My heart was with Bell. My loyalty and the life I always wanted was with Bell. But a special place was reserved just for Chevelle.

There was something I just couldn't put my finger on. Things would be fine while we were at work, but as soon as me, Chevelle, and Bell were in the same room, the dynamic changed tremendously. A deep jealousy was always in the air. Chevelle would lash out at both Bell and me in obnoxious and spiteful ways. I could see she was playing both sides. When Bella was not around, she would tell me things like, "If it wasn't for that baby, I wouldn't even fuck with her." Behind my back, I could feel that I was getting the same treatment.

I originally thought that she was secretly in love with me and hated seeing Bell and me together. I think that is true to an extent, but there was a whole other side to it, and I had no clue. Chevelle was bisexual. During this time, I would get 3 A.M. job calls to pick up cute Mexican strippers and escorts. I always made these bitches ride in the back seat like I was a chauffeur, even in my personal ride. This was a show of deep respect for my boss. I wouldn't even speak to these bag chasers. I wasn't trying to have them get the wrong idea and tell Chevelle that I was getting out-of-pocket with her hoes. She knew the way I did business, and she respected me for it.

Chevelle was totally mobile. She would target junkies and we would "trap" out of their crib. Moving around was a stealthy tactic that kept the cops guessing. When you were moving, the jakes didn't know where to set up surveillance. This would cause havoc for the person whose house we took over. The traffic was insufferable, the late-night partying had the neighbors thinking that Led Zeppelin was staying in the apartment upstairs. When citizens got restless, when the trapping became too much for the hood, we split. On to the next spot. Leaving the junkie a broke hardcore meth fiend, and in big trouble with the neighbors. All part of the game, heartless and uncaring.

There was one place that became legendary within our circle. There was a chubby White girl who lived at Willows Apartments, just a few minutes' drive from Oakbrook. Chevelle got this chick super strung out and made a move for a total takeover of this poor girl's apartment. The girl's grandpa paid her rent and her children stayed with some relatives, as she was a total mess. Chevelle got her own bedroom and would force anyone who was buying drugs or partying to stay chilling in the chubby girl's bedroom, right across the hall from Chevelle. There were too many drugs being stored in Chevelle's safe to allow free rein of the place to a bunch of junkies. Everyone had to be in one spot, always, to be held accountable.

This place was right next to the strip club and directly across from a gas station. It was a madhouse. Bella never hung out over there too much. She would much rather get high and stay at Oakbrook. It was far too dangerous of a situation to have the baby in. But what mattered is that Chevelle had a new trap house to do business in.

#

Bella and I started fighting relentlessly. I was obsessed with her, and I knew the feeling was less than mutual. She had this one younger friend that would come over. She was about twenty years old. A slinky little synthetic marijuana and ice addict that was also a crazy sex fiend. The chick hit on my father the first five minutes of meeting. Bella and her were best friends. Bella would get together with this girl and totally change on me. They would sit and make fun of me while I was in the room, whispering and carrying on. I hated them both during these moments.

I built a deep resentment towards Bella. Her little sister

was also evil at times. She hated seeing us living together. She was overly jealous. She had plans to cause major problems in our relationship. This was how I found out that my worst nightmare was true. One day, Brittany came over for a three-day bender. We were all up for far too long.

Brittany decided to tell me in front of everyone, "Yea, don't you know they used to call her Hotel Bell."

I sat confused. Her sister explained with laughter that Bella used to be a motel massage therapist who serviced rich older men for cash. Now I knew why she was well versed in a massage that always concluded with a sexual ending. She was a pro.

My heart fell onto the floor in a thousand pieces. I walked down the hall, leaving my audience, and wept as I smoked as much ice as I could fit into the pipe. This revelation was one that cut me in half. Debilitating, every breath I took from then on was laced with shame and regret. I was in love with a whore and there was no going back. This was also the start of an abusive rollercoaster that would prove to have destructive ramifications later.

It turns out that Bell had left the professional life sometime before, but she was still a honey catcher who had no problem sucking the life out of the men she seduced. She brilliantly played the good girl who was in a major drug addiction. She had already lost three children because of her ice habit. An incredibly sad soul who could never see a way out. She was trapped in a life that made her act in wicked and selfish ways. It does that to all of us. We lose who we really are and become something so dark and evil that we never dreamed it possible. It was how these bewitching women survived.

Pandora's box now open, I started to look for things that were unthinkable. I didn't trust Bell one bit from this point on and I started to open my eyes to exactly what our relationship was; at the same time, I closed my eyes just enough to continue in the relationship. An extremely twisted, drug-induced life that just wasn't dosed with reality. The whole thing was completely sick and codependent.

The fighting became violent. I would stay up working for a week straight, always playing catch up to fund this habit of ours. I would behave annoyingly and Bell had no problem telling me. She also had no problem punching me square in the face. I would be so tall on ice that I would talk nonstop about pointless and ridiculous things. She hated me; I could feel it. I would even say to her, "Bell, why are you with me? You don't even like me as a person." She would always say I was crazy and insecure. She was right on both fronts.

I hated myself. In my mind, I was still the three-hundred-and-eighty-pound revolting blob that couldn't look at himself in the mirror. How could a flawless creature like Bell love a massive pile of shit like me? My mind was warped by self-hatred and loathing. There were so many new failures and shameful acts stacking up in life that I just didn't want to be alive, more now than ever.

#

The argument started at dawn during dark morning. We had both been up for days. The stress of the drugs, no sleep, and huge risks were taking their toll on me. Some big weed dealers contacted Bella on Messenger and I happened to be snooping and found it.

"You're a fucking whore, worthless!" I screamed at her as I sat in my dad's office. I was an extremely angry man. Shamefully, I had begun to verbally abuse Bella. I sat on the expensive mahogany piano bench that matched my grandpa's pride and joy.

"I am a whore, Boston?" Bell said with wells of tears in her big, beautiful eyes.

I felt like half a man after a bullshit comment like that. She left the room pissed. I sat and lit the pipe, exhaling a massive cloud into the air. She returned as the buzz of the ice was still fresh in my cranium.

The room was dark, the large computer desk behind me riddled with drug paraphernalia and empty meth baggies. Just feet away, my dad was getting ready for work with his bedroom door open. Bell had a jump rope in her hand with big hard plastic handles and a black plastic rope that connected the two ends.

"You wanna run your fuckin' mouth, man?" Belle said in an aggressive tone.

She stood above me like a nun about to correct a student. Her face was twisted and villainous. She raised her hand as a shadow hit the wall, that of a killer holding a butcher knife in a Hollywood movie. I heard her grunt as she took a full swing, the business end of one of the handles cracking me on the side of my eye socket. My orbit started to swell immediately, blood streaming down my face, dripping onto the filthy beige carpet that was caked with dog hair. I sat with a blank stare, keeping my hands on the top of my thighs. She started whipping me with all her might. Bella was furious with the world, and me. I felt years of frustration and abuse leaking out of her. All the drugged-out boyfriends, the yelling, the sexual degradation she had endured, all being taken out on me, in this one explosive moment.

Bella had one man that she dated give her a third-degree burn on her soft little face with a red hot pizzle, punishment for using behind his back. These past scars were all elusive and buried, she'd had enough. When I called her a whore, the pot boiled over. I loved her so damn much. It was a sick and twisted love that consumed me. Here was the most beautiful creature I had ever seen, unleashing a therapeutic beating on me with a piece of workout equipment.

If this were what my Bell needed, I would let her punish me. If whipping me made her feel some sort of comfort or release, then I was willing to endure the abuse. I looked her in the eyes as she beat me for a good three minutes flat. That's a hell of a long time if you start your stopwatch. Especially if you're getting your ass whipped with a switch.

The lashes were getting further apart and weak. I didn't lose eye contact with her gorgeous brown peepers for one second as she unloaded her pain onto me. Bell, now panting and sweaty, lowered her hand and let out a grunted sigh. Her arms now at her side, still holding the jump rope, my Bella looked at me crying.

"Are you done, Bell?" I said morosely.

She started to sob and stormed into my bedroom. I heard the bed depress as the baby wailed in his Pack-N-Play.

I stood to my feet, head ringing from the contusions I had just received. I walked into the hallway bathroom and flipped on the light. There was a big mirror mounted there. The bathroom wallpaper was a bile yellow, peeling down in big strips. The floor was tiled, a white and green pattern, half scraped up from the flood my dad had caused. I felt like I was going to vomit. The toilet had not worked for a long time. I looked down to see a brown-caked film around the screws of the commode. The smell of urine and blood filled my sense of smell. Bell had never attempted to clean this room, no amount of drugs could motivate you for that job. I had my hands on the counter and looked up into my reflection. Rose-colored rivers poured from a deep gash in the outer corner of my eye socket.

Streaming down my face to my arm, blood rolled down till it splattered on to a vile floor of bare cement.

I threw up in the sink. Half clogged, I filled it with water to wash away the chunks of undigested candy and carrots. I knew I had a concussion; my eyes didn't look or feel right. The water sat standing high near the flood rim of the faux granite fixture. Big chunks of food and bile bubbled in the water above the center of the drain. I let it be as I lifted my blood-soaked t-shirt over my head. Deep lashes in my shoulders revealed valleys of blood. Canyons of pain riddled the milky-white flesh of my shoulders and back. Sore red skin was rising, feeling inflamed and on fire. I was a man broken physically, emotionally, and spiritually. All at the hands of my Bell.

I put the bloodied shirt back on and quietly walked into my bedroom. I changed the baby from his soaking diaper. This and an empty bottle were the source of his screams. I held and comforted him, feeding his empty belly until he fell fast asleep in his Pack-N-Play. I laid on the bed, spooning my girl from behind, holding her in my loving arms as she sobbed in silence. This was love in the game. We understood each other's pain. We forgave the insanity of our partner, knowing they would forgive ours. Only someone that has experienced this hell would understand, and for the nonaddict, this is what ice does to relationships.

#

Back at our new storefront, the chubby girl's trap at The Willows, things were jamming. Chevelle told me she had a busy afternoon ahead and wanted me to work all day. There were so many things going on that she felt better if I was with her even in between runs. The number of hot rails homegirl had started doing was unprecedented. Everyone's drug use around the squad started to get way out of hand. People were acting squirrely.

The first time I had met Chevelle, she made a scary admission while we were on the front porch of her house. She pointed up to the transformer on the light pole across the street and said, "You see up and over there, look near that box, that's where they'd put one of the cameras." She was talking about the police. She was saying that they had set up surveillance on her at one time.

We made some deliveries, ran errands, got as high as possible. You know, a typical Monday. Chevelle was dating a new man and I had to take him and his kid to a church service near Downtown. He was enormous, the largest cholo I had ever seen.

This dude was a reputed crack dealer and hustler from an exceptionally bad and well-known hood near City Hall. He and his boys were known for posting up in front of the traps, conducting business, and smashing on anyone who got in their way.

Coasting down the Crosstown Expressway, he spoke to me for the first time since we met. A man of very few words. He had the body of one who would compete in a Strong Man Competition. Over six feet tall, huge muscles, and donning a long beard and crew cut. Intimidation at its finest. His street name, which I won't even use a fake one, was that of fear and pain.

"Ya know, I hurt people for a living," he said in a serious and blunt manner. "If you ever need anything handled, you can pay me, I'll take care of it." He spoke these words with no expression.

A random and chilling offer, I guess he was trying to drum-up business. I was relieved when I dropped him off. There are some people so dark, you can feel the evil dripping off them.

A few days later, Chevelle went to collect. This little asshole named Juan tried to rip her off on a fronted eight ball, not paying her in the agreed timeframe. He ran a well-known trap near Del Mar College. Some jobs she wouldn't use me for. If there was a major crime being committed or some gang shit that I had no part of, she would use one of her other homeboys. She didn't want to involve me in anything real serious, outside of the drug dealing.

So she took her boyfriend as the muscle. Out of the two, she was more feared. They went up to the red wooden front door of Juan's trap. A single-story house with white vinyl siding. A single tree with a hangman's branch that stuck straight out, lots of vegetation. They "kicked door", shattering the frame where its deadbolt once clung for dear life.

Chevelle went inside and had a chat with Juan. She took what he owed her, plus the rest of his dope, and a pair of Gucci frames that he loved dearly. Chevelle was so feared, that this known drug-dealing gangbanger, a known associate of a violent Mexican street gang in Corpus Christi, could do absolutely nothing about it. She kicked homeboy's door, took all his shit, and wore his damn seven hundred dollar Gucci's out of his house and all over town. No one said boo. She was a bad bitch.

Chevelle had guns. She wouldn't pack them though until it was time to use them. When there was a threat or beef in the mix, the Queen Bee had the steel. She liked her nine-millimeter best. Chick was a thug. And here she was, rolling with Bosty Cakes. I just didn't fit in. I could see if I were a crash dummy or someone she was using, but I got paid big. I couldn't even add up the dope she was paying me if I tried.

#

This is when shit changed. This is when the whole friendship and arrangement started to crumble. It took a while, there were peaks and valleys, but this was the beginning of the end. God's Plan. Thank you, Jesus for protecting me through this next part.

You guys remember the fuzz watching from the light pole? Well, they were back, we just didn't know it yet. See, Bella was a very paranoid girl. Rightly so, she smoked mounds of dope, and the men she had been bedding down with since a young age were some serious gangsters. When she was seventeen, she was dating a fifty-five-year-old man, a shot-caller in a major crime organization. She was used to looking over those sexy shoulders of hers. She was quiet, always observing her surroundings, soaking up the bullshit around her.

My Bell was obsessed with CI's and snitches. I thought she was spun out and talking out of her ass. Truth be told, homegirl knew her shit. She had spent so much time pillow-talking with criminals, hanging in traps and motels, she had the skinny on everyone in the game. Some of her paranoia was drug induced, but most of her knowledge was real. She could smell it on people.

She hated me around anyone in the criminal element. Bell never wanted me hanging out at chubby girl's pad. Mostly because of the train of unknowns running in and out of there. She would tell me things like, "Boston you're gonna get in big trouble doing this shit." Knowing full well that if I didn't, she would be history, as that is how I scored for her, getting the quantities of meth she had grown accustomed to. Her concern was a strange mix of sincerity and lies.

One night I was at the chubby girl's place. Chevelle was no longer dating the massive cholo but had another boytoy she was banging. He was chilling in the secondary bedroom. Sitting across from him, the fool had a huge bulge on his ankle under his jeans.

"Hey, what's with the beeper?" I asked him.

He had an ankle monitor on and it was after dark. Normally I would mind my business, but after nine that night, this kid could bring the heat down on our trap. Those things are made in Israel, precision with the GPS. When you go out of your front yard, it alerts the police, beaming your location to the station, and they come to pick you up.

"Don't worry, homeboy," he retorted.

He smiled and lifted his pant leg, revealing the monitor covered in aluminum foil. Dude had found a way to trick the satellite system.

He told me that if you put foil on at a certain time, the signal gets bounced back and reads that your home, also blocking future signals from detecting that you left home. Brilliant criminal minds fill the Corpus streets. If they only used half that bullshit for good, then they would be millionaires.

The vibe was a little too strange for me, so I took off. I was in the cab and decided to go work with some regular customers to get my money right. I had to earn. I needed some things dope couldn't get me, such as diapers, smokes, and a few other things. Hours went by, I was downtown and now had a pocketful of bread. I got a frantic call from Chevelle, she was with someone on South Padre Island Drive and got a flat tire in the parking lot of a mattress store. I was on my way, just like that. Whenever she called, I dropped whatever it was and I went.

Pulling up, there was something way off. I was in a minivan that night. I slid in and parked under the sign of the store. Chevelle was there, the tire was in mid-change by a strange guy in a flashy car.

"Hey, you ok?" I questioned from the driver's side window.

"Yea, Bosty Cakes, we got this," she said.

She was laughing it up with the dude, not paying much attention to me, who just drove across town to help her ass, so I got a little heated.

"Yea, call me when you got a paying job, huh?" I said with an attitude. The van's tires peeled out of the parking lot, and I headed for Oakbrook.

The next day I got a call from Chevelle that she was coming over with a friend. I never asked her questions, but for her to come over to my house with someone new was out of the ordinary. They pulled up about thirty minutes later.

She entered the front hall of Oakbrook first, her fat frumpy friend in tow. He had a purple hair color. He wore a black wrestling t-shirt with holes in it, jean shorts, and cheap Walmart tennis shoes. It was the same guy who was changing the tire from the night before, only this time he looked much, much different. This time he wasn't in a forty-thousand-dollar Dodge Charger and he looked like shit.

Chevelle went right into the kitchen and set a bag on the counter near the stovetop.

"Bosty, is there anyone home? I got a treat for you!" Chevelle exclaimed.

"Nah, there ain't anyone home, what kind of treat?" I snorted back.

She proceeded to pull out a sandwich bag full of White-girl! Bella hated it when I fucked with any drug besides ice. I was already crazy enough; she didn't need me on anything more than my drug of choice.

"This is my new friend, Mario," Chevelle said with a

smile.

I reluctantly shook his hand. I didn't like the homeboy. He had this cheap dangly earring in his left ear. Between that, the purple highlights, the fact he was forty-seven years old and one hundred fifty pounds overweight, he also looked like he was in full makeup for a TV show. Something about him was totally ingenuine.

"He's gonna cook some shit, Bosty. Mario knows how to cook crack. This shit is as puro as it gets," Chevelle said with total confidence.

Chevelle took out a digital scale from the bag. She weighed out one perfect gram of some strange looking cocaine. Scaly and bright, it shined like a star in the Montana night sky. The shit twinkled. I'd heard stories of fish scale before but had never seen it in real life. Something like this is cut directly off the key in Peru.

"Wanna do some hot rails, Patty?" Chevelle smiled.

"Yea, some big mother fuckers. I wanna die today," I returned like fire on a battlefield.

Mario took the shit, some baking soda, and a pot, and went to work. Chevelle laid out some massive lines of crystal on an octagon-shaped tray with a clear plastic pane as its bottom. It was see-through, like a window.

On a separate plate, she formed out fat gaggers of the magic coke she had brought with her. Using a razor, she straightened the lines and cut a plastic straw. Out came the soldering torch. She filled it with a cheap yellow can of butane fuel. She stuck the nozzle in the bottom of the torch and with a "thunk" the gas started to fill the tank within the handle.

As the pot on the stove boiled, he swirled a small mason jar with the wintery mix inside. His eyes wide and wanting, the mark of a true junkie. I hated him more with every second. He was a crack addict. You could see that in his eyes as he cooked. What was Chevelle doing with this shit bag? This was way out of character for her. She heated the stem. The hot rails burst into the air, filling the room with a thick yellow smoke you could barely see through. It was my turn. Right away, as soon as I was done with mine, I dipped down and blasted the coke. I couldn't breathe; I felt like there was something wrong with me. I stood still for a minute thinking I had just overdosed. The mix of the two drugs was enthralling, a stimulant cocktail of epic proportions. Soon as I could move, I moseyed on over to the stovetop to watch Mario finish the cook.

      He scraped the rock out of the bottom of the cooking jar with ease. They were placed on the tray that was to sit on top of the digital scale. Chevelle hit the power and it read at absolute zero. She placed the tray on the scale, and it read exactly one gram.

      "What the fuck is that shit?" I asked in horror. I couldn't believe my eyes. I watched the pre-cooked weight of the coke; it was one gram. Now totally pure, it weighed the same. The coke this bitch had brought to my house was one hundred percent pure.

      "Chevelle, where the fuck did you get this shit? It's pure, nobody gets pure coke." I asked.

      "Don't worry about it, Bosty," she said in a strange, yet almost sad voice.

      Mario couldn't wait to smoke some. She had promised him the product of the cook, a bone to the little doggy for his job well done. She was going to have him cook the rest of the product in the sandwich bag, selling the hard for a big profit.

      He bumped his ass over to the bathroom inside the laundry room. Apparently, he didn't feel right hitting his crack pipe in front of anyone. He had taken a dime worth to roast, not a large rock by my standards. I heard the lighter flick, followed by a crackling hissing sound. The smoke blew through the door jamb that leads back to the kitchen. He emerged with his eyes wide, looking twisted and more awake than humanly possible. The guy was a shit show, peeping out my kitchen window, acting like a tweak box. I wanted him to get out of my house in a big way. My poor fathers house!

I was coked-up and out of my mind from the line I snorted, but you know damn well I was hitting that crack pipe. I had to try it. After all, they used my stove to cook it.

"Gimme that fuckin' pipe, man," I barked at Mario.

He reluctantly handed over his piece. I snapped off a good size twenty rock, double what he smoked. I was already zooming from the powder and the hot rails, but I hit that thing like Ike hit Tina.

Soon as I exhaled, Bell came around the corner. I lowered the crack pipe to my side in shame, as the blast coated the fluid surrounding my brain matter. I was speechless.

"You're an idiot," she said angrily.

I handed the dolt back his burnt-up pipe and felt my mouth go numb. That's never happened before, a hit so pure it made my lips undetectable to the touch.

I told them they needed to bounce. There was an eerie feel in the room. Where did Chevelle get that coke? Who was this homeless-looking crackhead that she just met out of the blue to help her change a tire at random? All this left a bad and very numb taste in my mouth…no pun intended.

#

Things started to pick up. Chevelle was as paranoid as she was busy. Her ironclad rule that I only work for her was in effect more so now than ever. She was getting very mysterious and leery of outsiders suddenly. Everyone was a potential snitch. But she trusted me back from the first time I ever had her in my car.

There were five of us in the little tuna can flying down Holly Road in Corpus. We approached the stoplight at Ayers Street near the freeway. The light was green. However, I knew that light well from being a cabbie. I was doing the speed limit as we approached the crosswalk. The light turned yellow, and I pumped the brakes hard to the floor. Tires screeched.

"What the fuck is wrong with you, pinche guerro?" Chevelle said with murder in her eyes.

We had over an ounce of ice on us, that's some serious time. Especially for her, who had already been to prison twice. At a complete stop, I raised my hand with a pointed index finger to the intersection just across the road, without saying a word. She glanced her eyes, and right there were two of Corpus Christi's finest in a black and white SUV.

"Good eye, Bosty Cakes," she said in relief.

See, that light turned yellow to red in the bat of an eye. Chevelle had seen this during my halt, and knew if I had run that light, we would have all been in orange in the Downtown county jail. That was our first delivery ever. That is why she trusted my skills.

My job was to watch our six, look in the mirrors at all times, and see the things that no one else could see. I had to be clairvoyant in my hustle. Always looking into the future, Zoltar of the open road, an iced-out Miss Cleo. They depended on me, in freedom, in horror, in hell. I was a safe passage for the lost and downtrodden junkie dealer. I was the way home.

#

We started noticing tails everywhere we went.

At first, it was Bell and me, rolling around and seeing white cars that seemed to follow us everywhere. With methamphetamines, you must discern fact from fiction. The drug plays tricks on the mind and makes you see and hear crazy things, especially after long bouts of insomnia and hardcore use. I blew her off, "Bell, your outta there; you're high chick," I said. I paid her paranoia no mind, Bella was always talking about the Fed's, CI's, and snitches. But sometimes the crazy person is telling the truth. Eventually, even I was starting to see that we were being followed. It worried me in the back of my mind.

One night, the Channel Six News did a puff piece on this new Jeep that the Corpus Christi Police Drug Task Force had purchased. It was "murdered out;" that's when the car has black paint, black rims, smoked-out headlights, all-black everything. This Jeep was equipped with all kinds of surveillance gizmos and other bells and whistles. It could even hear you if you were in proximity.

They showcased this new weapon on live TV for every criminal and wheelman to see. I couldn't figure out why they would show-out this Jeep that was supposed to be there to build cases on people involved with the drug trade in our city.

We woke up to what Bell was saying. I made Chevelle aware of the spooky things we were seeing, such as the white cars and strange vehicles driving by my dad's house. She was not wanting to hear it. There was something bubbling below the surface of it all that left me very uneasy. We had a good size drop to do on Leopard Street. We came around the beltway doing about eighty miles an hour. I was slipping and trying to get off the road with the shipment as soon as possible.

A very dark feeling hit me, spiritual in nature. I had Chevelle in shotgun and two others sitting in the back. Everyone but me had lit smokes and the music was loud. I glanced in my driver's mirror and saw a black blob screaming up from behind us at ninety miles per hour.

"Everybody clip those smokes. We got company," I said with authority.

I turned the music off and eased back down to the speed limit without trying to seem too obvious. My heart began to beat out of my chest, high as a kite, watching the emergence of a perfectly clear image of an all-black Jeep lurking up beside us. We sat still, no one even took a breath, hands ten and two on the wheel, everyone wearing a belt.

The Jeep pulled right alongside the Mitsubishi, stomping on its brakes to match its placement with ours on the road. The windows so tinted that they looked like onyx mirrors. There was no way you could see through. That's illegal in Texas, by the way.

That detail, along with some other very distinct markings that I had seen on TV the evening before, revealed that this was, without a doubt, the Drug Task Force in their newest ride. The vehicle steered alongside us for what seemed like an eternity. You could feel the eyes of a detective burning through the pitch-black glass and into my skull. Just then the Jeep's driver hit the gas and darted past us, right through the red light at the end of the off-ramp on Leopard Street.

"Ok, we're good," I said panting.

They knew who we were, they wanted us to know who they were. They wanted us paranoid and tripping out so they could catch us slipping. We dropped the drugs and I pulled into the next gas station.

"What the fuck is going on Chevelle? This is some 'French Connection' shit. Is there something you need to tell me?"

She replies, "No Bosty, your outta there bro, chill the fuck out."

She was blowing my admission off with a quickness. We drove home in silence. I dropped the crew off at her house and headed for Oakbrook.

#

Some nights were magical, no fighting, gazing at the stars in the picnic spot under the tree. I held love in my arms as silence gripped the night. I enjoyed watching the movement in her eyes as she looked to the moon, gripping the cosmic things with her thoughts. She was beautiful. A street-strong sassy mamma, captivating and special. Her problems were overshadowed by my stupidity. She didn't love me, not the way I wanted her to, but I'd take her any way I could get her.

The little boy was looking at me as his dad. The bond I fostered with this child was heartfelt and amazing in every way. I still made no recollections of my own children, but in my warped mind, I was becoming a family with Bella. We were junkies and acted as such. There were drugs at my dad's house nonstop, around the clock. All the cash I had was going to baby supplies and smokes, everything else was dope. Bella had food stamps and the bills at the house were paid. I estimated the dope tab was almost four thousand dollars a month at this point. A tough nut to crack every month, for sure.

We were no kind of parents. The baby cried a lot, he got yelled at often by certain people, and things were too chaotic to be raising a little boy within our home. I was constantly getting into fights with Bell for smoking meth in front of the child. I feared that if anything were to happen and Child Protective Services were dispatched, they would drug test the baby and he would be torn from our arms.

That's what the reality is of being a parent in the ice game. A constant threat of losing one's children. The danger, the dope, and the malnutrition. I've seen starving kids with dirty diapers. I have seen abuse, rancid conditions, and worse. I would have never let that happen to him. I couldn't. Chevelle wouldn't have it, either. She was friends with Bell only for the baby. She loved the little boy like it was her own child. When we started to have disagreements in front of the baby, Chevelle approached me to have Bell sign some lawyer's drawn-up papers to take the rights away from Bella.

I was furious. *Who did this bitch think she was?* At the end of the day, we couldn't take care of him properly. However, neither could Chevelle. She had more money, sure. However, she was doing thirty hot rails by lunch every day. She was as big of a mess as anyone.

#

All this time, I was still making deliveries with Chevelle. We would have anywhere from one to nine ounces of ice on us sometimes. I knew we were being followed, and Chevelle was now a believer herself. I don't know what happened on her off time, but she had come to the realization that something shitty was going on. Nevertheless, this next event happened without Chevelle in the vehicle.

Bella and I were in the Mitsubishi. The white cars were following us again. This time, Bell was armed with a pad and paper.

"Boston, they are following us, man," Bell said in fear.

"Come on Bell, this is bullshit," I barked back.

She wrote down a plate number while we were on the southside of town, not far from Oakbrook. About an hour later, we were parked at McDonald's on Leopard Street, all the way across Corpus. She pointed at a white Ford Focus. The same exact car we had spotted earlier. I'll be damned! The plate numbers matched.

Bell shouts, "See Boston, I told you, man! They're onto

us, we gotta get back to the house."

We knew someone was doing something shady. Either one of us were, or a person we had been selling to. No matter how you sliced it, we knew the cops were watching. What were we supposed to do? Stop working? Stop using? Hell no. That was laughable, there was no way we could stop. "I Always Feel Like" by TRU was in constant rotation as we drove during this time period. This was Master P's ode to being watched by the police.

We were mocking the Drug Task Force, letting them know that we knew we were under surveillance. Just like in the movies, I used my savvy driving skills to lose tails, including parking garage run-throughs. I felt like Joe Pesci in "Casino" when the Feds were clocking him. I was high and out of my mind. But the cops are not to be played with. Our arrogance was a twisted way to deal with the stress of what was going on.

I was very scared during this time of my life. I was in way over my head and things were not looking like they were going to change on their own. The cab was a refuge. Things seemed like they stopped when I was in the taxi. Bella was drawing more distant all the time. Something was going on behind the scenes.

Chevelle was having Bell over for massages all the time, and Bell was coming back with large amounts of dope. I would risk my life in prison doing jobs all day and make less than Bella did for a thirty-minute massage. In my heart, I knew what was going on, I just didn't want to believe it.

One night, while across from the chubby girl's trap house, I sat in my taxi alone at the gas station. In between calls with nothing to do, I sat people watching through the huge plate-glass windows of the convenience store.

There were a lot of stories about the Drug Task Force

on the street. There were tales of a very tall agent who looked like a pro-football player. A no-holds hardcore dude who turned ice heads into confidential informants like pimps turned out sixteen-year-old runaways.

I peered in at the table inside. Mostly people ate cheap gas station hot dogs and chicken legs there during their lunch breaks. Today there were three men in business casual attire. Black slacks, Polo golf shirts, and shiny black dress shoes. All normal, except for the fat homeless guy in a "Stone Cold" Austin t-shirt breaking bread with them. I observe things, after all I was going to be a cop when I was nineteen, remember?

The three professional-looking men got up and left the table first. The fat guy fell back and waited till they exited the store. As they flung the glass door to the gas station open, I was shocked to see brass badges hanging from their belt loops. On the other side, Glocks. These guys were cops, one of which was the top narcotics officer in our city looking like an overworked Terry Bradshaw.

I pulled out my phone and snapped some photos of the three men getting into a smoke-grey Dodge Caliber. They pulled out and went on their way. Then it happened. That fat homeless guy? It turns out it was that bag of shit, Mario. The same guy Chevelle met at random when she had a flat tire. The same dude who was cooking a batch of already pure mystery cocaine at my crib. He came out front looking around like he was waiting to get smoked, head zipping from side to side as he puffed half of a cigarette he found in the community ashtray.

I snapped a clear, undeniable photo of the prick. I made sure it was clear as day and then I rolled down my window.

"Hey, you bag of shit! Hey Mario!" I shouted.

"Oh, hey bro, what's up," he said, acting like I didn't just insult him.

"Hey man, I know what time it is bro, and I am telling Chevelle. Watch your back."

I was angry. I knew that he was a snitch, and I could prove it. Chevelle wasn't in on it. You could feel it in the air. The only thing she was guilty of was being off-guard and letting someone in the camp that she shouldn't have trusted.

Mario looked petrified. He was busted. He tried telling me he was there panhandling for a beer to drink. Where was his fancy Dodge Charger that he was in when he met Chevelle that first night when she had the flat? His story didn't match up. Never mind I had photos of him having a snack with three of the top narcotics agents in the Corpus Christi Drug Task Force. There was no way he could talk his way out of this one. I sent the photos to Chevelle and called her right away. I scheduled a sit-down in person, so we didn't discuss this event over the telephone.

At first Chevelle lashed out at me, but quickly thanked me for the heads-up. I was just about done with this shit. The heat around this broad was like a brick oven and I wasn't trying to be a deep dish by no means. I needed to think of how I was going to reestablish myself with old clients, and fast. One thing was for certain. With Bella in the balance, my dope earnings couldn't hit one hiccup or she was history. I couldn't lose her. One sided or not, I loved her. Or so I thought at the time.

#

Days went by, the tails were still there. I was avoiding Chevelle as much as possible due to the huge risks that were involved. Bella refused to stop doing the massages. Her side hustle was far too lucrative. I accused her of having a relationship with Chevelle and she went crazy on me. She told me I was high and paranoid, the whole nine. She was gaslighting me. Making me feel like I was the one who was out of line, even though all the signs were there that she was the one stepping out on the relationship.

One night, Chevelle called me for a very odd job. She wanted me to drive four hours to Austin with her sister to go pick up her kids. She was to pay for all the gas and road expenses, as well as give me an eight ball of dope. This was an ice-free ride, no risks, and at the time, I needed the dope bad. I was to go to her house, drop Bella and the baby off, pick up Chevelle's sister, and hit the road.

We took off at about one in the morning. The sister and I chatted small talk. I got the feeling that Chevelle pulled some jailhouse tweaker shit on me by having her sister flirt with me. I don't know why people pull stuff like that in the game, but they do. She wanted to see how faithful I really was to Bella. That's why she supplied the five humongous hot rails to me before we departed. On the way up, we were making small talk when the sister made a stunning admission.

"What, you don't know they fuck round?" She said with a grin. "Everybody knows that son, you living under a rock?"

I couldn't believe my ears. I wanted to kick her out, turn around, go back to the house and kill them both. It was then that it dawned on me that my best friend, my boss, was having an affair with my girlfriend. That's what the sister said anyway. Why would she lie?

This whole trip was set up so they could have time alone. Around this time, I was watching Bella like a hawk. I was already limiting her to where she could go and how much time she could spend with Chevelle. I was heartbroken. I played it cool for the rest of the trip and returned by dawn. I collected my dope from Chevelle, and we went back to Oakbrook to have one of the most horrific fights of our relationship.

I knew in my heart what was going on. The rumors that

other guys were smoking her out while I was at work, the foreign baggies with markings from strange dealers. I knew she was cheating on me and just never wanted to see it. All the risks, the way I loved her unconditionally, it all meant nothing to her. My soul was shattered. In the middle of this sick fight we had, I was smoking the Quag. I packed over a gram in the bowl, and I was taking hit after hit without stopping. I was trying to overdose in front of her.

"Boston. What are you doing?" she said with concern.

Then she motioned for me to let her hit it. We took massive hits, going toe to toe, in this twisted grudge match, trying to purposely have a couple of heart attacks from the drug. We screamed and there were punches thrown, by her as usual.

I went to the office and sat with the pipe, reloading another full gram inside. Chevelle screamed up the driveway and got out of a strange, borrowed car. Bella had called her and told her I was beating on her, a ploy to get picked up and taken to dope town for a vacation. I stormed outside, holding the water pipe in my hand, in full view of all my neighbors.

"You are fucking dike bitch! I should kill you for being with her!" I screamed at Chevelle with murder in my eyes.

We had a heated exchange. Lots of denials, finger-pointing, and accusations. I am so blessed that neither one of us had a firearm during this event.

Right or wrong, this was a shockingly dumb move on my part. Chevelle could make one phone call and I would be handled. She was a dangerously jealous and angry person. Factor all those hot rails in there and we are looking at a powder keg that would blow the roof off this mother.

They got in the car and left. This was Bella's famous trademark. If she wanted to leave, she picks a fight, then three days later, she returns. "Boston, can me and the baby come inside," she would say with a bashful face. She knew I was weak. I absolutely could not say no to her. This started to happen all the time. Chevelle wasn't the only one she would go to. There was someone different every time. She would come home, lie to my face, and I would promptly let her back in, knowing damn well she was sleeping with another man for drugs the whole time. I loved her unconditionally, remember? That means no conditions. Pure love where no matter what my Bell did, she could always come home to my loving arms. Some call it sick and they are correct.

#

About a week later at my dad's house, after Bella had already come home, and after watching quite a few strange vehicles passing by, Bell pointed out that there was a van outside, just sitting on the grass near the road. I had been up smoking all night. Wearing my boxers and a wife-beater, I marched outside with rage in my eyes. I was stopped dead in my tracks, cold fear poured over my whole being. It was a van that read "ACME PLUMBING" with no phone number on the side. In Texas, that's illegal, unless of course, you're the cops.

"Hey man, who are you guys?" I shouted.

I was fed up with the surveillance and the unknowns of who these people were that were following us. As soon as I was about to pound on the windows, two strange-looking men looked up and left tire marks as they peeled away.

This was the final straw. I couldn't do it anymore. This was my exit from Chevelle and all that came with working for her. I was done in a big way. The last thing I needed was to be implicated in a major dope case and be charged with participating in organized crime. That will put you away for quite some time.

I called the boss and cut ties. Just like that, it was over. I took my foot off the gas and did the bare minimum, just enough to keep us high. Just enough so my love wouldn't walk right out the door. I was on thin ice, in more ways than one. The following weeks were filled with guilt trips and insults. I couldn't provide like I used to. I was scared to my core by the heat that was on us, and I wasn't going to risk it, not even for her. Soon as I quit driving for Chevelle, the tails, the heat, everything went away. Bell kept talking to her, even as my feud with Chevelle ignited. When she would come over to hang with Bella or drop off dope, she was exceptionally aggressive and sassy. We began to fully hate one another. I told Bell at one point that Chevelle was no longer allowed over; any meetings after that were done behind my back.

#

I was in the cab like a madman, driving regular paying jobs and doing whatever quiet hustles I could just to keep the pipe full. That's when the calls personally asking for me started to come into dispatch. It was a crazy white boy who was requesting me for a lift. This was the second time I had driven for this guy. The first time was on my very first day of work for this company, and I had noticed the camera cutting on when he entered my cab. I rolled up to the location, he opened the door, and sure enough, the camera started rolling right when his ass hit the seat. I was worried but wasn't quite sure if I had reason to be.

I stayed silent and kept moving. I wasn't involved with his deals. We didn't speak in the taxi; he only requested me so he could pay me in dope. Then it happened. Five nights later, I picked him up once again. This was trip number three. Just as the last time had happened, his ass hit the vinyl…say cheese, homeboy.

I was panic-stricken. The first time, you don't count, the second is a coincidence, the third time that camera rolled, well that is a pattern. I was street smart; I knew what time it was. This had nothing to do with me. They were watching him. This cab company was rumored to work with the police. I was merely a tool to drive, no knowledge of what was taking place behind the scenes.

When the ride was over, I went off camera to collect payment and had a warning for "White Boy." I told him, "Hey bro, every time you get in this taxi, they start rolling candid camera, three times now. They are watching you, bro. Don't take this company anymore, no matter what."

He looked kind of puzzled and concerned. He heeded my warning and never took the company again. I am sure it sparked suspicion in him about me. True blue though, I had his back, I gave him a big heads-up. That was the last time I drove for him in any way, shape, or form. The game was getting crazy.

#

I loved Bell with all my heart. But our relationship was crumbling by the minute, and my soul was dying. It was August 24th, 2017, Hurricane Harvey evacuation day. The massive storm loomed over the Gulf of Mexico, headed right for The Body of Christ, Texas. The feeling was frantic in the meth world. Everyone scrambled to score anything they could before the bold winds blew The Sparkling City over like a house of cards.

Barry was going to ride out the storm at the house. Bella, the baby, and me were going to head to her family's cabin north of San Antonio. Fleeing seemed like the only option at the time. This storm was enormous, and they were expecting destruction. The whole city was leaving in droves. The storm approached so fast and made a turn at the last minute that only allowed hours for us to get out of town. So, we searched for dope.

White Boy was an easy option. He picked up my call and we made an appointment for him to serve us. No clue what we were about to walk into, we headed over to the familiar address to score an eight ball. As we pulled up, I thought it was a joke. A string of cars ran a mile long on the quiet suburban street where his trap existed. All waiting to be served like drunks at a fast-food drive-thru after the bars closed.

Cars that were fancy and hooptie alike sat and waited with drooping faces. Zombies patiently awaiting a feast of brains as they pouted and snarled in their rearview mirrors. The White Boy wasn't "curb serving." He was making everyone go in the trap, one by one, to obtain the fiery shards that he exhumed from a hole in the wall of his bedroom closet.

I sat in the Mitsubishi and counted seventeen cars and trucks waiting to buy drugs on this particularly strange day. The cops were far too busy for our dope games during the evacuation. The arrogance and flamboyance in which White Boy was serving was a straight slap in the face to all who observed. A group of neighbors gathered on the front lawn right across the street from the front door of the trap. Three White men and one terribly angry Black senior citizen gentleman. They stood, arms folded, looks of resentment on frightened faces as they watched one of the biggest illegal ice operations in the city flourish just feet from their homes. The old Black man, wearing an aged scally cap, shook his head in disgust as people funneled in and out carrying large quantities of methamphetamines. You could tell they had already complained to the cops, and nothing was being done. I will never forget that look of helpless-laced rage as long as I live.

We waited for what seemed like forever, then I was

called into the house by some degenerate ice head who worked as a lookout. I ran in and out as fast as I could. Remember, we had the baby with us. A true junkie move; shame was a constant part of our life.

We followed her family to the cabin in a caravan. I had been up for a week, and I was falling asleep at the wheel the whole six hours it took to get up there. At one point, I was going so slow, Bell's uncle stopped for gas and accused me of being high. Obviously, he was right. I felt like trash as he lectured me. Associating with Bell was to be guilty, as far as her family was concerned. She had burned them since she was a young girl. The lying and, the cheating had taken its toll on already strained family ties. We were junkies, and they knew it. It was the saddest thing I had ever seen, the lack of trust for my Bell. The whole family scorned, they spoke to her in nasty and spiteful tones. The effects of her then seven-year hardcore meth addiction ruined her within her own bloodline.

We were crammed into a two-story cabin in the middle of the woods. The second floor was an attic space with a low roof where most of the twelve people we traveled with laid pallets on the floor as bedding. The ceiling was made of naked plywood with pointed ends of nails showering through. Large cedar beams stood in the middle of the room acting as braces for support. They created a hardship of obstacles as we lurched in and out of bed. There was a smell of must and mold from unused air that sat stagnant for too long, as no one had been there.

At breakfast, we descended a wooden ladder to the first floor. Thick wood planks and more plywood gave the room a feeling of a "do it yourself" project, amateur in nature. There were men, women, and children crammed in like sardines. Close quarters gave Bell and I little space to hide our ominous addiction. Bell cleaned like a sexy Cinderella as her cousins and Aunts sat on their backsides. She was a servant, paying penance for her life of sin she inflicted on everyone. I sat back and watched her take passive-aggressive verbal abuse from the whole family. At certain flashpoints, I wanted to kill every one of them with the broom handle. That was my girl, junkie or not, and I truly hated how they treated her. They all watched from the ratty old couch that sat up against the one conjoined wall. There was a tiny bathroom off to the other side of the wall which she also cleaned.

The storm hit on August 26, 2017. We didn't have cell service, so we listened to radio news reports about the mayhem taking place in our beloved home city. The tall pines swayed above the cabin, the ground a mulched earth of deep brown, sandy, and filled with dead needles of seasons past. The crisp air of virgin woods filled strained lungs. For the first time in a long time, I felt peace. I wasn't hustling or performing illegal activities. I wasn't looking over my shoulder, waiting for the law to snatch me up and put me in chains. It was calm during a great storm.

We snuck to the mildewed attic where there wasn't a soul present. We fired up the potent meth we scored from White Boy back in Corpus. We blew the smoke into a toilet paper roll filled with dryer sheets. This was to mask any chemical smell, as well as hide the clouds bursting into the atmosphere. This had to happen. We couldn't abstain from using, I was getting visibly ill from the lack thereof.

It was a shameful walk back downstairs, high and guilty. We were morose. The night crept in like the stormy gusty wind that rippled within the aging pines. The family let me man the grill, an honor in the Mexican culture. I think this time it was just that nobody else felt like cooking. I was a bumbling fool to these people, gawky and loaded.

    The time away from Corpus made Bell sweet and motherly. She held my hand in the Mitsubishi after dinner. Everyone sat around the fire as we laid up in the car with the front seats back. Secretly toking away until the midnight hour struck. Bell signaled me to get out and follow her down the slanted, curvy path to the riverbed. The trees blew with hurricane-force winds as we glided arm in arm into the pitch of the forest.

    Bell's hair, fine and flowing, along with her white wife-beater, daisy dukes, and chanclas on her sexy tattooed feet made her a certified Latina fox. We had sunk into the valley at the bottom of a great hill. We had found a hardtop path that was paved by the wildlife department. There were magnificent trees standing a mile high above, stumps as wide as pastures. Gargantuan root systems exploded out of the bronze earth, a witchy feel as shadows danced in cumbia.

    Bell stood under a colossal pine, a tree so big it looked as if it were transplanted from the Redwoods in California. Under starlight, I gazed into brown eyes, her face angelic and smooth. I touched her cheek gently as the wind entangled her with a soft essence. Her head tilted down, shy and meek, her soul bled into mine as I kissed her. My hands ran down her sides, touching thick tan legs, intense kisses of the French persuasion swept us both into romantic places of folly. The woods engulfed us. Two lovers enchanted in the freedoms of nature, life but a dream from which we shall never wake.

    Croaking frogs and the rushing sound of a deep stream exhaled us into the night sky. An arrangement of worship that only God could compose. Fireflies sparkled as Bell's clothes slipped to the surface of the summer earth. The heat between two lovers ignited a passionate reaction. A sultry cadence of two hearts beating in the August wind. I melted as I loved her with every fiber of my energy. Biting her neck, Mexican pastry that melted like cotton candy in a carnival of lust.

The breasts of the goddess cascaded upon the pale white flesh of my chest. My threads were now torn off and discarded onto the bank of the mighty river. I became a snarling beast as I laid the cocoa skin of her back upon the earths floor. The pain of the stone piercing her skin made her moan in subservience.

She lay in wait, heart racing as penetration created soul ties that neither of us had ever experienced. Like virgin creatures, roaming fields of uncharted planetary dominance. She gasped as control wreaked havoc on her femininity. A once-mighty deity, now just a concave girl lost, one controlled by reverence for her master.

The cloud cover above lit up with natural electricity. A strange grey light raining down on us as I invaded her senses. On top of her, I looked down, only to see her truths through her iris. Loving eyes throwing a hex, as if a Haitian priestess to a sacrificial lamb. The transfer of the dominant and submissive roles exchanging between us during that very moment. The trees of the forest stood as pillars, watching the lovers as they wound in their sexual drive. A séance that conjured spirits from another dimension. An unseen world now breaking through all courses of space and time.

Embracing Bell, her moans echoing against the bedrock, flowing river sounds crackling in the distance. I lifted her up and forced her back against a tree stump. Lifting her legs with strong arms, reentrance splattering surprise all over her face. The storm swirled in a cyclonic motion.

The scene set, a lone wolf howls at a lunar ball burning above, our love finishing before the end of his cry. We collapsed to the forest floor, broken and distressed. Bell's heart beating out of her chest plate and onto mine. I loved this woman more than life itself. Holding her in my arms, all her iniquity floated away like a paper boat down a storm drain. All the cheating, the lies, as if it never happened. For the moment anyway. We walked back up to the cabin, drenched in the evidence of love and sweat.

The next morning, we packed for departure. One last walk to the river revealed the motion sensor cameras we made love in front of. Perched up in the trees, there they sat. Daylight shedding truth onto the watching eyes of whoever sat behind the monitor, in some far-off office of the Wildlife department. A happening we laughed about for a long time.

#

Upon our return home, we found Oakbrook intact with Barry lounging with the dogs, watching Matlock on TV. One of his favorites. Port Aransas was completely washed away. The old house I once lived in with my wife and kids floated down the street. The cab company was calling, dying for drivers. Off I went, back to the grind in those dirty Corpus streets. No sleep for the wicked.

I arrived at the cab stand and found sheer panic. There were a million calls stacked and customers had been waiting hours to be picked up. There was money to be made and I wanted every cent I could get.

The Crown Victoria's tires rolled along like pinwheels, onyx and gleaming. The city was a dark shell of what it once was. Residual rain bands clipped our town, making the dirty windshield almost impossible to see out of.

Crime was alive and well as the rest of the city remained safely in their homes. Power outages and pandemonium ruled, causing an apocalyptic appearance everywhere I drove. The end times had come to Corpus Christi, Texas. The days and weeks following Harvey looked very much like the city had fallen. The damage to Corpus proper was not that bad. Towns like Rockport, Port Aransas, Ingleside, Aransas Pass, and others were suffering from total devastation. When a natural disaster occurs, one thing is for sure, the criminal element will take full advantage of the chaos.

FEMA stepped right in and began offering assistance to the displaced. A huge chunk of government funds was released to those in need. The jackals roamed in packs. Every booster, identity thief, and dope dealer in proximity came out to play in the rain. The local motels were now taking government vouchers. A food stamp for housing, basically, that assisted the displaced by giving them free lodging. Every junkie loser in Corpus Christi signed up and defrauded the US Government for every red cent they could get.

#

I was working around the clock doing hotel pickups for hookers and dope dealers, fiends and hustlers. It was as ugly as it gets. That's where I met Mimi. She was taller than me. Her hair was platinum blonde and down to her ass. She was thick and sassy, a trailer park diva from Flour Bluff who sold ice all day, every day. I was angry at Bell, and for the first time ever, left her at Oakbrook to go smoke ice in a motel room. Flour Bluff's raunchiest. Here is the story of how I met Mimi.

I had got sucked into a check cashing deal earlier on this day. I cashed some questionable checks into my account for some tweaker that I had met while on a job. I was desperate for the drugs, and I went ahead and did it while knowing full well the repercussions. I didn't care. I had reached a crash dummy status. The sad part was, I knew I was a crash dummy and did the suicide mission anyway.

I scored a quarter ounce of shards and headed to the cheap motel. You pull into the parking lot, and the one-story brick structure was an L shape. Rotted shingles on the roof, frosted-over windows, filthy and streaked. Drunks and Mexican construction workers from out of town sat drinking tallboys and smoking Marlboro Lights while shirtless. Hookers strutted around in bicycle shorts and t-shirts with holes in them, covered in sores. The place was hell on earth. Flour Bluff's version of Leopard Street. It's the last stop on the train to hell.

I went to meet Scott, a full-blown heroin junkie. He begged me for a place to hang out and party. I obliged, as I thought he was funny. I was angry once he arrived because I soon realized I wasn't going to be able to get rid of him in order to smoke meth naked while watching porn. I had bought a nice glass water bong at a gas station. They sell meth pipes in corner stores all over our great city. I started smoking like a complete nutcase. I burned through two grams of fire in two hours.

We were super-duper spun. Scott said he knew this girl down the way named Mimi. He called and invited her over. The room had cream walls with gaping punch holes in them from past domestic disturbances. The floor was a grey stained carpet, matted with dropped whiskey and semen.

The queen size bed had a green and red floral bedspread, the type that felt like sandpaper and fleas when you had it over you. A musty smelling dinge filled the air in the devil's condo. The bathroom was tiny with a pink shower that had standing water and human hair in the drain, giving it the feel that Satan had vomited Pepto Bismol all over the place.

Mimi walks in. "Hey y'all, you guys' smoking?" was the first words out of her mouth. The tall blonde's hair was flowing, oily and thick. Her gaudy gold jewelry made her look cheap. She had on black tights and yes...a maternity shirt. The broad was eight months pregnant! Like nothing, she walked up, and I handed her the glass meth water bong. She ripped three consecutive clouds and put it on the cheap Seventies wood nightstand next to me.

"What is your name, handsome?" She gave a massive grin. Her sneer revealing a mouth full of chipped, black, and broken teeth.

We all talked and laughed for a while, and Mimi retired back to her room under the false promise she was to bring some "Bluff Rats" back for us to have sex with. A Bluff Rat is a female from Flour Bluff, one who is a glorified, ghetto-fabulous, trailer-park bag chaser. They will do just about any nasty sex act in the book if the pipe is smoking. I really didn't care either way since I never cheated on Bella no matter how angry I was at her.

They never showed. Scott was on the Jones for some tar. He looked like a clam with legs. Remember that cheap hot dog stand where I picked up the lady in the wheelchair? How could you forget, right? Well, we went to score some black tar smack from a Mexican dealer right quick and headed back to the motel.

Scott went down to Mimi's room for some fun at the expense of FEMA. I went back to my spot. This motel was a place of folklore. It was rumored that those holes in the walls were strategically placed peeps, equipped with small cameras that watched and recorded people doing drugs and having the kinkiest motel sex you can think of. There were rumors of this happening all over in the ice game. Later this would prove to be shockingly true.

Scott returned with some fresh needles. I wasn't into smack, nor did I like it. But this night I took a taste. I was extremely depressed over Bell, my sexual brokenness, and the drug use in general. I had him cook me up a decent shot, nothing I couldn't handle. I decided to "skin-pop." In the heroin world, that's when you don't put the needle in your vein, but a fleshy tissue like the tummy or shoulder. I shot the shit into my stomach. There is not a rush with a skin-pop. It's a slow-creeping burn. One where your pupil's pins close slowly and the death churns in your innards.

I sat in my chair watching porn. High on opiates and flying on crystal meth. Not quite nodding yet. But soon after, my eyes got exceedingly heavy. I woke up in the daylight hours. I was all alone in the room. My head was pounding as if I had been hit with a baby sledgehammer, like some Texas Chainsaw Massacre type stuff. There was no blood. Whatever was causing my pain was internal. All the dope and my bong were missing. I had put them on the back of a milk carton. Good as gone. I started to stagger around like a man in the throes of a stroke. Heart pounding in my temples, I vomited on the rug. Anger came over me. I walked to Mimi's room to look for Scott. I got to the room and confronted them both. My Texas ID, Cab ID, TWIC card. All of it was somewhere with the dope and bong in outer space by now.

"What the fuck did you do to me, man!" I shouted at Scott.

Mimi defended him and tried to convince me I just went to sleep naturally. I don't sleep, not even on smack. *Something was far off*, I surmised as I headed back to my room.

I knew they had drugged me. A homeless-looking man came to my room looking for dope. I let him in, as he looked eerily familiar. I sat back in the chair and listened.

"Man, you were fried last night," he choked out as he sipped a beer.

The man was an old scumbag. He wore a ratty knit cap

and had a beard that was soaked in drool. Mind-bending thoughts from the night before jarred me to my core. I was in horror as the memories started to play, as if I were seeing them for the very first time. I was in a closet with some girls and this bum who sat before me. I remember coming too and quickly standing up. My penis hard in a skinny looking Mexican woman's mouth. She had sores oozing a yellow greasy puss down her cheeks. She was naked and smelled like feet. I saw the bum with an equally grotesque fat woman getting relief from her hand just a foot away.

"Where the fuck were we last night, man?" I asked in a rage.

"We went to Robstown to score, you let me drive," he said.

I never, ever let anyone drive my ride. I was slipping. I was breaking cardinal rules that I had laid down soon as I got in the game. Robstown is a dreadful little place thirty minutes outside Corpus, run by smack and Mexican prison gangs. I asked him about the details of the sex party we attended. He explained that we were at a trap house scoring tar. We were in the closet because he let the two junkie hookers shoot up some of his dope. The girl I was with was sick for sure. Her bones were sticking out of her skin. She was at the late stage of some deadly disease that I didn't want to investigate.

I hopped into the Mitsubishi, and I was gone with the wind. Pulling into Oakbrook to have a fight with Bell. She was furious. My phone was off all night. I am surprised I returned with one at all. The car too, for that matter. She punched me in the face as I entered the hallway. My head instantly felt like it was a pumpkin exploding from the deer slug of a twelve gage Mossberg pump.

The baby was screaming. He had no diapers. The

bedlam of my life. It was all too much to take. I walked past Barry's bed. He stared at me and told me, "I am seriously worried about you, Boston." I just grunted and stepped over the dying dogs as I headed for the shower. Piping hot water was always a fix. The steam rose and fogged the bright yellow paint of the walls. The fake marble of my dad's shower was black and light gray. I stood under the heavy flow of cleanliness. The water burning my flesh to a lobster red. I sat and stared at my penis, scrubbing it with apricot foot scrub to dismantle the AIDS virus that surely lurked inside the tip.

After about an hour in the pressure cooker, I looked under the sink and pulled out a bottle of Isopropyl Alcohol. I doused my abused death stick in the burning flames of the liquid. As all junkies do, I came up with a sure-fire home remedy for a lethal risk I took the night before. Rubbing alcohol does not cure HIV. I never got the memo.

#

Back to work. We needed diapers, smokes and most importantly, ice. I told Bell I was going in and I would drop off some dope as soon as I made enough to score. Then I popped back in the door and said, "Oh yea, diapers too." She hated me. I hated me. I wanted to drive my car head on into an eighteen-wheeler on the highway. But I didn't have the guts.

An hour later, Chevelle called me furious, "You are fucking bag of shit junkie, you can't even get the baby diapers?"

She despised me, but she loved the baby and always came through. After all, she was secretly sleeping with Bella and would do anything for the little boy. Life was crashing down. I really, truly wanted to die. I was waiting for the massive heart attack to claim me in my sleep. But that would have been far too simple.

#

A week later, the cops called about the fraudulent checks I had cashed after the hurricane. They left me a voicemail telling me to come down to the station. I had to do something. Snitching is a foolish idea. You can get killed in a heartbeat. So, always quick on my feet, I called my bank and got a second chance loan. This is where I took full responsibility for the checks, to the tune of eight hundred and fifty bones. I did it without the law getting involved so that the bank would not press charges. The fuzz still wanted to question me about who I was with inside the bank.

Bobby the Fed Thomas was the scum of the earth. Corpus Christi's most notorious check casher, identity thief, and counterfeit money man. He was known to run with those pieces of trash, Leon and Tony. He was an average height dude. He dressed nicely and smiled like the devil himself. A real smooth-talking conman that could sell ice to an Eskimo...no pun intended. He had sandy hair, medium length, always combed perfectly.

When I met him, I had no clue who he was. After we cashed the checks, right before I bounced to the motel, we stopped by Oakbrook. He brought a big black duffel bag inside with him. We had the garage door open; it was around ten in the morning. There were about five of us smoking ice out there when Bella came to the doorway of the laundry room.

"Boston, what the fuck is Bobby the Fed Thomas doing here?" she questioned loudly.

Bell's comment was asked while she stared right into his eyes. A direct insult to him, a signal to go. She called me into the house and told me that the man I just cashed hot checks with was a well-known confidential informant. Not only to local cops, but you guessed it, the Federal Government. Bell knew him from the game. I got the feeling that she spent some time with this kid in a motel room, and after that, I wanted to kill him.

I stormed to the garage "We gotta go, bro!" I said this with force.

I looked down and he had a money printer, ink, and money paper. All the trimmings to print counterfeit US currency. I told him to pack it up right away.

Bella was furious. Standing there screaming "You see what your dope-fiend shit brings to our house!"

I tore out of the driveway in reverse. I had to drop him off. I just brought a notorious snitch to the crib. He had with him objects that would one hundred percent land us in Federal Prison, being questioned by the Secret Service. I had to get him out of there.

"Boston, what are you doing later?" asked the Fed. "If you come to pick us up , I will print ten grand for you. We're going to go to a bunch of strip clubs to drink, pass these bills, the mall, all that."

I fluffed him off by telling him I would return in a couple of hours. This was the guy the cops were preparing to question me about. He came inside my bank with me. He had insisted he come with me. It didn't fit. He knew he would be on camera.

I went in to face questioning. I had already taken out the loan, but the cops didn't know it yet. They started to show me pictures and ask how I knew the guy who passed me the checks. They alluded to the fact that Thomas was a known check thief.

He stole these checks from an eighty-year-old woman. He took twelve in all, clearing out her life savings. He had done it to multiple people this last run and the cops were looking to send him up the river.

What a scumbag. Ruining what's left of an eighty-year-old lady's life, all in the name of getting high. I hated cashers. I hated identity thieves, the scum of the earth. Always were, always will be. I told them I had taken a second chance loan from my bank, before I got into any kind of storytelling. I knew that they couldn't touch me at that point, as I had taken full responsibility. This was a multiple felony charge in Texas. The detective called the bank and verified.

Right before they let me go, one of the detectives asked me, "Bornagain, what do you do for a living?"

I answered, "I am a cab driver."

The two detectives looked at each other with a chilling surprised expression. They both faced forward, and the inquisitor asked me, "So you're the cab driver, huh?"

It was like they were in the know about something I wasn't. Like I had been spoken of behind closed doors. I was freaking out.

"You're free to go, Sir," a third detective said as he entered the room.

I was Swayze...ghost.

They had him dead bang, they told me all about it. They didn't even need my testimony, they just wanted to give me a look. It scared me half to death. The walls were really closing in on me. The driving, the criminal activity, all of it. If you are implicated in an organized crime case, all they must do is link three entities to form a conspiracy. A RICO charge is Federal and it's no joke. I wasn't trying to get into some John Gotti trouble over some shards.

I was wrestling with the idea of dropping out of the game one hundred percent. I felt an impending doom and evil all around. But the drugs had me paralyzed. I could no longer make the choice to quit. How else was I supposed to support an enormous habit the size of mine and Bell's?

#

God is real. This is the part of the story where things really start to get even crazier. Yes, it gets crazier than what you have read. What happens next is where you must decide what you believe in your heart. See, God will step in when you're going so fast that you can't pump the brakes yourself. I was clearly living a life with Satan. The drugs, the sex, the evil that surrounded the whole meth lifestyle, the occult, the pornography.

I was deeply broken and lost since I took that first drink back in Reading, Massachusetts. I was cursed with the spirits that afflicted me since before I was born. They came to light when I was a young boy and manifested loudly after that first joint on the train tracks, on that fateful and snowy afternoon. God saw me struggle for years with the demons, failing the twelve step programs. My whole life was a torture chamber. I just wasn't going to "get it." I was too dumb, too arrogant, and too unwilling. I was living in the fast lane, and I loved every second, while at the same time wanting to die. Death was the drug. I didn't care if I took my last breath in my sleep. That was the End Game anyhow. The ultimate objective since my wife left with my little angels.

I was staying up now in full week blocks, not drinking water sometimes for five days in a row. I was having episodes of great confusion. Losing my keys and throwing famous tantrums, screaming and yelling.

I was driving around the clock again in late September of 2017. One night, I found myself waking up as if I were slapped with a sandal in the back of the head, driving at eighty miles an hour and headed directly for the sharp turn onto the Harbor Bridge.

I woke up from a lethal sleep, saw the speedometer, and there I was heading directly into a wall. I slammed the brakes to the floor and took the ominous turn at over sixty miles an hour. Screeching tires and grinding metal noises, I almost defecated in my board shorts as I corrected my path and headed over the bridge. I pulled over off the North Beach exit and puked my guts out in a gas station parking lot. A near-fatal accident. *What in the world woke me up at the exact time that I needed to hit those brakes? Who was watching over me?*

About a week later, I was coming off shift. I found myself coming to, passed out behind the wheel of a taxi at the intersection of South Padre Island Drive and Weber Road at a red light. A very busy intersection. Commuters whizzed in front of my cab on their way to work at seven in the morning. My foot rested right on the brake pedal. One shift, one breath. or slip of the foot and I could have been in a major T-Bone accident. Once again, I lifted my weary head, checked my surroundings, and pulled away as if nothing had happened. In the times of cell phone cameras, no one sent in a picture to the Channel Six News? I was in the middle lane, fast asleep with cars on both sides and behind me, and no one even batted an eye. A taxi driver passed out would be front-page news for sure. Again, what was protecting me?

#

I had a sit-down dinner with Mimi in the Bluff about getting my ID's back. I knew she was in on it, but she swore she wasn't. She was an ice dealer. A pregnant one at that, and she was wanting me to do some side work with her. Bella was pissed about mine and Mimi's little date, as she called it. We sat down at a place that had a deck overlooking the flats on the bay. Mimi was really pregnant. The waiter looked shocked when she ordered a strong Long Island iced tea. He looked at her abdomen and she cut him off before he could say a thing, "I have a massive tumor, it's a medical condition. So, watch your mouth." He left to get the drinks and she smiled that seductive blacked-tooth grin, with the glee of a schoolgirl. She proceeded to have at least three strong Long Island's and started to pop bars, or two milligram Xanax pills that would knock out King Kong Bundy. She was a beast, partying for two.

I drove for her nonstop for a week straight. Dropping dub sacks of ice to the bottom of the barrel tweakers all over Corpus Christi. She was hanging out with some real dirtbags that always tagged along for the ride. I struck up a great friendship with Mimi at this time. She was the funniest girl I had ever met. A cut above a Bluff Rat, a real White gangster bitch. She would fight at the drop of a hat, even nine months pregnant. I thought she was going to drop that baby in my ride while we were trying to drop a sack. She was cutting it real close. I would always tell her, "Hey Mimi, you think it's time to retire?", as I pointed to her pudge. She was eating pills and smoking ice nonstop.

#

I was about to have sex with Bell late one night, around three a.m. She was sliding on some thigh-high patent leather "fuck me boots" when Mimi rang the Bat phone.

"Boston, I need you to come right now. I got kicked out, I got ice, I need a ride, like now!" She was frantic and shouting into the phone.

I told her to hold up, and then I went to the Bluff to scoop her up. Bella was pissed. I was almost out of dope, so the timing was perfect. Bella would shut up when I returned with a forty of shards.

I picked Mimi up; she was outside of some trap house yelling at this dealer over God knows what. She had so much luggage with her, I thought she was moving to Zimbabwe. I packed the trunk full of crap and we hit the road.

Now, I leave out a lot of nights in this book. There is no way I could fit in all the crazy times, memories, and sexual trysts. So, there are some aspects that I must explain. One of which is that when I would hit the bridge to go to North Beach, I would call Shorty every single time. He ran that part of town, and I would visit him every time I went, cab or not. However, remember Bell putting those boots on? Well, I was in a big hurry to get back home, so I skipped calling Shorty. We hit the bridge and made our descent into the back streets, and here is how the trilogy of death started.

Rolling up to the Days Inn, it was a humid Corpus night. The witching hour, three in the morning, not a beam of sun in the sky. The only thing close was the yellow and white neon hotel logo, burning bright on the sign above the Mitsubishi. The parking lot was plum full of cars, out-of-town workers, hookers. Everybody was either fast asleep or hiding. There was an electric feeling to the air. Not of doom, but the hairs on my head stood up like a cat in the presence of a dark spirit.

I popped the hatchback and lowered both back seats. I then started to unload Mimi's belongings. She had rented a third level room at the motel using a FEMA voucher. Mimi waited in the car as I went up to the room and dropped off all her stuff, since she was about to drop the placenta right there on the hardtop. After the final trip, Mimi made her way up to the room while I was to grab the last of the things and meet her when I was done. I turned around with one large duffel bag of clothes on my shoulder. Walking toward me, I saw a familiar face. It was Cara, Shorty's wife. She approached with a sour look on her face.

"Hey Cara, what's up?" I said with a big smile.

Cara just walked by, growling something I couldn't make out. I went on my merry way up to Mimi's room on the third floor. I didn't pay the sighting any mind, as Shorty lived three blocks away.

The building was three stories, white stucco with steel railings on all the breezeways. There were two matching exterior stairwells. There was a rectangular shape entryway one on each end, giving guests access to their floor without going into the lobby below. I hit the left exterior stairwell and climbed the mile-high structure until I reached my destination.

The motel room was clean, not a roach trap. It was a family joint, corporate and sanitary. There were maroon floral rugs and crisp beige curtains on the windows near the door. A flat-screen TV, a mini-fridge. This place might as well have been the Ritz compared to where I had been partying these days.

Mimi sat on one of two queen size beds, lighting a bowl, summoning the dark ones. The air in the room dropped to a cold, icy depth. All I could think about was getting home to my Bell, but a little nightcap wasn't going to hurt, would it?

The flames grew high, the pyre of souls danced between, there was a feeling of evil that I just could not shake. A turmoil of the unexplained, something looming in a dimension untouchable and unseen. My spirit was uneasy.

I bid Mimi farewell as I gripped the stone-cold handle of the motel door. We were done with the session, and I saw no need to prolong my trip. The air was a wall of water, typical humidity for a Corpus Christi night. My feet shuffled across the cream paint of the breezeway, staggering a bit as I got my bearings. I hit the exposed staircase, one hand on the steel railing as I made my descent.

Making it to the second floor, heading down, watching

my feet. A presence emerged. Heavy stomping and the sound of the steel rails clanging with vibration. I looked up and saw Shorty. He was wearing baggy jeans and a polo shirt. Short and menacing, Shorty had a devil's glare in his eyes that chilled me to the bone. I stopped dead in my tracks, frozen like a glass statue. My very breath halted as he accosted me in the dark October night.

    Shorty had his right hand in his jean pocket. He got within arm's reach of me, between the second and third floor. That staircase just became the loneliest place on earth. Slow-motion frames, I felt like Shorty and I were the only two people in the world. It was almost as if we had met on some belt of stars in deep outer space. Real fast, I realized this meeting was far from friendly. Shorty looked like I had never seen him before. His face twisted, contorted, and jaw jerking. His eyes wild as a rabid raccoon caught in a snare. He was growling and salivating buckets of spit.

    His foot stepped up onto the stair below mine, giving me no space for movement. He levitated to my height in just a fraction of time. His hand pulled out of his pocket. A glimmer of shiny chrome shot light into my eyes.

    As the pistol emerged, I saw thick bullet casings fly up into the air. It was a frame-by-frame playback, every flip and movement of the bullets shot fear inside until they clanged down the staircase below. Movement snapped into real-time. I felt the cold steel of a .357 magnum against my eyelid before I could make a move. Shorty took his thumb and propped it on top of the hammer. He cocked the firing pin back, a sound that ground into the back parts of my brain. The vibrations of the cylinder revolving bellowed in my heart. His hand was shivering like an alcoholic starved for a drink. I immediately recognized he was so high on ice, he may just splatter my brain matter out of the back of my skull by accident.

"Shorty, I don't know what I did man, but I didn't do it," I said with a cry.

An image of my youngest daughter, my baby, came into my mind. Her smiling face and pigtailed hair made me feel some sort of tranquility. A peace I was not expecting.

"Boston, you better not be fucking my wife! I'll smoke you Boston, I'll fucking do it, man!" Shorty screamed this while pushing his gun into my eyeball.

He meant business, far beyond that. I had never come face to face with the Spirit of Murder. Yes, the Spirit of Murder. An individual demon spirit that floats around looking for a weak tormented soul to infect. These spirits travel in gangs named Pride, Rebellion, Anger…Murder.

My right eyelid was glued shut by the shaking barrel of a loaded, cocked, hair-trigger .357 magnum. There is no feeling like that on earth. One flip of the finger, one false muscle movement by a demented and deranged man who was high on drugs, could have exploded thirty-five years of thought onto the white canvas below. Suicide was scary, but violence? When violence rears its head, it's a whole new type of death chamber. One that I didn't want any part of.

Just then, a miracle moment that I will remember until my last breath. A door flew open, a large shadow broke the plane of the flood lamp that illuminated the crime scene. An angel sent to spare me from a murderous death.

"Hey, what the fuck are you guys doing? It's four a.m.!"

It was a man on the second floor. Awoken by the tormented shouting of my attacker, he jawed something loose in Shorty that would save my life. Shorty dropped the hand cannon to his side and looked me directly in my eyes. The Spirit drained from his eyes like water in a bathtub. You could see the expression on his face change, shape and demeanor returning to normal. The hotel patron shook out whatever was inside Shorty. He returned to a normal man, my friend, in the blink of an eye.

"Go back inside, I am just looking for my wife," Shorty told him in a calm tone.

The awakened hotel guest slammed the cheap aluminum door.

"Boston, Cara is around here, man. You better not be fucking her!" Shorty exclaimed.

"Shorty, I think she is on the second floor. I was helping a client to her room on the third floor because she's knocked up." I retorted, speaking about Mimi.

"Ok, we'll see what time it is White boy," Shorty grumbled.

He took the gun and jabbed it in my ribs, now a little less threatening and thinking a tad more clearly. He marched me up to the third floor and we knocked on Mimi's door.

Shorty shouted through the motel window. Mimi saw the gun through the peephole and refused to open the door. Can you blame her? Shorty verified my reason for being at the Days Inn and lowered the gun.

"Why didn't you call me, motherfucker? You always call. When I saw your car here, I thought you were hiding something. She and I had a fight a few hours ago and she bounced on me."

Shorty was acting as if nothing out of the ordinary had taken place. The fact that he almost blasted my dome all over the floor at the Days Inn was not even a big deal.

I was high, drained, and shaking like a leaf in the wind. I could barely open the flimsy door on the toy Mitsubishi. I drove home in a shocked state, every breath felt like a gift, trotting down the freeway back to my Bell.

#

Things at home were not good. The next week was a cluster of arguments and a disappearance by Bella. My heart was breaking like Waterford Crystal in a storm drain, clanging down the grate on the avenue of broken dreams. I was falling off. Love was draining from the relationship, a sinking Titanic that was bound for the depths of the abyss below. This affected my hustle, creating an instant hardship. I was falling short every night. That only added more strain to the one-way love story that I was clinging to like a drowning man on a life preserver. The woman I loved was inching away from me minute by minute and there was nothing I could do.

The night with the gun to my eyeball was the night that sent shockwaves through everything I knew as reality. My faith, my mind, my whole life as I knew it was about to get switched up. You know what they say…in the blink of an eye. Well, mine was heavy, and when I woke, the world just wasn't the same. The next chapter is where it all changed…again. Another night for the books.

Chapter 6

Angels and Signs

It was exactly seven days from the night I had the cold chrome barrel of a .357 magnum pointed into my eye socket. I was a freight train bound for death, and I could have cared less. God will put situations in your life to slow you down. For this driver, it was all systems go, throttle wide open, the road to hell alone and forlorn. I was on a four-day bender. The bubbling quag and the blowtorch flames created a symphony. The dark spirits danced around me in the office on Oakbrook; a few quick wakeup blasts to get me in the mood for mayhem and I was off.

    I cut through the living room, where I spat some obscenities at Bella. Homegirl was getting lazy on me, and tonight was the night she was to clean the crib. She had been smoking a lot of weed these days. Most likely to numb the feelings she had about living with a man she loathed. I seeped into the old looking kitchen with glassy exhausted eyes. Something was different. I could run for a week with no sleep. I guess my lifestyle was catching up with me. That and the extreme emotional stress of the relationship falling to pieces. On the brink, I mustered up the courage to grab my keys and face another night in the terror dome that is Corpus Christi.

    The glassine baggy glimmered in sunlight that was gleaming through the kitchen blinds. A big dime nugget of bud sat within. Bella left her stash of hydroponic weed on the counter near the microwave as she sat playing with the baby in the next room. Stoned, and not caring if I fell off the face of the earth, she didn't see me grab the broccoli as I stuffed it in my white ankle-high sock.

I headed to the Mitsubishi, a man on a mission. A thirty of glass sat in the pack of Marlboros nestled in my cab bag. I was almost dry, so panic hit me like Tyson on a third-rate bum. I had to find some ice right away. All my connects were out of product. It happens like that sometimes. A period where every scumbag in town would be hard up for a hit and all the dealers would be waiting for a new batch to come in. This should tell us that one main source supplied the whole underbelly of the city. Pretty scary thinking all the dope is controlled by a select few.

The cab stand was jammed packed. Seemed like every cabbie in town was out to make some serious paper. It was seven p.m., and the start of the shift was sunny and bright. I stood at the counter waiting; the mouthy overweight Mexican girl who dispatched all the calls threw me the keys to a Crown Vic. I loved this car. It took off like a bullet and turned on a dime. I felt like a cop in some action-packed movie every time I drove her. I did my preflight inspection, and I was headed Downtown.

It was a balmy October night in the Year of Our Lord 2017. As the sun drained into the Corpus skyline, I sat making frantic calls to every drug dealer and hooker in town. I was coming up empty. The place was as dry as a ninety-year-old nun during Lent. I couldn't find ice if I was an Eskimo.

The shiny paint on my cab was festive and glowing. The interior was the intense dark version of navy-blue leather that you typically find in cop cars. The original lining where one of Texas' finest once sat and drove, taking handcuffed bad guys like me off to jail. I thought of a place that I might could score some ice off the street. I hadn't been to this spot in an awfully long time. I had to use my nose to score, and what better venue than the inside of my cab. I needed to hit the hood and make this happen. Daddy got to eat, and I knew just the place to start looking.

Mary Street was the most well-known hooking track for street walkers in the city. Mesquite trees lined a trash-filled two-way where middle-aged married men came to cruise for ten-dollar head and drugs. A plethora of toothless hags in halter tops and filthy fake leather boots strewn the sidewalks covered in dope-laced sweat. The smell of black tar heroin and strawberry body spray from the dollar store wafted the city air like a putrid perfume. I was right at home.

I began picking up flags. I was purposely looking for people who needed rides as they walked down the sweltering hot hardtop tainted with sin. I was desperate, all sense of brains left me as my one-track mind led me full speed down "Dope Street." I picked up a skanky Mexican prostitute in her fifties. Her smile was jagged. She was accompanied by a non-English speaking Mexican national who wreaked of Steel Reserve and tobacco.

"Where's the cold at?" I barked with no fear.

She smiled that black-toothed grin at me and cackled. "Well, Weto, we can swing by my homeboy's house and ask him if he is holding," she snarled in a broken accent.

She was wearing a pair of black stretch capris and a rainbow-colored top that only covered her small, but perky, breasts. She was clearly not wearing a bra. Her nipples stood erect from the air blasting out of the vents in the old cop car, turned street chariot.

The wrinkles of her sun-damaged skin told the stories of ten million packs of Virginia Slims and countless sexual assaults from her time on the streets. Her hair was a reddish-brown mix of cheap hair dye that she most likely shoplifted from the local grocery store. She had big, matted bangs to her eyes, her hair-do so tall it almost hit the roof lining of the taxi. She looked like a Mexican Peggy Bundy. A distraught voodoo doll with black-tar-laced puncture wounds that ran clear up her boney aging forearms. The look of disease and dismay made my stomach turn sour as a green apple Four Loko.

"Hey, I gotta handle this business, Weto. My homeboy charges me twenty dollars for the room. If I give you an extra ten, can we do it really quick in here?"

She wanted to get this guy off right here in the cab. She was a prospect to score, so regardless of the camera, I pulled into the back of an abandoned convenience store in the middle of the barrio and threw it in park. The Mexican national had this dumb bewildered look on his face as we sat in wait. She muttered something in Spanish as she started rifling through her maroon velvet purse. He took a small bag of what appeared to be coke out of his shirt pocket. He had to be thirty years old. A migrant worker, drunk in some little bar in the hood and looking to get his rocks off. He did a couple blasts off a dingy key as his jelly balls rolled in the back of his head.

He dropped his pants, exposing a pathetic-sized Vienna sausage. Whether it was the coke, the booze, or Mother Nature playing a joke on him, I will never know. Abuela slid a ratty-looking Trojan on him and started giving him the first part of the half-and-half he had ordered. She was charging him forty dollars for the works.

His sweaty hand made an imprint on her hair as she slurped on him. The gagging sex-fueled noises that came from my back seat aroused me. I was revolted with myself for where my meth addiction had taken me in life. Once again, the taxi was providing live porn for my viewing pleasure. She moaned and snapped her eyes up at him, croaked out some more Tex-Mex Spanish that I couldn't make out. She sat back and peeled her putrid capris to the floorboard, the elastic sticking to her slimy skin; hours of walking will do that to a girl. She sat on top of his manhood, riding him. Her skin from her buttocks hung down in drapes. Whatever sickness she had looked to be shedding pounds off her like she had Richard Simmons as a personal trainer.

The novelty of the strange sex wore off as soon as the musty, pungent smell of her tainted vagina filled the cab like a can of tear gas. Again, I would have stopped her, but she could be the connect I needed for the ice; nothing was going to come between me and getting high. Speedy Gonzalez let out a gargling sigh and it was all over. They both got dressed as I punched in the address to the trap house she was headed to in my phone's GPS.

We pulled up, she paid me for the ride and the ten extra dollars for the unconventional sex I provided shelter for. After this business was settled, she went in to see if they had what I needed. Moments later, she emerged empty handed, trying to sell me some brown or hard rock cocaine.

I politely declined and was back to square one. I inched off the curb, devastated and disgusted. I just watched a couple of elderly farm animals have full-blown sexual intercourse in my back seat for nothing.

By the time I hit Mary Street, it was a dead zone. Not a hooker was stirring...not even a mouse. The smell of the broad's innards reminded me of some sort of grotesque Thanksgiving dinner thrown by the family in the Texas Chainsaw Massacre. It was making me to feel nauseous, so I pulled over to buy one of those green Christmas tree air fresheners and Lysol to spray away her fluids from my seats.

After I cleaned up, two shady looking Black guys approached me for a ride to a local strip club off Staples Street. The whole way there, they were talking right out in the open about drugs, and I didn't stop them. I asked one of them for some ice and he whipped out a pouch full of black tar.

"Hey white boy, I got that brown that will make your head spin like a top."

The two mutants slapped five and giggled like two conspicuous busybody schoolgirls. Disappointed again, I dropped the pair off thinking that our whole exchange was caught on full audiovisual. *How could I be this stupid? I never acted like this in the office.*

I waddled into a McDonalds parking lot just up the street when an interesting looking Mexican kid in his twenties flagged me down.

"I need a ride to Kostoryz," he said.

"Hop in, homeboy," I said with a smile.

I could smell the ice on him. Surely my luck was about to change. It took me all of three minutes on our trek to the southside to ask him where the meth was at.

"I don't got any on me, homeboy," he said. "My friend got some off of Staples on the south, I can hook y'all up."

This was odd, and even more risky. But this is where my addiction had taken me. Scoring from strange street dwellers in my taxi...on camera.

He made a phone call to his connect and set up the deal. I was to meet him in a couple of hours at a gas station right off the highway. I killed some time having coffee. I picked up some southside calls and posted back up within arm's reach of this deal that was to take place. At around eleven o'clock, my eyes were like lead balloons. A dense fog rolled in like a cloud of thick pea soup that formed a wall of clouds, overlying with the deep darkness of the night made it impossible to see three feet off the windshield. I was fading fast, but I couldn't dip into the last of the meth I had in case the exchange didn't happen. I would need enough to get me and Bella through the night till someone familiar could drop off a much larger payload.

    I planned on scoring and flying to Oakbrook to beam up on my midnight lunch break. I had placed an order for a teener. A teener is one and three quarters of a gram. Plenty to get us through the night if the product was halfway decent. So, at eleven thirty, in the rolling clouds that set just off the hardtop, I drifted into the unknown. It could have been a setup, a stickup, the cops, or it could go as planned. The latter was my hope. So, I hit that gas.

    I passed Kostoryz on South Padre Island Drive shortly after. The feeder road sat just below to my passenger side. I started drifting into sleep. The distorted wail of a car horn woke me from a dead sleep. I jerked the wheel just in time to correctly reenter my lane. I came inches from sideswiping a little blue Ford. The driver was so close, I could clearly see their teeth and grimacing face as they flailed their hands in the air. I gave a half-hearted wave as they gave me the bird.

    I continued the path to the deal, shaking my head back and forth to stay awake. One eye closed, I squinted in true Mr. Magoo fashion. I sped over the exit on Weber Road. I was two exits from the buy; I had to keep going. Thoughts of pulling over and doing the rest of the ice ran through my mind. *Nah, I can make it, I got this.* Famous last words.

    Another car horn snapped me from slumber, another angry driver swearing their head off as the fog shielded them from my identity. I doubt my license plates or cab number were even visible. I was now passing Everhart Road; one more exit and I am home free.

A catastrophic smashing noise woke me up for the third and final time that night. My eyes glanced down at the speedometer as I realized I was airborne. Both hands clenched the old steering wheel, white knuckles locked around the vinyl ripples where fingers gripped. I was mid-air, going seventy miles per hour. I had jumped a massive curbstone, sending me flying over the feeder road to my right. I locked up the brakes before the lumpy, unaired rubber of my tires even hit the ground.

Life went into that ever so familiar frame-by-frame slow-motion film that I had experienced exactly one week prior when I had a .357 magnum squished into my eyeball. I hit the dividing strip of grass on the highway. The cab slid slightly sideways, fishtailing like a barracuda heading for its prey. The deflated wheels hit the asphalt, locked like a chastity belt on the king's daughter. A slow roaring screech and plumes of thick black rubbery smoke puffed up around the cab as I stared down a huge concrete sign reminiscent of a mighty Redwood tree. Its white neon light glowed like the bulb of a lighthouse guiding me to my final resting place.

I stared directly at the column; this is when time stood still. I had three flashes; three very clear, long thoughts that will be with me forever. The first flash hit, and the frame froze. I saw my little one again. A different pose, this time it was of her great big smile when she was just a wee baby. I saw the big hoop earring's mamma put on her as she wore daddy's black wool knit cap. Her massive smile and big chestnut eyes, her soft Mexican Irish skin, her gentle glow. This all soaked into my mind.

I felt an overpouring of love, the feeling of family and pure happiness returned for the first time since I lost them long ago, before I abandoned them and fell apart. There was no guilt or shame. It was calm, warm, and inviting.

The second flash was much more vulgar and abrupt. I had one thought as the cab zapped just a touch closer to the massive structure. *Oh shit, that's concrete.* I could literally hear my own voice in my head. The car was now skidding in micro frames toward the curb and giant sign that loomed in the wall of fog. It was this moment of awareness that I knew exactly what I was about to be pinned to. I could smell the rainy musk of death coming off the paint and through the air vents. I was inhaling the grainy, sand-like texture of the pole my head was about to be catapulted into.

The third flash?

Well, that one was where I accepted my death. Millions of memories and short movies burst into my mind like the Fourth of July fireworks. I saw myself as a young boy playing in the yard with my ma, back in Reading, Massachusetts. I saw all my friends, the laughter, the good times. I saw my career in Port Aransas. I saw Bella and the baby. And finally, I saw Barry on the golf course smiling at me as I hit my most famous shot ever at Brentwood Country Club in Keene, NH.

He talked about that one for years. I had the overwhelming feeling of forgiveness as I got right with Jesus. I had lived enough for ten men. I was ready to go home. As short as my life had been, I was ready to die. The relief that embodied this experience was like an elephant standing up and then off my chest. Losing my family killed who I once was. It was here when I realized my pain from losing them truly was the reason for the suicide solution I was looking for in meth. I was at peace with departing this world, and the feeling that Jesus was about to receive me had overwhelmed me. I was truly sorry for all I had done during these split seconds, and I had told Him just that. I asked for forgiveness.

The front end hit the curb that separated the street and the parking lot where the sign sat like a weeping willow tree. A chilling scene that stared me down like a twelfth-grade bully at three o'clock. The taxi was once again airborne. It looked like a gargantuan Halloween pumpkin soaring as a rocket through the foggy October night sky. Clarity in motion. It was in this dense midflight epiphany that I felt the presence of two angels. Now I am not crazy, so relax. I didn't see or hear anything. I just look back in hindsight and feel that whatever was in that cab with me at that moment were angels. I felt as if two sets of fingers plucked my shirt, one on each shoulder, between their index finger and thumb. I had on my seat belt, as always. However, I felt a feather-like levitation lift me out of the seat merely one inch off the navy-blue leather just before impact.

I was wide awake and braced for myself. An incendiary flash of hot white light erupted within the taxi. The concussion was like Hiroshima. The sound of twisting and crunching steel berated any sense of hearing that I had left. Elevated off the seat, I felt my entire body jerk against the belt, followed by a snapping noise as if a Rottweiler was chewing on a plate chicken bones.

I felt the cab touch the ground as my vision returned. A metallic scream reminiscent of the Twin Towers coming down on 9/11 shrieked all around me. I heard a loud crash on the roof of the taxi. The whole sign bent over and crashed right on top of me. The impact was so prevalent, it shook the neon sign till it snapped and timbered onto the roof of the car.

I looked around and realized the cab had literally imploded like a tin can all around me. The engine was sitting in the passenger seat. Blue smoke from 10W-30 motor oil billowed into my nostrils. The cab was engulfed in smoke and sparks were exploding on the dash. A firebrand of items burned on the floorboards. My breath was short, not just from the introduction of a chemical assault, but the realization that my rib cage had snapped like tinder.

I flipped the belt off and flung open the bent and folded door of the driver's side. I gagged out tar and phlegm-filled goo onto the pavement beside me. I moved to emerge when I saw that my left foot was trapped under the seat of the Crown Victoria police model. The reinforcements they make to the police interceptor package saved me. However, the seats were almost flush with the floor. My heel was shattered and mashed. I ripped my own leg out, revealing my tattered broken sneaker. They were grey and covered in blood. I sat for a minute as I picked the shards of broken windshield glass from my eyelids.

At this time, I noticed that there was a deep laceration the size of an inchworm on my right pinky finger. It was puzzling. It started to squirt blood out like table wine at an Italian eatery. The wound sprayed hot iron-filled blood that covered the smashed-in windshield. The rays of neon light poured through the broken glass, now tinted with my coagulating lifeblood. It illuminated the smoke-filled front seat like some crime scene in a bad Seventies horror movie.

Blood shot forward and splattered onto the hot motor that sat next to me in the passenger seat. It smelled like someone was grilling a fillet mignon at some twisted psychotic barbeque. I vomited as I fell onto the parking lot beside me. I sat in chunks of puke and stomach bile as my body went into shock. Fear that the cab would explode sent me to my broken feet and I started pacing in circles about thirty feet from the wreckage.

I was in a lit-up strip mall and nearly dead. I had just hit a twenty-thousand-dollar sign, wrecked a ten-thousand-dollar taxi, and was covered in blood. Not exactly how I planned my night. Good Samaritans started showing up to the scene. *The dope!* I hobbled back to the smoke and flame-filled cab to retrieve my bank bag in a last-ditch effort to eat the thirty dollars' worth of glass that was inside before first responders showed up on the scene.

People were holding me back as I fought to find it. The point was moot. The smoke was too thick, and I was far too blinded by the glass in my eyes.

"There are people in there," I shouted.

I was trying to come up with an explanation for these people of why I tried to get back into the inferno. Just then the ambulance, fire trucks, and yes...the police showed up on the scene.

I was walking in circles again saying, "Oh God, oh God," over and over when the police made their first contact with me. A big Mexican cop put his hand on my shoulder, and it all got a little too real. I completely passed out onto the pavement. I came to moments later with five of Corpus' finest standing above me, asking if I was ok. They asked me what my name was, but I couldn't speak. I was in full-on shock mode as blood gurgled out of my hand and the wounds on both my legs.

One cop started to pat me down to look for my ID, and that's when it happened. I remembered Bella's weed. I forgot all about it till the cop pulled it from my sock.

"This piece of shit is high!" he yelled out to his partners.

The polices officer's tone went from sympathetic to hate in two seconds flat. They then all started chattering and clambering as they hurled insults towards me.

"How many other people are in the cab?" shouted an EMT.

They quickly put out the engine fire and realized I was

all alone. All I could think about was the dope in my cab bag. I was on my way to prison for this. I darted to my feet and went toe to toe with the Mexican cop.

"Boy, you're on drugs, huh?" he sneered.

I looked that man directly in his eye. I was about to tell him the absolute truth and that goes a long way with cops. They can tell when you are lying.

"Look, man, that ain't my weed, that was my girl's. I took it off the counter so she wouldn't get too lazy to clean the house. You are gonna test me anyway, you won't find weed in my blood, I swear."

That was me trying to do damage control.

They sat me down on the pavement on my ass. What happened next shocked me in every way. The Mexican cop ripped the baggie open and dumped the weed in the bushes and threw the bag in a nearby receptacle. The cops all just looked at each other and talked in some strange telepathic cop language that I couldn't even fathom to understand.

I was put in the back of an ambulance and rushed to the hospital. I sat back on the gurney as the red and blue bubble gums plastered my blood-soaked face. An EMT told me to "Hang on" as they bandaged my wound to stop the blood from shooting out like a geyser. They wheeled me into a freezing cold ER and back into a stall. I was immediately surrounded by doctors and nurses and my police escort was told to vacate the room...for now.

They shoved a massive rig into the vein of my forearm. I loved shooting up in that one, a guaranteed hit every time. I called it Babe Ruth. They started a morphine drip right away and I was jammed. They asked me a million questions about the pain, allergies, and more. I could have cared less. That dope hit my brain and I became an instant comedian. I had the whole hospital staff rolling with laughter. Typical me behavior. Every now and then, I remembered I was just in a horrifying life-threatening accident in the cab company's vehicle where drugs were found on my person. Oh yea…and the over half a gram that was still in my cab bag. The meth that could land me in prison.

Not long after, my ex-wife showed up from Port A. I don't even know how they got her number. Then Barry and Bella showed up on the scene. Seeing Bella and my ex-wife interact was legendary. Bella showed up disinterested and irritable. It was a nuisance that I had just almost died. How dare I need her by my side. I was so high that I didn't care. Everyone except Bella sat around eyeballing me and acting dreadfully concerned. My dad was about to start in on me when the doctors came in and demanded X-rays. They were worried that I was bleeding internally and could die right there on the table.

My dad had to get back to the house. I assured him I was going to be just fine, and he took off. The girls stepped out as the doctors prepped the X-rays. My ex-wife had just got done toweling off the blood from my tattooed legs, as Bella sat and played with her hair, zero concern whatsoever. I sat alone, perched up in a hospital bed. It all started to hit me, even though I was high as a kite and in complete shock. I was realizing what I had just done, and it scared me to death.

The curtain divider peeled back. I felt like Oz as the boney fingers of a shadowy figure stoked from behind the void. It was an EMT.

"Hey Boston, we found your bag with your ID and everything in there."

The guy threw my cab bag at me and hit me dead in the chest. The bag slid down and fell right in my lap. I was shaking as I looked inside. There were the smokes. I cracked the lid and sure as shit, the dope was sitting right where I left it. I scrambled to hide the bag under my pillow before the doctors came back in.

My boss at the cab company came in next. He informed me that I was not going to be charged with anything. Not even a speeding ticket. I looked at him in disbelief. It all started to come together through the fog…no pun intended. The cab company had so much political pull in town, the cops were just going to sweep the whole thing under the rug. The news could have shot the story from their rooftop, but they were told it was not to run. There would be no bad press for this livery service, at all costs. The city couldn't be in fear that they had junkie cab drivers ferrying innocent families all over town. They didn't even test my blood. They would have found a small meth lab in my platelets.

However, the owners did hear about the weed. The guy told me that I would most likely not have a job when the sun came up. He shook his head in disdain and walked out the door. This is when Bella, my ex-wife, and the doctor came back into the room. The lady doctor watched as my ex-wife showed meaningful concern for me, and then watched as Bella took fifty dollars off my lap and went to go with her friend to get fast food.

"Let me get this straight, you're the ex-wife, and that's the girlfriend?" the doc said in question. My ex-wife shook her head in agreement with a look of horror on her face.

I told my ex that I was leaving.

"Boston, you could die, what the hell is wrong with you?" she stammered fearfully.

I played along and acted like I would stay overnight, if she would agree to leave. I knew Bella would be back soon. I grabbed my bag, ripped the IV out of my pulsing vein, and hobbled out of the emergency room doors before anyone knew any better. There was no way I was going to let the cops bust me with the dope, and absolutely no way was I going to get rid of it. Bella picked me up and off to Oakbrook we went. We smoked the dope as soon as we got home. A deep resentment grew inside me for the way Bella treated me. So cold, so hateful. This event opened my eyes as if I had just woken from a long slumber.

Waking the next day groggy, and in a ten on the pain Richter scale. I couldn't lay on my back without choking up a clotty piece of fragmented tissue. I tried to stumble to the bathroom and felt broken pieces of bone in my heel shifting around under the skin.

Something inside me was not the same. I felt strange and amphibian, as if I were able to live underwater but allowed on land just long enough to get what I needed to survive. I was disoriented. At the same time, I felt oddly awake. I retracted from all human contact as the day went on. I felt my sanity starting to slip away.

I was seeing a flashing sign in my head. A recurring thought that kept repeating *The Big Event* over and over. I thought I was on my way to the loony bin. I didn't say anything to anyone about this. I thought maybe I had a blood clot in my brain. After all, I left the hospital before any of the test results or X-rays came back.

Bella and I were in a constant quarrel. It got so bad that she took off with an alleged friend. Just like that, she and the baby up and left. I walked around like a zombie. After three days of her missing from my world, I found an address on someone she was believed to be with. I was in the projects off Agnus Street pounding on doors at eight on a Sunday morning.

Looking like a cop, hobbling around on one foot in the projects, and kicking at people's doors is a good way to get shot.

I never found her. I went home alone and was hurt beyond repair. She returned, like always, with the baby in her arms, begging to come back in, and as always, I let her. I was too weak to say no to Bell. My rage grew as I intensely questioned her about who she had spent the last three days with. That night I got dead drunk. I couldn't stand the pain. My side was splitting. She let me pass out on the concrete floor and I stayed there all night. I woke up hacking my lungs up, literally. I told her I needed to go to the ER right away and she told me to drive myself.

When I got to the ER and told them about the accident and my leaving against medical advice. They rushed me right to the back and ran all the tests. When the doctor came in with the X-rays, I was clutching my ribs. He was an older gentleman with snow-white hair. His white doctor's coat flapped at the tails as he slapped the results up against the lit board.

"Oh my God," he exclaimed. I had never heard a doctor react that way. "Mr. Bornagain, I don't know how you're walking around, your ribs are in half, they are not even touching."

He asked what had happened. He explained to me that the seat belt that had saved my life had also sawed all five of my ribs completely in half. It would be six weeks before I felt any kind of relief and months before I would be anything close to healed.

He gave me thirty Norco's, which I promptly traded at a Flour Bluff trap for some heroin. I smoked some off tinfoil in the parking lot at Walmart and headed home. Now the flashing sign in my head was repeating *find the others*. I was panicking from these signs I was seeing. *What did they mean? What was happening to me?* That night in the cab had shown me one hundred percent that God was real.

Bella took off once again. It was over. I waited for three days and decided that I had to rip off the band-aid. She was literally breaking my heart in two almost all the time. Something within was not the same. Something overcame me, feelings of freedom and change. I did something I would have never done before. I drove to the long-haired plug that started it all. I had packed up every stitch of Bella's clothes and found a girl in the parking lot of the trap. I gave away everything Bella owned.

I knew her love for material possessions would be enough to make her so mad that she would never return. So, I turned the page. I had this great internal need to go in another direction. At the same time, she was "The Greatest Love of All" and I knew I was about to go through devastating loss and pain. I felt then that I would never fall out of love with my Bella. Things in life don't always go the way you want them to, and I accepted this as something that just needed to happen.

She called a day or so later wanting to get her things. As planned, she was furious. The highchair and the baby's toys sat just as they were left. I couldn't bear to say goodbye to him. I couldn't even look at the "Thomas the Train Engine" that sat on the dining room table as I paced the hall. I felt I had made a massive mistake. I should have just let her come home.

Then, emotionally...I snapped.

#

Bella and the baby were long gone. Only Barry and I remained at Oakbrook, and by this time he was terrified by the unrecognizable madman that used to be his eldest son. I sat paralyzed under a Wiccan October moon. Perched in the picnic spot that Bella and I once knew as our safe place within the madness of our addiction.

Pale rays of light bounced off my skin as I sat in awe of the devil. The accident made God's presence known in undeniable ways. For the first time in my life, I knew God was real. The image of Jesus was in my mind's eye almost every waking moment. The car crushing around me, the flowing blood gushing from superficial wounds, it was all too real. I was spared that night. The thoughts of the angelic creatures, invisible and sweet, touched my heart in ways untold.

The week before, the gun trembling on my eyelid, flashed in my mind with terror. A force much greater than myself was with me, saving me repeatedly from sure death. There was no denying that my universe had just expanded into the infinite. The impossible became possible, the fear of death retreated like a failing army in Moscow snow swells. I was now certain that there was an afterlife with spirits and angels. This was also the night that I realized that Satan was before me in a shadowy encampment.

The events leading up to this night of enlightenment helped me see that if the Lord was this close…so was the Serpent. In my addiction, I was servile to the clawed beast that ruled the air. The meth was a gate, one that I had blown wide open on both sides. Being this receptive to the spirit world had become the most uncomfortable feeling I had ever known. The sign in my head saying "The Big Event" and *"Find the Others"* was now becoming noticeably clear. I was being sent messages from an outside force. Knowing God is real will do things to your reality that shatter any perception of life as you know it. This was the night my journey to God began.

Living on the fault line of good and evil. Straddling love and hate, truth and lies. Walking hand in hand with the Father and the enemy, both at the same time. I started to feel the first throws of the tug of war between Jesus and Satan, both engaging in a cosmic showdown where my soul hung in the balance. Real thoughts spun in my mind…*Why me? Why was my life getting so much attention from the Creator and His nemesis?*

    My cell rang and snapped me out of the catatonic state I had fallen into. It was Captain Cook's girlfriend, Rockstar. They now lived out in the woods in Aransas Pass. She explained that they had been in a fight, and she needed a ride to a friend's place before the situation escalated.

    I was literally broken in half, in mind and body. Every breath felt like a saber slicing through the layers of fat and muscle tissue in my torso. I agreed to go get her and downed the tail end of the liter of rum I was guzzling on the front lawn. I made the trip with one eye open, again I had been up for three days and was passing out from true exhaustion.

    It was about a thirty-minute drive that felt more like an eternity. I scooped blondie up, dropped her off not too far from her little trailer in the woods, and started to make my way home. By the time I hit the Harbor Bridge at North Beach, I was a man incapacitated. Once again, the nose of the Mitsubishi pointed skyward, gas to the floor, and eyes closed shut. By God's grace, I came up over the watermark fast asleep but driving straight.

    Drunk and dead to the world, I can only imagine that the tiny black car floated right at the absolute peak of the massive bridge. I woke to a horrendous screaming noise followed by the tinder of metallic sparks shooting up from the curbside. I jerked the wheel, overcorrecting and catapulting me across the double yellow line and into oncoming traffic. Luckily it was three in the morning and there weren't but two trucks on the road. I cut right and made it safely into my lane just in the nick of time, the passing horn of a Dodge wailing as he missed me by mere feet.

My hands clutched the wheel as I shouted obscenities into the rearview mirror in total disbelief. My forearms tense from gripping as I shook in fear. I remember glancing at the speedometer as an instinct when I sideswiped the curb. I made contact at the top of the Harbor Bridge at over eighty miles an hour. I was drunk, so pulling over at this hour was not an option I wanted to explore. Driving drunk causes impulsive and absurd decisions. My thought process was that I didn't want a jake to pull up with flashers on and send me off to County. I stayed the course a whole twelve and a half miles to Oakbrook.

I leapt out of the seat and hit the flashlight on my phone so I could assess the damage. Blinding white light splattered the onyx paint as I stood crouched in the driveway. Looking on, I had expected to see the whole right side of the car smashed in and scraped from the concrete wall that I thought I had nailed. It was pristine. The door was unblemished and intact. I slid the light from my cell phone in the direction of the small tractor-sized tire on the Mitsubishi. Long rubbery shreds intertwined with radial bands of steel that hung near the cement. I stood to my feet, pausing, and at that moment, after an almost thirteen-mile drive…the tire deflated right before my eyes.

I looked at the date on my phone. It was exactly seven days from the major cab accident that nearly ended my life. Three times in exactly three weeks, God spared me from sure death. This was no mistake. It was as if the same angels that were in the taxi that night had been floating next to the little car, holding the puncture wounds of the tire, keeping it inflated as I found my way home.

I stumbled through the door of Oakbrook in shock. My

life was contaminated, a murky clouded string of events and near-death experiences. The angels were all around me. Protection in legion, my own supernatural Secret Service trotting beside me in battle. Addiction is war, and from what was happening around me, someone in big places had my six. I praise Jesus for that.

#

I woke up hungover to an empty house. I changed the tire in the baking South Texas sun as I smoked a fat bowl of crystal. With sexual thoughts driving me like a dogsled team in the Iditarod, I started making calls. All thoughts of God were laid to the side. I was on the path to the worst hell-drenched period of my life. With Bella gone, I was now a single meth addict with nothing to lose. All bets were off.

Things from here on out get very dark, very strange, and very gross. Stay tuned passengers, things are about to get a little crazy…no pun intended.

Chapter 7
Till the Wheels Fall Off

Now out of a cabbie job, the Mitsubishi was the main source of income for my insane lifestyle. I was hell-bent on getting laid at every turn. I started making the rounds at local trap houses and drug dens to work, score, and pick up unsuspecting sexual partners. I was totally free from any kind of a monogamous relationship at this point. My sexual behavior was becoming daunting folklore. I had no shame in my speech with the messages I would send and the freaky sexual practices I was engaging in.

I was broken. Bella was all I could think about. What were she and the baby out there enduring? As bad as our relationship was, I cared. I saw her face everywhere I went. I'd hear the baby laughing down the empty hall at Oakbrook in the wee hours of a starlit night. But I was alone…all alone.

The guilt I would feel was momentary; I was injecting my penis in any 98.6-degree piece of meat that would have me. I was never wearing a jimmy. I was into having raw, unprotected sex with strange women wherever I went. All I had to do was keep lighting that glass bulb and the panties would drop every time.

#

I was kicking it at the crib more frequently since I lost my job at the cab stand. The train of junkies coming in and out of Oakbrook was becoming something of a Hollywood movie. Bitches with bags…that warning Captain Cook dropped on me some time ago was really starting to ring true. They were funneling in and out every three days like Alaskan salmon during spawning season. I was completely lost.

Three in the morning was always a strange time. On this night, I got a call from Chevelle. "Bosty Cakes, I need you to do a job for me. I will pay you whatever you want, there is no one else I can trust on this one."

She was frantic. She wouldn't tell me over the phone what the job was going to be. Chevelle and I had been through a lot of frightening nights together and I couldn't let her go this one alone. When she showed up, I could tell right away that she had been doing hot rails the size of the California coastline. We got in my ride, and she went through the whole scenario.

There was a guy named Tampa who lived not far from Oakbrook. A higher-level dealer that Chevelle knew. It sounded like some deep-seated gang shit that I was not to know and never quite understand. So, she left the details vague. However, the meat and potatoes were that he had been arrested twice back-to-back and called her for a front on some dope. This was unthinkable, seeing as he was a supplier. Why was he calling her for a half ounce of ice?

She had confronted him over the phone hours earlier about some rumors that he had been snitching to the task force. She was to go to his house, drop the dope, and feel him out on some things during what was sure to be a heated sit-down. The drive over was made in silence.

She directed me to pull up to a curb one street behind Tampa's house. I knew the spot from past business we had done months before. The engine purred like a Himalayan cat as Chevelle stared at me with welled up eyes. I had never seen this woman so visibly shaken in all the time we had shared together in the car.

"Bosty, this is some serious shit, baby. I seriously may not come out of this place alive." She said this with grave seriousness in her voice.

She gave me instructions to circle the block and keep an eye out for her. I was to dart in and scoop her up as soon as she hit the street.

She cocked a nine-millimeter pistol and tucked it into her gangster jean jacket as she rose to her feet. "Be careful Bosty Cakes, watch your back, they could try to smoke both of us."

My jaw dropped as she waltzed through the bushes and hopped the fence into his backyard. Wild thoughts ran through my mind. *How the hell did I get mixed up in this? What was I thinking?* My loyalty to this woman after all the foul shit she did with Bella behind my back was pure stupidity. But that's just who I am. Chevelle needed me, and that was that. When she called, I was there for her...period.

I was instructed to go to her mother's and tell her what had happened if she hadn't returned within thirty minutes. Telling a mother that her daughter was dead in some gangland drug shit gone wrong was not on my bucket list. I was there to do my job and get us home safe, and that's what I fully intended to do. I circled the spot like a hammerhead around a chum bucket. Wide high eyes peeled as I passed the dealer's house that was strewn with closed-circuit cameras.

The clock was running down. There were two minutes

left before I was about to leave. No sign of Chevelle as my heart beat out of my chest. I couldn't just take off without my friend. I couldn't do it if I tried. Just then, a hand ripped open the door to the Mitsubishi.

"Let's go, Bosty Cakes." It was Chevelle.

"What the fuck girl?" I said with rageful fear in my voice.

She had popped out of nowhere. She refused to tell me what had gone down in the meeting. We got back to Oakbrook and there was a car waiting for her in my driveway.

"Chevelle, this is a one-time thing. I can't do this kind of shit with you anymore," I said in a serious tone.

"I know Bosty, thanks for being a down-ass nigga." She got out of the ride and slid right into the passenger seat of a brand-new Maroon Chrysler 300.

That would be the last time I would see her for a long time. There was a fifty/fifty chance that she was going to die that night. There was a good chance they would smoke me just for driving her. That's how fast it happens out here in Crook City; they pull up to your door, unload a magazine, and your front-page news. Closed casket shit.

#

My drug use was becoming more insane by the day. The needle was starting to become my weapon of choice due to its sexual advancements. I was scoring at a trap in the Bluff at a little trailer park off Waldron Road. It was a busy little place run by a husband-and-wife team. Whisper was in his fifties.

He had throat cancer. At some point, they operated and cut a gaping stoma into his windpipe. It left him speechless. He could only whisper, mouthing deep words in your line of sight. He was a good dude; give you the shirt of his damn back, salt of the earth type.

He was married to Mammy. A cool older hippy chick who ran the house and the operation with a soldier's precision. They were a pair of old-school hustlers. They stayed in their lane and were genuinely good people. I never met anyone with a negative thing to say about the two.

The trap was a baby-blue single wide with a detached wooden staircase that reached a matching deck at the top, near the white aluminum front door. There was a padlocked gate on the porch with a guy who stood guard twenty-four hours a day, seven days a week. This trap was a stone's throw from the Flour Bluff Police Substation. Nestled perfectly in plain sight. The traffic in the Bluff was nothing out of the ordinary, as it was a small quiet suburb of Corpus, separated on all sides by the ocean.

I started going to this pad because of its cozy, inviting environment. The guard would let you in the front door and you would instantly be home. The carpet was a dark-blue shag job. To the left was a kitchen area cluttered with anything from full soda bottles to motor parts, and everything in between. It was cluttered but clean. The middle of the trailer was the living room. A comfy sitting area with an old cloth fiber couch of navy and gold. A small oval and cherry coffee table sat dead center. Handheld blowtorches and cans of cheap butane fuel littered the tabletop in typical tweaker fashion. There was a big flat-screen TV that could have anything from Saturday morning cartoons to hardcore porn with nun's squirting, depending on the time of day and the clientele working the remote.

The third section of the house was the back bedroom. It had a fold-out futon and some scattered kitchen chairs. The floor was hardwood, and the walls were decorated with old concert posters and twang from the Seventies. The doorway to get in had psychedelic multi-colored beads that you would walk through to enter.

To the right...well, that was the most special part of the whole place. A part that never changed, no matter what time of day or night, no matter what holiday or special event that was taking place in the much-forgotten world outside...Mammy was in her recliner.

Mammy's recliner was baby blue. The kind of color you would see on a ruffled shirt, in some bad early Eighties horror movie about zombies killing everyone at the prom. She was a short little woman with extremely long, pitch-black hair. Her face was perfectly wrinkled and warm. She had deep dark eyes and small lips that came to a subtle point. She wore a flowing black dress that flared out on the ends. Her house slippers matched her midnight dress with fluff and blooming texture. A dark wood chest sat on the floor. Something you would find on a pirate ship steered by Captain Jean Lafitte off the Texas coastline.

"Hey Boston, how are ya, doll," Mammy said with a smile.

"Gimme an eight ball, Mammy, and I am gonna need some help too," I said with enthusiasm.

I loved having a skilled professional shoot me up. It took the pressure of missing away, only the pure enjoyment of the minty rush remained on the surface. I scooted up a chair to Mammy's recliner. She made small talk as she opened her pirate chest full of underworld treasure. The booty within was eclectic as it was illegal.

"Ya know Boston, I give a free rig to anyone who buys from me. Clean shit, there is too many people getting sick out there in the street."

Mammy was the den mother for all of us tweaker junkies in the Bluff. Her skin was a canvas of tattoos. Her tattoos revealed a tale of exactly what generation she came from. The story of a cool Mother Earth hippy type, having been broken badly by society. The game took its toll on her. She was a survivor, to say the least.

  She pulled out five brand new UV-100 long point needles from the chest. A small box with a card catalog. It had divided sections of pre-weighed bags of ice within. She pulled a perfect three-and-a-half-gram ball out and placed it on the small table that sat on the floor.

  "Ok baby, I need you to start pumping your fist. Go ahead and tie off with your belt," she spoke with affectionate authority.

  I stripped my belt off and sat down. I wrapped it around my arm tight, just above the elbow. I made balls with my left fist as the circulation was cut off from my veins. The bulbous blue vein protruded out of my milky-white flesh. Mammy was just about done mixing a half-gram shot of pure fire. She grabbed my arm with one aging, gentle hand. Her skin felt as smooth as a piece of sea glass.

  I hated long points, as you could feel every micro inch of surgical steel sliding into your skin. When it popped through the vein, it made a snapping noise within the body. A puncture vibration you could feel in your teeth. But Mammy was an artist. She now took aim. She jabbed the rig into my arm with the fervor of an expert marksman. My blood streamed out and into the register of the needle. It filled the first eighth inch of the yellowy clear liquid I wanted in my body. She drew back the plunger. Crimson incantation, the flood of maroon made my penis instantly hard. I knew what was about to come to pass.

  She started the injection. A hydraulic maneuver that plunged pure chemical as thick as maple syrup directly into my bloodstream. I watched with ferocious vision as the rubber plunger slid down toward the bottom. It was like watching the ball drop in New York's Time Square. The warm flow of love ran from head to toe, passing through my tonsils like I had drunk a shot of eucalyptus. I coughed like a man in one of the last stages of a cancer dilemma.

As she ripped the syringe from my arm; I hopped to my feet. I did my signature jumping up and down move, almost smashing my head through the famously low fiberboard ceiling of the trailer. I couldn't bring myself to sit down. Mammy let out a giggle as she watched me wiggle like an overdosing circus geek. I attempted to speak as I grabbed the remaining four pins and the dope off the tabletop.

I glided through the beaded divider and shuffled my balloon-like feet into the living room. This is where I found Whisper tinkering with some post-apocalyptic gadget that I didn't even pretend to comprehend. I grabbed the pipe off the table and clinked an enormous shard down the stem and into the bulb. I picked up a long cylinder blowtorch that looked like a lightsaber from the movie "Star Wars."

I flicked my thumb upwards and began melting the ice down as I rolled the pizzle like a freaky tilt-a-whirl. I blew out a massive plume. My eyes felt like they were floating in midair between the sockets. I passed both pieces to Whisper. There were a few stragglers making their way to the session for some free therapy, including a couple in their twenties, ragged and homeless looking.

Whisper had a huge hole in his throat, remember? So how was he able to hit a meth pipe in the first place? Well, this was one of the most rad things I had ever seen. He took an old turkey baster and whittled the opening so the end of a standard meth pipe would sit in the tube airtight. On the opposite end, where the squeezer was removed, sat a much larger circular opening that fit snug around his leaking stoma.

He lit the torch and rolled the turkey baster in half moon turns. Once removed, a stream of toxic methamphetamine smoke streamed out the gaping hole in his neck. There are some things you just can't unsee. I always ended up cringing when I found myself on his left during a smoke session.

There is nothing like shooting up and smoking after. You get that major rush of the injection, followed by the pulsing buzz that it gives you next. You also get the euphoric brain blast that the pipe offers, the longer-lasting barrage that sticks to your ribs. The best of both worlds, like chocolate and peanut butter. I nodded farewell and headed back home to Oakbrook to watch hardcore porn on the DVD player. I had what I needed for the next seventy-two hours of sad self-sexual abuse. And I loved every oily second of it.

#

Time marched on, the clicking sounds of days passing by. Sleep was a foreign institution, only passing out from total exhaustion or the occasional Xanax bar. There were no days off. The risks were now becoming huge. I became less interested in the safety of my passengers and far more interested in the meth-induced sexual rage that was deep within me. I knew God was real, but the lure of the devil was far too great.

My bedroom looked like it was inhabited by a young Jeffrey Dahmer. Countless empty bags of ice, porn magazines and DVD's, syringes and burnt up aluminum foil. These all made it virtually impossible to walk without stepping on something that you wouldn't want any part of with a sober mind. My father and I barely spoke. I was scary in every way, shape, and form. The walking dead; a putrid depiction of an addict. I had bruises all over my body from stabbing myself with dirty used needles found on the floor.

      Knocks on the front door at Oakbrook were now a common occurrence. Strange travelers on the underground railroad of meth were showing up for free room and board. My father was footing the bill for everything. People ate his food, used his water and electricity. Items were constantly coming up missing. I would hear him start to swear and I knew…they had taken something else.

      My dad was drinking a lot during this period. Who could blame him? He was watching his junkie son go insane right before his eyes. I found myself behind the wheel, not only for work, but to cruise the slime scene, meeting any vulnerable woman that would let me insert my penis into her.

      This was my tour of hell. I recall specific moments; one is a vivid memory where I was naked. The blowtorch ignited, heating the pipe as the porn roared on my old television. It was a conjuring of demons. I knew I was summonsing a sexual being to possess my mind and body from the spirit world, unseen and destructive. I got excited knowing the insane perversions that were about to occur on my bed, even though I was alone. I was cracking up mentally. The spirits were real, but the thoughts in between my ears were starting to worry me.

      Extreme paranoia was setting in. The early stages of meth psychosis were beginning to take hold. I was hanging out with nothing but strange women. Somewhere along the line, I got it in my head that I had made some enemies in the tweaker counterculture. They are world famous for gang stalking people when they are high out of their minds. Once a mark was made, the antagonists would start playing mind games with their prey, confusing and terrifying them. This is not a phenomenon; this practice was very scary and, above all, very real. The problem is, when you're high, you never know what a fact is and what is fiction. The drug is a perfect lubricant for lunacy.

Double-talk and coded speech were a common tactic for the mental war waged on people in the game. Developed by the US military as an interrogation tool, tweakers found it amusing and vengeful to carry out such missions on weak-minded targets as revenge, or just plain amusement.

I started meeting a lot of women "by chance". A girl standing on a corner with a set of trash bags would find herself in my car. After a short talk, we would be at Oakbrook getting high and having sex. These bag chasers would stay for about three days. Now, it wasn't the drugs running out that would have them leave. It was me throwing them out. I started to believe that these chance meetings were by no chance at all. I started to think the girls were sent.

I had it in my head that my imagined enemies were paying drug-addicted women to meet me, have sex with me, and then do a one-eighty on me and torture me mentally. After three days of hardcore methamphetamine use, the girl and I would start the back-and-forth banter. We would both let on like we knew more than we did about the other. The crazy double talk and accusations would start hurling. At first, I would get overly angry and throw the girl out, on to the next one, and repeat. Yet, I am a huge jerk. I think I am a comedian and hate losing at anything. Eventually, instead of throwing them out, I decided I was going to make them want to leave.

This became a sadistic game of cat and mouse. A meth and sex-fueled dance that was all part of an underlying mental illness, brought on by years of heavy stimulant abuse and lack of sleep. These girls just wanted to party and have a place to stay. They were now bedding down with a madman, involved in some far-off hallucination that only existed in my head. The funny thing was, every single woman that I thought was sent by an unknown enemy would play along.

It was every three days like clockwork. Months and months of hard drug use, sex and now a sick game of mental torture back and forth between me and my temporary lovers. The mental illness brought out my raw and funny personality, a natural ball-buster I was. The jokes were exceedingly funny with each girl hurling a dirty dozen right back at me with perfect comedic timing. I refused to let them sleep. I started to act like the uttermost annoying human on earth. The end goal was to get them to leave, all on their own without me having to throw them out. This was the birth of *Them/They*.

Them/They was how I referred to the unknown financier that was sending these women to torture me. I would tell the girls, "I know *They* sent you. I know you are working for *Them*." One girl, who got to her wit's end, just flat out asked me, "Boston, who the fuck is *Them/They*?" I didn't have that piece of the puzzle worked out yet. All I knew was that even for a dapper dude like me, I was getting to sleep with far too many good-looking women for it to be free. *They had to be hired help in a sadistic plot to drive me insane. They just had to be.*

Looking back, it is sad to see that these poor women were so deep in their addiction that they would subject themselves to three full days of pure craziness just for a place to stay. At this point, I wasn't even working that much. The bare minimum to score drugs. That was it. A perfect storm was forming. Now, almost all the women I met at random would also be the ones supplying the drugs. I had the ride, the house to crash at and they had the pussy and the dope. To me, it was a little too good to be true. Guys like me just didn't run into these beautiful women for free sex and meth. *They were one hundred percent sent. But who was funding it all…and why?*

The three in the morning fighting and insanely loud

ball-busting sessions must have been like a prison camp for my father, who was now spending all his time drinking in his room when he was not at work. The poor guy was a prisoner in his own home; all the while paying all the bills and feeding every homeless drug addict in Corpus that I decided to let in the house. The fights with the women would sometimes get out of hand. My jokes would strike a deep nerve. Next thing you know there was a lady screaming and throwing dishes off my skull, bouncing off my hard head and crashing onto the floor. Barry was breaking up extraordinarily dangerous and violent domestic disturbances on a regular basis.

The house was falling apart. My dad was drinking any money that didn't go to bills. I was making less than nothing and feeding a massive meth habit. A roof leak in the baby's old bedroom started to form a hole in the ceiling. No one in the house paid it any mind. Our addictions blinded us to the reality that the castle was crumbling around us. The concrete floors were exposed. The darkness in my grandparents' old house was far beyond a lighting problem. It was a spiritual darkness foreshadowing the death that was about to be in the air. A haunting curse, generational and present. With dark days looming, our little psychotic family pushed on. Survival was a luxury. We were floating through our fragmented life, hanging on to our disease.

#

My ex-wife had been making the car payment for months. I was so strung out, I couldn't make a two-hundred-dollar payment, not even once. The finalization of my divorce was about to go through the court system, and she was done paying for anything I had. Little did I know, she had stopped paying months ago.

The bank that had the loan on the Mitsubishi started

calling me, as my ex-wife had given them my number. I dodged them at every turn. It didn't hurt that at this time I was changing phone numbers more often than El Chapo. They sent third party messages through my ex that they were interested in finding the car and starting the repossession process. That car was everything to me. It's how I survived. It's how I scored. Losing it was not an option. I was so behind on the payments, there was no way to get my head above water. Never mind I couldn't put the twelve bucks together to get a replacement license from the DMV.

I was seeing life through voodoo goggles. A strange thick air surrounded my every thought; concave senses of reality clouded any judgement I had left. The Sparkling City was a trash heap, the devil's playground where I roamed with no fear and an insane mind. The following events are important...so pay attention, passengers.

#

Bella and her friend had been getting super-duper fucked up about a month before our breakup. I hated this bitch that she was rolling with. A short, skinny, Mexican bag chaser with a big mouth. We hated each other right from the jump. I was at work when it all got cooked up...and I ain't talkin' about dope this time.

I returned home early one morning, at about half past seven. I walked in the door high as a kite. I found my Bell on the corner of the bed, baby fast asleep in his Pack-N-Play. Baby girl was sobbing as if someone had died.

"Bell, honey, what's wrong? What the hell happened?" She had uncontrollable cries, and salty tears in her eyes.

"I know everything, Boston. I know everything!" She was choking on her words so badly she could barely speak. "You're a fucking cop!" she screamed.

I was blown away. Me, of all motherfuckers, was absolutely, one hundred percent, not a damn cop. "Bella, what in the fuck are you talking about?"

Bella started to go through the whole thing, blow by insane blow. I was still together mentally at this point of my life so what I was about to hear was BANANAS.

Bell recalled that her and that little bitch friend of hers were smoking shards in my dad's office. They had been combing social media all night long, looking at people's profiles. That's when they found Clyde. Clyde was a guy who lived in the Bluff. A guy about ten years or so my senior. He was on the USS Cole when it got bombed by the terrorists. This guy was ex-special forces. Short, stocky, had a crew cut like mine, and most importantly, he was White.

Somewhere during the night, they concocted this hair-brained theory that Clyde was now a post-military DEA agent. Clyde was commissioned by the US Government to go under the knife for elective plastic surgery to look younger. He was being sent on a mission to take down the whole ice trade in Corpus Christi. She blubbered on about how Clyde was made to look about ten years younger. A twist was that Clyde was now me...undercover. She went on and on before I finally interrupted.

"Bell, lemme get this straight. I was Clyde, who had plastic surgery to look like and become me, so he now is me, as an undercover crimefighter from the future?"

She then threw in that my dad was also an agent who was in on the whole thing. All the family pictures surrounding her in the office, my life with my children, any shred of proof totally contradicting this crazy theory was thrown right out the window.

"Bell, you might as well have told me Martians just

landed on the front lawn. Baby, I think you need to get some fucking sleep."

I put her to bed and laughed about this event with Barry for about two hours after she had dozed off. Just remember this part of the story...later, it may be gravely important.

#

Long sleepless stretches and weeks of profound sexual bondage had criminalized my every fiber; the wheels of my ride, rolling in the rain, speeding through the streets where insanity became my master. My appetite for strange sexual encounters drove my every decision. I found myself on the northside, also known as The Cut. The day before I had been pulled over by CCPD for rolling through a stop sign. I was slipping. I had to dump seventy dollars' worth of dope into the prop water I kept in the front seat for this kind of event. The water bottle was solely kept for diluting the dope I had on my person in the event of a traffic stop. The fuzz didn't even end up searching me. I was furious at myself.

So, on this night, I had a seventy-dollar bottle of water with me. I was already high, the allure of the all Black, crime-ridden streets of The Cut had me mesmerized. I rolled through the half-abandoned, trash-riddled neighborhoods, peering into back yards of the numerous and terrifying trap houses with glee. A White boy solo, catching hateful stares from dark and mysterious faces.

That's when I saw her. A thick Mexican honey, big thighs and long brown hair. She was walking alone and flagged me down as I pulled up beside her. "Hey, can you give me a ride?" I nodded a happy hello; she hopped in, and we started on the road to nowhere.

After some small talk, it was plainly clear that she was

sent by *Them/They*. She was interested in partying back at my place, so Oakbrook was the next stop on the itinerary. Within minutes her clothes were off. Two strangers brought together in a twisted plot by the unknown force that was behind every sexual encounter I was coming across.

It's an odd experience to totally mistrust someone, and at the same time to be so sexually weak, you go ahead and have intercourse with them anyway. The recall of her smells and movements revolt me. The pulsing sexuality, the slurping and pounding is reminiscent of two farm animals feeding some sick primal urge to conceive.

My bedroom was sweltering. The filthy comforter caked with lint and empty drug baggies from binges past. The molten air poured from the heating duct above. I looked down as gallons of meth-laced sweat dripped in her eyes like a Peruvian waterfall. Her moans were demonic and docile. The building orgasm in my groin exploded without notice, deep within the confines of her birth canal. We sat drenched, panting in some vile bi-racial fantasy only *Them/They* could have written.

I extracted my penis from her bodily tissue. Horrifying amounts of unknown menstrual blood and semen flowed from her open chamber. I was covered. I stood up and threw on my clothes without so much as a wipe down. I could feel the O-positive beginning to dry and flake off my skin within seconds.

"You wanna get high?" I asked.

Her response was way off script from *Them/They's* usual program, "I only smoke rock, baby. Why? You got some hard?"

Her query was not of the meth world. How is this even possible? Them/They were starting to throw curveballs. They knew I was onto them, somehow. How in God's name did Them/They know what street I would turn down? How have they been putting people in my path around every turn? I had to start investigating.

All I had was the bottle of water with the ice diluted in it. I popped the top off and explained to this nameless mutant that the concoction would have her on some far-off planet in no time. It was a stimulant, like coke. That's how I sold it. My plan was to get her high and talking. I had some questions I needed answers to. *A little ice just may get Them/They's plan to backfire right in their face.* She took a huge guzzle out of the bottle. She almost puked all over my already ruined carpet.

"What the fuck is that? Are you trying to poison me, White boy?" she gasped.

I ripped the bottle from her chubby brown hand. I gave her a devious smile as I chugged more than half of the heavily laced liquid. The burning carbons in my throat were reminiscent of mimosas made with ninety-four octane gasoline.

Within thirty minutes of ingesting the poisonous venom, we both started to act in peculiar and paranoid ways. The woman was pacing the room in circles. She had transformed into a life-size rodent, a gerbil that was trapped on some imaginary wheel. *I had to get her out of my house fast.* I coaxed her back into the Mitsubishi and headed back to The Cut.

She peeled herself off my seat and into the flood of a streetlamp. She stood shaking and speechless. The lost vacant look in her eyes was harrowing. I dropped her at the exact location where *Them/They* had injected her into my life. Yet she looked as if she had never seen this strange and foreign land.

I leaned over and slammed the passenger door closed. The quaking shivering pile of Jell-O that resembled the female I had picked up only hours before vanished from my rearview. A ghost, an apparition that faded out of sight with just the right amount of distance and darkness. The amount of crystal meth she had ingested would have left even a seasoned tweaker catatonic. I chalked this one up as a big win. *That should show Them/They who they were messing with.*

I couldn't tell anyone about Them/They. Afterall, anyone could be in on this. At the very least, I can't risk sounding crazy. That's how these people design these attacks. They know once you start to ask for help, the people in your life will just write you off as insane. I had to go this alone.

The meth I had ingested from the bottle was not seeming to let up. When taken orally, the drug has a long-lasting, mind-bending effect. Hallucinogenic in nature, it twists reality, leaving the user with a slow buzzing noise that vibrates through the whole body and brain.

Three days later, I found myself behind the wheel: seventy-two hours of driving with no food, water, or sleep. I was a nervous wreck. I was still so high from the meth-laced drink that my left foot was bouncing off the clutch, making it almost impossible to shift gears. My mother texted me saying she had wired me two hundred through Western Union. I pulled into the grocery store and inched my way nervously up to the counter. It was fifteen minutes before the business center opened. I stood in wait with eyes glued to the clock as if I were awaiting the arrival of some alien spacecraft.

Once the worker called me forward, I fought with everything I had to pick up the pen off the counter and fill out the necessary paperwork to receive the funds. After four attempts, the pen dropped, my hands shaking like a victim of advanced Parkinson's Disease. The older grey-haired women thought I had some life-threatening medical issues. She took mercy on me and with loving eyes she picked up the felt-tip pen and guided my hand through my signature. She then filled out the rest of the paperwork and handed me the money. She had no clue that my physical state was altered by an illegal dangerous street drug. She also had no clue that I was about to get behind the wheel of a moving vehicle.

#

A few days later, I finally came down from the overdose. I ran into this guy who lived on the same street as Bella. They were friends with benefits for a long time. He got her high, she got him off. He was also seeing Bella's much younger sister. In the meth world, the sisters were rumored to have shared men many times in the past. It was a sick thrill that they both got from sharing sexual trysts. I never gave in. All the times Bella's sister would make comments, make gestures while visiting Oakbrook, I always remained true to Bella.

I picked him up and did a small job for him. We went on a quick dope run and he was to pay me some pebbles for my trouble. Along the ride, I got a sense that he was insulting me in that strange, meth-world double talk. I had the notion that he was making fun of me under his breath. I was paralyzed by the dope I had smoked earlier that day. My insecurity in the conversation forced me to just let it go.

I dropped him off and stared into the window at Bella's family's house on the corner lot. A strange resentment mixed with pain bellowed in my guts. I drove home in severe agony from the splintered ribs shifting under my t-shirt. I stopped and got a liter bottle of cheap rum. I was self-prescribing again.

The more I drank, the more furious I got. The face of the guy on Bella's Street kept projecting into my thoughts. The replay of him laughing at me had my stomach smoldering. An ulcer-like feeling that had my fists clenched and pacing. I was walking around Oakbrook, cursing and plotting. I had snapped.

The bottle was empty, and it was time to go make a precisely clear point that was a long time coming. I knew he had slept with Bella behind my back. He was always smoking my dope, acting like my friend. While I was at work, he was nailing her in my bed.

I drove over to their street in a blind rage. I had been keeping a stainless-steel butcher knife in the compartment on the driver's side door. The knife was a foot long, razor-sharp, and chrome from top to bottom. It was nightfall and the beams of my headlamps were now pointing directly at his front door. I threw it in reverse and backed up. I darted forward at ramming speed. I jumped the curb as I plowed into this guy's front lawn. I laid on the horn and started screaming. It was around ten at night, and the Mexican neighborhood was sleepy.

"Boston, what the fuck are you doing man?" he shouted from the open door.

The neighbors were now looking on as my silhouette stood to rant, one finger pointing at him, the other hand wielding what looked like a small medieval sword.

"You're going to wake up my dad, man," he shouted. He was pleading with me to calm down as I hurled death threats at him. "Come to the back, let's smoke a bowl."

That's all I needed to hear. For the next few minutes, I calmed down. I was dead drunk and not trying to hear it. He lit the pipe for a few minutes. Soon as the bowl was done, I walked off with no explanation for why I had shown up there looking to murder him.

I got into my ride and headed down the road. I didn't make it two home-lengths before I saw her. Bella's little sister was twenty-three. She was wearing daisies and some sexy sandal heels with straps that wrapped around her gorgeous brown ankles. She was thick as molasses, short and stacked like a deck of hot cards. She had on a white tank top with something written on it in Spanish. She was hot as a tamale. Her flowing curly hair made her look like a mature Latina Shirley Temple. She turned, I gazed at the profile of a hood rat. Juicy big lips painted red, smacking gum, and rolling her long, torturous tongue.

"What's up, Boston?" she said in her devilish, seductive voice.

"Get in," I slurred. Turns out she was drunker than I was. "You wanna go back to the crib?" I asked.

"Sure," she said.

I asked her where Bella was, and her sister, who was always trying to ruin the way I felt for Bella, was happy to tell me. "She's staying up the street with some other guy," she said.

I demanded to see Bella, I had to know who she was with. I wanted to see her and the baby. Her sister directed the trip up the street, maybe two blocks or so. Bella was staying in some ratty corner house in a garage that had been turned into a makeshift apartment. Her sister went in to go tell her I was outside. She returned alone. Bella refused to come see me. I was heartbroken all over again.

I pulled away, knowing full well what was to happen next. An evil seduction, one in the devil's plans since day one. The carnal attraction between myself and the sister of my lover. A betrayal in some Shakespearian play, written in the stars a lifetime ago; in some star-crossed destiny that would fuel hell's flames, and change the course of our souls forever.

We pulled into Oakbrook, shattered. We spilled into the laundry room sharing the drunkest of kisses. I picked her up by her thick thighs and gently placed her onto the dryer. The same dryer I had made love to her sibling for the first time. She was a much younger, servile version of the woman I loved. Sex became a weapon for us both, our shared hatred for Bella turned to a sick passionate trance that left two bodies reeling in sexual desire. She hated her sister. Bella, a little prettier, always got the guy first. This was vengeance for years of overshadowing her, a lifetime of one-ups and "I told you so's."

Tonight, she would take the lead. The one man that she could never sway, the man who loved her sister in poetic and dreamy ways, would succumb to her temptation. This wasn't lust. Her body spoke like a beatnik in front of some jazz club microphone, spilling out heroin-laced heartbeats, one syllable at a time.

We fought to catch our breath as I peeled her down to her sports bra. Thick Mexican curls jaded my heart. I couldn't relax, the wild between us roared like Serengeti lions. She moaned as I bit her cocoa-cream skin. She was a bit darker, a bit more shrouded in mystery than her sisterly counterpart. She was a meth-game sex diva. A wild-hearted youth with the sexual experience of a seasoned porn star. We both shared the hurt, the rage, and broken emotion that Bella inspired with her wicked ways.

We were now both naked. Sweaty, drunk, and dripping in love, I picked her up like a trap house bride and carried her across the slimy threshold to the bedroom. I sat her young flesh on the edge of the bed. I explored her tonsils with thick fatherhood; a sick dance, the perfect mixture of caring and sweet lovemaking, swirling with sexual punishment, and hate for the blood that ran in her veins.

My fingers clutched her thick Bo Peep curls as I ferociously gagged her with pride. She was eating up the abuse like a starving jackal in the plains. Feasting on the second-hand scraps that were left behind. She picked the bones of love clean, her mouth a cavern of primal sexual pleasure. White fingertips tortured the erected flesh of her breast. Nipple play had her squirming like a worm on the end of a serrated hook.

I sat between her silky young legs and spread her like a pad of Nutella. I started working into her insides with great care. Her palms were flat on the wall behind her. She moaned as the number of digits multiplied within her uterine wall. As tight as she was, the vengeful thoughts wouldn't allow me to stop until my whole fist was deep inside her body. Big doe eyes awake with pleasure, her pupils rolled into the back of her head like a demon-possessed villager.

The evil air of betrayal was in the environment. I spun her to her knees and entered her like a bull mastiff. Two street dogs pounding in the heat of a dark evening. Her long curls now had a purpose. Wrapped around the wrist of her much older and controlling lover, I used them as leverage in a sadistic plot to break her sexually. My movements were meant to inflict pain as much as I aimed to please.

The arch in her back was a half-moon, as I stared at her sexy foot soles in the twinkle ambiance of my bedroom. Her moans were animalistic. I lunged forward and choked her with my whole right palm. Her blood vessels constricted as she squirted her evidence on my shaft. Asphyxiation made her weak, a good pet that was now housebroken in the lair of shame.

A ferocious occasion, her first insemination by a Caucasian steed. I quaked on dominant knees as I orgasmed in her, raw and unprotected. I knew she wasn't on birth control; the thought of creating a forbidden life inside her turned me on even more. The vengeance placed in her womb would serve a damaging purpose.

As a meth machine, I remained hard as I slammed her on her aching spine. Her feet behind her head, I entered her used hole once more to inject her with the sin awaiting within my loins. We were covered in sweat, grunting like two caged circus tigers. I thrust as deep as the flesh would physically allow as I climaxed directly in her fertile reproductive ventricle. Booze and rumors leaked from my lips as I kissed her deep one last time. I remained in her as every vaginal muscle gripped my tool, extracting every drop of bodily fluid I had to offer. Temporary lovers left shaking, legs twitching with emotion and physical trauma.

    The drive back to her house was silent. This was of Satan. No matter how little Bella would care, what we did was wrong in biblical ways. It's hard to put into words the feeling you get when you try to impregnate the love of your life's younger sister. I dropped her off without so much as a goodbye. I watched her body ping-pong from side to side as she stumbled up the driveway. Her balance was affected not by the alcohol in her blood, but the sexual abuse she had just endured at the hands of a madman. My pride swelled as much as my penis as I pulled away from the curb.

#

    I was sinking deep into madness. My father had bought the food to cook for Thanksgiving dinner. For over ten years, I always cooked for the whole family. My dad loved it when I cooked anything. I learned at a young age to throw down in the kitchen. I enjoyed seeing the smiles on people's faces when they ate the food I prepared. The parts of me that I still loved were decaying by the second. He got up and started knocking on my door at ten in the morning. I was smoking shards and watching hard-bondage porn while masturbating. I couldn't pull myself out of the moment. On meth, one may find themselves stuck for hours, sometimes days, in a trancelike state or some wasteful tweak. During this same period, I had become stuck watching porn with headphones on in the middle of the dining room at Jack in The Box up the street from Oakbrook. I had to text the girl that was in my bedroom to come peel me off the seat and walk me back to my car. I just couldn't get free as I stared at my own car just feet away. That's where this drug takes you.

      Every thirty minutes, he would knock, and every thirty minutes I would tell him to fuck off, that I would be out in a little while. The concern and hurt in his voice made me well up and sob. I just couldn't stop. The insanity, the drugs, and the porn would not allow me to open the door. I was in a prison run by demonic forces. I finally got up sometime later and went out to start dinner. It was three thirty in the morning. My dad was fast asleep. I robbed him and myself of a Thanksgiving memory that I will never get back. To this day, I can't let that one go. Looking back, this wasted Thanksgiving should have been a precious day. One that I would cherish. I fucked it off to smoke ice and jack myself swollen. Sometimes you don't get to redo these mistakes. Sometimes, there is no making things right.

      My father had gone through one cancer surgery the year before. His kidney was removed, and he just had his checkup for his one-year remission. He got news saying he was cancer free. He was extremely worried about me. He listened to me for hours as I would speak about Jesus and the angels in the cab that night. He was the only person on earth I could confide in. I told him of *Them/They* and their evil plot to torture me. My dad listened as I laid it all out. With all he saw, the women and the goings-on, he told me flat out, "Boston, I am not saying you're wrong, there are some pretty strange things happening around you." Even someone on the outside could see the possibility that there was a dark force putting these women in my path.

      Barry was miserable at this point. He called me into his

bedroom on a cold winter night. "Boston, I don't feel so good, my toes are completely numb, man." He went to sleep, and I stayed up smoking huge amounts of ice until the sun dripped through the corroded bed sheet that was tacked to the window of my bedroom. He screamed for me; I have never felt the fear in my father's voice that I heard that morning. I ran to him, he was staring at me with wild, fearful eyes. "Boston, I can't move my legs, I can't feel them." After a few moments of shock, I called another close family member, and we got Barry to the hospital.

  The doctors found a massive tumor on his spine. It was pinching the spinal column to the point of paralysis. At its size, it was too dangerous to operate. They explained that he would need to undergo radiation treatments to shrink the tumor before any exploratory options for a surgical procedure could even be discussed. He was paralyzed overnight.

  My dad demanded to go home. The house was in shambles. Divorces, alcoholism, and drug abuse had taken its toll on our family. We were drinking and using to forget the hand that life had dealt us. Living that way, we spent every extra penny on getting wasted. Every facet of our life crumbled like sandcastles in the waves of some far-off beach, a family vacation we forgot to attend. The house was a dilapidated mess. The floors stripped, holes in the sheetrock everywhere, and the damn dogs.

  The dogs were so old that their bladders were a constant urine stream onto the aqua green rug in my father's bedroom. Matted tumbleweeds of dog hair rolled around as if the place were some twisted ghost town. They lived every waking moment in my father's room and never left. They ate, slept, and went to the bathroom out of his sliding glass doors, when they could make it.

Dragging him inside from his Mercedes, I hoisted this paralyzed two-hundred-pound man, my father, up into my arms and carried him one hundred and twenty feet through the grotesque pet-polluted dungeon that we called home. I laid him on the bed and went back out to the car to get all the supplies that we had picked up. We were dead broke, so it wasn't much. His pain pills, some ice cream, that kind of thing. I was in complete denial, I couldn't lose Barry, this was not an option. We had a family meeting right away. I was voted to be Barry's fulltime live-in provider. We couldn't hire an outside person for many reasons. The big one was that if an outside health care provider were to come into the home, they would legally be obligated to report the below-par living conditions to Adult Protective Services.

So here we were, Barry and I, alone to battle spinal cancer by ourselves with no money. I was in complete shock at the whole situation. So, I tucked him in, made a phone call, and went down the street and scored. It was a quick handoff, two minutes at most, and I ran home to be by his side.

I smoked a massive bowl in my water bong and decided to go sit with him for a while. He was scared. A man who loved to golf, swim, and dance his whole life, now told he was bedridden. I was a full-blown IV meth addict with no medical experience, in the throes of methamphetamine psychosis. But I punched in. This would prove to be the toughest job I had ever had in my life, and that says a lot.

Nothing was prepared. I got him an empty gallon jug of water from the kitchen. This was to piss in until I could find a way to get the proper medical supplies. A few hours of watching "Matlock" and he had to take his first trip to the bathroom. I picked him up under his arms and used every ounce of energy I had to lift him up securely. I stood on the putrid carpet, aqua and stained brown with dog urine and balls of old hair. I walked backward, him wearing his all-black Champion sweatsuit that he loved so much. I could hear my Adidas Shell Toes sloshing through deep puddles of piss. The stench was enough to make you vomit. I almost tripped over one of the blind, dying old dogs as I dragged my paralyzed father to the toilet in his restroom.

How did life get like this? I was numb to the conditions of the house until this moment. I screamed at the dogs to move, without trying to upset Barry too much. He was moaning in pain and very scared. We were both new to this "not being able to walk" thing. I sat him down on the toilet and pulled his bottoms off. He was terrified that I would drop him. I stood in the main bathroom area, outside the door to the toilet. The floors were stripped to bare to the concrete, as was most of the house. A massively elevated marble bathtub, that was once pristine, now had a beige and dark brown brindle coloring. An exposed plywood step sat underneath. My grandparent's house was beautiful before the madness. Not so much now.

To the left was a matching brown brindle stand-up shower. There was a glass door that leaked water onto the floor when the shower was on, covered in soap scum and dirt. While he was using the restroom, I thought to myself, *He can't be here like this*. He called when he finished and I sloshed my way back to his bed, him in my arms. I had to think of a plan to fix up the damn room and make it sanitary for my dad to live in.

I made sure he had everything he needed, then went into my room and mixed up a massive shot of ice. I was fading fast, and I needed some of that Go-Go Juice to stay awake during the long night ahead. I was now paralyzed myself, just in a completely different way. It took me a good fifteen minutes before I started to cry, once the grim reality set in that my father, who I loved with all my heart, my best friend in the whole world, was going to die.

The next few days were terrifying. You never realize how often someone goes to the bathroom, needs things, or depends on themselves, until you're thrown into a situation like this. The work was around the clock. I was making him his meals, all the toilet trips, and keeping him company. There was just no time to sleep. And I had to work; just the bare minimum driving, enough to get what I needed to survive.

This first week, I was getting my feet wet. I was testing the waters to see just how long he could be left unattended. The whole thing made me sick. I just couldn't do without. Barry knew when I left exactly what I was going to do. I started only doing southside dope drops and doing them for pennies on the dollar. My phone would ring. Someone would need to go drop some product. I would drive from point A to point B, and then I would fly back home. I felt as guilty as can be, every single time. I was constantly worrying in my mind, *what if something were to happen while I was gone?*

Over the next week or so, Barry got angry and started fighting me on everything. The dogs were the biggest topic. He refused to put them down so I could redo the room. I bought a shampoo machine at the pawnshop and cleaned his rugs. I dumped gallons of black water from its tank, out the door to the backyard that was connected to his room. I scrubbed the bathroom with bleach and did the best job I could with what we had.

Barry was getting restless. He knew how severe this sickness was and wanted to enjoy the short amount of time we had left. I was the opposite. As sick as I was, I was telling him he needed to eat healthy and start mentally preparing for the massive uphill battle ahead. He didn't want to hear it. We went to the grocery store. He wanted to get some beer and cigarettes. I pulled up and put him into one of the motorized shopping carts. My father was a man with pride. It was so sad watching him well up as he sat in that cart, legs motionless and weak. I put a case of Budweiser in his cart, and we checked out.

#

I was shooting up as often as I could. Things were deteriorating as weeks passed. I was meeting women left and right off dating apps and social media. They would come right over to Oakbrook and most of the time, they would bring dope. *Thank God for Them/They, if it weren't for them sending these women, I would have been up shit creek.* At least, that's what I thought was happening at the time. Sure, the girls would change up on me, as always. Sure, I would act so obnoxious that they would leave. But like clockwork, one would go and another one would show up just in the nick of time.

My mental state was folding like a cheap lawn chair. The house was becoming more evil every day. The haunted room had people spooked. More and more visitors at Oakbrook were refusing to come back because of the evil presence in that house. The look, the vibe, the things taking place inside, they were a little too spooky for people to deal with. I could feel the presence of the devil in everything I did. The drugs, the sex, my everyday life. Even caring for my sick father was a demon-tinted chore. I had never seen someone dying right before my eyes, and I was starting to break.

He would cry my name from his bed every few hours. I would pause the porn and get dressed long enough to go in and take care of business. My guilt was eating me alive. It was impossible for me to sit and watch TV with him. I used to love laying in his big king bed, watching old TV shows, and laughing with him. Nowadays, I would go in, do what I needed to do, and find myself choking back tears the whole time I was with him. He was wasting away. Dropping weight overnight, twenty to thirty pounds in what seemed like no time at all. My drug den was the only escape I had from the reality of his death. The meth, the demonic sex…it was a sweet release.

#

I ran into Heidi at a local trap right down the street. I was scoring one morning, getting ready for my day, and figured I would get my medicine early. We got in my car and headed home.

Heidi didn't blink at the condition of the house. She was used to the drug life. She was forty years old with big, thick, long curls, a fine Mexican Mamacita with the biggest green eyes you ever saw. Her thighs were plump. She was wearing black tights and a razor-sharp t-shirt, and as always, she was smelling good. She went into Barry's room right away to introduce herself. You think I am crazy? Heidi was bonkers.

She loved injecting meth; she had an eighty-year-old sugar daddy from a neighboring city that would drive in and give her cash for dope every few days. He couldn't get it up, so she would just let him lick her occasionally and the gravy train continued. Heidi quickly became my girlfriend. She had a bad habit and hung out with some well-known drug dealers from down the street. The problem was when they would get done using her body, they would throw her out because she acted so crazy. This is what I was about to get stuck with.

I started to get jealous daily. She would want to go over there, service the main guy, and come back with the dope. My twisted heart had feelings for her pretty fast and I hated it. Most times, I would just turn a blind eye, and smoke and shoot half the dope she would come home with. One night, Tony offered me an eight ball to drop her at a motel so he could sleep with her. I couldn't do it. I had never directly pimped out a woman I cared about before, and I didn't want to start now. I knew she was a whore, but I couldn't directly participate. It was too much of a scumbag move, even for me.

Heidi started spending a lot of time with Barry. She was taking it upon herself to care for him. I knew there was more than kindness in her black heart. These people are vultures. They will use whatever they can to get ahead. He owned the house, and he was dying. I was sure there was a dark, wicked motive there. But underneath it all, she was a very spiritual person. She had a direct link to Jesus, and I had seen it with my own eyes. She sang worship music beautifully, she loved the Lord, and she was one of the worst meth addicts I had ever seen. She began to lay hands on Barry and pray frequently. He never spoke of God, and this made him feel extremely uncomfortable. He even pulled me aside and banned her from his room. I always thought that was funny.

Heidi and I would have the hottest sex imaginable. Straight evil with a twist of Cain. I played games with her; I would have both of us naked on the bed in my room. We would mix up a couple of overdose size shots and get ready to fix, nude. The game was one where we would shove the needle in our veins, draw back the blood and inject it at the same exact time. As soon as that overwhelming rush would hit our brains, soon as the demon took hold, we would attack each other. The kissing was lustful and wet, the sex was a marathon...hours, sometimes days long and sickly perverted.

On a few occasions, the injecting got so serious, the sex so dangerous, I had to talk with her after, and on my own accord, apologize to her for how atrocious I was in bed. She didn't mind one bit. The thing about meth, it's all about pushing the boundaries. How much can we do? How crazy can we get?

How dangerous can we live? So, she was fine with it. Every oozing second.

#

My birthday in 2018, was one of the darkest days of my life. It was one of the most horrifying moments in time I had ever lived through. My mom had sent me a good chunk of birthday money via Western Union. I ordered a quarter ounce of a fire batch that I had heard hit the street just hours before. I knew Heidi was working with *Them/They* and it was irking me. I decided, after all this time, to pick a fight with her. I went and grabbed the dope, and what is to happen next, you can decide for yourself. It happened just the way I say, one hundred percent true. Was it the drugs, was it an act of God? The choice is yours passengers.

I returned to Oakbrook around six in the evening. with a payload of strong shards. I went in, checked on Barry. Heidi was at his bedside talking. He said, "Happy Birthday, Boston," and I started to cry as I walked away. Heidi and I went into my bedroom and fixed up a couple of shots to get this party started. I began with the double talk right away, and she was an expert at returning it. My dad had to break up the verbal arguments from his bed three times by midnight. I was threatening to go shoot up in front of him, to teach *Them/They* a huge lesson. I was acting nuts. Thank God, she talked me out of it.

Around one in the morning, I went out and had a piece of Oreo Ice Cream Cake in the kitchen. When I returned, Heidi really started running her big mouth. I went to my top drawer and continued to talk shit to her as I pulled apart the guts of a brand-new syringe. I had the quarter ounce in one hand, the plastic tube of the syringe in the other, with the plunger sitting on the top of the nightstand. I was arguing with her, "Oh yea Heidi, Ok, you wanna see crazy, I'll show ya crazy." As I was saying that I was digging the top hole of the syringe into the full bag of glass, thus filling it with heavy thick stones of crystal meth.

    I continued to argue with her as I took an eyedropper full of water and began dropping teardrops over the stones in the rig as if I was fixing a mixed drink on the rocks. I put the very end of the plunger into the setup. The fix was now in. I started to shake the needle up and down, back and forth, melting the thick poisonous rocks within its chamber. It was s hundred units of jelly, as much as one could fit into a syringe. Most likely a gram of very strong meth. It's a shot that would make your heart explode.

    I flexed my pale white arm into a fluttered pink mass of tension. The bulbous vein popped out of hiding like a gangster on the run. I looked at Heidi in her big green eyes, the surgical steel poking through my insidious flesh, pulsing and fair. The blood shot into the register, polluting the yellow dope film that filled the cylinder. I started to shake as I plunged the fire into my soul. Halfway through, I started to lose my eyesight. I screamed, a vicious roar, a lion quaking in flames. I pushed as hard as my body would allow. When the shot was finished, I ripped the bloody apparatus from my cold and clammy skin, throwing it on the filthy carpet, which was once beige and graced the floors of my grandparent's abode.

    Heidi looked on horrified, trying to make sense of the furious suicide attempt that just took place before her. I approached her with sexual disciplinary action. Tearing her top off with my teeth seemed relevant, infliction of fear was pertinent in my dominance. She was elated with fear; my saliva was beastlike and demonic. I kissed her with a loving hateful emotion, one that can barely be described in writing. I wanted to marry her as much as I wanted to spill her blood onto the mattress. *What was taking hold of me?* I felt as if I was in a scene from "An American Werewolf in London."

My fingernails felt as if they were growing in painful, alien-like strides. I felt myself becoming something grossly different, a metamorphosis into a beast. Elongated frightful hair sprouting from my once human skin. I was a man no more. The growls that came from deep within my torso startled us both.

"You got a demon in you," Heidi gasped out.

She was a healer spiritually. She knew the wickedness within my spirit, she knew it was not even me. There was something else in the room controlling my body and movement like a sadistic puppeteer.

"Your eyes have changed, Boston; you look like a reptile."

I spat at her to shut her mouth. The degradation between us only seemed to turn her on even more. The evil in this kind of sexual experience is unspeakable. It lures the participant deeper into what appears to be a good time. It's part of a spiritual death and snare that only Satan can conjure.

I finished deep inside her, a panting broken shell of a man once living. Now possessed by some dark, glowing force of evil. I sat on the edge of the bed, unapologetic and proud. She was whimpering, almost crying in pain from what I had just administered.

"Are you done, Boston?" she asked.

"Baby, big daddy is just getting started." I was smirking as I plotted my next maneuver.

What happened next is up to the reader to decide. I have a picture from this night, one where my eyes prove to be not my own. I worked up another seventy units of ice. Heidi was pretending to sleep as she wanted no part of what was about to be. I sat on the edge of the bed and fixed myself like I had a thousand times before. Then...black. It always goes to black.

I woke on my knees, looking out the reader's nook in my bedroom. The sheet was pulled down, the city street exposed to my fearful, weeping eyes. It looked like the money shot from "The Exorcist" with the flooded streetlamp hitting a dismal backdrop. I had no clue how I had gotten there. Heidi was behind me screaming. This kind of terror is something of folklore, and somehow, I was very calm, docile in nature.

I stood to my feet and assured Heidi that I was ok. "What the fuck happened?" I asked in a panic.

"I took it from you, Boston, I took it from you," she screamed.

"Heidi you're crazy, shut up," I sneered at her.

The poor girl was spooked something silly! Like she had witnessed a slaying in the Hollywood Hills. Something out of "The Wonderland Murders."

She explained that I had fixed, stood up, and overdosed in mid-stand. She described my lifeless body, lying face down on the corroded carpet. She used all her might to flip my carcass onto its back, where she placed her palms over my heart. She described the death leaking up in reverse, into her arms as she absorbed the sickness from within me. She took it. I looked at her in bewilderment. I blew off her admission as she laid on the bed. I nestled beside her and tried to make sense of it all.

She passed out from exhaustion. I had fixed the bedsheet over the window so no one could see into the madness. The twinkle of the Christmas lights allowed just enough site for me to be riddled with anxiety. I stared at the popcorned ceiling for what seemed like an eternity, then it happened.

A wall of heat hit me like a tidal wave. I felt warm fluid

pouring from some unknown source beside me.

"Heidi, what the fuck is going on, girl?" I shouted.

She moaned beside me like a cow giving birth. There was heat flowing from her body like a cheap plug-in radiator in some abandoned crack house. I leapt to my feet and hit the light switch on the wall. What I saw next haunts me to this day.

The light exploded into a reality untold. The mattress looked like a human sacrifice had taken place, once a virgin bride sliced into thin pimento arranged by a sadistic killer. Heidi laid almost lifeless, like a doll speaking in some foreign tongues. Her language wasn't that of demons but driven by some far-off spirit, summonsed to deliver a message of doom.

Her nightgown was a river mouth of blood. Her insides poured onto the once semi-clean sheets. She was bleeding out before my eyes, minstrel and thick. I panicked as I ran to get Barry's keys. The Benz was blocking me, so I decided not to waste one second. "Dad, I gotta go, this bitch is dying on me." His eyes were filled with fear. Another stress that was not needed in the life of a dying man. *What the fuck was wrong with me, exposing my father to this kind of shit show?*

I hoisted Heidi up into my arms, blood gurgling from her pulsating loins. She bathed me in iron as I stumbled to the black SUV in the driveway, just outside the door at Oakbrook. She was speaking to me as if I could understand her foreign lips.

"Love, love, love," she mouthed in pain.

I hit that gas. The tires of the Benz gripped like puma paws in some far-off jungle landscape. I shredded through the night, blasting down Saratoga Boulevard like a bat out of hell. I screamed into the ER entrance just after four o'clock. I ran into the lobby, leaving my almost deceased partner in the passenger seat.

"We got a bleeder," I screamed.

The hospital staff ran outside as if they were rushing to the aid of some superstar patient. Heidi was at the front of the line, and why not? She only looked like someone had put a sawed-off shotgun in her hoo-ha and pulled the trigger.

They rushed her to the back of the emergency room. Doctors and nurses were yelling, IV drips and drugs being ordered with a lightning quickness. This girl was dying...but why? To my surprise, they assumed I was her husband and let me stay to watch the whole murderous scene unfold. Her blood pressure was sky high, well into the two hundred range. Heart attack zone. Her body temperature was 103.3. The broad was roasting like a deluxe prime rib in a brick-laid oven at Boston, Massachusetts' north end during Christmas.

They poked and prodded, sticking her with all sorts of vile pins; a Mexican voodoo doll, beautiful and bloodless. She stared into my eyes as if these were her last moments. I held her hand like a loving husband awaiting the birth of some demonic Rosemary's baby. Then, we were alone.

Whatever cocktail the medical experts gave her seemed to be working. Her temperature had dropped to normal, and her blood pressure went to a regulatory model. She sat panting and covered in sweat. She looked like the little girl in "Interview with a Vampire." She even had the fangs to match. She never stopped talking, as if she were possessed.

When staff returned, I felt as if I had just witnessed a cannibalistic feast. A ceremonial murder of an innocent child, or far worse. I was emotionally spent.

"What the hell happened to her?" I asked.

"Well, she was experiencing heavy menstruation. She lost a lot of blood, but it looks like the proper medication has it under control," the doctor said. I was too high and dumbfounded to put up any kind of rational fight. They simply gave her the discharge papers and sent us on our way.

I pulled the Benz up. She was waiting in a wheelchair. Within forty-five minutes of arrival, we were ready to go home. I couldn't believe what had just happened. The short drive home was in dead silence, no pun intended. I lifted Heidi into my arms and carried her across the fecal filled threshold that was Oakbrook. Thoughts roared through my mind: *How in God's name did this happen? What really caused this horrific and near-deadly event? Did she really take the death from me? Was Heidi the healer that she's always claimed to be?*

She laid on the blood-soaked mattress once again. With a glance, she would say her first words in English since the possession.

"I told you I took it, Boston."

I stroked her sweaty mane with gentle love and care. "I know you did, baby. I love you, Heidi."

Some drastic part of my soul knew she was telling the truth.

Heidi was an IV meth user that never sat still in one place for more than two days at a time. This girl stayed lifeless in bed for five cycles. Only rising to use the bathroom or throw up. I brought her water and food and she touched none of it. Going back and forth between her and Barry was mentally taxing on all levels. I didn't know which one I was to find dead first.

I had to leave to score early on the sixth day. I figured if she wouldn't eat or drink, the least I could do was bring her some medicine. When I returned, Heidi was gone. Without a trace, she disappeared from my line of sight and out of my heart. I loved Heidi for saving me. She took the death from me that night. I shot up one-hundred-and-seventy units of jelly and lived to tell this frightening story.

#

I was slipping into madness deeper by the second. I was fetching Barry's beer and cigarettes daily. I would sit with him in a pair of these old, brown, leather office chairs in front of his king-size bed which faced the TV. The stench of the dog urine and feces was enough to gag a maggot. The two dying dogs were rotting at our feet, but he refused to euthanize them. He feared if they died, he would soon follow. The TV tray that doubled as a table between us held a nearly full ashtray. Butts of old soggy Marlboro Reds overflowed the stinking nicotine trap with a horrific aroma.

A ratty used Styrofoam cooler held his cold Budweiser, the only comfort left for a dying man. As much as I wanted to throw it all outside and call someone for help, was there really anything I could do? We were abandoned. Left to die by the outside world. A destitute old man, penniless and poor left with his dying drug addict and sex-freak son. The scene made a Rob Zombie horror flick look like an episode of "The Mikey Mouse Club."

We stared at the TV and tried to make small talk, all the while ignoring the cancer-ridden elephant in the room. The dog urine leaked from their ancient bladders. Thick smoke clung to once-white, now nicotine-stained walls. If hell had a look, this was the view. If it had a smell and a feel, this was surely it. Trips to the bathroom were appalling. I was having to give my dad laxatives to ease the flow from within.

One such trip from the shower to the bed proved murderous. I was to hoist him from the chair. He was naked and freshly clean. When I lifted him into my arms to perform the swivel lift, he defecated liquid all over the mangy aqua carpet. He started to cry in my arms. The pungent, acidic foam that lingered below had me tearing up. The fumes collided with the dog piss immediately, causing me to shudder and gag.

"I am so sorry, Boston," Barry yelped.

"Dad, it's ok. It's a normal thing when you take that medication."

I tried to make him feel better. His baby was now holding him like a child, and it killed him. It was time to begin the treatments for radiation. We still had no chair yet, so I would deadlift this man and carry him over hundred and twenty feet out to the Benz. He was terrified I would drop him. That was never an option. No matter how high, strung out, or sick I was, I loved this man far too much to let that happen.

The doctor had me hoist my father up onto a medical table. I laid him flat on his back in his sweat suit. No matter what the condition of the house, I always had him bathed, in clean clothes, and his hair looking like a million bucks. They lifted his shirt and put an X dead center on his chest. That's where they were going to shoot the radiation treatment into his torso. It was almost a fake feeling, the whole experience.

It always took about ten minutes for the doctor to examine him and leave the room. But getting Barry ready was a three-hour chore for this bullshit treatment that everyone knew was pointless. This cancer was aggressive, and it was eating him alive. I started to fear that maybe none of this was real. *Was Them/They behind all this? Maybe Barry wasn't so sick after all?* The wheels of lunacy started to turn in my mind. I was breaking. Looking back, seeing my father die before my eyes combined with the drugs…it was all causing me to lose touch with reality.

#

One night I was laying in my bed. It was about seven as the South Texas sun began to drain into the backdrop of a deadpan horizon. An insane lightbulb went off in my head. *Heidi is pregnant* rang in my thoughts like the Liberty Bell. I rushed into Barry's room to find him watching "Matlock."

"Dad, I got to find Heidi! I think she needs me."

He played along, what else could he do? He was scared and paralyzed and knew there was no stopping that freight train once it got going down the tracks.

I took the last eight dollars he had and the Benz. I was going to find the healer at any cost. I fully believed that Heidi was pregnant with our child. So off I went, into the night, no clue where to begin my search.

I started at the local trap where she was known to frequent. I found Jay, a homeless deviant who was rumored to be her cousin. He gleefully hoped in, seeing an opportunity to rob a clearly disturbed drug addict. I was an easy target for such a bottom feeder. He was far more malicious than I originally thought.

Jay was a sinfully short Mexican. His face was worn from years of giving head in city parks and smoking synthetic weed under the hot Texas sunlight. He wore tight jeans and ratty old cowboy boots, most likely stolen from the Goodwill Donation Station. We bullshitted as the Benz rolled aimlessly through the city on a search for a pregnant Heidi. His red and white checkered pearl-snap shirt smelled of vinegar and dick. He made me want to vomit at the sight and smell of him. An infested drug prostitute in my dad's Benz was now my tour guide through hell.

I told him of my dilemma. He played it like an Oscar-worthy actress. He started to point me in all sorts of directions. I didn't listen much. I was using my inner compass, and though insane, it told me to follow the light. I would see the glimmer of a streetlamp, or sometimes just the reflection of light off a bad paint job on an Oldsmobile would do the trick. Wherever God's light pointed, we went.

I ended up Downtown. I was off Agnus Street, at some abandoned tow yard behind The Prop Shop, an old boat propeller repair business. The lot was almost vacant. It was surrounded by a chain link fence with two chain gates, attached by a rusty padlock at the front. Matt was there at the entrance, a short White male with an eerie 5150 tattooed under his right eye. That's the call sign for police in California when the subject in question is known to be criminally insane to authorities.

I got out and signaled Jay to follow my lead. It was pitch black now. Only the flickers of gas release from the refineries and roaming flashlights in the distance broke the plane of sight. I bantered to the rear of the Benz. I lifted the sleek, black tailgate and dug into the beige clean wool of the boot. I lifted out a perfectly new shiny chrome tire iron from the hidden compartment for flat-tire repairs. Jay stood puzzled as to what my next move was. I locked up the ride and headed to the entrance to make our presence known.

"What? You got goin' here," Matt said with authority.

"My girls up in there, and I am going to get her," I said with no qualms.

He looked over his shoulder into the almost empty lot. There stood about ten junked-up, half-chopped Cadillac's and one dismal and haunted-looking trailer home.

Around one of the cars, stood seven tough looking Mexican gang members. And that's when it dawned on me. *This was all a damn put on. Another scene set by none other than Them/They.* With no fear, I ducked under the chain link fence and headed in to find Heidi, tire iron in hand. I cruised right past the thugs, tattooed from head to toe. They sat shocked. This White boy must be so insane, they best not get in his way.

Afterall, I had followed "the light" to this lot. *It was God, Them/They, something outside of myself that had guided me to find Heidi this fateful night. She was in that damn trailer, and I was going in to get her.* I strutted right past them; Matt and Jay following behind like two stray dogs. I walked right up to the haunted trailer and pounded on the flimsy aluminum door like I was a damn cop.

 Boom. Boom. Boom.

 The door swung open as a single exposed lightbulb swayed from a frayed wire that ran from above. "Who the fuck are you?" said the almost movie-worthy little Mexican hooker that came to answer. She stood all of four feet, wearing a gross Pearl Jam t-shirt and no pants. Her vagina in full view, hairy and unkempt.

 "My girl is up in this trailer, and I am coming in," I smirked.

 She cracked a smile and said, "Ok White boy, I will tell you what, put the club down, and I will let you in, your girl ain't in here."

 So, I laid the shiny metallic hammer down on top of an orange five-gallon Home Depot bucket that sat near the door, and in I went.

 The chick handed me a flashlight, almost on cue. There were no other lights in the deep rectangular trailer. I flicked my thumb upwards, the light began to strobe, almost like…A MOVIE! There were filthy pink panties and dirty clothes all over the counters as the light from the flashlight flickered in my trembling hand. I started my way to the back bedroom of the dilapidated structure. There was a musty old flannel curtain that separated me and the abyss that laid ahead. The drops hit an old oil pan that caught rainwater of days past. My hand touched the lumberjack pattern of the old curtain, and I slid it along the rusty shower curtain rings that were fastened to its top.

On the bed lay a lifeless Mexican girl. Her legs were covered in black tatts. Two massive dragon patterns swirled up her thick thighs and met white cotton panties. She had no top on; her nipples danced in the flashing illumination of the broken flashlight. It wasn't the healer. Now what? I retreated to the front of the trailer where the hooker waited with a shit-eating grin on her hairy face. Her long greasy hair made me sick.

"I told you your bitch wasn't up in here, White boy."

I couldn't even respond. I was speechless. The whole scene was larger than life. I was so scared I could barely place a rational thought. I clicked off the flashlight and stepped down the makeshift staircase. The gang members all laughed in unison, a macabre folly in a terrible nightscape. I hurried back to the Benz, Matt and Jay following once again.

We filtered under the chain link, and I opened the doors to the Benz.

"She ain't here," I bantered.

I started the truck, and now myself and two deranged passengers were on our way back to Oakbrook to get high. My newfound friends were demonic. Matt had a deep southern drawl, one from a poor southern state. He sounded like Glenn Danzig, Johnny Cash, and Spike Jones all had some sick lovechild.

I drove home in excess speeds of eighty miles an hour or more. The trip is an estimated twelve miles or so on the Crosstown Expressway. We arrived home and went through the garage door and in through the laundry room. I went to check on Barry and returned quickly to the table near the kitchen area. I didn't trust these two for obvious reasons.

The bowl was lit, and the conversation took a psychedelic turn. My head spun as Matt, in his strange southern accent, spoke of "The Prince," a novel he was recommending for its subtle text in warfare. The two spoke of the apocalyptical end of times. Nuclear holocaust and the end days. My breath was short, as the drugs only furthered this already insane trip into the beyond.

Just then Jay grabbed a sketch pad and pencil off the counter and sat back down to draw. He began telling some double-sided riddle as the pencil ran across the page. It was surreal.

He drew the famed Payasa, the Mexican female clown with diamond eyes. The pencil sounds were like a disturbed beehive. A muzzle of angry wasps crackling in rage. My eyes darted back and forth, a futile effort to remain in mental control.

Matt glided in his speech at the same time, an almost preplanned assault on all my capacities. Strength, feel, and smell, all ravaged by the drugs and insanity of the dark situation at hand. It was a nightmare coming to life, jumping off the page in black and white terror. A vaudeville replica of a life once lived, consisting of clowns, laughter, and tears. I was the source of the giggles this time, and I hated it.

Just then Jay turned the picture upside down, revealing a whole new Payasa, a whole new story, an inverted new climax. How could he draw this so fast?

"We gotta go," I choked out with my last breath. The two didn't want to leave, but I insisted.

Jay signaled to an old wooden box that sat on the floor near the haunted room on the way out. "Boston, that's where the demons are trapped. Remember that."

I was to let the two off about five blocks up the road in

some swanky neighborhood on the southside. I couldn't get to the drop point fast enough. The demonic duo had to go, and fast. We pulled up to the house and time didn't exist, only the thought of freedom from these two serial torturers. They got out of the car, and I sped away as soon as the last door to the Benz closed. I peered in the rearview in terror as they became ant-sized replicas of humans. They were gone, now I can get back to Barry.

    A few blocks later, I turned left onto Everhart Road. I was to go a few lights up, hit Saratoga Boulevard and I was home free.

    Now, I was a professional driver. Even high, crazy, whatever, I could spot a major mechanical problem a mile away. I was heading to the light on Saratoga when the Benz started to shift in ways never felt before. A grinding sound, the feeling that the truck was top-heavy. It started to flop from side to side, reminiscent of an old Western wood-wheel wagon.

    There was something very wrong with this situation. I was about as high and paranoid as one could possibly be, and I needed to make it to Oakbrook. The problem persisted as I leaped onto Saratoga for the home stretch of the journey. I was only going about five miles an hour as I glided around the turn onto Oakbrook Road. I pulled into the driveway like a wounded man. The grinding was as loud as gunfire when I came to a complete stop.

    Once again, I found myself with my cell phone in hand, ready to assess the damage from another dangerous trip. The glow of the phone screen hit the onyx paint like a spotlight in a prison break. It was the back-driver's side tire. What I saw next would change the game. I placed the light of the phone where the lug nuts would normally be. The trunks of the nut rings were bare in four out of five spots. The last lug nut was hanging by a thread. Smoke was billowing off the steel. Someone had removed all the nuts but one.

Those lugs were specially locked on that make and model of Mercedes. The only possible way someone could have removed those lug nuts was with the special key. Just then my mind shot back to the orange five-gallon bucket. The trailer behind the Prop Shop. The lug wrench I had used as a weapon was the only answer. Those motherfuckers tried to kill me!

I drove almost thirteen miles, at speeds over eighty miles an hour, with one damn lug nut sitting between me and a sure-to-be deadly accident. What the hell had happened? In hindsight, it was the angels all along.

In my mind though then, it was *Them/They. How could they pull off such an event? What kind of trick was this?* Only one answer came to mind as I walked back into death on Oakbrook that night. *I was in a MOVIE!* It all started to make sense.

Barry was faking cancer. The girls coming in groups of hundreds with free dope. The near-death accidents, the drug dealing, all the crazy, skin-of-my-teeth situations where I had come out unscathed. This was a damn Hollywood production! Now I had to figure out the Who, the Why, and the How I was selected to be in such an obscene movie.

I checked in on Barry and told him we needed some new nuts for the Benz. He didn't really say much; the pain medicines had taken effect for the night. I was back to the war room to spark a bowl and go over all the particularly important details in my newfound situation. *Why was there a movie? Why was Them/They filming me? What the hell could the plotline be in such a sex-crazed, drug-fueled extravaganza?*

The answers were out there. I just had to find them. *Who was in on it?* I started to pick apart every relationship, every scene, and every player that could be involved. I couldn't believe what I was discovering. All the puzzle pieces began to fit perfectly. I was the star. So, buckle up, passengers. This is where shit starts to get really, interesting.

Chapter 8

Movie Magic

Plagued with obscure creeping thoughts as I awoke from a nightmare. Sweat beaded down my skin as I sat up directly in bed. I was passing out more than sleeping nowadays. Momentary lapses in consciousness happened more slumber. Meth has a way of making life a large dream. One vibrant motion, always ending in a future fix, too little and short in stature. There just isn't a life worth living between hits. The smoke is fuel to keep your eyelids from setting adrift. Every heartbeat was a burden, every twitch an instant from disaster.

The Movie was now an obsession. *Them/They* had been outed. At least in my mind. I formed a hypothesis that all my cohorts, friends, and family had to be in on this grand design. My daily struggle was now with the "actors" I met. Everywhere I went…every drug dealer, every person at the store…everyone was suspect.

I would have people over as I watched Barry. In a normal conversation, my guests would always have a snide comment about something that happened deep within the privacy of my bedroom. These people would have knowledge of the kind of porn I had been watching the night before. Some detail of the gross sexual tryst that took place just hours before; things they just shouldn't and couldn't know.

This is when I became hip to the hidden cameras in

Oakbrook. In the tweaker world, there were stories of the hidden mini cameras everywhere. The ones used to record people having sex and use blackmail footage to extort the rich and unsuspecting victims of the night. This was the only way these creeps could know the things they knew about me.

As days went on, I got used to the fact that I was always on camera. Fights would erupt with Barry almost on the hour. I knew he was in on it. They got to the old man! Always a sucker for the mighty dollar, they were able to buy him off. I formed a theory that they had my old man on a liquid diet, shedding pounds off him as if he were a big-time Hollywood star that needed to lose weight for the leading role that would land him an Oscar.

The biggest fights happened when Her Highness Heidi returned to play her part. She sauntered in like Elizabeth Taylor. A diva queen on the set, always demanding and vile in her delivery. She warmed up to Barry real nice this time around. I walked into his bedroom once when things got a little too quiet. I found the little bitch laid right next to my old man in the bed. Since he was in character and supposedly paralyzed, there wasn't much he could do to entertain her.

"Bitch, what do you think you're doing?" I spat.

"Nothing Boston, just sitting here talking with your dear old dad," she oozed.

This immediately made me crazy. I started throwing glass objects, smashing old furniture and more within seconds. I was in a full-on fit as Barry begged me to calm down. I told Heidi to "beat feet with the quickness," and she barked at me:

"I am not going anywhere, you crazy motherfucker. Your dad will have to throw me out,".

Right then and there, I wanted to kill her. On this day I'd had enough of *The Movie*. I had been up for a solid week, I couldn't remember my last meal, and I was itching to get high. Heidi and I stood toe to toe on the saturated aqua rug, piss on our feet, and stinking.

I made the mistake of getting up in Heidi's face. I pointed my index finger right against her cute little nose and told her "Get the fuck out."

Just then she retracted her claws on her right hand like a velociraptor. She took her manicured index finger and shot her nail right through the jelly of my baby-blue eyeball. I felt her nail withdraw from my eye socket. A stream of warm blood flowed from my lower eyelash down to my face. I traced the path with my finger and examined the red paint that now covered my hand.

"You fucking cunt!" I roared.

At this moment blood came running out of my left nostril like a faucet. The clotty mess ran down the back of my throat, prompting me to vomit all over the dogs that sat below. The poor dogs and that poor damn rug.

We all went into shock as I began to bleed like a gunshot victim. My father screamed in terror. I grabbed my eye; it felt as if I had been hit with a ball bearing in a slingshot at a high rate of speed. Heidi ran out of the house, knowing full well that I was about to smack her skull with an antique lamp. Her role in *The Movie* was over far as I was concerned.

I looked at one of the hidden cameras, "If you bring that bitch back to shoot another scene, I am going to kill her!"

My father postured and continued to collaborate with *The Movie* as if I was a madman. He was sticking to his guns, never letting on that there was a full-length Hollywood picture being shot in our once quiet home. The guy was the Iceman, unbreakable, even in scenes of great stress and impromptu violence. *What a first-time performance*, I thought to myself.

I marched after Heidi in a rage. When I found her in the driveway, she was nonchalantly talking to the delivery driver and signing for the brand-new wheelchair that we had ordered for Barry just days before.

The delivery guy asked, "Hey man, are you ok?"

With blood still gushing and covering my face and hands, I snickered and then blurted out, "Nerf gun accident."

He didn't think it was too funny, but all I cared about was if the audience at home was getting a chuckle. If I was going to be in a movie, it was going to be a hit comedy show.

The funny thing about being in this type of movie was it turned into a "me against the world" mentality. I came to the determination that this was the first reality show of its kind. One where the star didn't know he or she was being filmed and everyone else was in on it. It was surely nothing like I had ever seen.

Over the next few weeks, I developed a character to play. I named him "Daryl." I never called myself by this name; but I needed a go-to persona to be able to act out scenes with any mysterious person I ran into in my day-to-day life. I built the framework of Daryl from the annoying character I used on all the women that *Them/They* had sent leading up to this point. Daryl was the biggest jackass on the face of this earth.

My love for movies and TV had been a huge part of who I was since I was eight years old. I enjoyed all the old comedies, action movies like "Predator" and more. I am a naturally funny dude, so improv comedy came easy. Soon enough, I was finding out that I was a damn professional. I would tuck Barry in after his daily appointment; then off I would go out into the world to see what kind of scene *Them/They* had planned for that afternoon.

Suddenly, what was once a fearful sequence of events,

now became a welcomed game. I was about to be a big Hollywood movie star. A damn dream come true for a thirty-five-year-old nobody in Corpus Christi, Texas. I tossed around the idea that I may be stuck in this reality TV show for a while. But then I would think, *no way.* There is only one entity on earth that could pull off this type of elaborate production. The executive TV world was small. This had all the hallmarks of Tinseltown. Every trap house, liquor store, and fast-food joint I walked into seemed to be full of a cast of waiting actors, all anticipating my arrival and waiting for their cue.

#

I had just wrapped a three-day pile-up of bad actors and loose *Them/They* women that I had emotionally destroyed back at the house. I sent every single one of them packing, tails between their legs and at a loss for words. I felt untouchable. Heidi had taken off about a week or so prior, sighting that "I was too much to handle." *Rightly so because Daryl was on his game. Them/They had barked up the wrong tree with me. If they wanted to shoot a movie, they were going to earn it.*

Them/They became the enemy. The unstoppable force with an unlimited budget sent to torture me day after day and film it. A grand plot to shoot an epic reality-style movie, where the hero was an unsuspecting victim.

The three days prior was madness at Oakbrook. Flashing back, there were countless screaming matches. Jokes on point in ruthless and furious roasts towards the actors who came to take on yours truly. They all lost in a big way. There were fistfights, excessive drug use, and sexual situations that would make Ron Jeremy blush. All on camera for all the world to see. I had no shame. I figured they would have to edit out the rough parts. At least put those pixel jobs over my junk, as they did in MTV's "Jackass" when Johnny Knoxville ran through the supermarket naked.

I would invite them over, or they would just show up. *Them/They* obviously had a script they followed. But they also rolled with the punches. No matter what road I would take, no matter what kind of casting curveball I would throw at them, they had it covered. I tried to piece together how they sent the extras on board, such as the passersby's I encountered in public with small speaking roles. I remembered from my research into film that there had to be a waiver. It was a release that actors and film participants signed to release their image to be used by the production team. It could also be used to bind these actors to a confidentiality agreement, one where they were gagged on the discussion of any knowledge of the film and its financers.

The waiver theory made sense with the fact that none of the main actors, like Barry, would discuss any details of the film. They were being paid. Handsomely. They couldn't go against the agreement they had signed without being sued for millions of dollars. They were only human, after all. They took the money! Who could blame them? *But my own Dad? How could he betray me in this way?* After being his son and best friend for over three decades? I thought it was a greedy and shallow move on his part to sell out the way he did. *And to fake cancer for a movie? What a heartless bastard.*

So, there I was. A marked man. Every person in my life, systematically bought off by this faceless Hollywood machine. Even the citizens of this great city were all in on it together, clearly being paid in hundred-dollar cash payments by production grips to make my life a living hell. *And for what? A damn movie? Well, when in Rome, I guess.* I may have been an uninformed target, but I might as well enjoy the ride to superstardom.

My comedic stylings were even surprising me. I would

find myself in a strip mall parking lot screaming jokes out to a random passerby; or in the Walmart electronics department standing on a counter doing a full stand-up comedy routine for all the shoppers in the store. Hell, we were on camera, weren't we? I had crowds of people busting a gut wherever I went. Here is where I pieced together that *The Movie* was hacking into the mainframes of all security cameras. Stores, traffic infrastructure, anywhere there was a camera, there was *Them/They*. I called it "The Eye in The Sky." An ode to one of Barry's favorite groups "Emerson Lake and Palmer." That song was a hit. Barry was a notorious B-side man. *Always a rebel, that one.*

  I started to take unexpected detours to throw them off. After that epic three-day win streak with the whores at Oakbrook, I decided to walk on foot to go pick up the Western Union money my ma had sent me from Myrtle Beach. When I was crossing the street to the grocery store, I noticed people in cars pointing at me as if they recognized me. Suddenly, I felt like I was John Lennon in the heyday of the Beatles. When I would get close to the car, they then would pretend not to notice me. Kind of like if John Lennon was on vacation, and they didn't want to come off as starstruck. I entered the store proudly and in character. There were a thousand people inside, shopping and going about their business. Not all of them were in on it, but some were, for sure.

  I made a beeline for the counter at the business center. The girl behind the counter was barely eighteen. A gorgeous half-Black, half-White goddess with the cutest face and thick Shirley Temple curls. Eyelashes so long, you would think they were Venus flytraps. She wore a bright red grocery store shirt as part of her uniform. She looked as if they had pulled her off the set of some reboot of "Saved by the Bell." A real class act. She could have easily been Miss Teen America. Her cheekbones high and sleek, her eyes big and cocoa.

"How can I help you today, sir?" she asked in a cute, high-pitched voice.

And here is me doing my best Rodney Dangerfield, acting a total ham. "Well honey, I am here to pick up two hundred smackaroos, Western Union please."

She met me with a giggle, almost looking directly into Camera One, hidden somewhere behind the floral department. "Of course, sir, could you please fill out the proper paperwork, so I can further assist you?"

She was such a doll. A little young for me, but this was The Movie...anything could happen, right?

"Sure, Sure, Sure baby, you got a pen for this proper paperwork?" I rattled off like a young Jackie Gleason. *He was The Great One, ya know?*

"Why yes sir, here you are," she said in a professional manner.

So, I am filling out the papers, right? And I got it into my head to do a little ad-lib dialogue with this A1 actor they had selected for this scene. *Hey, let's give the chick an opportunity to shine a little, huh?*

I leaned into whisper something to this mocha-latte mamacita. I signaled her with my index finger to come in a little closer, like I wanted to tell her a secret. She leaned in, smelling of diamonds and fresh-cut strawberries.

"So hey, are you rooting for the good guys...or the bad guys," I asked softly.

She paused.

Then, without skipping a damn beat, she looked left, then right, as if to see if anyone was listening from the outside, as if she didn't want to get caught breaking a contract.

"Well, we're rooting for you," she said quietly and smoothly.

We both sat back up onto the balls of our sneakers. We each had a surprised, joyful look on our face. And just then, we both burst out in uncontrollable laughter. She started to giggle. Then as she was counting out fresh twenty-dollar bills, she spoke clearly and professionally again:

"Ok sir, that's $200 today, is there another transaction I can help you with?" she smiled with her perfect pearly whites.

"No honey, but I'm gonna save you a seat right next to me at the premiere," I hummed in a jolly voice that, again, was only fit for Rodney Dangerfield.

#

My dad appeared to get worse by the second, and being the good son I was, I took care of him to the best of my ability. I wasn't one hundred percent positive that he was faking it. I loved him to death and no matter what, I was going to be there for him. The Lord started to make his presence known in bold ways during all this madness. I became militant in my love for Jesus Christ. Still getting high, living side by side with the Serpent, I began talking about the Lord to anyone who would listen.

Can you believe, after all the insanity, after all the sex, drugs, and hallucinations, the thing that got my whole family to turn on me, was my love for the Lord? I was speaking about the angels in the accident. I was going all over town, in the miscellaneous trap houses, and drug spots preaching the word of God to any open ear, high or not.

The wheelchair for my father became a symbol. It was pain, love, and dedication all rolled into one…no pun intended. *It was how we rolled at Oakbrook nowadays.* I got him up, got him bathed, and changed. I was a cheerleader as much as I was a caretaker.

"Dad, we can do this, we are gonna fight this all the way!" I refused to give up hope as *The Movie* played out. We were going to show the world the power of love, from a son to his dying father. So I was covered either way.

As Jesus began to touch my heart, I felt the urges of sexual immorality leaving me. I was becoming pure, in some strange drug-induced sanctification process. My shift turned from wanting to have sex all the time, to wanting a loving and nurturing marriage. The stage was set. I had so many women in my recent past. Now, I had the intense need to marry one of these women. I started to feel like the plotline of the movie was leaning into a wedding scene that would then end the whole story. A wedding day surprise where everyone would pop out, the movie finally revealing itself and all its characters. My new bride and I, riding off into the sunset in a brand-new sports car.

Now, who would this girl be? I started to get messages from actors wherever I went that there was a mysterious lover from my past, secretly lying-in wait, for the magical day where it would all come to pass.

This is where I started to go on missions. I would leave the house as often as I could, to pursue new avenues for the script. Everywhere I went, I felt like the movie was steering me in a new direction. All leading up to this marvelous wedding, a new life with the woman of my dreams.

Of course, there was the obvious, my Bella, the object of my affection. There was Heidi, the healer. Was she just playing the part of a crazy person to throw me off? There was Bella's younger sister. What a plot twist that would be? Was she secretly in love with me this whole time? Was I in love with the wrong sister all along? There were about ten more possibilities that ran through my mind, day and night.

#

I sat in my room one night well after Barry was asleep. This was the night that changed my life forever. This wasn't anything to do with no damn movie. Didn't feel like it then, and looking back, it sure as hell doesn't now. There are some things, some vulgar displays of power, that are undeniably real. Too grotesque and omni to blow off as some cheap special effect or prank. This was the night the Dark Prince of the Air made his presence known in a major and terrifying way.

Enter new actress. She hit me up through a dating app on my phone at night around ten. I was curious to see who *Them/They* were sending me at such a strange time of night. I was grasping at straws to find any sort of answer that would lead to the end of this torturous film. I responded, pretended like I was interested, and left to pick her up about thirty minutes later.

The Benz flew down Crosstown, with me completely unaware of the events that were about to take place, like an unsuspecting lamb being led to slaughter. She was at a rathole just off Baldwin Avenue. A Mexican hood just south of Downtown.

When I leaned over to pop the passenger door for her, I knew something was off. As her ass glided across the beige leather stitching, the air pressure within the Mercedes spaceship dropped dangerously low. Her grin was vile and despondent.

"So baby, you ready to party?" She let out a laugh something like Heath Ledger's version of the Joker.

She was chubby, long brown hair and a blemished mess for a face. She was oily and unbathed. Not anything like what *Them/They* had been sending around. The presentation was way off and out of character. *I think I may have intercepted a real-life bag chaser. One desperate for a fix and looking to screw. What the hell have I gotten myself into? I needed to stay on the script.* Anything other than the mission was a huge waste of time and resources. It was too late now; she was in the ride and ready to go. I couldn't just drop her off on the side of the highway. *Who knows, maybe this was some sort of a massive smokescreen that would pan out into some valuable information?*

We entered Oakbrook soon after. The chick didn't bat an eye at the condition of the house, which told me that she was either an actor or deeply disturbed. We went to my bedroom and talked for a good hour or so. A little bit of Daryl started to come out. Sheer frustration from not knowing if she was in "the know" or not. I was trying to tip the scales mentally in my favor and figure out a way to escape this nightmare.

She took her top off and started to masturbate in front of me. I was genuinely uninterested in sex for the first time in as far back as I can remember. My newfound love for Jesus, mixed with the smell of body odor coming from this girl, made for a very unromantic evening. I was out of dope, and to my amazement, she didn't bring any. I gave in and had some uneventful, boring sex with her.

This girl was mentally ill. There was something very dark and downright evil about her. I think her laugh is what tipped me off. It felt as if there were long yellow fingernails being raked across a dry chalkboard every time she cackled. After we finished, I made my way to the kitchen to find a liter bottle of cheap rum that I had stashed for emergencies such as this one.

I sat under the beaming light, almost like an extraterrestrial spacecraft was about to land in my grandparent's kitchen. My back was to the deep avocado porcelain sink. The countertop wrapped around to my right as I faced the opposing wall. The range top of the stove sat just to my right hand. It was a jet-black ceramic job, four knobs that controlled the heat settings perched closest to me. She stood with her arms folded, resting her elbows on the island counter on the other side of the range.

I sipped the rum as this bitch made loony girl small talk. Nothing too crazy, it was the calmest I had seen this broad since we met. At least I was getting a break from that maniacal laughter. I started to catch a buzz, warm and sour. I hadn't smoked meth in almost eight hours, and I was craving. Totally clear-headed and bored, I couldn't wait to drop her off and get back to the real business at hand.

I stared at her as she yapped about nothing. The air became thin and cold. A clear temperature drop turned the air frigid in a matter of milliseconds. I began to see sharp panes of hot white light appear behind her. Thin elongated frames, large rectangles of flashing energy that moved off her shoulder and to her immediate left. The mass of electricity took a blob form, almost human and tall in stature. It paused only a second as it turned and flew down the hall towards the bedrooms.

I couldn't believe my eyes. I looked at her and shuddered, almost unable to speak.

"Di, di, did you see that?" I stammered.

The women looked at me with wild eyes, the size of milk saucers, and weepy.

"No, but I felt it," she said.

As soon as the last word flung out of her mouth, I looked down and to the right. A hissing noise alerted me to the range top. Out of one of the range knobs came a billowing pyre of sparks, three feet high. Sparks that looked exactly like the hot white light that appeared behind the girl only moments before.

When the sparkler-like energy receded back down into the range, we both ran down the hall as fast as we could. I ended up crashing into Barry's room, waking him from a dead sleep.

"Dad, I don't know what the fuck happened down there?"

He looked at me in terror at first. Then just chalked it up to me being high. He called me crazy a few times before I hobbled into my room, a catatonic mess.

The woman and I sat in silence for a good three hours after this event. Not one word was spoken between us. We were paralyzed from fear.

"Stuff like this just happens," she said.

I looked at her furiously. *Shit like this doesn't happen to me*, I thought. As soon as I could muster up the courage to wander out into the dark driveway, I took her home.

There was a recurring thought that kept running in my mind for three days after this evil event. *Whatever it was, it knew who I was...and it didn't like me.* This is when I drew the conclusion that this had nothing to do with *The Movie*. This was Satan. Not a demon, not a spirit, this was pure evil making itself known in my life.

My dad had arranged for an electrician to come out to the house to fix the range top. Whatever had happened that night fried all the wiring to that appliance. It cost one hundred and eight-five dollars to fix. This was a turning point. The moment that I knew I was living a little too close to the devil.

I was about to be shown some mysterious things, aside from my role in the movie. Besides being in a reality movie, I was on a simultaneous spiritual journey that would blow the human mind. I was starting to transform into the character I was to play for the remainder of this shoot. The devil present, I knew the loving arms of the Lord were also with me. The feeling that I was about to do humongous things for Christ became overwhelming. Why else would the enemy, Satan, show me such personal attention?

I was no longer a stranger to the supernatural world. But I was about to be taken on a detour through a new part of hell. I still don't know the purpose of this trip to this day. I do know that it was the catalyst to the separation point between my dad and me. My family was furious with the condition of the home, and rightly so. They were also about done with, as they put it, my declining mental state. One close family member dropped by specifically to drive a colossal wedge between Barry and me…and boy, did it work.

There was a lot of screaming and yelling. It was a typical Bornagain fistfight in the making. Insults being hurled, spit being spat, a traditional Irish family holiday, sans the booze. Before this person stormed off, I was told I had to leave by noon the next day. I was being replaced. My caretaker services were no longer needed.

Barry was so tired of me, *The Movie*, and Jesus at this point that he happily agreed to the change in management. How could I blame him? I was dying before his eyes, as he was dying before mine. The last thing the poor guy should have to deal with was a big and fat burden like me. Let's face it, *The Movie* was a crazy experience. If he was in on it, the least I could do was play along. If this was the script, I was going to be onboard one hundred percent.

#

Remember my first plug? The long-haired guy in the Bluff? Well, I went to see him on the eve of my exile from Oakbrook. I figured I would score some quality shards and have one night of peace before things really got interesting.

Everything was business as usual until Marty Milford showed up. Marty was a well-known computer hacker and identity thief in Corpus. I never had the pleasure of meeting him in person. He was most famous for being the hacker who blew open the police department's mainframe. He supposedly ripped off all sorts of proprietary information and exposed the department's online confidential information for all to see. He was your perfect, class-act, tweaker, shit-bag extraordinaire.

He was a tall fella, about six feet with tight denim jeans, a brown button-down shirt, and some black restaurant shoes he bought from Academy Sports. He had sandy blond hair and a crew cut hairdo. He had a good potbelly and looked like a twisted, bad acid trip version of Bart Simpson. *Not someone you would want to babysit the kids anytime soon, that's for sure. Well, maybe after a few CPR courses, but not now.*

"What be your name, big fella?" Milford asked with a sneer.

"I'm Boston, a pleasure to meet ya," I said in complete sarcasm.

I was only going off what others told me about Milford leading up to this meeting. It appeared the whole thing was a build-up so I could meet this very interesting character from *The Movie. I mean come on...hackers, police mainframes busted wide open. Nice try, Them/They.*

Milford was the most annoying person I think I have ever met. I don't know if it was his slouchy appearance, my lack of sleep, or the total disdain I had for the color of his cheap button-down, but he irked me something fierce. I sat back and smoked a bowl as I took him in. I observed this creature as one would an animal you were about to adopt. I wanted to see just how long it would take before I wanted to kill him. Something told me that I better get used to this clown. *Afterall, it was no mistake that he just popped up out of nowhere. This was going to be a big scene. I would bet my life I am going to get stuck with this asshole in some way.*

I listened to this baboon for a good hour as he used the term "Fucked off" like it had an expiration date. See "Fucked off" can mean a slew of things. It is the tweaker equivalent to the Italians "Forget about it" once made famous by "The Sopranos". It can mean, you screwed up. It can also mean that you got someone high that normally does not do so. It can mean that you wasted a large sum of money, and so on, and so on. He had a certain way of saying it that made me want to jab a Phillips head screwdriver into his eye socket. *"Fucked off"…over and over and over again. This was going to be a pleasure having Daryl make him go insane. Every minute of it.*

After about two hours, I found myself with him and this massive pit bull named Boomer in the Benz on the way back to Oakbrook for my final night on the property. *What else did you expect? This is a damn movie.* Barry was not too happy that I had brought home strays. Milford and I got higher than a B-52 in the kitchen just before he went into his big spiel. He took off his shirt, revealing a ton of third-world tattoo work. He went into this super dramatic speech, pointing to each one, telling the harrowing tale of its origin and meaning. I wanted to vomit in my mouth.

Milford went on for hours on that insane diatribe. The time to twilight was growing short, as was my time on Oakbrook getting as thin as the hair in a Rogaine commercial. I couldn't figure out his role in *The Movie* yet; I could only feel the looming moment of my refurbished life headed my way, like the freight train coming down those snowy tracks all the way back in Reading.

That's when he spoke of our next destination. Crack

Mansion. *What in the world was I getting into?*

#

As the sun evaporated the dew on sunburnt grass blades, Milford schooled me on this world-famous house just off Ocean Drive. He spoke of a free society of meth and sex. The place was run by this eccentric old man they called The Wizard. I had heard rumblings of this Mansion for years now. I pictured a Draculin vampire orgy. Naked women covered in blood, something out of Bram Stoker's wildest nightmares. The place was known to be frequented by crazy swastika disciples and bands of gypsy bikers.

There were stories of large batches of dope being cooked there by some mean mothers that you did not want to cross. Legend has it that once the dope was finished, they would hold a ritual. A proverbial black mass over the piles of crystallized shards. I've had bitches' pillow-talk such stories to me on Oakbrook. A high priest in the black arts, donning a full cloak, speaking some far-off devil language, blessing the ice before it was shipped to traps all over this city. Spooky shit, not something you read about in the Caller Times, Corpus Christi's local newspaper. These were underground stories. The hood fables that are spoken by vampires with blood on their breath.

Milford looked me dead in the eyes and asked, "Boston, you wanna come and stay over there?" He explained that he was running the floor. He was the warped and perverted host. The master of ceremonies to this funhouse of sin. He showed the patrons a good time. He coordinated the sex with hookers, the drug dealing, and all other perversions that took place within its four slimy walls.

Well, hell yeah, I was going to go. I gave the nod and packed my shit. *Looks like The Movie has one hell of time planned*. I was broke. I hadn't earned any dope in God knows how long. I was running off the fumes and handouts of the *Them/They* party train. Bart Simpson assured me that when we got there, we would get high, settle in, and I would help him by working the front door. That's how I was to earn my keep.

I said goodbye to Barry; my family was to arrive anytime now, and he would be in good hands. I was sad to leave. I could tell he was sick, and I teared up as I closed the door. *I love my dad so much. Even if he is in on this whole fiasco, parting ways with him is killing me.*

We started our trip on foot. I was hoping *Them/They* would arrange some sort of a by-chance pick up for us on our fifteen-mile hike to The Mansion. Milford made some calls on the way, and surprise, surprise, we got picked up! We pulled up to the home just after dusk. It was a bluish grey two-story grandeur of Ocean Drive homes. The front yard was perfectly manicured. A winding brick walkway with twinkling lights led up to a Victorian-style door made of cherry and stained glass. A sectional drive sat on the right side of The Mansion, running to the rear and joining a lofty back yard. We didn't have to knock. Charla, a curvy hooker with jade eyes and a folded red and white bandana top welcomed us as part of a very sexy greeting process.

The home had mahogany flooring. The front hallway had a low ceiling that opened up into the great room. A massive living area had a slate billiards table with a red felt top. An imposing stone fireplace ran up the center wall. It was covered in the front by a glass frame fire protector with gold trim, and next to this sat a log holder. A humongous black leather sectional encompassed the entire room. Ample sitting room for epic-size sessions, reminiscent of a drug-ridden Woodstock festival.

The great room had cathedral ceilings painted white

with dark wood trim. There was a band of hippies lounging around as Milford and I strutted in. A very young-looking, rail-thin chick sat on a heroin nod. Her sexy legs wrapped around the jeans of a half-naked street performer with long, curly, black hair and a full beard. He sat strumming a guitar in his hands.

A red-hot meth pipe was being passed around with a blowtorch. The party was in full swing, and my eyes had seen the glory. I was in awe of this elaborate drugged-out production. This was Broadway on speed. I was waiting for the prostitutes to break out into song as they cruised through the living room.

The wizard floated into the room like a king holding court. He introduced himself right away.

"I'm Jerry," he said.

"This is Boston," Milford spat.

I shook his hand. He had to be six and a half feet tall with long snow-white hair and a matching long beard. He had on jeans, a Jan Sport backpack, and a white tee with a Hurley surfing logo front and center. His eyes were of diamond and pearl, his energy magnetic and sound. He was a presence like I had never felt. Captivating and strong. He was like a mystical Manson-type character that commanded respect from all his followers.

The Allman Brothers Band's "One Way Out" blasted on the house PA system. There was an opening into the kitchen area. A massive Viking commercial range and oven sat on the wall, and a stainless-steel hood system rounded out this first-rate eatery. A small island separated a tiny dining area that had a small wooden table. The whole joint had massive white tiles with black grout on the floor.

There was a bedroom with two French doors to the left

in the hallway. From there, huge windows overlooked the back yard and hot tub area. The back-bedroom wall ended at a door. With small arch-type woodwork, it looked like it belonged in a castle. It had black cast-iron handles with straps. I was daydreaming of fairies and sprites dancing in a lagoon of lily pads behind the walls and garden of this mystery bedroom. But, it housed Mary, a fifty-year-old hooker with a heart of gold.

She flung the door open on cue. "Where the fuck is my damn pipe?" she questioned in a deep Texas accent. She shared the back apartment with her very sexy daughter, Maggie.

There had to be thirty people at the Mansion on this night. Milford showed me to our room. The stairs circled in a spiral formation to the top floor. There were three bedrooms and a nook up there. A hot lesbian couple had the bedroom that shared a wall with ours. We had a queen bed, a table with five stolen laptop computers, and one ridiculously cute walk-in closet. I was to sleep on the floor.

Camilla was rail thin. She had Mad Max hair, shaved, and a devil's smile. I knew her from around the way. When she popped into our bedroom, I was elated.

"Boston, what the fuck are you doing here, baby?" she said.

We shot the shit for a few, and she proceeded to bust out some blue biker dope and syringes. *Did The Movie get to Camilla too? Well, in any event, we are about to get weird.*

She was a phlebotomist. She fixed up a massive shot for me. The strongest floater dope around. I didn't even feel the brand-new sword slide into my vein. The fix was over before it began. I was jumping up and down, coughing invisible flames onto the Iranian rug below. Milford cackled as I did my funny dance for a good two minutes.

I sat dazed, "Spill the Wine" by The Animals blared on

the house speakers. There was a felt puzzle-style picture on the wall. It was framed with cartoon characters all over it. It was a "Where's Waldo?" style print set in downtown New Orleans. It spoke to me in triumphant voices, star-glazed eyes ran from top to bottom.

Some real-life women came into view, enchanting me as they walked past. One small Asian girl put her hand on my shoulder and led me down to the nook at the end of the upstairs hall. She was four feet, eleven inches with pin-straight, long, jet-black hair. They called her Ling Ling.

She had a bowl in her hippy-print fanny pack. We started smoking and chopping it up, sitting on a feather-top mattress which laid directly on the floor. There was a brilliant duvet cover of maroon and gold dripping off the mattress. I felt as if I was melting into stratus clouds as the smoke slid out of open nostrils.

What the hell was Ling wanting with me? I mean, God, she is beautiful. Her slanted eyes were exotic and fierce. She leaned in and kissed me, unannounced and sweet. Ling wasn't much of a talker. *The Movie was probably saving a bundle not giving her any lines.* She was a sexy mime, tugging on the ropes of my heart, beautiful and classy.

The meth coursed through my blood, attaching to every capillary and vessel. I slid into paradise as Ling undid the string on my white and baby blue board shorts. Her thick Asian lips slid up and down my shaft as the room spun, open air, no doors or partitions. It was one of the most surreal experiences to date. We parted ways immediately after, never to speak again, not even a sigh.

Going downstairs, I ran into a hodgepodge of unsavory characters. A Mexican rock-n-roller and his three sons were sharing a downstairs bedroom tucked off the kitchen. He sat in the kitchen smoking ice with his sons. *Two generations of tweakers, getting high as kites out in the open.*

The mansion was total freedom. A true stop on the meth underground railroad. A smoke-filled speakeasy. A refuge for anyone in the game that was tired, broke, or in need of a hot meal. Well, that's how they sold it at least. It was really a major drug spot. Local dealers would literally post up, spend a few days selling ice, and then go take the weekend off with the wife and the kid. You could bet your bottom shard that every bag chasing honey in the Coastal Bend was going to be there with bells on.

Then you had your true-blue hookers. Yea, the real kind, that charged paper money. There were all races and colors of transsexuals and females. It was a hoe rainbow up in that place. Rule of thumb, if you had a vagina and if you stayed the night, you had to be willing to bed down with The Wizard. And the word on the street was…well, he liked it weird.

After eleven at night is when it started to get interesting. Milford found me, "Boston, time to get to your post; you're on the door."

Milford schooled me on my job requirements. The cops were at The Mansion every few hours. They were always scoping for stolen vehicles, serving warrants, or just answering your average noise complaint. There had to be a century on duty to watch the kitchen side door for the fuzz. The second part was to weed out potential troublemakers before they got in. If you were to smell too much booze, see any weapons, or just get a gut feeling, then you were to deny access to the party.

The third part was to act as an auxiliary bouncer just in case something pops off. It was no easy task. You are hired to potentially get in the mix with skins, crazy bikers, streetfighters, and anyone who could be packing heat. Not long after this night, I saw a man get picked up by two mansion staff, see-sawed, and thrown right through the plate glass window in the breezeway. The door was no place for the squeamish. At any moment, there could be blood.

It was about three days in, and it was four in the morning. The Wizard had ordered a burger and it was our turn to fetch. Urie was a Russian immigrant who turned crackhead overnight. He had some serious job in the underworld because the dude hit rocks like he was in a chain gang. He insisted on taking me.

So, the good guy I am, I didn't put up a fight. I was most likely going to get high for free, and maybe even a free meal! Camilla had literally just injected me with a shot. She handed me the rig so I could give it one more use later that night.

My Spidey senses went off. At the last minute, I decided to tuck the syringe and dope under Milford's mattress. I never liked to ride dirty, and something told me taking the pin would have been downright dangerous. So, we headed downstairs, Milford behind us so he could lock up as we left. Urie hit the door and got into a pearl white Lexus. He was acting out of pocket inside the ride, tearing apart the console and opening the glove box. I watched through the door's window before I went outside. I finally walked out, and, for some reason, Milford followed. When we looked up, Urie was being shaken down by CCPD.

There were two lawn chairs outside in the driveway for the door personnel. Someone saw the commotion and locked the door behind Milford. The cops sent a bull over to tell us to take a seat. First, they thoroughly patted us down for contraband, then up against the side of the house we sat, sitting there like we were in deep shit with the principal. A huge flood light shone directly down and into our eyes. *It really put the pressure on.*

"What the fuck are you boys up to tonight, Milford?"

The beat cop knew him. By name. We were in deep shit. They didn't find anything on us, so the grilling was to begin.

"You guys know that the Lexus is hot?" said the officer.

"No man, I don't even know that dude," Milford choked out.

"Well, he is in deep boy. Possession, GTA, among other things," said the cop.

We just sat in silence for a few minutes before I decided these cops were just actors. *The whole thing is part of the damn movie.*

"Hey man, I don't know any of these people, I got left here like a stray by a so-called friend," I said like a smart ass. The cops told me to clam up.

They hauled Urie off in cuffs as the wrecker pulled the Lexus off the elongated driveway.

"Mr. Bornagain, you are now in the book. You are forever linked to The Mansion for as long as you're in Texas. When we run your name from now on, it will show that you frequent this shithole." The cop was making it clear that I was now branded as a tweaker for as long as I lived.

They chopped it up with Milford for a few minutes. They gave him kudos for not being such an asshole these days. They gave us a staunch warning and, just like that, they were gone. I almost threw up when they pulled out of sight. Movie or not, I was almost busted with a rig and a thirty of fire. If I hadn't put it under the mattress when I did, I would have been Tostitos.

Ten minutes later, it was game on. The funny thing about the game is that it desensitizes you to danger. I have mentioned before, back in the day, I wouldn't even drive with a pot roach in the minivan. Now I am rolling around with duffels, loaded sets of works, and pistols. I was not the same person I once was. I had completely changed overnight. I had been hardened by the game after only a year and a half in. Nothing shocked me, not the sex, drugs, or the violence.

I was talking about God with everyone. You would think that a bunch of drug people wouldn't wanna hear it. But not the tweaker counterculture. That's all people want to talk about. The conversations always turn very spiritual after a few rolls of the bowl. People with all sorts of views, anything from Jesus freaks to devil worshipers, and beyond. There were witches, card readers, and all types of occult people at The Mansion. The fact was most people were having a major Jesus experience.

I was finding out what "Find the Others" meant, one of my signs after the wreck. I was meeting a ton of people, all loving Jesus with two common threads. One was a near-death experience. The other was meth. We would sit by the door at The Mansion for hours, talking about God, the visions, and the experiences we were having. It was a great way to meet people when I got off my shift to invite them up to my room and chill and talk.

To be honest, I was expecting a far worse crowd. The week prior to my arrival at The Mansion, a particularly dangerous gang was banned from the house. There was an 86'd board in the kitchen. If your name was on that list, you were not to get in the house under any circumstance. At that time, the board was full, and it was a who's who of Corpus Christi's most wanted on the list.

It was extremely tame compared to what I had pictured in my mind. I thought I was going to walk into a scene of "From

Dusk till Dawn," Cheech Marin screaming about "snapping pussy," and vampires ripping people's throats out. It was more like an episode of "Murder She Wrote," only the Angela Landsbury character would have been a hooker. But boring, nonetheless.

    Tony had stopped by to visit me. It was late and they called him back to the castle room, the back apartment, for what they liked to call "The Static Box." Tony went in and they shut the door behind him. I was curious about what the hell was going on in there, so I took a seat at the small table off into the dining room to listen. They had a box in the middle of the room. It looked like one of those old-timey radios you would see pre-WWII.

    Legend had it that the older hooker that lived back there had a boyfriend who liked to talk to demons. The box was the gateway, the channel if you will, where these supernatural persons without bodies would speak through. As I sat and eavesdropped, you could hear them talking to the air.

    They were asking the demon questions about the past, present, and future. They were addressing this spirit as if it were a person that was once alive. It was a legit séance. The questions got darker and more sinister by the second. You could hear the boyfriend talk about shooting up. He was a drummer and a terrible heroin junkie. He was asking the spirit to prompt him and guide him through the fix. After a long pause, as my ear was now at the door, you could hear the crackling in the airwaves as a loud voice said "Puuuuuuuuush," clear as a bell.

    After a long interrogation, I got out of Tony that the boyfriend had a loaded rig of brown. It was lodged in the man's main artery in his stomach, and when the demon said "push," the man did. The spirit was used to guide him in the shooting-up process. I was chilled to the bone as Tony spilled all the gruesome details. Again, there was something about this event that had me feeling like *The Movie* was miles away.

Later that night, I was walking into the great room when I stumbled upon Bingo. Bingo was the sweetest girl you could ever meet in your whole life. She was five feet tall with long dark black hair and just the right amount of thickness. She had Christian worship music on the big stereo. She sat alone with big salty tears streaming down her cheeks. She was a Mexican lady with small kids at home. Like most of the girls out here, she was a mom. Those moments when you're super high, the wrong thought about your kid, just at the wrong time, could send a person into a full-on tailspin. During these moments, all the drugs we do to forget our families while we are MIA seem to just amplify the pain.

She sat in total heartbreak, at the same time in complete joy for her love in Jesus. Her palms to the sky, Bingo praised the Father like a church-going fanatic on Easter Sunday. She sat and talked with me for about an hour or so, about her marriage, her "real life," as we all called it.

I bid my farewell and went upstairs to shoot some ice in my arm.

#

Two nights later I got off shift at around five in the morning. Milford was gone for the night, and I was on watch for the belongings to our room. I unlocked the cheap padlock on the door and swung it open. The room was dark, all except for the five laptop computers that sat on the table up against the wall that faced the front yard of The Mansion. The room was aglow with the LEDs of the stolen merchandise. I closed the wooden door behind me and fastened the padlock we had on the inside. This time to keep unwanted guests from coming in while I was fixing.

I sat in a wooden chair as I mixed up the shot. I didn't even flip the light on; I wanted to keep as low a profile as I could, so I didn't have to share with anyone else. I didn't even want to risk someone seeing the light under the door. It took me a few minutes, but I sunk in, plunged, and retracted all in good time. I was stoned. I stared at the screens in front of me. My first opportunity to really look around since I entered the room.

The screens all had five smaller screens within. They were small cubes like you would find on a closed-circuit TV for a security system. I leaned in and squinted my amazingly high peepers. I couldn't believe my eyes. There were bedrooms. All the fucking bedrooms of people that had no idea they were being filmed. One man jacking off. A Black couple having sex. One lady picking her nose. A hot younger broad laying naked, talking on the phone. I was horrified. This was what I had heard about all those times. The urban legend that hackers would hide small hidden battery-operated cameras in your room, film you, and later use it as a blackmail or a torture tool. *This is exactly how The Movie is spying on me.*

I scanned my eyes under the table, and sure enough, the whole thing was being recorded to a hard drive DVR that sat just below the computers. Now I knew for sure that Milford was a major player in *The Movie*. He wasn't just an actor; he was a full-fledged producer. I had some suspicion about other key players I had met along the way, too. *This was sick. Movie or not, there was a serious invasion of privacy going on.* It was then, I realized, that all that time I fantasized about doing webcams and becoming a real-life porn star., I wasn't too far off. *I had most likely starred in more films than Peter North.*

The next few weeks became hell.

Paul was a chubby Mexican in his late 20's. Neatly

trimmed mustache and clean-cut hair. He and I were now sharing the bedroom that the Mexican guy and his sons had vacated. *The Wizard had us spackle the walls and throw a fresh coat of paint on them hoes.* There was always a chore or a job to be done at The Mansion. If you were busted, had no money or dope for The Wizard, then off to chore duty you went. Got to earn your keep somehow…well if you didn't have a vagina.

I was now sharing the duties of Resident Chef along with Paul. All the while, still working the door at night. The Mansion was a commune. Different faces all the time. A revolving door of victory, relapse, and defeat. It was interesting watching dealers on a come up, people losing it all, and the reemergence of the addict after a long bout of sobriety.

Paul and I were being tested. For some reason, Milford and The Wizard had it out for Paul and me. Once the room was completed, there was a hazing period that began.

One in the morning wake-up, "Pack your shit, it's time to go for the night, guys," said The Wizard.

Paul and I were told to go outside and head away from the property. There was an old man they called "Grand Master," an ex-Olympic martial artist, now hooked on ice and riddled with cancer. When I hit the street, I was dazed with no clue why we were to vacate the property in such a manner. I got lost on a side street and there was Grand Master. He had a green laser pointer in his hand. He directed me from a block away and showed me a way to get out onto Ocean Drive.

#

I walked over twelve miles back to Oakbrook in the middle of the night. My feet were leaking puss from white blisters that had formed in my beat-up Adidas. I limped into the front door after almost a month of absence. I walked in to meet with Barry. He hadn't been happy with the new situation. He felt safe when I lifted him out of the chair. He loved how I took care of him and cooked for him. My family member that was on duty worked full-time with over-time hours. Leaving him for fourteen hours at a time and returning drunk when they did come home.

So, he asked me to come back and once again be his caretaker. Even crazy, I was better than the alternative. I agreed and went into the kitchen to heat up some leftover pasta he had offered me. I was starving; I don't think I had anything of substance in seven days.

My family member returned just as I sat the bowl of spaghetti on the counter near the famous avocado sink. He was pissed, something AWFUL! He told me I had no business at the house, that Barry didn't want me there.

I had been carrying a chrome tire iron from the Mitsubishi in my backpack. I had it on the counter within arm's reach. The family member lost it; he took my pasta fork out of the bowl and stabbed me directly in the forearm with it.

Blood shot out of the five-prong wound. I grabbed the lug wrench off the counter and chased him down the hall to Barry's room. A verbal sparring match exploded in front of a dying man. Barry finally made it clear that he had asked me to come back. The fool left and life went on.

The Mansion in my rearview for now, I went about my duties as caretaker, loving son, and movie star on the rise. My lunacy was evident to anyone I met. I was walking the southside neighborhoods and apartment complexes in complete psychosis. I was approaching citizens, thinking they were actors or fans in the making.

My character took on the role of People's Champ. My love for Jesus became a focal point in the script that I was now seeming to control. I would find myself on the bus, standing on the backseat, offering the rush hour crowd a fifty-thousand-dollar reward if they could properly identify *Them/They* and the Hollywood powerhouse that had me in its crosshairs.

I made Christ the center of my mantra. I would throw the peace sign, allowing for an epic shot, as I screamed "Let the light of the Lord be with you...all day, erry day!" I was coming up with taglines and branded catchphrases for my role. God Squad was another idea I had been telling people about in the streets. God Squad, to me, was a die-hard legion of my fans that would follow me into the depths of hell in my fight against *Them/They*.

I was wearing huge square sunglasses and a windbreaker suit with no shirt in the middle of summer. One pant leg up, of course. I had been wondering how on earth the crew was filming me as I walked down the street. *How did they know my location?* It then dawned on me that they were using satellite technology, fully equipped with microwave audio listening capabilities. *They could follow me anywhere, see and hear everything, till I entered a building or residence.*

I was a renegade, a comedic actor turned loose on the city with no repercussions for my actions. I thought the cops were all in on it, paid by Hollywood to let the madness ensue, all in the name of cinema. I was immortal, a king among poppers as I stalked city streets in one hundred percent humidity.

I started to become public enemy number one on Saratoga Boulevard. I was getting banned from eateries and stores for my crazy, over-the-top acting abilities. The cops started to take notice and they were not cordial. One day I got it in my head that the big wedding was to take place Downtown. So, I jumped on the bus and made my way to find the party with my new bride.

I walked into about five hotels, asking for the manager of the wedding department. I was trying to figure out which hotel the wedding was being held at and what name it would be under. I was leaking sweat from walking endlessly in the summer heat, covered in filth. I looked like a legit hobo. I entered a big hotel downtown in the evening at about half past seven. *This had to be the place! One of the largest wedding venues in Corpus Christi. Right on the water, perfect for a Hollywood wedding.*

The manager was a cute Black girl, most likely thirty years old, with a long straight-lace face and fake eyelashes.

"Can I help you, sir?" she said.

"Well honey, I am looking for a wedding being held here at the hotel. It's my wedding, kind of a surprise party if you know what I mean?"

I was clearly out of my element and totally out of my mind. She checked the roster anyway. Being it was a Tuesday, after hours, there weren't many names to look at in the book. She was extremely nice and helpful. Until two young, buff security guards met me at the door.

"Sir, you are going to have to come with us now," he said with authority.

"Hey man, I am the damn star of this show, go tell the crew I am here, will ya?" I was lost. They escorted me into the busy lobby near the packed hotel bar. There had to be two hundred people out there drinking, eating, and having a ball. I was convinced they were the crowd there to cheer me on for my big day.

They were not.

Four massive CCPD officers met me in the lobby. Security handed me off to them.

"Sir, we are going to ask you to leave the property right away." This Black officer had a bald head and looked like he played linebacker for the New England Patriots.

"Hey, I am here for my wedding, you know damn well *The Movie* is throwing this shindig," I said foolishly.

They handcuffed me on the spot and lifted me off my feet by my shackled arms. Thinking that I was on camera, I did my best Tony Montana impression for the massive audience at the bar as well as the security cameras.

"You ain't never seen a bad guy like me before!" I shouted and snarled at the patrons.

Off to Nueces County Jail, I went.

#

We pulled up to the motor pool near the side entrance of the jail. I was in line to be booked, feet and hands shackled like a common thug. They began to search us and ask our vital information when I broke out into some stand-up. The jailers seemed all smiles, busting out laughing and playing along. I had the inmates going crazy. People shouting from cells and holding tanks like monkeys at the zoo. It was quite a disturbance.

This little guy came over, top brass for the Nueces County jailers. He smiled in my face, signaled for the goons, and I was led into a back area where they housed suicidal inmates. This area had a camera that was notoriously turned off most of the time. This was so they could discipline the problem children without any threat of a lawsuit. I was cuffed behind my back, feet shackled. There were five of them. One jailer, who happened to be three-hundred-and-fifty pounds and six feet four inches, threw me to the cold, piss-stained concrete on the floor below.

I hit my head on the concrete. I saw blood leaking from my forehead. I started to scream for help. They held me down like an animal as this three-hundred-and-fifty-pound jailer jumped clean off the ground and landed his right knee on my left stack of ribs. The third time he jumped, I heard a tremendous crunch. *There's the Rottweiler chewing the chicken bones sound again.* He had snapped one of my ribs clean in half. That's what a big mouth gets you in the Crook City Jail.

    I was marched over to a holding tank in full view of all the inmates in Central Booking. The jail was at one hundred percent capacity and rowdy as an NYC biker bar on a Friday night. They threw me on the floor face down, bloody, and broken. The floor had blood, fecal matter, and urine all pooled just inches from my nose. I was cuffed and in deep suffering. Something told me *The Movie* wouldn't let this take place. *What good is your star if he is dead?*

    The lights stayed on all day and all night, bright as Fenway Park during a playoff Yankees game. People screaming, cops and jailers swearing at people. The lies being whispered between crooks dangled against my bruised earlobes.

    I was physically separated from others and in tremendous pain. I saw inmates peering through the bulletproof glass into my cell. In a situation where they would usually get great entertainment, they all felt bad for me. I must have looked like a mile-high pile of dog shit.

    The faces of passing jailers looked demonic. I screamed and cursed at them. These hoes weren't getting off that easy. They reentered for Round Two of the ass beating. They came in full force and used their tactical high-tech boots to smash my face. The waffle prints were imprinted on my face for a full week afterwards. One jailer took out a jail key. He sat on my back and dug it in my spine like he was paralyzing a prize pig at the county fair.

    The tip broke the skin; I felt my toes go numb. They left

me in a far worse condition the second time. I was wailing. I started to cry out to the Lord. I said, "Light of the Lord, Jesus Christ," over and over at the top of my lungs.

"Get that fuckin guy some help, man," I heard from the mouth of another White inmate from a neighboring cell.

People were really concerned about my life. Motherfuckers die all the time in Nueces County Jail. This was a seriously dangerous situation. I was in a pickle, and no one was going to come to the rescue. So, God is who I went to. Saying the sweet name of Jesus was the only comfort I had. I was detached from the world. I might as well have been on a lunar mission solo and running out of oxygen. I sat crying all night long. I legit thought this was it. *Not even The Movie can save me now.*

It seemed like days had gone by as I laid bleeding on the filthy concrete. But it was the next morning when they came back in. I was charged with criminal trespass. I was so injured that they decided to let me go. They threw me out the back door around ten in the morning.

I didn't even have bus fare to get home. My dad was paralyzed. I had been praying he called for help while I was in jail so that he hadn't been left all alone. I made my way home, bumming quarters to get on the bus back to the southside.

I finally walked up to Oakbrook around noon. Barry was in his office. He had wheeled himself in there to work from his home computer. I could barely stand up. *Whatever that guy did with that jailer's key really hurt me.* I sat in an office chair next to him and began to cry. I was at the end of my rope emotionally, physically, and spiritually. *The Movie* had taken a massive psychological toll on me. Months of brain warfare had me reeling. The thrashing I took didn't help one bit. On top of it all, I was ruthlessly strung-out and going through withdrawals.

Barry was in tears. I had never seen my dad this upset in my thirty-five years on earth.

"Boston, you need help, you are really sick," he said with welling tears in his beautiful blue eyes.

"Dad, I can't do this anymore, I know you are in on this whole thing," I screamed.

I went to the kitchen and pulled a razor-sharp fillet knife out of the butcher's block on the silk white countertop next to that damn avocado sink.

I stomped back to the office with the massive blade in my quaking hand. I was trembling with a cocktail of fear and pain. *I needed answers, and today I was going to force these motherfuckers out of the rabbit hole. Them/They wanted a war, they got one now.* I sat back down next to my dad. His eyes were wide with panic. A paralyzed man, nowhere to run and concern for his oldest boy deep within his heart.

"Dad, I am going to slice this vein wide open." I pointed to the massive artery that I liked to shoot up in on my forearm. "Dad, I am not fucking playing around, man. I need to hear about the movie NOW!" I exclaimed.

I will never forget the look on my father's face at this moment, sad and morose.

"Boston, there's no movie, I don't know what you have been talking about all these months, no one does. You are very sick, and we can get you some help."

I stared at him in disbelief. *He wasn't going to budge? Even with my life in the balance? They must have paid my old man a lot of money for this type of performance.*

My father's cell phone was right in front of him. My dad did not trust cops, so he called that famous close family member.

The guy answered his phone and started to scream his

head off when Barry told him I was threatening to kill myself in the same room as him. A few minutes later, the driveway at Oakbrook was crawling with cops. One had an AR-15 in his hands. They had the place surrounded, treating it as a full-on hostage situation.

I ran and barricaded the front door with a bookcase.

"If you come in here, I will slice this bitch wide open," pointing to my arm. "I just want to know about the damn movie, will someone please tell me?"

I was distraught. The cops were all screaming through the glass window next to the door. I ran back to the office to sit with Barry.

"Boston, please, give yourself up, we will get you help."

The cops shouted through the office window. "Sir, are you ok, is he holding you against your will?"

Barry looked at me. He was crying, I was crying. He shouted back, "No, I am OK, he is only harming himself," my dad shouted.

Those spoken words right there helped me dodge a felony kidnapping charge. I decided to give it up. I threw the fillet knife onto the office rug and told them I was coming out with my hands up. I did, only to be tackled like a Cleveland Browns receiver on game day. They put me back in the cruiser; now I almost knew *The Movie* wasn't real. Well, until I looked up and saw a cop with a glorified paintball gun. It looked comical.

Next, as I sat cuffed in the back of a CCPD SUV, a few nice cops popped open the door to see if I was ok. I had been home from jail less than an hour and I was about to go back. I went back into character. We can't waste the swat team footage, can we?

"Are you thirsty?" one cop asked.

"Hell yes I am, my favorite is in the fridge. I will take a Pepsi. No, make it two," I said with a smile.

He returned a few minutes later with my two Pepsi's. They even brought a bag of gummy bears I had on the counter. The cops started feeding me gummy bears as I was cuffed. He popped open a Pepsi and waterfall style poured some in my mouth. *What cops on earth act like this in a hostage and/or suicide situation? This was the damn movie. Looks like I got the answers I needed.* Well, it seemed that way at the time.

They explained to me that I was not being charged. They were going to take me to the Behavioral Health Unit at Memorial Hospital. When we walked into the unit, I was in full funny-man mode. I had the hospital staff and the cops all rolling with laughter. My comedy skills were shocking. I had been doing stand-up so much every day, I was a seasoned pro by now. Improvising off everything in the room. The staff and the cop all played along. This only fueled the idea that this movie was very real. *What a scene! The "Looney Bin" footage should be epic,* I thought to myself.

When I hit the waiting room for intake, there was something very different about this shoot. There was a man in a wheelchair. An old man who looked like he had a bad Hollywood makeup job. Full lips, nose, fake skin, all of it, even the bad silver wig. I went up to him immediately and started to perform at this "mental patient's" expense. I was convinced it was my old boss, the female that fired me and ended my career. *Looks like Them/They were hiring people from my past. Kind of a good move. On film, they could subtitle who it really was in real life...jokes on me.*

I was roasting this apparently mute patient at full volume. People were rolling. There was another patient, a Black guy also in what appeared to be full makeup, and he was clearly the protagonist in the scene.

"Will you shut the fuck up, some of us don't feel well," he clamored.

"Hey, let me get you a gun, Sanford and Son," I said like an asshole, insinuating he should go kill himself. These are the terrible things one says in addiction. Again, I was in full meth psychosis. I started to pick apart anyone I saw in makeup.

The nurse was furious, "Mr. Bornagain, there are suicidal people in this unit, you can't be making fun of people here."

"Ok Flow. Hey, would you be a lamb and fetch me an ice-cold Pepsi?" Again, like a real asshole. She looked like she wanted to kill me. I then proceeded to give the candy stripper my phone number and told her I will get her a part in *The Movie* if she acts correctly.

I was funneled upstairs to the real unit, as were the Black guy and my old boss in the wheelchair. *She was playing an old man who couldn't talk, how convenient! I was going to have fun during these scenes. What a depressing place.*

The walls were a drab mixture of white and baby blue. Everyone had on those terrible hospital scrubs made of blue paper. Those ridiculous matching blue socks with thick rubber treads on the bottom to prevent the zombies from slipping and falling to the floor.

I had been to a mental unit before; this same one to be exact. I knew some of the orderlies from years before. The jokes started up immediately. I was starting to feel like shit, and with no meth at my disposal, I did the only thing I could think of to get off. I picked a fistfight with the old Black guy. I threatened him, knowing full well that aggressive behavior would get me "The Needle," a toxic mixture of Thorazine, Ativan, and Benadryl. I was a live wire on this night, so they came over and hit me with a full rhino dart. I felt just like Will Farrell in "Old School" when he shot himself in the neck with a tranquilizer dart from the traveling petting zoo.

My brain went lucid. They laid me down on my bunk; my eyes felt like lead balloons. I went into a vivid dream. I was playing on the lawn back in Reading, Massachusetts. My dog and cat would wait for me at the bus stop every day. I saw them and called out to them in a child's voice. I stood just over three feet tall. There was no movie, no meth, and my parents were fine. I was playing with the toys my dad bought me for my birthday. Life was carefree and fun. I opened my eyes to the drab walls. When I realized where I was, I began to weep. *How the hell did my life end up here?*

As much as *The Movie* seemed real, part of me knew there was a possibility that I was mentally ill. It was the scariest thing on earth to think about. So, I put all my hopes in *The Movie*. If there was a movie, I was fine, rich, and my life was about to be forever changed when I got to LA.

The staff informed me that I was on a seventy-two-hour hold for suicidal threats. I was to undergo a full evaluation. I decided to leave *The Movie* out of the mix when I talked to the doctors. That could only complicate my release and my timeline to get high.

After the third day, I was released. The old man in the chair said to me as I made my exit, "Please don't leave me."

Like a great actor, I replied "Don't worry, I will come back for you all."

Epic in nature, I walked right out the door in my Adidas, sans the laces.

#

I made my way back to Oakbrook. I had a bag of dope on the front and already on the way. I went on a bender for a few days. There were women and ice and it all seemed to be provided by *Them/They.*

A few days later, Barry had to go to the hospital for an infection. He had a bedsore on his back that just wouldn't heal no matter what we did. He never came home. After a few days of silence, I made the determination that Barry had been shipped to Hawaii to play golf till the wedding happened. *Poor guy had been through hell. I don't care how much they were paying him; the guy needed a break.*

It was at this time that the silence of the house started to deeply affect me. I wasn't having guests over in his absence. I was scared and at my wit's end. I decided to reach out to Bella. I emailed her through social media. I explained that I loved her and the baby so much that I would take them any way I could get them. I must have reached her at a good time because she wanted to come right over.

She came and I told her that I can just be her friend, that I wanted her in my life, and explained that my dad would not be coming home for some time. I left out the jazz about Maui, Hawaii. She asked me if she and the baby could come to stay in the spare bedroom. I agreed right after she told me about her new boyfriend. *Sure, my heart snapped in half, but I could win her back. May just take a little time and finagling.* She showed up with a couple of strange dudes and a truck about an hour after she went to pack. Looked like the Clampett's from "The Beverly Hillbillies" were moving in. Her mattress, all her belongings, everything she owned was with her. *How could she pack that fast? Bell must have been waiting to go. She was part of The Movie after all.*

Bell left after unpacking and returned about five hours later with her new man. A scumbag ice dealer named Reynaldo. He came packing with at least one ounce of quality shards, so my reluctant handshake became warm and fuzzy. He tossed me a gram on the free. A show of good faith for letting Bella and the baby stay at the house. *If this asshole was going to be around, he better keep it coming.*

So, there it is, the return of Bella, "The Greatest Love of All," was back. Now I was questioning our whole relationship. *Was she sent from the start? How far back had this movie gone?* Breaking the fact to her that I had slept with her sister was not easy. *Lucky for me, she didn't care.*

Right away, Bella installed a security camera that pointed out to the driveway and Reynaldo started to trap out of Oakbrook with my full blessing. He was throwing me piles of ice as compensation. Bella was also stealing from his stash and giving me gram shards on the sneak, on top of what he was already giving me. I loved Bella with all my heart. It was impossible to see her with this guy. Then I figured out that he was an actor. *They were not romantic.* I was convinced they had never slept together.

I was seeing people in full Hollywood makeup everywhere I went. Even some of the people that were coming to buy drugs at the house. There were lines miles long to buy ice at Oakbrook. *Why not, the cops were in on the damn movie, no one was going to interrupt the shoot, right?*

This is when things took a strange turn. The songs on the radio were all sounding eerily like they were written about my life. *Number one smash hits on the radio, all must have been being released as part of the soundtrack to my life.* I suddenly realized why Bella had disappeared. *She was out of town, writing the hits!* I dreamed up a theory that my Bell was a ghostwriter for the Hollywood stars. She was the brains behind the music, and she had been out of town to write these songs for *The Movie*. She had to leave me, and this was her *stunning return to marry me and end the whole production.* I kept this find to myself, as I didn't want to ruin the end of the movie.

#

Bella and the crew left for a couple of days. I was most dangerous when I was alone. My frustrations with *The Movie* grew by the minute. I started to break things. I smashed every piece of crystal in the China cabinet. I began to think I had a superhuman power, one where I could touch something, and realize it's worth and value. Most things I touched in the house felt fake. I then realized that these things were all Hollywood reproduction pieces, made and switched while I was in the hospital for that three-day stint. *The great prank was exposed; everything in the house was fake! The reproduced items were all props, so when the madness ensued, none of Barry's family artifacts would succumb to the craziness of a drug-themed movie.* I started smashing everything in sight.

When Bella returned, there was shattered glass on every square inch of the twenty-two-hundred square foot home. The sound of shards snapping underfoot was present with every step taken…no pun intended.

"Boston, what the hell happened here, man," she said in a sweet voice.

Reynaldo muttered the words "crazy asshole" under his breath before walking into the spare room like he owned the place. Bella, being the doll she was, grabbed a broom like a ghetto Cinderella, and began to clear the way through the wreckage of my rage. She got loaded and cleaned for what seemed like a full twenty-four-hour period.

Reynaldo worked a day job at a satellite TV company. *The same company that was used to track me via satellite. Coincidence? I think not. A jab by the movie.* Everything was a coincidence, totally scripted to fuck with me.

When he was at work, I would hit on Bella. I loved her deeply and knew the whole relationship with that loser was just a put-on by *Them/They*. I would tell Bella my theories and thoughts about this whole movie, and she played along one hundred percent. Taking advantage of a mentally ill person was nothing to these people. Long as they had a spot to trap with lights, running water, and air conditioning they would do anything to keep the jig running.

One song that hit home was "Meet Me in the Middle" by Zed. It was number one on the radio while all this was going on. It talked about the broken dishes, the running taps, and the fighting in our relationship. I was positive Bella had written it for me. *An ode to our love, breaking down the walls, and offering up a solution to our heartbreak. She wanted me to "meet her in the middle."* I was convinced she had penned it. Even though today, I know for a fact that she never wrote it.

I walked into the laundry room as she was folding one day. She was looking like a whole snack with her daisy dukes' shorts and her white wife-beater tight as a snare drum. I put my hands on her hips from behind her and whispered in her ear, "Why are we wasting this love?" She received my words and nestled her head against mine. Even today it is tough to decipher what was genuine, and what was done to appease me for a free place to use drugs in. *My heart was hers, and I knew at the end of this insanity, she was to be my wife.*

#

I was still doing missions in the street, only now it was full time. I started to have clear brushes with the Lord. I know what you're thinking. *The Movie*, the superpowers, so surely the visions from God must be part of the illness too. Well, it wasn't. I believe that God was starting to reveal things to me. After my very real brushes with Satan, I think Jesus was making His loving presence known, and in big ways. I was dying, and my life needed to change. My real life, my real health, and my very real and massive drug problem all needed mending.

I was starting to give messages to people on the bus, the street, and beyond. Words of encouragement and hope. I would "know things" about perfect strangers and most times, I was spot on. I had people crying, cheering, and downright freaked out.

One such incident was in the morning around ten. There was a party at Oakbrook. I was walking through the house, a do-rag on my head, with a pipe and blowtorch in my hand. One of Bella's new friends, that I had never met before in my life, walked in the door.

She was wearing a pair of Pittsburgh Steelers slippers on her feet. She walked by me in the dark and crowded hallway near the bathroom. I pointed at the slippers as she grazed my shoulder with hers. "Hey, your dad says he loves you, and he misses you," I said with a smirk. I continued down the hall as I lit the blowtorch and took a massive blast.

Bell shouts out "Boston, stop it, you are freaking people out again." Just then the strange new girl spun around, huge wells of tears in her eyes. Her beautiful Mexican features in agony as she choked out, "Hey man, these are my dad's slippers, and he died last year." There was a house full of witnesses. You just can't write this stuff. Some things, the God things, are too good…even for Hollywood.

See, I think God uses mentally ill people as vessels for His work. The messengers that are written off as crazy also always have the most profound revelation to share. I think God does this because the world just isn't ready for what He really has to say. Messages of peace and love, equality and pacifism, are all too dangerous for the evil men who run this cruel world under the command of the enemy. He shines through, using people who are most time written off as mad or complete lunatics. So, don't laugh at the guy with the sign that says the end is near. Most likely...he is telling His truth.

I was having a revelation as I would walk down the hot, sun-drenched streets of the southside. One day, God's plan for the race was revealed. How He created us all different colors, like that of the spectrum. One, so He could make the world beautiful. The other...a test in our differences. To see how we would treat one another. A test that humanity is failing in massive strides.

Any hint of a racist bone in my body drained at this very place on Saratoga Boulevard. A revelation that to this minute has made me a much better human being, and a much more compassionate man of Christ. So, no matter what your views are on the status of my mental health during this time, good was coming out of this experience, long-lasting and biblical.

#

I came home late, high, crazy, and in my own reality. I closed the door to my room, the house silent as everyone had finally crashed. I heard the giggling first. I stood by the door, ears open in horror. I heard the slurping and moaning next. By the time the springs on Bella's bed started clanging, I was crying like a little bitch, tears streaming, and suicidal thoughts ruling my mind.

I sat and listened to Bella and Reynaldo making love for over an hour. *How could she do this to me? How could she rub my nose in this shit if she ever loved me at any point?* My heart shattered that night. I was never the same. Bella was the absolute love of my life during that time period. She destroyed my soul, leaving me heartbroken and dying within.

I decayed over the next few weeks. That's when Bella's sister showed up at Oakbrook. She was with this strange UFC fighter dude. They ended up getting into a fight two days later, and he took off, leaving her behind at my crib. Bella was consumed with her new dealer. My rage and resentment grew with every pulse of my heart. Bella was in my dad's grand bathtub, naked, when I entered the room to ask the million-dollar question.

"Bella baby, are you ever going to marry me?"

She looked at me with tears in her eyes and said a resounding "No, Boston."

Another blow to my already concaved, destroyed heart. I left the room and sat smoking for a good ten hours in solitude. That's when it hit me. I loved the wrong sister. I started warming up to her younger sibling just mere hours after Bella's admission.

She ended up in my bedroom to hop on some springs of our own. The ultimate revenge for us both. For me, this was a finger in the face for abandoning me. For her sister, the years of being shown up. The score was to be settled.

I made love to her while I was so high that I couldn't speak. It was a disappointing sexual experience for us both. She had no intention of being with me, as well. The love was absent, and for the first time I knew I wasn't to marry either one of the sisters. A dark shade came over Oakbrook.

#

A knock on the door revealed a very worn-out Tony. He looked thirsty and weak like he had been on a massive run for far too long. We sat in the office and talked about religion and war. I picked a fight with Bella as she sat in the spare room. The evil that came out of my vocal passage was malicious and to the point.

Bella came into the room and punched me in the face. I laughed as she retreated to her now private space. I was losing control of Oakbrook. The sisters, the crowd, was starting to overpower me.

The window was open as I talked with Tony. I felt the presence of the devil, and I spoke God's name. Just as I finished my sentence, the wooden door of Barry's office slammed shut.

"That's the Evil One, Tone," I said in fear.

Just as that statement was made, the door opened and slammed once more. It was clear we were being visited by a spirit. The same one that was in the electricity in the kitchen. You could tell the love for Jesus in the house was not welcomed. It had no problems letting us know.

Bella was playing along with the whole delusion of *The Movie*. She would admit that she's an actress, being paid to be on set. They all were. Almost every friend I had was going along with the crazy psychotic theme I had in my head. They were all stealing, partying, and carrying on all on Barry's dime.

The Big Bang happened. I came out of Barry's room in the morning at around seven about a week later. My hands were battered and bruised from punching holes in the sheetrock in frustrating moments of rage. The house was being systematically destroyed. I saw Bella's door open just a crack. I popped it open all the way in a rude, abrupt manner.

"Boston, get the fuck out of here, for God's sake," she spat.

She was smoking a bowl with Bugger; what a class act. He was tall for a Mexican. He stood six feet and three inches and over two hundred and seventy-five pounds. A big dude you did not want to cross. An associate of Reynaldo who had been coming and going as he pleased at Oakbrook for weeks now.

Bugger sat in a chair near the end of the bed, as Bella held a smoking meth pipe on the corner of the mattress. The baby was passed out near the wall on the very same bed.

"Bella, what the fuck? You can't smoke that shit in here with the baby. There is no window open or anything," I said in anger.

I loved that baby. The smoke was fanning into his little nostrils as he slept. Even crazy, strung out, and high, I was not a monster. I was always looking out for that kid.

"Hey man, why don't you mind your motherfucking business," said Bugger.

I cocked my head at him like I was Michael Myers from "Halloween." I smiled, nodded, and backed out of the doorway. Bella got up and slammed her door and locked it. My brain shut down; a rage of red came over me. Like a Brahma bull on parade in Madrid. I couldn't take it anymore.

The stress of *The Movie*, the disrespect of the inhabitants, the slime of my own skin all came to a breaking point as I stood in the dingy hallway. I turned around and slowly, calmly walked down to the kitchen. I pulled two, razor-sharp butcher knives out of the block on the counter...of course, near that damn avocado-colored sink. I walked back to the bedroom. There was a sheetrock wall next to the door. I don't know why I did what I did next, but I am still glad that I did. I put both knives in my left hand and proceeded to punch massive holes right through onto the other side. When there was a hole gaping enough for my face, I stuck it through. It was a scene out of the "Shining."

"Heeeerrrree's Boston." I screamed, "Bella, get that fucking kid out of there this minute!"

They both started screaming. I moved to the door. Now one knife in each hand, I looked menacing. I can only imagine the look in my wild eyes as I booted the door off the hinges with one foul thud. Bugger looked at me with terror. Bella screamed; the baby was now going berserk as he awoke from his slumber. I backed up as they ran out of the room. Bella ran from the house with the baby in her arms.

I was screaming, "I will fucking chop you both into pieces."

I stomped after Bella into the driveway. She was getting into Bugger's car, most likely stolen from his grandpa. I heard a snapping noise from behind me, back from inside the front doorway.

It was Bugger, the whole pile of him. He was breaking off a huge table leg from my grandma's antique credenza that sat in the front hallway near the window. It had a massive bolt sticking out of the top end. *That could do some damage.*

He held it like Babe Ruth would when he was about to knock one out of the park at Yankee stadium. He was inching toward me as I wielded two blades that might as well have been ninja swords. We did a strange dance back and forth.

"I don't wanna hurt you, Boston. Calm the fuck down, man," he said.

I replied with "I am gonna saw your fucking head off and roll it down Saratoga like a bowling ball. You stay the fuck away from Bella."

He took the table leg and whirled it at me sideways with both of his strong hands. The bolt ripped through my skin; blood was leaking out of my forearm in fountains. He ran past me. I had only dropped one of the blades, still had one left. He hurried into the driver's seat as Bella shouted "GO!" I stood on the passenger side, about five feet away. I chucked the knife at the windshield, leaving a long crack that ran up the middle. He threw it into reverse, backing up a good ten feet. I heard the screeching tires as my heart almost exploded. He had tried to hit me.

I dove into the bushes; he backed up and screamed down the road. The neighbors called the cops. When they arrived, it looked like a murder scene. There was blood everywhere. Ten cop cars pulled up to the scene. Of course, I thought they were actors. One had a Seventies porn mustache that I right away started to make fun of. I had to force them to take pictures.

I gave them Bella's name and they ended up threatening to arrest me for public intoxication due to my smart mouth. An aggravated assault with a deadly weapon, a baby being exposed to meth smoke, two massive knives sitting on the driveway. They did nothing; just drove away as if nothing had happened. This only further cemented the fact that they were paid off by Hollywood to turn a blind eye as to what went on at Oakbrook.

I went inside and began to tear up Bella's room in a rage. I smashed the security system. I took the massive antique mirror she had brought off the wall and smashed it into a thousand pieces. I poured BBQ sauce all over her high-fashion clothes. I ripped up her bedding and broke all her DVD's. I literally and completely lost it.

#

The next few days, I was alone with my insanity. I was crying uncontrollably from the seclusion when I took a statue and threw it through the picture window in the dining room. I cringed as the shards fell to the floor and out of the window frame. The sound of the breaking glass only fueled my rage more. I went into the kitchen and unloaded *The Movies* foul attempt on recreating my grandma's chinaware.

I smashed a hundred-piece set onto the kitchen floor. It

felt good to break things. *After all, it was fake anyway...right?* Now a massive hole into the world was poking through into the dining room. The air conditioning poured out into the hundred-degree Texas heat and hundred percent Corpus Christi humidity. I went to the thermostat and turned it down to sixty degrees. *Why not? Them/They were now paying the power bill on the set. I'll run the bill up to ten grand, Fuck 'Em.*

    I went on a five-hour rampage, destroying most of the house with my bare hands. There was glass everywhere. I had pulled out the pictures of my family from their frame. It was sad to look at all the descendants of the Bornagain family. I felt as if they were watching as I fell to pieces right before their lifeless eyes on the developed film prints. That's when I realized they were reprints that *The Movie* had made. I tore every picture up and left them on the floor in a mess. I tore all the clothes out of closets, drawers, and more. The whole house looked like a landfill. I was exhausted by the time I was done.

    I went on missions over the next few weeks. I was panhandling in front of stores for smokes. Hey, *Them/They* were sending some pretty generous actors my way. They would walk up with these sad eyes, looking at me like I was one of those kids in a "Feed the Children" commercial. They would buy me smokes, fast food, some even gave me cold hard cash so I could buy ice. *The Movie knew what I needed. They were stealing my idea...that God would provide.* The God angle was all me because I believed it with all my heart. That's when I started to make a lot of interesting finds in dumpsters and alleyways. TV's, leather coats, all kinds of items that I could trade for drugs later in the night.

    The pavement reflected lines of heat that sweltered upon my sunburnt face. I had been walking for weeks. Cuts from continually breaking windows and glass objects at the house riddled my already tormented body. I had infected cuts all over my feet, which were three times the size that they should be. Blisters the size of golf balls were on my soles, puss-filled and stinky. When I would get home, I could barely stand. When I took my filthy Adidas off, they would smell of rotten hamburger and feces.

I was wearing down. The more missions I went on, the more burnt my flesh became, the worse my mental state declined. I was knocking on people's doors. This is when I made a new discovery. *Them/They was using a color system!* Anything with purple or blue was a sure sign I should stop. These colors symbolized markers, telling me where to go, where to turn, and where to look for items on this fun treasure hunt. They liked to use Christmas wreaths and other unique items to entice me to a certain destination as well.

I felt as though everyone was whispering about me out in public. I was confronting the actors all over town, in eateries, on sidewalks, and beyond. I was getting into five to ten close-call fistfights per day. *But that's what they wanted. They were antagonizing me so I would snap and end up back in jail.*

The harassment from the Hollywood machine started to go to new levels. They had figured out that if they removed or drilled holes in the mufflers of the cars they were using and revved the engine as they passed by me on the street that it would drive me insane. It was working too. I was thinking of new innovative ways to oust them. I called the city and told them about *The Movie* shoot. I complained about the noise pollution they were creating with such tactics. I cited that this kind of noise disturbance had to be against city ordinance. *Well...unless they pulled a permit.*

I went on a mission Downtown to the City Hall one day. I went in and demanded to talk to the mayor. *I was going to get to the bottom of this. A production of this size had to have the county's permission to shoot such a high budget film within city limits.* So, the lady at the desk had me file a formal grievance. She pretended not to know anything and said the mayor was a man who saw citizens on an "appointment only" basis. *The damn movie had them sign the confidentiality agreements too. I was being stonewalled around every turn.*

When I removed myself outside, I was surrounded by a hundred homeless synthetic heads. I found this as a great time to shoot a scene. I got up on a ledge near the sidewalk.

"Hey, errybody! Synthetic marijuana is potpourri with bug spray on it, you fucking idiots," I screamed out to the crowd.

They all jeered and shouted threats at me. I continued to berate them for almost thirty minutes. City Hall security broke up an almost-fistfight and threw me right off the property. I panhandled some bus fare and headed home. *What a waste of a trip Downtown. The damn confidentiality waiver was brilliant for this type of shoot. They had thought of everything, they had got to literally everyone.*

I began to deteriorate physically. I was only drinking Pepsi, no water of any kind. It was during this time that I realized that I had not signed any type of agreement with the movie. When a product was shown in a film, they got paid by the company to show the product. I would hold up my Pepsi. I worked Pepsi into almost every scene verbally. When these bastards came to me to sign my release at the end, I was going to work in a deal where I got paid for every time, I had showcased the drink, in all its sugary goodness. It was brilliant; even now looking back, I would have made bank. Mentally ill people are not stupid, just misguided.

Everything around me was surreal. All the storefronts,

street signs, and advertisements in the windows seemed to be aimed at me. Subliminal movie messages, either directing me, poking fun at me, or other small tokens of terrible behavior. I pictured myself standing next to a store sign with a punchline for the film on it. *Them/They are filming me, and the audience getting a good chuckle at my expense. They thought they were so funny.*

#

The wind began to move in ways that were a little too coincidental. When I was supposed to turn left, the wind would suddenly change directions. When, according to script, I was supposed to go south, the wind would fight me from the north, as if to turn me back to where *Them/They* wanted me to shoot a scene. *Even for Hollywood, this was impossible...right? Not so fast...*

I remembered stories of a legendary weather control system that sat outside Nome, Alaska. A series of twenty massive radio towers on government land in the deep Alaskan tundra. They would shoot controlled radio waves up into the earth's atmosphere and heat up the ozone. *Something like that, anyways.* By doing so, the scientists for the US Government could control the wind, create storms, and other anomalies of nature. This was the real deal. HAARP was its official name. It was featured on "Conspiracy Theory with Jesse Ventura" on truTV network.

In this special, they had mentioned that Hollywood implemented the US Government's abilities in HAARP. They would use the system to control the weather on their shoots. If the scene was sunny, they got sunny. If it called for a downpour, they got buckets. I had also seen this on another show online, featured on "The Alex Jones Prison Planet" radio show. Watching and listening to these types of shows while doing illicit drugs is a dangerous mix, to say the least.

So now they had another fun toy to torment me with. One of epic proportions. The actors out in public were always saying "It's going to rain!" I concluded that if it did, *The Movie* would have to end. Coincidently, around this time in 2018, Corpus Christi was under an almost biblical drought. Crops were dying and there was a water ban in effect, so my odds of beating HAARP were not looking good.

#

I was dying. Every window was busted out at Oakbrook. The few people *The Movie* was now sending to help me all looked at me with fear in their eyes. Some played along more than others. Looking on in pity, they all felt sorry for me.

"When is your dad coming home? Do you really live like this?" were some of the common comments I was hearing.

Even though I destroyed her things, Bella would stop in to check on me every couple of days. She would bring me a cold Pepsi, and grams of Reynaldo's dope. *She was sent to bring me provisions. Maybe she was the one I was to marry? Why did the film want to torture me like this? Why did she want to torture me like this?* All I knew was my Bella cared for me.

#

I went to see Heidi at a local trap. I was walking everywhere; the Benz had a flat. I walked up the drive at Sherry's house in the afternoon at around four on a sweltering summer Monday. I entered after a quick knock and only Heidi was present. We went into the bedroom where I was to collect on an old debt the bitch still owed me. A forty of ice. She was acting strange. I knew she was a huge movie person. *Who knew? She could be the love of my life.*

She played around a bit before telling me she was going to take a quick shower. When she left the room, I sat on the floor among a huge pile of dirty clothes. As I lifted my head, I saw the clothes had all been starched and formed into insane life-like barnyard creatures. Llama's, dogs with faces, and the piece of resistance that was to poke fun at me. *A very evil-looking pig. The movie liked to poke fun at the fact that I was husky, as my Ma called me since a kid.*

      I had started to refer to *The Movie's* very elaborate and high-tech props department as the *Boys in Props*. I pictured a group of Hollywood nerds. Special effects gurus that were something like the puppeteers on the show "The Muppets" with Jim Henson. I pictured the makeup artists as specific characters with their own job to do. They were the guys who rigged the falls so that I plopped down right there in my path onto my butt. The guys who placed things just at the right spots so when I was dumpster diving, things would smash me in the face. *Very funny guys.* I had a big love/hate relationship with the *Boys in Props*. As much grief as they were causing me, as much hell these guys were putting me through, they were still very capable of shooting epic footage. For me, the funnier the movie was, the bigger it was going to be when it premiered. *I'd do anything for a laugh my whole life, and now…I was getting paid for it. Well, not yet though.*

      Heidi had to go get the dope from her regular trick down the street. She told me I had to wait outside. I was left to sit on the tree swing that hung from an old Mesquite tree outside Sherry's place. When I glanced up, I saw that Sherry's three little dogs were sitting in front of me, all lined up in a perfect row. Dogs I had known for over a year now, suddenly acting like Lassie. *Totally trained Hollywood pooches.* Foxy Lady was my favorite of the three dogs. She was the odd duck in the group. She was a miniature Collie that had stolen my heart long ago.

So, what did I do? A blistering forty-five-minute stand-up set for the dogs, that's what!

These trap houses all had hidden cameras and microphone systems covering their house, in the trees, and anywhere else that was good to get strategically placed shots. So, I knew we were about to get some insanely funny footage. There were neighbors outside as well. *Maybe we could get some real laughs for the flick.*

I talked to the dogs like they were my audience. I was saying things like "This is a tough crowd," and making a joke that these adorable pooches were going to be worse joke thieves than Carlos Mencia. That I would probably see Foxy Lady doing my routine on her next HBO special. I was roaring with laughter. Bending over in pain with joy. I was getting good at stand-up comedy, my lifelong dream coming to life before my eyes.

Heidi showed up with the dope not long after and I went back to the now ruined trap house in the Country Club Estates, better known as Oakbrook. I laughed as I entered the house. The windows had been busted out for weeks. *Them/They's electric bill was going to be 5 grand at minimum.*

The next few days were tough. No actors coming by to provide dope or money. *What was I to do?* I found a bunch of lemonade mix in the pantry. That's about all that was left for food in the joint. I got one of the only glass pitchers that remained and engineered a huge batch of ice-cold lemonade. I knew *Them/They* would send by a massive crowd if I held a lemonade stand at a comical thirty-five years of age. *This was an awesome idea.*

I went to social media for some free advertising. I set up a table and chairs, a money box, the whole nine yards. I posted pictures on every local yard sale page and sat and waited for my fortune to roll in. Nothing. I was out there for three hours. I got a lot of messages saying I was "sad" and "desperate.". *Idiots just trying to get a rise out of me for some footage. Not today, Junior.*

I decided to walk to Sherry's. That's when they threw it in my face. It was a Tuesday in the month of May. The kids weren't even out of school yet. It was in the afternoon at half past four. I walked down to the corner, and I almost lost my shit right there.

I saw the most epic, most grandiose, pink and white lemonade stand on the corner being run by little girls in white sundresses. Pink streamers blew in the exotic wind! I wanted to burn it down. *What a punchline. These assholes wrote into the script that I was to be put out of business by the damn "Fitzpatrick" twins down the street. Foiled by a couple of nine-year-old bitches and their mom.*

I stood on the opposite corner and screamed at them, "Very funny, lady. It ain't gonna be so funny when I come poison your cat." The Mother hustled the child actors into the house, and I decided to pack it up for the night. I put some stale rum in the lemonade and drank till I passed out.

#

Tony had shown up with some real scumbag looking check cashers, with Laurie being their queen. They sat around acting funny, double talking, and such. They wanted to party, even with all the windows smashed out. I let them stay the night. Then I got sick of them stealing checks out of my father's top drawer for future scams and I threw them out. *The checks were fakes from The Movie anyway. They were just testing my reaction for a quick test of my character.*

I threw them out at nine the next morning. I had to walk to the grocery store to pick up some Western Union my ma was sending me. She insisted my dad was in hospice care and I was crazy. I blew her off, knowing full well Barry had a nine iron in his hand in Maui. When I returned from the store, the Benz Cl 350, my dad's prized possession, was gone. I wasn't worried. *The Movie had come and got the keys out of my top drawer, and towed it to a lot somewhere, just to put a scare in me.*

The following week, everyone who came by told me Laurie had stolen it. Drove it with a flat, fixed it, and was now driving all over town, hitting licks, and committing crimes. *Yeah right! it was laughable.* I mean just the week before I took it for a spin on the rim in a rage at four in the morning. I had driven to Sherry's just a few blocks away, drunk on rum, and screamed up onto the lawn. I was pissed at Sherry's son for some reason. On the way home, there were sparks shooting out of the rim, so I knew it was nowhere near in driving condition. *Thank God the cops were paid off by The Movie.* I mean, imagine the Benz, sparks flying out everywhere, half past four in the morning, going ten miles per hour down the road with a drunk driver behind the wheel. *If this were real life, I would be in prison.*

There was a big rumor brewing at the trap houses within the ice community that I had killed my dad for his life insurance. People were saying that he was missing and that I was insane. *Another attempt to get me to snap, right?* They had people asking me left and right If I had buried him in the backyard.

#

I had no ride, no money, no dope. I was miserable. All I had was my phone. And on this day, I got the most terrifying phone call of my life. Well, I didn't know it until way later. I got a call from a kid I knew from Port Aransas. Not a drug guy at all. He was saying that they were shooting a porn film in Aransas Pass, Texas at a house he knew. There were going to be women, tons of kinky sex, and more. He scooped me up later that day, and we took the thirty-five-minute drive over to Aransas Pass.

We arrived at the house at dusk. A musty one-level ranch that had an evil feel as soon as you walked in. The owner was a three-hundred-and-eighty-pound man with a Fu Manchu mustache and overalls on. There was only him, the kid who picked me up, and myself. I felt something was off from the very start.

Over the course of the next two days, I was fed small amounts of dope at a time. Kid size portions that made me feel strange and trippy. I would keep asking where the porn shoot was and all kinds of other questions; and when I would ask to leave, out came the pipe. So, my addiction won, and I would stay.

Day three out in Aransas Pass was nothing short of grueling. I was dehydrated and felt like I had been dosed with a hallucinogenic. The rooms looked liquid and scary. The dark wood and low lighting all over the house had me petrified. I felt as if the two men were out to get me. The double talk was nonstop and horrendous. Things between us were starting to get the opposite of friendly.

I went into my best Daryl that I could muster, but I was just not myself in this state. These guys were making my life miserable. I was in the bedroom watching porn around five in the evening. I had complained that I needed to charge my phone. They laughed at me and brought me a charger. I had it on there for hours. When I went to check if it was fully charged, it was dead. I was sure it was charging; I had triple checked.

The short little rat-faced kid started to laugh

uncontrollably. He held up a small homemade remote device. He clicked it with his bony little fingers. He was skinny and rodent-like. He explained that he "fucked with people" with this device that he had made. He could remotely turn off the plug in the wall so people's phones wouldn't charge. This is when he started to get downright mean.

 He was a hillbilly type, White and scummy. Trailer trash. Even way back in my Port Aransas days, I didn't care for him. I had been begging him for two days to take me home, and every time, out came the dope and an excuse.

 The fat owner of the property was out back tinkering with some machinery, and the rat suggested we take a drive. Whatever was in this dope had me hallucinating. I had been up almost five days moreover. I was terrified, angry, and confused the whole time. The Rat kept telling me to make sure my location was off on my phone. I assured him it was dead, and he would burst out in a manic laugh.

 We cruised around the dark residential blocks of post-Hurricane Harvey, Aransas Pass. A town that still looked as if it were a post-war third-world country. This town was hit particularly hard.

 He started referring to some big names, in a menacing criminal organization within the drug game. One I had never worked for, not even once, because they were so scary. The type that would disappear you because they got high and paranoid about you, even if it weren't true.

 He kept making references and mentioning these guy's names. I had seen them around; I knew who they were, and I feared them. My hair stands up thinking of them to this day. He kept saying "informant, snitch," and dropping all kinds of code words that rang underworld bells. By the time we got back to the house, it was dark.

We went to the back bedroom. I couldn't speak at this point. The Rat started in on a tirade. He was acting even more foul and vindictive now, as if he hated my soul. He made a reference to a lynching as he pointed to the wood rafter above our heads. When I looked, there was a very real, very sturdy noose hanging from a beam. I was shaking. I felt like I was going to urinate in my pants.

I looked over into the closet. There was a dark blue fifty-gallon drum, a bunch of bulletproof vests, and boxes of rounds for assault rifles.

"We got enough shit here, to start a race war," the Rat said with an evil grin.

That's when it dawned on me. I was in a safe house for one of the most feared, ruthless, and dangerous organizations around. I threw up. The Rat started laughing as he patted me on the back. He signaled me that I had to follow him. We went to meet the fat owner in the overalls that was in the backyard. It was fenced in, with a mighty tree that was bent over from the storm not long ago.

There was a huge tractor sitting there, running loudly. The fat man was high up on the seat. The tractor was construction yellow and looked monstrous. I was speechless as the massive rusty claw dug into the damp summer earth. The shifting moans of the hydraulic pistons were burning in my ears. It was surreal; I was under the influence of some strong hallucinogenic drugs, not the sort I was used to. They had drugged me.

"You're the famous cab driver huh, the one that's helping a case get built?" said the Rat.

I couldn't even respond. Just then a ferocious realization came over me. I had a dead phone, no money, no friends or family. I took off running. I hopped over the wooden fence that leads to the front yard, and I was out of there. Tripping and paranoid, yes, but one thing was for damn sure. That motherfucking hole was being dug for me. This wasn't any movie. This was not a misunderstanding, and it was certainly no joke.

#

As I ran out of breath, I found myself walking down the dark main drag toward the nearest businesses. I didn't feel like I was being followed. It was over two miles of terror as I walked alone and mentally shredded in a light summer drizzle. I arrived and sat down on the curb outside McDonald's.

Not long after, it began. I started to recognize certain people from the drug game. Ugly faces of death and misfortune. Soon I realized I was surrounded. I made a beeline for the adjoining Walmart, as it was twenty-four hours. I needed a refuge in a huge way.

I made it to the cart lobby unharmed. A gang of criminal well-knowns were pacing the parking lot. The crowd grew over the next hour. They drove by taking pictures of me on their cell phones. They leered and snarled at me. One guy, a bald fifty-something, walked by and got close enough to speak.

"You know what happened to the owner of Walmart…he is pushing up daisies."

I recognized this scumbag from the Bluff. I was now terrified. At least the store was twenty-four hours.

I sat contemplating how I was going to make my escape. I went inside the store to the Walmart Business Center. There was a customer courtesy phone that was hung on the wall. I thought of anyone and everyone I could call, but not a soul came to mind. It was a sad day in the life of Boston Bornagain. The guy who had once carried two cell phone batteries because the calls were so plentiful. To be honest, I don't know if I would have called a homeboy into this kind of situation. Guns could pop, right there in the parking lot.

I recognized more big-name killers. One giant, he looked like he crawled off the screen of "The Hills Have Eyes," walked by me, glaring like a demon. There was a pad of paper lying on a counter just beneath the phone. I picked up a felt pen and scribbled a cryptic message. One that may very well be my last. "I didn't snitch" was all I could say. A last-ditch effort to the world that these monsters killed me for nothing.

I went back to the lobby and sat on a Walmart blue wire bench, freezing cold. I was exhausted, scared, and furious. The king daddy of them all walked in. A man who, when his name was spoken, would stop five o'clock traffic in the meth world. I couldn't believe my eyes. I had seen him around a few times. Most people didn't even know what this man looked like. He had a very sinister street name that I won't even dare recreate for this book.

He had very distinct and evil tattoos. He looked like a demonic version of Jax Teller from "Sons of Anarchy." When he passed by me, he gave me the wickedest murderous smile one could fathom. My legs were shaking, my mind shattered with terror. I could only sit there, like an overstuffed cup of green Jell-O. About ten minutes had passed. Satan reemerged into the lobby. This time he didn't even look my way, holding one plastic sack with two boxes of Teddy Grahams cereal inside. His lack of eye contact made me even more nervous. He didn't want to be filmed on security cameras, mean-mugging a dude they planned on burying later that night.

Two smokes remained in a crushed, sorry-looking cigarette package that rested deep inside my pocket. I decided that my heart needed a little break. I went outside and lit up. Cars drove by, sly stares of death within, gliding by like apparitions into thin air. I was halfway done with the Marlboro cigarette when I heard the most terrifying noise possible.

The chain system on the store's security gate was activated. Now at eleven, the store was about to close. The store was no longer twenty-four hours. All hope of refuge collapsed like Tower One on September 11. In a split-second decision to save one's life, I dove and rolled under the gate, and back into Wally World.

The manager ran up on me with a quickness, "Sir, what the hell do you think you're doing," he chimed.

He was a geeky White guy wearing a cheap clip-on tie and a plain white button-down. Now, this was a moment where quick thinking could save your life, and I believe that it did as I look back.

You very well can't rat and call the law on the most notorious gang in the game. Snafu moves like that will get you smoked like some country-style ribs on the Fourth of July. The Spirit of Jesus came into me, and I sobered up instantly.

"I am having chest pains, man. I think I am having a heart attack." I clamored.

The manager looked pissed. All the extra incident reports and right at quitting time.

"Alright, Susan call 911," he snapped.

Within five minutes, fire trucks and an ambulance came with their lights on and flooded the walls of the lobby, breaking through the mesh of the security gate, plastering the walls with red and white strobe lights. The EMS staff put me on a gurney and wheeled me out, throwing me in the back of the bus. Once in the back, they assessed me. I was hooked up to suction cups. My blood pressure was taken, and they looked at each other, puzzled as could be.

"Sirs are you under the influence of any drugs," said the

Mexican EMT.

"I did a bunch of meth earlier in the day. In certain situations, you just can't say too much, buddy" I replied.

He looked at me, then to the other worker. He got the point. He took mercy on me and decided to transport me all the way back to Corpus Christi from Aransas Pass. By the grace of God, for my situation, the hospital there had closed permanently after the hurricane.

We arrived at the hospital late at night. They took me out of the back of the ambulance and wheeled me into the ER. I was still petrified. They brought me right back to a room to be assessed by the physician and their staff. This cute blond nurse, chunky and sweet, came into the curtain's view. She sat down with a blood draw kit. We started chopping it up. I alluded to the fact that my life was in danger but didn't say too much.

She stared into my eyes for what felt like hours but must have been mere moments. She welled up and put her left hand on my shoulder. She asked, "Boston, are you a Christian?"

I didn't hesitate, "Yes Mama, I am." (It is common in South Texas for people of all sex and ages to call women Mama.)

She laid both hands on me and started to pray. She spoke soft words of safety and healing into my life. She prayed for a total transformation and freedom. She knew I was a drug addict by the condition of my punctured, ruined veins.

She walked out, and about thirty minutes later a young doctor came in, a White guy with a coat that matched his skin. He looked like he hadn't seen the sun in forty-seven days.

"Mr. Bornagain, from what we can tell, you are killing yourself." He was serious as a heart attack, no pun intended. "You are severely dehydrated, and your blood isn't looking good." He had a sad look on his face.

They gave me something to sleep, and I was out like a light. When I awoke, I was groggy with a film over my eyes. I walked out not knowing what time it was. By my estimates, the drugs wore off about an hour after I took them. When I emerged into the ER waiting room, I saw some familiar faces. These bastards had followed me!

I walked outside and saw that they had some men posted up at the double doors leading out to Ocean Drive. a massive dude, and a much more fearsome and lethal guy who was ironically short. I walked right back inside like Speedy Gonzales, not believing my eyes. I thought I had escaped the clutches of death back in Aransas Pass. I was dead wrong. I took a seat in a packed ER waiting room. I watched as the men inside stared me down, rolling their eyes as if not to be noticed.

It was then I knew I had to spring into action. I got up, walked outside, and right up to the dynamic duo. They were outside smoking. I knew the little guy was the shot caller, so I stormed up to him to clear the air.

"I think you guys got the wrong impression of me," I said. I was shaking uncontrollably. "Look, man, there ain't no paper on me, you got people who can check that out. I ain't never talked to the cops, not once." The Spirit filled me, it directed my speech, like a conductor of a truth symphony.

I looked directly into that man's eyes. I said, "You can tell when a person is lying, you can tell by the eyes." He looked directly at me as I spoke those words. He paused, took a long drag off the Marlboro Light he held smoking in his bony little fingers.

"Ok, what about the girl?" he said inquisitively. "You been beating on her?" He looked unhappy, to say the least.

"I love that girl more than life itself. I call her 'The

Greatest Love of All.' I would never touch her," I said truthfully.

The little guy looked at the big guy, and the big guy looked to the ground, and said "Ok, we will look into it."

Just like that, they left. I walked back into the lobby. The men inside left after a quick ring of one of their cell phones. My heart began to return to a normal pace. The air in the room changed, and I felt safe for the first time in four days. When I walked outside at daybreak, I was cautious and constantly checking of my surroundings so as not to have a revolver put to my skull. I headed back to Oakbrook. Alive.

#

The word on the street came to me fast over the next couple of days. Remember that crazy story where I was the plastic surgery pig? The crime fighter from the future? The one where Bella and her friend believed that I was a police officer who had surgery to look differently. Well, legend has it that Bella and her friend went to Crazy White Boy's trap. Bella unloaded the whole tale in a room full of high-level gang members. They heard the story, knew who I was, and they ran with it to spread the word through the drug world.

The next part happened when the story made its way to a clubhouse in the Bluff. The insane parts had fallen off the bones, like the meat on some pork ribs in the summertime. The information had unraveled. I was a cab driver, working with the cops as a confidential informant. I had got caught up and turned snitch for the task force.

The people who heard this were no joke in the drug world. They don't take chances. The other part the chick told these men was that I was beating on Bella during her last stay at Oakbrook. As we know, both stories were ass-backward and false.

What I found out next touched my heart. They had

checked it out and found no paper of any kind. A female in my life. A very special girl to me who was also involved in the drug world. She went to some high-level shot callers. She one hundred percent vouched for me as being legit. I heard from multiple sources that this was the part that saved my life and had the green light turned red.

It all just went away, like a teen pregnancy scare when little Suzie started to bleed. I came inches from being buried in a backyard in Aransas Pass, Texas. I would have been labeled a runaway tweaker, my children thinking I had just taken off, never to be seen again.

That is how easily you can disappear in the drug game, kids. Addiction, mental illness, none of that meant jack shit to these jokers. Afterall, we were all in the same boat, or world if you will.

#

Right after this scare of my life, I was back out on missions. I walked into the Whataburger on Weber and Saratoga. They gave you free water and I was changing my ways, trying to take better care of myself. Or maybe it was because it was free, and I was broke. Either way, six at night dinner rush was a packed house, I get up on a table and started to do some acting.

"Alright, everybody, this is a message to *Them/They!*"

The cops showed up almost immediately. Another three days in the nuthouse.

#

I had scored an eight ball for the first time in weeks. There were people in and out of Oakbrook without permission while I wasn't at home. I walked out onto the driveway on this day and found a pack of syringes just lying-in plain view on the ground. I picked them up, went in the house, and loaded them in Barry's little toilet room in the master bathroom. There was a cabin mate in there where I hid the rigs and the dope, under some old issues of my grandma's "Good Housekeeping" from the Eighties. I didn't want any house guests to get my stash.

I went out on a mission and came back home a few hours later. There was a crew of workers and four Corpus Christi City Marshals there with them. As I walked up, they informed me that the house's condition wasn't up to code. The heaping dumpster of trash in the driveway, the smashed-out windows, all the pictures torn up and floating in the breeze on the front lawn. It was a danger for squatting and a promotion of crime.

They were to board up my dad's four-bedroom house in the Country Club Estates. The neighbors hated me. I was out on the front lawn screaming every morning at three thirty while doing stand-up, "Hear Ye, Hear Ye, the court of the king is now in session." I would say that in an old English accent. Then I would do a routine for about an hour at the top of my lungs. You know…for the cameras.

They would stare out of the windows, watching as I lit a meth water pipe with a massive blowtorch. No cops ever came. *CCPD had to be paid off, and if the neighbors took the money to participate in the film, I was going to make their lives a living hell. I would make them earn that Hollywood cash.*

I talked them into letting me into the house while they worked. I went in and locked all the doors. I stepped into the bathroom where the preloaded syringes were. I sat on the toilet as the drilling began. It was an awful feeling, one of desperation and fear as the police boarded up my house with me inside. I shot up a massive load into the main blood vessel in my femur.

I was injecting crystal meth while the cops were just outside the structure. My eyes, feasting on chemical pride, I hid the junk again, and outside I went. I started to perform. One cop was playing along to a tee. I had them all rolling. We talked about old-style stand-up. My love for Rodney, Sam, and Andrew Dice Clay.

That's when they hit me. They had been running my name. I had a warrant from missing a court date on one of the many public intoxication charges I had leading up to this. I had to go to the city jail for a few hours and see a judge to reset my court date. I was furious; I had all that dope in the bathroom. I made them promise that they would give me a ride home, and off we went.

It was all fun and games till I went into the box to see the Magistrate Judge.

He was in a wheelchair. I was furious at the joke he was pulling, poking fun at the whole Barry situation. I started to scream at the judge, asking him if he was a real judge or an actor. Two massive jailers, ex-military, were ordered by said judge to take me out right away. They hoisted me up, cuffed me behind my back, picked me up off my feet, and hauled me away. When we got to the last cell in the row, they opened the steel gate and dropped me about four feet, directly on my cranium.

They twisted my arm like the twisty tie on a loaf of Wonderbread. I could feel the cartilage in my elbow detaching from the slick bone underneath the skin. I yelped like a puppy being burned with a lit cigarette. They exited my cell and made me wait five more hours to see the next Judge, under the promise that I would behave. *I did. I mean, come on, I had three grams of fire at Oakbrook that needed shooting.*

They let me walk out the side door of the city jail as is procedure, and what a shocker, I had to panhandle to take the bus back to the southside of Corpus Christi. I had to sneak around to the sliding door into Barry's room. Thank God it wasn't boarded up like the rest of the now rancid and condemned dwelling. I went inside and my dope was right where I left it. I couldn't find a vein after an hour of swinging into dry wells. I plunged the spear deep into the artery in my neck as I looked in the now shattered glass of the hanging mirror on the wall.

When the needle retracted, I couldn't stop the bleeding for over two hours. I thought this was curtains, as the dirty sock I used as a tourniquet covered the festering gape of the wound. The sock stunk of wine and corn chips. If I remember correctly, I also used it as a masturbatory cleanup cloth a few days before.

I went over and sat on the skeletal remains of my father's king-size bed. The floor was covered in trash, food, and broken glass. I was so high that I couldn't breathe. I was in the only room with frigid AC due to the broken windows. And BOOM...the lights dissolved to black. The power had finally been turned out. I sat in the desolate pitch black shooting up by candlelight until dawn. *Them/They finally gave in, I had won the war of the electric bill. Even for Hollywood, that bill must have been too high.*

#

The following days were dark and filled with the deep despair of a life in the twilight glow; the end felt near. I walked an average of fifteen miles a day on swollen and blistered feet. The vortex had me; I was in a vacuum of disaster and impossibility. I walked as Jesus did, going where the whispering wind and *Them/They* would take me. I was a champion of the people, starting to discuss political issues in the community on my soapbox. I was taking on the God/Tupac/Comedian role well. I would speak on racial issues; stand up to the police in front of crowds; really anything to take on The Man, whoever he was.

I was walking home late one night when the storm clouds swayed in from the east, looking as if they may penetrate the dry-caked mud and brittle grass, and end the longest drought in recent history for Corpus Christi, Texas. The thunder roared as my emotion grew as tall as a Midwest scraper. The sky began to open. The rain hit my white flesh as I bantered along like a wino on fire. The first drops of water were cool to the touch, an elevated environment, and the crisp spoils of victory dropped the atmosphere's temperature below what was normal.

It was raining! The movie was about to end, the money was about to be deposited! It was finally going to end. I was going to see Barry, my family, my children, and all my loved ones at the big party at some swanky Downtown hotel. Roll the credits, homeboy. This movie is a wrap.

Cats and dogs, the pouring of pure happiness came down in buckets as I walked home from Sherry's pad. Precipitation's glorious flow of grace and mercy. I was on top of the world. The cool water ran down into my shoes, soothing my hurt feet as I stomped in lake-size puddles. I entered Oakbrook as a champion that night. I went into my room by cell phone light to find some clean socks I had shoplifted. *I couldn't show up to this evening party as anything but fresh.*

Hours went by with no activity from *Them/They*. *Those bastards reneged on the Rain Clause?* I was furious. I stomped outside at three in the morning and screamed "I knew it, you no-good sons-a-bitches, you went back on your word." I crashed into a deep sleep after taking a bar of Xanax. I woke the next day in the afternoon at four. I walked aimlessly and ended up at Outback Steakhouse at around a quarter past six. It felt right, so I went in.

There he sat, a dim table off the side of the bar area. A

man with a bald spot in the shape of a horseshoe. He looked like a thinner, more put-together version of Dr. Phil. The man was in full makeup. I beelined my way towards him.

"So, what's the big idea, cowboy," I asked snidely.

"What are you talking about, Sir?" The man was puzzled. "I am James DeBrow," he said with a smile.

I retorted "I bet you are, you dumb son-of-a-bitch. You got more makeup on than Mrs. Doubtfire!"

"Young man, I don't have the faintest idea what you are speaking of," he said this in a terrible Southern accent. "Waitress, check please," he was trying to mosey his way out of the door.

I chased after him as soon as he left. We had an altercation by his car, one where he opted to call local law enforcement. I started walking away. I went around to the back of the steakhouse and acted as if nothing had happened.

When the cruiser pulled up beside me, I acted startled. "Son, were you causing a problem back there?" The officer shouted from his open window.

"That guy tried to grab my cock, Officer, so I left." He gave me a pep talk and was on his way.

There was a motel behind the restaurant. As I strutted through the parking lot, I ran into Malcolm. He was a thin young Muslim man. Maybe twenty-five years of age. I asked him for a smoke.

"Hey man, you got a place to stay? I can give you thirty bucks if I can stay the night." He spoke.

I replied, "Well, just so happens I do, good Sir. But I will need those thirty bucks upfront, if it's all the same to you?" *Simple as that, I collected the bread, and Malcolm was now an official cast member.*

On the walk over, I had the revelation that this was the

reboot of the classic Jim Carrey hit "The Truman Show." *How could I have been so forgetful? It's the exact plotline. They had selected someone from the meth world, because of the lubricant effect it has on one's mind. It is the perfect drug to keep the subject always guessing. The one drug that could pull the real-life, reality TV version of "Truman" off without a hitch.*

#

Malcolm and I entered through the back door to a powerless Oakbrook. We lit candles and sticks to find our way. I showed him to the office, as it was the most bearable of all the rooms left. Malcolm was fine with his accommodations. In fact, we got high, and he started telling me his background and religious views. His father was a prominent doctor, his mother was a stay-at-home wife. His family was from the country of Jordan. A son of Immigrants, Malcolm shared the same "Fight the Power" views as me. Rage Against the Machine was one of his favorite bands as well as one of mine.

We hit it off as best buds over the next couple of days. He even got the power turned back on in his name. *I love Malcolm, even though he is a major producer in this film. There is no doubt in my mind that M is top brass for Them/They. At least they cared enough to write me a buddy into the script. Took them long enough.* These types of thoughts about *Them/They* were constantly going through my mind at the speed of a bullet train. I could never quit thinking about *The Movie.*

As the days went by, Malcolm and I became close. However, my paranoia and frustration with *Them/They* had me acting a bit out of pocket. If we couldn't score, I blamed Malcolm. After all, he had all the power at his fingertips to make those kinds of dreams come true. One phone call and he could have blue biker dope delivered if he chose.

Almost every other night, I was throwing Malcolm out at knifepoint. Only for him to return the very next day and we would both act as if nothing had happened. A beautiful black cat started showing up at Oakbrook. She would crawl through gaping holes in the wall that were exposed to the elements. The place was collapsing at the seams. She was radiant, and the sweetest thing you ever saw. I would cry out to her "CAT". With an extreme pronunciation on the "T" at the end. That was her new name. Our iced-out mascot of sorts and she loved every minute.

One night I had a major issue at a burger joint on Saratoga and Weber. I had ordered a coke (they didn't carry Pepsi), and I got into it with a sixteen-year-old girl who was working at the register. The cops showed up in seconds on the north side of the building. I darted out the door on the south side and sprinted the two blocks back to Oakbrook.

I slammed the great oak door shut and latched it. Malcolm was in the office masturbating to porn when five cruisers screamed onto the lawn. I had just run from the police, a crime they do not take lightly. I got into form, facing the door. We had ripped the boards off days before this event so we could enter like human beings. Just then around ten officers emerged under the porch light, guns and tasers drawn.

"CCPD, open this fucking door right now!" the captain said.

His medals in full view, a show of force by a decorated officer, the large White general in the *Them/They* army proceeded to take a right tactical boot to the massive door, five kicks in all. The door wouldn't budge. Malcolm quickly got dressed and met me in the hallway.

I decided to open the door. When I did, I was jerked

outside by my t-shirt.

"What the fuck is wrong with you, boy?" a big Mexican cop shouted.

I was being interrogated. They accused me of running from them; I maintained that I never even saw them. I did have a big jump on them as I was turning the corner onto Oakbrook before the cops were even in shouting distance. They entered the home, and Malcolm, being the idiot he was, gave them the grand tour. There were needles, tinfoil full of dope residue, and thousands of empty meth baggies all over the floor. That's enough paraphernalia to put us away for ten years.

The only thing that saved us was that the house was so gross, the cops didn't even notice. The smell alone was enough to make you puke. They started to interrogate Malcolm while in the hallway. I was now cuffed and surrounded by cops.

"You better leave him the fuck alone, motherfuckers; that's racial profiling."

I was pissed. I went into a screaming ten-minute rage about September 11 and the spiritual divide, forever present in our great Nation.

I accused them all of being paid actors, planted by *Them/They*, just like the ones that did nothing about the Booger incident. *The whole department was bought and paid for. City officials at the highest level, allowing Hollywood to rear its ugly head in The Sparkling City by the Sea.*

For some reason, they took off the cuffs. Whatever Malcolm said to them worked. *Did he pull his producer card? Did he lie to them and tell them I was mentally ill?* In any event, they started to vacate Oakbrook like locusts that just devoured a crop in West Africa. The top cop was walking by me as they retreated and said in a gloomy tone, "I am going to alert Adult Protective Services." They disappeared like ghosts in turbulent clouds.

The next day I was dumpster diving all over Saratoga. I was finding all sorts of expensive items. Portable cell charging batteries, Italian leather coats, three to be exact. Kids' toys still in the package, one pair of Nike track shoes with spikes on the bottoms that were all sorts of ethnic colors of red, green, and gold. I touched them inside the bubble wrap they sat in. I immediately felt the value. I was convinced in a vision that they were once used by Usain Bolt during the Olympics. I had just hit a major *Them/They* payday. My thoughts raced, *What a gift from the gods of Hollywood! Bestowed upon me so I could reap rewards necessary to my survival.*

There were so many high-priced items, I had to steal a shopping cart from a department store. I walked down Staples Street as a winner on this day. My head held high. I may have had on an old t-shirt as a do-rag, but I rocked my style with pride. I was in character and loving every minute of it. I needed to flip this stuff into an eight ball. The problem was turning it into cash first. *I don't wanna get low-balled by the dealer, no half-price bullshit today. No Sir!*

I entered storefronts and real estate offices like a bull in a China shop. I instilled fear in the eyes of the local business community, as I acted my way through as an iced-out peddler. A stoned gypsy warrior, on a mission from God, to get high and hold court for all my subjects.

No one wanted anything to do with my stuff even as I dropped the prices through the floor. It was getting dumb. I was like a tweaker Marlon Brando, making offers to potential buyers that they should have never refused. I was offering prices bottom low at one point, just to test people. *The Movie must have instructed them not to buy anything from me. A big joke just to torment me*, I thought to myself. *Dropping all this high-*

end merchandise on me, only to have the cash carrot dangled just out of reach. It was a tortuous scene, and I was getting dope sick and angry.

I wasn't no junkie piece-of-shit. I was gonna show *Them/They* who they were fucking with. I took a stand. The people's champ, about to show out in big ways. *They can't buy me; I am way above their pay grade.* I entered the grocery parking lot at noon, sun baking through the top of my sweat-filled do-rag. *This was now a giveaway.* I approached a young Mexican MILF and her young offspring.

"Hey honey, this is all free, not a penny to you, ok? My gift to you, courtesy of the ugly Hollywood monsters!"

She looked at me like I was a vampire about to rip her children's scalps off and eat their brains. I pleaded with her to take the shipment as she damn near tossed the infant in its car seat. I was now sure the movie had people in place to refuse my blessings of the day. *Bastards. Every one of them.*

I stomped off like a toddler that just had his rattle removed by his hideous older brother. Pissed, tired, and on a mission of principle, I devised a plan to spit in the face of these demons. All to unfold, live on camera. Academy Award type shit that Jack Nicholson would die to perform. *I shot nothing short of epic scenes*, I thought as I headed to the Exxon, across South Padre Island Drive.

I had three dollars in my board short's pocket, leg tattoos glistening with perspiration. I laid the treasure chest outside the door so I could see anyone who was trying to catch me slipping and steal my finds. I went to the overpriced household item section of the store. I grabbed a cheap bottle of sub-par bleach. I paid, and then I was outside to burn Paris to its knees. The incendiary Napalm flares showed within my iris and smoldered in rage. I made my announcement.

"Ok motherfuckers, the moment you have all been waiting for, the king has arrived. Money don't mean shit to me. You wanna see something, you're going to see something from Boston today!" I flipped the cap off the bleach.

I was about to make a political statement for the people. I wanted the world to watch the power of Jesus, the passion of man, and the decline of materialism among the awakened Army of God's people. *Them/They wasn't going to get their shot, I was getting mine. I was the director of this film. I do what I want!*

I poured the bleach upon the high-priced booty I had cleverly collected. The chemicals bubbled upon the surface of the buttery soft leather that had been tediously stitched by Italian hands. The liquid seeped into the computer boards of expensive equipment, the faces of Micky and Minnie Mouse became distorted into melted piles of dark brown as the presence of dyes and colors drained from once-perfect toys.

I destroyed it all, in full view of the audience pumping gas into their vehicles. People stared in awe as I screamed, "God Squad, All Day, Erry Day!" I ran through the parking lot, doing a bull dance, like an NFL player who had just scored the winning touchdown at the Super Bowl.

I celebrated with the roars all the way back home, punching the air with my own hands. Horns were honking from Chevy's, there were booms from diesel duallies, and the screams of my loyal followers that were rooting for me, escaping open windows in the summer sun. I was now hobbling.

My feet were so damaged by the daily trekking, that I could barely stand, let alone walk. I hobbled miles up to Holly Road, where I took a left. I stopped at the local strip club begging for a ride. With no luck, I made my way to the gas station across the street from the chubby White girl's trap. The same gas station where I took the photos of that crack-coking police informant, Mario.

The cops were there as if it was scripted. They came up to me as I was sitting on the hardtop, taking off my rotten Adidas. They asked me what my problem was. One male officer, one female officer.

"Can you give me a ride back to Oakbrook?" I asked.

They laughed at me and told me, of all things, that they were not a "Taxi Service". You can't write this shit! *Well, I guess you could, if you were a Hollywood writer in some dark board room in LA, tormenting the soul of a meth-induced ill individual.*

They warned me, told me to move it along, like I was a no-good hobo. I was being persecuted by this neighborhood that I had known and loved for fifteen years. I was crawling on two feet when I passed a yard I knew too well. On Holly Road, a few weeks before, I had a shouting match with a local homeowner. He was on his lawn this day, sipping tea with his teenage daughters.

"Hey, what the fuck are you looking at, asshole?" he said with war in his eyes.

"Hey shithead, you don't want it with me, I am the king of this shit, I am the motherfucking star of this show!" I said with fervor.

The man came over in a rage and pushed me to the ground. A blue-collar Mexican type, longer hair, muscular, and in his fifties. He wore a grey tee and blue jeans. I fell over like a bowling pin on a seven-ten split. He was screaming at me. *I must have really made him furious last time. His insanity was terrifying. What an actor. He was like a local version of Danny Trejo from "Machete." They found a good one in him.* I stared up as he went and grabbed a huge yard stone from the border of the lawn.

"I'm going to fucking kill you, motherfucker. I will smash your fucking brains in!" he shouted.

My eyes were huge as I told him to fuck off. I had no fear. *This was The Movie, baby. I was too important, even for this Hollywood mishap who joined me on set, no matter how good he was. Anyway, he was most likely just a stunt man of some type.*

His teen daughters wailed, "Daddy no, Daddy no," as he juked his arms at me with the huge rock. He dropped it to the lawn, as they led him back to the porch, exasperated.

I got to my feet and shouted, "Fuck you prick," as I walked away. *All I do is win; he obviously cowered at the thought of murder. That, to me, was a big win for The Squad.*

#

I was broken physically. I got it in my head that if I made it out of the city limits, I would be able to escape *Them/They* by the way of the permits they must have had to acquire. *I doubt they pulled the permit for the movie in any other county.* So, I packed up some buckets onto a massive Bo Staff that I had found in my travels. More specifically, it was a shellacked Shillelagh stick, about five feet long. These can be used as walking sticks or in martial arts.

It was four in the afternoon and my feet were leaking blood and pus from infected corns and bubbling blisters. I was wearing a pair of black and hot pink board shorts and a brand-new white tee I had stolen from a dollar store, with no socks on my feet. On my head was a black t-shirt wrapped all the way around, a do-rag of sorts for sun protection, but more importantly…style. A massive pair of square sunglasses, jet black. I looked like I came out of a black hole in some far-off universe, Martian in nature.

I walked to the highway with the stick on my shoulders, buckets on either end, like a Chinese peasant working the rice patties on a morning in May. As I walked under the Texas sun rays, I realized that I emulated Christ. Crucified, walking in torment as the townspeople spat in my direction. I took off my shirt, left the rag on my dome, and headed south, Flour Bluff bound.

I was on a multifaceted trip, enduring troubles and persecutions in physical, geographical, and spiritual ways. It was as if the bible had met a Thompson novel. My life was full of fear and self-loathing. But at the same time, I was on the greatest spiritual journey. Full of Demons and Angels, darkness and light, Jesus and Satan. Vivid visions and revelations filled my mind's eye as I walked as Jesus did. I was swimming in every dumpster on the way. I found some puke-stained scrubs for nurses. Under the first pair, was a stack of brand new "Grey's Anatomy" scrubs. All colors and sizes. A nice find to trade my plug for some of his stash to sell. When I arrived in Flour Bluff, which is still part of Corpus Christi, and therefore Nueces County, it would be the halfway point to Kleberg County. *My great escape from the dreadful movie! It was time to cash in. The rain didn't stop them, so maybe this would.*

Darkness began to fall as I ran out of smokes. I ducked behind a hotel on the highway to smoke the last of the meth I had in a bowl I had stolen from Heidi. When I finished, I was dying for a cigarette. I turned the corner, and there she sat. An older blond lady, worn from the Bluff sun, having a Marlboro Light, sitting Indian style.

"Mama, can I have one of those?" I asked.

She replied, "Sure sugar, well, if you sit with me awhile."

I obliged. We talked for around thirty minutes. We discussed *The Movie*, life, and Jesus. In the end, she said, "You know what, take a pack, Sugar Plum. I just bought three." She handed me a fresh deck of smokes. *God had provided once again. Even if Them/They paid, God was still in command.*

I walked on, my feet buckling on the hot pavement below. I saw blood leaking out of a tear in the leather. I kept going, eyes on the prize, full of vindication, with millions of dollars at stake. "The Wolf of Wall Street" Ferrari was just within arm's reach.

The Bluff came up over the horizon. I had to cross the bridge, which was terrifying on foot, especially with two heavy treasure buckets and a Jesus cross on my back. *It was epic. The shots we were getting must have looked amazing. The grand sight of the cross, a man on a journey, against all odds, beating a Hollywood foe, with unlimited paper.* The words I muttered to myself were epic as well, looking back.

I found myself singing the haunting Bob Marley piece "Redemption Song" as I came off the bridge. I cruised down and passed a vile motel, the same one I got drugged and robbed at. I spent many nights in that drug den, hating myself and suicidal. *Look at me now. I was to be the biggest comedic and dramatic thespian in the country, possibly the world.*

I sang the most sublime tunes as I dreamed of what I was going to do with all this money. At the Walmart to my right, I lit a fresh smoke and laughed feverishly. I planned on plucking families out of homelessness. Changing real lives, not giving it to corrupt charities. I planned on putting kids through school, feeding, and clothing the homeless. See, the "character" of the people's champ was inside me. The lover, the comedian, and man of Jesus was really who I was and continuously strived to be. Masked for years by addiction.

Oh God...my children. I broke down and started to cry. A moment of reality we all have when we are out there doing the things we shouldn't be doing. One that drops you to the knees and makes you remember how fucked up meth has made you. A total God-smack. Mentioned before here, yes, but it's something that happens every few weeks as you drift in and out of consciousness.

I arrived at the long-haired plug's house soon after. We sat in the living room, a larger group than usual. That only meant more dope was being smoked. They offered me food right away. I had dwindled down to a hundred and seventy pounds, and for me, that's rail thin. *I was in the best shape of my life...I was husky no more.* I was killing myself by not eating and not sleeping. I estimate that during the time with Barry, I stayed awake for the better part of sixty days.

During this session, I sat next to the plug. Suddenly, he was in full makeup. He was making the exact movements as my younger cousin. Picking at his feet, laughing just like him. *Was this my younger cousin in full costume? I knew they were using voice boxes in the throat to change people's voices, but this one was good.*

I'd had a suspicion that they were flying in old friends, and people from Boston to star in the film, putting them in disguise. *What a great idea, all my loved ones surrounding me on the journey, and I had no clue. Well, at least that's what they thought, I am far too smart for that old gag.*

Suddenly, I was seeing that my uncle, my other cousins, and the whole family were in full makeup, made to look like real-life people that I had known from the Bluff. In other words, this was my family disguised as my druggie acquaintances. *What an amazing job, I got to hand it to The Boys in Props, they did a bang-up job on this scene.* I knew the place was crawling with hidden cameras, so I played like I didn't know any better. But I would make some references to our family vacation we had taken to Canada when I was just a kid.

The whole situation was so overwhelming, I was finding it hard to breathe. I was now making subtle jokes as if I knew what was going on, without saying it outright. We all laughed for hours. The size of the party dwindled down to me, the plug, and his nightly bag chasing honey.

The plug threw me out! He has never asked me to leave before. This must be some huge to-do in the script. Outside I met a homeless guy who is known for biking all over town. He told me to meet him on Red Dot Pier, which is on the bridge between Flour Bluff and North Padre Island. It was on the way to Kleberg County, so I said: "What the Hell." There must be something there for me.

I stopped at the Goodwill donation station in the Bluff, which was on the way to the Island. There was a mountain of merchandise outside, just sitting on the pavement. For the Bluff, that's a find. Usually, anything not nailed down gets stolen faster than it gets donated.

There was a whole box of brand-new purple t-shirts from some fishing tournament that happened a year before. I stuffed around twenty of them in the now empty buckets. I had traded all my findings for a little dope back at the plug's place.

I had a plan to go down to the pier and sell them for dirt cheap. *I was almost out of smokes, and I needed a damn Pepsi. If I sold them for ten dollars, I would be happy.* So, when I arrived at Red Dot Pier, I was elated that there was a massive four in the morning crowd fishing some monsters out of the Gulf. I started to perform stand-up right away. The crowd was busting a gut. I started to bat my eyes at this older Mexican woman. I tried to talk to her, but she didn't "speaka no

English." So, I chatted with her daughter for a few minutes and showed her the shirts. The daughter clambered off some Spanish to her ma and the deal was done. She took the whole lot for twelve bucks. *I'm rich, bitch.*

So now I got what I needed, and it was time to end this fucking movie. I couldn't get the unreal images of my family in full makeup out of my head. The idea was so big, the makeup and the voice-changing system were so state of the art, I started to think there may be something wrong with me. For the first time, I started to consider that I may be going mad as everyone had been saying for the past six months. That is the worst feeling I have ever experienced.

As I walked, I played the tapes back in my head. I started to go over all the situations that led me to believe that this was a movie. For an hour or more, I thought of all the crazy coincidences, the people in my life, all the stand-up, and more. *Yep, it was a movie.* In the back of my head, I knew I had too much invested in this thing for it not to be. *I mean I had destroyed a two hundred and thirty-thousand-dollar home beyond repair. It had to be a movie...or I was fucked.*

I made it to the JFK Causeway. It's a massive four-lane bridge that connects Corpus Christi's mainland, to the prestigious North Padre Island. There was no path to walk over the bridge on foot. I was at a roadblock...no pun intended. So, I did what any good actor would do. I hid the buckets on the side of the freeway and stuck my thumb out. I was hitching. That was my only chance to get over the massive body of water that was between me and superstardom.

It only took ten minutes to acquire a ride. A big dude in a tank top and a caterpillar mustache picked me up. He was in a red Ford two-seater headed to the exact beach that I was going to. *A coincidence? I think not!* He told me he would take me out there. He was sporting a neon green B.U.M Equipment tank top. I hadn't seen one since 1992. He had on a pair of American flag shorts and tan leather boat shoes.

We didn't say much. I was so grateful to have a ride. This man was saving me ten miles of walking on my now disfigured feet. I am sure he could smell my rotting wounds from my sneakers. I know I could. We pulled onto the sand not long after. *This was it. I had made it to Kleberg County. Them/They could never have gotten a permit pulled in this county, and I hadn't told anyone about my plans to go to Kleberg.* The weeks leading up to this, I had started to think that somehow, they had the ability to read my thoughts. I was going mad, and on that day, I was starting to realize it. So, I was trying to keep my thoughts contained, but it was too hard.

I was victorious! I had made it out of town, all on my own, using the small number of resources I had. At this moment, I felt free. I started walking on the beach on a blistering hot Memorial Day.

The "stay-cationers" and tourists were leaving in droves. Thousands of tents and canopies were being deconstructed as my slow walk to paradise took place. *No one was looking at me; no actors approached. I was finally in the clear. Them/They were in the lurch. I had made it!*

An old fat man was packing up his things with a woman who couldn't have been more than twenty-five years old. As I walked by, the old man told his playmate "I thought they didn't let the homeless out here, honey," and they both started deviously laughing.

I looked around with my arms to the sky and replied in a roar "Ladies, this is why it's important to stay in school, that way you don't have to blow your grandpa!" People that were around all started laughing uncontrollably, as the beach was still packed.

A few feet later, I took my shoes off. My feet were unrecognizable. It was as if a team of doctors sawed off the extremities I once knew, and sewn on a pair of hobbit's feet, black and covered in slimy blood, the kind at the bottom of a chum bucket. I was whimpering in pain. I have been in major accidents, been beaten brutally. I have been stabbed with forks and knives. Nothing I can remember compared to the excruciating pain as from these wounds. The sores were different shades of purple, green, and dark browns. The gaping wounds and cuts leaked an iron film that smelled of rotten seabass. I could feel my heartbeat in my toes. This was grounds for amputation. I had basically put enough miles on those Adidas to walk to Pluto.

I stood up with a scream, beachgoers were horrified by the site of my tootsie toes. One lady looked away and cupped her mouth. I began to trek toward South Padre Island, routing my way there through the beach. I figured that I could set up a makeshift camp once I was in the middle of nowhere and wait for *The Movie* to send the rescue party containing the woman I was to marry.

As I walked, my heart dropped out of my dehydrated sphincter. I caught the eyes of a tall White male, no shirt or shoes. He was on one knee next to an ice-blue Yeti cooler. He stared like a cyborg. An evil and familiar look that had the signature feel of…*Them/They*. I was devastated. *Hollywood was here. If they hadn't pulled a permit, they had followed me for my own safety. Either way, they were not making their identity known. The Movie wasn't to end.* I wept as the grains of sand entered toxic holes in my feet. Walking barefoot with dead feet and toes was not the smartest idea.

The massive tires of the truck driven by the United

States Parks Police at the Padre Island National Seashore tore through the sand. They skidded to a stop next to me, as the inferno above scorched my Casper-white skin. Under my eyes the skin had started to blister, and puss streamed down like clear Elmer's glue. I had a third-degree sunburn on every exposed part of my body. Thank God for my "do-rag" fashion sense that was protecting my head.

"Sir, we need you to take a seat next to the truck please."

Two very tall National Park Officers stood over me. They were wearing huge aviator Ray-Bans with pressed uniforms and jailer boots. The boots brought on an onset of PTSD instantaneously. The sight of law enforcement of any kind made me want to fly, with every fiber of my being.

"Sir, we had reports of you being aggressive with a man and woman just down on the beach."

That fucking old man. He couldn't take what he had been dishing out. He had to be an actor too! His BMW wasn't nice enough to score a young chick like that.

The officers stood me up on my demolished stilts. I winced in agony as they hoisted me into the back seat of the white pickup truck. The air conditioning felt foreign. The cold blast on my skin gave the flesh the consistency of overcooked bacon. Waves of pain hit me as I got comfortable in the strange temperature. The back door swung open. The officer gave me no option for what was to come next.

"We are taking you back to Corpus," the officers said with a vengeance.

I was devastated. "I can't go back there! I don't want to, just let me walk down the beach. I am not hurting anyone," I said.

"Look, kid, all that's out there is eighty miles of

wilderness. The coyotes will eat your carcass after you die of dehydration."

I had no choice in this matter. The truck barreled down dunes of May, whisking me away, back into the arms of *Them/They.*

#

They took me to the Bluff; an AR-15 was resting in a gun rack behind my skull. They dropped me off at the Flour Bluff grocery store. I nearly drowned in unromantic sorrow as the pickup left the scene. I hopped on a bus and tried to make my way to Oakbrook. I had my shoes off on the public transit, not the best idea. A Mexican couple began to fight with me over my mid-trip fashion decision. The tiny Asian bus driver looked in her mirror and began to spout at me in broken English, which was totally lost in translation.

A screaming match erupted between yours truly and almost every passenger on a very packed bus. The driver had turned around and sat at the store while she called CCPD. It seemed like I was making police contact every five minutes, at this point.

The police officer arrived. He was clearly ex-military. A big, burly, southern White boy type. Cornfed and not in a good mood. He jumped out of his cruiser and directed me off. Surprisingly, he didn't cuff me.

"Boy what are you doing," he asked.

I went into the whole song and dance. He couldn't take his eyes off my clubbed feet.

"Look, I need a ride home man, I can barely walk," I was pretty convincing, seeing as my feet looked like James Caan's in "Misery."

He was about to get off shift and head back to the Downtown station. He politely explained that CCPD wasn't a taxi service, as I fought the urge to throw a verbal haymaker. He took mercy on me and told me to wait in the back of the car as he smoothed things over with the tiny Asian bus driver.

"Ok, Bornagain, give me your address, I am taking you home." I don't think he wanted to do any paperwork.

We pulled up at Oakbrook. He sipped a coffee and laid into me about being a junkie. I guess it was obvious, huh? We parted ways with the promise that I wouldn't come out of the house. I had to tell a fib about how the house is under major renovation in order to justify the boards on the windows.

The power was out. I bantered over to put my feet in the filthy tub in Barry's bathroom. I got myself up to where I could swing my cramping calves over the side. My feet throbbed as if a '57 Ford dropped on them in a tire shop. I bent forward, anticipating the cold rush of cool, soothing water. I turned the spout left…nothing.

No power, no water, and no breeze in the house made Boston an angry boy. I had no dope and no smokes. I thought of slicing my wrists with a shard from the mirror, right there in the bathtub. The image of the reflective blade slicing into my artery was like a sleek suicidal dream. I could smell the iron rich blood draining the life from my blue eyes. I could see my spirit transcending up and out of my body, drifting to the location of my loved ones that had gone before me. *I want to die. Movie or no movie, I don't care.* I was all done living this way. I had the foot long and razor-sharp knife in my hand. I sat in the tub and laid my bare back upon broken glass, urine stains, and some mystery liquid that soaked my board shorts. The do-rag on my head stunk like musty death and depression.

I fell fast asleep before I could carve into my flesh, passing out from exhaustion and fear. I awoke the next morning at seven. Dope sickness had taken hold. My forehead swelled like a fresh-baked sourdough loaf, my pulse raced like Seabiscuit in the Preakness, my eyes were blurry and drained. I stood to my wounded feet, only to fall, lacerating the bottom of both palms on a broken mirror and beer bottle remnants.

I tried to walk to no avail. I made it to Barry's bed with the last energy in my soul. I wept most of that day and well into the sweltering night. A candle flickered as I laid on the mattress. A hole in the wall revealed the same face I had been seeing recently. It looked like a hockey mask, painted black, staring at me through the hole punched in the sheetrock. I couldn't move as the glowing eyes peered in, glaring from side to side. I was speechless. Thoughts of crawling into the bathroom to commit suicide were almost every few minutes.

I stayed off my legs all night. Over twenty-four hours of pure pain and misery. I defecated and urinated in my pants, all while I was awake. I laid in my filth like a feral hog in the Mississippi mud puddles. I got up and changed into some filthy duds, using a cum-stained t-shirt for a do-rag. I then threw on my sand-filled, disgusting Adidas, and headed for the door.

I stumbled all the way to Sherry's trap, where I knocked on the door to beg for some dope and water. Her elderly father answered the door.

"Hello, can I help you Boston?" he said in a sweet voice.

"Is Sherry home? I need to talk with her bad," I retorted.

"No, I am afraid she is out," he said.

That's all he needed to say. I lost control. I balled up my fists at this eighty-year-old elderly man. I started to scream, "I know you motherfuckers are all in on *The Movie*, old man. You tell them if they don't have some fucking dope for me when I get back, I am going to saw every one of their fucking heads off and shit down their necks!" I was murderous. In a homicidal rage. I felt myself slipping off the edge. This was different. I was like a cornered rat, ready to chew his own leg off to get out of a snare.

I stormed off the lawn as he slammed the door and latched it. I could barely breath as I headed to a grocery store on Weber Road. I needed something for my pain. I went into the store, looking like I had walked out of war-torn Somalia, bloody and high on khat. When I entered, I grabbed a plastic bag off one of the bagging stations at a closed register. I walked to the beer aisle and put five of the twenty-four-ounce cans of assorted malt liquors into the sack. And just like that, I walked out.

I made it to the side of the building and proceeded to chug the whole twenty-four ounce can in front of a car-full of kids and their parents. I left some of the swill in my mouth, so I could spit it all over the windshield as I walked by.

"Fuck you demons, staring at the homeless peasant," I growled.

They screamed. I must have looked like I had on a bad Halloween costume.

I walked around to the apartments behind the building. I knew some Black drug dealers that lived inside a mentally challenged woman's apartment. They had taken it over by force and were selling synthetic marijuana to low-grade clientele. She was a White woman in her fifties with a big afro of dirty, curly hair. She had makeup on her face that was fit for a clown, while wearing tight and inappropriate clothes. Today though, she was naked on the couch as I entered. Three men were having sex with her at one time as I sat looking on.

They let me smoke some legal in trade for one of my drinks. My eyes rolled; the poison was in full control. I went to the kitchen and pounded all four of my remaining cans in a matter of what seemed like minutes. I had to go. I was worth nothing to these people and the sight of them corroded any moral value left within my already decaying soul. I prayed to Jesus as I walked back to the store. A cold, brooding feeling came upon me as I linked up to the WIFI. I called my family for the first time in months. I needed help. This couldn't go on, not one more second.

"Boston, Dad's been dead for three weeks."

Something in their voice snapped me out from the spell of *The Movie*. I knew deep within my heart he was telling the raw truth as I hung up the call. I couldn't handle the terror that came over me. I headed back to smoke more with the demons I had just left. As I cut through to get to my hellish destination, Sherry and Randy appeared. Randy, a short little Mexican wannabe gangster, was wearing baggy jeans and a white wife-beater shirt. He had longish hair and a teenager mustache.

"Hey, motherfucker, you stay right here," he said as he ran to an upstairs apartment.

"Why the fuck are you threatening my dad, Boston," Sherry rattled in rage.

I just sat there, confused and dehydrated from the gallon of cheap alcohol I had ingested. I must have looked like death warmed over. I heard Sherry as she screamed in my face. I couldn't respond, it felt like I had separated from reality.

Randy returned with a Rambo-style serrated blade the size of Oklahoma in his right hand. "You motherfucker, Imma kill you for fuckin with my family."

Apparently, he was related. He put the blade to my throat; it was slicing its razor-sharp edge through my skin. I felt blood running down my chest.

"Do me a fuckin favor, you little cunt, do it" I spat.

This wasn't the fearlessness of being in a movie, where

nothing bad could occur. This was the pleading of a man who was begging to die in every way. I wanted him to spill my blood upon the lawn right there at the Watercrest Apartments. I wanted my soul to escape into the heavens above.

He pushed me to the ground and walked away in hateful bliss. *A pussy through and through, I knew he didn't have it in him. I wouldn't be that lucky.* I walked home in a numb, blood-soaked enigma. The sun was still pouring on my leaking skin. I walked into Oakbrook with plans to die and meant it.

I sat on the edge of my father's bed. I looked around and saw the ghosts from years ago. Him and I watching the Masters Tournament, drinking beers on New Year's, and watching the Patriots win a come-from-behind victory, with my only son there between us. Three generations of Bornagain love, celebrating with smiles as our team surprised the whole world. I wept uncontrollably.

I laid back on the bed, shirtless, and covered with coagulated blood. I thought I was about to die. I had never felt so weak in my entire life. I had been through a war; one that most people could never imagine. I was ready for Jesus to call me home, to be with my dad. My eyes closed like the doors of a school on its last day. And I was out.

#

My eyes peeled open as if super glued shut in the stinking summer heat. I sat up, like Linda Blair in "The Exorcist." I scanned the trash heap on the surface of Oakbrook's floors. Tragedy bestowed upon a dying man. The events of the last six months came pouring upon my mind like monsoon rains deep inside Indonesian jungles. The broken glass, piles of clothes and trash, hundreds of dirty syringe needles, blackened drug tinfoil, tampons, used condoms from strangers, and hundreds of empty beer cans. The feeling I had inside is indescribable. I was suddenly filled with the Holy Spirit, poured upon me, out of a golden chalice, bedazzled with rubies and emerald stones.

    I peered over to the cluttered nightstand. Within arms-reach was a sinister-looking knife, one that appeared to be of Arabian origin, the blade slanted upwards, and covered in rust. It was approximately one foot long. I reached for it like a drowning man for a life preserver. I grasped its weathered wooden handle and said, out loud, "This ends now."

    I had on a blue bathing suit, no shirt, and was covered in old blood. I had the despicable Adidas on my black, pulsating feet. I was engulfed in alcohol-laced sweat and unbrushed teeth. My hair was long for me. I looked homeless, broken, and possessed. I raged out of the front door, wielding the weapon.

    I stopped, grabbed a flat-screen TV that I had thrown through a closed window weeks before, and tossed it over the neighbor's fence, smashing it into the siding of their home. I walked as the "Terminator" would, two blocks, screaming and ranting at whizzing cars. I crossed the street on Senators Drive. A man in a pickup saw me shirtless and covered in blood. His big smile turned into a horrified glare as I balled my fist and made slashing movements in his direction. That's when I knew what had to be done.

    I stared down the burger joint the same way Tyson did McNeeley in the mid-Nineties. That's when I devised my plan. A final stand against *Them/They*. A farewell to my massive ice problem, the tortures of Oakbrook, and the inferno of hell that had become my life. Movie or no movie, this whole way of life was about to come to a freeze...no pun intended.

    I gripped the cold steel of the exterior door sometime after dinner. The blast of ice-cold air hit my battered flesh like a

Mack truck. The floor was brown tile with black grout. It was your run of the mill burger stand, nothing special. It had a kid play area separated by a glass wall, tables, a bathroom in the back. Another entrance sat directly across, to the north side of the building. I stood in the doorway of the south side of the entrance. There were three workers making food in the back, and at the counter was the rude, Middle Eastern looking girl who was the acting assistant manager. The same one who had called the cops on me a hundred times in the months leading up to this life-changing moment.

    I raised my hands over my sunburnt head, and at the top of my lungs, I shouted, "This is not a robbery, everybody get the fuck out of here." It was almost like they were waiting for me to come in, a pre-planned event, but there was no way they could have known. They leaped off hoofs like a mob of deer.

    I heard the back-door slam behind the four frightened employees. I knew if I caused a big enough disturbance, the cops would arrest me, and I could get clean in jail. My local rehab had turned me away twice in the month leading up to this event due to lack of bed space. I needed help, I knew it, and I had decided to take the system into my own hands. This is a serious social issue. For someone in the richest country on earth, a person who is begging for help, crying in the lobby of a rehab center, being turned away due to a lack of funding. The second trip I made to detox, I wept and begged them not to let me go back outside into the real world, my drug world. I told them, "I am not going to make it, something bad is going to happen." I was met with the famous "I am sorry sir, make an appointment and come back in two weeks". Once you leave, that needle goes back in your arm. You're spun onto Planet X, and months pass before you blink your tired eyes.

    I stood alone in the burger joint's lobby; the place was a

ghost town. There was a family that exited to the north as I held up the knife. A man, his wife, and a teen female around sixteen years of age. He had left a white envelope on the table. On it, in black magic marker, was written "Mr. Lopez." I strutted over to the table and picked up the package. I will never forget this for the rest of my life. I followed the family to their car. I shouted, "Mr. Lopez, here, I think you forgot this". He was in terrified shock. He extended a reluctant, trembling hand, visibly shaken by my actions and appearance.

He took the envelope, turned around, jumped in his vehicle where his family was waiting, and peeled out of the parking lot. I walked back into the establishment. This was all in full view of the security cameras. I decided to steal something so the charges would be serious enough to keep me for a month or two in jail. I needed a substantial time away from the streets.

I went behind the counter and poured a coke (again no Pepsi) and took a burger right off the line. The motherfucker didn't even have cheese on it. I had thrown the knife off to the side right after everyone had left, so it sat on the floor near the south entrance. I sat down and took one bite; through the glass on the north side, I saw the barrel of a 12-gauge shotgun come peaking around the corner.

I hit the deck. Something told me this wasn't going to be good. The stocky Mexican officer lunged inside like a viper striking.

"I will shoot you, motherfucker. Freeze, Freeze, Freeze!" at the top of his lungs. It was a strange experience, but I could feel this human being wanting to end my life. He wasn't just doing his job; it was much more than that.

He came over and put his knee in my back. The cuffs went on as I shouted, "I am not armed!" He lifted me up and took me out to his cruiser, throwing me in the back seat. The local news showed up right away. Two different stations, it seemed like a hundred people had gathered to gawk at me as I sat like a caged varmint. The parking lot crawled with investigative reporters, townspeople, and just about everyone I had terrorized in the neighborhood for the past six months leading up to this point.

I spat at the window, reminiscent of a young Tupac Shakur as he left court donning a Detroit Red Wings jersey and red bandanna to match. *I was making my last statement to the paid actors who took the money and made my life a living hell, the ones who sold me out to the Hollywood machine. A last "fuck you" as I shot my final scene on the set.*

The cruiser door swung open, "Bornagain, I almost shot you," the Mexican first responder said with a fearful look. He explained to me that he was at my neighbors, responding to an attempted break-in call. The TV that I threw over the fence had sounded like someone was trying to force entry into the home.

While on that call, the initial reports of an "active shooter" event came across the radio. So, when he came in hot like that, he thought I was inside smoking people with a pistol. He thought he was going in to save lives. That's the eerie feeling I got that he wanted to kill me. He would have been a hero, and maybe a part of him wanted to be.

"Hold tight, Bornagain. We are going to be taking off in a few minutes."

I saw the employees being interviewed by the cops; town folk giving statements to the media; the place was a full-fledged circus. I cried as I mentally said goodbye to Oakbrook, now unsure of the existence of *The Movie* or the whereabouts of my father. I was no longer sure of one thing in my life. I knew I had mentally snapped. I couldn't tell what fact was or what was fiction. I closed my eyes, listening to the hard-beating pounds of my broken heart, as the wheels pulled away from the curb. *One thing is for sure, I am in for one hell of a costume and scene change.*

Ok passengers, that was one hell of a ride, wasn't it? The meter is still running, the cab is gassed up, and we are about to put Oakbrook in the rearview. We must get some questions answered, don't we? Will we find out about *The Movie*? The identity of *Them/They*? What will happen to me in response to the burger joint heist?

Put on your seatbelts, brace yourself...next stop...Nueces County Jail.

Chapter 9
Orange is the New Whack

I was a high-profile case now. I had made the news in Corpus Christi, so this was going to be interesting. They led me up the ramp to the Central Booking area sometime before nine that night in the summer of 2018. The officers took me through to be frisked and do my fingerprints. The place was jam-packed on this hot summer evening. The heat of the night brings the worst out in people. Crime skyrockets: inmates come in droves.

On top of that, it was a Warrant Roundup Weekend, so the place was full to the brim with every type of low-life scumbag you can imagine. Remember the layout? The five holding tanks, the two suicide tanks, and a nurse's station? I was led up to the fingerprinting pad shortly after arrival. My thick white fingers blotted onto the ink, then rolled across a white card with my name and birthdate attached.

"Alright, Bornagain, follow me." The jailing staff knew who I was. They hated me from the jump, and that can be deadly.

I was put in Pod One this time around. They closed the heavy steel door behind me, as one of the worst periods of my life was to begin.

The holding cell's floor was a drab concrete grey. It had a stainless-steel bench attached to the wall that ran about two feet off the ground. The walls were cinder blocks and colored a dingy white. There were two toilets and a urinal. They had a beige paint job, with vulgarities, and police blasphemy carved in for all to read. The ceiling matched the cinder blocks, with a large grate that covered a ventilation shaft for the air conditioning system.

The temperature had to be in the low sixties. In jail, you wear what you came in wearing for at least three days before you go upstairs to the general population, and that's a minimum. I was covered in blood, with that stinking navy-blue bathing suit, no shoes, and the grossest, most wounded feet you had ever seen. I walked barefoot, pacing the cell's urine covered floor, exposing my cuts to the strange bodily fluids of criminals unknown.

I know that we will get this all sorted out soon. I won't be in here too long, maybe a couple of months for theft and disorderly conduct. Going to jail to get clean off the ice is an idea that looks great on paper. Once you get there, you start to realize that there had to be other ways. This revelation took place right as they were calling me out to make me aware of the formal charges being brought against me by The State of Texas.

"Mr. Bornagain, you are being charged with aggravated robbery, a first-degree felony, and three counts of aggravated assault with a deadly weapon, all second-degree felonies," the clerk said in a bored tone.

I was blown away. Those are just about as serious of charges as it gets. *This had to be The Movie. I only took a three-dollar burger and a Coke. I didn't ask for anything. I didn't come closer than thirty feet from anyone with that knife! Oh God, help me, please.* Part of me was sure the charges wouldn't stick. The other part was petrified.

Once back in the cell, I was surrounded by Mexican gang members. Profanities launched like NASA rockets, liars' tongues ruled by force, and desperation took hold like an Amazonian python strangling one of breath. I was the only "cracker in the box," the only faired-skinned male in the can of formally charged sardines. The jail was at over one hundred percent capacity, with over forty men packed into a grimy cell fit for half that number. The holding was hell on earth. Lights stay on twenty-four hours a day and seven days a week, the air is freezing, and the only thing on the menu is a Johnny sack. When the breakfast bell chimed on my first day, a brown bag was thrown on the floor at my feet by a trustee. A trustee is an inmate worker signed up to do chores, in turn getting time knocked off their sentence. A meal I would normally turn my nose up to, on this day was received like a ravenous dog. Besides the bite of the infamous burger, it had been now over one week's time since I had ingested anything other than malt liquor and speed.

My blood sugar was low, I was shaking, and the first signs of ice withdrawal were starting to make their way through the cracks of an already shattered exterior. I knew I had to survive. In Nueces County Jail, there is no room for weakness. The zoo is crawling with lions, circling, waiting to devour the sick gazelle that lags the pack. You had to be on point in every way. Not only ready for a physical confrontation, but mentally alert, watching every word, being strategic in speech, and never shedding tears.

The other inmates start to size you up right away, questions thrown about crimes and affiliations, who you roll with, and what your drug of choice is. They are looking for chinks in the armor, ways to prey on unsuspecting crash dummies, and means to steal food. Right away, you know where you are, you discover who you are, and you see who you're up against.

Opening the Johnny sack, I stuck my hand in as a starving man. I extracted a plastic-wrapped stack of bologna and cheese, a tangerine, and some mysteriously soggy dollar store cookies. Your only choice of beverage was water from the drinking spouts on the back of the toilet/sink combo. Not an especially comfortable situation to be coming off a seven hundred and fifty-day straight run on one of the most lethal drugs known to mankind.

I was trance-like. The sandwiches disappeared like a coin within the hands of a seasoned magician on Fremont Street in Las Vegas. Next, the baby orange, and finally, the wet cookies. In a matter of moments, all that was left was the two mustard packets they threw in for a garnish. The only reason those were not devoured was that I didn't have the energy to tear them open.

I had never been so tired in my entire life. I felt as if I had been in the deep jungles of Hanoi, shot and left for dead, bleeding and calling out for my mother. My mind was not present, I was weak in every way, and scared of my fate with the law and the buzzards that circled above me as I respired. I started to sweat out the chemicals from years of using. You could literally smell the camping fluid and lithium leaking from constricted pours.

I crawled onto the floor and hid under the bench. The stench of bare feet and corn chips invaded my senses. I stared at endless bare and infected toes as I began to detox. I crawled over to the stainless steel toilet and projectile vomited the only food I'd had in a week into the shit-caked bowl. The sight of the human fecal matter of strange addicts made me throw up the only bile I had left. This was day one…and death was looming.

I retreated to the cavern, under the cold steel of the bench. I sought shelter from the blinding neon above. My eyes pressurized; my forehead swelled like a watermelon in the sun. I stunk of body odor and loathing.

The bullshit stories, the gloating of crimes past, and the tales of sexual degradation swirled like a commode as I wanted to die. I wanted to murder every scumbag in the joint this day. Being outnumbered, I was basically useless in an altercation, so I decided to clam-up and try to get some rest.

I woke up a day later; I had urinated in my bathing suit. The fibers stuck to the concrete, like egg yolks that were shattered on the ground a day after Hallows' Eve. I was so dehydrated, it felt like I was pissing a yellow, glue-like substance from a narrow urethra. Medically speaking, I was close to death. The smells within the packed cube were something of slaughterhouse dreams.

I drifted in and out of consciousness, bands of sanity came in waves. Terror and filth consumed broken thoughts and visions. They say ice detox is all in your head. I can tell you, psychosomatic or not, the shit is as real as the guy who was sitting on the toilet in front of me. I can't describe this discomfort in the spoken word or written language. The flashes of hot and cold, the sour stomach, the dizziness of sight.

Inmates came and went. You had everyone from murderers down to drunk drivers all lumped into one stale pile. Now three of us Whites huddled into one corner, like rats in the sights of Mexican exterminators. There is not much violence in the holding pattern; it's upstairs where the politicking begins. This was a low-rent detox center for the city's most sad cases. The lawyer is for the middle-class and up, so there was no bail in sight for most of us.

Misery floated in the air with a frightening thickness. You were breathing hopelessness and fear. Surrounded by men, some facing formidably serious crimes, never to return home. The screams of the tormented filled the noise barrier.

Time had no place in the Central Booking area. You could ask the guards, but what the fuck does it matter what time of day it was? The lights remained on, and the steady stream of crooks remained endless, no matter the section of the day.

Windowless and secluded from the eyes of earth, we waited to be judged, all hope in the hands of an educated socialite in a black robe. A human being that has the power in one hand to set you free, and the other…to make sure you never see your children through anything but bulletproof glass for as long as you live.

Days went by, the next nastier than the last. No mat to sleep on, my bones felt as if I had been beaten with a barrage of aluminum baseball bats. I would fight to stand on those feet of mine. I would fall as the inmates laughed. I needed a wheelchair, only to be left unnoticed and forgotten.

A homeless man who had experience with the freezing air dilemma took the toilet paper and wetted a whole roll in the sink. He tore off chunks and threw them up at the vent, which was pouring freezing cold oxygen into the pod. He blocked the airflow. In a matter of hours, the soggy material would harden like a criminal paper-mache.

The cell immediately warmed up. All the inmates' moods changed, docile and sleepy. There was a glimmer of comfort as the massive guard came in to shake us down.

"You piece of shit, ok, now I am taking all the toilet paper. You wanna fuck around, we will fuck around!"

That's how they speak to you. They treat you in ways

that are subhuman. He left us with nothing to wipe ourselves with as a punishment for trying to survive. The cold in there is bone-chilling. It makes you feel like a piece of meat hanging on a butcher hook just before you are to be cooked and consumed.

Ice detox isn't a short one. It lasts for as long as two weeks, depending on the user's appetite. I was in for the full buffet of pain. Day five in the bottomless pit. I wasn't getting any better, in fact I was worse. My toes were infected. I sat Indian style looking at the quarter size puss bubbles and lacerations on purple and green skin. I should have gone to the hospital. They don't care in Nueces County Jail. People die there all the time, only to become a statistic of a "naturally caused death." The nurse was less than interested. My TB test came back negative, my blood pressure elevated, and she was ready to give me a clean bill of health.

"Bornagain, let's go, you're headed to 4R," the guard chimed.

It was an angelic voice this time. I knew upstairs, a shower awaited, along with hot food and a cot with a blanket. I hobbled out like an amputee. The guard helped me with a disparaged look of hate in his eyes.

I was marched down the hall through the booking area. I was led down a manila-painted walk to a set of stainless-steel elevator doors. We went to the basement where I was to be "dressed out." They handed me a pair of extra-large "oranges," which are what we called the matching orange top and bottoms. You know? The ugly jumpsuit uniform you see in the movies. We went back to booking, and I was to wait there to be called. Only a few more hours and I would be dropped deep into general population. I was to be injected into the incarcerated criminal element of Corpus Christi, Texas.

#

First, I was called into a tiny office in the manila hallway. I was to see the sergeant. I was questioned about my HIV status, gang affiliation, and my sexual preference. There are certain areas they put you if you are gay. I almost told them I was so I would have a fighting chance at survival. I opted out. Moments later, I was on my way to 4R. A locked-down transfer unit, one for confirmed gang members and transfers on their way to other pods. We walked in the pod God knows when. It was the first time I had seen daylight in five days. The pod had two sets of barred gates for security. You had to be buzzed in. The gates opened one at a time and the guard led me through. I had been given a bedroll along the way. It consisted of two plain white sheets, a pillow, and an unbelievably cheap wool fire blanket. It was so bad that it had tin strips in it, the kind you would find on a Christmas tree. Made in Bangladesh. Abrasive enough to scratch your flesh right off the bone.

The ceiling looked mile high, two tiers of cells, one top, one bottom. Forty-eight cells in all, two-man houses on the bottom floor, single cells on the top floor that were reserved for problem inmates that can't be housed in pairs. All the large areas of the jail were set up this same way. The difference was that 4R had no dayroom. It was a twenty-three-hour a day lockdown situation. You were to be let out once every twenty-three-hours with one hour to shower, use the phone, and exercise.

When I took my first steps into the pod, I was alone in the massive room surrounded by cells. Inmates were acting as primates. They sounded like monkeys, screaming and shouting threats and profanities at each other. Some of the worst inmates at the jail were here. This was the terror dome. There was non-stop screaming from cell to cell. Code words and primitive calls were used to communicate.

After a few hours of landing there, I started to see how it all worked. A person's name and then "lookout" was shouted to get that person's attention. For example, if I had a friend in Cell 48 way up top in the corner. He would scream "Bornagain, Lookout", and I would respond, and a conversation would take place.

I watched as the inmates "kited" items, such as letters and Coffee, folded up in a paper. They took a paperclip on a long string they had stolen or made from strips of trash bags. They would attach said item and toss it under the door jamb of a neighboring cell. Items could be passed down cell to cell until it reached its intended party. Not allowed for sure, but what is allowed in this shit hole?

See, food is currency during incarceration. I learned this on my first day at 4R. The king daddy of all the tradable items...coffee. Besides having a drug connection inside to real products, coffee was as close to drugs as you were going to get. Guys were making ultra-strong cups. Keefe was the brand. That yellow bag! It was a luxury to have the instant concoction.

A few days go by and...enter Wheezy! Remember my tattooed, pimp buddy from North Beach? Well, he was brought in on the exact charge that I was there on. Aggravated armed robbery. He pulled a funny stunt on a dude while he was shitfaced. Wheezy loved drinking Four Loko and smoking crack. He loved laughing and pimping hos. Addicted to the game, in love with the life, he was an iced-out superstar. I always had a blast with The Wheez. *The Movie is for sure in full effect now. I mean, what are the odds that Wheezy would be in the same pod with the same serious charges as me? Looks like the producers thought I needed a buddy, to guide me through my first major trip to the pokey.*

They put Wheezy almost directly above me, in a single-man cell. I think he told them something so he wouldn't have to have a cellmate. Wheezy is street smart. He had been down to prison twice before. He knew the system, the dos and don'ts, the ins and outs. He was one hell of a motherfucker to have on your team on the inside.

Wheezy and I conversed far into most nights that first week. I found myself barely able to stand, shouting through the crack in the sliding, steel, blue door that separated me from freedom. Every cell has a small rectangular window so that guards can do bed checks once an hour after lights out. Boy, did we laugh! We talked about *The Movie*, old times, and future dreams after the money came in.

As days ticked by, it was obvious *The Movie* had infiltrated the jail. *They have the camera system hacked. The whole jail is now an elaborate set. Where is my dad? Where is his Benz? Who is behind this production? It is brilliant. They must have paid the jail off to participate in the film.*

Occasionally, they let all the inmates out at the same time for recreation in 4R. We spilled upon the pod floor like Canadian geese at the lake. Human contact was rare, so everyone was politicking, laughing, and just shooting the general shit. I decided to take a shower. My first public shower of all time. Normally I would be mortified, ashamed, and probably even sad. But I had spent so much time on "camera," naked and having sex, that I had no shame to feel. I was used to being a porn star; a little rinse in the rain box wasn't a thing.

I stripped my orange attire off onto the concrete below. A room full of Mexicans stood staring at the huge Irish themed tattoos on my calf muscles. That could be a surefire invite for a beef. *I don't give a fuck though; I am a star. Untouchable Boston is in the building.* I wasn't sure who was an actor or not, so I treated every situation as an on-screen opportunity for greatness.

I started singing in the shower, in county jail, without a care in the world. They were for sure R. Kelly fans, as they applauded my rendition of "Bump and Grind" that I belted out at the top of my lungs. They forgot to give me a towel in my bedroll packet, so I used a wad of brown paper towels. Jail is one place that will teach you the things we think we need in everyday life are unnecessary products, sold to us by The Machine. You learn to live basic and invent out of necessity.

When I returned to my cell, I was called up by the brass. "Bornagain, pack your shit, you're going to the D unit."

I was to be moved to a whole new situation. I yelled up to Wheezy as I followed the guard out of the double gates. Well, I was off to D unit apparently, a tiny pod the size of a living room, with three bunk rooms and a TV dining area. I'd say about two hundred square feet of hell. When I arrived, I met the actors for this next short and scary scene.

Tug was a White dude who was short, stalky, and around twenty-four years old. He had been involved in a gangland shooting where everyone shot their guns and Tug was the lucky winner. The bullet he fired hit an innocent bystander, she died at the hospital. I later found out that he got life in prison. Tug was a character. He had a crew cut like me. He was clean-cut and gangster to the core.

"Hey, come here, lemme lace you up," Tug said.

He showed me to my bunk and began to school me to the common rules and regulations that these fellows lived by in such a small space.

"This toilet is to piss, last two are to shit. Don't fuck up when it comes to that, you will get smashed," Tug meant business.

There was an older cat who I didn't like him from the

jump. He was an older guy who I was convinced was a producer on *The Movie*. He started off telling me he was from...you got it, California. See what I am talking about?

There were a bunch of local Mexican gangsters. Cap was in on a serious enhanced charge. He was the leader, a higher-ranking member, who the rest followed as if he was king. He was only twenty-six, running shit in the small, high-tension pod. He had about five homeboys under him. Animal was a tall Black kid, looked like the rapper Waka Flocka Flame. He had a big forearm tattoo. *It must be as fake as his name. An actor, one hundred percent. He must be six foot three inches tall and is pure muscle. Good job by the casting department.*

Two more Black inmates rounded out the crew besides Animal. Both on murder cases and facing life. These dudes were no joke, well at least that's what it appeared. The thing about *The Movie* was, you just never know who's who. I treated it like a shoot. I sat at the stainless-steel dining table, peering up at the cameras. Perfect line of sight shots, easily hidden microphones, this set was perfect. A big flat screen TV sat on the wall; Cap decided what the crew was watching.

I watched as Cap made colorful necklaces. It's common in jail within the Mexican culture to wear Rosaries. Cap took an all-white, run-of-the-mill Rosary and melted crayons and inks into pools on a piece of cardboard. He colored each bead either green or purple. He made another one, red and white. He had all the colors of the rainbow. He was selling them for coffee, soup, and pastry. That's how you make a living, that's how you eat well on the inside when you have no one cutting for you on the outside. You hustle.

Everything was fine. The TV was showing "Whose Line Is It Anyway?" an improv comedy show, hosted by Drew Carey. I watched, as obviously the sketches were all directed towards me. A female guest star looked just like Heidi. I felt the sketches poking fun at me, trying to get me to explode. I knew they were zooming in on my face to get reactionary shots. *Hollywood is going as far as paying big-name actors to do scenes in this film? What is the budget on this thing?*

It reminded me of the porn I had been watching. *They were clearly filming scenes for Brazzers, a pornographic film company and using it to make fun of me by broadcasting the videos directly into my phone so I would see them when I got out. This was really funny.* I told Cap the story. I explained that when this was all said and done, I would be able to pull some strings to get him into a scene with Mia Khalifa, at the time, the biggest porn star on earth. Everyone huddled around the table as I informed them about the hidden camera and *The Movie* I was staring in.

I said, "Look, I know it sounds crazy, but trust me, when you see me on TV six months from now, you will say, 'I was locked up with that guy.'"

They were acting amazed. But I knew full well they are all part of the Screen Actors Guild of America.

#

Tensions started getting high between me and the guys. All of them. I was acting manic. I was still sick, and the laughter I was getting from my jokes was all that made me feel better. So, I was on, in a magnified version of myself. Animal especially hated me. This was when it became clear who the real hired protagonist was to be in this section of the script.

I started mouthing off to Animal, knowing there was nothing he could do. *He is an actor, I am an actor, what's the worst that could happen...right?*

"You better shut your fucking mouth, Boston," Animal sang.

"You know what, Animal? You ain't the boss of me," I retorted.

Some of the other guys held him back. His fury was a class act, performance of perfection. *This guy is good. A top-notch, unknown, found on some casting call in the San Fernando Valley.*

I started to get under everyone's skin. I was doing stand-up, acting out, making jokes about almost every one of them. The old man said, "You could get kited out of here." This is a process where the inmates as a group, with one hundred percent participation petition, could have you moved to another pod.

So, I went to Cap, "Hey man, that old man is a snitch."

I tried to use the street code to my advantage. There was a mini town hall meeting conducted and Old School, or School as they called him for short, came out on top. I was told to go back to my bunk to lay down for the night. Like a little kid in trouble, I was sent to my room for a time-out.

Later that night, I was trying to sleep. I was bunking with two murderers. It was set up for a three- or four-man tank, with two bunks on each wall. School and the two murderers were having a conversation as I tried to sleep. They just wouldn't shut up; I also felt the conversation was poking fun at yours truly. *I need to sleep. I must shoot all day tomorrow.*

"Can you guys shut the fuck up, I gotta work tomorrow," I said. The room erupted in yelling. The rest of the guys came to break up the obviously scripted moment. And as always, right on time, I was rescued by the cast. *Good job, boys.*

Everything had calmed down for about thirty minutes. Everyone was in their bunks. The tiny pod was now so silent that you could hear a pin drop.

"Goodnight, crazy," Anime said in a Walton's' style

goodnight John Boy.

"Goodnight, Wakka Flakka" I responded in the same tone.

Animal went insane. He threatened to kill me all the way from the last bunk room. I heard the pod rise out of slumber; the whole place ascended upon my bunk. There was screaming and yelling, Animal was trying to attack; it was a horror show of classic proportions. I wasn't worried. I just sat up in my bunk and laughed and shot some preverbal slugs at old Animal...*if that is his real name.*

A female guard came storming around the corner. I couldn't believe my eyes. She was a girl that had been at my house for a BBQ one time! *Typical Them/They casting. Always people from the past, you know how they do.*

"What the fuck is going on in here? Everyone back to their beds," she exclaimed!

The whole pod unanimously kited me out, and just like that, not twelve hours after arrival, I was back in 4R.

#

I hung with my new cellmate, Creeper. I was getting very frustrated. I was performing and acting to the best of my ability. They just wouldn't throw me a bone. I got it in my head that *Them/They* were putting me through a testing period. Having me "in chains" as Paul was in the bible would add a great God twist to the script, after all. I thought they were trying to use my love for Jesus to profit. It made me insanely angry.

As days ticked by, stuck in a two-man cell with Creeper, I began to get angrier accompanied with an overwhelming feeling of desperation. I was starving on the tiny rations handed out by the jail. I was telling Creeper, *Them/They needs to come off the cheap version of the script and come off the muscle with some commissary.* Creeper could never get any sleep, as I would do stand-up, social commentary, and sing Nineties songs into the wee hours of the night. For someone who lived the vampire life for two years, it was going to be tough to get me off the Team No Sleep schedule.

I was dead sick of the daily letdowns. I was waiting for them to come to my cell and reveal that I had passed the test and that *The Movie* was in fact in the can and finished for good. This was starting to feel just like the endless buildups to the wedding scene and all the daily missions that made it seem as if *The Movie* was going to end, but then it never did. It felt like the rain was pouring on my weary head with no end in sight. I couldn't take it any longer, so I came up with a master plan in case I was released. This was the birth of Plan Z.

Plan Z was my way of forcing *The Movie* into the light. I had always said, out in public and crying to the masses, "I'll go all the way up to and not limited to death to beat *Them/They*!" And I meant every word. *If these bastards wouldn't pay me what they owed me, I was going to make sure the torture stopped. I would make sure the people behind The Movie, the financers, and the unstoppable force that was Them/They, would do the rest of their lives in prison.*

I hatched the plan in the dead of night, scheming like a bank robber. So, I came up with a situational solution. I knew enough about conspiracy theories to understand how to bring the full-bore of the Federal Bureau of Investigations down on someone.

Here is how I was to bury *Them/They*:

When I was to get out of this hell hole, I would write 10 letters. All the exact same content, bone-chilling and fierce. I was to write about terrorism, that I was a homegrown terrorist convert to Islam and I hated the US Government. I was to pen a manifesto with an evil plan, describing a wave of attacks that I was to carry out with a group of other faceless boogeymen. I was to claim that I was working with a large cell in Texas. I was to tell of a series of future attacks at schools and nursing homes with plastic explosives.

I planned to take a two-gallon gas can to the La Palmera Mall in Corpus Christi, walk in without saying a word, and light myself on fire at the wishing well during lunchtime on a Saturday. Before torching myself to a charred black corpse in front of a thousand onlookers, I was to address the letters to major news publications. The Boston Globe, The New York Times, The L.A Times, The Boston Herald. I was to also send two letters to the FBI headquarters to separate agents. The letters were a warning that more attacks were truly imminent.

This series of events, matched with the deliveries of the letters, was a shoo-in to spark a major FBI investigation into my life. Upon investigation, the FBI should find proof of a major motion picture being filmed around my life. *The Movie* would be blamed for tormenting me to my death. *I was hoping that the producers, and all involved, including the major players on screen, would do prison time.*

My mind was buzzing with dangerous and suicidal thoughts.

I even felt that if my dad didn't love me enough to tell me, if the money was more important to him than honesty, then he deserved to go too. I was angry and hurt beyond repair. With the plan hatched, I had to run it by someone with a *Them/They* connection. This was in hopes that this actor would inform *Them/They* of my suicide plot, scaring the daylights out of them and forcing them to wrap *The Movie*.

It just seemed like it would never end.

#

I was staring at Creeper as he slept. When he opened

his eyes, he saw me standing there like a serial killer.

"Boston, wow bro, what are you doing," he said with surprise.

"Well Creep, my man, we gotta have a little chat this morning. I got the answer to all my problems, and you are going to listen, and listen well."

Creeper looked at me in horror as I laid it all out, in the voice of the maniacal character, Daryl, that I knew and loved.

"Would they really allow my children to see their father covered in napalm than end this thing," I said dramatically, knowing he was the right actor to get the message to *Them/They*.

I sat on the bottom bunk and started to sob. I cried "Why do *they* want to do this to me? I am a good person, I love my dad, I love my mom, I love my kids!"

As the tears streamed down my face, as my heart broke into a million pieces, Creeper came down off the top bunk and sat beside me. Here is this hardened ex-Mexican gang member, putting his hand on the shoulder of a crying White man, a stranger.

He told me "Boston, everything is going to be ok."

Creeper had been playing along with *The Movie* thing all week long. As I was crying, I had racing thoughts. *I fear you don't want to shatter my reality, and part of you is scared that I am a lunatic. I mean, who wouldn't, the story is very farfetched. That's how Them/They designed it to be. Who could blame this thirty-year-old guy for not believing that there is a hidden camera movie being filmed about his new cellmate? He thinks I am insane and doesn't want to hurt my already fragile mind. Thank God I knew the truth.*

See, Plan Z was the last resort, hence it's reference to the last letter of the alphabet. It was a surefire bet to get the FBI to investigate my life and expose *The Movie*. The perfect plan, where a tortured man in America uses the name of Allah to spark a major investigation. I was desperate at this point. I had one more tactic I was to try out while I let *Them/They* mull over the whole Plan Z ordeal.

I would become "Boston Bornagain from Corpus Christi." I would abandon the whole "Daryl" persona. I would deconstruct my own personality and become the most boring character of all time. A reverse of "Daryl," if you will. I started to work this character out, live, with Creeper as my only audience. *Well, him and the hidden cameras that were in the vents.*

I said "Creeper, I think I am going to be Boston from Corpus from now on. It will be like watching paint dry, Creep."

He looked puzzled. After about four hours of the drabbest and horribly bland conversation, Creeper snapped. He had so much fun with Daryl, he decided to tell me *The Movie* was real and reveal his part in the whole fiasco. He was cool like a cucumber when he pointed across to the new lawyer's office across the street. It looked as if there were flashlights moving in the pitch blackness of the room.

"Boston, it looks like we got company", he said with a smile.

I looked below and into the parking lot. I saw a car there with its headlights on, then off, then on. Someone was flashing their headlights for a loved one behind bars. *I figure it was Bella letting me know she was there and that everything was going to be ok.*

#

Fourth of July fireworks were popping over The Harbor Bridge. Electric skies opened, spiders of white, red and green blew up in the heavens above. I wondered where my kids were. *I know The Movie is making sure they are ok. They must have* them comfortable, safe, and with the information that Daddy was going to be the biggest star in the world...once The Movie was over.

I was moved to 4P.

4P was the real-deal Holyfield. I walked in midday with my bedroll. I was to be moved to Cell 21. The far back corner of the pod that was set up just like 4R. Forty-eight cells, upstairs there were one-man cells, downstairs there were the two-man cells. It was chow time, and I was about to get my first real lesson on what jail was really like.

This was a General Population unit. All the men could chill in the dayroom with the TV. There was a big empty concrete room for exercise. At the top of the room, facing the City Hall, there was a large window that was covered by a steel grate, open to air. For the first time in a month, I would be able to feel rays of the sun, smell the rain, and listen to the roaring thunder of the Lord in all its glory.

In the center of the pod, surrounded by cells, was a massive open area. White plastic folding tables were set up at mealtimes in the center. The place was bustling. There were all kinds of inmates. For the first time, I was to see whatever role that race played for me in incarceration. Every group had its own table. First the Mexicans. They ran shit. They outnumbered any other race in Nueces County three to one. All different gangs, all getting along for the most part, in the name of racial unity. They all broke bread together; rules ran by respect and valor. You had to be a gentleman in jail.

They wore rosaries and oversized uniforms, ordered once a week when it was time to change out into clean clothes. Yes, we only changed once a week. They were covered in tattoos, distinctive and dark. Prison-style black and white ink including 361 (Corpus Christi's area code), the Corpus Christi

Hooks' emblem (our national baseball team), huge great-white sharks, hammerheads, and more. They all had different meanings and ranks. Some wore a CHANEL tattoo, which is an interlocked CC, the logo for Coco CHANEL's company. The Mexican group of prisoners adopted it and made it a symbol of their people and love for their city.

They were especially respectful and clean people. They were cool with the Whites. You had to know what the social moray system was and who you could "fuck with." That's a term for deal with or do business with. The Mexicans were funny, cool peeps that loved dominos and spades, which are common jailhouse games to pass the countless hours inside.

The Mexicans stayed in their lane; they were massive but kept the lowest profile possible. However, they were the most hardcore when it came to politicking, which refers to the jail system and speech, how to solve problems, ranks pulled, or negotiating beefs between members. Shit, the outside, a lot of times, ran from inside, meaning the gang members in jail ran the deals on the streets. But you must understand, most of these gangs were established while in the Texas Department of Corrections. Nueces County Jail was just a midpoint between the streets and the big house, many inmates become gang members due to serving jail time. Upon release, they would then carry on this lifestyle on the outside. I got nothing but love for the Mexicans and their culture. I worked for many during my time as a cabbie; they were always cool, on point, and sane. Far as gang members are concerned, I think they are the coolest to deal with. Don't get it twisted, you fuck up with those guys, it's curtains. They will smoke your ass like a three-alarm fire.

Up next are the Blacks, who are the smallest by numbers in most any South Texas jail. Afros, dark tattoos, and huge muscles were the uniform. Not all had Afros, but I am sure the possibilities were endless. A short guy with big designer glasses ran shit over there at that table. Rumor has it, before he came to jail, this cat and his buddies were all smoking ice one night while they gangbanged a tranny. If you are straight, this is a no-no in the gang world. I don't know what gang he represented. Even if I did, I would never tell you, passengers...

The story goes that the tranny wanted more drugs than she already had, who the fuck knows though. Again, this is a rumor. She supposedly threatened to run and tell the whole neighborhood about the romp those guys did on her. This little guy went out to his Lincoln, got an AR-15, and then smoked the bitch. Shit like this happens every day in the ice game in Crook City.

The Blacks clowned a lot, made jokes, played a lot of cards with the Mexicans; they were just a laid back, cool bunch. A lot of seriously talented, unsigned rappers. I would listen to them spitting from their cells. Really good shit. Again, just like the Mexicans, they would whoop your ass if you got out of line. Coke is king in the Black community, so there were a lot of crack dealers and armed robbers in that sect. However, ice knows no bounds. It doesn't care what color you are; the White-trash Drug of the Ages has now spilled into the Black hood.

One thing that always puzzled me was one guy that rolled with them, a skinny White boy, big thick-rimmed glasses, and short hair. He had a black cross tattooed in the middle of his forehead. He sat with them as a full member of a reputed Black gang. He must have lived in a Black neighborhood his whole life. Grew up with those guys. To be a White guy in an all-Black gang was rare. He looked exactly like the kid from "There Will Be Blood" with Daniel Day-Lewis. I, from day one, referred to him as "There Will Be Blood," and he hated it. I would riotously laugh as he got insanely furious.

Then you had the Whites. Made up of about three different affiliations, it looked like a keg party at a trailer park. You saw swastikas and iron crosses, and you saw skulls and menacing words, all inked on the arms of some of the city's craziest gang members. Meth was the drug of choice of these master cooks, check cashers, and identity thieves. The gambit, the whole array of the criminal spectrum, sat with them.

I am White and I won't speculate anymore on these cats. I never worked for my own people. I had a rule not to. They were by far the highest, most paranoid, and ruthless that The Sparkling City by the Sea had to offer.

Now there was also a table for Solitos, a ragtag group of outcasts. These were the misfit toys of the North Pole that all hung together as one. Power in numbers, you know how the shit goes. It was mostly the gays that made it to Gen Pop, child molesters, plus the stragglers that no one else wanted to eat with.

You can still sit with your racial group if you're not a member of their gang. You must be legit, straight, and respectful. So, on my first day at 4P, that's what I did. You are to sit with the Solitos until you are called. Luckily for me, 4P was a movie scripted, iced-out all-star game. The Who's Who of the meth world was housed in this unit. I saw a bunch of familiar faces and was given the nod to come to sit down right away. Even though I never worked for the Whites, I partied with everyone.

My first evening on this pod was scary. This was the first time I had been exposed to a long term, Gen Pop situation in my life. My cellmate was a cool Black dude. We never really spoke much, which told me that he was not involved with *The Movie*. Singing voices floated and bounced off concrete walls. Street poets, serenading their own hearts, trying to find comfort in anything they could grab onto. By the time lights-out was announced after lockdown began, my nerves had calmed a bit. I am sure the singing helped. I got the first good night sleep that I'd had in years.

I woke up ready to perform. I started walking around the pod after the lockdown was over. I wanted to see what *Them/They* had for me. But I lost count how many times I was accused of being crazy. So, I went back to my cell to write a letter to Sherry; the mail was our only cheap way to communicate.

#

The day after I got to Central Booking, on my second day in the County Jail, the brass came to see me as I rotted under the bench.

"Bornagain, we gotta talk to you," the Sergeant said.

He informed me that Sherry and her pal, who threatened to slash my throat, were at Oakbrook, taking miscellaneous items out of the house. There wasn't much of value left in there after I'd had the nighttime Estate Sale, where I had put up the Halloween and Christmas lights to sell all my grandparents' antique furniture, thinking that *The Movie* was really buying it all. Sherry, one of my closest and dearest friends in the game, saw me on TV, went to my dad's house, and robbed me.

"They are not supposed to be there," I explained.

Movie or not, those motherfuckers had no business at my crib. That's lower than low. That was Barry's house. He was a citizen, and I had no way to handle it on my own. I was trapped, helpless, and completely powerless.

I wrote to her, forgiving her. I told her about the power of Jesus, how He could do anything, and that I loved her no matter what. I also told her to tell Foxy Lady "hi" for me. I needed the Lord in order to deal with the pressure of this whole situation. *The Movie*, the new environment, and all it came with. I had nothing. No money on my books, no way to make phone calls, I didn't even have a book to read.

#

My next-door cell neighbor was a guy they called King. A Black crackhead from Leopard Street. He was alright, a little mouthy, but hey, who isn't from time to time. King loved Jesus and gave me a ratty extra NIV bible he had in his cell.

"This will get you through the hard times. All the answers are in there, homeboy," he explained.

Wow, what a message! I then figured out that *Them/They* wanted me to read the Word. I had a revelation…no pun intended…that if I read the parts they wanted, this would all come to an end. I was to find a cryptic message of some sort. This was also around the time I figured out they had some sort of technology that could see what my eyes saw!

I went back to my cell and started in the Book of Matthew, the first book in the New Testament. Jesus was the theme of the script. *I may as well start off where He enters the story, right?* I read feverishly over the next few days. I never left my cell. I dug in that book like an Alabama tick thinking I would get to the point they wanted, and out would come the wedding party I dreamed of.

Nothing. But I started to get a triumphant peace and comfort in reading the Bible. I was a Catholic my whole life, and I can't ever remember cracking it open. As days melted, I began to have major revelations and insight while reading. I was growing to know the Father in new and huge ways like never before.

I was talking to the other inmates about God, and inside it is well received. They still looked at me like I was crazy, but when I talked about God, well, I was spot on. I felt almost human again. While discussing this one topic, people respected what I said. They listened and nodded their heads. It made me feel normal for the first time in a long time. I took my studies very seriously, totally separate from anything movie related. God was a real, personal, and a tangible source of love in my life. I would not let anyone pollute that for anything. I meant the God Squad stuff. I meant, "Let the light of the Lord be with you all day…erry day!"

#

I was starting to get flustered. I saw a new man on the pod. It was Buddy, my childhood friend, in full makeup. He was parading around as a Mexican. He was rubbing elbows with the shot callers in that crew. I approached him a total of three times. He acted like he didn't know me the first two times, then the third time, he gave me a wink. *It is my best friend, giving me a sign that it is, in fact, him.* I couldn't believe my eyes. As happy as I was to see him, I was furious that *they* would go that far. I was devastated that *they* didn't take Plan Z seriously. I stewed on this development for a few days.

Enter Wheezy, again. He came up to me and gave me daps and a big bear hug.

"Boston, I skipped bail on the robbery. I was Top Ten Most Wanted; did you see me on the news?"

Wheezy was happy to see me. In the back of my mind, I knew he was full of shit. *He is a high-level producer on this film, I am positive. It is all adding up. I had to make a move.* I went to "Buddy" and asked him about his "Hooks" tattoo.

"You know you can't wear that unless you're the real deal, right Buddy?" I said to him in anger.

"Who the fuck is Buddy?" he retorted.

My plan was to catch him slipping. "Ok, I have a

challenge for you. Let's go into the gym. I want to ask you a series of questions over a three-minute period. I want you to answer every question, and let's let the audience decide if you are who you say you are."

He looked at me and said, "No."

He stormed off in a big huff. *Typical "Buddy" fashion. Right, Buddy? Ha-ha.*

My idea was to ask rapid-fire questions, such as: What is your mother's birth name? What middle school did you go to? I was going to ask him questions, that would be easy for a person to answer quickly if they are who they said they are. I was dying to trip him up in front of the whole pod. *This could draw out The Movie from the hole they have been hiding in.*

Since he refused, I went to the top Mexican shot-caller in the unit. I said, "Look, your homeboy is not who he says. I wanna ask him some questions in front of the whole pod."

He replies "What? Look you're crazy, man. You're that motherfucker who thinks he's in a movie, huh? Look, fuck off with all that noise."

I was walking back to my cell as I injected, "Well, now we know you're on the take too. You guys are pathetic."

Between Buddy and Wheezy showing back up, and the revelation that the Mexicans were getting commissary items as payment for participation in *The Movie*, I snapped. I walked up to the guard picket. The guard had a booth in the middle of the Chow Hall. They sat just higher up than the inmates, sending a sociological message not to fuck with them.

"Look, man, if you don't move me out of here, Imma kill one of these motherfuckers," I said in anger.

"Are you sure you wanna do this, man? Come on Bornagain don't do this," pleaded the guard.

This guard was trying to give me a chance to retract my

statement. I continued onward on the path though. I was so angry; I knew I was about to lash out. He made a phone call downstairs, and I was locked in my cell to wait for my escort back downstairs.

This was one of the biggest mistakes I ever made while in jail. But I was deranged with illusions of *The Movie. It was Buddy! I was one-thousand percent positive. The makeup was great, the nose a little off, but it was him. I couldn't stand back and take this abuse anymore.*

Moments later, I was on my way back down to Central Booking.

Threatening the lives of other inmates is not taken lightly at Nueces County Jail. I was hauled downstairs, back to the holding tanks. I met with the brass and was told that I was to be put into segregation. A solitary confinement situation where I was to be put into a cell, by myself, twenty-three-hours a day lockdown. I had a talk with the Jail's in-house psychologist. The Dr. knew my grandpa, who was also in the field. She knew him from court cases, county functions, and other events in Corpus. She asked me a series of questions. I think I may have told her a little too much about *The Movie* because I was to do my solitary time in 2P. The medical unit.

The medical unit housed the sick, the elderly, the gay, and the pedophile. It was a unit for men who could not defend themselves. Why the hell was I being sent here? Well, it also holds the mentally ill. I was now deemed crazy by the brass, the medical staff, and the jailers. They walked me over to a top-floor cell. The door closed behind me; the feeling of a permeating dread spread through every nerve ending in my body.

Passengers, this is the most pivotal part of my gross tale of drugs, sex, and God. This is where I met the Lord, found myself, and finally got some answers. So, grab the "oh shit" handle, because the miracles are about to begin. Not that the guns, accidents, and near-death brushes were not enough for you. Well, here we go, buckle up. We are headed to solitary.

#

I sat on my bunk like a dog in the rain. Solitary is the most boring place on earth. You can hear the other inmates pacing the dayroom. Games of spades getting heated, old men yelling about some bullshit that happened in 1964, scuffles from some guys in wheelchairs over Matlock or Gunsmoke. It was me, God, and my ratty old Bible in the 8x10 hovel. After chow, the inmates were on cleanup duty. The smells of the chemical cleaners would hit the roaches, causing them to run. Massive palmetto bugs would crawl under the door jamb of my cell. I would find myself trapped with them, with nowhere to run. You would hear people slapping the walls with the cheap plastic orange sandals they issued us.

My heel was broken in the accident, it was never properly set. The healing was all fucked up. Standing on the concrete floor, all day looking out of my little square window, I found myself in excruciating pain. It was unbearable at points; my feet were still a mess from walking to Mars and back. The guards served my meals three times a day and I drank water from the back of the toilet. I was surviving, but that is all. However, you never think you can survive a situation till you are forced to go through it. The boredom is what can drive a man mad.

I timed my masturbation parties. When the guards were doing a medicine line with the nurse, everyone had to be locked up. So, once they passed my door, I would rub out two solid loads, just to pass time and take off some stress. They put me on some crazy pills. I started taking a well-known antipsychotic. I wasn't insane, clearly, but they helped you pass out for a solid eight hours. God knows I needed to catch up on some sleep. I was losing interest in jacking off. Without the meth and the porn, it just wasn't the same.

In the next few weeks, I got into that bible like nobody's business. I was reading the Word with heartfelt passion like never before. I started to form an intimate relationship with the Father. I grew to trust Him in many ways. I even started the process of thinking about my sexual immorality. That is a whole detox in itself. Can you imagine two years of yanking on yourself, till your junk looked like a piece of Kielbasa sausage, and nailing anything with a heartbeat? And then…nothing. It was very depressing. Like I had lost a lover or was grieving the death of a loved one. I had no female attention or contact. I was lost. So, I began to do what it said in the Book. And it was working.

Bella never showed up to visit. I would stare out my window on weekends, waiting for them to call me for visit, and like clockwork, I would get passed up like a fat kid in dodgeball. I was like an abandoned puppy, looking out the window, waiting for his owners to come home.

A few days later, I got called out of my cell during the evening at around seven. It was an odd time to be taken out. It was a weekday and meds had already come. *What in the world could this possibly be?*

They took me to the gate of 2P. I asked, "What is this about?"

"Lawyer visit, Bornagain. Shut up and let's go." the guard growled.

The guard was not in the mood. They took me out of the pod and led me down the hall to a tiny room. It was right near the rows of phones for visitation. I entered and almost hit my head; the ceiling was so low.

The room was soundproof. It had an almost wool sweater-looking material that covered the walls, ceiling, and floor. It was a dark gunmetal gray. There was a small stool with a circular seat for your ass. The room had a partition, half wool sweater and half bulletproof glass. There was a grated hole only big enough for voices to pass through. I waited for what seemed like two hours when he finally appeared.

He was a small man, about five and a half feet. He had medium-length snow-white hair. He was in his early Sixties, wore a charcoal gray suit, and a white button-down shirt. He looked exactly like Martin Scorsese, the director. He sat down and pulled some files out of a brown leather briefcase.

"Mr. Bornagain how are you tonight?" he chirped.

He was a happy man, extremely well spoken and well prepared. *He had to be an actor.*

"It looks like you are facing some very serious charges," he said.

We talked for a while, and I explained everything about *The Movie*, how Bella was paid one million dollars to be my girlfriend, and more. Near the end, he talked about an insanity defense. He explained how hard it was to win and asked if I wanted to try it.

I said, "Sure, I can pull it off." *I was an actor anyways; I could pull off the role of a lifetime.*

He told me the whole process, about the State Hospital and how I would need to go for a full evaluation. *I just wanted to get out and get my money. If the insanity defense were the way out, I would play the part.* When we parted ways after about an hour of talking, I was in good spirits. *It is time to suit up, for possibly the most important scene of my life.* I was taken back to 2P, and I fell fast asleep.

Inmates in the jail were barbers. Our hair was cut by trustees getting time off their sentences. They are only supposed to give standard trimmings with the clippers. If you bribed them with a soup or a honey bun, you could get a more elaborate doo. I had nothing but managed to talk the cool Black New Orleans native on duty into giving me a full mohawk, a cut frowned upon by the brass. I had a feeling this trustee wanted to "Stick it to the Man."

I was well on my way to looking nuts. In jail, you are limited on hair products among other things. I figured out that if I lathered a crazy amount of soap into my hair, it would stand straight up. *I was now rocking some bitchin' liberty spikes and feeling very punk rock.*

#

I woke one day to a concerning mechanical problem. The fountain in my sink stopped working. Normally, out in the free world, not a big deal. In here, that's where my drinking water came from, a little faucet fountain on the back shelf attached to the toilet head. *I had been giving the guards absolute hell for weeks. I had made enemies, fuck them, fuck they, and their sister. I made a formal complaint and waited patiently, only asking for maintenance updates every fifteen minutes or so.* The more you ask for something in jail, the longer you wait. You are no longer a human being. Your life means less than zero. You are now just a number, lost in a sea of orange with destitute last names.

On day two, I became thirsty and tired. I was already dehydrated. As you can imagine, I was avoiding drinking water. It's a gross spout in the back of a toilet, used by a million criminals before yours truly. Day three, I sit in bed, with moments of insanity raging. My mouth was dry as a wishbone. A film of white paste caked the corners of my mouth. My testicles hurt, and my back swelled.

The feelings of old from the cab and being a dehydrated mess once again. This is a bad sign medically. It could be deadly. *I cried out all night for help, not a soul came. Not even other inmates.* I was yelling so much in the days leading up to this, I was the Boy Who Cried Wolf.

Day four was torture. I was starting to hallucinate; it was like when I was drugged in Aransas Pass. The room swirled, spinning like drunk dreams. My urine was bright orange. During meals, they just ignored my pleas for help. They told me to "Shut your fuckin' loudmouth." This was a punishment for giving them lip. They will smoke you in Nueces County Jail. No fucks given for the inmate's human life. We were vermin.

I woke at breakfast on day five vomiting. I had nothing left to expel. A thick yellow ooze, reminiscent of eggbeaters out of the carton, leaked off my lips as I prayed to the stainless-steel god before me. It was when I flushed the toilet that it hit me. The animalistic instinct of survival kicked in, the water sound gurgling in my brain, sounding sweet and seductive. I looked up at the concrete desk near my bed. A large plastic coffee cup another inmate had gifted me out of pity, sat dirty and raw. I had a few bags of coffee that I had begged off a generous soul just before the water had gone off.

I decided to mix the coffee with the fecal water from the freshly puked-in toilet. I had a plan to catch the water as it ran out of the feeder hole, directly where an inmate's penis would point during a sit-down urination and defecation routine. I figured the cleanest it was going to get was right when it came out of the spout during a flush.

I put the rim of the cup under the hole and simultaneously flushed. Water poured out, grim and salty. My gut told me the jail's water system was not potable. Hepatitis and HIV-positive visions of inmates before me, staggering and vile in my mind. I pictured men shitting blood and liquid excrement out of infected anuses. I saw IV drug users spraying the feeder hole with a biohazard of bile. I saw male prostitutes, jacking off and throwing the venomous rags into the newfound oasis I had discovered.

I mixed the coffee in the liquid death with a spork. Chunks of something were floating like June bugs in a stagnant river hollow. I put the chalice to cracked, bleeding lips. Opening my throat wide as the Grand Canyon, water rehydrating near-dead tissue. My gag reflex reacted as I imagined hot chunks sliding down my sorry drab esophagus. I fought the urge to lose the payload back into the bowl. This was a life-or-death situation. It was already in my mouth, no turning back now.

I guzzled the bubbling witches brew fast as my body allowed. When the brown scum hit my guts, it burned and fizzled. I succumbed to a nervous breakdown in a momentary lapse of mental weakness. There is a unique feeling when one drinks toilet water in the Nueces County Jail. One of morose depression, a fight or flight judgment call where I decided to live.

I always live.

The shame of my situation hit me, as familiar as it was stained. I felt as desolate as when I was stabbing myself in repetition, a dull and used needle harpooning through already bruised flesh. Another dehydration situation, where one's veins run like a gazelle racing through June flowers while being chased by a cheetah. The moment of desperation when the last of the dopes at stake, and it's just a waste to ingest it orally.

The scissors clip off the strange blood-filled pin that someone had used days before, discarded on a bedroom floor in a trap. The petroleum jelly saturates the dirt-matted plastic, a syringe that had seen better days. Booty bump shame, as the rig is injected up the anal canal. The meth squirts into a rectum, virgin and raw, lying on one's stomach, the poison nearly expelled by the canal of its entrance trying its best to eject the gift. The body rejecting the household cleaners and carcinogens from the homemade meth. Yes, this was a familiar feeling. Where was my humanity?

You know kids, you never think you will shove a dirty meth syringe up your ass to get high when you're a kid. Sometimes life just works out that way. The booty bump, and the Nueces County Jail toilet water were a darkness, one and the same. It will bring you to a place mentally that you don't ever want to be.

Later in the day, God worked in His all too familiar and mysterious ways. An old man had gone into cardiac arrest and expired in his bed. Standard procedure when an inmate dies is the Texas Rangers interview any inmate that desires. And I desired in a big way. They interviewed me, heard about what I had just been through, and within ten minutes, I was moved to 4R. A working cell awaited me. A terribly angry Nueces County Jail staff escorted me, talking shit the whole way…no pun intended.

#

The same lockdown, different roach filled apartment. The mites ate the flesh from my pale ankles, as I came to realize I had been left for dead, no bond for Boston. All the three in the morning rides for free, all the money I spent, parties I threw, not one friend was thinking of me. When you go away as a member of the shallow ice underbelly, you have no real friends; you never had any.

Barry? God knows where he was. My family told me to

"fuck off," and blocked the jails wall phone number, never to be heard from again. All alone in the world, forgotten by anyone who I had ever known. Suicide daydreams ran amuck in a tortured soul. This is a moment of brokenness that you can never forget, no matter how hard you try.

I wrote my ma through my ex-wife. Weeks passed in silence. I had no one in my life, not even Catt...*how I missed that animatronic feline from Japan.* Crazy the things you learn to love when no love is present. Not long after, I had my first major court appearance. They led me down the long tunnel, the underground pathway between the jail and the County Court, shackled on a chain, connected to a file of other zoo animals. On our way to learn the justice system on the business end of the mighty gavel.

I donned a full mohawk, I looked like I slimed my way out of a dumpster at a punk club. I emerged into the courtroom and took a seat in the inmates' box, where the jury usually sits. I saw the females being led in right behind us. And who do I see?

Bella's younger sister, looking like a beauty queen. She was about to bail out, currently wearing the orange-clad costume, with shorter locks, and the cutest face you have ever seen. *This isn't a movie? What are the odds, that the love of my life's little sister, the one I slept with, would be seated right in front of me in the box at a major court appearance?*

"Hey Boston," she said under her breath.

We were not allowed to talk to the females, so we flirted in secret within full view of the court officials. The older female judge we had was all business, all the time. I rose to wounded feet as she graced us with her presence. *She did giggle when she looked at my choice of hairstyle, though.*

A few people went up before me. My lawyer walked in late. I was pissed, what a first impression for the judge. Little did I know, they were cool as the flip side of the pillow. They had a long-standing relationship. We went up and he asked her for a full psychological evaluation to be done on me. It was ordered and right then, it was done. I was to be seen by the County's top forensic psychiatrist. If deemed unfit for trial, to the State Hospital we go for round two of the process.

Back at the pod, the guys asked me who my lawyer was while I was being led up to my cell. When I spoke his name, the crowd gasped. Days later, I found out by chance that I had gotten the number two pay lawyer in our city as a public defender. I guess they have to do a certain number of free cases per year, and I had just won the lottery.

A letter from my ma came in the mail. Besides being hung up on by my other family, this was my first real outside contact since I got to jail. It had been months since I talked to anyone who I knew outside of the game. She told me she loved me in a long letter where I could see how her tears had dried on the page. My mother and I had a turbulent relationship for twenty years due to the divorce and other factors, some that led me to drink for almost three decades. I loved my ma, and she loved me. An Irish love that could never be broken.

I wrote the brass; I wanted to plead to get out of solitary confinement. *I must have pissed them off something royal, I never got so much as a note back.* I had heard that Laurie had gotten arrested while in my dad's Benz. They had found her driving it after months. *I think it was a plan to throw me off from my research on The Movie.* I went back up to my cell.

#

The next day I was told I was being moved back to 2P. When I arrived, I saw Whisper, the guy with the hole in his throat. How could you forget him, passengers? Whisper came up to the door of my cell and we shot the shit for a minute. *Wheezy was on the pod; it was a great set to be on, even though I was still in my cage.*

Guys would bring me coffee and snacks. This pod was a lot better than on the first floor. This was where all the action was. I wrote back and forth with my ma, and I finally got a phone number for her. I called her in the morning at half past four while out on recreation and she answered my call. We talked for the whole hour; it was strange to feel love after all that time. *She still thought I was "sick", but that was ok. As I said, the story was a whopper, and I understood that until The Movie wrapped, people would call me crazy.*

At the same time, I started to reconnect with my three children. Days grew less stressful in solitary. *Them/They* had less and less of a presence as life marched on behind the blue door. I found Ephesians 6:10. A scripture explaining the battle in the heavenly realms, the struggle between good and evil, God and Satan. Suddenly, a lot of things started to make sense. I read the whole book of Ephesians, repeatedly.

The game, the spiritual world, and the first-hand encounters with evil that I had experienced were all starting to mean something different. The things we see are temporary. The spiritual, the unreal to the human mind, is what lasts forever. I began to deepen my faith. I would read that scripture every day. Putting on the full armor of God, gaining strength in an impossible situation. God began to heal my heart. I would still cry for Bella every day. We were sick. I know she did me wrong. However, I did her wrong too. The game is chock-full of sins and mistakes. You are out of your mind when you are out there. I began to toss the idea around that *The Movie* was all in my head.

The further I got into that scripture, the worse the

pestilence was in my cell. Day by day, the infestation grew. I was waking up with roaches on my face almost nightly. The rat infestation in 2P was nothing short of a scene in the underground subways of NYC. Massive rodents would crawl under the cracks in the blue door after dark. Late one night, I felt a wrestling match on my groin. I woke up to see the red, glowing eyes of a beast. A rat the size of Master Splinter digging his fangs into the wool of my blanket. So ravenous, he was gnawing on the tin strips in the cheap Indian-made bedcover. I screamed. There is a certain trauma in these things. You will never know fully unless you have been there. Passengers...take my word for it. Stay out of Nueces County Jail.

#

I had my evaluation with the psychiatrist. I was already committed to the insanity defense. I soaped up the mohawk, headed to the lawyer meeting area, and put on the performance of a lifetime. I was like Robert De Niro. I had practiced for hours in the cheap, fake glass mirror above the rusted sink in my cell.

The doctor was horrified. By the time he was leaving, he was already on his phone. I knew then we were onto something. *If The Movie wasn't real, I had become one hell of an actor, no matter how you slice the bread. Technically, if The Movie was in my head, I was a crazy man, acting to be crazy. How could I lose?*

Some more weeks pass: trials of this magnitude take time. I was still deep into *The Movie*, but the seed had been planted that this may not be real. I was still performing, just in case.

I was still in solitary confinement. The walls were starting to close in and one day, I drank far too much coffee. I had a massive panic attack. I was screaming for Barry, and I couldn't breathe. I was having signs of a full-on heart attack, as far as I could tell. Of course, I was not checked out by a nurse, not that she would have done much to help outside taking my blood pressure. But with my drug use over the years, it was all too possible that I could have a heart attack.

The guard let me go into the gym, even though other inmates were in the dayroom. This one tall, blond, younger kid took mercy on my soul. I paced for over an hour, throwing a racquetball he had given me to take my mind out of the war zone. I was on a heavy round of pills after seeing the forensic psychiatrist. Pills that are worth money on the inside. My ma had started sending snaps for the books, but it wasn't a steady stream. So, I needed to eat. I was rail-thin for me; the pains of hunger that were with me took me to the point of lunacy. A starving man, eating leftover scraps from the other inmates who were kind enough to bring them to my cell, slipped under the same cracks that the rats came through.

Terrence was a big Black dude. He was bald, wore big designer frames of glitter and gold. He was about two hundred and seventy pounds; I heard he was one hundred and sixty pounds when he arrived at the gates. He was balling. Terrence had an older, White, sugar mamma he had seduced on the outside. Plus, his grandma was a multi-millionaire in the Corpus scene. The whole pod would watch as Terrence went to the store. The commissary cart was a rolling bodega of sweets and treats. All of us have-nots, the starving masses, would glare in jealousy as Terrence would spend hundreds twice a week. Cakes, cupcakes, hundreds of freeze-dried soups of all flavors, tuna, chicken and meat in pouches, among other goodies. Almost anything that you would find in a little corner store sat in three massive totes on his cell floor.

Terrence was in jail on a vehicular manslaughter case.

He was an awful alcoholic, in his late forties. Before incarceration, he had been drinking all night when he decided to go to the store. He got behind the wheel of a rented SUV and went for some smokes. He was a drinker, synthetic marijuana smoker, and a seasoned crack user. He was cruising a well-to-do neighborhood when it happened. Terrence went to grab for his last smoke in the pack, through his center console. He took his eyes off the road for just a second. He heard a thud. When he looked up, he saw nothing. He made his way to the corner store and parked. He was felony-style drunk on this day. He was soon surrounded by a murder of police, like crows surrounding crumbs in a city park. He was taken aback by the barrage of cops. He hadn't the faintest clue why this was happening.

    The story goes as follows. When he heard that thud, he was rolling through a crosswalk near the high school. Two teenage girls, around sixteen, were on the road. He hit them so hard, the girls' bodies were ejected into the neighboring corner lots. One left, one right. So, when Terrence looked in the rearview, all he saw was pavement.

    An accident so brutal, one girl had her faced almost ripped completely off, and the other? Well, she passed away not long after. This was not Terrence's first drunk driving offense. He had many. He was already a multiple felon. He had been to prison multiple times. Drinking and drugs in Crook City had struck again. The devil kills on the daily in this dark mysterious city in South Texas.

    He was a major high-profile case. All over the news. Every single time Terrence had a court appearance, the cameras were there, and so were the girls' families. Fathers with murderous eyes would cut Terrence in half with a glare. Terrence faced huge time in prison. Might as well bury a guy of his age under the prison when facing that much time. He would most likely never see the Harbor Bridge, or anything outside again, in anything other than photos sent to the Texas Department of Corrections by his loving grandma.

Facing a major sentence is no joke. The reality of the boring hell-ridden life ahead can drive a man mad. Anything to take the mind out of the bear trap is greatly sought after in jail. I was on Busbar, a calming drug; when snorted, it gave the user a filthy fifteen-minute high, something like a Xanax trip.

Terrence had buying power. There was an open offer on the table to anyone on Busbar to sell their pills to him. The price would vary, depending on supply and demand. Two soups or a honey bun was the going rate.

This was a very risky thing to take part in. It was an operation called "cheeking." The med cart would come to each cell. All forty-eight cells locked down with the men inside. The nurse would administer the inmate's medication, and a look under the tongue was then performed to make sure there is no funny business going on.

If you maneuver your tongue just right, you could swirl the pills into the side of your mouth, into the concave of the cheek. Once the nurse and guard went onto the next cell, one would spit the pills into a dry napkin from dinner. After meds, the buyer would come by your cell to make the trade. Deal complete. Terrence gets to escape his depressing fate for fifteen minutes, and you get to eat. Everybody wins.

Terrence liked me. He thought I was funny. We would joke from inside the cells during periods of lockdown. He really enjoyed my voice. I had started to teach myself how to sing while in solitary. I would belt out "Scream," the Misfits hit, sung by Michael Graves. I would sing this as a slow ballad. It was eerie, as it details the descent into bone-chilling madness. The echoes of the dark lyrics would float against the concrete walls, just as the ghosts of the inmates who died inside.

I began to cheek my pills. A scary practice. You could lose your meds and beyond as punishment. Losing your pills meant you wouldn't sleep; thus, you're doing double the time. That is just not an option. Terrence was buying pills from ten guys at once. A massive drug habit on dirty pharmaceuticals. When people couldn't cheek, and I was lucky, I would set the market price. One time, he paid me a whole bag of Keefe coffee and a honey bun. Unheard of. This was ten times the market price. That's the desperation of facing that kind of time. He had to have it, no matter the cost.

#

The next couple of months, the tank started to really bother me. The time in isolation was wearing on my soul. The place was full of child molesters. I could smell it on them a mile away. I hated being around the hurters of children. My faith and spiritual awakening had me sensitive to evil of any kind. I was aware of deep things.

The gym was tiny, my legs had begun to atrophy while in solitary confinement. I had become weak and frail-looking beneath the waist. I hated working out in jail. I would get jealous of the guys becoming bodybuilders while there.

Some time had passed in 2P. One day, the sergeant came to my cell. After ninety days in an 8x10 box, the brass at the jail had deemed me sane enough to leave my cell. I was let out into the pod at lunchtime chow. It was like crawling out of the grave.

As I walked out of my isolation, I was in a lucid state of shock. It leaves you weak in the knees to be around other people, even for just a moment, after so long in isolation. The novelty of false freedom wore off within hours. I did get to chill with Whisper and Wheezy, live and in person. That was a blast.

A preacher man and his assistant came to 2P. It was church service for the inmates, and I was in attendance. The service was going just fine. A little boring for my taste, but the guy's heart was in the right place. Then the preacher started to speak of "honey-tongued women," and the lusty traps they set. How men in our situation should avoid them at all costs. I couldn't help myself. With a full spiked-up mohawk, I interrupted his sermon. Today the preacher was going to learn a valuable lesson from the Spirit.

I looked at the man, hand up, as the other inmates hissed. Trying to shut the crazy guy from *The Movie* up. *Not today! You gonna learn today.*

"Yes, young man," he said.

"Shouldn't we lift her up?" I asked softly.

"What do you mean...lift her up?" said the preacher.

I returned with, "Shouldn't we search her heart, should we not, as men of Jesus Christ, go to her, comfort her broken heart, and find out why she is acting out sexually? Shouldn't we get to the bottom of the devil's plans and lead her soul to the Lord?" I said seriously.

The whole room was silent; my mohawk standing at attention. The preacher man paused and looked around the room for what seemed like an hour. He then looked to his assistant, and back to the inmates.

"He's right...the man is right in that statement," he said looking puzzled.

I sat back down on the concrete Indian-style as the man went on to give a blistering thirty-minute, Spirit-filled sermon on the power of the loving arms of Jesus. The Spirit had a message for that man, I was the vessel, all glory to the Highest.

I started to change, a healing of sorts, the beginning of

something great. The next spiritual hoop had been jumped through. I remember crying on my bunk. Singing "Wagon Wheel" by Old Crow Medicine Show, the only version that should be listened to of that song. That was the song that was to play during the wedding scene of *The Movie*, as I kissed my girl, my kids playing around us, Barry laughing with a cold beer, as they presented me with my check for *The Movie*. A new life, a new career, and a newfound love of Jesus, all in the sequel. Part of me was so sad because I had begun to feel as if it could be all in my head. I was about fifty/fifty when it came to the "Hollywood" conspiracy.

You start to see the genuine person of the criminals around you. These are real-life people, just as I saw the souls of the most-feared dealers in the front seat of my cab. The soul of a murderer is that of you and me. No different. Yes, in some cases, you run into the demonic. That sort will stand out right away, pure evil. I have met far more demonic child rapists in my travels than evil murderers.

One day, Terrence was drinking a bunch of homemade jail hooch. A home-brewed alcoholic drink made from water, sugar, and the oranges they served at lunch. He was getting lit in the gym. He was cutting up, laughing, joking, having the time of his life. Until things took an incredibly sad and touching turn.

The booze took hold of Terrence, opening up all his deepest emotions. He started to talk about the grim demons eating him alive on the inside. The things that had him lying awake at night, living in fear of the God who would judge him. He started off calm and low spoken.

"I was drinking man, I didn't mean to hurt anyone," he said in a depressed tone.

Terrence started to weep as he gave the chilling details

that I recounted earlier.

"She was only a fucking kid man, just a fucking kid. I wish I could trade places with her," he said as he unreservedly broke down.

He recounted the looks the fathers would give him in court. He was shattered in pain as he told his side of the story. The devil had Terrence. He was in the grips of a debilitating alcohol and drug addiction. The girls in the accident, the victims of his crime, were innocent souls. The grieving families were filled with anger and rage, and rightly so. This day though, I saw Terrence's guts. A birds-eye view into the man behind the high-profile case. I saw his heart and a glimpse of his damaged soul.

I have drunk and drove many, many nights. I drove high for two years without a day off. Look at the night of my accident on South Padre Island Drive. Someone could have easily been killed by me. For some reason, God chose Terrence and those girls to intersect, in the exact moments in time that transpired on that fateful day. He called one home and crippled another. Two innocent souls, and their loved ones were forever changed. Terrence was in limbo due to his addictions and his shattered soul. We will never understand how God works. His mysteries are unknown. His motives shrouded. One thing is for sure, that man didn't set out to kill. I could see it in his eyes.

#

Time bantered on in the cold recesses of 2P. Weeks flew by, one day melting into the next, as the bondage candles burned, dripping anticipation on the flesh. I grew worried about my case. Meetings with the lawyer man proved dismal. He spoke of fifteen-year sentences and the possibilities of a bleak and long-term prison stay.

An insanity defense was a rare and unheard-of

accomplishment in the criminal court system. From my understanding, one percent of people who apply get it in front of the judge. Twenty-four percent of that one percent get the "not guilty by reason of insanity" finding. I was facing a Goliath of criminal court case. My heart raced at lights out. When you start to think about a fifteen-year sentence, and what that really means, it is devastating, to say the least.

I had a weapon involved in my crime. That makes it what's referred to as an "AGG charge." An aggravated charge in the State of Texas means that if convicted, a man would be required to serve eighty-five percent of his sentence before ever even being considered for parole.

That's over twelve years of hard time in my case. My dog would be dead. My mother and father already ashes in the night sky. Even my youngest baby would become a young woman while I was trapped behind cement walls. Wrap your mind around those wounds for a minute.

Passengers, I was in a pickle. I was straddling the fence between insanity and total freedom. The barber came; I lost the mohawk, and I returned looking like the best version of me that has ever strutted around. That would be short-lived though. Ma was sending me money on the regular, and I was beginning to put on some lock-up baby fat.

The Movie still terrorized the backlot spaces of my mind. The replay of the mental tapes, the memories of the psychedelic experiences and dreams, all seemed too real and vivid to be fake. I still thought the TV in the dayroom was speaking directly to me. I thought the weatherman was sending coded messages from *Them/They*. The actors toned down. I felt as if they were retreating like the Nazi's in Paris. The players who once antagonized me were now docile forlorn creatures that suddenly seemed to find kindness and mercy in their hearts for yours truly. I was getting a break, one that my Irish heart needed, like water or food.

I was asked to step out of my cell. "Boston, you're going to 4P."

A return to the zoo. The racially divided fishbowl where lions roared, and gorillas roamed. *Ok, I was ready for some action. Hold the lights and cameras!* The medical tank, with its sick and old-timers, was starting to get mundane. I folded my bedroll and walked to the double doors at the mouth of the pod. Almost to the destination point, I intersect with Wheezy. Two samurais fresh from the game, buddies and brothers on an unbelievable trip, walking side by side to the crossroads.

"Where you headed, bro?" I asked.

"4P brother, where you headed?" Wheezy said.

"Bro," I cackled to the hanging lamps above. What are the odds my friend and I would be headed to the same pod...again? It could be *The Movie,* or it could be God serving up camaraderie to a broken man. That's for you to decide, passengers.

4P was a party. We settled in fast; lots of new faces graced the jungle within. Card games and dominos were constantly being slammed upon the cheap plastic tables. There were fights over the TV and raps being spit. We all made the best with what we had. A bunch of guys, some good, some bad, all trying to make it back home. All dreaming of a more fruitful way, a better life for our children. We were human beings. Not the lost souls in orange, the animals portrayed by mainstream society.

The first few days in the pod, I saw the drug game in action again. This time, I was allowed more access to the conversations taking place between the guys. I had stopped talking about the war with *Them/They*. I kept *The Movie* between me and the weatherman, as well as some smaller roles that a few actors still played. I was received as a new man, with new respect and a whole new experience.

I ran into a homeboy of my old dealer, Maybach. Through him, I made buddies with a lot of inmates. We played handball as hard as it gets. My broken heel was now protected by some cheap second-hand sneakers. I had traded two honey buns and three soups for them. What an investment!

The sports brought out my competitive nature. I felt like I was back on the field with the hood kids in Reading, Massachusetts, having the time of my life. It's the little things that get you through. The mid-day campfire politicking, the coffee sessions near the payphones. The loose, stand-up shenanigans of a multiracial cast of characters. I started to see beauty in the belly of the beast for the first time.

Those shit-talking guards, those racist ass judges, the whole derogatory system couldn't take who we were. Men praying, singing songs, expressing themselves through poetry and street music. It was an artistic community. Tattoo guns buzzed with a lookout stationed for the watchguards. Envelopes with Rembrandt quality drawings scribbled on the front in colored pencil for the girls back home, left alone by the ice game's shattering consequences.

Seeing the beauty in the different cultures was life changing. To see the love and respect for Jesus from the viewpoint of the Mexican culture; to consistently hear a male's perspective on the Father, our Lord. Watching the pain of the young Black male in America, the plight of those left behind by our country. Seeing the spiritual experiences of those facing the worst possible circumstances is an experience all in itself. A sure fate of doom where all one has left to hang onto is prayers that the angels will reach with merciful hands and unlock the gates to freedom. With God, all things are possible.

One of the guys I roomed with had his girl back home cutting for him on the outside. Baby girl was taking eight balls of strong dope, diluting them in syringes, and spraying the jelly upon greeting cards. The dope would dry into a visible stain. Then, he would tear the card into dub size doses and serve it to the paying members of the pod. Homeboy was going to eat, regardless. The buyer would in turn to their cell, eat the dried-up dope, ingesting the paper with some water out of the back of the toilet. Twenty minutes later, out came the mops and kill-shots.

A kill-shot is as close to porn as you can get in jail. This is where an inmate jacks-off to a picture and unloads their frustration. The celebrity most used in Nueces County Jail was Arianna Grande.

Poor Arianna, looking all cute on a lone bed, wearing thigh-high boots somewhere in L.A during a photoshoot. Most likely, she has no idea that the pictures from that day were being passed around between Black, White, and Mexican pervert gang members in the drug world at the Nueces County Jail in Corpus Christi, Texas. The picture could be traded for just one soup, allowing the inmate the inspiration for countless gooey orgasms spat out of the penises of the ice games most élite. Crook Cities' highest and horniest incarcerated animal population.

Pumping the toilet came to me via Busy. Busy was a light-skin black cat. He looked like a "Busy Bone," with a big Afro that he wore on top of his head in a bun, looking identical to Rick Gonzalez's character, Spanish, in "Old School."

Busy showed me that the girls were right above us. He came into my cell late one afternoon.

"Boston, you crazy motherfucker, let me use your

shitter," he said.

"Well, why Busy?" I demanded.

He laced me up on some important things really quick. He showed me that you could speak to the girls above us by pumping the toilet water out of the pipes, using your mattress and your knee. Once the bowl was empty, he took a huge stack of cups from the drinking coolers and poked holes in all the bottoms. He shoved the stack into the hole and started pounding on the stainless-steel toilet.

An angelic voice came chiming through the makeshift phone system.

"Hey, who's this?" she said.

The door was now wide open to meet girls for stimulating conversations. I was in awe of the jailhouse innovation that I was seeing. MacGyver-type people were in this place in large numbers. When Busy was done, it was my turn. A new girl comes on the line.

"Boston, it's me, Brittany." It was Bella's little sister! *Tell me this isn't The Movie.*

We chopped it up for about two hours. She said a bunch of sweet, meaningful words to me. Then a few days later, she went home. And just like that, she exited my life again. She did confirm that Laurie was upstairs being charged with the theft of the Benz. *At this point, I didn't know what to believe. What are the odds that she would be in the cell right above mine, at that exact time, and on that day?*

#

The food in jail is terrible. Watery spaghetti, frozen meatballs, and you better believe that all the meats of any kind are fake patties of soy. Guys make spreads, which can be a hodgepodge of soups, Cheetos, tuna, almost anything you can think of. Inmates made birthday cakes out of crumbled up cookies and other items. It was really terrible, but after a few days of no commissary, it tastes like a gourmet meal.

The holidays were hell on earth. Thanksgiving turkey, Christmas ham...all fake as a three-dollar bill. Dry stuffing and green beans in a sludge filled the stomachs of suicidal fathers who miss their children. The Chow Hall was dead silent on Christmas. No one would speak a word, and right after our meal, everyone went straight to sleep. It truly was a "Silent Night."

A Mexican from the 210 (San Antonio area code) was bumping his gums to one of the 361 boys. There were some words exchanged in the dayroom over some soups that were owed. The behind-the-scenes gang shit is unquestionably private, so this is the extent to what I knew. These two were given the green light to duke it out by the General of the Mexicans.

So, in 4P there are two places it can happen, the gym or the bathroom. The latter was chosen for this particular beef. I was in my cell with Wheezy and others, chopping it up, having coffee with Jolly Ranchers melted in it. We saw the two men enter the bathroom alone. A few minutes later, the 361 boy came out by himself, followed by some moans in the bathroom. The guard went in and called a code.

The pod was flooded by henchmen in a matter of two minutes. Every guard in the jail that was available came up to stabilize the emergency situation. Moments later, the 210 Mexican clambered out. He had a Spurs tattoo on the side of his neck, signifying his 210 click. He was holding the side of his face as blood poured out of his nose. That problem now settled, the 210 kid told the fuzz that he slipped and fell in the shower.

That's how shit works in County. You take your lumps, and you never tell. Otherwise, you get an S.O.S. (Smashed on sight). In other words, you would be targeted, and more than one person is going to whoop your ass.

To light cigarettes, or sticks of synthetic, you would get a lead. A lead is where you take some toilet paper and use it as a wick. A piece of pencil lead was then stuck into the wall socket, causing a spark. With the wick successfully lit, the inmate would run into the gym with his smokes and the party would begin.

There were some punks in 4P, gay inmates that would suck cock, and more, for a bag of chips. I have seen shit that blows the mind. Away from home, wives' out of sight, hardened gang members of all races were having secret gay sex behind bars. Not the most common practice, but it happens. I have witnessed punks going to sleep with straight inmates overnight in their cells. I feel the guard was compensated in some type of way. They wouldn't emerge till morning, always with something dripping from a sinful mouth.

One time there was a Black inmate, about nineteen years of age, who looked like a skinny Somalian. Blackest flesh I had ever seen. He was hanging out quite a bit with this fiery red-haired White kid who ran Solito. They were both straight men, really loud-mouthed and goofy. Typical kids. At nineteen, everyone's an idiot. They had clicked up with Tovar, a flaming gay Mexican Solito who was on the smaller size. Tatts were all over his face. His voice was high pitched and feminine. He was an exact replica of John Leguizamo from "To Wong Foo, Thanks for Everything! Julie Newmar." One day, Tovar came out of Cell 48 from upstairs, way up in the corner.

"Ok that's it, Imma put both you motherfuckers on blast!" He was pissed, acting like the typical diva that he was. "Look out 4P, these two motherfuckers were up in here drinking my cum!"

It was a packed house in the middle of the pod. Tovar came downstairs and recounted the past two weeks of events. Apparently, they were going up to Cell 48 and having graphic three-way sex. Blow jobs, anal, cum drinking, all of it. The crowd listened with sour stomachs as the nature of the encounters were described. He also informed everyone that these two young straight men had taken female names as part of their new sexual identities. One was Starr and the other was Heather. The accused came down in total denial. A Mexican cat, who was older and a seasoned shot caller, came and put his hand on my shoulder, as the nefarious argument flexed on.

"Boston, if there's one thing you learn from me, learn this...punks don't lie. When this comes up, and it does from time to time, the punk is always telling the truth, "said the shot caller. "Punks, nine times out of ten, have no reason to lie. When they out a straight lover, it's usually because of a scorned woman-type situation, or money is owed and not being paid".

There were tranny inmates too. Transsexuals' that may or may not have breasts. One thing is for sure, if you're on a male unit, you have a cock. Not all gay inmates went to the special tank. Some don't want to. I think they like the normalcy of Gen Pop and the other reason, they got off on turning on straight men and all the attention it brings them. A lot of times, guys had the gay-for-the-stay attitude, an out-of-sight, out-of-mind mindset, as if the rules of sexuality didn't apply on the inside. I never understood it. I can wrap my head around why a straight male might swing that way in a life sentence situation; or if they suddenly realized they were gay or bisexual. But this was County. The longest you can stay is for two years. Most inmates are there between one and nine months, tops. In the scheme of things, not a lot of time to hold out in order to get back to the little lady.

I saw one situation firsthand. A gang member at one of the tables, I won't say what race, was caught by a guard getting a sloppy blow job by a punk during nighttime bed check. The story spread around all over the jail, even to the outside. The newly gay gang member was ousted. He was thrown out of his gang for life. He was no longer able to sit with his own people. Off to the Solito table, it was.

In 4P, I was moved around quite a bit. I was asked to switch cells due to a racial issue, not a nefarious one though. I landed in Cell 24 with Marty, aged nineteen, but looking like a lost twelve-year-old. He was a kid at heart. He had extremely short reddish-brown hair, and he was full of life. We started to chop it up.

Marty was in for murder. The story goes that he was homeless. He was in the commission of a robbery of a homeless man. He took a stone and bludgeoned the male victim's skull. He was desperate and didn't realize how hard he really hit the man. He only got two dollars and six Marlboro Reds.

I spent a lot of time with Marty. I got the full introspective scoop of his life. He seemed like the sweetest kid on earth. He became addicted to ice, and it led him to the streets. It's no joke where the Crystal Ship will take you. Strange science fiction "Roswell, New Mexico" type of relationships carrying you to aimless points of destination, the actions of others always cloudy and with ulterior motives. Fact is, you can't trust your own mother on the shit, and nothing is as it appears. I was so sad talking to Marty. I would always share soups and candy with him. Anything I had, he had. He sat at the table with us Whites. He started working out when he got to jail. He put himself in a personal boot camp for prison. He knew he was on his way, and he wanted to be in tip-top shape for fighting.

We became fast friends. I watched for months as he battled to get a lower offer from the DA. When it was all said and done, one of the sweetest, funniest guys you ever met, got forty years flat. He was looking at getting parole in his forties. Another life claimed by the game and a young man lost his youth, what should be the best years of his life. This drug is of Satan. Period.

#

We went to court. I stood before the Judge, and she informed me that she was signing the order to deem me "unfit to stand trial." I will spare you the legal mumbo-jumbo, but basically, it means I was too crazy to understand the court process. My acting had paid off. I was off to Phase Two of this trial. I was put on a waiting list to go to the State Hospital in Vernon, Texas, a maximum-security unit near the Panhandle of Texas. I next had a quick court date, where my lawyer told me that the hospital would put me in classes to better myself. After this, I would be sent back to trial. This is a very vague description of what was to happen. I went back to my cell to wait for my turn.

#

Over the next month, I was having some bad days. The TV was still sending me messages. I was extremely paranoid about my trial and the sentence that loomed. My faith was being tested; I was so depressed. Once again, I was at the end of my rope, this time spiritually broken. I started to question God as I sat alone in my cell with the door closed. Marty was playing spades in the dayroom.

"Why do you do this to me? I love you so much, you are destroying me," I wept as I looked to the ceiling above. I perched on the edge of the bottom bunk and contemplated shaking my fist at the Lord and turning my back on Him. I was about to curse Him when it hit me like a ton of bricks. *Boston, if you do this…you have nothing left*. I lost everything a man can lose. My freedom and possibly, my sanity. If I gave up on my love for God, I would be eternally lost. I took some deep, calming breaths and chose to push forward.

A few weeks later, I went to see the Dr. It was a routine visit for medication. I explained the situation with my current "not fit to stand trial" status. What happened next was absolutely earth-shattering.

"Mr. Bornagain, there is over a year wait to go to Vernon," she said.

I fired off plenty of obscenities and the older Black guard that ran the mental patients hauled me back to the foggy depths of 4P.

I couldn't last that long in this place. The boring days, the food, and the rats. I would snap. I knew if I got too out of pocket, solitary confinement would be imminent. The next thirty days were a drab, nothing more than a series of trips around the sun. I moped around like a stoned housecat smelling his own shit, projecting sheer misery on anyone within arm's reach.

There were drugs everywhere. People nodding on black tar, smoking synthetic, and ice. Even in my depression, I opted out. I had done so many drugs in the two years leading up to this period of my life, and so much drinking for twenty-three years before that, I knew my body could not take one more trip in the Crystal Ship. Detoxing once was enough for me for a lifetime.

I was watching TV in the dayroom right before lights out. I stared up at the ten o'clock news. I zoomed in on that son-of-a-bitch weatherman on Channel Ten. I was telling him, out loud, that I was going to deconstruct *Them/They* for how they had shattered my once-promising life. He was mocking me back with his vindictive smile and scripted banter. I snapped and began screaming as I stormed out of the room like The Ultimate Warrior.

I returned to my cell with my mouth dry and my blood full of the poison prescribed by the Dr. I went to bed with the full intention of carrying out Plan Z with a calm and candid heart. My mind was made up. It was time to put Plan Z into action.

#

I woke on that Thursday. I sat up in my bed. My heart was still, peaceful and full. Marty was fast asleep on the top bunk, dreaming of his release, decades in the making, a future yet to take place.

I walked to the toilet to urinate. I flushed, and the civil war in my brain made a sudden and terrifying turn.

I examined the lines around my aging Irish eyes. Peering at myself in the cheap tiny square mirror above our sink that morning, I realized, *the things I have been thinking are pure imagination. This stuff was all...well, just not true.*

It was just all of a sudden, one hundred percent, obvious and clear that *The Movie* was all in my head. There were no actors, no producers, and no script. A wave of panic hit my soul in ways that are indescribable. I sat on my bunk, tears streaming from my Irish eyes, recounting the events and dreary happenings of the last year of life.

Passengers, imagine the feeling of seeing the truth of a life full of insanity, slamming the knowledge of an entire year of heartache down like a sledgehammer...all in one moment.

Barry was dead.

My grandparents' house was destroyed, foreclosed on, and lost forever, as my mother had told me weeks prior.

My family was indefinitely estranged for so many reasons. They robbed me of all the inheritance my father had left behind for me and my children.

I sold all my grandparents' antique furniture and irreplaceable family heirlooms in a nighttime estate sale, Christmas lights twinkling in the tree on Oakbrook.

My best friends betrayed, robbed, and abandoned me.

Remembering that I had slept with thirty-two women that year with no protection. They were, in fact, not part of a film and therefore not being screened for STDs. Nor were any of these women most likely on birth control. I had inseminated every last one of them.

The dirty needles I had been filling with shards found from that filthy carpet matted with dog hair. Needles possibly used by strangers and were definitely not movie props.

I hadn't been in my children's life for over a year and a half. I owed more than ten grand in child support.

All the establishments I had been banned from for life projected in my head.

The songs on the radio were not about me; the weatherman was not talking to me. My friends and my nemesis *The Boys in Props* were all a fragment of my imagination.

There was no fame, no money, no "Wolf of Wall Street" Ferrari coming my way. I was in debt, facing a possible ninety-nine years in prison, with no support system outside of my mother.

The courtroom drama of my life had just passed through while I was in a fog.

And by far, the most terrifying one of all...Bella never loved me. There was no wedding, and she and the baby were still out there existing in the recesses of the most dangerous game known to mankind.

Darkness fell upon my face, choking back the emotions of a dying man. The epicenter of the quake, the realization that my life was Ground Zero, the plantation point in a holocaust nightmare. Looking back, this moment would not only be a turning point. It would be one of the greatest miracle events of a certifiably insane man's life, and the restoration only made possible by the loving hands of God. When you are that deep in methamphetamine psychosis, there is usually no coming back. I went to bed talking to the weatherman, thinking he was talking back, and I woke up totally restored! It was a healing, the kind you compared to a man standing up and walking out of his wheelchair at a revival.

Passengers, anything you have read about *The Movie*, such as the actors, the sets, hidden cameras, and fake Hollywood prosthetic makeup was absolutely all in my head. The accidents, the brushes with death, and spiritual revaluation as well as the miracles, were all very real. The demons, the displays of vulgar power, and the menacing sparks...well, that's for you to discern.

I know the sparks coming from that stovetop were the real-deal Holyfield. I know I shot a hundred units of straight diesel jelly into the bulbous vein in my forearm. The self-destruction, sexual degradation, and pornographic religion that I worshiped was all-consuming and a facet of my real existence.

The love for my three children and all the miracles I had experienced were as real as the words on this page. Passengers, God is real.

I paced the gym circle for hours that day. Coffee cup in hand, keeping the harsh truths of my life close to the vest. What did it matter? The story was too big, too psychedelic to describe. Wheezy saw the change in me right away. It took weeks for him to address my mental illness. He was a true friend and brother, always caring for my fragile mind. Our friendship started out in the game, one where he would have robbed me in a New York minute. As we remained clean, under some of the most stressful situations a person can face, we formed a true bond. A real friendship that had meaning and value. It was no question that Wheezy, and I were meant to take the jail journey side by side. God knew that we both needed a buddy, as we both faced ninety-nine.

Now completely my old self, I called the lawyer. There was no way I was going to wait a year for the trip to Vernon. I wanted a new evaluation. When I called him, he informed me that he had already put in the request. He had heard about the year-long wait and decided that there were other ways. He was tight with my judge. I just didn't know how tight.

I had been in Nueces County Jail for eight months now. My dreams were a sweet escape from the hindering thoughts of those dreadful days under the spell of that damn movie. Projections of my father before he passed, the children, and ghosts of a life once forgotten always left me smiling as I woke, the muscles in my face flexing.

The happiest moments were the dreaming parts of slumber on cold nights. The rats, roaches, the devil were things of torment in my life. They were left miles away as I slept. Like a demonic antique clock every single morning, my eyes would open and peer down to the pumpkin-colored pants. The manic meltdowns were sun-up reminders that I resided in hell. The court case and the sentence were not going away. This insanity defense would most likely not even get in front of the judge.

I met with the forensic psychiatrist for the second time. This day I was a sane, docile, cardboard cutout, of the buffoon lunatic that had so recently donned a mohawk and wild eyes to see this very doctor.

"How are you feeling, Mr. Bornagain?" he asked.

"I am totally fine, doctor. I am facing a lot of prison time," I said with death in my voice.

"Well, there are other alternatives, Mr. Bornagain," he said quietly.

He asked me if I was having any hallucinations. He saw the total transformation within me, and he was shocked. I didn't gain any kind of hope from this conversation. I called the lawyer as soon as I got back to 4P.

"Mr. Bornagain, we are looking at a minimum of fifteen years in the Texas Department of Corrections. This is a very serious situation. I will be meeting with the DA soon. Be prepared to go to prison," the lawyer begrudgingly told me.

I hung up the phone a broken man.

#

Back on the pod, violence was the worst it had ever been. There was some gang bullshit going on, a warring of the rival factions disenfranchised by a shift in the power structure. First, a sizable alert for help came in the gym at 4P. Then, another pod had a major fight between six inmates. Lastly, an assassination attempt was made in one of the tiny tanks over in the C Unit.

In this last incident, a man was attacked in a small space, smashed on sight by the men he lived with. It was a bloody event that left the victim in a pool of blood. The jail had made the call and they moved every gang member of that race to different sections, strangling the problem with a brute force. I won't say what race these guys were, just know that it was no joke. It could pop off at any moment, anywhere, and anyone in the way could get it.

The funny part about Nueces County Jail was that one minute the laughs were billowing out, smiles, and happiness flowing from wounded hearts. The very next minute, fists could fly, and you see a man lying on the ground with his nose leaking out his brain.

There was one guard, a fat Mexican kid, who I apologized to for picking on him during the movie days. I had actually called him to my cell one night to test him. I had said, "When I get out of here, I am going to make a move on the White House; I am going to kill the president!" He had replied, "What do you want me to do about it." I always thought they were obligated to report a threat on the leader of the free world. Thank God this kid was a lazy son of a bitch. He actually turned out to be a pretty nice guy. The guards, for the most part, were pieces of shit. One kid tossed my whole cell just for leaving my door cracked two inches while I walked in the gym. He tore up the only pictures I had of my three children. The images that comforted a broken heart. I wanted to kill him.

Most of the jakes would respect you, as you did them. After I snapped out, I became really respectful and friendly, the model inmate. They all kind of liked me in a way, because as big of a pain in the ass as I was, I was wicked funny. There were a few guards that really took care of me, letting me have major slack at times.

My lawyer came to see me in the box. The diagnosis felt like murder. Things were not looking good. We had this hard ass motherfucker for the district attorney; the guy wouldn't budge. We had a court date set for a bench trial in two weeks. The truth was, I should be a candidate for probation. A first-time felon, no one came close to getting hurt, and the only property that was taken was a three-dollar burger and a fountain coke. Not even a Pepsi!

So, the sentence could be anything from ten years deferred probation to ninety-nine years in prison. Talk about a fucking gambit. There is a lot of room in between those punishments. The jailhouse lawyers in orange had come to the determination that probation was it, even though my lawyer heard fifteen years. Everyone said I was worrying for nothing. It's comforting to hear. Then someone would say the smallest negative comment, and it would send you back to your cell a shattered man. Ruins your fucking day, that's for sure.

When facing a massive sentence as I was, one becomes emotionally fragile. Like sea glass, looking smooth on the exterior but with just a tap, you could be reduced to grains of sand. I was walking with Wheezy almost all day, every day on the weeks leading up to trial. I would say all the time, as kind of a way to lighten the mood, "Wheezy, we got ourselves in a pickle this time." Wheezy would laugh his ass off. He had a lawyer, an expert at getting illegal search and seizures thrown out. I would constantly ask Wheezy, "Is the expert working his magic?" It lightened the mood a little. In reality, we were both scared shitless.

The day before trial was extremely nerve wracking. I bite my nails and always have, but this day there was blood drawn. Around four in the afternoon, I decided to give Martin Scorsese a call. I loved the guy. He was one of the top dog lawyers in Crook City, defending little old me for free. A defense that I later learned would have cost me fifty grand. Even if I were to go to prison, I knew I had the best possible defense that money could buy. He was a White terminator Johnny Cochran type of lawyer. How could you go wrong?

His secretary pitched the call back to him, my heart racing. Some questions were about to be answered. I knew he had met with the DA earlier in the day.

"Mr. Bornagain, how are you today, sir?" His voice sounded grim.

"So, what are we looking at, probation?" I asked with a heavy heart.

His reply was a shotgun blast to the face. "Mr. Bornagain, I have some bad news. The DA is asking for fifteen years in the Texas Department of Corrections. They rejected the insanity defense."

As I hung up the phone, I started to cry. I had seen many men come off that phone on these exact lawyer calls. I don't care if you're the leader of the Latin Kings or Pee-Wee Herman, when you get told that you are going down for a fifteen piece, you cry like a little bitch.

I went back to my cell. I took my white rag towel off the rack, sat on my bunk, and screamed into it. It was a death scene. Every terrible thing that I did, all the loss, grief, and all the misery in my life hit me in one fell swoop. I laid upon the cold compression of the rack. I fell fast asleep in the arms of Jesus. He was all I had left.

Passengers, pay close attention to what is about to happen. Next is an evolution of a legend.

#

What I experienced on the day of trial will blow the human mind. I hope the next part of this grim and honest testimonial shows you that we are not alone, and the ones we love never truly leave us.

I woke in the morning at seven o'clock on the saddest day of existence. The guards who came to my cell were sad and sympathetic.

"Good luck today, Bornagain I really wish you the best," one said sincerely.

I already knew my fate as I walked through the great double-gated exit of 4P. Fifteen years, in one of the most ruthless prison systems in the United States of America. I strangely had the acceptance of a weary Christian heart. My relationship with Jesus will never be accepted by the mainstream Joel Osteen types. I know a Gangster Jesus, one of love and compassion, one who goes to the dark places to save those He loves. The Jesus who found me in the trap house, under the streetlamp, and in the burning confines of a taxi. He came to me shackled in the motel rooms, with the prostitute and the homeless; that's the God I know, the Rescuer and Comforter of the broken-hearted. I had total faith that no matter what the sweet lady judge handed down; God got me.

 We took the elevators down to the basement. I was put into a holding tank that inmates stay in before they are taken through the rancid tunnel between Nueces County Jail and the place of judgment, we all feared. The hour-long wait was full of hope mixed in with criminal lies from the inmates at hand.

 Everyone innocent, everyone going home. All in all, no matter how you slice it, your boy here was on video with a knife, taking property in a local business. My goose was cooked. I just had to take this shit like a man and start my journey upstate. Jesus and I would be duking it out with the scariest gangs in Texas. Needless to say, I skipped breakfast so I wouldn't puke on my poor lawyer.

 The descent to hell began. The tunnel was about a quarter mile in length. Lights hung from a low ceiling on strings, bulbs burning like Jerusalem oil lamps. Ironically with twelve inmates shackled together, sullen and orange clad. Twelve diabolical, tangerine troops on their way to meet destiny. Irons tied together our shaking legs and trembling wrists as we walked connected, single file and strong. Not a soul spoke a word as we took our time trekking to judgment. The walls around us were white. The floor was a plain sidewalk-concrete shade, the kind you would see in Hades.

Leaky pipes above dripped a rusty pink sludge as the sounds of Chinese water torture sang death hymns and the blues. The sounds of the restrictive chains clanged, the stomping of feet, reminiscent of a Nazi March in WW2 Germany. Something in the distance on the left side of the wall caught my nervous attention. A black blob, blurry in the dim lighting of an abyss-style gateway to prison.

I could not believe my eyes as I walked past the object. Within a shackled arm's reach, I saw the same exact make, model, and color of the wheelchair that Barry owned at the time of his death. A tangible sign of God's existence, sitting on the floor. A moment of miracle brilliance where my dad shined through from The Great Beyond.

This wheelchair was in the middle of a tunnel escape, in the center of nowhere. No purpose for it being there. The feeling that "everything was going to be ok" flooded my heart like the acceleration on a 1991 Pontiac Firebird.

After getting off the elevator, we were marched into a full courtroom. Terrence's trial was taking place on this day. He had just been handed down a seventy-seven-year sentence. From what I was told, the largest nonlife sentence ever handed down by the Crook County Court. He was fat, in a tan and gold suit and tie, in full view of every camera the news stations had in their arsenal. He gave me a somber wave in his defeat. He mouthed the words, "You got this," as I waved my goodbye. I was to never see or hear from him again.

The minute the judge released everyone; the cameras receded into the lost beyond through the infested crowd of the courthouse. The court case everyone had come to see was over. Terrence was gone. My lawyer emerged upon the scene like Hunter S. Thompson in a stomping rage.

"Mr. Bornagain, let's go into the deliberation room."

We stood in a private room next to the jury box. I was awaiting the life-altering bad news when he blew my mind.

"We beat the case," he said laughing and jumping up and down.

I returned, "What do you mean we beat the case?" My attorney then laid out the miraculous happenings of the night before my trial.

My lawyer just happened to be at the DA's office after hours. They all worked late, a common practice. He was there on unrelated business and just so happened to have my file in his briefcase, as he was preparing for my bench trial the next day. The DA caseload, on that day, had been switched at random.

A new DA had taken my case last minute. When my lawyer became aware of the switch, he asked the new DA if they would be willing to accept my plea for a "Not Guilty by Reason of Insanity" finding. If found NGRI, I would be found innocent, not even having a felony on my record. There was to be a safety evaluation at the State Hospital in Vernon, Texas before I could be released. Nothing short of a miracle, the DA looked at my file and accepted. On the day of my trial, they would recommend to the judge that I was to be NGRI. The last hurdle was for the judge had to accept and sign the plea.

Moments later, we stood before the judge. I was shaking with fear. She heard the DA recommend the finding, and she addressed me.

"Mr. Bornagain, do you understand the terms and conditions of The State?"

I nodded and said "Yes, your honor."

She said some more that I couldn't make out with my bleeding ears. Hemorrhaging in terror, I watched as she signed the paperwork.

"This case is adjourned." She slammed the gavel, as my lawyer took my elbow and walked us back to the deliberation room.

When we got there, I was in a state of disbelief.

"What just happened?" I asked.

My lawyer explained to me that I had just won my case. I was found Not Guilty. It had stipulations attached, but we had won. This was a big, huge, enormous, win for the squad. "God Squad, all day, erry day!"

My lawyer explained to me that I was to go back to 4P and wait for my transfer to Vernon State Hospital. I was to be assessed for a thirty-day safety evaluation before I could be released. This was Mozart to my Irish ears. I was elated with what God had just performed in my life. My faith had never reached this type of pinnacle. I saw the mountains that could be moved by our creator. I had beaten Goliath, and all because of Jesus. I was led by a bailiff to a tiny box-style waiting cell near the elevators. The happiest one hour I had ever spent stuffed into a can like a shackled sardine.

The chains rolled and opened the second gate at 4P. I returned a champion, on fire and full of gusto. No fame, money, or achievement in the world could have compared to the victory freedom gives.

"I beat the case!" I screamed. The center of 4P was a packed house with Wheezy at the epicenter. The place erupted in applause. I felt like I had just won the esteemed academy award, the one I daydreamed about on the imaginary movie set I once roamed.

We went into a full celebratory mode. A full spread was made in my honor. A New York-style pizza made from a million soups and packaged meats galore. We ate like kings on the heels of one of the greatest underdog stories in Nueces County history. And we didn't even know it. Passengers, I'll get to all that down the road.

I had no clue how long the wait would be to transfer. As days went by, my anxiety was almost nonexistent. I prayed to God, thankful for the miracles He performed in front of my exhausted eyes. I was so grateful, crying as I read Ephesians 6:10 in my daily routine. What was to happen next was one of the best common-sense choices I was to ever make. One that saved my life, once again. All glory to God for allowing me to think clearly enough to make the right decision.

#

One of the leaders at my table came into my cell a few days later. "Boston, we need you to move cells. See, there is a guy who can cut holes in windows really good, they are going to bring up a bunch of dope. We want to get a piece of that."

He was trying to use me as a crash dummy. They wanted me to move cells so when the guy who cut the holes in the window got the delivery, they could stake claim to it because I shared a cell with the window cutter. Real jailhouse bullshit.

"I don't know man. I just beat my case, man. I don't want no part of it," I said. He looked at me in a hateful way. The pause seemed like a fortnight.

"Are you mad at me?" I asked. I was curious, seeing he was over six foot and pure muscle, and had the clout to snap his fingers and have me smashed on sight.

"Nah bro, we'll find someone else." He left my cell.

I was then to watch one of the worst jailhouse blunders in history. A ringside seat to stupidity. This is "Nueces County's Dumbest Criminals".

They found this White kid. He had long hair, a thin beard that ran the line of his cheekbones, and he talked like he grew up in Compton. He donned a huge tattoo on his belly that said somthing in an arch, kind of like Tupac's "Thug Life" ink. They got the guard to do the cell move under the guise of some manufactured racial tension. Once the switch was made, the operation went into overdrive.

Within two days, the holes were cut, and the hole cutter's old lady brought the ice, weed, and rolling tobacco down to the jail. It was to be fastened to a string made of old trash bag strips, like a fishing line. The trash bag fishing line was to be lowered down the four floors to ground level. A paper clip held the homemade basket that was to be hoisted back up with the goodies inside. The hole cutter's old lady also included a ton of rolling papers and ten crack lighters. All the instruments of a jailhouse party now to be at the fingertips of the craving and depressed masses on the inside.

The shit came in on Store Day. Everyone was balling and willing to spend good money. The dope was now in their possession. The crash dummy was to get a cut of the delivery as part of his participation in the crime. As soon as the goods hit the pod, everyone went into the gym and bathrooms and started partying. In the gym, the dummy hits a joint and while exhaling, he says, "We doing it big in the 361." The herb smoke mimicked a stratus cloud, billowing thick and yellow. It looked like the Corpus Christi Sharks arena football team was in a huddle in the corner. In full view of the cameras, everyone toked and snorted their way into blissful happiness.

All was going perfectly...until lockdown. The guard had us all rack up for shift change. During the beginning of the next shift, the new guard started his beginning-of-shift bed check. Those idiots in the cell that cut the windows decided to smoke one more joint before bed. In their cell, the guard sniffed. He then entered at once. He called for a code. Twenty officers showed up, ascending on 4P like a swarm of Africanized killer bees. Soon, I watched from my cell window as mattresses, kill shots, toilet paper, and more were all thrown out onto the tier, shakedown style. They had put some artwork over the holes in the plexiglass that they had sawed through. It was easily discovered by the brass.

The hole cutter and the dummy were whisked away to be questioned at Central Booking. These guys were in deep shit. I later found out that they were both charged with "Introducing a Dangerous Drug into a Correctional Facility" and "Escape." The Escape charge alone starts at a minimum of twenty years in Texas.

Just another day in Nueces County Jail!

#

A few days later, I was in line for the breakfast chow. Wheezy and I were chopping it up, anticipating the opening of the serving line.

"Bornagain…B and B… pack your shit, you're going to The State Hospital," the guard yelled.

Wheezy and I slapped a mean high five and I went to get my bedroll. Wheezy walked me to the gate.

"Wheeze, you're next to get outta this pickle, trust in God and the expert," I said.

We both burst out laughing. I promised I would write to my good friend as soon as I touched down at my new home. Vernon State Hospital, The State of Texas' only maximum-security mental health facility. The one joint that held the worst of the worst. Murderers, rapists, child fuckers, and more.

#

Ok Passengers, we are about to leave Crook City. I'll hit the meter on this crazy cab as we venture nine hours north to a little town outside Wichita Falls, Texas. This is a place like no other, chock-full of pain, misery, and sexual assault. I heard the food is better at The State Hospital, but the conversation is about to get a whole lot more interesting.

Next stop…Vernon Maximum Security Hospital for the Criminally Insane.

Chapter 10

Dark Days Asylum Nights

The wheels of the fifteen-passenger van began to roll away from Nueces County Jail just after six in the morning. It was Marcus, me, and a very senile, elderly man suffering from countless grim and emotional mental illnesses. Bewildered by sunlight and passing cars, I was seeing the earth for the first time in a long time. This was my reemergence into reality and the raw emotion of the fresh air entering my tragic and abused lungs. Walking out of those doors was indescribable. I was still in welcomed denial about the fact that I was being released. How was I to start a new life after this? My only comfort was the changes from within. I knew the ice was a thing in the rearview.

On the nine-hour journey to Vernon, Texas, I had a revelation. God had stripped me to my bare foundations so He may rebuild me into the man He always intended me to be. I was a clean slate. One with spiritual doors blown wide open. Once you cross into the realm, you can never return. Meth lifts the veil off eyes once deceived. Numbers and signs pop, things have meaning, and you see God in everything.

The hard-black plastic lining in the prisoner transport

van was abrasive. I tried to get some sleep to break the monotony of the grueling trip. It was winter and extremely cold. As I laid upon the cold floorboards shackled, I enjoyed viewing the dismal grey cloud cover as miles drifted by. Marcus had a high-profile case. He had stabbed four people where one had passed away. We had court together a few times. Two miracle NGRI findings in the same court, in the same week.

We were instant pals. The most normal guy you could ever meet. I didn't care what he did. He was judged by The State of Texas, and ultimately by God, so who am I to judge? Pretty sad The State of Texas is right under God for the judgement of its citizens. We had some sack lunches packed by the kitchen. Nueces County's last "fuck you" to its once faithful, fulltime residents.

We stopped at a gas station in some nowhere place where the people grimaced at the orange suits and chains. They let us use the bathroom once on the nine-hour voyage. I had put on a little weight; Ma was making sure I was eating well. It was me, some papers, and that ratty old bible that got me to know the Lord. We were well on our way, having already reached the halfway point to the supermax mental hospital where we were to live. The place was that of a legend. Andrea Yates once lived there; the woman made famous by drowning all five of her children, who was also found NGRI.

Passengers, this place was for the most evil. The ones that your grandma whispered about, the creatures your mom warned you not to talk to. This was to be hell. When I awoke, the great fence that surrounded the sprawling compound reminded me of a prison. Mile-high chain link topped with razor wire stared me in the face.

We were in the middle of a field, one that would fall into place on Mars perfectly. I pictured an escaped mental patient running on the horizon wounded after hopping the fence, all while being chased by the bloodhounds and goons. There was no running from this place. We were trapped.

Once the massive gate was retracted, the white fifteen-passenger prisoner transport vehicle parked near the door. When I stepped onto the hardtop, my head swiveled side to side. I scanned the grounds. It looked miles wide. The fence line was endless. The only point of reference was the four skyscraper guard towers, one at each corner of the earth. I waited for angel trumpets to sound as we were led inside a plain brick structure.

Once inside, an orderly met us at once. Shown to a small area, it looked like…well, the waiting room at a hospital. Big foamy seats that sat on the white floor. They were constructed so that if a person were to throw one, it would do minimal damage. The walls were a boring baby blue with hot, white, neon lights burning above. It wasn't long before the three of us were called down a long drab hallway and into the office of a nurse.

"Mr. Bornagain, here at Vernon we do an initial blood draw for the CDC. So, we will need to draw some blood," the nurse said routinely.

My greatest nightmare had become a reality. As she spoke those dreadful words, the frequencies in her voice would allude to boredom. But I got the message loud and clear, even though the fibers in her speech were frayed and cerebral. This was routine for her, but potentially life-altering for me. I was sure my blood was tainted by sin.

She tied my arm off as I sat in a lime-green phlebotomist chair. As the needle slung into my vein, the images of all the times I had fucked up flooded in my mind like a monsoon. The dirty pins off the floor in my room. The filthy unprotected sex I had daily. The bloody straws I had shared; the fistfights where blood transferred between tumbling bodies. Every maniacal mistake I had made, every questionable judgment, and all the risky behavior ran in my mind. I was to be tested for the full gambit, including Hepatitis C, and the granddaddy of them all...HIV.

I was positive I had Hep C...no pun intended. From my research, statistically the first-year needle junkie will have it over sixty percent of the time, and that is your cautious user. I was reckless, at best. The fear of the unknown results of a lab test was scarier than my trial. Ninety-nine years is nothing compared to the long, puss-filled death sentence that AIDS can provide.

They complimented the scare of a lifetime with not one, but two sacked lunches. Ham on white, two in each sack. Juice boxes, fit for a preschooler, and some gummy bears rounded out the post-jail feast. In spite of the shitty Nueces County sack lunch, we were eating as Henry VIII did. Full, dreamy, and docile, we were taken to the unit. Marcus went his way, and I went mine. I bid him farewell and looked forward to a warm bed.

The pod was made up of three spaces. There was a glorified living room with couches and TVs on the wall in each area. One section had a pool table with green leather and wood. The floors were the same manila gray tiles you would find in a mediocre high school in Iowa.

My eyes glared on the domain of the insane. What I saw jarred me. There was a nineteen-year-old man there for beating his mother practically half to death, and almost right as I arrived, he punched another patient. The man's eye concaved into its socket like a rotten pumpkin, soggy and horrid.

I got my first taste of the violent response by the staff. Right before the victim's body hit the floor, four orderlies and a nurse were there to intercept the assailant. The nurse had two syringes the size of hockey sticks in her latex covered hand. The orderlies tackled the man to the floor. He shouted obscenities while the staff tried to talk sense into him. One voice said, "Sir, we are going to put you back in the chair. You can go the easy way, or the hard way. Do you remember last time?" This was not his first rodeo.

Some more staff emerged rolling a gray padded chair on lawn mower wheels. It was clad with thick black nylon straps, buckles, and pins. It was a revamp of a medieval device. He was stripped to his unlaced Nike's and pushed down onto the gray mat of the seat. Four orderlies held him down as he spasmed and struggled, his muscles seizing and groaning as he shrieked and roared while being accosted.

The cap came off a needle the size of a yardstick. I watched the plunger move and the sedative cocktail of Thorazine, Ativan, and Benadryl squirting up mid-air. The chubby Mexican nurse chimed, "Sir, you need to hold still, I could hurt you." With no fear, she stabbed the meatiest part of his arm with the rig. His speech stopped on a dime and his eyes rolled back like a pair of turned-up deviled eggs. His neck went limp. They hit him with a knock-out dose of some of the strongest psych meds known to man. There were two trouble rooms on the unit. The man's lifeless corpse was wheeled into the room on the north side of the unit, barely breathing.

The door remained open; a full-time guard in a cheap classroom chair watched to see if his chest was still moving up and down. Later, I found out that people died all the time at this place. This was Deep Space Nine, the corner of the Milky Way Galaxy's furthest reaches; the place where no one can hear you scream. I knew then that I was on my own, no one was coming to the rescue.

I had a thirty-day stretch in a new, uncharted, and experimental environment. The rules and monsters were different from the County which I had just come from. They were not covered in tattoos, but real demons never are, contrary to societal rules.

I met her on the puke green of the couch. She sat small and meek. Her hair tied up in a bun, grey sweatpants, flip flops, and socks. She wore a pink t-shirt that read "Daddy's Little Girl". She looked like a twelve-year-old reject from an orphanage. Timid and silent, right up until she spoke.

"Do you have any snacks?" she said in an almost fake Ukrainian accent.

"No, I just got here," I murmured.

This was the closest I had been to a woman's body in ten long months. I wasn't paying the tranny's bags of commissary chips just to jack off to their tits in the County. So, this, for me, was my first real taste of a co-ed situation of any kind, in a long time. For a detoxing sex addict, it had been an eternity.

There was a presence about her that made my cock shrivel up like I had just dived into the South Sea. Something slithered deep within the woven knots of her wicked soul. I could see the claws of the beast resting on Daddy's Little Girl. The lyrics to "Cirice" by the metal band Ghost haunted my mind as I sat next to one of the wickedest human life forms in existence. This bitch wasn't there for being bipolar and depressed. You learn too quick where you are at.

This place was for the murderer, the rapist…the crazy cheeseburger thief. Can you imagine my pacifist free spirit around theses hounds of hell? Some were demonic, some were not. This is where the discernment of spirits was imperative to survival. I had this eerie feeling I knew who her "Daddy" was. I think I had some dealings with him in the kitchen at Oakbrook. She sashayed into her room just feet away, directly across from mine, with the TV area separating the male and female rooms. The rooms were set up as two-man quarters with twin beds, tile floors, and one window with reinforced bars. This place was evil encased in concrete.

I asked this tall, mad scientist-looking kid with big circular, wire-rimmed glasses, "Hey, what is that chick in here for? She gives me the creeps."

Jeremy explained to me the backstory of "Daddy's Little Girl". Apparently, she was in a musty two-bedroom hovel alone with her two toddlers, who were around two and four years of age. No one knows the why, but she got it in her head that her children were to die. It was bath time for the toddlers. She took a piece of plywood fiberboard as she entered the room with wild eyes, all the while calm as a cucumber. She placed the fiberboard on top of the bathtub. The infants instantaneously submerged into the warm water. "Daddy's Little Girl" sat atop the board, Indian style, as the pair fought for their young and desperate lives. She was deemed insane at trial, found NGRI, and could someday be released to walk among the living.

As romantic as my NGRI finding may appear, in my experience, a lot of the people that get that finding were let off too easy. In cases like this, the charges are not even listed as convictions. So, we have to take the good with the bad as a society. The view in the public eye is that when a person is insane, they would be better treated in a hospital than in a prison.

Passengers, in a little while, we will expose this whole facade as absolute bullshit.

#

Day two, I awoke for chow at six. I shuffled down to the

dining room. Yes, a dining room. How fancy! They were filled with four-person tabletops built in with circular seats, about ten in all. The serving line was exactly a scaled-down, miniature version of a school cafeteria. Two lunch ladies served fake bacon, powdered eggs, and biscuits. It wasn't the Country Kitchen, but this was not Nueces County Jail either.

The whole hospital was the same throughout. White tile floors with white walls just a shade darker. The halls all had thick wood handrails that ran the length of the hallway, more for decoration than anything else. The corridor, which led to the dining area, had artwork on the wall drawn by the drooling army of Zyprexa-eating vermin that I would grow to despise.

Just before lunch was the med line on the unit. All hats and hoodies were to be removed. This was some show of force by the powers that be so that no one skipped their meds. This was my second dose of pills on the unit. They called my name and I obliged. I usually didn't take my pills until bedtime. On this day, I expected that the doctors had added something new. So, I went and gulped back five large pills with a Dixie cup of water. I was fine for about twenty minutes. Then I suddenly and without warning went south.

I headed for my bed; I felt woozy, and my vision blurred. I stumbled like a drunkard stabbing through the saloon door of some eighteen hundred's mining town. Laying down, paranoid thoughts consumed my mind. I started to salivate buckets of thick salty drool. It came continuously and relentlessly. The spit filled my mouth and drained off my lips, soaking my pillow. I had heard there were drugs in here with this side effect, but this was extreme.

My pulse raced to the point where I could feel it palpitate against my chest plate. I had done every illicit drug known to man in excess since I was a preteen. Never have I felt this close to death in my entire life. There is something dirty and grim about hardcore psych meds. They make you feel as if you have been poisoned. A pollution of the mind that leaves you disoriented for days. The side effects of some of these toxins were mind-bending...no pun intended.

As a drooling, crawling pile of meat, I inched my way to the nurse's station. I looked like one of those double amputee zombies clawing myself across the floor on "The Walking Dead." The staff came to my aid right away.

I stammered, "I think I got the wrong pills. I think I am going to die."

I could barely get the words out. My breath was shallow and broken. They didn't even check my vitals. I was carried back to bed to sleep it off. Rolling the dice of life and death, hanging in the institutional balance.

I woke the next day, feeling as if the HIV death sentence I so feared would be a much-welcomed way to die. I shouldn't have spoken so soon.

"Mr. Bornagain, we need to take you to an appointment," the orderly said.

"Well, what for?" I asked in terror.

She returned, "Well, all we know is there was a problem with your blood work."

I was breathless and terrified as they took me to a transport van at the back of the unit. My death chariot awaited. I was shackled with a softer, nylon system. A sweet change from the cold steel of County. The mental hospital is just as horrifying as jail, it is just presented in a more sanitary way.

Off we went, wheels spinning to Wichita Falls, the closest town to my personal Mars. After listening to some idiotic trap house version of my favorite hip-hop music, we finally coasted into civilization forty-five minutes later. We pulled up to some tan-colored stone monstrosity in a strip mall. Big red letters on the sign read Cancer Center. One of my personal techs for the day went in first, while one stayed behind and kept me guarded. We were then waved through the waiting room, past all the waiting patients, as this seemed to be a special kind of appointment. The youngest person in the lobby had me by thirty years. It looked exactly like where I used to take Barry for his bullshit treatments that had no effect on him living or dying. Oxygen masks were in the nostrils of the praying and dying men in a heaven's waiting room. A depressing vibe, to say the least.

We walked back to the room to meet with the doctor, skipping the legions of sick left gasping for air in the waiting room. They sent in their own tech to do a blood draw. After a quick wait, maybe an hour, a doctor came in to see me.

"Mr. Bornagain, we found some abnormalities in your bloodwork. Upon further testing, we think your spleen is enlarged. We do not know the cause. Further testing will need to be ordered."

She informed me I would need to come back for an ultrasound of my liver. The main cause for the spleen to plump up is cirrhosis of the liver. It wouldn't shock me. I drank harder than almost anyone I know. I made Charles Bukowski look like Jack LaLanne. So, if this was the beginning of the end, I had to take responsibility for a life recklessly lived. Back to the unit I went with no real answers and the AIDS possibility still scaring me.

#

I had a lot of time on my hands for the past ten months. All along in my cell, especially in solitary, I was working on getting down to the root causes of why I drank and later drugged the way I did. I found the relationship with my ma was the biggest one. She loved me, but she had some issues. She also had major issues with my dad. I looked just like Barry, so it was easy to use me as a punching bag when he was not around. A lot had happened in my childhood in reference to this topic. I won't go into graphic details, and here is why, passengers. On this extensive spiritual journey, I have found that letting go is the most important thing we can do when we get clean. I held onto that fierce resentment like a drowning man on a life raft covered in thorns. It was bleeding me out. The more I fought, the more I bled. It was insanity. Sure, my mom was toxic in certain ways. But I should have just kept my distance, loving her from a safe and healthy place.

The second part was that I genuinely liked getting fucked up. I loved the sorrow, the dark dance, and the depressing times. I soaked up the sadness like a bar rag does gin at last call.

The excitement of the party life was the third reason. At first, it was the dive bars and clubs, the backyard BBQs, and being out on the golf courses. Later, I was enchanted with the romantic poeticism of drinking alone, the quiet of a motel room as I hid from my marriage or my problems in business. Drinking was a refuge that I thought would make me more creative. Unfortunately, drinking is a deadly experience. I based my drinking on a reward system. If I worked hard, if I had great success, then I deserved a drink. If I had a tremendous failure, I deserved a drink. I was Irish, that's how we dealt with the reward and the pain. I had a reason for everything. Once I got to jail, I started to realize that was a vice that I no longer needed in my life. Meth proved that I could stop drinking, crazy as that sounds.

Then there was ice. I first loved the porn and raunchy sex, for those were the spirits that possessed me into getting in the game. Next, I loved the cab driving and fast lifestyle. Being a part of the whole scene is just as addictive as the drug itself. Then it was the spirituality. The devil had tricked me into thinking that Jesus was floating somewhere in the bottom of that pipe. I had to look at my life honestly; I had to detox from the game. Going to jail showed me that every relationship from drugs was propped up on lies. The toughest one to let go of was Bella. I just wasn't ready for that. By this time, I was thinking clearly enough to decide the game was not something I was ever going to go back to. Period. Plus, after the insanity, the obsession to use was miraculously torn from my soul for the first time since I was thirteen years old.

 I spent my days walking the massive track with Jeremy and our big friend, Jason. They both worked in the library. Jason was a large guy. He had beaten his dad almost to death in some sort of a psychotic episode. His medication for bipolar was off-balance, and he lost it one night out of the blue. He got into a fight with his elderly father.

 Jason became a great friend. Jason was literally the most gentle, sweetest guy you could ever meet. We spent time talking about football and watching movies together. Wicked funny guy. We would usually laugh at Sarah. She was a thirty-something lady with a debilitating mental disorder. She was the most medicated person I have ever seen, with excessive drooling and closed eyes as she walked around nude in the TV room. We laughed only because we would be having a normal conversation while watching "Dancing with the Stars," and Sarah would appear between us on the couch, naked as a jaybird. Or was it a jailbird?

 "Hey guys, what's going on?" She would ask. She was a gawky, six-foot tall White girl with crazy black hair. The smell of her vagina alone would have us heading for the hills, dying of laughter.

Jeremy was that mad scientist-looking guy. He had killed the chief of police in his hometown. A traffic stop went bad, and, for whatever reason, he ended up smoking the old cop with a pistol he had in the console. He too had been found NGRI. One of the most docile, sarcastic, funny creatures I have ever encountered. Guys like that keep you sane. The environment around you can drive you nuts...no pun intended.

The crazy talk was the worst part of Vernon. I mean, you would be at a picnic table talking to one of the girls, and she would tell you her kids were being held captive and raped in China. It's all bullshit in her head kind of talk, but to hear it all day really starts to affect you. The graphic details of child rape are horrifying delusions, and for it to come up in a random conversation is beyond disturbing.

Next, was all the crazy real-life crimes you would hear about. I was sitting down, chatting with a girl I had just met. She was a normal run of the mill forty-year-old woman. For the State Mental Hospital system, she was kind of cute. You can't hug, kiss, or touch anyone whatsoever, but it is nice to chat with a person of the opposite sex. It gives you a feeling of normalcy in your life in a not so normal situation. Then, I asked her why she was there. She explained to me, without batting an eye, that she had gotten into an argument with her seventy-five-year-old mother and anally raped her with a pickle. I thought she was a delusional case with a vivid imagination. But not even close. Her tale was later confirmed as true by a staff member.

Some of the staff and patients at Vernon were having intimate relationships. There was this hot staffer. A tech with a booty the size of Arkansas, short brown hair, and a huge rack. She was a cute Mexican, well put together and sweet. She was bringing in cigarettes and weed for a guy she had struck up a relationship with. There was a rumor that this wasn't the first time she fucked around with patients at the hospital. Now, having an inappropriate relationship with a patient had stiff penalties with the law. You would be looking at jail time. I think these staffers that participate are not so much sucked into the relationships as much as they just get a cheap thrill out of it. And three to one, its women staff fucking around with male patients, rumor has it anyway.

The sexual relationship that took the cake during my time at Vernon was between two patients, Richard and "Daddy's Little Girl". Richard was a tall Black dude in his fifties. He was a quiet man of Jesus who played the organ in the chapel on Sundays. He was also an avid Satanist. Talk about being confused. He was about six foot two inches, two hundred and fifty pounds, and had a neatly trimmed beard. Richard was a real-deal serial killer. There were lots of them in this state hospital. He was accused of killing a string of prostitutes from Louisiana to Texas. His M.O. was to beat their heads in with a bowling pin, of all things. Then he would stuff a dead bird in the cadaver's mouth and dump their body in a densely wooded area. He had seven victims in all. Staff would confirm all these arrest stories. They had access to files with the criminal case details on each patient. They could get in major trouble under the HIPAA Act if it were discovered they were divulging confidential information on their patients, as it was highly illegal. No matter what kind of scumbags these people were, they had rights. I am not sure why staff risked their jobs the way they did by sharing information. I think there were certain ones that were addicted to gossip.

Richard had been dodging his trial for years, drawing out his insanity defense by purposely flubbing his competency test. That's what Vernon really was below the surface, a place the courts sent crazy people to get just un-crazy enough to stand trial. They would ask questions during the test like, "What is a judge?" or "What does a lawyer do?" If you passed the fifteen-question test, you were sent back to face your crimes. It's called being a 46B in Texas. Patients classified as 46B had not been to their trial yet, like Marcus and me. We were 46C's, already found not guilty, and only there to have a safety evaluation so The State of Texas didn't get sued if we were to reoffend.

    Well, the story goes that Richard and "Daddy's Little Girl" had established some sort of a romance. They would walk the massive two-mile track around the border of the hospital, near the fence line. They never held hands or kissed, but rumor has it that "Daddy's Little Girl" had given Richard a pair of her dirty, pink-laced panties, and he was caught jerking off into them. There were no consequences to this find because they couldn't prove where or who he got them from.

    Eventually, they found a way to sneak around to an area of the campus where cameras couldn't see them. Speculation was that staff had been bribed so that this peculiar couple could go undisturbed to have sex either in a closet, the bushes, or somewhere else. The location of the sexual act was not clear. The part that was clear was "Daddy's Little Girl" came from the doctor's one morning and she was pregnant. Staff confirmed this information to other patients, as did she. I asked her myself.

    She had been locked up a year already, and she was only a few weeks pregnant. That fully confirms that she had become pregnant within the walls of Vernon State Hospital. Not long after, Richard was sent packing to a different state hospital. He was sent to Rusk State Hospital in none other than Rusk, Texas, an even smaller and way shitter place to be. They even let the two lovebirds have a one-hour meeting to say goodbye before Richard was to ship out.

Passengers, just to summarize the whole fiasco, two mental patients got together and fucked in a maximum-security mental facility. Both were notorious and high-profile killers. She got pregnant, and we're about to have the "Seed of Chucky" in our state, Texas' first little serial killer baby. I wonder if the adoption agency the baby went to disclosed that little bit of information.

My lawyer had warned me that there was going to be full surveillance. It was rumored that the State Hospital system monitors and logs all behaviors of its patients, mining information and movements, and keeping track of a change in moods and actions, all so they could disprove people who are trying to fake insanity. "Playing the Role" was a popular tactic by felons to try and beat the system. I found it ironic that the man infamous in his city for being the "guy in the movie," a person who was paranoid about being watched by a system of cameras everywhere he went, was now being clocked by the eye in the sky.

There was a minimum of four cameras in each room. One in each corner, and some rooms had them dead center as well. They had night vision cameras in the two home theaters Vernon had built. Seating for about thirty, two decent size movie theaters were constructed to give its residents, well…a break from watching TV.

There were some classes at Vernon, but I wouldn't call them therapeutic. For example, one class was *Video Games*. One hour a day, patients could enjoy all the old Nintendo games, GameCube, and PS4. Not the most beneficial thing for a bunch of criminals attempting to be rehabilitated, but it got you out of your head for a little time each day.

The class I grew to loathe was art. The people in the State Hospital were sick. Legally disabled human beings that if, and when, discharged could pull a social security check from the United States Government. Boxes full of thick colorful crayons and pencils laid upon the tables in the dining hall. A cheap CD/boombox combo sat next to the teacher, constantly playing classic pieces from the Seventies. There were four stacks of paper laying there for you to choose from. All were traceable outlines of elephants, frogs, trees, and other generic shapes and creatures. We were to sit as if we were some heavily medicated kindergarteners trying to stay within the lines, while forced to stay within the walls.

The shame and self-hatred I experienced every day was paramount. Here I am, Boston Bornagain, once the top vacation rental salesman in one of the largest markets on the Texas Gulf Coast, doing an assignment fit for my firstborn son. Once I was the man responsible for the day-to-day operations at a six million dollar a year company. I was now reduced to coloring with a belly full of psych meds as "The Piano Man" played at high volume.

One cannot begin to explain the slow burn, the smoldering pool of kerosene within one's soul, building and heading for the flashpoint. I was a 46C. If I were to have any kind of outburst, I would be subject to further evaluation. If all I had to do was eat this putrid and rotten crow for a few more weeks, that's what I was going to do, and with a smile.

The first authentic piece of a carnivorous product I ingested since that fateful day in the burger joint, and even that is debatable. Jeremy and I would go to the canteen twice a week. If you were lucky enough to have money on your books, you could enjoy one of the best cheeseburger's money could buy even in the free world. I ordered extra bacon, extra cheese, mayo, and told them to drag it all the way through the garden. And on the side? A double order of chili-cheese tater tots. The canteen looked like a mom-and-pop restaurant, four-top booths with wood grain, a flat-screen TV on the wall, and a full counter to order from. It was a diner-style joint. The short-order cooks even rang a little chrome bell when your food was ready. It was a welcomed taste of home. Food is the only escape you have in a place like this. The madness in the speech of your peers is beyond belief. The soothing taste of bacon grease strangely comforts the soul as the world around you goes mad.

#

My second trip to the Cancer Center was terrifying. The fear of the unknown felt paralyzing and black. Once again, the cold gaze of the elderly in the waiting room doused me in shame. Something about the shackles, they looked at me like a murderer being led through the town square. Once in the back, I was to see a tech for an ultrasound on my liver. I laid upon my back, staring at a black and white screen, the kind where new mothers see an unwanted fetus in an abortion clinic. Also, the same screen that an expecting set of newlyweds view the heartbeat of the love that God has given them. Defining irony in almost every way.

For me, I was to see the tissue of the organ that has been in the crosshairs of a full-on alcoholic assault since I was thirteen. A life of damage and recklessness about to be viewed on closed-circuit TV. It was the eeriest feeling; with the same exact notion I had experienced in the tunnel on the way to face fifteen-years. I did the crime and I had to face the consequences. In my mind I knew I had hepatitis, and the years of drinking had surely led to cirrhosis of the liver. All in all, it was my fault.

Latex-laced fingers squeezed a tube of ice-cold jelly.

The farting noise prompting a chuckle from a man facing death. The tech's hands massaged the goo into the flesh on my right side.

A plastic, rubber instrument that came to the shape of a "T" was placed over my liver. I saw a blob on the screen. Only professional eyes would be able to determine my fate. She snapped photos; screenshots later to be viewed by an actual medical doctor, an expert in the field. I got up from the table feeling nervous. I had a flashing vision of my children. My babies appeared every time in my mind's eye when I was facing difficult life-and-death circumstances, lost on the street, in jail, and now. Was I about to die? After all that I had been through, I didn't want to meet an end like this. Another appointment was booked. The results would be in at that point. A complete diagnosis of my enlarged spleen, and its cause would be determined.

The doctors never said anything about HIV or hepatitis, and I was too scared to ask. So, the fear of the unknown still sat in the pit of my stomach every minute of every day. I started to question things about mental health treatment at the State Hospital. These past weeks, I had not received any therapy of any kind. No doctor in a room, no couch to lay on. This was a glorified daycare, for the state's most hated criminals.

I spent the following days going to ridiculous classes, walking the massive hardtop path around the grounds, and watching TV. They passed out snacks twice a day. Graham crackers, milk, Jell-O, and whatever else they had. My favorite was Rice Crispy treats. You were not allowed to share. However, a lot of patients were too sick to eat. The medications made appetites already thin go completely absent in a select few. I would stalk the room, begging for whatever I could get my hands on. Some nights, four snacks and four cartons of milk right before bed. The Dietician on staff told me the average weight gain for a new patient was between thirty and seventy pounds. After months of not eating for five days straight while in the game and the starvation at Nueces County Jail, I was basking in the double size portions and snacks. I was getting fat.

The maximum-security hospital didn't fuck around. If you acted up, you got the chair. I saw it used more than a few times. Patients feared the chair. Its constrictive physical properties were torture. The drugs would make the victim a zombie for at least one full day after being hit with, what we called, the rhino dart. Many times, I would see a wholly psychotic person think about popping off, go to stand up, only to sit back down and shake it off once the chair was threatened. The chair wholeheartedly worked to prevent outbursts; even the insane would think twice about going off on a disorderly tangent. Nurses had the rhino darts preloaded in the fridge at the beginning of the shift. Vernon was no joke, and the staff kept the residents in line to the point where, for the most part, it was safe and quiet.

About thirty days into my arrival, I was told I would need to pass what's called a DRB. The Danger Review Board was a group of doctors that sat in offices all over the state. As the convicted party, you would be inaugurated into a virtual courtroom, which is set up just like a real courtroom with pews, a witness seat, and an elevated position where the judge would sit. Everyone is in their own settings, as the courtroom is empty in real life. In place of a judge, the lawyers, and the other participants was a massive projector that stood behind the judge's bench that would project cubes, like a small TV within a TV, where the doctors that held your fate in their virtual hands would be broadcast via satellite. Daunting, to say the least, that you never get to personally meet some of the people that hold your life in their hands.

The DRB results determined if a patient was going to be deemed safe or unsafe to proceed to their next treatment phase. If deemed safe, one would be transferred to a lower-security hospital. In these less restrictive environments, phones were easily accessible, care packages could be received, among other perks. If you were to be deemed unsafe, it would be six more months at Vernon before your next review board meeting.

Judgment day was fast approaching. I met with a counselor and was told that I would be judged based on my behaviors since the arrival to my current setting. If deemed safe, I would be moved to the San Antonio State Hospital. He further informed me that I should be there for approximately two weeks before being released back into free society! I was ready to return to life as a born-again man, with a newfound relationship with Jesus Christ, and help others by telling my horrifying addiction story combined with a story of hope through our Lord and Savior.

I quickly lined up a place to stay upon my release. I found a little trailer home, as well as a job washing dishes for a friend of Wheezy's that owned a Mexican restaurant. I was all set! I planned on staying clean and was excited and ready to find my next path in life.

I stood before the DRB early on a Friday. A man in a pressed, white shirt and tie with big, framed glasses, and a mustache sat as the moderator. Two older female physicians and one male physician, all in different locations around Texas, reviewed my file before joining us for the virtual meeting.

"Mr. Bornagain, we have reviewed your behavior and all of the records from your primary doctor. We will now put to vote the decision to move you to a less restrictive hospital."

The doctors put the meeting audio on mute. After just a few minutes of discussion, they had reached a verdict.

"Mr. Bornagain, we would like to inform you that you have been deemed safe by today's Danger Review Board."

I was elated! I was on my way home. Almost a full year had gone by since my arrest and I was ready for a break in life. First, I would need to make a quick detour to the San Antonio State Hospital, but after what I had put myself through, two weeks would be a cinch!

I spent the next few days saying goodbye to all of my new friends at Vernon. Jeremy, Jason, and even the girl who anally raped her mom with the pickle! It was a bittersweet time; I hated leaving them behind in such a crazy place. But I was ready to get the fuck back to the free world. Or simply "the free" as a lot of us called it.

It was a strange feeling not being in the movie anymore. There had been months of looking over my shoulder while on the outside, as well as times of extreme paranoia and hysteria while in Nueces County Jail while still committed to the movie's truth. Once I was mentally released from the self-induced meth psychosis, I spent countless hours reviewing the events of my past, and even to this day, I am still trying to make sense of it all. That deep of psychosis, that massive of a spiritual journey, full of wonders, signs, and miracles, would leave anyone in a state of confusion. It all left my head spinning. To go to bed one-night crazy, and to wake the next sunrise completely healed, was insanity…no pun intended. It took a long time to really feel as if Them/They were a ghost of the past, a delusional fragment of a mind in lunacy. I trust and accept that God showed me an exceptional proportion of His wonders during my obsession with Them/They. I believe the whole psychosis was another dimension, an elevation to a new consciousness. Meth opened spiritual doors in my mind, allowing God to put me on a path to healing from my out-of-control and deadly addiction to alcohol, as well as an eventual complete healing from all addictions, albeit a dangerous one, and one that I stand firm in opposition of today. God works in mysterious ways, and what happened to me is beyond belief and not recommended or something I advocate for others to try. We each have our own journey. My journey through indirect spiritual dimensions allowed me to see the world through a lens where evil was apparent, and God's love was everything. The material things around us that we see as real are just temporary holograms on a passageway to the heavens. Life is nothing but a test to see who acknowledges God, and who allows pride to blind them to the Creator.

#

I had one of those famous sacked lunches with me for the trip to San Antonio, equipped with an extra vanilla pudding! The bus trip was short, seeing as I slept the whole way. The property was beautiful, gothic, and sprawling. Rolling green hills were lined with a brick structure that sat far off in the distance. A compound of Draconian proportions topped with a massive admission's building that looked like it was off the set of some well-produced horror film. Open since the eighteen hundreds, the practices and treatments for the mentally ill were that of an urban legend.

The horrendous history of San Antonio State Hospital followed the building to its present day. Stories of evil wicked physicians literally mashing out the frontal lobes of their patients were later confirmed by my doctor while in group therapy. Back then, San Antonio State Hospital was the trash bin where the states' super-wealthy threw their unwanted problems. There had been a vast spectrum of patients admitted.

Anything from slow and mentally challenged, gay, pregnant youth, to people with mental disorders were all gladly accepted and remained residents for an indefinite period of time.

Once these patients arrived, the medieval staff would strap them down, take a long instrument with a tiny hook on the end, and jab it into the hole where the tear duct meets the nose. They would thrust it side to side, tearing into the frontal lobe, pureeing the minds of the victim. This would leave the patient in a docile trance-like state for the rest of their life. Nowadays, they do the same thing, just with pills.

I entered the admissions building victorious. This was the final leg of the tour. I only had to make it two more weeks and I was a free man! The admissions process required another blood test, more questions, and as always, fear. You can never say you're truly free until the judge releases you on paper. So, I had to go at this in the right frame of mind, on my best behavior, and with the balls of a gorilla.

Another white, fifteen-passenger van took me from the admissions building to my new home at Crockett Unit. There were about eight units at San Antonio State Hospital, all set up exactly the same. Cookie-cutter buildings to house the criminally insane of the Lone Star State. It was a one-level brick building. Once inside there were two hallways, housing about twenty people on each side. The Crockett Unit was co-ed, men and women in dorms with the two groups separated by a Day Room.

I walked in with my duffel bag which was now full of civilian clothes. My ma had put money on my books at Vernon and they would take an order for a Walmart run. I had real t-shirts, basketball shorts, socks, and sneakers. I felt like the dude in ZZ Top's "Sharp Dressed Man" video. You know, after wearing the same orange jumper for almost a year, it felt good.

Walmart be damned, I was stylin' and profilin'.

I was shown to my room. Two windows against the back wall, a wood grain bench running underneath. A steel grate over each window. Four twin beds, with baby blue hospital blankets and cheap flimsy pillows. That was my set-up for the next two weeks. I put my belongings into the wood dresser and headed to the Day Room to meet my new playmates.

The first encounter was with a beautiful, young, Black female. She wore huge fake eyelashes, a sexy blonde wig, and was dressed exceedingly well for a mental hospital.

"Hi, what is your name?" She asked.

"I am Boston, can you show me around here?" I said in return.

"Sure, follow me," she said with the most perfect smile.

The Day Room was a big open space. White tiles shined on the floor, freshly mopped. A row of windows faced the front of the unit. There were wood-trimmed couches with an ugly green and white print pressed upon faux leather. Two separate TV watching areas were contained in their own separate row, one on each end of the pod. The TVs were encased in wooden entertainment centers. A pane of unbreakable plastic glass separated them from flying fists and other objects routinely thrown in rage.

The back wall was a nursing station. Maybe five feet deep, same white tiles with a green, wrap-around countertop that also sat behind fortified glass for the same flying fists and objects, only this was not to protect a TV, it was to shield the staff. The nursing area is where you would fill out written request forms, complaints, and to see the doctors for Treatment Team Meetings. The patient utilized this meeting to converse with their doctors, social workers, and other team players, as well as get updates on their open court cases. Opposite the nursing station was an office for the psychologist.

In the female hallway, there was a dining room. More white tiles, more big windows...see the theme here? This section overlooked the track and exercise area, which was outside. The dining room had a total of ten of the four-person tables, drab white tops, and heavy chairs that were not to be easily thrown. The stand-up fridge, which held the nighttime snacks, sat in the back corner.

In each hallway was a bathroom with a combination of a bathroom and shower. Each of these rooms were the size of a lavatory you would find in a mall or your local sporting arena. These rooms were the scariest places of all at San Antonio State Hospital. A checkered pattern of sadness had you traipsing on tiny green and white tiles multiple times a day. On one side were two urinals and four stalls that held stainless steel shitters, with the larger handicapped one at the end. The toilets were shallow causing a repulsive splash to strike you on your ass with every excrement. The flushes were bionic and powerful. On the other side was the place I feared most. The showers had six stalls, these deep concrete caverns with the same tiny green and white tiles from the floor. Lukewarm water ran out of chrome showerheads. You could hear the leaking drops from your bed like Chinese water torture come to life.

The first rinse I took in this dreary sexual bathhouse was putrid and dim. Inmate patients lived out gay sexual fantasies just by walking by you in the shower. My first night was a preview into the daily shame I was to feel as I cleansed my body, an action all humans should have the right to do in privacy. Every time one of these perverts would sneak a peek of my dick, it would take everything in me not to beat in their skull.

The second day at San Antonio State Hospital was a gut punch that still makes me cringe, even to this very day when I recall its events. I had my first Treatment Team Meeting. Dr. Kahn looked like an eighth-grade science teacher. She was a short woman of five foot, three inches. She had sandy, curly hair that went to her shoulders. She wore reading glasses upon her head. Khaki pants housed the biggest thighs you have ever seen. She ran the Crockett Unit as the Chief Psychologist and Unit Director.

My fate laid in the hands of this woman, one hundred percent. She was an expert on 46C patients and therefore, on safety evaluations. San Antonio State Hospital was not a hospital that specialized in NGRI cases; they were just getting into that area of expertise. So, this lady was brought in to establish and run the 46C model at the hospital.

"Hello Mr. Bornagain, how was your first night on the unit?" She asked.

"It was ok, I just can't wait to go home," I returned politely.

She looked at me puzzled like I was gravely mistaken about my situation. "What do you mean by that, Mr. Bornagain?" She asked.

In response, I said, "Well, my treatment team at Vernon said I would be here about two weeks, then I would go home."

She sat back and flipped her reading glasses onto her eyes. She looked at my chart and sighed. "Mr. Bornagain, I don't know why they have been telling people that up at Vernon. The process ahead for you statistically would be a three-and-a-half to five-year evaluation for someone with your kind of charge. This was a very serious crime we had here. We need to make one hundred percent sure that you are not a danger to the community before we turn you loose."

At that moment, I died. This revelation was one of the worst of my life. I couldn't last three-and-a-half-years in this place. No way, no how. The crazy talk, the perverts? I just couldn't face this reality. Not long after, we wrapped up our meeting. I quickly exited, grabbed the cordless phone, and called my mother.

I was crying, "Ma, they are talking three-and-a-half to five-years in here."

My mother was now weeping right along with me, "Oh my God, Boston, I love you, we will get through this, ok?"

I sobbed for over an hour with my mother. This is someone who had been my adversary. I had faced a lifetime of distress from her; yet, she was the only soul on earth to console me. She was all I had. She was the one person who loved me unconditionally during this insane and horrifying incarceration.

I gave her my address and asked her to send me a huge box of chocolate, candy, and other goodies. She knew that food would be the only security blanket I had, and I was in desperate need of a care package. In the weeks to come, I was to get the full experience of this lower security hospital. But on this day, neither of us knew yet of the murderous atrocities that were taking place within the walls of the Crockett Unit.

Days went by and all I did was watch TV, staying bored out of my mind, and terrified from all the fights I had witnessed. There were at least four good-sized fistfights a day on Crockett. Blood was shed, eyes blackened, and whistles blown. Whenever a fight would ensue, the first staff member to see it would blow a whistle that hung from a rope around their neck. The call for help was followed by a sea of techs in green hospital scrubs, running to aid in the takedown of the aggressor.

A major difference I noticed during my first week in San Antonio State Hospital was their "No Restraints Policy." The staff were not allowed to touch a client unless they were actively attacking another person. So, in essence you could beat someone senseless, hear the whistle, and when staff approached, as long as you backed off, you could simply walk away. There was no takedown, there was no chair. It would simply go in your file, and it would go against you in court.

This alerted me to some other shocking policies at San Antonio State Hospital that were created as a result of Texas laws regarding treatment of mentally ill patients. If a staff member were to put their hands on a client without it being in the commission of the patient committing a violent act, the tech could be charged with assault. This led to a culture of fear within the techs, and rightfully so. They couldn't even do their job effectively due to the bullshit laws written at the state level in Austin. This coupled with the "No Restraints Policy," created the perfect climate for violent and predatory criminals to wreak havoc without consequence. I found it to be a hundred times more dangerous in this lower security hospital than anywhere else I had stayed so far on this wild and debilitating journey. I was legitimately scared most days.

You could be at chow minding your own business when all of a sudden Connie, the hepatitis C infected prostitute, would walk up and break your nose. Maybe she had heard voices that told her you killed her children? Delusion was an everyday reality in the mind of the afflicted. In Connie's head, you were the enemy. She was right and justified in splattering your nose cartilage onto the floor. Connie would be talked to, her file noted, and next thing you know, she is on her way to noon meds. That's it. No cops, no repercussions.

If you were a victim of a violent physical or sexual assault at San Antonio State Hospital, the police could be called upon request. After waiting hours for them to show up, a report would be made that noted the incident and facts involved. However, no formal charges could be pressed until that patient was released. Upon the victim's release, in order for charges to be filed, they would have to go down to San Antonio Police Department headquarters to speak to a detective. Only then would formal charges be filed.

The thing to remember is that most patients will be at San Antonio State Hospital for years, not months. So, let's say for example, that "Jimmy" sexually assaults "Sally." She fills out a report at the hospital with the San Antonio Police. After the police leave, a year and a half go by. "Sally" has schizophrenia, and she is mentally low functioning; she suffers from memory loss and delusions. What are the chances that she is going to head down to file the charges after all that time has lapsed? Slim to none, at best. When she got there, would anyone take her seriously? The State Hospital system in Texas is the Wild West, and when on the inside, you better learn how to take it on the chin almost every day.

Sitting in the Day Room was like watching a psycho circus with no peanuts. It had a ringmaster, tigers, lions, and bears, oh my! It also had pedophile rapists. Many times, I would be sitting there, and I would look over at a chair in the corner. A male client, who knew full well what they were doing, would be jacking his dick off as the females made their way to the dining room.

Just like the commissary day in jail, there was store day at San Antonio State Hospital. I would watch the high-functioning criminals target the low-functioning, mentally challenged people. It was so sad to watch as these demons conned this poor person, with the mind of a child, out of all the snacks their family bought for them. It was like watching a flock of seagulls devour a dropped hotdog bun on North Beach.

The depression was draining and debilitating for me, in every way. I would find myself crying in the shower twice a day. I could literally feel myself slipping mentally during my first two months at San Antonio State Hospital.

I was totally sane in the throes of madness all around me. It was an assault of lunacy punctured with the absence of outside stimuli that could break the human spirit. The only tastes of home were my daily phone calls to Ma and my kids. Those phone calls were the only thing that kept me hanging onto life, and the hopes to one day make it home.

#

Then she walked into my life. A person that would teach me all about compassion, love for others, and the deep, dark places the mind can wander. Eve was a transgender male to female resident, my new roommate, and a person deeply affected by a grave mental illness. She was rail-thin with long dark brown hair that was shoulder length and crinkly-curly looking. She had burned it with high heat and chemicals. She wore old sundresses, shoes far too small, and women's panties donated by the hospital. They allowed her to live as a woman, and she was loving it.

The first few weeks, I would listen to Eve as she talked to herself on the edge of her twin bed. She bantered on for countless hours about the rapes she endured in the group homes where she had grown up. Early in life, her family discarded her back when she was still Doug. This poor, lost, little boy with the sweetest soul was deeply affected by schizophrenia and mental challenges. Doug was too much for his family to handle. Violent outbursts forced his family to give him up to the sacrificial altar that is the group home system. Doomed from the start, overdosed on psych meds, and subject to all kinds of abuse, Doug became Eve.

I would sit and talk with her for hours. She would burst into tears almost by the minute. It was in my nature to console her broken heart. After all, there was a human being, a child of God, within the tormented shell that most people could not see through. The nighttime was the hardest.

I was forced to learn to sleep in the same room with Eve while she screamed at full volume for most of the night. Sometimes I would be wide awake and see her pass out from exhaustion after hours of screaming. I would remain wild eyed as the hollowed cries of the tormented souls lingered in the sound waves. Ghosts of real-life people, overshadowed by demonic possession and the effects of mental illness, stayed lurking in the halls. Once again, I found myself on Team No Sleep. I was feeling my soul wearing thin. My will to go on was weak and fading. I was a hologram of the man who arrived at San Antonio State Hospital just a few months before.

#

I had a meeting with Dr. Holden, who was an older Black guy about seventy years old. He worked directly with Dr. Khan, the leading physician on my floor. Dr. Holden was my psychiatrist, the real MD that would sign off on my release. I went to Dr. Holden for some new meds. I could not sleep and was cracking mentally. Without Meth, going without sleep for more than three days could drive a person insane. I was living off months of broken sleep at this point. So, I begged him to have mercy on me, and he did. He switched me to some high-powered anti-psychotics; the main side effect was deep sleep. They worked well for the first four days. I slept right through the all-night screams just a few feet away, belted out by Eve.

As the drugs built up in my bloodstream, I was noticing some changes. The effects were becoming less beneficiary. I was starting to wake up in the middle of the night. The second thing I noticed concerned me the most. My dick was dead as a doornail.

On the first day that I detected this, I chalked it up to nervousness. The fear of getting caught masturbating in the shower, perhaps? Maybe the presence of men around me as I tried to make love to myself? Basically, I thought it had to be the environment around me giving me performance anxiety.

The second day of this discovery really had me worried. I used some lotion to spice things up a bit as I took a shower. Now passengers, by now you know I am a sexual mastodon. The one thing in life I have never had a problem with is getting a hard on. So, when I was beating it like it owed me money and there was no reaction, I began to panic.

By day three, I was angry and frustrated. I took five showers Nothing. It was like I was pawing at a lifeless Vienna sausage for forty-five minutes. I toweled off a broken man. I thought to myself, *if I can't make love, kill me now*. I can't describe the emasculating feeling you get when your manhood and sexual purpose gets chemically snatched away like a purse in Seventies' Harlem.

I wrote a request for an urgent meeting with Dr. Holden, but I wouldn't be able to see him until the morning. I kept at it thinking back to the nastiest most vulgar sexual experiences of my life. As you know, I had plenty in the "Spank Bank." The next twelve hours were a series of failed attempts to pump my pathetic dead member with blood that was just not present. I was suicidal. I had lost a normal body function, one that determined my love life and very happiness. I couldn't breathe. I guess sex is important to me. I think that much is safe to say, passengers.

At nine sharp on the fourth day, I stormed into Dr. Holden's office, "I am not taking these fucking pills, none of them. I want off all this bullshit now!" I exclaimed.

He looked at me and said, "Mr. Bornagain, what seems to be the problem? Are you having side effects?"

In response I said, "Side effects? My cock is like Kennedy. Dead!"

We talked in great detail about my erectile dysfunction. But this next part is the single greatest and significant turning point in the State Hospital story. The moment it all started to unravel.

I told him, "You know Dr. Holden, I don't need these pills. I was in meth psychosis. I have never had a problem before I did drugs or after I snapped out of it in jail."

He looked extremely puzzled. He asked, "Are you telling me that you were on drugs at the time of the crime?"

I responded, "Yes, and the seven hundred and fifty days leading up to the crime. I told the doctor, the court...everyone knew that."

He was amazed. He explained to me that any type of drug use of any kind disqualified you for an NGRI finding.

He immediately called in Rochelle, my social worker. She is the woman who would talk directly to the courts. She was a smug little woman with puffy blonde hair. She was a bit chunky, and she always wore black dress slacks, black mid-pumps, and flowery blouses. She looked like an antique pin-up, one that had been through the ringer from years of drinking and aging too fast. She was pissed, to say it mildly.

"This is impossible, Mr. Bornagain. This just doesn't happen."

I chuckled while saying, "Well, obviously it happened. I

am sitting here, right?"

She didn't think I was funny, not in the least. We had an in-depth conversation. My heart raced as I recounted all the details of my trial while she took notes for my file. She looked decidedly concerned.

After I finished my long story, she told me, "Mr. Bornagain, someone like you should not have been found NGRI. I need to take this information to the courts. We need to see what this means for your evaluation and how we will move forward."

I just couldn't shut my mouth, "Well, my lawyer gave me the option. He told me to sign the papers, and I would be out in thirty days. What would you have done?"

She looked at me, as Dr. Holden cringed, and said, "Well, I would have told the truth. I would have taken the prison sentence."

I was now the one who was pissed, "If you sit here and tell me that you would have taken fifteen years in TDC over coming to a hospital for thirty days, I'd say you're a Goddamn liar."

She sat back in her chair, her back arched like the back end of her seat was a cactus. A screaming match ensued. Dr. Holden broke it up, "Look, we need to confer with the courts on these new developments, Mr. Bornagain. This is going to be something that markedly changes the trajectory of this case. In the meantime, I will take you off all these medications. We will monitor you very closely and see how you act. If nothing happens, we will leave you off the pills."

Dr. Holden had spoken. He was the be all, end all when it came to my treatment. Not Dr. Khan, and certainly not Rochelle. Dr. Holden was the alpha and omega.

So, it began. I was one of the only patients ever to not

be on any medication of any kind at San Antonio State Hospital. As the days ticked by, my mind, soul, and my cock were all back to normal and in standard working condition. I was off the Lithium, Zyprexa, Seroquel, and whatever else I was taking.

After being clean for about seven days, I felt like a million bucks! Every day, as I continued to sit out during med line, I began to see myself as a champion in my own eyes. I wasn't crazy and I was going to prove it. I was going to get the fuck out of San Antonio State Hospital, by any means necessary.

As my mind cleared from the toxic zombie drugs, for the first time in years, I felt like myself. I dare say the best version of me that there had ever been. It was around this same time that the violence and mayhem really started to go wild on Crockett Unit. The bleak dispiriting conditions really started to surface, and I started to see how it all really worked.

#

Juan was a guy from a little town outside San Antonio. He was a full-fledged member in a ruthless Mexican prison gang. He was "Playing the Role" to beat three major dope cases. Him and I became the greatest of friends. He was your typical standard dude trying to beat an enhanced twenty-five to life sentence for dealing ice. Sad to say, he had been set up by his much younger girlfriend. She was busted first and turned snitch. She agreed to give him up and in turn, she was released unscathed. He was out on bond on the first charge, but he decided to continue hustling. He was an IV user, and an addict will always go to what they know. Addicts simply do not possess the functionality to learn a new way to make a living while using. He couldn't just leave the money, the drugs, or the pussy. The game had Juan by the balls. He didn't know yet that his girl was in fact, the confidential informant. As far as he was concerned, she was still on the team at that point.

She made a call and set him up again. When they came to the crib, she let them in, and he got snagged for three ounces. Now he was out on bond for two arrests, and they ended up finding an eight ball in his pocket during a routine traffic stop. He was toast. In Texas, three felonies of the same pedigree start at twenty-five and go up to life.

He was forty-seven years old. If he did the minimum, it would be ballgame for him. There is no short way home on a sentence like that. If convicted, he would be an old man when released. Juan was playing crazy the best he could in the hopes he would get an NGRI finding. Little did he know, he was already disqualified. He was a 46B, as were most at San Antonio State Hospital. The 46B inmates had yet to go to trial. They were only at San Antonio State Hospital for competency classes. Every one of them still had to face the judge, a portion of the process I somehow skipped, saving me years of my freedom.

I would listen to Juan for hours as he held high hopes for beating his charges. Our friendship was sad and depressing, as I knew he was marching closer every day to the end of his independence, freedom, and life as he knew it all because of an addiction he needed help with. Destined for a cage and lack of the sun, I would always agree with his predictions of hope, lifting the spirits of a dead man walking.

Most 46B patients were arrested on an aggravated assault charge. Most of the time, they were unmedicated, mentally ill, homeless people that would spit on or assault a peace officer. In Texas, this carries 2- 20-year prison terms. These peoples were the mindless moneyless masses that lurk in homeless shelters, under dark bridges, in the bushes, on side of the street with a sign, and in camps on the outskirts of town.

For the very first time, I started to really realize where I was. The state-run hospital was getting over a grand a day for each client. There was a total of seven units at San Antonio State Hospital, and in each unit, there were forty residents. We are talking about some serious cake, guys! I calculated it to be over seventy-three million dollars every year. This place was a "for profit" holding center for The State of Texas, all in the name of the criminally insane. No treatment for illness was even attempted outside of medication. There was no real therapy, addiction treatment, job training, or money management and life skills classes. No one gets better in the State Hospital system in Texas, and my eyes were wide open.

#

The craziness was now at a flash point. Eve had been acting out quite a bit. She became a tornado, total destruction of anything and everything in her path. She was stomping through the Day Room, screaming and hollering, four or more times a day. I would find myself calming her down and taking her back to our room to pacify her. I did this primarily so that the techs wouldn't have to clear the lobby for the safety of all residents in the unit. That would be a process that would force everyone out of the TV areas and into our rooms for at least an hour.

I was called to see Dr. Khan. She informed me that part of being on a 46C evaluation was to see how well I listened to directions. She said that Eve was what is called "an attention seeker." That she throws tantrums to gain the attention of her peers. She schooled me to the fact that I was in fact hindering Eve's treatment by drying her tears at every opportunity.

On my end, I just saw my roommate in complete and total distress and was trying to help the staff and the other residents by preventing the lobby from needing to be cleared. However, Dr. Khan held all the cards for my fate at this point, so I needed to listen and take to heart her advice and instructions.

I was ordered to stop talking to Eve at once. A redirection that I had no choice but to follow. Eve was my roommate and friend, and she was used to our companionship. I felt terrible. She would speak to me, and I had no choice but to give her cold, one-word answers. A few days went by like this, and then the investigator came to see me.

I guess the story goes a little something like this. Eve was furious that I had abruptly and with no explanation stopped being her friend. She got the bright idea to call the San Antonio Police Department and report that I had brutally raped her in our room. I am a 46C. While on this type of safety evaluation, any kind of allegation or altercation that occurred could prevent me from ever leaving the State Hospital system. They could end up holding me for the maximum sentence of my original crime. In my case, if San Antonio State Hospital wanted to, they could keep me for the rest of my natural life or ninety-nine years. Though I was found not guilty, the NGRI finding had all sorts of traps and pitfalls that Martin Scorsese had no knowledge of. The NGRI finding is so rare that not many lawyers in the court system know the ins and outs of mental institutions. He was the best lawyer money could buy but the information about how all this worked was just not available.

Thank God in this instance, the cops did not believe Eve. They walked away knowing it was all bullshit. She accused someone of rape every five minutes out in the free world. They knew her track record as an attention seeker, manipulator, and liar.

So, after the staff pulled the cameras, I was totally exonerated. However, the accusation still went in my file as an occurrence. Even something that was proven to be one hundred percent false, still ended up in my jacket in black and white.

Passengers, can you see how fucking scary this situation was? If the smallest thing happened while I was a 46C, there was a huge probability that it would cost me years, if not the rest of my life. Even if it was not my fault.

#

James was a Black man I knew from 4R, the lock down unit at Nueces County Jail. He was a Herculean muscular guy in his late twenties. He had a Hitler mustache, one patch of hair on the middle of his upper lip. He had no other hair on his entire body. Completely and totally smooth chocolate skin. It was rumored he suffered with a long-lasting case of syphilis that left his hair follicles unable to grow.

He was one of the most violent and dangerous criminals I have ever met. We verbally mixed it up one night as I was being walked by his cell while still in Nueces County Jail. I will never forget those eyes. The cold gaze of a man gone mad.

James was transferred to San Antonio State Hospital, and when he came onto the unit, things really began to get crazy. He was constantly causing problems, threatening staff, and other clients. He had gotten into three violent altercations in a short amount of time. Mental institutions are just like any other large group setting, where we would vibe off of each other, our energies and personalities.

Once you get a couple bad seeds, they change the ambiance of the whole place. Violence feeds off itself. The demons in the room stalked in gang formation. Once James entered the picture, the brutality skyrocketed. Eve was furious all the time now, throwing trash cans and screaming. She even pummeled one of the nurses in the face so hard that it knocked her out cold. Too bad the enforced plastic barriers didn't protect her. These poor nurses really had no protection and no way of defending themselves unless they wanted to risk catching an assault case.

A sixty-nine-year-old man named Phil was even punching women in the face. I mean, constantly. He was also famous for pulling his penis out of his diaper while sitting next to the young girls in the Day Room. He would tug on that dead piece of wrinkled sausage till a tech would redirect him. The girls would run away, terrified. He did this day-in and day-out.

Huge fights started to erupt almost on the hour. The whistles would blow, and the place would be stormed with staff from every unit. Things were seriously dangerous. Juan got into a major fistfight in a bedroom over some gangland bullshit with another Mexican. Blood was everywhere. He hurt his back to the point where he needed physical therapy. Unfortunate.

The climate in Crockett was desperately dark. I felt as if I lived in a war-torn country, in the midst of a bloody battle, unholy and unforgiving. The place just had a very dark and eerie feel to it. Something was building, unstoppable and evil in its purpose.

#

Then I got called to the cancer center in San Antonio. I was brought over to the hospital by Clara, one of the nicest staff members I had met to date. She regularly comforted the broken-hearted souls at San Antonio State Hospital. We went in to see the doctor around two in the afternoon and my mind was blown apart by what I learned.

The doctors at the cancer center in Vernon had sent down my charts. Turns out I didn't have cirrhosis of the liver. The doctor at the cancer center in San Antonio consulted with me after we got the results of the new bloodwork. She sat down in the chair right in front of me in her office.

"Mr. Bornagain, you used to drink quite a bit, didn't

you?" She asked.

"Yes, I would drink an eighteen pack of beer and ten shots of Jager a night, seven nights a week, for about eight years before stopping."

She responded, "That explains it. Well, most of it. Mr. Bornagain, why did you quit drinking?"

I told her that I started smoking meth and that is what caused me to stop drinking altogether. She looked at me in complete bewilderment.

"Mr. Bornagain, by our best guess, at one time, you had a nearly failed liver. In turn, your spleen was enlarged. When you stopped drinking, the liver healed, going completely back to normal. The spleen does not heal as fast as the liver does. You were acutely close to death. Between the testing we did, and some guessing on my part, if you hadn't started smoking methamphetamine and halted the drinking right when you did, you would have been in a box, in the ground, in about thirty-ninety days. You are a very lucky man."

She went on to explain that my latest blood work showed that my blood count was only one point below normal. If I were to abstain from drinking for the rest of my life, I would live an entirely normal life. I was healed. She also explained to me that my blood was free of hepatitis, and all other STDs and bloodborne pathogens.

The weight of the world was lifted off of me on this day. God once again showed me his omnipresent love for me and His ability to perform miracles in larger-than-life ways. The life of recklessness I had lived was not only forgiven by the Father but healed by Him too. I was covered in the blood of Jesus. I began to cry, right there in front of the doctor. Passengers, I am living proof God is real. I think this occurrence alone proves that. Statistical impossibilities made possible by the Creator.

The doctor even told me they don't know how to explain why I didn't have cirrhosis of the liver.

I went back to the Crockett Unit recharged and full of faith. God was working in big ways, including ways I wouldn't see until the dramatic conclusion of this amazing story. Passengers, wake up. Things are about to get interesting, even for this whopper of a true tale.

#

James cornered me in the Day Room. "Come on, you fuckin cracker," he said in a rage. Big veins began to protrude from his smooth hairless skull. He pumped his fist, lunging at me as if to get me to flinch. I was a 46C, remember? I couldn't do a motherfucking thing to defend myself. Dr. Khan had informed me that as a 46C, even under attack and being beaten to death, if I were to push my attacker even so much as in self-defense, it would be another ninety-day evaluation. I would rather have let James kill me than do one more day at San Antonio State Hospital than I absolutely had to. Fighting was just not an option. No matter what.

Thank God the techs came to my aid, as they were my only hope. Belinda, a short woman of about a hundred pounds, talked the hulking giant off the ledge of murder and five male staff showed him back to his room. Later that night, he threatened to kill Laura, a thirty-five-year-old Mexican 46B. She did nothing offensive, but James had the spirit of murder in him. Someone was going to get hurt.

I made a formal complaint to Dr. Holden. I told him that James is going to kill someone in this unit and it's going to happen soon. He assured me that the other physician on the unit who saw James had put an order in to switch his meds, and that he should calm down once that began. However, that was not the case. The next day was a moment in time that will be burned into my memory till the day I leave this world.

Alexa was a skinny, lesbian, Mexican chick. She was about five feet, seven inches and one hundred forty pounds. She had cheap home-grown tattoos recklessly drawn anywhere there was skin. She was a delusional aggressive girl with severe bipolar one disorder. She was frightfully hallucinatory but for the most part, a sweet soul.

She was wearing some basketball shorts, a black t-shirt, and a pair of Nike sandals. As always, she wore her thick, coke-bottle glasses with circular lenses. She was sitting underneath one of the great trees in the recreation field, over by the track. There was a red metal swing just to her left side. I was on the track walking when I saw it happen.

I heard a massive crack. The same sound a baseball makes when coming off a Louisville slugger at Fenway Park as it heads for the great big green wall named the Green Monster in good sportsmanship.

When I looked up, I saw Alexa laying on the grass, green blades squished all around her with a pool of blood running from her nose. James was towered above her as he kicked her square in her face, over and over and over again. I counted six brutal full-on, no hesitation, complete follow-through kicks to her jaw. There were no techs in sight. As a 46C, I ran up to the scene powerless. If I decided to step in, I would be done for. And what good am I to my family, my loved ones, and myself if I stay locked in a mental institution?

Just then, the whistle blew. Mateo, a tech, was a huge guy, but he was flying down the hill. He slammed into James and tried to tackle him. Mateo was unsuccessful, as it seemed James was built like a concrete wall. Mateo squared off with the brute. James pounded him square in the chin. They started wrestling, Mateo using whatever breath he had left to blow on the whistle that remained in his mouth, out of pure desperation.

      Twenty techs must have responded to this ferocious attempted murder. I had just witnessed this man damn near beat this girl to death right before my eyes. After the mass of techs arrived, James just ceased the assault and was allowed to walk right back onto Crockett, as if nothing had even happened. The twenty techs followed him, like an entourage assisting Mariah Carey in her heyday. I followed the parade back inside.

      I stood in awe as James looked at the group of twenty green-clad employees and hurled insults and threats towards them. Out of fear of losing their job and the prosecution for assault themselves, they stood back and did nothing. How does this type of scenario help anyone? How is this productive mental health care? James certainly wasn't getting the help he needed, and now there was a new victim of his and nothing was going to be done about it.

      I timed this event once we got inside. James was allowed to stomp around the Day Room and male hallway for over forty-five minutes. The whole time, other patients were within arm's reach of this wild man who could singularly overpower any person in the building. Everyone's life was in danger. And the staff couldn't do a damn thing about it for as long as he wasn't attacking people. There was obviously not a plan in place for this type of situation, either because they didn't care, or because it goes against policy, I do not know. But it seems reasonable, if the staff can not physically protect themselves and their patients, there should be a master plan in place to quickly and immediately remove the dangerous individual. Instead, the staff has to try and convince the person to go to segregation willingly and without force.

The EMT's finally showed up to transport Alexa. This whole time, she had been gushing blood in a wheelchair in the women's hallway, propped up like a corpse at an open casket funeral. Lifeless and unconscious. She was rushed to the hospital, as they finally were able to convince James that he needed to go to the behavioral unit to be segregated. He went as peacefully as one could after nearly taking the life of another human being for absolutely no reason. They asked him why he attacked the woman. His response was, "She looked at me funny." At San Antonio State Hospital, a wrong look, or the perception of a wrong look, could get you killed in a heartbeat.

#

Crockett was a warzone due to Eve, Phil, James, and others losing their shit in the Day Room. The place was in total chaos. There was constant screaming, throwing of chairs, among other things. The staff continued to just stand by, helplessly watching as the inmates literally ran the asylum.

I was reaching my breaking point. The fever in the room ran high. We had a new problem patient, a six foot and two-inch-tall transsexual kleptomaniac. She was stealing everything out of people's rooms. Her third day in, she had robbed about six people. She was of Mexican descent, ginormous, and she had long black hair down to her back. She wore a ratty red hoodie with peeling screen print that ran down the side. She had on a pair of funky purple women's jeans that seemed to be at least five sizes too small. She wore a double-D size push up bra that gave the ogre the appearance of having Dolly Parton tits. Out of the neck of the filthy white tee, underneath the red hoodie, was the biggest bush of Robin Williams pubes you could imagine. Chest hair like I had never seen. I use the word "she" very loosely with this transsexual from Transylvania.

Not only was she stealing property. She would walk up to people in the dining room, and just start forcibly eating food right off their tray. It was starting to cause a major problem. On top of all that, she claimed to be mute, using sign language to communicate. Well, really just pointing fingers at food items and other things she demanded. She also grunted for emphasis. It was the perfect storm for an ass whooping.

The day before, I received my cell phone in the mail. The Treatment Team was fucking livid. See passengers, if you can't tell by now, I am one smart cookie. I read the Client's Rights handbook minimum of a dozen times. I noticed a loophole. You could have a smartphone as long as you had the camera taken out of it. So, I had my ma get it done and she had mailed it in. I had full service, text, and internet access.

It did take weeks for them to allow me to have it in my possession, but they couldn't deny their own rules in black and white. This would later turn out to be the worst mistake these assholes had ever made, so stay tuned.

So, I now had the smartphone, and boy, did I love it. The rule was that I had to turn it into the nurse's station at lights out and let it charge overnight. I could also charge it anytime I wanted during the day or leave it up there for safekeeping while I showered.

The second day I had the damn thing, I got lazy. I tucked it under some clothes and my ratty old jail bible and went to do a quick five-minute shower. I wasn't even going to flog the dolphin this time, just a swift in and out rinse. When I returned, you guessed it, it was missing. I knew exactly who I needed to kill. I stomped up to the nurse's station and made the initial report. They shut down the whole unit to look for my property.

I cornered the tranny while she was in the shower. I

knew she was the one who stole it. "Look man, if you give it back right now, I won't say shit to the staff, I will tell them I found it in my room. It has a code on it so you can't even use it." She looked at me with her full five o'clock shadow, massive hook nose, and with a cock the size of a kielbasa swinging between her knees. I almost couldn't keep a straight face. A guy with a porn star pipe, a donkey's dick, that wishes he didn't have it. Ironic, don't you think?

Staff came in and intervened just in time. I was about to choke her with that fire hose that she wished was a vagina. I wanted to beat her to death with a bar of soap in one of my gym socks my ma had bought me. When she got out of the bathroom, they had the wand out. It was one of those metal detector devices that you would find at the gate in an airport or at a dance for high school.

They searched her room and belongings, they searched her person, and they found nothing. An hour went by, and they searched every single person on the unit, except one.

Ignazio was another mute, only he was the real deal. He looked like he stepped off the set of "Lord of the Rings." He was a deeply disturbed pervert, the kind that would jack off with a whole bottle of shampoo. They would have to interrupt his five-hour self-love sessions to let him know chow was ready. They used the wand on his pants pockets, and sure enough, my cell phone was in there. I tell this story because this was the straw that broke the camel's back. The tranny handed it off to this clearly incapacitated stooge right before he went in the shower, leaving Ignazio to take the blame for the theft. Just another normal day in Crockett.

I wanted to murder the immoral ridiculous klepto but because of my 46C status, I had no choice but to just take it as it came. This event had really pushed me to my limit. I was tired of the weary loathsome behaviors and insane talk. I was repulsed by my peers, though I was sympathetic to the sick, there is only so much a man can take.

As soon as I opened my eyes, the bullshit on Crockett was underway. The next day at breakfast, I waited in the Day Room for the show to begin. Eve was in full certifiable character. Phil was screaming, squalling, and threatening the nurses. He was a short, elderly, Mexican man wearing a straw hat, the kind a scarecrow would wear. His body was ravaged by years of heroin addiction and psych meds. He was drooling and wearing the stolen sneakers he took from Ignazio. This unit was off the chain and only getting worse by the second.

Phil proceeded to get into my face, "Hey Papa, you wanna get outta here and go get some beer and cheeseburgers?" Phil asked.

He was riddled with dementia; the poor bastard was most likely never going to leave the State Hospital. I just ignored his offer and went to chow.

The vibe in the dining room was that of "The Purge." People were verbally assaulting one another, the big tranny was stealing muffins off the trays of unsuspecting victims, and someone threw their powdered eggs up against the window that overlooked the recreation yard. I stood up, dumped the contents of my tray into the trash like a good boy and went to go sit in the Day Room.

I was sitting on a big lime-green foam seat near the nurse's station on the back wall, close to the entrance to the women's hallway. I had on my black hoodie, a pair of basketball shorts, and a pair of fresh jet-black DC skate shoes that my Ma had mailed to me. I was reeling. I was ferocious. See passengers, being totally sane, not on meds of any kind and in a psychotic environment at the State Hospital in San Antonio, can really break a coherent rational person.

The depression of seeing the most despicable human behavior, the public masturbation, the violence, and sexual assault, the insane talk at every waking moment of every day, the neglect you witness, public urination, the shit-filled diapers abandoned on the bathroom floor, all this chips away at the human mind. I was mentally broken at this moment. After everything I went through, all the loss, pain, the dehumanization of my soul as a man who had once been loved, I had finally had all I could take.

Not long after everyone emerged from breakfast, the Day Room was full of criminal minds. Smeared lipstick faces by women who woke up and were inspired to paint clown makeup on their face, creating demented looks of madness on themselves. The screaming of a mentally tormented transsexual in black and white-checkered leggings. A completely bald woman pounding on the Plexiglass windows, roaring about her children that she had abandoned. These were all in my TV room, except it wasn't a horror film I was watching, it was real life. My thoughts were now corrupt with homicide and hatred. There was no Jesus in this corroded heart of mine. It was as if the pot boiled over, the oily water hitting the range procuring smoldering smoke that rose into hell's kitchen.

That's when I rose to my finally healed feet. A show of force that would forever change the course of my life. Right as I was contemplating murder, it was as if the Holy Ghost poured into me, out from a clay jar, and saturated my soul. I began to roam the Day Room, stomping up to the mental monsters. I proceeded to shame them one by one. A snarling animal beast laying down verbal law in a psychedelic mindfuck type of way. I pictured Jesus turning over the tables of the money changers. I wasn't out for blood, but a point was going to be made. Things needed to change on the Crockett unit and there was no time like the present.

Saliva dripped from my foaming mouth of war and my big blue eyes transformed into laser beams, I was in their faces, screaming at patients, and yelling through the nurse's station protective glass window.

"Why do you let them act like this? How dare you let them, how dare you!"

Without warning, every ounce of rage instantaneously drained from my spirit. The whole room grew quiet and meek. All at once, it was if I had held up a mirror to the madness. Even the truly insane, crazy ones saw their actions for the very first time. I had snapped the catatonic back to reality. God saw fit for an explosion in me. This was the point of no return. I had crossed the line. Once the model 46C client, I now had a major outburst of biblical proportions on my record. It felt so good, though. I felt alive in ways that are indescribable. To release the tension valve that masturbation, drugs, nor any other action could honestly and truly release. The verbal expression of rage, the true feelings I had for ages, coming out all in one dose. It was liberating to a point of exhaustion. I sat back into the green foam chair as the pod looked at me silently.

It's an esoteric feeling when the eyes of thirty criminally insane souls gaze upon you as if you were the crazy one. The look of shock and dismantled reality upon their bewildered faces was almost comical. The shameful stares that my speech had surfaced was liberating in a way, like maybe I had got through to someone. I sat panting, salty tears flowing out of tired Irish eyes. The head nurse on duty that day was Alice. She was a mousy but very sexy woman with sandy blond hair to her midback. Circular framed lenses upon her thin white face. Her navy-blue scrubs contoured a pair of perfect size C breasts and globe shaped booty. She was hot. Unfortunately, we didn't get along. Now she had reason to drop Thor's hammer.

"Mr. Bornagain, what the hell is wrong with you? You can't be acting like that to other clients!" Alice yelled.

"I can't take any more of this. You people let madness take place all day, every day. Some of us have to live here and some of us are not insane. Order needs to be restored!" I said with authority.

She went to the med line and fired off some orders to the tech that runs that process. She returned, "Mr. Bornagain, I am going to medicate you. You can take the pills, or you will get the needle."

This was fucking bad for me. If I were to get a dose, forcibly or not, I was subject to do more time. It could set me back pretty far. I was already staring down a three-and-a-half-year minimum evaluation. I just couldn't do one more day than absolutely necessary.

Alice, by the grace of God, stormed out of the nurse's station, "Mr. Bornagain, I am going to give you one more chance to calm down. You think you can do that for me?"

I looked at her like a man on the cross. I begged for mercy, "Yes, Alice, for you, I will shut my mouth," I said somberly.

My panic-ridden body immediately began to relax as she explained that she was not even going to chart the incident. She understood my take on this crazy place. Alice hated Crockett as much as I did. In all reality, the people that work there are living there and in a terribly similar situation as I was. Totally sane and unmedicated, these healthcare professionals and angelic techs all go through the same trauma I was going through. Day in, day out. She saw the hurt and degradation within my heart. The painful world I was forced to reside in.

And with the Spirit flowing within her, she took mercy on me as Jesus had many, many times before.

#

The techs were a refuge. There is no way to thank those people for what they did for me while at San Antonio State Hospital. I would have conversations with them for hours. The only sane topics, commentary, and comradery I had.

Outside the high-functioning patients, the techs were all that allowed me to stay in touch with humanity and the person I once was. It's easy to succumb to insanity when being exposed to the craziest environment possible. Picture the most deranged conversation you have ever had and times that by ten on LSD. That is your typical conversation at San Antonio State Hospital.

About an hour later, Alice approached me whispering, "Mr. Bornagain, there are a lot of people that look up to you here for the compassion you have for others and the way you have endured this. We know you shouldn't be here. Look, if you don't like what you see, write a serious letter to the administration and I will hand deliver it to the "White House." Alice was an angel on earth, and you will soon see how God worked within her.

The White House' was something of a fable. It was actually the main administration building that sat way up on a green hill overlooking the grounds of the insane. This is where the big man himself sat. The top doctor on staff, the one man who had the power to waive his pen and set you free. At the time, I didn't even know such a being existed. I just knew some high-ranking authority sat in that boardroom up there. When Alice finished speaking, a holy lightbulb went off in my head. I was to write a letter. Looking back, this letter was one that would change my life forever and once again prove that God was in fact real.

#

A few hours went by and Dianne, a sexy little meth head in full on psychosis, decided to take a steamy shower. She was thin but stacked with long black hair. She was half White and half Latina. She had a pretty face and a pension for turning tricks.

He stalked her for days. I saw it with my own eyes. His sexual rage and urges building like an orgasm like a man in a porn theater. He watched her as she left her room in the girls' hallway to go to the shower, shampoo basket in hand. He waited until the perfect moment arose.

The stars aligned, the universe was in place, and on board for God's plan to start unfolding. Ishmael was an ex-college professor and wrestling champ who had endured multiple head injuries throughout his life. The bashing turned his brain into mush. He was now known as a rapist and sexual predator. Ishmael was famous for publicly masturbating, grabbing of client's breasts, and walking through the Day Room totally nude. He was a short man in his fifties with a hunched-over stature, curly stringy black hair combed over to the right and greasy as a pile of McDonald's French fries. He loved to wear donated sweat suits, gray and drab. He wore orthopedic shoes just like your grandpa might wear during the twilight of life. And oh God, those fucking tighty-whities. I can't tell you how many times he appeared in the Day Room in those snow white, but shit stained, underwear…with a full boner.

Ishmael was White, but almost looked Hungarian. His face had a dark tint with a beak for a nose and the biggest mouth full of rotten yellow chiclets you had ever seen. He was a vampire. The kind of man who would corner an eight-year-old girl in a bathroom stall and go right into her Strawberry

Shortcake panties. A legend of a boogeyman that you only hear about on the six o'clock news. These are the monsters that walk among us in the shadows of every city and every sleepy village across this land. The devil is as real as God and at times, he creeps from hell to snatch the innocence of our young.

Ishmael, just like James, was at San Antonio State Hospital on a serious sexual crime and awaiting trial as a 46B. I wanted to kill these child molesters and rapists that roamed the male hallway. I loathed their presence in every way. Between 2P and San Antonio State Hospital, I had crossed paths with many legitimate demons. I could almost see their crimes written on their faces and in their body language. As these men would pass me in the Day Room, I could hear the whimpering pleas of the preteen girls they had molested. The screams of the little boys they had abducted and anally raped in trap houses, and the suicidal confessions of the innocent family members that they had violated for years, using their position as family to guilt their victims into pulling down their pants. I constantly thought of my own babies out in the world unprotected from the beasts. I cried every day knowing that my addiction was the sole reason for my incarceration and absence from their little lives. This is where addiction can lead you, friends. So please beware, young passengers. That first joint, those good times, that first beer, and those hard drugs can lead you right here to the reality in this book.

Ishmael stalked Dianne into the women's bathroom. He was the lion waiting to devour, sent by Satan. The firsthand account of what happened next came to me straight from the victim. Dianne got out of the shower and began to towel off. The generic white rag they give us is tiny, nothing like you ladies are used to at home. She looked up and saw Dracula fangs dripping saliva onto the white and green tile below.

"Take it off baby, let me fuck you," he snarled.

She cried out, "Help me! Please, somebody fucking help me! RAPE!"

She recounted how he pawed at the towel with his boney nicotine-stained fingertips. The only veil from her shame torn to the floor, she stood there naked. He pinched her hard nipples, the cold in the room making her body react in natural ways.

"Give me that pussy, little girl. I wanna get you pregnant," Ishmael said in a creepy Ted Bundy voice.

She persistently cried as he groped her dripping wet skin. His vile hands searching her flesh for non-existent pleasure points. The whistles sounded like angel trumpets from the four corners of Crockett Unit. The stomping of Ked's and Nikes cascaded the Day Room as a sea of green uniforms ran by like the Arizona winds. They couldn't even touch the bastard as he walked out of the bathroom. That fucking "No Restraint Policy" allowing monsters to initiate victims like this was some high school hazing gone horribly wrong. Shame on you, son. You are grounded for a week. That is basically the equivalent to this evil policy which allows wickedness to run wild with no real consequences.

Ishmael strutted back into the Day Room, rubbing a full hard-on. As he walked by a beautiful tech, he grabbed her ass with both hands and stroked his penis against her scrubs. She was a faithful married woman; I could feel the horror and shame in her soul as he stuck out his tongue to lick her face.

Then this mother fucker just sat down in those ratty tighty-whities with skid marks on the seat as the techs frantically arrived back at the Day Room to confront him and protect the others. They finally brought the chair out and he agreed to go peacefully. So, there was no punishment. Only a trip to the Behavior Health Unit.

The chilling part was that Dianne decided not to make a formal report. Her past trauma, experience with the system failing her, and the daily derogatory experience of the ice game had left her desensitized to rape and sexual assault. Later on, I found out that since she never told the police, this crime was as if it had never happened. Ishmael's original sexual assault charge was actually dropped by the courts, for whatever reason, and this man was set free shortly after. If Dianne had confidence in the system, this barbarian would not have been set free. There is no way the courts would have thrown out his original case if he had a pending case for the same charge in the State Mental Hospital. I watched him get transferred to a noncriminal, non-forensic unit and soon he walked out the doors to molest and rape again. An unsuspecting city left in the crosshairs of one of the most dangerous sexual minds ever stamped out by Satan's assembly line. The system creating more victims, once again.

This event awoke a sleeping giant within your boy here. I now had the ammunition for the gun I was about to point at the White House at San Antonio State Hospital. I had seen enough, and the ball was now rolling in one of the greatest underdog stories of all time. It was me against the State Hospital System. A plot now hatched where I would become a champion of the people; I would rescue the forgotten masses, and hopefully secure my own release. I was taking on The Machine, one that could potentially hold me captive till my last breath under the iron that was a 46C finding in Texas State Law. God was with me, and what happened next was all the Spirit.

#

I grabbed a pen and a pad of yellow-lined legal paper. I

looked up at the clock, the big hand sat on the one. The well of ink started to drain upon the paper below. Out poured words recounting the tales of sexual assault and violence inflicted upon the voiceless. It described the neglect and other atrocities that I witnessed firsthand within the four walls at San Antonio State Hospital. I gave names, dates, and times. I enlightened them to the fact that I had been keeping a journal of everything I had seen. It explained that I was a man not on any medication of any kind. That I had run a six million dollar a year company and knew many influential people in the Lone Star State. After even more details and sightings of the evil and corruption within the walls of San Antonio State Hospital, I ended with a not-so-veiled threat. One where I was to take my journal to the local and state media, thus exposing the State Hospital system for what it really is with all its greed and lies. I knew this was a for-profit entity that housed the sick like cattle, all in the name of the almighty dollar and on the citizens of Texas dime and time. I reminded them that I had a cellphone.

 I looked up and the large hand of the clock sat on the two. The Holy Spirit had allowed me to pen one of the most well thought out, powerful letters I had ever seen, and certainly ever written, in only five short minutes. Four pages in all. It was compelling, factual, and well written. For a man who only went to the tenth grade and hadn't paid attention in school since fifth grade, it was a masterpiece.

 I read it through once not believing my eyes. I folded its contents and sealed it. I placed it into an envelope I had gotten from Alice and handed it in to the nurse who promised to personally deliver it to the White House. This letter was personally addressed to the top executive in charge, with hopes that it would send shivers up his spine and put into motion a life-changing set of events. Not only for me but the mentally challenged family in the Crockett Unit that I had grown to know and remarkably love in compassion.

I was five months into a three-and-a-half-year evaluation at the minimum. The courts were now aware of the mistake that took place in my miracle trial. My councilors and treatment team were to inform me that, though the courts were not happy, it was signed into law. There was nothing that could be done due to "Double Jeopardy." I could not be retried or resentenced for the same crime twice. I called Martin Scorsese and verified this new information before I was able to sleep a full night for the first time in months.

However, the hospital could still keep me for ninety-nine years. I had just sent a letter to the god of San Antonio State Hospital threatening the evil empire and promising to tear down the house of cards in the name of change. I had fired the opening shots in a war that no one saw coming. This letter began a cause-and-effect reaction within the building. And one week later, it happened.

"Boston, they are about to move you, bro." A gentle giant, he reminded me of a Mexican Buddy. He was a tech on Crockett Unit. He was lacing me up, forewarning me of a chess move being made by the brass.

An hour later, I was told to pack my shit and I was off to Fannin Hall. Before I moved, I chopped it up with Mexican Buddy in secret. I was curious as to why I was being moved to a unit with only males. Mostly all child predators, murderers, and people not suited to be in the presence of the female species. At first glance, we both speculated that it was in direct retaliation for the letter. In all reality, this chess move was already the checkmate I had been dreaming of.

I sat at the front door of Crockett Unit, angry and betrayed. I was full of rage, and planning on filing a formal complaint for retaliation against the hospital. That's when I got called in to see Dr. Holden.

"Mr. Bornagain, I want to discuss this move the hospital has decided to make," Dr. Holden carefully said. We talked for about twenty minutes. He elaborately detailed out how this was not going to affect my future release, how my files were to be transferred over, and my new doctor would be made fully aware of my docile and respectful nature while on Crockett.

I asked why I was being moved and Dr. Holden responded, "Well, sometimes the top people make decisions based upon beds and other factors."

I knew he was being gagged by the White House and I knew what the "other factors" were. He couldn't tell me the real reason why.

He wished me well and Dr. Holden said his final goodbyes as I was led out by Mexican Buddy to my new home at Fannin Hall. It was a short walk, maybe a few hundred paces, but it felt miles away from the madness of Crockett Unit. When I was led through the gate, the tiny yard space for clients was eerily quiet, especially after the instability and insanity of my previous residence.

A rod-iron gate opened into a space that had a backyard feel to it. A red metal two-person swing sat near the front of the property. A mighty mesquite tree, indigenous to South Texas, towered over the secluded area. A lone dilapidated basketball goal sat unused with a faded ratty ball, frayed from water damage. I walked past inmate clients feeling the cold stare of curiosity as fresh meat descended onto the unit.

"Mr. Bornagain, welcome to Fannin Hall. Let's take your things and get you settled in. Your new doctor would like to speak with you," the headmistress, Ms. Jackson, stated.

Ms. Jackson was a bonafide Black princess. She had short dreads and cherub cheeks. Her eyes sparkled with compassion and love. Her zealousness and commitment for people, and especially her patients, shone through like a nighttime diamond, twinkling and radiant. She was in her forties, but she looked twenty-five to me!

I dropped my paper bag suitcases and was taken into one of the most paramount meetings of my life. A smug little man sat before me. Maybe five foot, three inches on stilts, sporting medium brown hair, and a sharp spear-like nose. He wore an inexpensive pink button-down shirt, the kind that had me questioning his sexuality at first glance. His eyes were beady and bulging. I think we will call him Dr. Nogood.

"So, Mr. Bornagain, why do you think you have been moved," Dr. Nogood said in a cheerful yet evil tone.

I returned, "Well, one of two things. Either the rape allegation Eve made or the other is the letter I wrote to administration."

He looked at me with a smile; Nogood then gave an answer that truly shocked me, "The hospital has reviewed your case, Mr. Bornagain. Upon review, we feel that you just do not belong here. Your case was mismanaged by Nueces County, and we feel you would be better suited in a drug treatment facility in your home county. You are to be discharged almost right away, in about thirty days. As long as there are no incidents of any kind, you will be going home."

He explained that he was going to recommend a drug treatment program at the same facility that had turned me away twice for lack of a bed. The facility that left me to take my recovery into my own hands. He told me that on paper, I was going to be listed as having no Axis One diagnosis. My records would only show that I suffer from methamphetamine substance abuse.

I knew the letter was the reason. They are the largest organization of no-good liars I had ever seen...no pun intended.

He sent me away as a champion. There is no way to describe what it feels like to come from behind against all odds and beat Goliath to his knees. I basked in the glory of my success at actually beating the system at its own game.

I called my mother, "Ma, I am going home in thirty days!" I shouted.

"Son, what the hell are you talking about? They said three and a half years," my ma said in her thick, sweet Boston accent. I told her the whole story, how the gamble had paid off and they were going to release me. She couldn't have been happier! The nightmare was finally over.

Passengers, I think you know me pretty well by now. I am one hell of an extreme motherfucker. I don't do anything small. When these next events took place, I just couldn't shut my Bostonian big mouth. It was time to win...BIG.

#

I had to make it thirty days. That was it. Sit in front of the TV, shut up, and watch the days melt away, like crystal shards in the pizzle of time until my exit date finally arrived. But I started to notice some very unsettling things. There were multiple clients that had not changed or showered in months. Other clients would tell me about this one particular guy, "Johnny hasn't showered or changed in ninety days." The smell of urine would steam from stained brown jeans, the fumes visible to the naked eye. He wasn't the only one though. There were people with unbrushed teeth, uncombed hair, and body odor that would knock you right over. It made me sick that San Antonio State Hospital would let this continue on unchecked.

I asked Ms. Jackson why this was being allowed to

happen. She explained to me that clients had so many rights that they were unable to force them to shower. I felt depressed over this, it truly felt like a tragedy. It was a double-sided coin with these patient protection laws. The lobotomies were a thing of the past, but Client's Rights ushered in the age of neglect into the State Hospital system. The same place laws were written in Austin that brought us the "No Restraints Policy," now protected clients to such an extent that they were being harmed. Nobody was getting the help they needed, many were growing worse, and the ill-fated became victims with no one to turn to.

  I sat and played chess with an elderly man in a wheelchair. Everyone called him Rabbit. It was sort of a tongue-in-cheek joke because of how unlucky he was. We sat for hours as he mapped out his innocence. How the lesbian sheriff in a small Texas river town had it out for him. He said the sheriff had a thing for his then wife. He detailed how he told the sheriff to fuck off and how she hatched a plot to frame him. His wife was found strangled with a pair of her own panty hose behind a ramshackle seedy trailer that they owned. One wild, slightly confusing tale.

  "How did you get that phone in here, young fellow?" Rabbit asked.

  I told him how I read the Client's Rights book and found a loophole. As I spoke, all the men of Fannin Unit huddled around as I held court. Some had cheap flip phones that the hospital had told them was their only option. In the following days, many of them ordered camera-free smartphones. I explained to them the importance of having a direct line to the media and how staying in touch with family during their time here would hold the hospital accountable for their treatment. The guys listened as I detailed the events that surrounded my early release, how much of an impact a piece of paper and pen can have on their treatment at San Antonio State Hospital. A newfound hope began to build and grow in the eyes of the inmates.

The letter had opened this floodgate inside of me, I needed to write. It wasn't something I chose, it chose me. I started to express myself in short stories. I wrote about the harrowing tale of my life and the gut-wrenching events that had taken place in the most recent years. I detailed my days as a cab driver and a lot of the crazed stories that you have read here.

It dawned on me I had this smartphone which gave me access to certain websites. I began posting my short stories on social media and recovery pages in order to get feedback. Truth be told, I used social media as a way to record my writing into the cloud since I didn't have an actual computer to save it on during my incarceration. I may be the first person ever to write the framework for a book using social media. I have not heard of anyone else doing this. However, I don't want to break the damn internet by claiming I am a genius. Passengers, that would be overconfident, wouldn't it?

I was releasing one piece a day, writing them in forty-five-minute periods each. The Spirit was guiding me, stroking the keys. I had discovered my God-given gift of writing at thirty-seven years old in a mental institution for the criminally insane. I couldn't believe the response I was getting. Friend requests came in bundles by the hour as people found a liking for my insane and dangerous life and my street-smart style. I put one of my more disgusting stories about booty bumping ice into the comment section of the post of one of the largest hardcopy Christian magazines on earth by complete accident.

The editor for the "Testimonial Department" contacted me. I thought it was a scam at first, only to find out the publication had over two million social media likes. They were the real deal. I gave them permission to comb through my writing on my page. Surprisingly to me, they went ahead and wrote a story about my life. It was to go out in the July 2020 issue in hardcopy worldwide. I thought that was pretty cool.

#

Marcus, my buddy I rode up to Vernon with, walked into Fannin Unit. Seems as if God was providing another pal for me to ride out the end of this journey with. He was a short, stout fella. The circular rimmed glasses must have been in style at this time because he had that type also. He was funny as hell, loved playing video games, just a real cool cat. Genuinely, one of the nicest guys I had ever met. They allowed us to order takeout on Wednesdays at the Fannin Unit. The catch was you had to eat whatever you ordered in one sitting. So, me and this kid would order around eighty dollars of Chinese food and seriously eat the whole damn thing in one sitting. Our weight was definitely going up like the stock in Pornhub during COVID-19.

I was having a blast, knowing that my time was coming to an end at the San Antonio State Hospital. I entered into the Work Program. I would go to Bowie Hall every day to wipe down the walls, tables, and chairs. We made a whopping seven dollars and fifty cents per day. Bowie Hall was a computer lab and recreation unit. Clients would go there a couple times a week to get onto the internet, watch movies, and my favorite, play ping pong. I was the undisputed champ; only one staff member was ever able to give me a run for my money. This guy actually beat me more than I beat him. It was like watching a clip out of "Forrest Gump."

I had created a dating profile for myself. I was probably the first person in the State Hospital history to get on a dating app while an active resident. I had this idea that if a woman could love me at San Antonio State Hospital, she could love me anywhere. At the time, the show "Love After Lockup" was huge. I watched it religiously in the Day Room at Crockett. I titled my name on the app, "Love After Lockup," just like the popular show. Hey, for my situation, a little novelty couldn't hurt. Riding off the coattails of a popular TV show didn't seem like a bad idea at the time, and I am obviously not so prideful as to pass up on a great pun for myself. It was absolutely insane the number of emails I received. What was even crazier was the number of women that agreed to come meet me at a mental hospital for the criminally insane. I really wanted to meet the girl I was going to marry while still locked up. Not so the fictional movie would end properly, either. I just wanted to get my life back to what it once was.

    The women that would come see me were in two categories. The first were the absolute saints. Amazing women that didn't judge me for where I was currently living, my past, or the events that led me there. The other...these bitches were crazier than anyone I knew in the hospital and should likely switch places with me.

    The more women I met, the more it made me realize I was still madly in love with Bella. I had thought about that woman from the time I woke up till the time I went to bed for two and a half years. It was time I reached out to her to see what had happened with her. I got in touch with her through social media. It turns out that "The Greatest Love of All" got herself cleaned up around the same exact time that I went to jail.

    We started talking every day, building a bond again. I saw a totally new girl. One full of life, going to church, and lightyears away from the evil game we once lived in. I was in love on a whole new level in just a matter of days. I told her

Barry had passed away. I mentioned that I had found almost eleven thousand dollars of my inheritance and when I got out, I would be starting a brand-new life with a nice car and new apartment.

That part was all true about finding an inheritance; I know that sounds odd. In a complicated deal, some of the foreclosure money from the house was given to a family member that my father had already paid cash under the table. So, I was all set. I found where the money was at, told this person how to get it, and they did it for me. The check was cashed, and was there, waiting for me to be released.

#

There was a young White guy who was twenty-six years old that came out of some county jail and onto the unit at Fannin. He had a full beard down to his chest, piercing eyes, and a wild mind. He had gone mad some time before from smoking synthetic marijuana.

Right away, he started defecating in the Day Room. Some type of defense mechanism so other patients wouldn't attack him. That's what one of the tech's whispered to me anyway. He had a massive bandage on his foot, but he was getting into fights almost every day. He was a notch up on the looney meter. A major problem for the unit. He would spit on the floor and piss in bottles right in front of everyone as we watched TV. It was becoming unbearable.

I wrote a series of three letters to the administration about the neglect I was seeing at Fannin. I wrote about the need for change in Austin at the state level. I passed along the information that patients were not bathing or changing clothes on this unit, although they should have already known. Word trickled down that the White House was growing angry with me. Yes, I had won by solidifying my early release, but I couldn't just allow these men to be abused, not on my watch. These people were disabled to the point that they could not speak up for themselves. I could no longer sit back and watch the decay of the men I lived with.

Charles was a tech up there with Ms. Jackson on the cool. I would talk to him for hours. He was a soul that helped get me through a lot of hard times. It was still madness at San Antonio State Hospital. Having a sane person to talk to was always a nice change of pace. I had Marcus to chill with but in a lockdown situation like this mental institution, I would take as many sane people on my team as I could get. Charles saw me bribing patients like John to take showers and change clothes. In five minutes, I used a two-dollar bag of candy to successfully convince John to take a shower and change.

Charles agreed that there were ways around Client's Rights, such as bribery. In my letters, I detailed how much money the hospital was taking in per day. I pointed out that it would cost them pennies to buy a freezer and fill it with ice-cream sandwiches to coax problem clients into personal hygiene habits with the promise of a treat.

There was a four-time convicted rapist named Lavonne. He had been so extremely dangerous that he was sent to Vernon from the prison with an ankle monitor on. The first time I met him at Fannin, I wondered why a man that was already locked up needed an ankle monitor. Turns out that if Lavonne ran, the State didn't want to take any chances. If he did manage to escape, they needed to be able to find him as quickly as possible before he hurt someone. The part that puzzled me was how a man so dangerous could pass the DRB and be stepped down into a lower security hospital. Also, how are you too dangerous and crazy for prison?

Lavonne was rumored to be a pedophile and a sexual

deviant. This was the face of the devil living at the Fannin Unit. Lavonne was having homosexual relationships with as many men as possible on the unit for well over a year. Staff knew, the doctors knew, everyone knew. I started to notice that some of the more mentally challenged men were following him around like puppy dogs. I started to keep a close eye on this scumbag.

He was a creepy Black male, noticeably light skin, short and fat, with huge swollen ankles. He had salt and pepper hair, cut almost bald. His face was scrunched up like a bulldog. He worked with us at Bowie Hall in the mornings. He always wore a hoodie as he played countless hours of spades with the guys, gambling Dr. Peppers and bags of Doritos.

I saw that the bathrooms were now locked at night. One of the tech's spilled the beans on an orgy story in the bathroom a couple days after it all went down. It involved two severely mentally challenged men named John and Ramiro.

I was angry. I put on my Nancy Drew backpack and started a little investigation of my own.

I interviewed techs on the low to learn the whole story. Late one night, one of the techs went into the north side hall bathroom to do a headcount. He heard moans coming from the shower stalls in the communal space, which was already creepy enough on its own. Upon further investigation, he discovered Lavonne, John, and Ramiro having an oral and anal sex orgy. Nauseated and repulsed, he broke up the party and sent them to their rooms. He charted the event and promptly reported it to the doctors. Nothing came of it. Not even the required Adult Protective Services investigation. The families of the mentally disabled men were never called, and proper STD testing was never done. Well...that is until my loud Irish ass got involved.

I talked to clients who knew the victims a little better than I did. What I found had me Boston-style furious. It turns out that Lavonne had been bribing these mentally challenged patients with sodas. He would offer them three Dr. Peppers each to suck his dick and more in the restroom. This had been going on for months. These men were adults by birthday standards. But knowing them personally, they had the minds of an eight or nine-year-old child. All they heard was "soda" and they were sold, sucked into Lavonne's deviant world of foreplay and oral sex...no pun intended.

 I went to the staff and told them I was going to write a letter. I told them I wanted a full investigation on the sexual crimes taking place by Lavonne. He was a sexual predator on the loose in a unit of severely disabled men. It had to end. They blew me off and swept the whole thing under the rug. So, I did the next right thing. I bribed Ramiro with six sodas to give me his older sister's number. I had heard them talking frequently on the phone, so I knew she loved him and would raise hell in a situation like this. Before I called her, it was brought to my attention that John was in fact HIV positive. He had tested positive on his entrance blood test to San Antonio State Hospital. He was a known male prostitute.

 Ramiro's sister was horrified. She began to cry as I recounted the details of what I had discovered. I told her that I wasn't in the room, but had received my information from reliable sources, and it was worth her calling the administration building. And boy, did she! In big ways. She also called the media and some people at the State level.

 My next move was to look up Lavonne's arrest record online. What I found blew my motherfucking socks off. He had raped an eighteen-year-old girl and three older women and had been convicted of all four crimes over the span of his life. He had also raped a man while in TDC, but the guy never pressed formal charges.

I found open court documents where his doctor from prison was quoted saying, "Lavonne is so dangerous, that he has violent sexual thoughts every moment he is awake." I called a meeting in the Day Room with all forty men in Fannin. I figured if the hospital wouldn't protect these men from Lavonne, I would.

"Look out Fannin, I have in my hand the full arrest record of Lavonne. He is a rapist and known sexual predator. Even his own mother said in court that he should never be let out." I went on a twenty-minute attack that told the men to watch out for themselves and each other, to report any sexual assaults they may have seen, and to basically not fuck with Lavonne. The pod was in an uproar as Lavonne sat dazed, staring at me like he wanted to kill me. He knew I was causing a major problem for him, and he didn't like it.

The next morning is when it popped off. I came out for the Sunday morning meeting. This old male nurse that wore a set of scrubs that read "Can't Poop, Tell the Nurse" on the front, came every week for this meeting. He talked about things like STD's and well, not being able to poop. He also gave us ice-cream sandwiches. After he was done with his speech and the ice cream had been devoured, about twenty of us guys sat in the Day Room, which was set up exactly like the Crockett Unit. We all were thoroughly enjoying ourselves, just lounging around and playing cards.

"You motherfucker, you goin' around sayin' I molested those motherfuckers!" Lavonne shouted at me from a table in the middle of the room. He was squirting spit out of his wretched bulldog jowls.

I looked him dead in the eyes and replied, "Not today demon, I know who you are, the rapist of women and the hurter of children. Fannin Hall will be your brothel no more!"

His response stunned me. "I was going to be a preacher when I was younger."

I fired back in rage, "Devil man, the only reason you would become a preacher is to take advantage of children."

He erupted in anger, standing to his feet. The whistle blew. The signal for help was felt and heard throughout the unit. Ten techs came into Fannin to help break up the explosion. I just sat smiling at him, as he seethed and writhed. This made him lose his demonic mind.

They tugged him away as I gave my little speech, "I am writing a letter to the administration. I will detail this whole crime. I call for justice against this man for his crimes, and this corrupt administration for the cover up that happened here!"

And so, I did. A five-page article was penned later that night and turned in for delivery. I had been making copies of every letter I had written. So, I threatened again to go to the media. I emailed all the local news stations in San Antonio. The administration was fuming on Monday. Adult Protective Services came down and interviewed everyone involved. The lady from Client's Rights came down to interview me. Nothing really happened, but it put the fear of God in those at the White House. The media can't report on anything inside the hospital because of HIPPA laws. I needed to find a story they could verify.

#

The potential spread of HIV. The cover up of the sexual assault, against the mentally challenged. This was a massive scandal the hospital did not want on the front page. I discovered that the hospital was selected by the State to be the next to receive a three hundred and twenty-million-dollar grant for a new state of the art building. There were fifteen or so private stakeholders that had a vested interest in the project.

Any bad press would be devastatingly costly.

Dr. Nogood informed me that the judge had turned down his recommendation for drug treatment. He said I was still to be discharged, but it was back to the drawing board as far as my after-care plan was concerned. See how he earned his name? This was done just to delay my release. Well, not if I could help it. I was now in the mindset that anything that happened on Fannin was going to be a letter-worthy event. I was going home win, lose, or draw.

I got a text from Bella late one evening. She said she wanted me to call her, and for her, that was strange. I rang her phone through social media, and she picked up on the second ring.

"Hey Bell, how are you sweetheart?" I said in a Boston accent. I had told her about the money, I had told her about the book I planned on writing.

This is what she said, "Boston, look, I have always loved you. I know you're the guy I want to be with one hundred percent. I wanna get married."

I was taken aback. My dream had come true, until she said the next part, "Boston, why don't we give the book the ending everyone will want to see, The Greatest Love of All?"

I knew it was all bullshit at that very moment. But my heart wouldn't allow me to see it just yet. So, I said, "Hell yes!"

The next day she requested to video chat with me. When we got on, we talked about the apartment, the car, and her and the baby coming to stay with me right away. I looked at my Bell with a bursting loving heart. After the long absence, then seeing her face again and the greed that lay beneath the surface, I knew she wasn't the one. I saw that all she wanted was the money. We stopped talking after that video chat. As much as I saw the truth in her, I think she saw how much she didn't love me.

I had loved her every day since she had left. I could never face the fact that she was gone. It was the single most painful thing I had ever gone through. All the accidents, jail, the mental institutions, none of it compared to losing Bell. So, I prayed for three full days. *Lord, please take this love for this woman away, out of my heart forever. Why would you put that kind of love inside of me for her?* Praying and asking, over and over again.

On the evening of the third day, it hit like a beam of light through the barred glass of the window. God showed me how Bella only looked to me when she needed something. It is like when we only look to Him in times of peril or need. He put that supernatural, unconditional love for Bella in my heart so He could teach me a lesson, one to make me see how He looks at us. He looks down in unconditional love as the world rotates day in, day out. He looks at us as I saw Bella. And we only look back up when we need something. When we do, He cries out in joy. At this moment, I realized that I should be looking to God at all times. Loving Him back the way He loves me. He is the greatest Teacher the world has ever known. He used the flesh, the one thing He knew that would grab my attention and utilized it to show me one of the mysteries of life. I am forever grateful for the pain. There is always purpose in pain.

Nogood was calling me almost every two days at this point trying to get me to explode. One meeting I remember was in front of about fifteen social workers, techs, and other hospital staff, including a couple cool Black females. He was ranting about my case and going on and on about how I should have never got an NGRI finding. At one point, he shushed me when I was speaking. No one, and I mean no one, shushes me.

I raised my index finger and thumb and interrupted

him abruptly, "Don't speak to me like that."

He was startled by the tone in my voice. He sat back in his chair, speechless. In a calm voice as I sat back in my chair, folded my hands, and repeated myself.

"Don't...speak to me...like that." The females in the back were smirking.

Dr. Nogood blurted out, "Well, you should not even be here."

I looked at him, and in front of the whole Treatment Team, I said, "I should be here because the Lord sent me here to see the atrocities within the four walls of this place. He saw it fit to send me to change things...and I will."

The whole room was pin drop silent. Now, it's not a good move to talk about God in a mental institution; that can hold you for the next ninety-nine years of your life. So, with one statement, I clarified my position and mental stability.

"I am spiritual, not crazy. There is a big difference."

The Black women in the back almost erupted in laughter. I could see a familiar look in Nogood's eyes, the same exact one Lavonne had given me that day I outed him to the whole pod. It was the look of an evil man in the presence of justice.

#

Passengers, do you remember that twenty-six-year-old kid, the one who pooped in the Day Room? Well, I had started to take an interest in him. He was being neglected by the nursing staff. That bandage on his foot was leaking a bloody, brown mix. I could tell it hadn't been changed in days. I knew how to bargain with the mentally ill quite well at this point, so I made my move.

I offered him two bags of peanut M&M's with a soda if he agreed to take off the bandage and give me a peek of the wound beneath. He was elated and off came the filthy rag.

What I saw had me gagging. A scoop, inches deep and three inches long, was festering green and purple. It was a faucet of sickness. The smell of a four-day-old salmon carcass came fuming into my nostrils, full of ammonia.

I immediately called the head nurse over to shame her, "Why the hell does this man's foot look like this? This dressing hasn't been changed in days." I was so angry.

"Mr. Bornagain, we can't do anything. This man has Client's Rights to refuse a dressing change. He won't let us," the nurse explained.

The kid was refusing treatment. Under Client's Rights, they can't treat wounds or anything else without the permission of the client. These are people that can't make choices for themselves. I looked up the law and definitions of being "disabled" in The State of Texas. It clearly says that disabled people under law can't make certain decisions on their own specifically such as hygiene, among other things.

So, Client's Rights was written by some guy in a boardroom in Austin who most likely never spent one night in a state hospital and was dictating how these people were being medically treated as they resided in hell. There was a thick red line running up the young man's leg. This indicates that the infection was spreading, and he may have blood poisoning. He was in real danger of losing his leg and possibly his life. I had to do something.

Again, Ma came through. I bribed the kid with ten sodas to get his dad's phone number. The son of a bitch wasn't as crazy as I thought, he drew a hard bargain. He finally played ball and once I verified the phone number was legit, I paid him in Dr. Pepper and Fanta.

I rang the man in the afternoon. I started by saying,

"Sir, I am a fellow client here at San Antonio State Hospital with your son. He has a gaping wound on his foot, and they are not treating it properly because your son has the right to refuse treatment. I am scared he is just days away from losing his foot."

The man was shocked that his son was even at San Antonio State Hospital. He knew he was in jail but had no clue that he was now living in one of the state's mental facilities. So much for that emergency contact bullshit. The dad explained to me who he was, where he was from, and some other key information. It turns out this kid was from right around Crook City. His dad was no stranger to the game. A real streetwise character. Above all, the family had resources.

He explained to me that he and the kids' grandma had a lawyer on retainer. I told him that he needed to get his son to fill out a release form so the hospital could legally speak to him about his son's treatment. Once this form is filled out, the family has a right to call and be involved. I went into detail about the severity of the wound and the frequency of the dressing changes, which I was now keeping a written log.

The family called the White House, the media, and most importantly, a lawyer. This red tape bullshit takes a lot of time. So, I did what I knew to be most effective, I bribed the guy. Every day, I was shelling out bags of chips, soda, and candy so the kid would let staff change the dressing and clean the wound.

I wrote a five-page letter to the administration. I once again threatened to take my first-hand account to the news media. I took a stand against the medieval practices at San Antonio State Hospital and told them I was the reason for the family becoming aware of the issue. Just like the letter I wrote to them about the Lavonne scandal, I took the credit. Like a terrorist organization, after a major suicide bombing in the Gaza strip. I wanted to let them know...Boston was the source of all their newfound problems.

Over the next few weeks, the wound got better. It healed in a miracle fashion, returning to a normal looking foot. To this day, it amazes me that a group of nurses and doctors, who took an Oath as my grandpa did, could sit around and watch a twenty-six-year-old man lose his leg. A situation that was preventable by offering an incentive in the form of a snack to a problem patient. When a man is bringing you over thousand dollars a day, I think the least you could do is treat him properly, no matter what it takes.

#

I put a call into "Martin Scorsese." This is what he told me, "Mr. Bornagain, they are trying to release you, but they wanted you to go to some rehab facility. The judge heard this and denied it. She says it's against your constitutional rights to send you anywhere after you have been deemed safe, and you have. They sent a letter saying so. They also said you have no mental defect, or disorder."

It all came together. I was being kicked out before I even got to Fannin. He told me the timeline of the letter the doctors had written to the courts. It turns out that first letter that God wrote through me was the single thing that sparked my release.

I had made friends with a woman who worked for the hospital. I was at the fence outside about a day after I called my lawyer, and this is what she said, "Mr. Bornagain, you scared some people. Three days after you wrote that letter, there was a secret meeting at the White House. During that meeting, it was determined that you needed to go. Whatever was said in there, it put the fear of God into them. There is one doctor up on the hill who has the power to release any patient, at any time, for any reason. He wrote the letter that set you free."

See, they couldn't release me before I hit the six-month mark on a Felony One charge evaluation under Texas State law. So, they decided it was time for me to go, and that they were going to move me to Fannin in a holding pattern for the rest of the thirty days till I hit the sixth month mark. Fannin was a much quieter unit than Crockett Hall. There was almost no violence, no madness, and no opportunity for my ball-busting ass to see things I shouldn't. It just turned out that by chance, everywhere I went there was something popping off.

By now, I should be gone already. However, they didn't want to just let me go free. So, they were cooking up a plan to get rid of me, but at the same time, making it impossible for me to go home a free man. That's why they were suggesting a rehab facility. The judge had already got the letter and decided I was to go home. So, behind the scenes, the hospital was looking at housing options for me to be released to. There is a policy in place that if a person is indigent, as I was, and had no place to go, the hospital was to find them a place to stay before they were put back into the community.

I had no clue all of this was going on. Passengers, this is the point where I should have just shut my mouth and go home, right? Well, we all know that shit is not what happened.

Dr. Nogood called me into the tiny nurse's station around six in the evening. I was followed by this skinny tech; he looked like he was a cop in the movie "Super Troopers." He was cool as fuck. Tall and thin with short, brownish-blond hair and a pencil mustache to match. He was a man in green, a friend. He was another guy like Charles, who silently cheered me on as I fought the machine. He had to sit in on this meeting as the security guard in case I decided to attack Dr. Nogood.

"So, Mr. Bornagain, I wanted to explain some terms with you. Under an NGRI, a 46C finding, you will be required to see a doctor once a month, a social worker once a week, and be drug tested for the rest of your natural life, ninety-nine years."

He said this with the evilest of smiles. Then he continued as I sat there stone faced, but in full acceptance. Nogood went on, "It looks like you are going to be released soon. They are just working on the final details, finding housing and such."

I interrupted him, "I found some interesting facts in my research Dr. Nogood. I saw the timeline of the letter that was written for my release. It was written before I had even met you. You are my primary doctor, the only person who should write such a letter. Did you write it?"

Now, in the days leading up to this, he had fucked up. He had said that he was the one who released me and wrote the recommendation letter. They are so used to dealing with highly medicated, mentally challenged people that they weren't expecting such a level-headed and bold question. It was like Lex Luthor and Superman had a baby.

He was speechless. I reminded him of his admission that he'd said he wrote the letter. When confronted with the facts, and that I had knowledge of the behind-the-scenes meetings, he just didn't know what to say.

Then he spoke, "Well, I don't know who wrote the letter."

I loved watching this worm squirm on the end of the hook, so like one of the "Super Troopers," I proceeded into battle, "Sir, it appears to me that a doctor who has never met me, nor even looked at my files, has written a letter regarding my care. In fact, was a physician at this hospital releasing a Felony One patient, sight unseen? Is that the case here, Sir?"

He was looking scared at this point. All he could grumble out was, "Mr. Bornagain, I don't know who wrote the letter."

I pressed on, "Wow," drawing my wow out extra-long, "This looks pretty bad for you guys. I mean, I am not positive on what happened yet, but you can see what this looks like, right Dr. Nogood?"

He was visibly shaken at this point. But I wouldn't let up, "I think you were told by the administration to simply keep me quiet and get rid of me as fast as possible. I think you are scared of someone there if you ask me. I mean, why else won't you tell me who signed the letter setting me free?"

He fired back, "Mr. Bornagain, what does all this matter to you? You making a big deal on something like this would only hurt your release, you know that, right?"

I knew I had this asshole and the entire damn hospital on the ropes. So, me being the prick that I am, I decided to shoot some more slugs his way, dead center, "Well, when it comes to threats, here is my stance. Letting a Felony One patient go without ever speaking to them is a pretty big risk to take. Let me ask you, Dr. Nogood. Would you sign off on a patient with a crime of that stature to go home, without ever meeting them in person?"

He returned immediately, "Absolutely not."

And with that I made my point, "Well… it looks like someone did, and I am going to find out who. Then you, him or her, and this whole place is going to be on the KSAT-TV News. I don't care if I have to spend the rest of my life in this place, what's right, is right."

Dr. Nogood was a wintery mix of steaming mad and terrified. He knew that after talking to my lawyer, I had discovered that whoever is in charge at the White House had, in fact, set me free before I had ever even walked onto Fannin Hall, without ever so much as meeting me.

Then I asked, "So will you get me a copy of this mystery letter?"

He looked at me and flat out told me, "No."

I had done a lot of reading in that Client's Rights handbook. I practically had the whole motherfucker memorized. So, what I did next really ruffled the feathers of Nogood and the whole damn Whitehouse.

I said, "Dr. Nogood, I am going to walk out of here and fill out a request form. I am going to summon all of my medical records, which I have full right to do under the Client's Rights subsection called Open Records. I will be able to see every letter, and every chart, pertaining to my case indefinitely."

His face looked like I had just taken a shit in the punch bowl, at the San Antonio State Hospital Christmas party. He spouted, "Do that, Mr. Bornagain. This meeting is now over."

This was scary as hell. I had just threatened to blow the whole corrupt system at San Antonio State Hospital wide open. They knew I had access to the files and the knowledge of what to look for. If this got to the media, it would be a mess. They just couldn't explain it away.

There is something enormously powerful about the pen. I had a letter signed by a strange doctor up on a hill. One which set an armed robber free without ever meeting him. I bet the stakeholders in the new construction project wouldn't like this to be on the front-page newspaper and blasted all over social media.

#

The next time period to follow were dark days and asylum nights, indeed. I felt the hatred in the daggered eyes of the staff. Anyone that outranked the techs now saw me as the enemy. They were all briefed on my meeting with Dr. Nogood, and they were instructed to have zero verbal contact with me. I had staff members literally run behind the nurse's station when I went to approach them.

"So, what is going on with my discharge housing plan?" I would always ask. That's if I was lucky enough to corner an unsuspecting social worker in the hall.

I got the same answer every time, "I don't know, I will have to ask Theresa, up at administrations."

I started to ask questions like, "Well, you are my social worker on the unit, you should be handling my release, and reentrance into the community, right? That's what you told me when I got here. So why is there some mythical creature, in an administration building, running my case? I have never even seen what this person looks like." That's right about when the social worker would mentally implode and scurry away, like those Nueces County rats that I grew attached to and loved.

The days were long, and the stonewalling was omni. I felt a grim black cloud forming as my social worker approached me for the first time since the open records request, "Mr. Bornagain, I am really frustrated, as are you. I have put applications in for every halfway house, assisted living program, and homeless shelter in Corpus Christi and not one will accept you."

I was getting furious. This close to release and all that was keeping me behind the gates was a spot to live. So, I made the truth be known.

"Look lady, I got eleven grand sitting out there waiting for me. If I can rent a place to live, and show you a lease, will the hospital agree to let me go?"

She returned, "Well yes, I don't see why that wouldn't work."

Then she went on her way. If the hospital knows you have a large sum of money, they can seize it. So, I kept my inheritance money close to the vest for as long as I could. Looking back, the mystery of why even homeless shelters had all turned me down was proof that God had a plan.

I called the family member that was holding my money. We were a year apart and truly close even though we hadn't seen each other too often over the years. I loved her more than anyone else at this point. When I talked to her last, I had blessed her with twenty-seven hundred out of the eleven thousand dollars that remained of Barry's money. That left me around eight grand to start a new life. It was time to cash in.

I had called with no luck for two days. Finally, when she did pick up, the bullshit started. "Look, I got arrested, I had to spend a little bit of your money, Boston."

I knew she was lying. I could tell by the shaky tone in her voice. "Well, how much?" I asked.

She spat back, "Well, a couple thousand."

I was pissed but asked anyway, "A couple thousand, on top of the money I gave you already?"

"Yes, but I will pay you right back." She spoke.

I was really spread thin at this point. I only had six thousand now to get a car and rent an apartment. I told her sternly, "Look, I need you to send me a bank check for the six thousand dollars to my unit right away. I am days from being released."

She agreed to overnight it to me, and we got off the line. Boy, I was worried.

I was working hard, wiping down the walls at Bowie Hall with a baby wipe. I could taste the free world like a Fenway frank on opening day. Time seemed to stand still. After an incarceration of this magnitude and the nature of its happenings, one waits on the edge of their seat like a movie goer at showtime.

A few weeks before, my new roommate had threatened to kill his wife and child on a phone call in the Day Room.

"Listen you fucking cunt, I am going to get out of here and fucking kill you and the baby!"

He was a bag of shit. Everyone in the Day Room had heard the threat. Including a large, Black male tech. He charted the incident, and my roommate told me they had threatened to take his visitations away. All in all, it was another incident swept under the rug by the brass at San Antonio State Hospital. I guess they just couldn't be bothered with the necessary paperwork.

This new roommate was a short, wire-thin, Puerto Rican-looking rodent. He had the hair of a Black man, and at times wore clothes like Spanish from "Old School." (That actor is going to love this book; plugs for days!) My roommate's skin was pale; he looked mixed. He had vampire teeth; long fangs mixed in a pile with chunky, misguided hunks of enamel. Their color was the exact shade of the yellow that one would find on a Spicy McChicken Sandwich wrapper at McDonalds. Tinted with off-white and in some spots, the shade of nighttime. His face was long and thin.

 Tales with years of childhood abuse and demonic torment toiled upon the contours of his flesh. His matted hair was black and puffy. The attributes that haunted me more than anything else were the dark, maleficent circles under his eyes. An afflicted mind and corroded soul, he was a demon to say it politely.

I would listen to him on the cordless phone as he sat on his twin bed abusing his family, "You fucking fat bitch, no one out there is going to want you. I am that nigga, you understand me?"

I wanted to murder him. Especially when he would cut into his young son. "You listen to me! You're my son, you do as I fucking say, Goddamn it!"

This went on for weeks. My fantasies of strangling him as he slept grew more vivid by the day. He came to our four-man room one night, disoriented and bizarre. I knew the tell-tale signs all too well. My time in the game gave me an eye for drug use. Especially synthetic.

He sat and fell over onto his pillow, letting out long sobs. That drug has a way of taking the user into the dark recesses of the mind. Bringing out sorrowful spirits and memories of doom. I saw it from a mile away. I guess he had just been in the shower moments before. Throwing the same type of spastic, pathetic fit and staff was hip to his use. Two techs came in and thoroughly searched his area. I saw the hand of one tech pull a full bag of legal out from the cupboard. Later, it was known that the same girl he had been threatening was the one handing him bags of synthetic and ice at their forty-five-minute make-out sessions in the visitation room. Love is strange in the game.

After work one day, I sat under the mesquite tree in the yard at Fannin. I was on one of those red-wire benches that matched the two-person swing near the fence line. That's when Nosfuratu appeared out of nowhere. I looked up and saw the slimy fangs of the cannibal before me.

"I am gonna get the fuck over the wall, man," he said. I looked at him like he was, well…crazy. No pun intended.

"What do you mean, bro? You want to get another charge? You will be an escaped mental patient; they will have the bloodhounds looking for you," I said with gusto.

"Nah man, I am going to go see this guy that owes me

twenty grand real quick, then I'm outta here."

He had to be delusional. Like everyone else in this place, living in fantasy and talking shit out of his boney little ass. I watched him mosey on over to the fence line. He tried to holler at this thick, sexy Black girl who worked as an occupational therapist. She had thighs that you would see in a "Cash Money" video. He had less than no chance, seeing he was in a mental hospital and looked like Count Chocula. So, I walked back inside and went to go write on my bed. As I would get lost in the craft, an hour or so would pass by before I even looked up again.

Marcus pops his head in my room. "Hey bro, that motherfucker hopped the wall."

I leapt to my feet, and we stormed into the Day Room to find pandemonium. The facts were already swirling about my roommates daring midday escape. Story has it, he coaxed two mentally challenged men, one being John, the HIV-positive male prostitute, to let him stand on their backs. He climbed up the human-made steps and dunked over like a young Michael Jordan in his heyday.

The staff had not been outside watching the patients. It wasn't the tech's fault. San Antonio State Hospital is famous for negligently understaffing its units. They have a massive turnover rate among the guys in green. I mean, who wants to live in a mental institution for twelve hours a day, getting spit on and punched for twelve dollars an hour? There just weren't enough scrubs on the floor to keep an eye on all of us.

The pod was in chaos. I had never seen anything like this. This was early afternoon, and we all awaited the news reports at six like a pack of starving wolfhounds. We gathered around the TV as if World War Three was about to unfold live. Six o'clock came and went and there was no mention of the daylight jailbreak. This was an escaped mental patient, awaiting trial on five or more felony charges, including a family violence charge. And not one news outlet had picked up the story. That's when I had another lightbulb moment from Jesus.

"The hospital must not have reported it to the media," I told Marcus. I hurried over to the corner couch so no could see what I was to do next. I messaged the KSAT-TV newsroom through social media. I simply put, "Do you guys want a story about an escaped mental patient at the State Hospital?" I waited, and in about ten minutes, a producer in the newsroom messaged me back. "We have to verify a story like this. How do you have knowledge of this alleged escape?" So, I explained to him that it was my roommate, and that I was on the inside. He came back with, "I don't believe that you are really inside the State Hospital. They don't have phones in there." So, with some quick thinking, I responded by dropping a GPS pin, right from Fannin Hall, and a message that read, "I have my phone." He messaged back immediately. He said he wanted the homeboy's name, and he would look into it.

This kid who escaped was crazy. I had heard with my own ears how he talked to his woman and young kid, and I said, "fuck 'em'." This little stunt would have a dual purpose. One, it could save the lives of two innocent people. Two, it could be the hot knife that cut through the red-tape bullshit at San Antonio State Hospital. I didn't tell a soul of my plan till later that night.

When the lights of the TV began to twinkle at ten o'clock, I let Marcus in on my little secret. "I was the one who called the news, this is going to be big," I said. Marcus just looked at me with a smile. The next thing you know, there he was, plastered all over the TV screen. An escaped patient at the State Hospital. The biggest story of the night. I went to bed with a plan in mind.

I woke up and headed to the Day Room with a pad and a pen. I had written eleven letters to the White House in all. I left out some in order to protect the innocent. Those stories far too graphic and far too obvious who the victims are to disclose here. This final letter would be my twelfth and final communication with the god of San Antonio State Hospital. To this day, I have never found out who that person is. One thing is for sure, he knows who Boston Bornagain is.

I prayed to the Lord as I penned a six-page manifesto to the powers that be. I explained that I was a witness to the escape, the events leading up to its inception and afterwards. I told them that I would testify for the families of the victims in the event that anyone was killed while this man was on the loose. The hospital's failure to report such an escape to the media may very well have botched an apprehension early on by police, thus preventing any harm to the innocent. I said if anyone were hurt, the hospital should be sued in a two-hundred-million-dollar lawsuit and clearly, they would lose.

I detailed my knowledge of the threat my roommate, the escapee, had made on his family not long before, and the hospital's negligence in acting appropriately. I made them aware of my eye-witness account of the hospital staff finding drugs in the room of the escaped days before he hopped the wall.

I also told them I was outside moments before the escape and saw firsthand his mental state prior to him climbing over the wall off the backs of the innocent, and that there was no staff overlooking the clients. I made a grim promise in this letter that this was not the last they were to hear of Boston Bornagain.

It was early and I marked the letter "ESCAPE: URGENT INFORMATION." So, shots fired. I took full responsibility for the news story in the hopes that it would push me out of this portal to hell I had wandered into about six months before. A few hours were all it took, then Dr. Nogood made a house call.

I sat in the boardroom once again with about fifteen staff around me. I was all smiles as Nogood gave me the news.

"Mr. Bornagain, we are just waiting for the housing plan to go through, and you are to be released. We need to have a place for you to go before the courts will release you." I started in on him about the escape and how I had called the news; he threw me out of the meeting by force. I am sure a strict gag order was in place for all staff. So, that was that.

I went out and called the family member about the whereabouts of my money. I hadn't received any calls back, which was worrisome. I thought maybe there was a problem with my mail, and that was why I had not received the check the next day.

After ten or so calls going through to voicemail, I decided to call her mother, "Boston, I think she spent all the money. I am sorry honey; I think she has a major problem."

I heard this woman's words and I wanted to die. I was so close, I could feel the ocean spray, the sound of the gulls upon my ears as I reentered Corpus Christi.

"What the fuck do you mean she spent the money?" I screamed.

The eyes in the Day Room fixated on me as I lost my shit. We had a two-hour long conversation. I hurled lots of hateful words and made some loosely veiled threats about regaining my inheritance.

So, after all this, ice was not done fucking with my life just yet. Turns out that she was spun out on meth and spent almost eleven thousand dollars of my money in under thirty days, after I had given her almost three thousand dollars for her troubles. Another instance of the people closest to me leaving me for dead. I was devastated, lost, and scared. My ticket home snatched right out of my hands. I needed a miracle, and I felt I may have used all those up.

    I sat in front of the TV for the rest of the day. I wanted to die. Now with the hospital wanting to fuck me worse than ever, I had no clue what was going to happen next. There was no shelter or program in my county willing to take me in and no money to rent a place with. I was fucked. Then I remembered Jesus.

    I texted the family member who robbed me. I told her I was sorry for saying such hateful words to her mother out of anger. I asked myself that all too familiar cliché, "What would Jesus do?" So, I did as I thought he would want me to. I told her I knew what it was like to be out of control on meth. I understood where she was coming from and that it was only money. I asked her to help me show the world the power of forgiveness and the amount of love within our family. Together, we could teach people that God was real.

    About two minutes later, she blocked me. Her mom stopped answering my calls and texts not long after, and that was that. I sat on the couch defeated. Now I couldn't even forgive someone the right way. I had acted in a way that not many people, outside of the living Jesus Christ and his true followers, would have.

    And it still just wasn't good enough. I figured the shame of the betrayal, mixed with the fact that if I was released, I was going to live under a bridge was just too much for them to continue to face me. They didn't even offer to let me come live there till I got on my feet. At that moment, the last living members of the blood Bornagain family went up in smoke, as far as I went anyway.

I had never felt so low in my life. I started feeling really sorry for myself around half past nine at night. By nine-fifty p.m., I wanted to die. That's when Rabbit rolled by in his wheelchair and the Lord spoke through him. He screamed to someone else across the room with a big smile, "Ya never know when God will open the door and let ya walk the fuck on outta here." He wasn't speaking to me, but what happened next would change my life forever. That message was clearly meant for me.

The ten o'clock news opened with a special story, one about the State Hospital and all its creepy little secrets. They told of the nine escapes in the last two years. One was about a man who had hacked his wife up and was found wandering the unsuspecting streets of San Antonio. A lot of these stories went unreported to the media. It showed all the police calls, assaults, the violence, and other crimes that the San Antonio Police Department was forced to respond to. It showed a piece of broken-down fence, not the one my roommate went over, but it made the story far more effective. Finally, it ran into the story of my roommate who had escaped and the fact that he was still at large.

Just as the story ended, I heard the wall phone ringing. No one was picking it up, so I went over to answer, "Hello, Fannin," I said.

"Hey, is Nosfuratu there?" It was a female voice asking for my escaped roommate. She told me that she was the girlfriend, the victim of the family violence case that he was locked up for. She was never alerted by the San Antonio Police Department that he had escaped. At least, that's what she told me anyway. I told her to go look up the story from the day before up on YouTube. She hung up the phone in a somber mood. Finding out the father of your children was about to go down for a twenty-year minimum sentence on an escape charge must be a real downer.

#

I went to work the next morning at Bowie Hall while feeling in limbo. I didn't know what was going to happen next, or how this plot was going to unfold. I was there for about an hour when she appeared. It was my social worker from Fannin.

She had a stack of papers and folders in her hands, "Mr. Bornagain, it is my sole job today to get you out of here."

She was the most nervous I had seen any San Antonio State Hospital employee since my first day here. She was to have me fill some things out online using the computer lab. Just so happened the internet went down moments before, so she had made a call to IT support.

She didn't know I could hear her from the other room, "Look, I have to get this guy out, like…now. I need this internet fixed. Yes…YES, I need him discharged, like…yesterday. This is coming from the top."

I wanted to blow my load all over the damn keyboard. I knew this was about to get good; but once again, I had no idea how big God really is.

She enters the computer lab once again, "Ok Mr. Bornagain, we are working on your release; we are looking into Pathways for you."

Pathways is a damn homeless shelter. Pretty luxurious, right?

I said, "That sounds perfect."

At this point, I would sleep on the floor of a peep show to get the fuck home.

The news story from the day before was the last straw. Nogood called me in and told me they called an emergency court date; it was set for this coming Friday. The judge was to hear my case and sign off on the final terms and conditions. Thus, signing into law my release and allowing me to go home. I was so excited. Sure, I was going to be homeless, but there are worse things you could be.

I called Ma, and she arranged for three hundred dollars to be waiting for me when I got out. Plus, I had the whopping one hundred bucks I had stored in my account from working at Bowie Hall. So, I figured I would have some money to eat and get started out in the free world.

Rabbit and some of the other guys didn't believe that I was really leaving. It's not every day that a person takes on the monster that is San Antonio State Hospital and then just walks out the door years early. I was just sitting around waiting to see if Pathways was going to accept me. It was now Thursday, less than twenty-four hours before my court date.

Here comes the social worker stomping through the Day Room, another stack of papers in hand, "Mr. Bornagain, Pathways has rejected you."

My heart sank to the floor.

And then she spoke again, "We are going to release you on your own accord."

I couldn't believe what I was hearing. From my understanding, no one gets released onto the streets from a mental institution. It's an almost unethical practice. They wanted me gone so bad; they were willing to drop me off with no plan for me in place. I told her that I agreed to terms and signed some bullshit papers. She went back into the nurses' station.

I spent the rest of the evening celebrating and saying my goodbyes to Charles, Super Troopers, and the rest of the gang at Fannin Hall. I pre-packed my bags by ten at night and went to sleep. I have to admit, I was a bit nervous. More than anything, I was ready to go the fuck...HOME!

I woke early and had chow with Marcus. I couldn't believe it was finally over. The order that Dr. Nogood had written for my aftercare was in the hands of the judge. He wrote that one personally. I was to see a state psychiatrist once a month, a social worker once a week, and be randomly drug tested for the rest of my natural life of ninety-nine years. I was ok with it. Somewhere along the way on this crazy spiritual journey, God had taken my addiction. The drug dreams, the cravings, and the obsessive thoughts were all gone.

To me, this addiction was like having stage four lung cancer. The whole world, all the second opinions of doctors, everyone saying I am a dead man, and POOF. I was completely healed. The major spiritual revelations, the visions, feeling the loving hands of God, mixed with the tangible miracles that were undeniable left me changed. I could never go back to that lifestyle. I am forever grateful to the Lord for what he did in me. I had zero intention, nor the want to ever return to a life in the ice game. I made up my mind a long time ago, I was going to help my brothers and sisters up and out of the flames of hell.

I had been tossing around the idea about turning my short stories into a book. I knew that God didn't perform these miracles, give me the amazing gift to write, and this amazing story for nothing. If there was any doubt in my mind about turning my life story into a full-length bio, what was to happen next cemented into my mind that it must be written.

Court was at nine in the morning, sharp. I knew things took a long time at the San Antonio State Hospital, so I sat tight and waited for them to call me for my ride home to Corpus Christi. They never drove people to their home city. It was unheard of for the San Antonio State Hospital to transport a client in a van two and a half hours away. They seriously wanted me gone.

Two o'clock rolled around and I started to get extremely restless. The transport driver was on standby and kept coming to check if the court had called giving the nurses station the green light for my departure. I must have called my lawyer, "Martin Scorsese," a hundred times. His secretary kept telling me I either missed him or that he would call me back.

Finally, at half past four, thirty minutes before the court was to close for the day, I got in touch with him, "Hello Mr. Bornagain. There has been a little problem with your release today. I can't talk too much about it at the moment. The information is sensitive and it's better if you didn't know at this time."

I almost threw up on the Fannin floor, "What do you mean?" I asked in tears.

He said, "Mr. Bornagain, everything is going to be fine. You just have to trust me on this, ok?" He told me there was a new court date on Monday morning at nine.

The weekend was a suicidal mindfuck. I ate more candy than one should in a lifetime. Marcus, who I had given all my leftover goodies to before I was to leave, took mercy on me and gave them all back. I stuffed my face with cupcakes, chocolate, and anything else I could get my hands on. Don't judge me, I am an emotional eater. The hours ticked past in what seemed like yearlong blocks of time. It didn't help that I had Rabbit talking smack to me with his long gray hair that filled out a black knit cap like OJ wore. He kept telling me, "I don't think you are gonna get outta here, youngster." Every little comment of negativity threw me miles off track. Just like before my trial, I was a fragile, shaky bowl of green Jell-O, in fear of the unthinkable, just plain scared.

I sat packed and ready to go at a quarter past nine in the morning. Ms. Jackson had received a call from the administration department that told her to have me ready. She was an angel. She packed me up a bunch of extra socks, a coat from the donation pile, and gave me a brand-new duffel bag to put all my stuff in. "No patient of mine is going to hit the street carrying paper bags," she said. She wished me well and assured me the ride was coming, that I was going to do great when I got home. I grew to love some of the people at the San Antonio State Hospital. The ones who got me through the impossible nights. The screaming, the violence, and perverse sexual situations. The angels that worked there were the only reason that I came home in sound mind.

"Mr. Bornagain, you need to call your lawyer," said a voice from behind. It was my social worker in the door jamb of the nurse's station door.

My heart sank as I dialed the 361-area code. "Hello Mr. Bornagain. Ok! You are going home. The judge is signing off on the documents as we speak. I can't talk about what happened in court on this phone call. I want you to call me as soon as you are off the bus and out of earshot of any hospital employee," my lawyer said, shrouded in mystery.

I waived to the guys and walked out the door as cheers erupted behind me. You can't write this shit, for real...except I did. My life is, well...like a movie. We entered that same old hospital van that took me to the Cancer Center, and we were soon barreling down the highway back to Crook City, the place where this whole magical story began.

#

On the way home, I decided I was going to write a book about the whole damn experience. At the time, my short stories had gained me almost two thousand friends on social media.

The article was to come out in the Christian magazine. I remember thinking, "I better get a damn website built soon." See, I made the magazine promise to plug the writing and put the link in the article in order for me to agree to the story. I dream of helping others out of addiction. I had a crazy idea that I would apply to work at the same drug treatment facility that turned me away twice; the one that didn't have a bed and pushed me to pull the greatest "Hamburgler Heist" in the history of the world. Even if I had to mop the damn floor in that place, it would make one hell of a story. On this same ride, I thought of some names for the miraculous story that I was to pen about my life and all that had happened. I kept seeing one title…Fire and Ice: The Meth Bible. I was happy for the first time in years. God, He had one more miracle for me. He chose to have my lawyer, "Martin Scorsese," hand me the gift.

The two techs that drove me knew who I was. The legend that was Boston Bornagain had been floating through the halls at the San Antonio State Hospital all week. I was the guy who took on Goliath and won.

One of them said, "Well Mr. Bornagain, we wish you well on your travels. You did it."

I looked at him as I pulled my brand-new duffel bag from the van and said, "God opened the doors to hell. I was just the guy who walked through 'em."

The van pulled away, leaving me staring at that same ominous clock while gazing towards the City Hall. The same one Wheezy could see from 4P. Even today. My home boy is still there as I write today, two years later.

I got on my cell phone and called my lawyer, "Martin Scorsese." His secretary patched the call through, and here is what he said, "Mr. Bornagain, are you alone?" I answered in the affirmative. He continued, "Ok Mr. Bornagain, the reason you had to sit up there all weekend was because on Friday, I went before the judge and told her we were not going for all that aftercare jazz. She told me that if I would go back to my office, and draw up a new order, she would sign it. So, I did and today she signed your release into law. There are no conditions, no doctors, no social workers, or drug testing."

I was dumbfounded. I asked, "Sir, what are you telling me?"

He paused, then said boldly, "Mr. Bornagain, I am telling you that you are a free man. No felony record, no stipulations. You are a free man as if this crime had never happened."

I nearly collapsed. I damn near kissed him through the phone. When I hung up, I was in a blissful trance.

So, there I was on December 16, 2019, in Downtown Corpus Christi. A duffel bag and four hundred dollars to my name. I had nowhere to go, but there was nowhere I couldn't go. The sky was the limit, and the road...well it was wide open.

Chapter 11

Epilogue:

The Open Road

Relax passengers, this next part of the Journey won't be a long one. The meter is not going to be cheap; you have been on this ride for a hell of a long time. Well, here it goes. Oh, and put your seatbelt on. The last thing I need is for the damn cops pulling us over, ok?

I was standing at the City Hall with my bags containing all that I owned in this life. I called my ma just to let her know I was free. She was in tears, happy ones, for the first time in as long as I can remember. I had a homeboy from Corpus that I met in the San Antonio State Hospital. I had texted him earlier for a ride and he finally texted me back. He was on the way to get me. I watched as the homeless toked on legal and sparked ice blowtorches all around me. That's when it hit me. I needed to start documenting my journey.

I was going to get a new phone. You know, a normal one with a camera in it. Then I was going to start shooting footage, showing the world that drug addicts don't have to smoke ice no matter the circumstances, even being homeless. My buddy picked me up in his old red Dodge truck. He couldn't let me crash at his place at the time, so I asked him to take me to a hotel. I have no clue why, but my heart led me to the Bluff, of all places.

I wanted to go back where this dreadful portion of my life began. The one place you shouldn't go if you were me. I wanted to show myself that the miracle God performed was in fact real. I rented a ratty motel room for sixty-five dollars a night. I took my first private shower in over a year and a half, and walked up to the local cell phone store.

I got a brand-new phone, one with a camera. I spent far more money than one should in my situation but filming this portion of my life was priceless. I walked the run-down sidewalks in the methamphetamine capital of earth. The streets felt different because I was not the same. I met my children a few moments later and hugged them for the first time as a free man in almost two years, the tears cleansing a part of my soul that I had no clue existed. We ate a nice meal, talked of the future, and what was to come.

It was bittersweet, as I saw the years of emotional abandonment within their eyes, and it was all my fault. They were scared of me, after all those times I never showed. The times they had to see me dressed as a pumpkin through the glass, and not on Halloween. This was going to be a process, but that was ok. We said our goodbyes, and I assured them that Daddy was all better.

I walked back to the motel room in wonder. The bustling street sounds and honking of horns throttled me. The city streets I knew like the back of my hand, all of a sudden felt Martian and strange. I stopped and got a pack of Newport's along the way. I hadn't smoked in eighteen months. I was an idiot to start back up. In reality, I needed a little something to calm the nerves as I reentered the atmosphere.

When the door closed behind me, I felt refreshed. The

stark realities of freedom hit me like a Wade Bogg's line drive clear into the outfield. I decided to call a friend I had met in my travels. A good girl never mentioned in this book before. She wasn't into drugs; she never danced in that sick ballet we call the ice game.

I was hanging out, contemplating my next move. I had just over two hundred and fifty bucks, a pack of Newport's, and a dream. I had my writing, the passion it brings that bursts from my heart that I couldn't live without now.

It is a new hunger, as strong of a need as food and water. I began to tinker with the keys on my phone. That's when a message came in on social media.

It was Buddy! I couldn't believe my eyes, what timing! We talked about my release for a few minutes. We chopped it up about old times, and then he asked, "Boston, where are you staying, a motel? You got no place to go tomorrow?" I told him my situation, and he said he had to call me right back.

I went outside the room and shot my first social media live. This was all new to me; I don't recall it being out before I went away. Kind of like the drink White Claw. That was some bullshit that I saw on TV and literally laughed to myself, *that shit will never catch on*. I come home and dudes are drinking the shit like it's as manly as Jack Daniels. Oh, how the world has changed. On the Live, I told everyone of my friends that I was free. I explained that I was homeless, but I was going to show the world, "We Do Recover." So, the journey began. My first declaration as an ice-free warrior of God, in the free world! It felt good to shoot that video. I told everyone that I was going to write the story detailing my life. A task that I could not wait to start.

I went inside and sat on the bed with my friend, smoking cigarettes and having a normal, sane conversation.

Wow, that was amazing!

Then I saw Buddy calling me back, "Boston, I booked you five nights at a place called North Beach."

My all-familiar haunt was foreign to Buddy. How fitting he blessed me with a place to stay in one of my most notorious drug hangouts. It was as if God was taking me on a tour through Hell, only now equipped with that fancy armor of His that I had read about all those times in Ephesians 6:10.

God was working in huge ways. That same night, only moments later, I got a message from Erica. A wicked old buddy of mine from Reading. She hung with us hood kids all the time. She asked how I was doing and where I was staying. I told her that Buddy had blessed me with a motel for five nights on North Beach. We hung up, only for her to message me a confirmation number twenty minutes later. Erica had blessed me with five more nights! God just kept the miracles coming.

So now I had ten nights and two hundred and fifty dollars. Ample time to figure out a place to stay. The next day, my friend took me over to North Beach. I checked into the motel. It was a palace compared to the place in the Bluff. It was cheaper too. We got settled in; she never left my side as she cared for me and didn't want me out there, scared and alone. By this time, I knew full well that God had my back.

That's when Ma called. We talked for a little while, and then she hit me with it, "Boston, I really think you need to write this book. I have read your work; you have got to write this story. Don't just talk about it like everyone else does."

Her words rang true, I knew this amazing story needed to be told. But I needed a computer to do it on. Ma came through once again, like always, "Boston, I sent you five hundred dollars to Western Union. Go get you a little computer and find a place to stay with the rest of this money, and I will send more in a couple days."

So that's what we did. We drove to Walmart, and I bought a zip drive and the computer that I am typing this on right now.

I sat in front of the computer nervous as a whore in church. Writing a book like this was not going to be easy, and I knew it. However, as Bukowski once said, "If you find yourself staring at the screen, thinking for hours, don't write." Well, that's what I think he said. As soon as I started to tap the keys, love poured from my fingertips. I recounted the story of a group of young boys, and the love they shared in Reading, Massachusetts. So, it began, "Fire and Ice: The Meth Bible" was underway and I was the happiest I had been in my whole life.

Days went by. I wrote feverishly as we sat in that little motel room with an ocean view. Just my friend and I, writing unforgettable moments in the book of my life. I set up a meeting with some guys at a recovery-based living house in Corpus Christi, off Airline Road. I was set to interview with them the day the motel money was to run out.

After a quick meeting, I was welcomed as the newest housemate at SS. The guys there welcomed me with open arms. I tinkered around for a few weeks and decided to put in an application with the corporate office in Dallas of that treatment center that turned me away. I was hired at the interview, right there on the spot.

I got off the hour and a half long bus ride from my new house. I walked through one of the worst drug areas of "Crook City." Leopard Street was the area where I once stalked the night as a cab driver. It was now the path I walked to help the afflicted. I was hired on as a tech for nine dollars an hour. You don't get into that type of work for the money, that is for sure.

One of my greatest friends and a new brother from

South Shore joined me in the fight against the devil at the treatment center. We were working mostly on the same shifts, preaching the name of Jesus and the miracles He performs.

I met all sorts of interesting people in early recovery. Souls I will never forget as long as I live. I told this incredible story in condensed form, leaving out the sexy parts, of course. I reminded the clients how lucky they were to not be turned away. The brass at the rehab knew my story. They knew I was turned away. They knew about the news stories of my arrest online. Hell, I told them in my interview.

I even spoke the name of Jesus to the guy who hired me. I was almost too honest if there is such a thing. I went into this job totally transparent. With the thought in mind that if God wanted me there, He would make a way. And He did. So, my brother and I went to war on the floors of that treatment center. People would try to walk out, and we gave them hope. Together, we comforted the brokenhearted and preached the Word with the spirit of God at the helm.

It was such a privilege to see the Lord at work. I received great joy and fulfillment during my time working at this place of healing. It was always on my heart that this job would be only for a season. I started to see that the claws of corporate America had infiltrated the once locally owned rehab. Not long before I started to work there, a major corporation had bought the treatment center and turned it into a business.

I sat in the Dayroom where I worked one night and saw Barry's ghost smiling at me near the bookcase, where he once handed me my birthday present back in 2010. This was well before my arrest, when I was able to get a bed and was a patient there.

I walked over to the bookcase and picked up a copy of "K9", starring Jim Belushi. It was that old inside joke we had when I was growing up. He looked just like the actor. I think that was my dad shining through, telling me that he was proud of me.

The place was wearing on me for some strange reason. Looking back in hindsight, it is clear. I was working too much at the job and not enough on the mission. Though my work at the treatment center was important and glorified the name of Jesus, it wasn't what God wanted me to do. This book needed to be written, this story needed to be told. It shows how addiction grabs you. The parties, the laughing with friends, the first memories where you have sex with your high school sweetheart after a couple of beers. No one ever thinks that the innocent fun we have in our youth can turn into the dirty needle dances we do in trap houses while in the clutches of the demon beast.

Addiction is an inviting Jerusalem tulip. Before you know it, it turns into a Venus flytrap that you can't escape. People may say this piece glorifies drugs, and I will agree that in spots it does. If doing drugs and drinking started off in horror, no one would do it. This book is the story of Satan and all his evil schemes, how we need to tell our young that he exists and what he looks like. Pretending the devil does not exist is the main thing we do that the devil loves the most.

As my time grew near a closing point at the treatment facility, another miracle took place. After only thirty days of my brother and me preaching the truth inside the four walls of the corporate rehab, a client appeared. She came up to us as we stood near the double glass doors of the courtyard.

She came up and said this, "Hey guys, me and the others want to start a bible study."

I looked at her angelic face, a girl no more than twenty-five, as she handed me a piece of lined paper. On it were the names of almost every patient at the facility. Every last one of them were starved for Jesus and craving hope.

This showed me that God is needed in a big way in the recovery world. To preach the name of Jesus inside the culture of a corporate facility was not welcomed. Multiple times we were told to "Tone it down or watch out." That's when I decided that before they could fire me for speaking His name, I would gracefully bow out. My work was done there in only thirty days, almost to the day. I had seen what I needed to see, and I left.

I was baptized on New Year's Eve of 2019. This cool church in the Bluff did the honors. I was actually only free a couple weeks when this happened. It was before the treatment center, but the Spirit is telling me to share it now, so I will.

We went to baptism class, me and the same brother I worked at the treatment facility with. When it ended, we had an hour to kill before the actual shindig popped off at the church. So, we decided to go get coffee at the little shop next door owned by the pastor.

When we walked in, I heard a distinct keyboard solo. The song was haunting me as I approached the counter. I asked the male barista if that was "Riviera Paradise" by Stevie Ray Vaughan? I already knew it was, I just couldn't believe it. The barista confirmed for me that it was, and it was playing on SiriusXM.

"Riviera Paradise" is an obscure cut. An instrumental that Vaughan did on one of his last albums. My dad would listen to that song on loop, driving me nuts many nights. I had never heard that song anywhere else besides when I was with Barry. It has no words, no commercial appeal. Hearing it on the radio in rotation is like winning the lottery.

To walk in at that moment, minutes before I was to die in the flesh and be saved in Christ, was a sign to me. It was God using Barry's memory to shine through at just the right moment. I walked back to the church bawling my eyes out. I had my brother in Christ to witness this event.

Once I was dunked and baptized, I was left to remain on the stage to get a Word of prophetic nature. A very large man from out of town, rumored to have charismatic gifts, stood up to address me, "I just want to say, I have an overwhelming feeling that God is very proud of you and what you are doing." He put down the mic and walked away.

See, God will speak to us if we listen in the right way. A lot of people will be furious if this book is published. I am not the perfect Christian by any means. I have never claimed to be, and never will. I am a Spiritual man, one who was saved by Jesus in the streets of hell. He met me in unique ways that I will never forget. He was with me as I walked with the serpent, gaining information for this very tale.

I will be a target for Christian hate and many other forms of persecution. The way I talk about sex and the Lord in the same breath. The way I can speak of drug use and the spiritual awakening within. This is my life and the way I experienced the loving hands of the Father. Some people go their whole life without thinking of the Creator. If I had to walk through hell to feel His touch directly, I would do it all over again. Twice on Sunday.

I left the recovery house to live with an old friend. She took me in when no one else would. She was my neighbor all those years ago when I lived in Port Aransas. God put her in my life at just the right time. I would have been on the streets if it weren't for her. She is a sister to me. The sister I never had, and an adopted sister in Christ. Some people may have taken our relationship the wrong way, but we have the deepest bond of sibling love.

While living at her house, I shot videos as I became a

rising star in the recovery world. I wrote love poetry and honed my craft as an author. I was working at a gas station up the street to pay the rent. And then it happened.

The call I feared the most, "Boston?" It was my ex-wife.

I asked, "Is my ma dead?"

She returned, "I am so sorry."

As I took the call, this once fulltime hopeless alcoholic had an eighteen pack of ice-cold Michelob Ultra in his hands, stocking the cooler at work. Instead of walking out with it and drinking a six pack in the back of the store, as he always would have, he asked his boss if he could go home to grieve the death of his mother. I rode my peddle bike down The Island's back streets, along the Corpus Christi coastline, crying my eyes out for the women I loved so much.

After all that turbulence, I get to say that my ma died knowing I was clean. She left this planet only when she knew that her oldest son was free, safe, and happy. I loved my ma.

Passengers. Do not get unbuckled just yet. We are about to hop in the Crown Vic once again. This time we are going deep into Washington.

True adventure, true miracles and one hundred percent true love is waiting for us 2000 miles away! Boston Bornagain was a new man. God may just have a "new woman", and that wedding we have all been waiting for just around the bend. We are leaving Corpus Christi, The Body of Christ Texas, and headed for Moses Lake Washington. "By Chance"

The End

Made in United States
Orlando, FL
05 December 2023